T0336755

Recent Advances in Ambient Intelligence and Context–Aware Computing

Kevin Curran
University of Ulster, UK

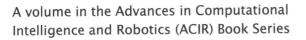

A volume in the Advances in Computational
Intelligence and Robotics (ACIR) Book Series

Information Science
REFERENCE
An Imprint of IGI Global

Managing Director:	Lindsay Johnston
Managing Editor:	Austin DeMarco
Director of Intellectual Property & Contracts:	Jan Travers
Acquisitions Editor:	Kayla Wolfe
Production Editor:	Christina Henning
Development Editor:	Erin O'Dea
Typesetter:	Amanda Smith
Cover Design:	Jason Mull

Published in the United States of America by
Information Science Reference (an imprint of IGI Global)
701 E. Chocolate Avenue
Hershey PA, USA 17033
Tel: 717-533-8845
Fax: 717-533-8661
E-mail: cust@igi-global.com
Web site: http://www.igi-global.com

Copyright © 2015 by IGI Global. All rights reserved. No part of this publication may be reproduced, stored or distributed in any form or by any means, electronic or mechanical, including photocopying, without written permission from the publisher. Product or company names used in this set are for identification purposes only. Inclusion of the names of the products or companies does not indicate a claim of ownership by IGI Global of the trademark or registered trademark.

Library of Congress Cataloging-in-Publication Data

Recent advances in ambient intelligence and context-aware computing / Kevin Curran, editor.
      pages cm
 Includes bibliographical references and index.
 ISBN 978-1-4666-7284-0 (hardcover) -- ISBN 978-1-4666-7285-7 (ebook) -- ISBN 978-1-4666-7287-1 (print & perpetual access) 1. Ambient intelligence. 2. Context-aware computing. I. Curran, Kevin, editor.
  QA76.9.A48R43 2015
  004.01'9--dc23
                                          2014036868

This book is published in the IGI Global book series Advances in Computational Intelligence and Robotics (ACIR) (ISSN: 2327-0411; eISSN: 2327-042X)

British Cataloguing in Publication Data
A Cataloguing in Publication record for this book is available from the British Library.

All work contributed to this book is new, previously-unpublished material. The views expressed in this book are those of the authors, but not necessarily of the publisher.

For electronic access to this publication, please contact: eresources@igi-global.com.

Advances in Computational Intelligence and Robotics (ACIR) Book Series

ISSN: 2327-0411
EISSN: 2327-042X

MISSION

While intelligence is traditionally a term applied to humans and human cognition, technology has progressed in such a way to allow for the development of intelligent systems able to simulate many human traits. With this new era of simulated and artificial intelligence, much research is needed in order to continue to advance the field and also to evaluate the ethical and societal concerns of the existence of artificial life and machine learning.

The **Advances in Computational Intelligence and Robotics (ACIR) Book Series** encourages scholarly discourse on all topics pertaining to evolutionary computing, artificial life, computational intelligence, machine learning, and robotics. ACIR presents the latest research being conducted on diverse topics in intelligence technologies with the goal of advancing knowledge and applications in this rapidly evolving field.

COVERAGE

- Computational Logic
- Cognitive Informatics
- Algorithmic Learning
- Heuristics
- Neural Networks
- Machine Learning
- Computational Intelligence
- Fuzzy Systems
- Add/Edit Topics Covered
- Artificial intelligence

IGI Global is currently accepting manuscripts for publication within this series. To submit a proposal for a volume in this series, please contact our Acquisition Editors at Acquisitions@igi-global.com or visit: http://www.igi-global.com/publish/.

The Advances in Computational Intelligence and Robotics (ACIR) Book Series (ISSN 2327-0411) is published by IGI Global, 701 E. Chocolate Avenue, Hershey, PA 17033-1240, USA, www.igi-global.com. This series is composed of titles available for purchase individually; each title is edited to be contextually exclusive from any other title within the series. For pricing and ordering information please visit http://www.igi-global.com/book-series/advances-computational-intelligence-robotics/73674. Postmaster: Send all address changes to above address. Copyright © 2015 IGI Global. All rights, including translation in other languages reserved by the publisher. No part of this series may be reproduced or used in any form or by any means – graphics, electronic, or mechanical, including photocopying, recording, taping, or information and retrieval systems – without written permission from the publisher, except for non commercial, educational use, including classroom teaching purposes. The views expressed in this series are those of the authors, but not necessarily of IGI Global.

Titles in this Series

For a list of additional titles in this series, please visit: www.igi-global.com

Handbook of Research on Advanced Intelligent Control Engineering and Automation
Ahmad Taher Azar (Benha University, Egypt) and Sundarapandian Vaidyanathan (Vel Tech University, India)
Engineering Science Reference • copyright 2015 • 567pp • H/C (ISBN: 9781466672482) • US $335.00 (our price)

Handbook of Research on Artificial Intelligence Techniques and Algorithms
Pandian Vasant (Universiti Teknologi Petronas, Malaysia)
Information Science Reference • copyright 2015 • 694pp • H/C (ISBN: 9781466672581) • US $345.00 (our price)

Emerging Research on Swarm Intelligence and Algorithm Optimization
Yuhui Shi (Xi'an Jiaotong-Liverpool University, China)
Information Science Reference • copyright 2015 • 341pp • H/C (ISBN: 9781466663282) • US $225.00 (our price)

Face Recognition in Adverse Conditions
Maria De Marsico (Sapienza University of Rome, Italy) Michele Nappi (University of Salerno, Italy) and Massimo
Tistarelli (University of Sassari, Italy)
Information Science Reference • copyright 2014 • 480pp • H/C (ISBN: 9781466659667) • US $235.00 (our price)

Computer Vision and Image Processing in Intelligent Systems and Multimedia Technologies
Muhammad Sarfraz (Kuwait University, Kuwait)
Information Science Reference • copyright 2014 • 312pp • H/C (ISBN: 9781466660304) • US $215.00 (our price)

Mathematics of Uncertainty Modeling in the Analysis of Engineering and Science Problems
S. Chakraverty (National Institute of Technology - Rourkela, India)
Information Science Reference • copyright 2014 • 441pp • H/C (ISBN: 9781466649910) • US $225.00 (our price)

Insight Through Hybrid Intelligence Fundamentals, Techniques, and Applications
Neil Y. Yen (The University of Aizu, Japan) Joseph C. Tsai (The University of Aizu, Japan) and Xiaokang Zhou
(The University of Aizu, Japan)
Information Science Reference • copyright 2014 • 314pp • H/C (ISBN: 9781466648722) • US $195.00 (our price)

Global Trends in Intelligent Computing Research and Development
B.K. Tripathy (VIT University, India) and D. P. Acharjya (VIT University, India)
Information Science Reference • copyright 2014 • 601pp • H/C (ISBN: 9781466649361) • US $235.00 (our price)

www.igi-global.com

701 E. Chocolate Ave., Hershey, PA 17033
Order online at www.igi-global.com or call 717-533-8845 x100
To place a standing order for titles released in this series, contact: cust@igi-global.com
Mon-Fri 8:00 am - 5:00 pm (est) or fax 24 hours a day 717-533-8661

Editorial Advisory Board

Siobhán Clarke, *Trinity College Dublin, Ireland*
Lorcan Coyle, *University College Dublin, Ireland*
Willie Donnelly, *Waterford Institute of Technology, Ireland*
Jesús Favela, *CICESE, Mexico*
Michael Friedewald, *Fraunhofer ISI, Germany*
Lidia Fuentes, *University of Malaga, Spain*
Diego Gachet, *European University of Madrid, Spain*
Nikolaos Georgantas, *INRIA Paris – Rocquencourt, France*
Hani Hagras, *University of Essex, UK*
William Hazlewood, *Indiana University, USA*
Juan Carlos López, *University of Castilla – La Mancha, Spain*
Diego López de Ipiña, *University of Deusto, Spain*
Malcolm McCullough, *University of Michigan, USA*
René Meier, *Trinity College Dublin, Ireland*
Nuria Oliver, *Microsoft Research, USA*
Paolo Remagnino, *Kingston University, UK*
Fariba Sadri, *Imperial College London, UK*
Christian Tchepnda, *France Telecom, France*
Reiner Wichert, *Fraunhofer IGD, Germany*

List of Reviewers

Adel Al-Jumaily, *University of Technology, Sydney, Australia*
Joan Condell, *University of Ulster, UK*
Jean-Pierre George, *IRIT – Université, France*
Tom Lunney, *University of Ulster, UK*
Dan McCormac, *Dublin Institute of Technology, Ireland*
Maurice Mulvenna, *University of Ulster, UK*
Gerry Parr, *University of Ulster, UK*
Gokmen Zararsiz, *Hacettepe University, Turkey*
Liangpei Zhang, *Wuhan University, China*

Table of Contents

Detailed Table of Contents

Chapter 1
    Aodhán L. Coffey, National University of Ireland Maynooth, Ireland
    Tomás E. Ward, National University of Ireland Maynooth, Ireland

Home-based therapy will need to play a huge role in the future if we are to achieve effective and cost-efficient forms of rehabilitation. Creative solutions are already being implemented by researchers with the development of revolutionary applications for healthcare leveraging commercially available technology. In this chapter, the authors endeavour to contribute to this goal, describing their ongoing contributions through the application of combined ambient and wearable sensors for gesture-based environmental control. The authors describe in detail the development of three novel systems: an autonomous sensor glove that classifies hand gestures and controls Infrared (IR)-based devices, a smart watch that recognises motion gestures to interact with Radio Frequency (RF) controlled devices, and a hybrid (sensor glove and LEAP motion controller) sensor solution for achieving high fidelity hand and finger motion capture/playback with applications for virtual ambient systems.

Chapter 2
    Alessandro Testa, Institute of High Performance Computing and Networking (ICAR), Italy
    Antonio Coronato, Institute of High Performance Computing and Networking (ICAR), Italy
    Marcello Cinque, Università di Napoli Federico II, Italy
    Giuseppe De Pietro, Institute of High Performance Computing and Networking (ICAR), Italy

The problem of failure detection in mHealth monitoring systems is becoming more critical, and the use of wireless technologies and commodity hardware/software platforms pose new challenges to their correct functioning. Remote and continuous monitoring of patients' vital signs aims to improve the quality of life of patients. Such applications, however, are particularly critical from the point of view of dependability. Wireless channels can be affected by packet loss, and cheap and wireless-enabled medical devices can exhibit wrong readings, inducing the medical staff to make wrong decisions. In this chapter, the authors present the results of a Failure Modes and Effects Analysis (FMEA) conducted to identify the dependability threats of health monitoring systems and a set of services and monitors for the assurance of high degrees of dependability to mobile health monitoring systems. Moreover, the authors describe a case study realized to detect failures at runtime.

Chapter 3

Aaron Bond, University of Ulster, UK
Kevin Curran, University of Ulster, UK

Rheumatoid arthritis affects around 1% of the world's population. Detection of the disease relies heavily on observation by physicians. The effectiveness of these kinds of tests is dependent on the ability and experience and can vary depending on the observer. This chapter aims to investigate the use of Xbox Kinect camera for monitoring in rheumatoid arthritis patients as a cost-effective and precise method of assessment. A system has been developed that implements the Kinect sensor for usage in a hand recognition and digit measurement capacity. This system performs the tasks usually completed by a physician such as digit dimension monitoring and exercise observations. With the system being designed to be portable and easy-to-use, it is an ideal solution for both the physician monitoring patients in a clinic as well as posing a possible solution for patients wishing to monitor their own condition in their homes.

Chapter 4

A. M. Middleton, National University of Ireland Maynooth, Ireland
R. P. Harte, National University of Ireland Galway, Ireland
T. E. Ward, National University of Ireland Maynooth, Ireland

This chapter reviews Ambient Assisted Living (AAL) in the context of movement-based rehabilitation. The authors analyse the need for AAL solutions and how they can overcome many of the drawbacks associated with traditional rehabilitation. They discuss the benefits and challenges of rehabilitation within the AAL paradigm and the well-known benefits that the telerehabilitation and telemedicine models have already established. The authors review the top ambient technologies in use today, detailing their advantages and shortcomings. The review focuses primarily on areas such as motion capture, serious games, and robotic rehabilitation. The authors carry out a structured search of two well-known databases to find the most recent advances and present the most interesting lines of research and development. Finally, the authors discuss the review findings and draw conclusions on the future of personalised rehabilitation within an AAL paradigm.

Chapter 5

Nigel McKelvey, University of Ulster, UK
Kevin Curran, University of Ulster, UK

Teamwork is an important aspect that should be provided by both employers and employees. This chapter proposes relating this ethos to an educational environment in order to foster encouragement among students. Students demonstrating professionalism can provide important discussion points that can help the class environment run more efficiently. When issues arise in a class, students learn not to hesitate in speaking up. Many co-workers fail to work as a team because people do not voice their opinions on certain matters. Learning how to voice that opinion can aid students/employees in progressing an assignment without hindering any other processes. This chapter outlines how to incorporate teamwork into IT educational environments in order to encourage students to engage more with the process. It also gathers information based on student, staff, and industry surveys and strives to highlight the importance of teamwork as a skill essential for IT graduates.

Chapter 6

Mobile application development is relatively new and has seen growth of late. With this rapid expansion, there are growing pains within industry, as the usual time given to the evolution of an industry to learn from past mistakes has been significantly shortened and is even going on within the currently saturated market. Because of this, inexperienced developers are attempting to design applications based on what is of yet a shady set of design principals. This is providing problems during the development process and can be seen to be stifling innovation, as many developers have yet to get a grasp on the shift between traditional software engineering and what it means to implicate these designs on a mobile device. This chapter analyses these difficulties in depth, as well as attempting to draw solutions to these problems based on development in the context of the characteristics of mobile devices.

Chapter 7

The recognition of human behaviour from sensor observations is an important area of research in smart homes and ambient intelligence. In this chapter, the authors introduce the idea of spatio-temporal footprints, which are local patterns in space and time that should be similar across repeated occurrences of the same behaviour. They discuss the spatial and temporal mapping requirements of these footprints, together with how they may be used. As possible formalisms for implementing spatio-temporal footprints, the authors discuss and evaluate probability theory, fuzzy sets, and the Dempster-Shafer theory.

Chapter 8

Over the past years, ambient intelligence has infiltrated our lives through various home applications, enabled by the decreasing size and cost of computing technology. While in transport or industry, its presence has become second nature; some areas, such as our bedroom, have remained fairly untouched. Since our bedroom hosts the beginning and end of our daily activities, it needs to assist us in the recovery and preparation of daily activities. Therefore, it holds an enormous opportunity for AI applications, which do exactly what is needed: sensibly assist the user, learn his preferences, and react to his/her mood and needs. This chapter outlines the different ways of assisting the user in his/her intelligent bedroom: ways to monitor health, improve both physical and mental recovery during the night by automatically optimising the environment, as well as automate a number of tedious tasks that reoccur at every start and end of the day.

Chapter 9

Jonathan Weinel, Glyndŵr University, UK
Stuart Cunningham, Glyndŵr University, UK
Richard Picking, Glyndŵr University, UK
Lyall Williams, Glyndŵr University, UK

This chapter considers the technological feasibility of the Holophonor, a fictional audio-visual instrument from the science fiction cartoon Futurama. Through an extended discussion of the progression of visual music towards interactive models, it was proposed that the Holophonor is an example of an ideal visual music instrument and could be constructed in the near future. This chapter recapitulates the key features of the fictional instrument. An evaluation of the technological feasibility of building a real-world version of the Holophonor is then given, with reference to existing technologies. In particular, it is proposed that the Holophonor's ability to respond to the emotional state of the performer may be facilitated by drawing on approaches from HCI and affective computing. Following this, a possible architecture for the Holophonor is proposed.

Chapter 10

David Lillis, University College Dublin, Ireland
Tadhg O'Sullivan, University College Dublin, Ireland
Thomas Holz, University College Dublin, Ireland
Conor Muldoon, University College Dublin, Ireland
Michael J. O'Grady, University College Dublin, Ireland
Gregory M. P. O'Hare, University College Dublin, Ireland

Autonomically managing energy within the home is a formidable challenge, as any solution needs to interoperate with a decidedly heterogeneous network of sensors and appliances, not just in terms of technologies and protocols but also by managing smart as well as "dumb" appliances. Furthermore, as studies have shown that simply providing energy usage feedback to homeowners is inadequate in realising long-term behavioural change, autonomic energy management has the potential to deliver concrete and lasting energy savings without the need for user interventions. However, this necessitates that such interventions be performed in an intelligent and context-aware fashion, all the while taking into account system as well as user constraints and preferences. Thus, this chapter proposes the augmentation of home area networks with autonomic computing capabilities. Such networks seek to support opportunistic decision-making pertaining to the effective energy management within the home by seamlessly integrating a range of off-the-shelf sensor technologies with a software infrastructure for deliberation, activation, and visualisation.

Chapter 11

Mobility has become an omnipresent part of our modern IT society. Alongside the general taxonomy of mobile users, terminals, sessions, and services, there are also more specialized forms of mobility. Context-Awareness Supported Application Mobility (CASAM) or "Application Mobility" is one such form that is explored in this chapter. CASAM builds on the idea of using context to move an application between different devices during its execution in order to provide relevant information and/or services. The authors use a concept-driven approach to advance mobile systems research, integrating it with a more traditional user-centric method and a case study, further exploring the concept of CASAM. To empirically situate our design work they conducted an empirical study of a home care service group serving the Swedish municipality of Skellefteå, followed by an exercise in matching the properties of the CASAM concept in relation to problems within current workflow.

Ambient Intelligence (AmI) promotes the integration of Information and Communication Technologies (ICT) in daily life in order to ease the execution of everyday tasks. In this sense, education becomes a field where AmI can improve the learning process by means of context-aware technologies. However, it is necessary to develop new tools that can be adapted to a wide range of technologies and application scenarios. Here is where Agent Technology can demonstrate its potential. This chapter presents CAFCLA, a multi-agent framework that allows developing learning applications based on the pedagogical CSCL (Computer-Supported Collaborative Learning) approach and the Ambient Intelligence paradigm. CAFCLA integrates different context-aware technologies so that learning applications designed, developed, and deployed upon it are dynamic, adaptive, and easy to use by users such as students and teachers.

Following the expansion and mass adoption of Online Social Networks, the impact upon the domain of Social Network Analysis has been a rapid evolution in terms of approach, developing sophisticated methods to capture and understand individual and community interactions. This chapter provides a comprehensive review, examining state-of-the-art Social Network Analysis research and practices, highlighting key trends within the domain. In section 1, the authors examine the growing awareness concerning data as a marketable and scientific commodity. Section 2 reviews the context of Online Social Networking, highlighting key approaches for analysing Online Social Networks. In section 3, they consider modelling motivations of networks, discussing models in line with tie formation approaches. Section 4 outlines data collection approaches along with common structural properties observed in related literature. The authors discuss future directions and emerging approaches, notably semantic social networks and social interaction analysis before conclusions are provided.

Chapter 14

Albert Brugués, University of Applied Sciences Western Switzerland (HES-SO), Switzerland
& Universitat Politècnica de Catalunya – BarcelonaTech (UPC), Spain
Josep Pegueroles, Universitat Politècnica de Catalunya – BarcelonaTech (UPC), Spain
Stefano Bromuri, University of Applied Sciences Western Switzerland (HES-SO), Switzerland
Michael Schumacher, University of Applied Sciences Western Switzerland (HES-SO), Switzerland

The development of pervasive healthcare systems consists of applying ubiquitous computing in the healthcare context. The systems developed in this research field have the goals of offering better healthcare services, promoting the well-being of the people, and assisting healthcare professionals in their tasks. The aim of the chapter is to give an overview of the main research efforts in the area of pervasive healthcare systems and to identify which are the main research challenges in this topic of research. Furthermore, the authors review the current state of the art for these kinds of systems with respect to some of the research challenges identified. In particular, the authors focus on contributions done regarding interoperability, scalability, and security of these systems.

Chapter 15

Jonathan Weinel, Glyndŵr University, UK
Stuart Cunningham, Glyndŵr University, UK
Richard Picking, Glyndŵr University, UK
Lyall Williams, Glyndŵr University, UK

This chapter discusses the progression of visual music and related audio-visual artworks through the 20th Century and considers the next steps for this field of research. The principles of visual music are described, with reference to the films of early pioneers such as John Whitney. A further exploration of the wider spectrum of subsequent work in various audio-visual art forms is then given. These include visualisations, light synthesizers, VJ performances, digital audio-visual artworks, projection mapping artworks, and interactive visual music artworks. Through consideration of visual music as a continuum of related work, the authors consider the Holophonor, a fictional audio-visual instrument, as an example of the ideal visual music instrument of the future. They conclude by proposing that a device such as the Holophonor could be constructed in the near future by utilising inter-disciplinary approaches from the fields of HCI and affective computing.

Chapter 16

A public display that is able to present the right information at the right time is a very compelling concept. However, realising or even approaching this ability to autonomously select appropriate content based on some interpretation of the surrounding social context represents a major challenge. This chapter provides an overview of the key challenges involved and an exploration of some of the main alternatives available. It also describes a novel content adaptation framework that defines the key building blocks for supporting autonomous selection of the Web sources for presentation on public displays. This framework is based on a place model that combines content suggestions expressed by multiple place visitors with those expressed by the place owner. Evaluation results have shown that a place tag cloud can provide a valuable approach to this issue and that people recognize and understand the sensitivity of the system to their demands.

Chapter 17

The Northern Ireland pre-school curriculum promotes educational development through enabling learning environments and active learning through play and exploration. Enabling learning environments are rich in books, pictures, signs, symbols, rhymes, and multimedia technology. Through play and exploration, children are engaged in activities that interest and preoccupy them. The resources that are used as a context for play have an important bearing on the depth of learning experienced by a child. According to the Early Years Foundation Stage, from age 40 months, a child's literacy and numeracy can develop rapidly with the support of a wide range of interesting materials, activities, media, and technologies (Department for Education, 2008). The aim of this project is to create the "SmartFun" literacy and numeracy E-Learning application. "SmartFun" is a fun, engaging environment to promote the early learning of letters and numbers for pre-school and primary one children.

Light therapy is applied as treatment for a variety of problems related to health and ageing, including dementia. Light therapy is administered via light boxes, light showers, and ambient bright light using ceiling-mounted luminaires. Long-term care facilities are currently installing dynamic lighting systems with the aim to improve the well-being of residents with dementia and to decrease behavioural symptoms. The aim of this chapter is to provide an overview of the application of ceiling-mounted dynamic lighting systems as a part of intelligent home automation systems found in healthcare facilities. Examples of such systems are provided and their implementation in practice is discussed. The available, though limited, knowledge has not yet been converted into widespread implementable lighting solutions, and the solutions available are often technologically unsophisticated and poorly evaluated from the perspective of end-users. New validated approaches to the design and application of ambient bright light are needed.

Claas Ahlrichs, University of Bremen, Germany
Hendrik Iben, University of Bremen, Germany
Michael Lawo, University of Bremen, Germany

In this chapter, recent research on context-aware mobile and wearable computing is described. Starting from the observation of recent developments on Smartphones and research done in wearable computing, the focus is on possibilities to unobtrusively support the use of mobile and wearable devices. There is the observation that size and form matters when dealing with these devices; multimodality concerning input and output is important and context information can be used to satisfy the requirement of unobtrusiveness. Here, Frameworks as middleware are a means to an end. Starting with an introduction on wearable computing, recent developments of Frameworks for context-aware user interface design are presented, motivating the need for future research on knowledge-based intuitive interaction design.

Preface

INTRODUCTION

The subject matter of this book is based around Contextual Computing. Contextual Computing (aka Context awareness) is the ability for a device, object, or service to be aware of not only the user's surroundings but about the user, their views, behaviours, and their interests (Deak et al., 2013). They adapt their functionality and behaviour to the user and his or her situation. To do so, they need context information about the user's environment (e.g., about different kinds of real world objects). It is about improving the quality of interaction with the user or the object. It is akin to giving the object intelligence to obtain information on the user and use it to enhance the user's experience. Contextual computing is different from the simple sensor-based applications seen on smart phones today. Instead of the user having to go and look for something like hotels, this device would already know what kind of hotel you are looking for by using the information gathered on what hotels they have picked in the past and what facilities they used (i.e. swimming pool, spa) and suggest hotels nearby based on those preferences.

Context relates to both human factors and physical environment factors. Human factors include information on the user: this is their emotional state, their habits, and interests. It also includes the user's environment (e.g. their group dynamics, social interactions, and co-location of others). It also takes into account the user's tasks (e.g. engaged tasks, general goals, and their spontaneous activity). These categories help define the person involved with the object. The physical environment factors include location (e.g. the user's absolute position, relative position) along with co-location and infrastructure (e.g. the users surrounding resources for computation, communication and task performance [Deak et al., 2014]). Physical conditions as in light, pressure, noise, and atmosphere of the area also play a role. Typically, these models contain data about real world objects and virtual information objects that are relevant at a certain location. The main purpose of a context model is to provide dynamic context data at runtime on request for different applications.

CREATING COMPELLING USER EXPERIENCES

Ambient Intelligence plays a major role in today's world. To create compelling user experience requires a great deal of research into the understanding of consumer behaviour and needs. Convenience is the number one achievement when creating a device. Less complications means it is more appealing. The key to making context work is when the design is people-centred. This will work out what they want, what their preferences are, what target market is out there, and whom to aim for. This is very important when creating and device as well as creating experiences for the customers. Context-awareness can make computing devices more responsive to individual needs and help to intelligently personalize apps and services (Deak et al., 2010). Ideally, future computers will become adapted to a person enhancing their lifestyle and helping them make important choices. There are many examples, such as by using information gathered on your location and your previous preferences of food they can guide you to a restaurant nearby which can accommodate your preferences. It can improve health and fitness by taking all the information about activities, eating habits, and giving guidance and recommendations to suit each user. The remote control of a TV could be used in contextual computing scenarios by identifying the person that is holding it and displaying options suited to that viewer (Feng & Curran, 2009). Contextual computing is aware of its environment and circumstances and can respond intelligently. A future Internet capable of embracing this concept and delivering context-aware services to users and artefacts elevates this to a persuasive sensing and acting knowledge network. This would be a network able to make decisions, actuate environmental objects, and assist users. The future of computing is all about devices that will not only be smarter than today's devices but will also be more aware of the habits and day-to-day lives of their users. Context-aware computing has not found commercial success, but as phones get smarter and tablets become popular, the company hopes users will have a device where apps disappear and become part of the gadget's intelligence (Schacter et al., 1993).

ACTIVITY RECOGNITION

A key research area within Contextual Computing is Activity Recognition, which involves combining the hard senses, which are accelerometers (measuring relative motion), location sensing, ambient light, and ambient audio, with soft senses, which include device activity, social networking actions, and calendar data. Knowing and combining these senses will help the research team reach their goal of transforming a computer into an intelligent assistant, which will intelligently guide, instruct, encourage, inform, and support the user's activities in a personal way. There are many ways this form of context awareness could be useful. Technologies involved for this awareness are wireless communication, speech recognition, image processing or recognition, motion detectors or sensors design, parallel processing, a computer network, and an operating system (Furey et al., 2011; Dreyfus, 1979).

Activity recognition aims to recognize the actions and goals of one or more users from a series of observations on the users' actions and their environmental conditions. Using hard sensing and soft sensing the device is able to carry out the activity fusion algorithm that enables the device to help the user in different situations. For example, if a person had diabetes, the device could tell if the person has taken their medication, if they are sleeping and eating, and if they are doing well. This is done through activity recognition using hard and soft senses (Kleindorfer & Martin, 1983; Agre & Chapman, 1990). The goal is to enable computers to have similar capabilities as humans for recognizing people's activities (Condell et al., 2012). If we develop computers that can reliably recognize people's various activities, we can dramatically improve the way people interact with computers, and we will have a huge impact on behaviour, social, and cognitive sciences (Carlin & Curran, 2014; Moravec, 2010; Knox et al., 2009).

BOOK OVERVIEW

In "Combined Ambient and Wearable Sensors for Gesture-Based Environmental Control in the Home," Coffey and Ward claim that home-based therapy will need to play a huge role in the future if we are to achieve effective and cost efficient forms of rehabilitation. Creative solutions are already being implemented by researchers with the development of revolutionary applications for healthcare leveraging commercially available technology. In this chapter, the authors endeavour to contribute to this goal, describing their ongoing contributions through the application of combined ambient and wearable sensors for gesture-based environmental control. The authors describe in detail the development of three novel systems: an autonomous sensor glove that classifies hand gestures and controls Infrared (IR)-based devices, a smart watch that recognises motion gestures to interact with Radio Frequency (RF) controlled devices, and a hybrid (sensor glove and LEAP motion controller) sensor solution

In "Services and Monitors for Dependability Assessment of Mobile Health Monitoring Systems," Testa, Coronato, Cinque, and De Pietro outline how the problem of failure detection and management in mHealth monitoring systems is becoming more and more critical and the use of wireless technologies and the adoption of commodity hardware/software platforms poses new challenges on the their correct functioning. Remote and continuous monitoring of patient's vital signs is the target of an emerging business market that aims both to improve the quality of life of patients and to reduce costs of national healthcare services. In this chapter, they present the results of a detailed Failure Modes and Effects Analysis (FMEA) conducted to identify the typical dependability threats of health monitoring systems and a design of a set of services and monitors for the assurance of high degrees of dependability to generic mobile health monitoring systems. Moreover, they describe a case study realized to detect failures at runtime.

Bond and Curran in "A Camera-Based System for Determining Hand Range of Movement Measurements in Rheumatoid Arthritis" discuss how rheumatoid arthritis affects around 1% of the world's population. Detection of the disease relies heavily on observation by physicians. The effectiveness of these kinds of tests is dependent on the ability and experience and can vary depending on the observer. This chapter aims to investigate the use of Xbox Kinect camera for monitoring in rheumatoid arthritis patients as a cost-effective and precise method of assessment. A system has been developed that implements the Kinect sensor for usage in a hand recognition and digit measurement capacity. This system performs the tasks usually completed by a physician such as digit dimension monitoring and exercise observations. With the system being designed to be portable and easy-to-use, it is an ideal solution for both the physician monitoring patients in a clinic as well as posing a possible solution for patients wishing to monitor their own condition in their homes.

In "Rehabilitation Systems in Ambient Assisted Living Environments," Middleton, Harte, and Ward provide a review of Ambient Assisted Living (AAL) in the context of movement-based rehabilitation. The authors analyse the need for AAL solutions and how they can overcome many of the drawbacks associated with traditional rehabilitation. They discuss the benefits and challenges of rehabilitation within the AAL paradigm and the well-known benefits that the telerehabilitation and telemedicine models have already established. The authors review the top ambient technologies in use today, detailing their advantages and shortcomings. The review focuses primarily on areas such as motion capture, serious games, and robotic rehabilitation. The authors carry out a structured search of two well-known databases to find the most recent advances and present the most interesting lines of research and development. Finally, the authors discuss the review findings and draw conclusions on the future of personalised rehabilitation within an AAL paradigm.

McKelvey and Curran in "Developing Team Work in IT Education to Foster Student Engagement" posit that Teamwork is an important aspect that should be provided by both employers and employees. This chapter proposes relating this ethos to an educational environment in order to foster encouragement among students. Students demonstrating professionalism can provide important discussion points that can help the class environment run more efficiently. When issues arise in a class, students learn not to hesitate in speaking up. Many co-workers fail to work as a team because people do not voice their opinions on certain matters. Learning how to voice that opinion can aid students/employees in progressing an assignment without hindering any other processes. This chapter outlines how to incorporate teamwork into IT educational environments in order to encourage students to engage more with the process.

In "Common Problems Faced when Developing Applications for Mobile Devices," Curran, Carlin, and McMahon discuss how mobile application development is relatively new and has seen growth of late. With this rapid expansion, there are growing pains within industry, as the usual time given to the evolution of an industry to learn from past mistakes has been significantly shortened and is even going on within the currently saturated market. Because of this, inexperienced developers are attempting to design applications based on what is of yet a shady set of design principals. This is providing problems during the development process and can be seen to be stifling innovation, as many developers have yet to get a grasp on the shift between traditional software engineering and what it means to implicate these designs on a mobile device. An outline is given of the possible benefits and drawbacks when creating a native, Web-based, or hybrid application for a mobile device, and potential revenue streams and business models that developers can use to monetize their applications are also discussed.

In "Human Behaviour Recognition in Ambient Intelligent Environments," Guesgen and Marsland discuss how the recognition of human behaviour from sensor observations is an important area of research in smart homes and ambient intelligence. In this chapter, the authors introduce the idea of spatio-temporal footprints, which are local patterns in space and time that should be similar across repeated occurrences of the same behaviour. They discuss the spatial and temporal mapping requirements of these footprints, together with how they may be used. As possible formalisms for implementing spatio-temporal footprints, the authors discuss and evaluate probability theory, fuzzy sets, and the Dempster-Shafer theory.

In "Ambient Intelligence in the Bedroom," Van Deun, Willemen, Verhaert, Haex, Van Huffel, and Vander Sloten discuss how Over the past years, ambient intelligence has infiltrated our lives through various home applications, enabled by the decreasing size and cost of computing technology. While in transport or industry, its presence has become second nature; some areas, such as our bedroom, have remained fairly untouched. Since our bedroom hosts the beginning and end of our daily activities, it needs to assist us in the recovery and preparation of daily activities. Therefore, it holds an enormous opportunity for AI applications, which do exactly what is needed: sensibly assist the user, learn his preferences, and react to his/her mood and needs. This chapter outlines the different ways of assisting the user in his/her intelligent bedroom: ways to monitor health, improve both physical and mental recovery during the night by automatically optimising the environment, as well as automate a number of tedious tasks that reoccur at every start and end of the day.

Weinel, Cunningham, Picking, and Williams in "Holophonor: Designing the Visual Music Instruments of the Future" consider the technological feasibility of the Holophonor, a fictional audio-visual instrument from the science fiction cartoon *Futurama*. In a previous book chapter ("Holophonor: On the Future Technology of Visual Music"), the Holophonor was used as a means through which to consider the next steps for visual music research. It was proposed that the Holophonor exhibits many of the ideal qualities that should be sought in a visual music performance instrument. An evaluation of the technological feasibility of building a real-world version of the Holophonor is then given, with reference to existing technologies.

In "Smart Home Energy Management," Lillis, O'Sullivan, Holz, Muldoon, O'Grady, and O'Hare outline how autonomically managing energy within the home is a formidable challenge, as any solution needs to interoperate with a decidedly heterogeneous network of sensors and appliances, not just in terms of technologies and protocols but also by managing smart as well as "dumb" appliances. Furthermore, as studies have shown that simply providing energy usage feedback to homeowners is inadequate in realising long-term behavioural change, autonomic energy management has the potential to deliver concrete and lasting energy savings without the need for user interventions. However, this necessitates that such interventions be performed in an intelligent and context-aware fashion, all the while taking into account system as well as user constraints and preferences. Thus, this chapter proposes the augmentation of home area networks with autonomic computing capabilities.

In "Application Mobility: Concept and Design," Johansson and Wiberg discuss how mobility has become an omnipresent part of our modern IT society. Alongside the general taxonomy of mobile users, terminals, sessions, and services, there are also more specialized forms of mobility. Context-Awareness Supported Application Mobility (CASAM) or "Application Mobility" is one such form that is explored in this chapter. CASAM builds on the idea of using context to move an application between different devices during its execution in order to provide relevant information and/or services. The authors use a concept-driven approach to advance mobile systems research, integrating it with a more traditional user-centric method and a case study, further exploring the concept of CASAM.

In "CAFCLA: A Framework to Design, Develop, and Deploy AmI-Based Collaborative Learning Applications," Garcíaa, Alonsoa, Tapiaa, and Corchadoa discuss how Ambient Intelligence (AmI) promotes the integration of Information and Communication Technologies (ICT) in daily life in order to ease the execution of everyday tasks. In this sense, education becomes a field where AmI can improve the learning process by means of context-aware technologies. However, it is necessary to develop new tools that can be adapted to a wide range of technologies and application scenarios. Here is where Agent Technology can demonstrate its potential. This chapter presents CAFCLA, a multi-agent framework that allows developing learning applications based on the pedagogical CSCL (Computer-Supported Collaborative Learning) approach and the Ambient Intelligence paradigm.

In "Contemporary Gold Rush or Scientific Advancement: A Review of Social Network Analysis Approaches and their Impact," Quinn, Chen, and Mulvenna outline following the expansion and mass adoption of Online Social Networks, the impact upon the domain of Social Network Analysis has been a rapid evolution in terms of approach, developing sophisticated methods to capture and understand individual and community interactions. This chapter provides a comprehensive review, examining state-of-the-art Social Network Analysis research and practices, highlighting key trends within the domain. In section 1, the authors examine the growing awareness concerning data as a marketable and scientific commodity. Section 2 reviews the context of Online Social Networking, highlighting key approaches for analysing Online Social Networks. In section 3, they consider modelling motivations of networks, discussing models in line with tie formation approaches. Section 4 outlines data collection approaches along with common structural properties observed in related literature. The authors discuss future directions and emerging approaches, notably semantic social networks and social interaction analysis before conclusions are provided.

In "Current Trends in Interoperability, Scalability, and Security of Pervasive Healthcare Systems," Brugués, Pegueroles, Bromuri, and Schumacher discuss how *the development of pervasive healthcare systems consists of applying ubiquitous computing in the healthcare context. The systems developed in this research field have the goals of offering better healthcare services, promoting the well-being of the people, and assisting healthcare professionals in their tasks. The aim of the chapter is to give an overview of the main research efforts in the area of pervasive healthcare systems and to identify which are the main research challenges in this topic of research.*

Weinel, Cunningham, Picking, and Williams, in "Holophonor: On the Future Technology of Visual Music," discuss the progression of visual music and related audio-visual artworks through the 20th Century and considers the next steps for this field of research. The principles of visual music are described, with reference to the films of early pioneers such as John Whitney. A further exploration of the wider spectrum of subsequent work in various audio-visual art forms is then given. These include visualisations, light synthesizers, VJ performances, digital audio-visual artworks, projection mapping artworks, and interactive visual music artworks. Through consideration of visual music as a continuum of related work, the authors consider the Holophonor, a fictional audio-visual instrument, as an example of the ideal visual music instrument of the future.

In "Smart Displays in Ambient Intelligence Environments," Ribeiro and José outline that a public display that is able to present the right information at the right time is a very compelling concept. However, realising or even approaching this ability to autonomously select appropriate content based on some interpretation of the surrounding social context represents a major challenge. This chapter provides an overview of the key challenges involved and an exploration of some of the main alternatives available. It also describes a novel content adaptation framework that defines the key building blocks for supporting autonomous selection of the Web sources for presentation on public displays. This framework is based on a place model that combines content suggestions expressed by multiple place visitors with those expressed by the place owner.

In "A Literacy and Numeracy E-Learning Mobile Application for Pre-Schoolers," McCarroll and Curran discuss how the Northern Ireland pre-school curriculum promotes educational development through enabling learning environments and active learning through play and exploration. Enabling learning environments are rich in books, pictures, signs, symbols, rhymes, and multimedia technology. Through play and exploration, children are engaged in activities that interest and preoccupy them. This chapter outlines a "SmartFun" literacy and numeracy E-Learning application. "SmartFun" is a fun, engaging environment to promote the early learning of letters and numbers for pre-school and primary one children.

In "Light Therapy in Smart Healthcare Facilities for Older Adults: An Overview," van Hoof, Aarts, Westerlaken, Schrader, Wouters, Weffers, and Aries discuss how light therapy is applied as treatment for a variety of problems related to health and ageing, including dementia. Light therapy is administered via light boxes, light showers, and ambient bright light using ceiling-mounted luminaires. Long-term care facilities are currently installing dynamic lighting systems with the aim to improve the well-being of residents with dementia and to decrease behavioural symptoms. The aim of this chapter is to provide an overview of the application of ceiling-mounted dynamic lighting systems as a part of intelligent home automation systems found in healthcare facilities. Examples of such systems are provided and their implementation in practice is discussed.

In "Context-Aware Mobile and Wearable Device Interfaces," Ahlrichs, Iben, and Lawo begin by providing an overview of recent research on context aware mobile and wearable computing. Starting from the observation of recent developments on Smartphones and research done in wearable computing, the focus is on possibilities to unobtrusively support the use of mobile and wearable devices. There is the observation that size and form matters when dealing with these devices; multimodality concerning input and output is important, and context information can be used to satisfy the requirement of unobtrusiveness.

CONCLUSION

We are not yet at the stage where wearable computers are able to take the place of our mobile phones, but as the miniaturisation of computer chips and components continues, we are getting very close to mass consumer products on the market. Meanwhile, curved screens allow us to embed mobiles into clothing and furniture, ushering in a ubiquitous world of communications. Ultimately, that appears to be how the industry views market demand: for devices that "disappear" into our surroundings and just "know" what to do in order to make our lives more bearable, more productive, and more creative. It may be that is what we actually want; it may be that advances in technology lead companies to develop solutions that entice us into believing it is what we want. Either way, why carry it when you can wear it? Sounds simple when put like that.

TARGET AUDIENCE

The target audience is under-graduate and post-graduate students and researchers in an IT-related discipline.

Kevin Curran
University of Ulster, UK

REFERENCES

Agre, P., & Chapman, D. (1990). What are plans for? *Robotics and Autonomous Systems*, 6(1), 17–34. doi:10.1016/S0921-8890(05)80026-0

Carlin, S., & Curran, K. (2014). An active low cost mesh networking indoor tracking system. *International Journal of Ambient Computing and Intelligence*, 6(1), 45–79. doi:10.4018/ijaci.2014010104

Condell, J., Curran, K., Quigley, T., Gardiner, P., McNeill, M., & Winder, J. et al. (2012). Finger movement measurements in arthritic patients using wearable sensor enabled gloves. *International Journal of Human Factors Modelling and Simulation*, 2(4), 276–292. doi:10.1504/IJHFMS.2011.045000

Deak, G., Curran, K., & Condell, J. (2010). Evaluation of smoothing algorithms for a RSSI-based device-free passive localisation. In *Advances in intelligent and soft computing* (pp. 59–66). Berlin: Springer-Verlag; doi:10.1007/978-3-642-16295-4_52

Deak, G., Curran, K., Condell, J., Bessis, N., & Asimakopoulou, E. (2013). IoT (internet of things) and DfPL (device-free passive localisation) in a disaster management scenario. *Simulation Modelling Practice and Theory*, 34(3), 86–96. doi:10.1016/j.simpat.2013.03.005

Deak, G., Curran, K., Condell, J., & Deak, D. (2014). Detection of multi-occupancy using device-free passive localisation (DfPL). *IET Wireless Sensor Systems*, 4(2), 1–8. doi:10.1049/iet-wss.2013.0031

Dreyfus, R. (1979). *What computers can't do: The limits of artificial intelligence.* New York: Harper Colophon Books.

Feng, W., & Curran, K. (2009). Enhanced WiFi location sensing with activity data. In *Proceedings of Intel Conference 2009 - Intel European Research and Innovation Conference 2009*. Intel Ireland Campus.

Furey, E., Curran, K., & McKevitt, P. (2011). Probabilistic indoor human movement modeling to aid first responders. *Journal of Ambient Intelligence and Humanized Computing, Ambient Intelligence, and Humanized Computing, 3*(2), 20–28. doi:10.1007/s12652-012-0112-4

Kleindorfer, J., & Martin, J. (1983). The iron cage, single vision, and Newton's sleep. *Research in Philosophy and Technology, 3*, 127–142.

Knox, J., Condell, J., & Curran, K. (2009). An ultra wideband location positioning system. In *Proceedings of TAROS 2009 - The 10th International Towards Autonomous Robotic Systems (TAROS) Conference*. University of Ulster.

Moravec, H. (2003). Robots, after all. *Communications of the ACM, 46*(10), 56–68. doi:10.1145/944217.944218

Schacter, J., Chiu, C., & Ochsner, K. (1993). Implicit memory: A selective review. *Annual Review of Neuroscience, 16*(1), 159–182. doi:10.1146/annurev.ne.16.030193.001111 PMID:8460889

Chapter 1
Combined Ambient and Wearable Sensors for Gesture–Based Environmental Control in the Home

Aodhán L. Coffey
National University of Ireland Maynooth, Ireland

Tomás E. Ward
National University of Ireland Maynooth, Ireland

ABSTRACT

Home-based therapy will need to play a huge role in the future if we are to achieve effective and cost-efficient forms of rehabilitation. Creative solutions are already being implemented by researchers with the development of revolutionary applications for healthcare leveraging commercially available technology. In this chapter, the authors endeavour to contribute to this goal, describing their ongoing contributions through the application of combined ambient and wearable sensors for gesture-based environmental control. The authors describe in detail the development of three novel systems: an autonomous sensor glove that classifies hand gestures and controls Infrared (IR)-based devices, a smart watch that recognises motion gestures to interact with Radio Frequency (RF) controlled devices, and a hybrid (sensor glove and LEAP motion controller) sensor solution for achieving high fidelity hand and finger motion capture/playback with applications for virtual ambient systems.

INTRODUCTION

Computing technology is pervasive, each decade bringing smarter, cheaper and more powerful devices to the market place. It may be hard to believe but by today's standards the computer NASA used to put a man on the moon is no more powerful than some pocket calculators (Hall, 1996). It is estimated that there are approximately 2 billion personal computers (PCs) actively in use as of 2014, with countless more office based and autonomous systems in use world-wide (Gartner, 2012). Indeed, computers have become much more than simple tools of labour and now play

DOI: 10.4018/978-1-4666-7284-0.ch001

Copyright © 2015, IGI Global. Copying or distributing in print or electronic forms without written permission of IGI Global is prohibited.

an active role in how we live, socialise and even identify ourselves. The internet has created a global connectedness of unimaginable proportion allowing us to instinctively interact with systems, purblind to the reality that such information might be stored on a machine half a world away. The last decade saw the introduction of new technology that challenged the very way in which we conventionally use computers, with innovations such as touch screens and voice/gestured based control. Today, powerful computers exist all around us and in the most unexpected places; smart watches, smart phones and now even glasses are packed with tiny advanced sensors that can tell us everything from our global geographical position to where the nearest bus stop is. Subsequently, human computer interaction (HCI) has become a major field of study in computer science, with researchers attempting to answer the question of how best to interact with these emerging systems. A key vision for HCI is the development of ambient intelligence environments, that is, immersive electronic environments that are sensitive and responsive to the presence of people.

From the perspective of healthcare, there is great potential to utilise this emerging technology to improve the efficacy of home-based rehabilitation. While not applicable to all illnesses, this technology can play a major role in assistive healthcare, offering enhancements to unsupervised forms of physical therapy in the comfort of a patient's own home. We live in a time of unprecedented global aging. The number of people worldwide age 60 and older is estimated at just over 810 million as of 2012, by 2050 this figure is projected to reach 2 billion (Kinsella K., 2009). In other words, in just over four decades the proportion of older people in the world will double from 7% to 14%. This rapid aging is a testament to development. People are living longer because of better nutrition, sanitation, medical advances, health care, education and economic well-being. However, an aging population is also a call for concern. Longer life doesn't necessarily

coincide with quality of life; in fact many chronic illnesses such as cardiovascular diseases, diabetes, cancer, epilepsy and respiratory disease have age dependent risk factors. The truth is healthcare systems internationally are struggling to meet the demand of both new and recurring patients. This is evident from the fact that health spending is rising faster than incomes in most developed countries (Kea, Saksena, & Holly, 2011). As a direct consequence, governments and healthcare agencies are focusing on technology as a means to cut costs and improve quality of care.

Home based therapy will need to play a huge role in the future if we are to achieve effective and cost efficient forms of rehabilitation. Creative solutions are already being implemented by researchers with the development of revolutionary applications for healthcare leveraging commercially available technology. In this work we endeavour to contribute to this goal, describing our ongoing contributions through the application of combined ambient and wearable sensors for gesture-based environmental control. We describe in detail the development of three novel systems; an autonomous sensor glove that classifies hand gestures and controls infrared (IR) based devices, a smart watch that recognises motion gestures to interact with radio frequency (RF) controlled devices, and a hybrid (sensor glove and LEAP motion controller) sensor solution for achieving high fidelity hand and finger motion capture/playback with applications for virtual ambient systems.

A NOVEL SENSOR GLOVE FOR GESTURE BASED CONTROL OF INFRARED BASED DEVICES

Body language (kinesics) and in particular hand gestures play a significant role in the efficacy of human communication, providing reinforcing visual imagery of what we are trying to convey verbally. Naturally then the use of hand gestures could also provide an attractive alternative for interacting with computer systems (Murthy & Jadon, 2009). Sensor gloves exemplify the aspiration of developing low cost, immersive human-computer input devices and subsequently many novel sensor gloves have been developed with a wide range of applications. Sensor gloves have been designed as interfaces for virtual reality (Guo & Song, 2008) and gaming (Liarokapis, Macan, Malone, Rebolledo-Mendez, & De Freitas, 2009), as a tool for learning sign language (Ellis & Barca, 2012) and even as an experimental tool for developing music through motion capture (Costantini, Saggio, & Todisco, 2010). There has also been keen interest in sensor gloves from a healthcare perspective, with many researchers realising the potential for non-invasive hand impartment assessment (Micera, et al., 2003), remote monitoring of the usage of a paretic hand (Simonea, N., Luo, Jia, & Kamper, 2007) and the ability to add context to otherwise mundane and tedious physical exercise programs (Jack, et al., 2001).

We developed an innovative sensor glove with a novel approach that compliments conventional physical therapy programs for people recovery from movement weakness after stroke. Our design couples therapeutic exercises with environmental control, through a system incorporating infrared (IR) communication technology and sensor based gesture recognition. The glove system aspires to promote the repetitiveness deemed necessary for encouraging motor learning, through the practise of functional movement synonymous to activities of daily living. Essentially, the sensor glove system can be programmed with a set of pre-recorded hand gestures and IR codes. Each gesture is paired to a unique IR code that is transmitted on recognition of that gesture. For example, one hand gesture might trigger an IR code that turns on a television; another hand gesture might change the channel.

Hardware Design and Development

Most sensor glove are designed as novel peripheral input devices only doing the most minimal, if any,

on-board computation themselves and instead rely entirely on a host machine (PC) to make use of the acquired sensor data. The design novelty of our sensor glove is that it functions autonomously, acquiring sensor data, classifying hand gestures and wirelessly transmitting control signals and or sensor data using on board hardware, independent of a host machine. To accomplish this, the glove incorporates a powerful micro-processor, five independent sensors, a high density light weight battery power supply and two independent wireless communication systems (IR and Bluetooth). Such design considerations allow our sensor glove to be used as an agile unconstrained controller, freeing the user from the typical confined and tethered user interaction space of a desktop. The sensor glove system was designed around a standard, knitted fabric cotton glove. We chose cotton as it is comfortable, cheap and pliable, being easy to attach sensors and other electronic components to. It was also designed with adjustability in mind as the chosen cotton fabric is inherently elastic allowing it to stretch to accommodate different size hands. The flex sensors are strategically fixed to the glove only at the tip of the finger, with the remaining body of the sensor guided by elastic through holes at each of the finger's phalanges. This mechanism allows the rigid flex sensors to tightly following the curvature of the fingers as they bend without compressing and opposing movement, see Figure 1.

The sensor used for acquiring finger position is a bi-directional flexible bend sensor (Flex Sensor – Spectra symbol Corp, Salt Lake City, USA). This sensor exhibits a varying resistance that is proportional to its bend, with a nominal resistance of 10k ohms at rest and its resistance decreasing with the angle through which it is bent. In order to sample and subsequently quantify this physical change property of the sensor we need to convert the resistance into a varying voltage. This is accomplished by incorporating the sensor into a standard voltage divider configuration, with the output going to an analog-to-digital converter

Figure 1. Sensor glove

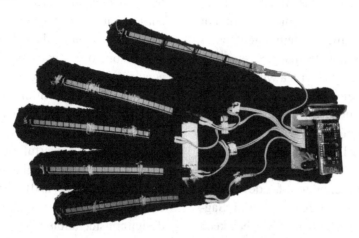

(ADC), see Figure 2. A voltage divider circuit and ADC channel are required for each flex sensor, totalling 5 for our design.

In order to remove the dependency on an external PC, we based our system around a powerful embedded microprocessor, the PIC16f688 (PIC16f series, 8 bit microcontroller, Microchip corps, USA). We selected this microprocessor as it has the necessary functionality and additional internal hardware required for our sensor glove design requirements. That is, five dedicated (ADC) channels, three digital I/O pins, one of which has pulse width modulation (PWM) support required by the IR LED and the remaining two having uni-

versal asynchronous receiver/transmitter (UART) support as required for the embedded Bluetooth module (HC-05 Bluetooth Module - Guangzhou HC Information Technology Co., Ltd.). The chosen PIC16f688 is a suitable microcontroller meeting all the above requirements; however an alternative equivalent microcontroller would suffice. The entire system is powered by 5 VDC, using a 3.3 V DC lithium polymer battery and a step-up DC to DC converter (NCP1402-5V, ON Semiconductor Components Industries, USA). The complete hardware schematics are shown in Figure 3. We advocate the replication of our system.

Finger Position Estimation

Though the human hand is extremely complex, natural gestures made with the fingers are for the most part simple and are well captured by the flexion and extension of the fingers. Hence lateral movement (movement along the axial line) of the fingers can be ignored. To estimate finger position, a two stage calibration method is used to determine the maximum and minimum sensor values (X_{max}, X_{min}) for each flex sensor, corresponding to the angles ($\partial_{max}, \partial_{min}$) of the open hand and closed fist, respectively. A linear mapping system is then used to map the intermediate

Figure 2. Flex Sensor voltage divider configuration

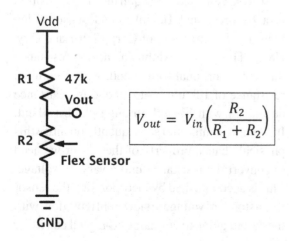

$$V_{out} = V_{in}\left(\frac{R_2}{R_1 + R_2}\right)$$

Figure 3. Electronic schematics for glove system

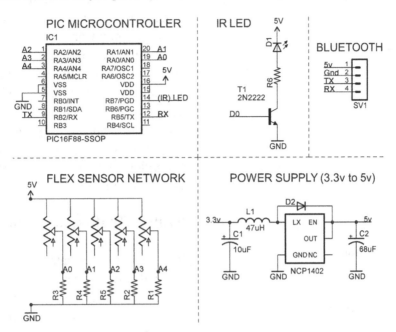

flex sensor value $x_i(t)$ for each of the five flex sensors ($x_1,\ x_2,\ x_3,\ x_4,\ x_5$) to its corresponding finger's angle of flexion $\partial_i\left(t\right)$, for each of the five fingers ($\partial_{little},\partial_{ring},\partial_{middle},\partial_{index},\partial_{thumb}$).

$$\partial\left(t\right) = \partial_{min} + \left[\frac{\left(\partial_{max}-\partial_{min}\right)}{\left(x_{max}-x_{min}\right)}\right]\left[x\left(t\right)-x_{min}\right]$$

(1.1)

Gesture Recognition

Hand gestures are recognised in real time using a simple template matching technique that compares attempted gestures against a table of pre-defined gestures stored in memory on the microcontroller. To ensure a detected gesture was actively attempted by the user and not just part of some natural movement (such as arm movement while walking) each gesture is encapsulated by a proceeding and succeeding static pose that initialises the gesture checking routine, see Figure 4.

A pose P is defined as,

$$P(t) = \left[x_0\left(t\right), x_1\left(t\right), x_2\left(t\right), x_3\left(t\right), x_4\left(t\right)\right] \quad (1.2)$$

where X_i is the value of the *i*-th flex sensor at time *t*.

The microcontroller continuously monitors incoming sensor values, creating pose candidates and searching for the framing pose which at the start of a gesture is considered the "proceeding pose" and at the end of a gesture is termed a "succeeding pose". When it finds a match corresponding to the proceeding pose, it then starts buffering the next (*N*) consecutive poses until either a timeout occurs or the succeeding pose is captured. If a timeout is detected, the sensor glove simply dumps the captured poses and returns to its previous routine. If instead the succeeding pose is detected within the time limit, the microcontroller stops buffering poses and proceeds to check each of the buffered poses against a gesture lookup table. An intermediate pose $\left(p\right)$ matches one of the pre-defined poses (g) if the sum of the Euclidean distance (D) between each element of those poses is less than or equal to some error threshold E, (Equation 1.3).

$$D = \sum_{i=0}^{5} \sqrt{\left(g_i - p_i\right)^2} \qquad (1.3)$$

$$f\left(D\right) = \begin{cases} 1, & D \geq E \\ 0, & otherwise \end{cases}$$

where,

f(D) is a matching function.

Transmitting (IR) Codes

We conducted a series of tests with healthy users to validate the operation of our system. This included the programming of a series of unique hand gestures and commands which were uploaded to the sensor glove. Users were given the glove and asked to attempt each of the gestures in order to control a TV. The preliminary results were promising, with users finding the glove system intuitive, responsive and fun to use, with little or no training requirements other than learning the relationship between gestures and the corresponding control commands. Users also reported that the glove was comfortable, easy to don and doff and that using it as was an enjoyable experience. These results are promising, as the devices usefulness as a healthcare apparatus is contingent on practicality of use and gratification of use. The next step in validating our device will be to conduct a pilot study with both patients and therapists, to investigate the practicality and usefulness of our system as a tool for promoting exercise and hence improving adherence to physical therapy routines for patient with neurological movement disorders.

System Testing and Validation

In the case where a match is found between an attempted pose and a pre-defined pose, the index of that pose in the gesture lookup table will be used to retrieve its paired IR code, from an additional table. IR codes are transmitted using pulse distance encoding following the NEC infrared transmission protocol (Semiconductors, 2013). The NEC protocol was chosen as it widely used by commercial IR products and for which command codes are freely available. This design consideration allows our device to interact with many commercial based home entertainment systems, including (TV's, DVD players and radio/CD players).

Figure 4. (a) proceeding pose, (b) attempted pose and (c) succeeding pose

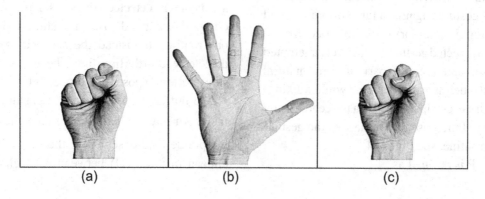

GESTURE BASED ENVIORNMENT CONTROL USING A SMART WATCH (CHRONOS EZ430)

Wearable sensors systems endeavour to create a harmonious medium through which humans and computers systems can interact, in an intuitive and instinctive manner. Gestures can communicate a complex variety of thoughts and emotions. A simple wave of the hand can be either dismissive or affable depending on how it is cast. Given the wealth of information that can be conveyed in such a natural and intuitive manner, gestures provide an attractive alternative to cumbersome interface devices for human-computer interactions. However, a pragmatic solution for (HCI) that is suitable for everyday interactions should be inconspicuous when not needed yet prominent and highly accessible when required. Our previously described sensor glove is a good solution for interactions within the comfort of one's home but it is too delicate for outdoor excursions and might bring unsolicited attention due to its unusual nature. Aware of this problem, companies have started to design more fashionable technology, attempting to disguise the technology in contemporary designs, such as bracelets (apple's iBangle), necklaces (CSR's pendant) and watches (pebble's smart watch). While all of these devices have great potential, the smart watch is of particular interest for the application of (HCI). While early models were little more than smartphone accessories, offering convenient notifications at a glance, modern smart watches are the epitome of wearable technology, boasting powerful embedded computers and an arsenal of sensors. Smart watches are located in a prime position to retrieve valuable position and acceleration data from a user's hand movements. They are fashionable, discreet and powerful with great potential as a ubiquitous controller for smart environments.

In this work we endeavour to contribute to the practicality of the smart watch as a device for advanced human-computer interactions. We describe our contributions towards implementing gesture-based environmental control of radio frequency (RF) controlled devices (i.e. remote controlled lighting systems, gates, garage doors etc.) using Texas Instruments' Chronos ez430 watch. Towards realising this goal we describe an easily replicated, open-source solution for capturing RF signals and a procedure for imitating such signals with the Chronos watch. We describe our own custom designed remote RF switch, capable of wirelessly switching (on/off) low current appliances. And we discuss the implementations of gesture recognition on the platform.

Hardware: Chronos eZ430 Watch

The eZ430 Chronos watch (Texas Instruments Incorporated, USA) is a highly integrated, wireless development system posing as a watch. It incorporates an on-board 3-axis accelerometer, pressure sensor, temperature sensor, battery voltage sensor, 96-segment LCD and a sub Giga Hz wireless transceiver, see Figure 5. In addition, the device can also be paired wirelessly with external sensors including heart rate monitors and pedometers.

Given the high density of its functionality in a compact fashionable watch, the eZ430-Chronos has great potential as a tool for ambient healthcare monitoring or equally as an interactive wireless controller for ubiquitous computing systems. The watch comes with a USB based wireless access point allowing it to be connected directly to a PC. Out of the box software allows you to stream and plot accelerometer data in real-time, emulate user defined keyboard shortcuts using the watch buttons, wireless control PowerPoint presentations and motion-based control of the mouse. However, the real potential of the Chronos watch lies in its programmability, allowing developers to build custom wireless smart applications. To accommodate this, the Chronos watch is complete with a reference design and a well-documented API. Not surprisingly, there has been much interest in the watch from tech enthusiasts and researchers alike with many interesting applications being developed. One project looked at using the Chronos as a novel computer-input device that acts as a high-precision mouse with unique snap-to-click technology (Toole, King, & He, 2011). A series of office based "stress relief" games have been developed using the Chronos' accelerometers to discern movement patterns from the wearer and to augment this motion onto mini games (Qian & Cui, 2010), (Lin, Yuen, & Barth, 2008). There has also been considerable research applications developed for the watch. (Nordin A., Chee, Addi, & Che Harun, 2011) describes a wireless health monitoring system, developed in LabVIEW which is able to transmit and receive a patient's body signal wirelessly to an EZ430-Chronos watch. (Uslu, Altun, & Baydere, 2011) describe a technique for indoor human activity monitoring and position tracking. Bersch et al described a novel fall detection technique for the elderly (Rakhecha & Hsu, 2013).

It is also worth highlighting the difference in functionality between the glove system previously described and the wrist mounted sensor technology represented by the Chronos. The glove system allows patterns of finger position and their sequences to constitute a gesture. The Chronos is different in a complementary way as it provides an inertial sensor solution that allows the acceleration of the lower arm and the wrist in particular to be monitored as a source of gesture for environmental control. The combination of both technologies provides a very comprehensive wearable solution for rich gesture driven control in a smart environment. The rehabilitation potential of such technology especially in terms of the occupational therapist perspective is clearly significant and worth pursuing much further.

RF Signal Capturing

The use of the radio frequency spectrum is highly regulated in most countries with strict guidelines governing there usage. A specific band called the industrial, scientific and medical (ISM) radio band is reserved internationally for such purposes. Despite the intent of the original allocations, the fastest-growing uses of these bands have been for short-range, low power communications systems and as such specific portions of the (ISM) are dedicated license-free. The pertaining frequencies are dependent on geographic location. Accordingly, there are three separate versions of the Chronos watch which differ only in their radio's operation frequency (433,868 and 916) Mhz respectively.

Figure 5. eZ430-Chrono watch

CC430F6137 MCU

<1GHz RF
433, 868 & 915 MHz

2 Wire JTAG Access

96 segment LCD

Buzzer

3-Axis VTI Accelerometer

VTI Pressure & Altitude Sensor

Temperature Sensor

Voltage & Battery Sensor

CR2032 Battery

For the same reason, consumer devices utilising RF communication such as automotive, alarm systems, home automation, and temperature sensors are also restricted to one of these three bands. This greatly reduces the complexity of designing an RF signal analyser. Furthermore, while there are many modulation techniques available that could be used in the transmission of signals, in practise most commercial products use a form of modulation called amplitude-shift keying (ASK) (Rouphael, 2008). Amplitude-shift keying (ASK) is a technique that represents digital data as variations in the amplitude of a carrier wave. While there are alternative modulation techniques, (ASK) seems to be the most frequently used in commercial products, as it is the simplest and most cost effective form of modulation for low powered, short distance devices. An illustration of (ASK) is given by Figure 6.

Given the limitations discussed above, a simple single frequency RF capture device can be built using a standard off the shelf OOK/ASK receiver module, such as the RF Link receiver (RWS-371, Wenshing Electronics CO., LTD.). The frequency of which should be selected depending on your region.

A simple circuit can be built only requiring the addition of a 2.5mm mono jack plug, a resistor and a 5 VDC power supply. Power can be obtained from any suitable source (USB, battery, etc.) however for completeness we have included a simple 5 volt regulator (LM7805, Fairchild Semiconductors) and a nine volt battery in our schematic, see Figure 7.

A simple length of single core wire will suffice as an antenna, measured to ¼ the wavelength of the receiver frequency. The wavelength (λ can be calculated using equation 2.1.

$$\lambda = \frac{c}{f} \qquad (2.1)$$

where, c = speed of light f = signal frequency in Mhz.

The above device can be plugged into any standard PC sound card in order to digitalised and record the resulting demodulated signal. This implementation leverages the sound cards high speed analogue to digital (ADC) sampling rate (e.g. 48,000 Hz), guaranteed to be higher than the demodulated information signal. Any freeware audio software can be used to record and analysis

Figure 6. OOK/ASK modulation scheme

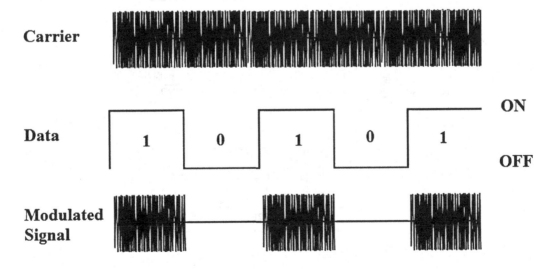

the resulting data. We recommend Audacity, as it is a powerful, open-source and freely available software tool for sound recording and editing. Using Audacity we can easily capture our remote controls signal, hone in on the information and extract the RF codes. The resulting signal will be displayed by audacity in Transistor-transistor logic (TTL) format which can be converted directly to binary (visually), see Figure 8.

Emulating Captured Codes with the Chronos Watch

In order to emulate the captured signal with the Chronos watch we first need to configure the watches C11011 radio to match the characteristics of our signal. This is a tedious process requiring the configuration of over 50 individual registers on the eZ430 microcontroller. Fortunately, there is a software suite (TI Smart RF Studio) which can generate the necessary configuration values for us once we know some vital information about the signal, i.e. its baud rate and frequency.

The signals bit rate (b_r) is easily calculated using equation (2.2), knowing the sampling fre-

quency used in Audacity (f_s) and the number (N) of sampled points contained in a single TTL bit of the signal. From this, the baud rate can then be calculated using equation (2.3).

$$b_r = \frac{N}{f_s} \qquad (2.2)$$

$$Baud\,rate = \frac{1}{b_r} \qquad (2.3)$$

The final piece of information needed in order to emulate the captured signal is to rewrite the signal in byte format. As the Chronos watch's application programming interface (API) describes a function for transmitting data which takes a sequence of bytes as its argument. To obtain this format we first convert the TTL signal into its binary equivalent, partition the resulting binary sequence into bytes (8 bit segments) adding additional zero's as needed (i.e. if our total signal length is not divisible by 8).

Figure 7. Wireless capture device

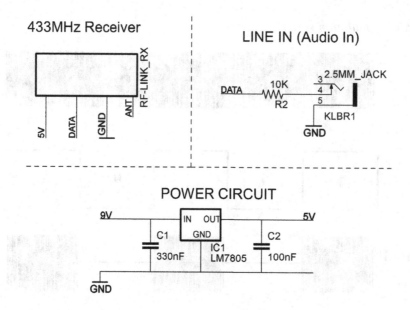

Design of a Custom Wireless Switch

This section describes the development of a custom designed remote switch that can control low current, 240V appliances, for example a standard desktop lamp. While there are commercial products available for this purpose we instead developed our own, aspiring to create an affordable, adaptable solution that could be used as a flexible platform for further research and development. The remote switch is based around a miniature, 5 VDC double coil latching relay (NEC EA2-5TNFG, NEC corp. Tokyo, Japan). Incoming RF signals are detected and demodulated using an ASK OOK 434Mhz receiver module (ET-RXB-10, EEant Technology CO., LTD, china). The resulting extracted information signal is passed to an embedded microcontroller, the PIC16f688 (PIC16fxxxx, Microchip technology Inc.) which buffers the incoming data, parses it and extracts the information signal. See Figure 9.

We developed our own simple asynchronous transmission protocol for use with our RF switch, consisting of 3 bytes, described by Figure 10. With this configuration we can communication with 32 (i.e. 2^5) uniquely addressed switches, issuing 8 (2^3) unique commands. This protocol is flexible and can easily be scaled to accommodate additional devices and commands. Additionally, error detection bits could also be incorporated in order to reduce transmission errors and encryp-

tion could also be incorporated. A suitable baud rate was selected to be 1200 bps for our device, as this rate is easily replicable with the Chronos watch radio.

After an information signal is extracted, the PIC microcontroller checks if the address matches its own address (configured using address switches, see Figure 9). If the addresses match then the corresponding command code is looked up in a table stored in memory. For example, the command '001' might set the relay to its open state, command '010' might set the relay to its closed state and command '011' might instruct a delay of 25 seconds before toggling the relays current state.

Gesture Recognition

We implemented a crude mechanism for recognising two basic gestures using the Chronos watch. The first involves detecting a 'double clap' gesture which corresponds to two sequential sharp spikes in the accelerometer data across all three axes, within a very short time window. The second involves detecting a 'wave' gesture which is characterised by the repeated reversal of the sign of the accelerometer sensor reading across the axis orthogonal to the watch face.

Figure 8. Example of an RF signal captured using Audacity and its superimposed binary representation

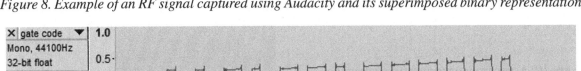

System Testing and Discussion

To test our entire system we wired up a standard 240V AC desktop lamp to our wireless switching system. We configured the switch with a unique address ('00001') and loaded two standard commands codes into its memory ('001 – Open switch', '010 – Close switch'). On the Chronos watch side, the radio was configured to match our protocols specifications and the wireless switch's address was set. The two commands codes were matched up to our gesture recognition routine, equating a 'double clap' with code 001 and a 'wave' with code 010. Preliminary tests exceeded expectation with the switching system working up to a distance of 50 feet and through multiple walls. We tested the efficacy of the system under many conditions including purposely sending erroneous codes and addresses from the chronos watch, which where correctly ignored by the switch. We also tested a series of undefined hand gestures in an attempt to falsely activate the switch, without avail.

In its current state, this system already represents the fundamentals of both ubiquitous computing and ambient intelligence. However, to be useful as a device for ambient intelligent interactions we would require a much more robust gesture recognition procedure. Recognising more complex hand gestures with a single 3-axis accelerometer is a challenge. Even the simplest of gestures, such as tracing a circle with one's hand is difficult to repeat exactly. A good recognition algorithm needs to be robust enough to detect the same gesture in the present of discrepancies, such as slight timing and scaling errors. For example, a circle gesture should be detected regardless of how large it is or how long it takes to trace. Fortunately, many diverse approaches to capturing and classifying hand gestures based on a single 3-axis accelerometer have been developed. The most

Figure 9. Electronic schematics of custom RF switch

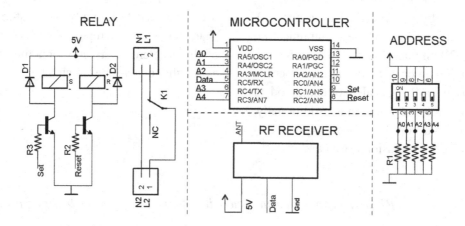

Figure 10. Asynchronous transmission protocol

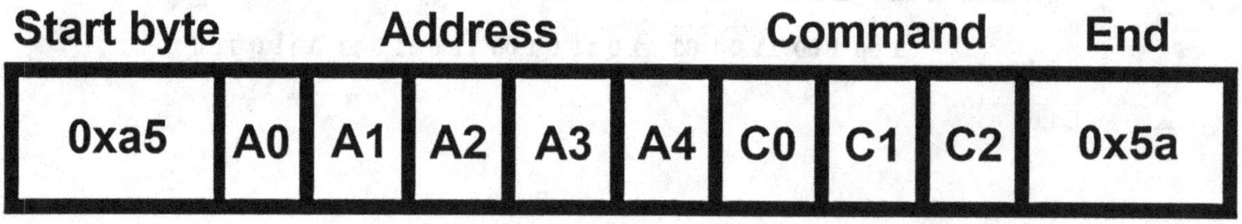

Start byte	Address					Command			End
0xa5	A0	A1	A2	A3	A4	C0	C1	C2	0x5a

prominent of these are dynamic time warping (Akl & Valaee, 2010), hidden Markov models (Nickel & Busch, 2011) and naïve Bayesian classification with feature separability weighting (Long, Yin, & Aarts, 2009). Recently, work has been done to compare two of these approaches for discerning gesture motions with the Chronos watch, (Mace, Gao, & Coskun, 2013). The results of this work are promising showing classification accuracy as high as 97% for a series of tested gestures.

In future work we intend to incorporate such techniques into our system, realising the potential for sophisticated gesture recognition. From a healthcare perspective, we could generate reports on the use of the paretic hand, monitoring how well patients perform gestures during activities of daily living (reaching to grab object, turning knobs of appliances, opening jars of food and stirring, mixing food etc.) in a non-invasive manner. Additionally, we can couple hand gestures and RF commands in an identical manner to that used in our sensor glove system (Part 1) for promoting additional use of the paretic in the home setting. There is also room for improving the usefulness of our wireless switch by incorporating additional hardware such as a transmitter and a current sensor. This would allow for two way communications between the sockets and the watch opening up interesting opportunities for ambient intelligent home based monitoring. For example, we could log information about the individual power consumptions of appliances, and relay warnings to the watch when an unusual activity is noticed, such as an appliance being on at night-time when it is usually off, or a change in the power consumption of a device, perhaps an indication that it is damaged.

A HYBRID SENSOR SYSTEM FOR HIGH FIDELITY HAND MOTION RECORDING AND PLAYBACK

Virtual reality (VR) (i.e. computer-simulated environments) is set to play a huge role in the next generation of human computer interaction technology. In 2014, we are currently awaiting the release of commercial VR headsets, including the much anticipated Oculus Rift (Kushner, 2014). Such devices enable advanced low-latency positional tracking allowing for the accurate mapping of your real world head movements into the virtual world, shifting and modifying your viewing experience as if you were really there.

Body tracking and in particular hand tracking can further enhance a user's experience of immersive VR allowing them to not only move around in a virtual environment but also to interact with it in a natural manner. Subsequently, VR headsets are often coupled with other wearable sensors such as sensor gloves and motion capture suits. Given the total immersive-ness in a digital environment, there is great potential here to develop ambient intelligence into the virtual environment. However, capturing the full three dimensional motion of a hand in a cost effective and non-invasive manner is a complex problem. Sensor gloves are exceptional at capturing fine finger movement, cheaply and effectively. However, most sensor glove designs lack the veracity to make them useful for monitoring the full range of hand motions, principally; translations and rotations of the hand. Developing an autonomous, integrated solution to such a problem is challenging. That said, there have been commendable attempts at embedding additional sensors (accelerometers, gyroscopes, and altimeters) into the standard flex sensor based glove for this exact purpose. However, this class of sensors use a local inertial-frame for reference, which suffers badly from integration drift. To reduce this drift, existing algorithms make use of gravity and the earth's magnetic field measured by accelerometers and magnetometers respectively. These components themselves are sensitive to local magnetic interference and require further compensational mechanisms. Quite quickly our once nimble sensor glove can become heavily populated with external sensors, increasing its cost, power requirements and agility of the device.

The software complexity also increases, requiring additional routines for acquiring and processing each of the newly added sensors and in some cases the implementation of computational expensive filtering algorithms, which have a severe impact on the responsiveness of the glove.

Subsequently motion capture is typically acquired using an external camera or similar vision based device. The motion of an object from the camera perspective is used as a relative measure based on a static reference frame i.e. the camera's fixed position and field of view. One device that excels at this form of tracking is the LEAP motion controller (Weichert, Bachmann, Rudak, & Fisseler, 2013), a relatively new innovative approach to hand motion tracking, Figure 11.

The LEAP aims to make motion control ubiquitous, with a small device designed to be placed on a physical desktop, facing upward. It uses two monochromatic IR cameras and three infrared LEDs. The LEDs generate a 3D pattern of dots of IR light and the cameras generate almost 300 frames per second of reflected data, which is sent to the host computer, where it is analysed by the Leap Motion controller software. Using this approach the LEAP successfully tracks both translational and rotational hand motion, fluidly and at very high frame rates. However, it is not without its limitations. Visual forms of motion capture suffer from an alternative class of problems, mainly that of visual occlusion. We found that while adept at hand tracking, the LEAP is poor at tracking finger positions, as the fingers become occluded from view when they are bent and flexed. This is problematic for healthcare applications, as accurate finger tracking is an important component of most exercises routine, such as pinching, or picking up an object.

In this work we describe our attempts to develop a hybrid sensor system which combines our previously described sensor glove and a LEAP motion controller for high fidelity, full hand and finger tracking. A system diagram of the entire system is presented in Figure 13 for reference. We believe such systems will play an active role in the future of healthcare, enhancing unsupervised forms of therapy through immersive interactive applications.

Initial Investigation

An initial test of combining our sensor glove (described in Part 1) with the LEAP motion controller was disappointing. The LEAP struggled to track the hand while wearing the sensor glove, further testing confirmed our suspicions that the black matt coloured fabric used as a base for our sensor glove was absorbing too much of the infrared light emitted by the LEAP. This is problematic, as the LEAP essentially detects objects based on how they interact with and deform the projected 3D pattern created by its three IR LEDs. Subsequently we experimented with different types and colour material that would better reflect the IR pattern. We found that the best tracking results were achieved using a high-visibility, reflective, fluorescent yellow glove. This material reflects IR extremely well, with the results being indistinguishable to that of tracking a naked hand with the LEAP. Subsequently, we rebuilt our sensor glove using this new material as a base.

Software System

We developed a windows form application named 'Ditto', written in C# to create a virtual environment (VR) for use with our sensor glove. The software system essentially amalgamates the otherwise independent sensor glove and the LEAP controller, augmenting their independently acquired motion data onto a realistic 3D model of a human hand, Lib hand (Sari, 2011). Lib hand is an open-source permissively licensed portable library for rendering and recognizing articulations of the human hand. To render and animate the hand we leveraged Ogre3D (Object-Oriented Graphics Rendering Engine), an open-source,

Figure 11. Leap motion controller

scene-oriented, real-time flexible 3D rendering engine.

Hardware Integration

Interfacing the LEAP controller with our software was facilitated by an extensive, well documented application programming interface (API) allowing us to easily detect and track hands within the LEAP field of view. The LEAP controller is integrated with our system over USB using a virtual serial port implementation. Our sensor glove communicates wirelessly with the software system through an embedded Bluetooth module, as described in section 1.a. On request, the software system instigates a virtual serial port connection between the PC and the sensor glove with data being transmitted in packet format, following a custom designed protocol in which sensor values for each of the 5 fingers are transmitted at a rate of 1000 samples per second. Once connected, the sensor glove continuously streams data to our software system. When configured both the sensor glove and LEAP act as autonomous entities,

grabbing new sensory data and piping it into the software system through their own independent virtual serial port connections.

Augmenting Finger and Hand Movement onto a 3D Model

To accommodate any discrepancies in the two devices acquisition speed, the software system was designed to be event driven. When new data arrives either from the LEAP or the sensor glove a software routine collects it, unpacks data and buffers it. After a set amount of time (20ms) the buffers are filtered using an averaging filter and the resulting data from both the LEAP (hand position and rotation) and the sensor glove (finger flexion's) are applied to the hand. Moving and rotating the model hand around the VR environment is trivial, as OGRE contains high level functions for applying rotation and translations of the objects orientation and position. Manipulating the fingers of the model hand in a realistic manner is accommodated by a digital skeleton structure that is built into the model hand. This form of modelling is known as rigging and is a popular technique used in animation and gaming. This allows us to simply apply rotation operations to each segment of the finger, in order to mimic fine finger movements, see Figure 12.

Capture and Playback System

To add some basic and useful functionality to this platform we integrated motion capture and playback functionality, based on the widely used motion capture format, the bio-vision hierarchy (BVH) format. The BVH file format consists of two parts where the former section details the hierarchy and initial pose of the skeleton and the latter contains motion data. There are many benefits to recording data in this format, mainly it is highly portable and can be played back on any open source BVH player. Also, the BVH format describes the underlying skeleton structure of the model and records the relative positions of each bone and their joint values with respect to their parent. This means that the motion is not captured relative to some reference point and subsequently we can change our perspective during playback, allowing us to view the recorded motion from different angles.

Applications

From the perspective of healthcare, there are many applications of this technology. For example our system could be used by a patient when practising exercises prescribed by their therapist. On completion, they could then send the recordings of the sessions to their therapist, who with the addition of any open source BVH file player could playback and review the exercises. There is also potential for much more sophisticated applications. The Ogre3D graphics rendering system which we integrated into our system offers great flexibility for a developer, allowing importation of most well-known 3D model formats. Hence, interactive objects can easily be added to the

virtual environment, facilitating the development of intelligent interactive environments. For example; a simple paper tossing game could be implemented in which the user has to reach for, pick up and throw a virtual piece of paper into a rubbish bin. Reaching, grasping and coordination are important functional movement that are integral to many activities of daily living, which most rehabilitation programs endeavour to incorporate. A simple scoring mechanism, adding competition to the game might encourage more replay-ability in which users try to beat their best scores or timing. Behind the screens, each movement made by the user can be tracked, recorded and quantified, allowing for a semi-automated assessment of recovery over time.

Virtual emulations of real world assessments protocols could also be developed using our platform, such as the Fugl-Meyer (Gladstone, Danells, & Black, 2002) or nine peg-hole test (Olindo, Signate, Richech, & Cabre, 2008). The benefit of simulating such protocol are many, including; automation/standardisation of testing and allowing the patient to test themselves in the comfort of their own home rather than making an inconvenient visit to a clinic.

CONCLUSION

Computer technology is advancing at an ever growing rate, with technology becoming smaller, smarter and more powerful with each new innovation. Technology truly is everywhere, we carry it with us, we rely on it, it cuts our grass, washes our clothes, entertains us, feeds us and even helps us socialise. It is also becoming more portable with the recent development of smartphones and smart watches we carry with us incredible computing capacity. However, regardless of how smart the technology becomes we still find ourselves struggling to use it. Older people in particular struggle with new technology, finding it hard to adapt to new ways of doing things. That said there are

Figure 12. Illustrating the internal rigging system used in LibHand and a sample point showing the moments of rotation (dictated by arrows)

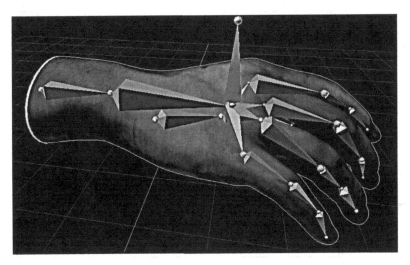

times when the rest of us just want a computer to do something simple and become frustrated by how difficult they can be to instruct. How often have we caught ourselves shouting at a machine, perplexed by how capable it is, yet ignorant to our desires? Born out of this frustration a new concept in computing is emerging, known as "ambient intelligence". Ambient intelligence is best described as an electronic environment that is aware of and sensitive to the presence of people. The electronics and computer systems required to support such environments exists today, with the ubiquity of embedded sensory systems, smart devices and computer systems, interconnected by the internet.

In this body of work, we present some of our recent efforts towards developing new and innovative ways to interact with these ubiquitous systems in an attempt to develop ambient intelligent solutions. We are particularly interested in such environments from the perspective of healthcare as we believe they represent great potential for realising effective home based rehabilitation systems for stroke and other illnesses with elements of movement weakness. We believe that such technology can play an active role in elevating the burden on healthcare systems international by supporting the

paradigm shift towards home-based rehabilitation. Advocates of home rehabilitation publicise the many benefits to such a move, including; reduced nosocomial infections and hospital acquired illness, reduced costs for both the patient and the tax payer, and the convenience of quality care in the comfort of one's own home.

Systems such as our sensor glove and smart watch might offer new exciting ways for people to practise beneficial, therapeutic exercises as prescribed by their therapist. It is important to note that these devices are not intended to replace the need for conventional therapy but instead to be used as ancillary devices with the intention of supporting and enhancing recovery. Research shows that patient adherence to physical therapy reduces when they leave primary care i.e. hospitals and clinics. This paradox can simply be attributed to the fact that in the absence of professional supervision patients find their exercises difficult, unrewarding and frustrating, and subsequently switch to using their unaffected hand. Our systems were designed to encourage the use of the paretic hand through the novelty of gesture-based environmental control while performing functional movement used in the activities of daily living. We hope that there might also be auxiliary benefits to using our

Figure 13. System diagram

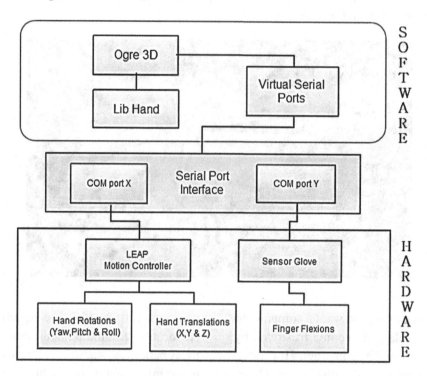

devices, such that the newly acquired functional control over their environment might improve a person's sense of ability and independence. Much further work is required towards investigating such benefits and both of our wearable devices require pilot studies with patients and therapists in order to investigate their suitability and merits as devices for healthcare.

Virtual reality systems are fast emerging as the latest form of human computer interaction, boasting new immersive ways to interact with computer systems and to explore virtual environments. The benefits of VR and its potential for developing content rich, interactive environments are exciting, as are its applications for healthcare. VR represents the possibility of coupling interactive games with otherwise mundane and tedious exercise programs. Our combined hybrid sensor system pertains to the needs for accurate, cost effective full hand tracking systems, which we believe will play an active role in the future of

healthcare. We designed our software system using open source libraries and free-licenced content in an attempt to develop a relatively cheap motion tracking system making it accessible to researchers and potential users.

We advocate the replication of all of our described systems and have subsequently released our designs and software, which are available on request. We hope our work might inspire and encourage other researchers.

REFERENCES

Akl, A., & Valaee, S. (2010). Accelerometer-based gesture recognition via dynamic-time warping, affinity propagation, & compressive sensing. In *Proceedings of International Conference on Acoustics, Speech and Singal Processing* (pp. 2270-2273). IEEE. doi:10.1109/ICASSP.2010.5495895

Costantini, G., Saggio, G., & Todisco, M. (2010). A data glove based sensor interface to expressively control musical processes. In *Proceedings of International Conference on Sensor Device Technologies and Applications*, (pp. 217-220). Academic Press.

Ellis, K., & Barca, J. C. (2012). *Exploring Sensor Gloves for Teaching Children Sign Language.* Advances in Human-Computer Interactions.

Gartner. (2012). *Forecast: PC Installed Base, Worldwide, 2004-2012.* Gartner, Inc. Retrieved from http://www.gartner.com/newsroom/id/703807 .

Gladstone, D. J., Danells, C. J., & Black, S. E. (2002). The fugl-meyer assessment of motor recovery after stroke: A critical review of its measurement properties. *Neurorehabilitation and Neural Repair, 16*(3), 232–240. doi:10.1177/154596802401105171 PMID:12234086

Guo, S., & Song, Z. (2008). VR-based active rehabilitation system for upper limbs. In *Proceedings of IEEE International Conference on Automation and Logistics*, (pp. 1077-1082). IEEE. doi:10.1109/ICMA.2008.4798757

Hall, E. C. (1996). *Journey to the Moon: The History of the Apollo Guidance Computer.* American Institute of Aeronautics and Astronautics.

Jack, D., Boian, R. M. A., Burdea, G. C., & Poizner, H. (2001). Virtual reality - enhanced stroke rehabilitation. Transactions on Neural Systems and Rehabilation Engineering, 308-318.

Kea, X., Saksena, P., & Holly, A. (2011). *The Determinants of Health Expenditure: A Country-Level Panel Data Analysis.* Geneva, Switzerland: World Health Organization.

Kinsella, K. H. W. (2009). *International Population Reports.* Washington, DC: U.S. Census Bureau.

Kushner, D. (2014). Virtual reality's moment. IEEE Spectrum, 51(1), 34-37.

Liarokapis, F., Macan, L., Malone, G., Rebolledo-Mendez, G., & De Freitas, S. (2009). *A Pervasive Augmented Reality Serious Game.* Games and Virtual Worlds for Serious Applications.

Lin, K., Yuen, F., & Barth, T. (2008). *The Punch Meter.* Retrieved from http://processors.wiki.ti.com/index.php/The_Punch_Meter

Long, X., Yin, B., & Aarts, R. (2009). Single-accelerometer-based daily physical activity classification. In *Proceedings of International Conference of Engineering in Medicine and Biology Society*, (pp. 3-6). Academic Press.

Mace, D., Gao, W., & Coskun, A. (2013). *Improving the accuracy and practicality of accelerometer based hand gesture.* Santa Monica, CA: International Conference on Intelligent User Interfaces.

Micera, S., Cavallaro, E., Belli, R., Zaccone, F., Gulielmelli, E., Dario, P., et al. (2003). Functional assessment of hand orthopedic disorders using a sensorised glove. In *Proceedings of IEEE International Conference on Robotics and Automation*, (pp. 2212-2217). IEEE.

Murthy, G. R., & Jadon, R. S. (2009). A review of vision based hand gestures recognition. *Internation Journal of Information Technology and Knowledge Management*, 405-410.

Nickel, C., & Busch, C. (2011). Classifying accelerometer data via Hidden Markov Models to authenticate people by the way they walk. In *Proceedings of International Carnahan Conference on Security Technology* (pp. 18-21). IEEE. doi:10.1109/CCST.2011.6095941

Nordin, A. M., Chee, P. S., Addi, M. M., & Che Harun, F. K. (2011). EZ430-Chronos watch as a wireless health monitoring device. In *Proceedings of International Conference on Biomedial Engineering*, (pp. 305-307). Kuala Lumpur: Academic Press. doi:10.1007/978-3-642-21729-6_79

Olindo, S., Signate, A., Richech, A., Cabre, P., Catonne, Y., Smadja, D., & Pascal-Mousselard, H. (2008). Quantitative assessment of hand disability by the Nine-Hole-Peg test (9-HPT) in cervical spondylotic myelopathy. *Journal of Neurology, Neurosurgery, and Psychiatry*, *79*(8), 965–967. doi:10.1136/jnnp.2007.140285 PMID:18420728

Qian, K., & Cui, C. (2010). *Chronos Tennis*. Retrieved from http://processors.wiki.ti.com/index.php/Chronos_Tennis

Rakhecha, S., & Hsu, K. (2013). Reliable and Secure Body Fall Detection Algorithm in a wireless mesh network. Rochester, NY: Department of Computer Engineering, Kate Gleason College of Engineering, Rochester Insitute of Technology. doi:10.4108/icst.bodynets.2013.253528

Rouphael, T. J. (2008). *RF and Digital Signal Processing for Software-Defined Radio*. Newnes.

Sari, M. (2011). *LibHand: A library for Hand Articulations*. Retrieved from http://www.libhand.org/

Semiconductors, V. (2013). *Data Formats for IR Remote Control* (Document Number: 80071). Retrieved from MCS electronics: http://www.vishay.com/docs/80071/dataform.pdf

Simonea, L. S. (2007). A low cost instrumented glove for extended monitoring. *Journal of Neuroscience Methods*, *160*(2), 335–348. doi:10.1016/j.jneumeth.2006.09.021 PMID:17069892

Toole, J., King, A., & He, L. (2011). *MSP430_Flying_Mouse*. Retrieved from MSP430_Flying_Mouse: http://processors.wiki.ti.com/index.php/MSP430_Flying_Mouse

Tran, N. X., Phan, H., & Dinh, V. V. (2009). Lecture Notes in Computer Science (Vol. 5611). Springer Berlin Heidelberg. doi:10.1007/978-3-642-02577-8_30

Uslu, G., Altun, O., & Baydere, S. (2011). A Bayesian approach for indoor human activity monitoring. In *Proceedings of International Conference on Hybrid Intelligent systems* (pp. 324-327). Melacca: IEEE. doi:10.1109/HIS.2011.6122126

Weichert, F., Bachmann, D., Rudak, B., & Fisseler, D. (2013). Analysis of the Accuracy and Robustness of the Leap Motion Controller. *Sensors (Basel, Switzerland)*, *13*(5), 6380–6393. doi:10.3390/s130506380 PMID:23673678

KEY TERMS AND DEFINITIONS

Ambient Intelligence Environment: An environment which is sensitive and responsive to the presence of people, through electronic means.

Assistive Healthcare: The practise of maintaining, increasing, or improving the functional capabilities of individuals with disabilities.

Autonomous System: Existing or capable of existing independently; not needing a host computer; self-contained.

Gesture-Based Environmental Control: The interpretation of natural hand gestures and body language by a computer system for the intentional control of one's personal environment.

Home-Based Rehabilitation: An individualised rehabilitation program for patients, which facilitates learning and their return to previous activities and lifestyle, in the comfort of their own home.

Human Computer Interaction: The study, design and implementation of how humans interact with computers.

Microcontroller: A multipurpose, programmable device that integrates a central processing unit (CPU), which processes digital data according to instructions stored in its memory, and provides results.

Sensor Glove/Data Glove: A wearable input device for human-computer interaction worn like a glove. Typically used to capture physical data such as finger flexion or position.

Ubiquitous Computing: The presences of computer systems everywhere, constantly connected and available; widespread.

Virtual Reality: A computer generated simulation of a 3D environment that can be interacted with through specialised electronic equipment.

Chapter 2
Services and Monitors for Dependability Assessment of Mobile Health Monitoring Systems

Alessandro Testa
Institute of High Performance Computing and Networking (ICAR), Italy

Marcello Cinque
Università di Napoli Federico II, Italy

Antonio Coronato
Institute of High Performance Computing and Networking (ICAR), Italy

Giuseppe De Pietro
Institute of High Performance Computing and Networking (ICAR), Italy

ABSTRACT

The problem of failure detection in mHealth monitoring systems is becoming more critical, and the use of wireless technologies and commodity hardware/software platforms pose new challenges to their correct functioning. Remote and continuous monitoring of patients' vital signs aims to improve the quality of life of patients. Such applications, however, are particularly critical from the point of view of dependability. Wireless channels can be affected by packet loss, and cheap and wireless-enabled medical devices can exhibit wrong readings, inducing the medical staff to make wrong decisions. In this chapter, the authors present the results of a Failure Modes and Effects Analysis (FMEA) conducted to identify the dependability threats of health monitoring systems and a set of services and monitors for the assurance of high degrees of dependability to mobile health monitoring systems. Moreover, the authors describe a case study realized to detect failures at runtime.

1. INTRODUCTION

Health monitoring systems have been shown to be effective in helping to manage chronic disease, post-acute care, and monitoring the safety of the older adult population. They can help older adults slow progression of chronic disease and ensure continued recovery after being discharged from an acute care setting. The implementation of such systems is gaining an increasing attention in the academia and the industry, also due to the increasing healthcare costs and the aging of the world population (Hao et al., 2008).

DOI: 10.4018/978-1-4666-7284-0.ch002

Copyright © 2015, IGI Global. Copying or distributing in print or electronic forms without written permission of IGI Global is prohibited.

To this purpose, cabled measurement equipment is already used to guarantee reliable and robust control of vital signs. However such systems complicate patient autonomy and mobility. Hence, wireless technologies and mobile devices are starting to be applied to build more comfortable and patient-friendly health monitoring systems (Paksuniemi et al., 2006).

Nevertheless, the use of wireless technologies and the adoption of commodity hardware/software platforms, such as smartphones, pose new challenges on the correct functioning of health monitoring systems. Wireless channels can be affected by packet loss, due to shadowing and absence of signal coverage. Smartphones can be subjected to unpredictable failures, which could affect the correct functioning of the system. Finally, cheap and wireless-enabled medical devices can exhibit wrong readings and temporary disconnections from the so-called Body Area Network (BAN (O'Donovan et al., 2009)). These issues may induce the medical staff to take wrong decisions, e.g., to administer wrong dosages of medicine, which can happen to be fatal for the patient.

For these reasons, the problem of failure detection and management in health monitoring systems is starting to be addressed in the literature, especially for mobile systems. However, several studies are based on simplistic failure assumptions or on basic fault-tolerance schemes (such as, sensor redundancy), which are not assured to cover all possible failure scenarios. For instance, sensor replication is ineffective against smartphone failures.

To overcome the limitations of current solutions, in this paper we propose the design of reliable mobile health monitoring system, based on the configurable and the automatic deployment of system monitors, enriching the task of vital sign collection with the ability of detecting failures at runtime, hence enabling the realization of dependable health monitoring services. Differently from the previous attempts in the literature, we base our design on the results of a detailed Failure Mode

and Effect Analysis of a typical mobile health monitoring system (Cinque et al., 2011) (Cinque et. al., 2012).

The FMEA allowed us to identify the failure modes of the main components composing such systems, by taking advantage of our past experience and detailed field studies on the dependability of mobile devices, wireless communication technologies, such as Bluetooth, and wireless sensor networks (WSNs). The characterization of the failure modes of the system components allowed us to identify the main responsibility of system monitors, along with their placement in a typical mobile health monitoring architecture. The driving idea behind our design is to keep monitors transparent to application developers, allowing them to implement dependable health monitoring applications only by using high-level collection and delivery services. Such services are in turn conceived to exploit the underlying system monitors to detect the failures and potentially react to them. In order to let the solution be adaptable to different application needs, monitors are conceived to be activated and configured automatically, based on a high-level and system-agnostic specification of the desired dependability level.

The rest of the paper is structured as follows: The related work is presented in Section 2; Section 3 describes the typical architecture of a mobile health monitoring system, while in Section 4 we discuss about the results on the realized FMEA. The proposed monitor-based dependable architecture is presented in Section 5. Section 6 presents a use example of a monitor. Finally, Section 7 reports our concluding remarks.

2. RELATED WORK

Currently, the research is progressively recognizing the need of novel solutions to build dependable health monitoring systems. These solutions mainly focus on two key issues: node failures and wireless network interference.

Regarding node failures, the power consumption of battery driven devices represent a remarkable issue, which is a limiting factor for long-term monitoring. Although the emerging of new technologies (Kansal et al., 2007) and new standards like the bluetooth low-energy profile, this issue cannot be considered definitively solved (Zhang et al., 2009). For this reason, the system must be able to detect low battery levels and to migrate onto spare devices.

In addition, both WSNs and BANs may suffer from intentional or unintentional node removal or unresponsive nodes. While in WSNs, this issue can be resolved with new path discovery or redundant paths, in BANs this may cause the loss of important vital signs being monitored by the failing sensor. A combination of node redundancy and multi-sensor data fusion was one of the solutions proposed to face these issues (Baskiyar, 2002)(Curiac et al., 2009). The introduction of redundant sensors measuring the same vital sign avoids the loss of any vital data if a node becomes compromised or faulty. In addition, they can serve to facilitate multiple paths when the routing becomes an issue.

Interference has the potential to cause significant delays and data loss and is a major concern with all wireless devices. Medical devices can interfere with each other in the BAN as well as being subject to environmental noise. This is due to the lack of harmonious regulations and standards, as demonstrated in (Hanna, 2009) (Spadotto, 2009). A solution would be to eliminate the wireless aspect of the intra-BAN network (Chen et al., 2011) (Hanson et al., 2009). BAN systems such as *MIThrill* (Chen et al., 2011), *SMART* (Chen et al., 2011), and *MobiHealth* (Van Halteren et al., 2004) all employ a wired connectivity between sensors and the aggregator. However, these solutions strongly limit the usability of the system, especially for elderly people, and makes it hard to interconnect all the sensors to commodity mobile devices, such as patients' smartphones, hence requiring ad-hoc aggregating devices which increase the overall cost of the system.

Some proposals in the literature have employed techniques to provide some form of fault tolerance to monitoring systems. *iROS* (Ponnekanti et al., 2003) uses an Event Heap for communication between various entities. The EventHeap is based on the tuple-spaces model proposed by Gelernter for *Linda* (Gelernter, 1985). Arnstein et al. propose a project (Arnstein et al., 2002) to enhance the robustness of ubiquitous systems by providing transaction-level persistence and support for disconnected operations. But the project does not address device or application failures.

Chetan et al. highlight the various challenges and issues that confront fault tolerant pervasive computing (Chetan et al., 2005); also, they propose some solutions to these problems but they do not address the specific issues of health monitoring systems.

Health monitoring systems within closed environments can be conceived as a special case of Ambient Intelligence (AmI) systems. Currently there is still a lack of a commonly accepted architectures to build dependable AmI systems. This issue was first considered in (Simoncini, 2003), where the author points out that the concepts of "architecture" and "system" need to be redefined in the context of AmI, in order to properly define dependability attributes, threats and means.

In (Bohn et al., 2005), authors define a dynamic AmI system able to adapt itself to the current situation. They claim that, in order to guarantee dependability requirements, the system architecture has to be manageable, controllable and it has to provide means for the prediction of the system correctness at runtime. In (Nehmer et al., 2006), authors proposed an integrated system approach for living assistance systems based on ambient intelligence technology. They claim that the construction of trustworthy, robust, and dependable living assistance systems is a challenging task which requires novel software engineering methods and tools, and novel approaches for dependable self-adapting software architectures, able to react to changes due to frequent failures and reconfiguration events, which become the norm, rather than the exception. In addition, self-adapting multi-modal human-computer interfaces must be devised, since even the wrong interaction with humans may represent an obstacle for the dependable operation of the system.

Georgalis et al. argue that the most important architectural property in an AmI architecture is the fault-tolerance (Georgalis et al., 2009). The fault tolerance, in the context of an AmI architecture, has to be able to isolate failures, to eliminate single points of failure, to restart failing services before that are used by the clients, and finally to provide mechanisms for notifying the fault level about the irreparable failure of a specific service.

Coronato and De Pietro (Coronato & De Pietro, 2010) pointed out that the design of Ambient Intelligence applications in critical systems requires rigorous software-engineering-oriented approaches. The authors proposed a set of formal tools and a specification process for AmI, which have been devised to lead the developer in designing activities and realizing software artefacts.

In (Duman et al., 2010) it is defined an Ambient Intelligent Environment (AIE) as a multitude of interconnected systems composed by embedded agent with computational and networking capabilities which form a ubiquitous, unobtrusive, and seamless infrastructure that surrounds the user. These intelligent agents are integrated into AIEs to form an intelligent "presence" to identify the users and be sensitive and attentive to their particular needs, based on a publish-subscribe communication infrastructure. The intelligent agents are dynamic and capable to keep a high level of dependability of a network structure preserving the resilience and the fault tolerance. They suggest, as future work, to investigate the proposed AmI system in a truly distributed and real AIE with a richer set of sensors and actuators.

Some solutions focus on the dependable delivery of data. In (Chakraborly, 2007) authors propose a trust-based routing protocol able to ensure the delivery of event data from sensors to actuators in a Ambient Intelligence environment even in the presence of faults; the dependability is measured in terms of a trust value for the node. It is also performed a security analysis of the effects of malicious nodes.

Several new mHealth monitoring systems have been proposed in literature focusing on security and privacy issues but not on dependability issues within a WBAN (Lin et al., 2013)(Yan et al., 2010) (Triantafyllidis et al., 2012).

In (Lin et al., 2013) the authors present a new kind of mHealth monitoring system that is based on cloud computing; the paper is focused on security and privacy concepts since the authors design a cloud-assisted privacy preserving mHealth monitoring system to protect the privacy of the involved parties and their data. However dependability requirements such as coverage or connection resiliency are not considered.

Also in (Yan et al., 2010), it is implemented and evaluated a WBAN-based e-health monitoring system which is sensitive to security and privacy issues; it is proposed a mixed localization algorithm based on received sensor data and received signal strength indicator (RSSI) that is exploited to perform passive localization of monitored elderly people. However, the proposed system does not take in account failures like a packet loss or isolation of part of a WBAN.

Triantafyllidis et al. present the design and development of a pervasive health monitoring system integrates patient monitoring, through mobile wearable multisensing devices, and status logging for capturing various problems or symptoms met. The authors focus on security issues of a gateway device disregarding any failure that could occur in a WBAN that is the source of needed data.

There is some mHealth monitoring system based on reasoning techniques. Benlamri and Docksteader design the Mobile Ontology-based Reasoning and Feedback (MORF) health-monitoring system, which monitors a patient's health status using a mobile unit. Unlike previous cited papers, the system uses ontology based context model to process and determine a patient's health status; the system can process the incoming sensor data by means of ontologies and various reasoning methods. For this feature, this work is similar to our but also in this case no dependability assessment is performed.

Sneha and Varshney investigate an approach based on mobile ad hoc network to address the challenge of enhancing communication dependability in the context of health monitoring; they propose power management protocols to overcome issues of low battery power management of patient monitoring devices increasing communication dependability. They assert ensuring reliable end to end communication in a mHealth monitoring system is a critical requirement. However, their research is based on dependability issues that affect this kind of systems; also this work is far from our aim since only power consumption is considered as dependability parameter while we consider also coverage, connection resiliency and packet loss. Moreover they consider end-to-end dependability and not within a WBAN.

Therefore, several mHealth monitoring systems have been proposed in literature but dependability assessment remains an ongoing challenge.

Despite the presence of these reported solutions, several unexplored issues can limit the adoption of mobile health monitoring systems, such as cellular network connectivity, smart phone failures and many others. Each failure mode in turn needs proper countermeasures to be handled at runtime. Thus, not only a more comprehensive view of the failure modes of these systems is needed, but even a new architecture provided with monitors to observe the behavior of the system and to detect and mask the occurring failures.

3. MOBILE HEALTH MONITORING SYSTEMS

In the last years, several health monitoring systems have been proposed in the market. Among

different implementations, we chose three of the most popular and presenting a sufficient variety of characteristics to conduct our experimentation: the *MedApps System*, the *Nicolet Ambulatory Monitor System* and a system used by the *Center for Technology and Aging*.

The *MedApps System* (Dicks, 2007) provides a healthcare connectivity platform that delivers scalable and flexible remote distribution using cellular, wireless and wired technologies with cloud-based computing. This system can work with multiple internal and external devices. Patient data is collected, analyzed and forwarded, via cell phone to servers, guaranteeing a more robust picture of the patients' health.

The *Nicolet Ambulatory Monitor System* (Carefusion, 2011) combines a flexible, high quality diagnostic unit, ideal for patients of all ages. It is a flexible, robust system specifically realized to provide the requirements of long-term monitoring. This system diagnoses patients' cerebral function (premature neonates to older adults) monitoring continuously ill patients at risk for brain damage and secondary injury.

Finally, authors in (Center for Technology and Aging, 2009) discuss two areas of opportunity for remote patient monitoring: i) Patient Safety and ii) Chronic Disease Management and Post-Acute Care Management. In alignment with the mission of the Center for Technology and Aging, they focus on technology-enabled innovations, such as wireless connectivity, mainly aimed at improving the health of older adults and promoting independent living in community-based, home, and long-term care settings.

Observing the underlying architectures of these systems, we can assert that a mobile health monitoring system is usually composed by a number of sensors (medical devices), a gateway device (a handheld device) and a medical station; typical communication means are Bluetooth (within the Body Area Network - Intra BAN communication), WiFi and cellular (external to the BAN - Extra BAN communication). Vital signs are sensed by sensors (i.e. oximeter, electrocardiogram - ECG, insulin pump, etc.) and transmitted to a mobile device over a bluetooth network. Afterwards, data are sent to a remote station deployed, for an example, in a hospital by means of either a WiFi or a cellular connection (the medical center location).

In this typical network, we can note that possible failures can occur in medical devices, in the bluetooth communication, in the mobile device, during the WiFi/cellular communication and finally in the local monitoring station of the caregiver.

Figure 1 depicts the components of a generic mobile health monitoring system.

4. THE FAILURE MODES AND EFFECTS ANALYSIS (FMEA)

4.1 FMEA Fundamentals

Failure Modes and Effects Analysis (FMEA) is a teambased, systematic and proactive approach for identifying the ways that a process or design

can fail, why it might fail, and how it can be made safer (Latino et al., 2004). To properly evaluate a process or product for strengths, weaknesses, potential problem areas or failure modes, and to prevent problems before they occur, a FMEA can be conducted. The purpose of performing an FMEA, as described in US MIL STD 1629 (Department of Defense – USA, 1980), is to identify where and when possible system failures could occur and to prevent those problems before they happen. It represents a procedure for analysis of potential failure modes within a system for classification by the severity and likelihood of the failures.

An FMEA provides a systematic method of resolving the questions: How can a process or product fail? What will be the effect on the rest of the system if such failure occurs? What action is necessary to prevent the failure? To realize a FMEA, the system is divided in components/ functions that are divided in subcomponents/ subfunctions; it considers a table in which the rows are composed by the subcomponents/sub-functions and the columns represent respectively

Figure 1. A mobile health monitoring architecture

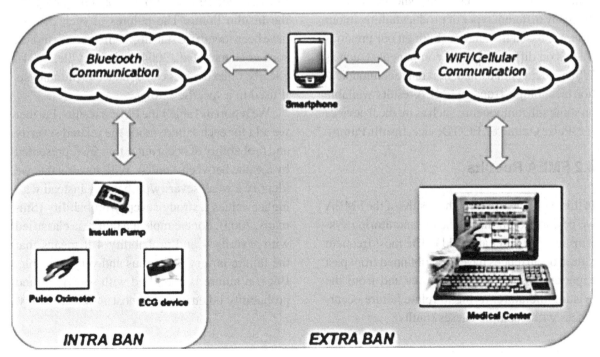

the failure modes, the possible causes and the possible effects. If a particular failure could not be prevented, then the goal would be to prevent the issue from affecting health care organizations in the accreditation process. The FMEA team determines the effect of each failure by failure mode analysis and identifies single failure points that are critical.

It may also classify each failure according to the criticality of a failure effect (severity) and its probability of occurring (probability). There are some motivations why this analysis technique is very advantageous. FMEA provides a basis for identifying root failure causes and developing effective corrective actions; the FMEA identifies reliability and safety critical components; it facilitates investigation of design alternatives at all phases of design; it is used to provide other maintainability, safety, testability, and logistics analyses. FMEA is thus part of a larger system of quality control, where documentation is vital to implementation.

Since FMEA is effectively dependent on the members of the team which examines the failures, it is limited by their experience of previous failures. If a failure mode cannot be identified, then external help is needed from consultants who are aware of the many different types of product failure. In our case, we based the analysis both on our previous studies on different system components (such as WSNs, smart phones, and short range communication technologies) and on FMEA results available on some subcomponents, such as medical devices (i.e. Pulse Oximeter, ECG Device, Insulin Pump).

4.2 FMEA Results

In this section we present the results of the FMEA we performed on mobile health monitoring systems in (Cinque et al., 2011). The most frequent failure occurrences have been obtained from past experiences on real architectures and from the existing literature, trying to relate failure occurrences with potential causes (faults).

Considering the general architecture, we omit the Medical Center location, since we assume it to be more reliable and under the direct control of the medical staff, who can immediately intervene in case of failures (e.g., they can connect to the system using a different machine). Hence, we want to focus on the components which have to be used by patients, who might not be technology experts and who need to rely on a monitoring system able to work even in case of accidental failures.

To perform the FMEA we identified four components/functions (Cinque et al., 2011): the node (i.e., the sensor used to monitor the patient), the Intra BAN communication, the Extra BAN communication, and the gateway (i.e., the smartphone of the patient).

Eight sub-components/subfunctions have been identified for the node component: the sensor board, the power supply unit, the CPU, and the OS (such as (Qnx., n.a.)(Threadx. n.a.) which are used in medical devices) are the general components of a node, and their analysis is based on our previous study on sensor networks (Cinque et al., 2007a). In addition, we considered the failures of some specific medical devices, such as the ECG sensor (divided in the ECG Device Adhesive, the ECG Device Electrolyte), the patient cable, and the Insulin Pump. The failures of such devices have been identified starting from existing studies, such as (James et al., 2004)(Sommerville, 2004). Clearly, other devices can be added to the analysis if used in a specific setting.

We report in Table 1 the FMEA results. Further we add for each failure mode the related severity and probability of occurrence that are represented by a value between 1 and 4. With lower value we identify a weak severity/probability instead with higher values a strong severity/probability (Stamatis, 2003). For example if a failure is classified with severity 4 and probability 4 it means that the failure is very dangerous and very probable. But if a failure is classified with severity 1 and probability 1 then there's almost nothing to worry.

Table 1 is structured by seven columns. Every row contains the description of a single failure mode. So, considering a possible failure mode that may occur in the health monitoring system, we identify from left to right the component (and the subcomponent if it exists) interested by failure mode, the failure mode, the possible effects of failure, the possible cause of failure and finally the

Table 1. Failure mode and effect analysis of a mobile health monitoring system

Component	Sub-Component	Potential Failure Mode	Potential Effects of Failure	Potential Causes of Failure	Sev.	Prob.
Node (the Medical Sensor)	**Sensor Board**	Stuck at Zero	The device is out-of-order it does not deliver any output to inputs	Sensing hardware	4	2
		Null Reading	The device delivers null output values	Sensing hardware	4	4
		Out of Scale Reading	The device delivers no meaningful values	Sensing hardware	3	4
	Power Supply	Stuck at Zero	The device is out-of-order; it does not deliver any output to inputs	Natural energy exhaustion	4	4
		Reset	The node resets itself to its initial conditions	Anomalous current request that cannot be supplied by batteries	3	1
	CPU	Stuck at Zero	The device is out-of-order; it does not deliver any output to inputs	Micro-controller	4	4
	OS	Software Hang	The device is powered on, but not able to deliver any output	Operating system's corrupted state	4	3
	ECG Device Adhesive	Incorrect reading	Wrong data values, irritation or rash of skin	Skin contact	2	3
	ECG Device Electrolyte	Incorrect reading	Wrong data values, irritation or rash of skin	Skin contact	2	3
	Patient Cable	Discontinuous readings	Noise, wrong data values	Defective wire	2	2
	Insulin Pump	Insulin overdose	Low blood sugar levels (hypoglycemia) which can be quite dangerous	Incorrect sugar level measured	3	4
		Insulin underdose	Patient at risk: sugar accumulates in the blood	Incorrect sugar level measured	1	3
		Power failure	Desidered dose was not given	Natural energy exhaustion	2	2
		No delivery failure	Desidered dose was not given	Corrupted rewinding mechanism	4	3

continued on following page

Table 1. Continued

Component	Sub-Component	Potential Failure Mode	Potential Effects of Failure	Potential Causes of Failure	Sev.	Prob.
Intra BAN Communication	**Transport and Routing**	Packet Loss	The radio packet is not delivered	Packet corruption	3	2
				Buffer overrun		
		Isolation	The node is not longer connected to the sink node	Failure of all forwarding nodes	4	2
	Bluetooth Stack	Bluetooth stack failure	A Bluetooth module (e.g. L2CAP, BNEP, etc.) fails	Bluetooth stack's corrupted state	3	1
	Bluetooth Channel	Header corruption	Header delivered with errors	Packet corruption	2	1
		Header length mismatch	Header length deviates from the specified one	Packet corruption	2	1
		Payload corruption	Payload delivered with errors	Packet corruption	3	1
Extra BAN Communication		Data Delivery Failures	The network is not able to deliver the required amount of measurements	The number of failed nodes is more than a given threshold	3	3
		Cellular/ WiFi network unavailable	Monitoring stopped	Area without cellular/ WiFi signal	4	3

continued on following page

severity and probability of occurrence, to highlight the more dangerous and frequent failures.

All of these analyzed failures cause abnormal vital sign readings, or even it can happen that a value is not received at the Medical Center location; in this case an inaccurate monitoring is provided, potentially resulting in a significant hazard to patients. Health monitoring systems must be aware of all the possible failures, in order to react to them or, at least, to detect them. For instance, in case of failure detection, a possible action can be to call to the patient's home or to call to an emergency contact to suddenly check the patient status and restore the normal operation of the system.

5. THE PROPOSED SERVICES

The problem of architecting mobile health monitoring systems with predictable and verifiable dependability properties still represents a critical open issue. The problem lies in the highly evolvable and dynamic nature of such systems, which, coupled with the unpredictability of hardware and software faults, exacerbates the definition of fault tolerance means, and compromises the application of fault forecasting techniques, due to the non-reproducibility of their behavior. In other terms, mobile health monitoring systems do not allow the application of techniques based on the a-priori knowledge of the system itself, even

Table 1. Continued

Component	Sub-Component	Potential Failure Mode	Potential Effects of Failure	Potential Causes of Failure	Sev.	Prob.
Gateway	Device (The Smartphone)	Freeze	The device's output becomes constant; the device does not respond to the users input.	Systems corrupted state	3	3
		Self-shutdown	The device shuts down itself; no service is delivered at the user interface.	Natural energy exhaustion or self-reboot due to corrupted state	4	2
		Unstable behavior	The device exhibits erratic behavior without any input inserted by the user	System/Application corrupted state	4	2
		Output failure	The device delivers an output sequence that deviates from the expected one	System/Application corrupted state	3	4
		Input failure	User inputs have no effect on device behavior	System/Application corrupted state; Natural energy exhaustion	1	1
	Bluetooth Application	Inquiry/Scan Failure	The scan procedure terminates abnormally	A Bluetooth module fails or device out of range	2	3
		Discovery Failure	The discover procedure terminates abnormally	A Bluetooth module fails or device out of range	2	3
		Connect Failure	The device is unable to estabilish a connection	A Bluetooth module fails or device out of range	4	3
		Packet Loss	Expected packets are not received	Packet corruption	3	1
		Data mismatch	Packets are delivered with errors in the payload	Memoryless channel with uncorrelated errors	3	1

because, being these systems relatively young, there are no field failure data or experience reports available on their failure behavior, apart from the high-level FMEA reported in Section 4. Given the high dynamicity and heterogeneity of these systems (which behavior is strongly influenced by the mission they need to accomplish), we note that the knowledge on the system behavior needs to be acquired during the actual execution of the system, and to be adapted continuously to current system dynamics. This allows the tailor the intervention of fault tolerance means based on the current situation (what we call situation-aware fault tolerance).

In this section we present the proposed monitoring services conceived to build dependable mobile health monitoring systems, able to automatically detect failures and potentially react to them. The services are discussed with respect to a reference mobile health monitoring system, depicted in

Figure 2. First we present the services offered to applications, and their role. Then, we introduce the concept of monitor and describe the monitor components introduced in the system.

The system is structured in four main parts: Intra-BAN, Gateway Services, Medical Center Services and External Applications.

5.1 Intra-BAN

The Intra-BAN is a particular network constituted by a set of biomedical sensors that communicate among each other and with the gateway. Being the majority of wireless medical devices available today equipped with the Bluetooth communication technology, we assume that devices are discovered with the Bluetooth Discovery service. Vital signs are then collected by means of the Bluetooth Connection service.

5.2 Gateway Services

The services offered on the Gateway side (mobile) are summarized in the following:

- **Bluetooth Connection:** This service provides the Bluetooth communication between a medical sensor of the Intra-BAN and the gateway device (i.e. a PDA, a notebook, etc...)
- **Bluetooth Discovery:** This service is used to discover the medical devices in the Intra-BAN.
- **Wifi Discovery:** This service is used to verify if there is an access point for the WiFi connection.
- **Wifi Connection:** This service provides the WiFi communication to transmit the data stream to the medical center.

Figure 2. The proposed service schema

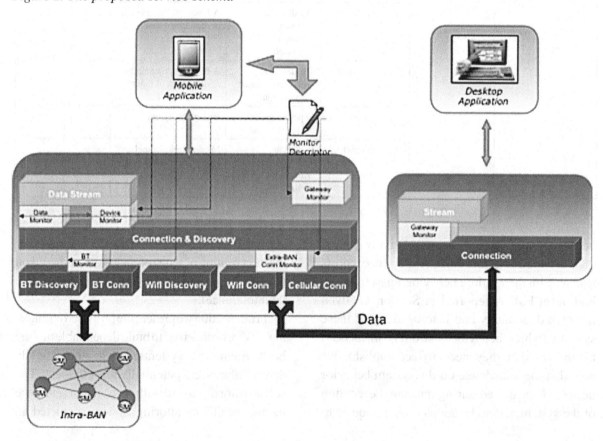

- **Cellular Connection:** This service provides the cellular communication (GPRS, UMTS, etc...) to transmit the data stream to the medical center when a WiFi access point is not available.
- **Connection and Discovery:** This service is placed at an upper layer and it has the role to hide to applications the details on the communication technology (Bluetooth, WiFi and cellular). Further, it provides technology-agnostic discovery services, which are then specialized for Bluetooth and WiFi.
- **Data Stream:** It provides streaming services for vital sign data to the application.

5.3 Medical Center Services

The services offered for the Medical Center side (desktop) are:

- **Connection:** This service provides the needed communication interface to receive data from the Gateway and to send commands to manage the monitoring.
- **Stream:** It is the service that dialogues with the desktop application of Medical Center. It reports the data acquired by the medical devices.

5.4 External Applications

Finally, we have to consider external application for both side (mobile and desktop). These applications generally include the GUI used by patients (on the mobile side) and by the medical staff (on the fixed side), and implement application specific data interpretation and reporting functions.

5.5 Monitors

Once introduced the general services of the mobile health monitoring system, we enrich the system with failure detection capabilities. To this aim, we introduce the concept of System Monitors.

A monitor is a service instantiated on-demand on the basis of the failures that have to be detected. By means of a Monitor Descriptor file (i.e. a XML file), the developer can set the failures that he wants to observe. This file is provided to the Mobile Application that, in turn, dynamically creates the requested monitors, which run in the background and are managed transparently from developers.

Monitors can act as lightweight model-checkers supporting formal runtime verification as shown in (Coronato et al., 2011).

Specifically, we introduce the following monitors to detect the failures reported in the FMEA study conducted in the previous section:

The Sensor Monitor is deployed on the medical device and it detects all of the failures that occur in a medical sensor node (ECG, Pulse Oximeter, Insulin Pump, etc...). This monitor can be considered as a failure logger for the medical device, since it can store the state of the node before of the failure, and report it to the gateway when the device is recovered. Since in the industry market there are medical sensors equipped of operating systems and programmability capabilities (i.e. TuffSat Oximeter (ThreadX, n.a.)), we can consider the possibility to add sensor monitors to the future releases of such sensors. On the other hand, the implementation of such monitor is already feasible in commodity WSN nodes, such as Berkley Motes (in (Salazar et al., 2010) authors identify a set of wireless sensors – IRIS, MICAz, TELOSb, SHIMMER and Imote2 - used for capturing and transmitting biomechanical and physiological signals, among other data related to healthcare, sports, motion capturing)

The Bluetooth Monitor detects the problems related to the Bluetooth connection such as, connection failures, Bluetooth channel failures and Bluetooth stack failures. It can also verify if there are problems during the discovery and inquiry phase of the medical devices equipped with the Bluetooth technology.

The Extra-BAN Monitor checks the availability of the WiFi and Cellular connections. It can be

Table 2. Failures detected by the monitors

Monitor	Detected Failures
Sensor Monitor	stuck-at-zero; software hang; reset; power failure; isolation
Bluetooth Monitor	connect failure; bluetooth stack failure; header failures; payload corruption; inquiry/scan failure; discovery failure
Extra-BAN Monitor	cellular/wifi network unavailable
Data Monitor	packet loss; data delivery failure; data mismatch
Device Monitor	incorrect reading; discontinous reading; out of scale reading; null reading; insulin under/over dose; no delivery failure; device unavailable
Gateway Monitor (mobile-side)	self-shutdown; input failure; output failure; freeze; unstable behavior
Gateway Monitor (desktop-side)	gateway unavailable

efficiently used to manage the handoff process between the two technologies. For instance, in the case of a patient leaving home, this monitor detects the WiFi connection failure and requires the establishment of a cellular connection. In contrast, when the patient comes back home, the Extra-BAN Monitor reveals the availability of the domestic network and switches from the cellular connection to a WiFi connection.

The Data Monitor checks if there are anomalies in the data stream acquired. For example, during the monitoring, some packet can be lost or a data delivery failure can occur.

The Device Monitor detects mainly if a medical device is unavailable. In this case, to better analyze the failure it is necessary to require extra information to the Sensor Monitor. Other failures that can be detected by this monitor are incorrect/discontinuous/out of scale/null reading failures and some failure related to a specific medical device (for instance, for insulin pump, it can control the injected dose, whereas out-of-scale readings can be detected for the ECG, depending on application specific threshold values specified in the Monitor Descriptor file).

The Gateway Monitor is present both in the Gateway and in the Medical Center. The aim of this monitor is to check if the gateway operates correctly. The Gateway Monitor in the Medical Center can only detect if the gateway becomes unavailable but it cannot know the cause. Instead the Gateway Monitor in the mobile side, can keep track of occurred failures, such as a freeze, self-shutdown, etc, following for instance the logging approach proposed in our earlier work (Cinque et al., 2007b).

6. USE OF A MONITOR

We have physically deployed a WSN topology in our lab to detect failures at runtime (Figure 3). We have designed and implemented a system monitor with the aim of detecting failure events from the real-world WSN. The monitor runs on a machine and listens for packets coming from all sensors through the sink node of the WSN. The detection of events (such as the stop of a node) is performed assuming that each sensor sends packets periodically, with a known rate, which is common to several WSN applications. Hence, for every node, the monitor sets a timeout, which is reset each time the monitor receives a packet from the given node. If the timeout expires for a node X, the monitor generates a Stop(X) event.

The use of time out may also detect temporary disconnections or delays. In this case, when packets from a node X are received again after a stop, the monitor generates a Start(X) event. Clearly, different failure detection approaches could be used as well, however this is not relevant for our experiment and out of the scope of the paper.

The monitor has been implemented as a java application running on a server (a Pentium 4 machine in our case) and connected via USB to a MIB520 Base station by Crossbow. As sensor nodes, we have adopted Iris Motes by Crossbow equipped with ZigBee RF Transceiver and TinyOS 2.0 operating system, running the BlinkToRadio application, just to perform a periodic sensing and sending of packets of all nodes to the sink.

7. CONCLUSION AND FUTURE WORK

The advent of AmI systems applied to critical application scenarios, such as mobile health monitoring, requires facing new dependability threats that may arise during the functioning of the system and that may result fatal for the health of the patient. Moved by these considerations, in this paper we propose the design of an innovative mobile health monitoring system, based on the configurable adoption of system monitors, conceived to detect the failures occurring at runtime, and hence providing a means to react to them in due time, preventing catastrophic consequences. The responsibilities of the monitors in terms of the failures they have to detect, are defined starting from the results of a failure modes and effects analysis, which allowed us to focus on every single

problem that may occur on these systems, and to define exactly where to deploy the monitors in order to deal with given failure modes. The approach can be used iteratively, to extend the system with further monitors or to readapt the existing ones, as soon as new failure modes are found. Future research activities will deal with the realization of a prototype system including the defined monitors, in order to assess on the field their capability at detecting the type of failures identified in the conducted failure mode analysis.

REFERENCES

Arnstein, L., Grimm, R., Hung, C., Kang, J. H., LaMarca, A., & Look, G. et al. (2002). Systems Support for Ubiquitous Computing: A Case Study of Two Implementations of Labscape. In *Proceedings of the First International Conference on Pervasive Computing (Pervasive '02).* Springer-Verlag.

Baskiyar, S. (2002). A real-time fault tolerant intra-body network. In *Proceedings of Local Computer Networks,* (pp. 235-240). IEEE.

Benlamri, R., & Docksteader, L. (2010). Morf: A mobile health-monitoring platform. *IT Professional, 12*(3), 18–25. doi:10.1109/MITP.2010.3

Bohn, J., Coroama, V., Langheinrich, M., Mattern, F., & Rohs, M. (2005). Social, economic, and ethical implications of ambient intelligence and ubiquitous computing. In Ambient Intelligence. Springer.

Figure 3. Failure detection by means of monitor

Carefusion. (2011). *Carefusion nicolet*. Retrieved 2011 from http://www.carefusion.com/medical-products/neurology/neurodiagnostic-monitoring/eeg/nicolet-ambulatorymonitor.aspx

Center for Technology and Aging. (2009). *Technologies for remote patient monitoring in older adults*. Center for Technology and Aging.

Chakraborty, S., Poolsappasit, N., & Ray, I. (2007). Reliable Delivery of Event Data from Sensors to Actuators in Pervasive Computing Environments. In *Proceedings of 21st Annual IFIP WG 11.3 Working Conference on Data and Applications Security (DBSec'07)* (LNCS), (vol. 4602, pp. 77-92). Redondo Beach, CA: Springer.

Chen, M., Gonzalez, S., Vasilakos, A., Cao, H., & Leung, V. C. (2011). Body area networks: A survey. *Mob. Netw. Appl.*, *16*, 171–193. doi: 10.1007/s11036-010-0260-8

Chetan, S., Ranganathan, A., & Campbell, R. (2005, Spring). Towards fault tolerance pervasive computing. *IEEE Technology and Society Magazine*, *24*(1), 38–44. doi:10.1109/MTAS.2005.1407746

Cinque, M., Coronato, A., & Testa, A. (2011). A Failure Modes and Effects Analysis of Mobile Health Monitoring Systems. In *Proceedings of the 2011 International Conference on Systems, Computing Sciences and Software Engineering (SCSS), part of the International Joint Conferences on Computer, Information, and Systems Sciences, and Engineering (CISSE 11)*. Academic Press.

Cinque, M., Coronato, A., & Testa, A. (2012). Dependable Services for Mobile Health Monitoring Systems. *International Journal of Ambient Computing and Intelligence*, *4*(1), 1–15. doi:10.4018/jaci.2012010101

Cinque, M., Cotroneo, D., Di Martinio, C., & Russo, S. (2007a). Modeling and Assessing the Dependability of Wireless Sensor Networks. In *Proceedings of the 26th IEEE International Symposium on Reliable Distributed Systems (SRDS '07)*. IEEE Computer Society.

Cinque, M., Cotroneo, D., Kalbarczyk, Z., & Iyer, R. (2007b). How do mobile phones fail? A failure data analysis of symbian os smart phones. In *Proceedings of Dependable Systems and Networks*, (pp. 585–594). IEEE.

Coronato, A., & De Pietro, G. (2010). Formal design of ambient intelligence applications. *Computer*, *43*(12), 60–68. doi:10.1109/MC.2010.335

Coronato, A., & De Pietro, G. (2011, July). Tools for the Rapid Prototyping of Provably Correct Ambient Intelligence Applications. *IEEE Transactions on Software Engineering*, 20.

Curiac, D., Volosencu, C., Pescaru, D., Jurca, L., & Doboli, A. (2009). A view upon redundancy in wireless sensor networks. In *Proceedings of the 8th WSEAS International Conference on Signal Processing, Robotics and Automation (ISPRA'09)*. WSEAS.

Department of Defense – USA (1980). *Us mil std 1629 1980: Procedure for performing a failure mode, effect and criticality analysis, method 102*. Author.

Dicks, K. E. (2007). *Telemedicine 2.0 has arrived. Future Healthcare Magazine*.

Duman, H., Hagras, H., & Callaghan, V. (2010). A multi-society-based intelligent association discovery and selection for ambient intelligence environment. ACM Trans. Autonom. Adapt. Syst., 5(2).

Gelernter, D. (1985, January). Generative communication in Linda. *ACM Transactions on Programming Languages and Systems, 7*(1), 80–112. doi:10.1145/2363.2433

Georgalis, Y., Grammenos, D., & Stephanidis, C. (2009). Middleware for Ambient Intelligence Environments: Reviewing Requirements and Communication Technologies. In *Proceedings of the 5th International on ConferenceUniversal Access in Human-Computer Interaction. Part II: Intelligent and Ubiquitous Interaction Environments (UAHCI '09).* Springer-Verlag.

Hanna, S. (2009). Regulations and standards for wireless medical applications. In *Proc. of the 3rd Int. Symp. on Medical Information and Communication Technology.* Academic Press.

Hanson, M., Powell, H., Barth, A., Ringgenberg, K., Calhoun, B., Aylor, J., & Lach, J. (2009). Body area sensor networks: Challenges and opportunities. *Computer, 42*(1), 58–65. doi:10.1109/MC.2009.5

Hao, Y., & Foster, R. (2008). Wireless body sensor networks for health-monitoring applications. *Physiological Measurement, 29*(11), R27–R56. doi:10.1088/0967-3334/29/11/R01 PMID:18843167

James, C. B. H., Cook, R. & Konwinski, J. (2004). *Failure mode effects and criticality analysis (fmeca).* Home ECG test kit.

Kansal, A., Hsu, J., Zahedi, S., & Srivastava, M. B. (2007). Power management in energy harvesting sensor networks. *ACM Transactions on Embedded Computing Systems,* 6.

Latino, R. J. & Flood, A. (2004). Optimizing fmea and rca efforts in healthcare. *Journal of Healthcare Risk Management, 24*(3), 21–28. doi: .10.1002/jhrm.5600240305

Lin, H., Shao, J., Zhang, C., & Fang, Y. (2013). Cam: Cloud-assisted privacy preserving mobile health monitoring. *IEEE Transactions on* Information Forensics and Security, *8*(6), 985–997. doi:10.1109/TIFS.2013.2255593

Nehmer, J., Karshmer, A., Lamm, R., & Becker, M. (2006). Living assistance systems: an ambient intelligence approach. In *Proceedings of 28th International Conference on Software Engineering (ICSE'06)* (pp. 43-50). ICSE. doi:10.1145/1134285.1134293

O'Donovan, T., O'Donoghue, J., Sreenan, C., Sammon, D., O'Reilly, P., & O'Connor, K. A. (2009). A context aware wireless body area network (BAN). In *Proceedings of Pervasive Computing Technologies for Healthcare,* (pp. 1-8). Academic Press.

Paksuniemi, M., Sorvoja, H., Alasaarela, E., & Myllyla, R. (2006). Wireless sensor and data transmission needs and technologies for patient monitoring in the operating room and intensive care unit. In *Proceedings of Engineering in Medicine and Biology Society,* (pp. 5182-5185). IEEE.

Ponnekanti, S. R., Johanson, B., Kiciman, E., & Fox, A. (2003). Portability, extensibility and robustness in iROS. Pervasive Computing and Communications. 11-19.

Qnx. (n.d.). Retrieved from http://www.qnx.com/solutions/industries/medical/

Salazar, A. J., Silva, A. S., Borges, C. M., & Correia, M. V. (2010). An initial experience in wearable monitoring sport systems. In *Proceedings of Information Technology and Applications in Biomedicine (ITAB),* (pp. 1-4). IEEE.

Simoncini, L. (2003). Architectural Challenges for "Ambient Dependability". In *Proceedings of Object-Oriented Real-Time Dependable Systems.* IEEE.

Sneha, S., & Varshney, U. (2013). A framework for enabling patient monitoring via mobile ad hoc network. *Decis. Support Syst., 55*(1), 218–234. DOI: 10.1016/j.dss.2013.01.024

Sommerville, I. (2004). *Software Engineering* (7th ed.). Pearson Addison Wesley.

Spadotto, K. M. S. E., & Hawkins, J. (2009). ICT convergence, confluence and creativity: The application of emerging technologies for healthcare transformation. In *Proc. of the 3rd Int. Symp. on Medical Information and Communication Technology*. Academic Press.

Stamatis, D. H. (2003). Failure mode and effect analysis: FMEA from theory to execution (2nd ed.). ASQ Quality Press.

Threadx. (n.d.). Retrieved from http://www.qnx.com/solutions/industries/medical/

Triantafyllidis, A., Koutkias, V., Chouvarda, I., & Maglaveras, N. (2012). A pervasive health system integrating patient monitoring, status logging and social sharing. *IEEE Transactions on Information Technology in Biomedicine*. PMID:23193318

Van Halteren, A., Bults, R., Wac, K., Konstantas, D., Widya, I., Dokovski, N., et al. (2004). *Mobile Patient Monitoring: The Mobihealth System*. Academic Press.

Yan, H., Huo, H., Xu, Y., & Gidlund, M. (2010). Wireless sensor network based e-health system implementation and experimental results. *IEEE Transactions on* Consumer Electronics, *56*(4), 2288–2295. doi:10.1109/TCE.2010.5681102

Zhang, Y., & Xiao, H. (2009). Bluetooth-based sensor networks for remotely monitoring the physiological signals of a patient. *Trans. Info. Tech. Biomed., 13*.

KEY TERMS AND DEFINITIONS

Ambient Intelligence: The field to study and create embodiments for smart environments that not only react to human events through sensing, interpretation and service provision, but also learn and adapt their operation and services to the users over time.

Dependability: Dependability is a measure of a system's availability, reliability, and its maintainability.

Failure Analysis: The fault analysis is a top down, deductive analysis in which an undesired state of a system is analyzed combining a series of lower-level events.

Health Monitoring: In information technology and multimedia terms, health monitoring refers to the technique to check patient's vital sign by means of remote communications.

Monitor: A device used for observing, checking, or keeping a continuous record of something.

Resiliency: An ability to recover from or adjust easily to misfortune or change.

Wireless Sensor Networks: A network of RF transceivers, sensors, machine controllers, microcontrollers, and user interface devices with at least two nodes communicating by means of wireless transmissions.

Chapter 3
A Camera–Based System for Determining Hand Range of Movement Measurements in Rheumatoid Arthritis

Aaron Bond
University of Ulster, UK

Kevin Curran
University of Ulster, UK

ABSTRACT

Rheumatoid arthritis affects around 1% of the world's population. Detection of the disease relies heavily on observation by physicians. The effectiveness of these kinds of tests is dependent on the ability and experience and can vary depending on the observer. This chapter aims to investigate the use of Xbox Kinect camera for monitoring in rheumatoid arthritis patients as a cost-effective and precise method of assessment. A system has been developed that implements the Kinect sensor for usage in a hand recognition and digit measurement capacity. This system performs the tasks usually completed by a physician such as digit dimension monitoring and exercise observations. With the system being designed to be portable and easy-to-use, it is an ideal solution for both the physician monitoring patients in a clinic as well as posing a possible solution for patients wishing to monitor their own condition in their homes.

INTRODUCTION

Rheumatoid arthritis (RA) is a chronic disease that mainly affects the synovial joints of the human skeleton. It is an inflammatory disorder that causes joints to produce more fluid and increases the mass of the tissue in the joint resulting in a loss of function and inhibiting movement in the

muscles. This can lead to patients having difficulties performing activities of daily living (ADLs). Treatment of RA is determined by physicians through x-rays, questionnaires and other invasive techniques. An example of this would be angle measurements taken using instruments such as tape measures or a dynamometer to measure grip strength. There is no cure for RA but clinicians

DOI: 10.4018/978-1-4666-7284-0.ch003

Copyright © 2015, IGI Global. Copying or distributing in print or electronic forms without written permission of IGI Global is prohibited.

aim to diagnose it quickly and offer therapies which alleviate symptoms or modify the disease process. These treatment options include injection therapy, physiotherapy, manual therapy (i.e. massage therapy or joint manipulation) and drugs which can reduce the rate of damage to cartilage and bone. These treatments are assisted by patient education. Patients are shown methods of Joint Protection, educated in the use of assistive tools to aid in ADLs and shown altered working methods..

Solutions designed to facilitate and aid diagnosis of vulnerable patients – ones which are in chronic or debilitating pain, for example – face an array of unique requirements. Rheumatoid Arthritis affects around 1% of the population (Worden, 2011) and causes synovial joints in affected areas to become inflamed due to extra synovial fluid being produced. This can lead to a breakdown of the cartilage in the joints and can cause the bones in the joint to corrode. As a result, patients commonly exhibit deformation in their fingers and joints; as well as note regular and occasionally disabling pain (Majithia & Geraci, 2007). Typically, assessing patient mobility is a case of factoring in the patient attending their local medical practitioner for tests or treatment. This can become difficult however if a patient has limited mobility. For a patient who is suffering RA, it is possible that their disease is afflicting more than one set of joints in their body. Also, having the disease increases the risk of osteoporosis in the patient due to the nature of the disease and the medication they are required to take (Handout on Health: Rheumatoid Arthritis, 2009). In effect, this can mean that the patient would require home visits more commonly than a patient who is not suffering joint pain. Physicians required to visit the home of their patients in order to assess the current disease progression and possible treatments must have access to portable equipment. Therefore the equipment used must be mobile, easily set-up and be an inexpensive product. Portable low cost equipment does exist that aids treatment at home, however these methods have their own limitations

that must be considered. The Jamar dynamometer has proven to be an inexpensive and reliable gauge of grip strength, providing data used in assessment. However, in patients with decreased mobility, a grip strength test would prove to aggravate their symptoms and increase levels of pain. This option is also open to false reading from patients not willing to exert their maximum grip strength due to the uncomfortable nature of the test (Richards & Palmiter-Thomas, 1996). There appears to be a lack of a measurement device that can record patients' treatment progression that is portable, cost effective and which has maximum consideration for patient discomfort level.

Healthy joints require little energy to move and the movement is usually painless. However for RA patients their joints have a thickened lining, crowed with white blood cells and blood vessels. Movement of affected joints not only causes bone erosion but also triggers the release of a chemical within the white blood cell causing a general ill feeling (Panayi, 2003). This secreted substances cause the joint to swell, become hot and tender to the touch while also inducing varying levels of pain. Increased swelling, triggered by the white blood cells response causes joint deformation. Severe joint deformity can render traditional methods, such as the manual devices mentioned earlier, ineffective. However it also presents limitations for the proposed advance methods currently being developed. The glove method requires the patient to fit their hand into a standard size glove. This method fails to address the fact that RA patients do not have standard joint movement; therefore maneuvering their hand into the glove could cause unnecessary pain and discomfort. Additionally a standard glove does not accommodate for joint deformity, especially not the extreme deformities that are symptomatic of RA. The difference in finger and joint size is also not considered. RA patients usually have symmetrical joint deformity, i.e. if there third knuckle on their right hand is affected then it is likely that the same joint on the left hand will be affected (Panayi, 2003). Expanding this example, if the same joint on both hands is swollen then the glove would either fit appropriately to the swollen joints or the surrounding joints. This increases result variability as hand movement cannot be standardised. In order for the glove method to accurately measure joint movement and limit discomfort a custom version would be needed for each patient. This would not be a viable option since the progression of RA would require patients to have multiple gloves fitted.

Current goniometric tests are not repeatable and are subject to human error (Condell et al., 2012). This can lead to adverse effects on the patient treatment. However, proposed solutions in the areas of glove-based measurements fail to address the fundamental issues like patient comfort and differing hand sizes. Moreover, the cost incurred with these solutions renders the systems impractical. In order to maximise patients comfort during testing, an external non-contact device is needed for RA patients. This is one of the proposed benefits of a potential computer based camera system. The patient would perform movement tasks but they would not be restricted by any outside materials. Movement would be recorded digitally aiding treatment analysis. The Kinect's versatility and cost effectiveness address accessibility issues. It would be a beneficial, portable piece of equipment that could be purchased by physicians and also patients. Therefore patients could carry out movement tasks daily; the results would be recorded by the camera and a computer. The data could then be assessed by the physician at a later date. A continual data supply would aid treatment planning and could also indicate differences in movement throughout the day. Providing a fuller grasp of movement functionally that is not currently assessed, due to the time restrictions of appointment allocations for patients.

The primary aim of this research therefore was to assess the viability of a camera-based software system for the real-time and historical measurement of hand movement and deformation in RA patients. Its development proposes a viable gain over current goniometric measurement methods. Existing methods and approaches to digitally measuring hand dimensions and movement have failed to address the key issues surrounding RA treatment. While these solutions seek to allow automatic and accurate measurement, many use non-commercial hardware and rely on proprietary software which can be very expensive. Similarly, these devices tend to be highly technical and require the supervision of a trained technician. The hand recognition and measurement system outlined here is a user-friendly alternative to current goniometric measurement methods. It will attempt to overcome challenges and limitations of other physical systems and establish the best solution to the common issues.

BACKGROUND

Measuring hand movement in this context refers to the ability of a given system to determine finger-digit movement in relation to the rest of the hand. Some methods may also allow for automatic detection and measurement of swelling and deformities of the hand. These characteristics are essential when tackling the development of a system aimed at assessing the symptoms and progression of an RA patient. When visiting their doctor, the patient will have their movements assessed in the areas where their RA is affecting them. The physician will check for the presence of finger-thumb drift, swan neck/boutonniere deformity, as well as Bouchard and Heberden nodes (Rheumatoid: Hand Exam, 2011). The examination consists of a patient placing their hand flat on a table (where possible – depending on patient discomfort) with their elbow and wrist resting flat. Using a goniometer, the physician examines (in degrees) extension, flexion, adduction and abduction of the proximal interphalangeal (PIP), metacarpopalangeal (MCP) and distal interphalangeal (DIP) joints of the fingers (Arthritis: Rheumatoid Arthritis, 2008). This determines thumb-index finger drift (position of index finger away from thumb) and palmar abduction (de Kraker, et al., 2009). The measurements are all documented in handwritten forms and are recorded to aid future assessments. These readings are all influenced by physician training and observations therefore they can vary between examiners.

Physical Goniometric Methods

Current goniometric methods for monitoring and assessing joint mobility and deformity are mostly analogue. Among the measures and practices used to establish the patient's disease activity are several self and physical assessments. These are essential for the continued treatment of RA in a patient, allowing the physician to determine joint-protection exercises as well as potential medicinal treatment in the form of anti-inflammatory and auto-immune medications. Measurements of a patients hand is recommended to be taken at regular visits to their doctor (Handout on Health: Rheumatoid Arthritis, 2009). These assessments can include hand measurements, blood tests (among other lab tests), and X-ray imaging of the affected hand.

A sphygmomanometer is used to assess a patients grip strength in their affected hand. This is achieved by inflating the cuff of the device to a standard pressure in a rolled manner, then having the patient grip the cuff in the palm of their hand. After the patient has squeezed the cuff, the physician can take a reading of pressure which can be used to indicate patient's grip strength (Eberhardt, Malcus-Johnson, & Rydgren, 1991). However, using the modified sphygmomanometer can proved misleading results. This instruments pressure gauge is activated when the patient squeezes the air filled compartment (Ashton & Myers, 2004). The limitation of this being that patients will larger hands will have artificially lower pressure readings than patients with smaller hands. This is due to the variance in pressure applied over the surface area (Fess, 1995).

The Jamar dynamometer is seen as a reliable alternative to the modified sphygmomanometer. It is a hydraulic instrument, functioning within a sealed system. It measures grip strength in kilograms or pounds of force (Ashton & Myers, 2004). Its versatility, simplistic functionality and cost effective features makes this method easily accessible (Fees, 1987). It has been found to provide accurate readings and the results are reproducible (Hamilton, Balnave, & Adams, 1994). This is an additional benefit the Jamar dynamometer has over its mechanical counterpart the Stoelting dynamometer. This mechanical method measures tension when force is applied to a steel spring and is not viewed as a reliable measurement (Richards & Palmiter-Thomas, 1996).

In assessing the patient's discomfort, the physician must rely on several questionnaires in order to gain an understanding of disease progression. The Stanford health assessment questionnaire, for example, is designed to assess the average morning stiffness the patient feels in the affected joints of their hands (Eberhardt, Malcus-Johnson, & Rydgren, 1991). This is measured and recorded in minutes and is used to gain an understanding of how long it takes for the patients joints to loosen and become supple again. Similarly, the patient is assessed on their experience of pain levels since their previous examination. This is done through a questionnaire in which they must evaluate their pain levels and discomfort over the preceding period. Another assessment of this form is comprised of several questions regarding ability and pain when performing ADLs. Commonly, the ADLs which are assessed include "dressing and grooming", eating, cutting and preparing food and general hand control over cups and jars (Eberhardt, Malcus-Johnson, & Rydgren, 1991). Patients are also assessed using the Visual Analogue Scale to measure their level of pain and discomfort. This consists of a line, marked on one side as "No pain" and on the other as "Worst pain imaginable" and patients are asked to mark a spot along the line which reflects the current feeling (Schofield, Aveyard, & Black, 2007). Similarly, a Health Assessment Questionnaire is designed to establish the patient's ability to perform daily tasks, with each question grading their capability using a "four-point grading system". This measures their "daily functionality level" (Fries, Spitz, Kraines, & Holman, 1980).

As a result of RA, joints in a patients hand and fingers can suffer bone erosion to varying degrees. In order to measure and document this, the patient will undergo radiographic tests in the form of X-ray imaging and MRI scans of the affected areas. This shows how the bones in the patients hand are affected and can be measured over a period of time to show disease progression and activity. Another method which has the potential to highlight key areas of bone-degradation and joint swelling is an ultrasound imaging of the affected hand. This offers a less invasive method of assessing bone density and level of swelling in the patient. However, Chen, Cheng & Hsu (2009) have shown that "prognostic value of MRI is not directly transferable to Ultrasound" and therefore it is, not yet, an adequate option for assessment.

Typically, several clinical tests are performed to establish the disease activity level; including urine, blood and other tests. From these tests, the patients Erythrocyte Sedimentation Rate and C - reactive protein results are established (DAS Booklet - Quick reference guide for Healthcare Professionals, 2010). In patients with rheumatoid arthritis, the C – reactive protein and ESR levels are used as a measurement and indication of inflammation in the patient's joints (Black, Kushner, & Samols, 2004).

Camera-Based Movement Detection

There are many options when attempting to determine a movement of a subject via camera-based methods. Providing a system with "computer vision" and allowing it to assess variables such as movement, size and depth of an object, is the goal in camera-based solutions. Some camera based-solutions require proprietary hardware, while others are able to utilise common devices and already existing technologies.

OpenCV is a cross-platform function library focusing on real-time image processing. The aim of this library is to supply an application with "Computer Vision", the ability to take data from a still or video camera and transform it into new representation or decision (Bradski & Kaehler, 2008). By taking pixel location and colour information, the library builds an image matrix which it uses to "see". OpenCV was originally developed and released by Intel. Since its release in 1999, the library has allowed a method of tracking motion within captured video and given developers the ability to discern movement angles and gestures. Also, in terms of utilising images and making a decision, here it refers to the ability for any given system to then automatically determine people or objects within a scene. Functions like this are possible with statistical pattern recognition, located within a general purpose Machine Learning Library (MLL) included in the library. This allows for implementation of many features including Object Identification, Segmentation and Recognition, Face Recognition, Gesture Recognition, Camera and Motion Tracking (Chaczko & Yeoh, 2007).

OpenCV is optimised to run on Intel-based systems where it finds the Intel Performance Primitives. Bradski & Kaehler (2008) note that while the library consistently outperforms other vision libraries (LTI and VXL), its own processing is optimised by about 20% with the presence of IPP. The OpenCV library works well with installed camera drivers to ensure that it functions with most commercially available devices. This allows developers to create applications and rely on non-proprietary, widely available camera equipment. Therefore cost and development become a lot more practical for potential developers. Furthermore, in relation to potential environments and scenarios in which applications may be deployed, utilising existing cameras and commonly available devices means that applications can be implemented in a wide array of locations.

The Prosilica GC1290 system is a product designed to facilitate the measurement of a hand for patients with RA (GigE Vision for 3D Medical Research, 2010). Designed by threeRivers 3D, the device is intended to monitor the joint swelling in a hand by recording changes in the volume of the patients joints. A metal frame (80cm high, 60cm wide and 40cm deep) houses a total of four cameras and scanners. Two 3d laser scanners project patterns and grids onto the patient's hand which is then returned in order to create a 3d representation. The laser scanners are equipped with a monochrome camera in order to record this image and identify the laser grid. A colour camera picks up a standard image and is used to monitor joint deformation, while a thermal imaging camera detects joint inflammation. There is also a device intended to measure thermal information located near the hand rest; this is used to provide reference information: ambient room temperature, patients general thermal information.

All data taken from the device is recorded and displayed in real time in order to minimise problems such as motion blurring because of hand movement. This data is then processed by proprietary software packaged with the device to display this information (at 32 frames per second) to the patient and the physician. The software system used is also deployable to all major operating systems (GigE Vision for 3D Medical Research, 2010). With the range of information gathered by this device, it would allow physicians to gather very specific and relevant information on a patient; and process it in a relatively short period of time. Similarly, using a device which outputs measurements on a patients hand standardises the procedure and readings; making them more assessable. This is because the information gathered by the device is statistical and provides a quantitative assessment of disease progression. Furthermore, this limits human error in measurements taken and does not

rely on the physicians judgement. The Prosilica system does have some drawbacks, however. Since the device is bespoke it is not commercially available but is designed for medical use. This results in the device requiring direct contact with the manufacturer. This also has an adverse effect on the affordability of the device. The device itself is relatively large, consisting of the aforementioned cameras and frame. While the device could be suited for use in a doctor or physician's office or surgery it would not accommodate home visits and physician mobility. In cases where a physician is required to perform a home visit to the patient, it is not feasible that the device could accompany them due to size and associate cost.

Glove-Based Systems

As an alternative to current goniometric methods, there have been many investigations into glove-based technologies. These aim to assess a patient's finger and joint movement in order to aid in diagnosis and treatment of RA. Existing glove-based solutions, use varied methods of reading joint mobility and tension. Among the technology used are sensors using magnetic technology, electrical resistors and contacts or LEDs with flexible tubes (Dipietro, Sabatini, & Dario, 2008).

Previous research into the use of glove-based technologies has shown the 5DT Data Glove to be among the most accurate versatile gloves available (Condell, et al., 2010). It utilises fourteen fiber-optic sensors; with two sensors per digit and one sensor for each knuckle on the patients hand. It also has a tilt sensor mounted on the back of the hand to measure the orientation of the patient's hand. The sensors on the glove work by measuring light travelling through the sensors. As the patient moves their hand, the stress on the sensor changes, altering the amount of light passing through the receiver.

The glove is produced by Fifth Dimension Technologies and allows for accurate measurement of hand/finger movements; passing the information via USB to either the bundled software or software developed to utilise specific aspects of the glove. To accomplish the creation of custom software to utilise the glove, it comes with a cross-platform SDK in order for developers to make better use of the data they are able to collect. However, this glove is only beneficial if the hand to be tested is always going to be either the left or right hand of a patient. Since the glove is designed to fit only one side of the patient, a new glove must be used should the measurements being taken be desired from the other hand. Furthermore, if the measurements are to be taken from a patient with a different sized hand than the glove which is available, a more suitable one must be found.

Dipietro et al. (2008) also found that the most accurate results were read from the device when the cloth of the glove fit the patients hand well. Were the cloth too tight, the glove would restrict movement in the patient and give readings which were more extreme than the actual movements. However, if the glove material was loose on the patient, readings were not representative and were less than the actual movements. While the glove allows for highly accurate information readings from the patient's hand; it has some problems which are intrinsic to its design. Gloves like this one are designed to measure hand movements and gestures while the software has been designed to incorporate that use into hand assessment tools for RA patients. One of the main symptoms of RA is hand and finger deformation along with "periarticular osteopenia in hand and/or wrist joints" (Arnett, et al., 1988). Combined, this results in limitations to hand movements and articulation. Thus, the finger and wrist articulation which is needed in order to manoeuvre the hand into a glove can become painful and difficult.

USING THE KINECT

A Kinect Sensor is the medium chosen to receive the images of the subject's hand. The Kinect is currently available in two models; the "Xbox 360 Kinect" and the "Kinect for Windows". Both models are functional with a Windows-based PC and can utilise the Kinect SDK released by Microsoft. The Kinect for Windows has been modified to allow for readings to be taken much closer to the device than allowed by the Xbox 360 version. This ensures a greater accuracy of data taken from the subject. For the purpose of this design the software will be designed to work with both the Kinect for Windows and the Xbox 360 Kinect; allowing users to utilise whichever is more accessible with the knowledge that Kinect for Windows readings will be more accurate at closer ranges. The Xbox Kinect was used due to affordability and accessibility of the device. However, all code produced can run on both platforms as much of the business logic which handles transferring information from the device to the development computer is achieved through drivers and image-processing libraries like the Kinect SDK. This abstraction allows for maximum versatility in the system.

The Kinect is a device which facilitates the translation of real-world objects and motion into 3d representations. The basics of the device were initially developed by PrimeSense, who later sold the technology to Microsoft. The device utilises a number of sensors in order to accumulate input which can be compiled into a digital representation. It has one camera which allows for input in the infra-red (IR) spectrum which returns a depth map. This map is transmitted from an IR transmitter located next to the IR receiver and consists of a projection of dots onto the target area[1]. Also, the sensor contains a third camera which receives standard RGB (human spectrum) input in order to gain a colour image of the target area. The colour input camera receives information at a resolution of 640x480 pixels while the IR receiver gathers input at 320x240 pixels. Both cameras run at 30 frames per second. The field of view on the depth image is 57.8 degrees (Limitations of the Kinect, 2010). The device also contains a microphone array for receiving sound input (which can allow

Figure 1. Microsoft Kinect for Windows

voice recognition and commands). This consists of 4 microphones placed along the bottom of the Kinect. Lastly, the Kinect features a motorised base. This base allows for targeting of the sensor bar; adjusting its position to acquire the best perspective of the target space. This base allows for manoeuvring allows for a total alteration of 27 degrees vertically in either direction. All of these features of the Kinect make it capable of processing an area to determine distance to an object as well as colour and audio ambience.

While a standard camera with computer vision software may be able to determine objects in a space, it can become difficult if there is a lack of colour differentiation between the object and the surrounding space. Tölgyessy & Hubinský (2011) assert that with the extra cameras and sensors, performing tasks such as image segmentation becomes a lot easier, especially with the distance threshold which can be assigned to the input. This allows unwanted background data to be filtered out and reduces the noise in the input. Microsoft has also released an SDK which contains drivers

and other files associated with producing an application utilising the Kinect. The SDK allows for the device to be used with a Windows 7 operating system and supports C++, C# and Visual Basic programming languages. Along with access to the raw sensor information the Kinect is gathering, the SDK also allows for skeletal tracking (identifying humans and human gestures) via bundled libraries (Ackerman, 2011).

One of the main advantages of the Kinect is the accessibility of its hardware. The Kinect is a relatively advanced device allowing for computer vision. By combining advanced hardware with a commercial price-point and making an SDK available, Microsoft have allowed developers to capitalise on the capabilities of the device at relatively low cost. This promotes its use in varied environments since maintenance and cost are comparatively small when regarding other advanced computer vision utilities. The device is mobile too. The Kinect sensor was designed and built for home use, making it reliable in many conditions. For optimal functionality, the device requires standard room lighting. It requires that the room be lit well enough that the standard RGB camera can pick up information but also not so bright that the IR patterns become indistinguishable (Carmody, 2010). A downside of the system is that for accurate readings, the subject must be at least the minimum distance from the device. This minimum distance for the Kinect sensor is 0.6m and the maximum range is variable between 5m – 6m (Limitations of the Kinect, 2010). However there is an inexpensive add-on for the Kinect which acts as a zoom lens, reducing the minimum distance required. We utilised Connector/NET to integrate a C# system with web-based MySql database implementation. This was the preferred option of database technology as the web-based data access allowing remote tests feeding back to a centralised database and hand readings are never stored locally but on a web server. The system only measures hand data when all 5 fingers are present and readable by the program. This ensures accuracy since the hand has to be properly oriented in order for the fingers to be recognised.

We establish a single finger width as shown in Figure 2. This process ensures that each finger examined by the system is assigned to a relevant local variable and thus can be analysed and stored based on which part of the hand object it belongs to. Employing this method will also mean the readings from the fingers are as accurate as possible no matter the orientation of the hand.

The system uses several supplementary software frameworks in order to receive and analyse information from the Kinect sensor. The Kinect sensor reads the scene and this image and depth information is passed from the Kinect to the OpenNI framework via a set of 64bit PrimeSense drivers. The CandescentNUI implemented in the main C# program then accesses the OpenNI data stream and constructs it into usable objects for use by the hand recognition system. The graphical user interface (GUI) is constructed using Visual Studio 2010's designer and XAML code. The type of interface created is a Windows Presentation Foundation (WPF) project which allows for efficient form navigation in the form of XAML "pages" which can be linked to and navigated away from. This layout allows the system to retain a sense of being light-weight and efficient since the pages are only loaded as-and-when they are needed and are not causing too much background processing. Furthermore, the GUI is developed in such a way as to be approachable and easy to navigate for any user since a main objective of this project is to test viability of patient home-use. The Connector/NET addition to the C# project which allows integration with MySQL also facilitates quite functional MySQL statement writing. We set the maximum depth range for the Kinect sensor to receive data as 900mm; this is chosen because at ranges close to and above 900mm, with an image resolution of 640x480 pixels, hand and contour information

Figure 2. Finger width measurement process

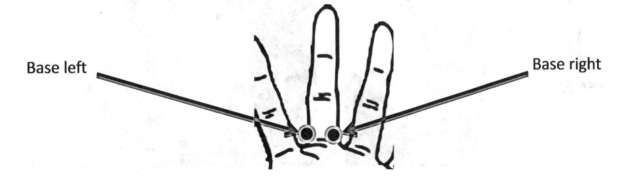

becomes very difficult to establish and the integrity of the data is questionable. The CandescentNUI code which is used for the majority of the hand recognition returns detailed information back to the recognition interface. In the system, a listener is set up to handle new frames of information being returned from the Kinect sensor. In order to give feedback to the user of the computation that is being performed on the image data being received, we add a raw data window which contains much of the pertinent information involved with the hand recognition. This window may be presented in either RGB (full color) image format or a black and white depth interpretation of the data. For the purposes of this system, it is more effective to show the depth data since it gives a better idea to the user of the location they need their hand to be in order to achieve optimal readings as shown in Figure 3. Now, when the depth data is being analysed by the system we can automatically pass it forward to the interface of the system in order for the user to observe the changing depth and finger recognition information.

The location of the cluster information and finger information overlays align much better with the depth data than with the RGB. This is due to the location of the two cameras which receive this information being located slightly separately apart. The data generated by Candescent allows for the hands on screen to be enumerated and for each hand to have a number of "finger" elements. Within these objects numerous pieces of position and depth data are accessible. In order to establish which finger the data is associated with, we must first determine which finger is which in the hand object. To achieve this, a method utilising the logic of finger position on the X axis is used. This code is run for each finger. This code is utilised in the case of the left hand being presented as the thumb in that context would be the digit located furthest along the X axis. This is run for each digit and as it is assigned, it is removed from the hand object; allowing the system to re-enter the hand object and assign any unassigned fingers. Each finger has a "BaseLeft" and "BaseRight" property as well as a "FingerPoint". Each of these objects has an X, Y and Z (depth) value. It is from these that we are able to determine dimension data and whether the users hand is positioned correctly for optimal readings to be taken. Optimal position for

Figure 3. Sensor depth data and RGB with finger recognition

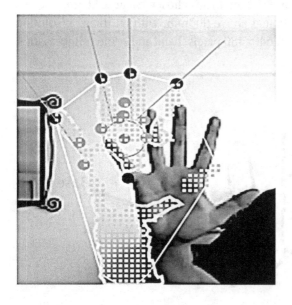
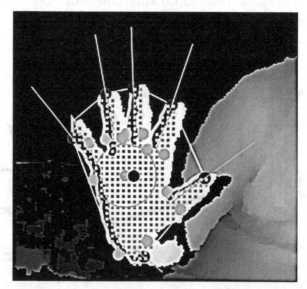

readings is determined by taking the Z value for the left-most digit and Z value for the right-most digit and comparing them. Using this method we can establish horizontal tilt of the hand and can formulate an algorithm which will alert the user if their hand is positioned too far skewed on the X axis.

We compare the left-most and right-most digits and use a threshold of 4% +/- each other to allow for some tilt of the hand. This has been assessed to be the most effective range since it allows enough range of movement that the hand does not feel stiffened in order to be read but maximises the integrity of the hand data. This is especially important in this project since it is quite possible that a sufferer of rheumatoid arthritis will have difficulty orienting their hand to an exact location in order for the system to assess it. Using this method, the user is afforded quite a lot of freedom of movement. The base left and base right values of an individual finger may have different Y axis values since the hand can be tilted to many different orientations and the system will still detect it and analyse the data. To overcome this, the finger width must be determined by using Pythagoras' theorem to determine the distance between the two points.

As seen in Figure 4, the distance on the X axis between the two points can be determined as "B". When the distance on the Y axis is also determined we can use it as "A" and find "C" through Pythagoras' theorem: $c^2 = a^2 + b^2$. A similar method is implemented in order to determine the height of a given finger. Since the finger can be oriented in a number of different fashions (similar to Figure 4 the Y value of the finger point is not an adequate reference to the height of the finger from its base. For this reason, the Pythagorean theorem is again utilised in the following fashion detailed in Figure 5.

Since we have already established finger width, we can half it and use it to determine a base value for a triangle. By taking getting the difference between the "BaseRight" and "BaseLeft" values we can construct a base line for the triangle to be used for the Pythagorean theorem. The "B" line referred to in this code snippet is the straight line distance between the lower part of the triangle and the top; effectively giving the second side of the triangle. The *"Math.Abs()"* function here is the method for returning an absolute value which is part of the Math library of C#. The purpose of this is to always return the difference between the

Figure 4. Finger width Pythagoras Method

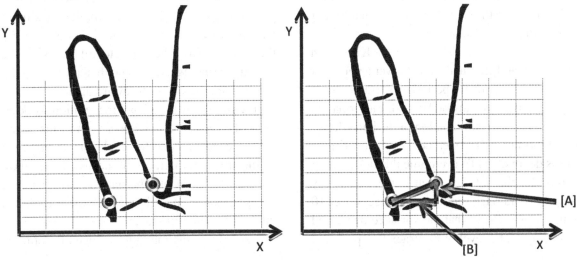

Figure 5. Finger height measurements

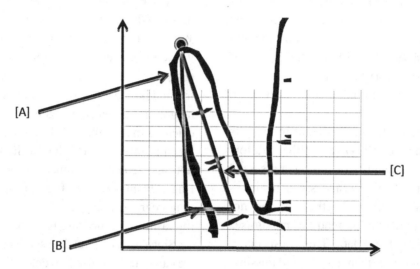

two values, instead of a negative value which may happen if the hand is presented in an orientation other than that which the system was intended to handle. The system can return the height of the finger, no matter the orientation of the hand. If the hand in an ideal orientation, the distance from base to tip on the Y axis would be suitable for determining the finger's height. However, since the fingers can be oriented at many angles diverging from the palm of the hand, this function utilises the midpoint of the finger to construct a triangle to use the proven method noted above. The midpoint is constructed by adding the two co-ordinate values of the "BaseLeft" and "BaseRight" and dividing it by 2. From here the triangle is created in a similar fashion to that utilised above.

The information received from the Kinect can be variable at different distances over a period of time; i.e. at 50cm over a period of 30 frames there may be a variance of around 10% in the information received due to a combination of the hand detection algorithm and the method wherein the Kinect senses depth data. To overcome this, a sampling method for the data has been implemented. By sampling data retrieved from the fingers over 10 frames it was found that the variance decreased in readings. The level of accuracy this provided

was determined to be adequate on the testing device (Xbox Kinect sensor) and would be more than enough on the more powerful Kinect for Windows device.

EVALUATION

The user can utilise the system to perform and monitor exercises in their hands. The data recorded from these exercises is potentially useful to a physician and is therefore recorded to be viewed at a later date. The exercises performed can be on either hand, (which the user must specify before proceeding) and includes determining maximum flexion on the finger muscles. This is assessed by the user stretching their hand to full extension, the system beginning a timer and then prompting the user to flex their fingers inward again.

Figure 6 shows the hand recognition working even when no fingers have been found. This allows for the exercise code to check for the presence of the fingers at extension and when they have not been found it but the hand is still visible it establishes that the full hand has been clenched into a fist. The time taken to perform this exercise as well as the maximum range of motion is

Figure 6. Hand at full flexion

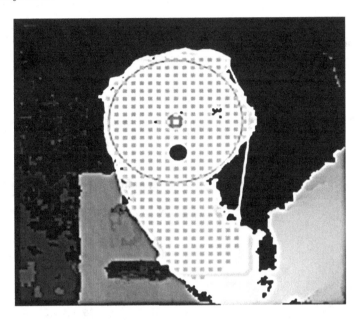

Figure 7. Exercise time taken message box

potentially useful in establishing a treatment plan for the patient and is stored with the rest of the user's information in the database.

The main landing screen after login is shown in Figure 8. The "Begin Test" button shown in this page will start the finger measurement process. Before it starts the functions necessary to measure the hand, several checks are performed to make sure that the system is accepting all the necessary

data. Firstly, it will establish whether or not the user has selected a "Hand to test" so that the fingers on the hand can be correctly identified later. After, the system can begin to show information to the user in the form of the raw depth image previously shown in Figure 3. From here, the finger recognition and dimension determination begins. When the data is constructed by the system it is displayed on screen for the user (see Figure 10).

Figure 8. Main interface

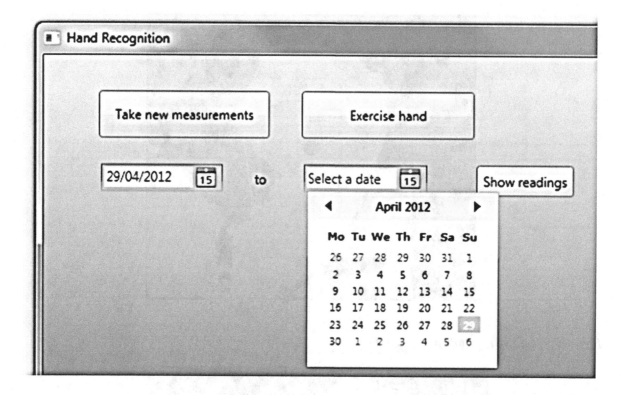

Figure 9. Finger measurements results

Tests were performed to assess the real-world dimensions of the digits on each finger independently and then compared these to the readings output by the system. The tests were then performed at optimal range, too close to the sensor and then far way to determine the scale of results depending on distance to the sensor. The system was used to determine height and width of digits on a specified hand. To compare this set of results, physical measurements were taken of each digit using a ruler. These results were tabulated as "expected" results and measured against results output by the system. The results of these tests are put together as a series of graphs in order to visually display the effect of range on the data taken from the sensor. The first set of results, measuring the width of digits on the right hand, is shown in Figure 10.

As can be seen the results from this test, system readings vary only slightly at the optimum range

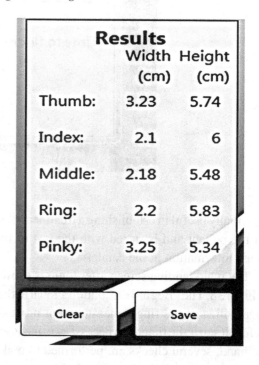

Results	Width (cm)	Height (cm)
Thumb:	3.23	5.74
Index:	2.1	6
Middle:	2.18	5.48
Ring:	2.2	5.83
Pinky:	3.25	5.34

Clear   Save

Figure 10. Width of digits on right hand

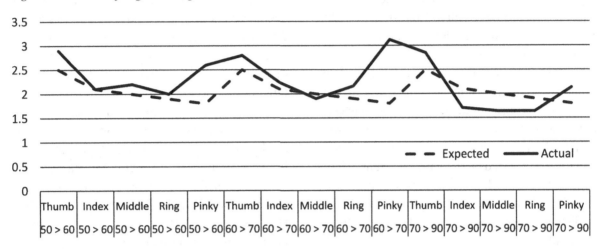

of 50 > 60cm from the sensor. With some outliers, the readings remain consistent until outer limits of range at ~80cm. Furthermore, as a result of this test it can be determined that most variance occurs within the recognition of the pinky finger on the right hand. The results of this test remained more constant than were initially expected to be. Consequently, this adds to the integrity of the data at all readable ranges from the Kinect sensor. Next tested was the width measurements taken of the left hand. Once again, the physical measurements of the left hand were taken and compared against

the width measurements established through the system. The variation of these results is shown on Figure 11.

Variation in these results is similar to the results shown on the right hand. As can be seen, at optimal range the data interpreted by the system is very reliable. With the distance between the sensor and hand increasing, so does the level at which the results fluctuate. Once more, the readings are most varied in the mind range (60 > 70cm). This was found to be true of the readings for the widths on the right hand also. When the variations in the

Figure 11. Width of digits on left hand

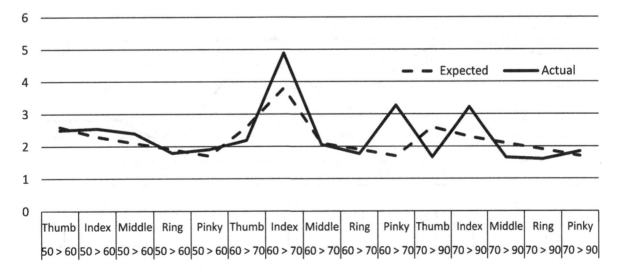

digit widths had been determined, the next step was to compare the results of the finger height measurements. This was done by measuring the fingers on each hand in a similar fashion to what the system is intended to do. By taking the centre point of the digit then using a ruler to go from base to fingertip, a physical, real-world value was determined. This value was then laid out in a table and used for comparison with system-generated values. First tested was again the right hand. Similar to the width tests, the hand was placed at different distances from the sensor to test effects of distance on reading accuracy. The values from the right hand are shown in Figure 12.

While the variance in width measurements remained relatively consistent throughout the distance tests, finger height measurement showed much more varied results. As seen in these results; at optimal range, digit height is established very accurately. However, these tests prove that for digit height, distance is a very important factor.

These tests must be compared with the results of the left hand testing in order to be substantiated. Figure 13 shows the results of these tests.

Through this second set of height results, we can determine that the behaviour of the first test is replicated. As the distance from the sensor in-

creases, the data variance increases. This variation becomes very high at the extreme ranges such as 70 > 90cm and renders information invalid.

From these tests we can determine that the optimal range for the Kinect when finding digit height falls between 50 > 60cm distance from the device. Figure 14 shows this range in a visual diagram. Within a range of 0 to 50cm, the information from the Kinect sensor is not efficient enough to rely in for accurate data. At 50cm the data becomes usable and reliable for accurate readings. However, as the distance from the Kinect increases, the data becomes less and less accurate; finally resulting in the data being unusable again.

The ability for the system to determine individual fingers was tested. The aim of this test was to ensure that the system can pick up a hand without needing to identify finger elements (i.e. a fist). It was also used to test if the system can pick up a hand showing only a sub-set of fingers (i.e. a raised index finger). To accomplish these tests, the measurement process was run with the right and left hand testing scenarios. Through this raw data window we can determine when the hand has been recognised by the system as it overlays a cluster image on the raw data. Furthermore, when a finger has been recognised, a "fingertip point"

Figure 12. Height of digits on right hand

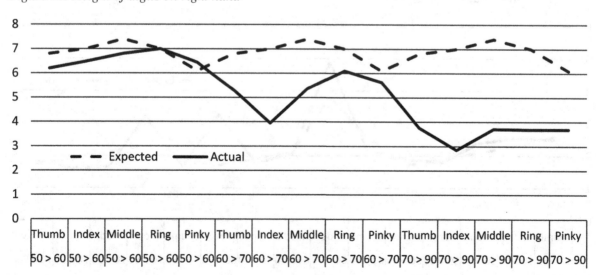

Figure 13. Height of digits on left hand

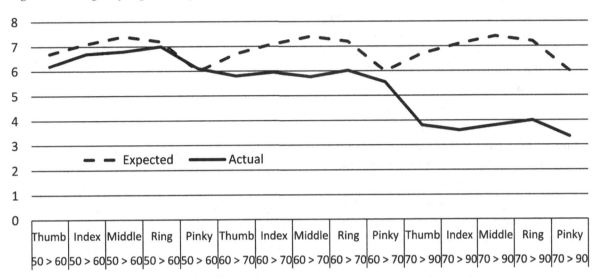

Figure 14. Kinect optimal range

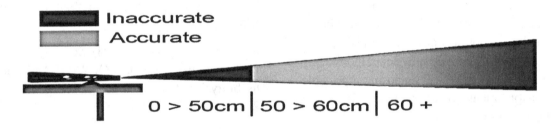

is added to the overlay. By monitoring this when the sensor is presented with a hand clenched into a fist and a hand which presents only the index and middle fingers, we can assess whether the system will work with only partial readings. It was found that the system could determine that a hand is present even without all of the fingers showing. This functionality is utilised in the hand exercise section to establish the time a user takes to complete tasks. This testing validates the readings returned by the exercise section of the system.

The system was also tested in a number of adverse conditions such as poor lighting and range diversity in user location (too close, too far from sensor). In terms of these requirements the system performs well. Since the Kinect itself works with infra-red light rather than standard image recogni-

tion, it is functional in very dimly lit scenarios. The only adverse condition in terms of lighting is when the Kinect sensor is introduced to a room with direct sunlight which can interfere with the infra-red recognition. Similarly, the system has been developed in such a manner that the range of user motion is accounted for programmatically; handling poor hand orientation on-the-fly where possible and displaying notices to the user otherwise.

CONCLUSION

The detection of progress in the treatment of Rheumatoid arthritis relies heavily on observation by physicians. The effectiveness of these kinds of tests is dependent on ability and can vary depending on the observer. The adoption of a camera based system is a step towards providing a less subjective analysis of the range of movement in patients. We outlined here a system which integrates an off-the-shelf Kinect sensor for usage in a hand recognition and digit measurement capacity. This system repeats common tasks usually completed by a physician (or specialised nurse) such as digit dimension monitoring and exercise observations. Measurements taken include digit width and height as these can be accomplished different distances from the Kinect and in varied environmental conditions. Physicians can also monitor patients over time without requiring multiple appointments where the measurements are taken manually. Ultimately, the system shows that it is possible to use a Kinect-based solution in many scenarios which call for regular observation of a patient with RA. With the system being designed to be portable and easy-to-use, it is an ideal solution for both the physician monitoring patients in a clinic as well as posing a possible solution for patients wishing to monitor their own condition in their homes.

Next we hope to monitor the resting angles of joints in the hand and comparing to the fully flexed angles of joint movement. While the system handles patient exercises and provides useful data; this could be extended to accommodate the treatment plans provided by a physician. The user could perform joint flexion and extension exercises day to day and over a period of time the physician could build a model representing their range of movement. This would be benefit to a patient as it would result in a full documentation of their condition, rather than the physician taking measurements weeks apart at different appointments.

REFERENCES

Ackerman, E. (2011, June 17). *Microsoft Releases Kinect SDK, Roboticists Cackle With Glee.* Retrieved from IEEE Spectrum - Automaton: http://spectrum.ieee.org/automaton/robotics/diy/microsoft-releases-kinect-sdk-roboticists-cackle-with-glee

Arnett, F., Edworthy, S., Bloch, D., Mcshane, D., Fries, F., Cooper, N., & Hunder, G. (1988). The American Rheumatism Association 1987 Revised Criteria for the Classification of Rheumatoid Arthritis. *Arthritis and Rheumatism, 14*(2), 315–324. doi:10.1002/art.1780310302 PMID:3358796

Arthritis: Rheumatoid Arthritis. (2008). Retrieved December 08, 2011, from American Society for Surgery of the Hand: http://www.assh.org/Public/HandConditions/Pages/ArthritisRheumatoidArthritis.aspx

Ashton, L., & Myers, S. (2004). Serial Grip Testing- Its role In Assessment Of Wrisy And Hand Disability. *The Internet Journal of Surgery, 5*(1), 32–44.

Basili, V., & Selby, R. (1987). Comparing the Effectiveness of Software Testing Strategies. *IEEE Transactions on Software Engineering, 21*(3), 1278–1296. doi:10.1109/TSE.1987.232881

Black, S., Kushner, I., & Samols, D. (2004). C-reactive Protein. *The Journal of Biological Chemistry, 279*(47), 48487–48490. doi:10.1074/jbc.R400025200 PMID:15337754

Boehm, B. (1988). A Spiral Model for Software Development and Enhancement. *IEEE Computer, 12*(3), 61–72. doi:10.1109/2.59

Bradski, G., & Kaehler, A. (2008). *Learning OpenCV: Computer vision with the OpenCV library. Sebastapol*, CA: O'Reilly Media, Inc.

Carmody, T. (2010, November 5). *How Facial Recognition Works in Xbox Kinect*. Retrieved from Wired: http://www.wired.com/gadget-lab/2010/11/how-facial-recognition-works-in-xbox-kinect/

Chaczko, Z., & Yeoh, L. (2007). *A Preliminary Investigation on Computer Vision for Telemedicine Systems using OpenCV*. Swinburne, Australia: 2010 Second International Conference on Machine Learning and Computing.

Chen, Y., Cheng, T., & Hsu, S. (2009). Ultrasound in rheumatoid arthritis. *Formosan Journal of Rheumatology*, 1-7.

Chung, L., Cesar, J., & Sampaio, J. (2009). On Non-Functional Requirements in Software Engineering. *Lecture Notes in Computer Science, 28*(3), 363–379. doi:10.1007/978-3-642-02463-4_19

Condell, J., Curran, K., Quigley, T., Gardiner, P., McNeill, M., Winder, J., et al. (2012). Finger Movement Measurements in Arthritic Patients Using Wearable Sensor Enabled Gloves. *International Journal of Human Factors Modelling and Simulation, 2*(4), 276-292. DOI: 10.1504/IJHFMS.2011.045000

Condell, J., Curran, K., Quigley, T., Gardiner, P., McNeill, M., Winder, J., & Connolly, J. (2010). *Finger Movement Measurements in Arthritic Patients Using Wearable Sensor Enabled Gloves*. University of Ulster.

Conger, S. (2011). Software Development Life Cycles and Methodologies: Fixing the Old and Adopting the New. *International Journal of Information Technologies and Systems Approach, 8*(3), 1–22. doi:10.4018/jitsa.2011010101

DAS Booklet - *Quick reference guide for Healthcare Professionals*. (2010, February). Retrieved December 08, 2011, from National Rheumatoid Arthritis Society: http://www.nras.org.uk/includes/documents/cm_docs/2010/d/das_quick_reference.pdf

de Kraker, M., Selles, R., Molenaar, T., Schreuders, A., Hovius, S., & Stam, H. (2009). Palmar Abduction Measurements: Reliability and Introduction of Normative Data in Healthy Children. *The Journal of Hand Surgery, 8*(4), 1704–1708. doi:10.1016/j.jhsa.2009.06.011 PMID:19762165

Dipietro, L., Sabatini, A., & Dario, P. (2008). A Survey of Glove-Based Systems and Their Applications. *IEEE Transactions on Systems, Man and Cybernetics. Part C, Applications and Reviews, 22*(4), 461–482. doi:10.1109/TSMCC.2008.923862

Eberhardt, K., Malcus-Johnson, P., & Rydgren, L. (1991). The Occurence and Significance of Hand Deformities in Early Rheumatoid Arthritis. *British Journal of Rheumatology, 34*(5), 211–213. doi:10.1093/rheumatology/30.3.211 PMID:2049583

Fees, E. (1987). A method for checking Jamar dynamometer calibration. *Journal of Hand Therapy, 16*(1), 28–32. doi:10.1016/S0894-1130(87)80009-1

Fess, E. (1995). Documentation: Essential elements of an upper extremity assessment battery. In J. Hunter, E. Mackin, & A. Calahan (Eds.), *Rehabilitation of the hand: Surgery and therapy* (4th ed., pp. 185–214). St. Louis, MO: Mosby.

Fries, J., Spitz, P., Kraines, R., & Holman, H. (1980). Measurement of patient outcome in arthritis. *Arthritis and Rheumatism, 14*(3), 137–145. doi:10.1002/art.1780230202 PMID:7362664

GigE Vision for 3D Medical Research. (2010, May 13). Retrieved from Allied Vision Technologies: http://www.alliedvisiontec.com/us/products/applications/application-case-study/article/gige-vision-for-3d-medical-research.html

Hamilton, A., Balnave, R., & Adams, R. (1994). Grip strength testing reliability. *Journal of Hand Therapy, 7*(3), 163–170. doi:10.1016/S0894-1130(12)80058-5 PMID:7951708

Handout on Health: Rheumatoid Arthritis. (2009). Retrieved from National Institute of Arthritis and Musculoskeletal and Skin Diseases: http://www.niams.nih.gov/Health_Info/Rheumatic_Disease/default.asp

Limitations of the Kinect. (2010, December 17). Retrieved from I Heart Robotics: http://www.iheartrobotics.com/2010/12/limitations-of-kinect.html

Majithia, V., & Geraci, A. (2007). Rheumatoid Arthritis: Diagnosis and Management. *The American Journal of Medicine, 44*(2), 936–939. doi:10.1016/j.amjmed.2007.04.005 PMID:17976416

Panayi, G. (2003). *What is RA?* National Rheumatoid Arthritus Society.

Rheumatoid: Hand Exam. (2011). Retrieved December 08, 2011, from Clinical Exam: http://clinicalexam.com/pda/r_hand.htm

Richards, L., & Palmiter-Thomas, P. (1996). Grip strength measurement: A critical review of tools, methods and clinical utility. *Critical Reviews in Physical and Rehabilitation Medicine, 32*(1), 87–109. doi:10.1615/CritRevPhysRehabilMed.v8.i1-2.50

Roman, G. (1985). A Taxonomy of Current Issues in Requirements Engineering. *IEEE Computer, 28*(4), 14–21. doi:10.1109/MC.1985.1662861

Schofield, P., Aveyard, B., & Black, C. (2007). *Management of Pain in Older People.* Keswick: M&K Publishing.

Tölgyessy, M., & Hubinský, P. (2011). *The Kinect Sensor in Robotics Education.* Bratislava: Slovak University of Technology. doi:10.1016/j.talanta.2011.09.055

Wiegers, K. (2003). *Software Requirements.* Redmond: Microsoft.

Worden, J. (2011). *Rheumatoid Arthritis.* Retrieved from BBC Health: http://www.bbc.co.uk/health/physical_health/conditions/in_depth/arthritis/aboutarthritis_rheumatoid.shtml

KEY TERMS AND DEFINITIONS

Cloud Computing: Cloud computing describes a new supplement, consumption, and delivery model for IT services based on Internet protocols, and it typically involves provisioning of dynamically scalable and often virtualized resources.

Kinect: The Kinect is currently available in two models; the "Xbox 360/One Kinect" and the "Kinect for Windows". Both models are functional with a Windows-based PC and can utilise the Kinect SDK released by Microsoft.

Multitenant Architectures: Many companies share the same infrastructure within the Public Cloud, and the term given to this is Multitenant Architectures.

OpenCV: OpenCV is a cross-platform function library focusing on real-time image processing. The aim of this library is to supply an application with "Computer Vision", the ability to take data from a still or video camera and transform it into new representation or decision.

Quality of Service: This is a measure of network performance that reflects the network's transmission quality and service availability. QoS can come in the form of traffic policy in which the transmission rates are limited which guarantees a certain amount of bandwidth will be available to applications.

Rheumatoid Arthritis (RA): RA is a chronic disease that mainly affects the synovial joints of the human skeleton. It is an inflammatory disorder that causes joints to produce more fluid and increases the mass of the tissue in the joint resulting in a loss of function and inhibiting movement in the muscles.

Router: A device or setup that finds the best route between any two networks, even if there are several networks to traverse.

Sphygmomanometer: A sphygmomanometer is used to assess a patient's grip strength in their affected hand. This is achieved by inflating the cuff of the device to a standard pressure in a rolled manner, then having the patient grip the cuff in the palm of their hand.

ENDNOTES

[1]   Night Vision with Kinect Nightvision Infrared IR http://www.youtube.com/watch?v=-gbzXjdHfJA&feature=related.

Chapter 4
Rehabilitation Systems in Ambient Assisted Living Environments

A. M. Middleton
National University of Ireland Maynooth, Ireland

R. P. Harte
National University of Ireland Galway, Ireland

T. E. Ward
National University of Ireland Maynooth, Ireland

ABSTRACT

This chapter reviews Ambient Assisted Living (AAL) in the context of movement-based rehabilitation. The authors analyse the need for AAL solutions and how they can overcome many of the drawbacks associated with traditional rehabilitation. They discuss the benefits and challenges of rehabilitation within the AAL paradigm and the well-known benefits that the telerehabilitation and telemedicine models have already established. The authors review the top ambient technologies in use today, detailing their advantages and shortcomings. The review focuses primarily on areas such as motion capture, serious games, and robotic rehabilitation. The authors carry out a structured search of two well-known databases to find the most recent advances and present the most interesting lines of research and development. Finally, the authors discuss the review findings and draw conclusions on the future of personalised rehabilitation within an AAL paradigm.

INTRODUCTION

By the year 2020, it is estimated that 29,000 people per year in Ireland will suffer a stroke (Institute of Public Health Ireland, 2012). Across the European Union 2.11 per 1,000 children will be born with cerebral palsy (Oskoui et al., 2013). These figures, coupled with the multitude of people who acquire brain and spinal injuries every year, suggest a need for quality rehabilitation therapy that can be delivered where the patient needs it when they need it, without placing burdensome

DOI: 10.4018/978-1-4666-7284-0.ch004

Copyright © 2015, IGI Global. Copying or distributing in print or electronic forms without written permission of IGI Global is prohibited.

costs on the healthcare system. In this paper we present and discuss an approach that couples the pervasive computing elements of ambient assisted living with movement-based rehabilitation.

Ambient Assisted Living (AAL) is a technology framework designed to unobtrusively assist the user and allow them to accomplish goals in their day-to-day activities. These technologies come in many forms. AAL typically involves the use of sensor networks (Cavallo et al., 2009), smart fabrics (Harms et al., 2009), monitoring equipment (Fleck and Straßer, 2008) and robotic agents (Linder et al., 2013a) all operating within a home environment. AAL systems have been used for activity monitoring (Adami et al., 2010), fall detection (Lombardi et al., 2009) (Leone et al., 2011), medication management (Pollack et al., 2003) and surveillance systems (Fleck and Straßer, 2008). The data from these systems can be collected and transmitted remotely where it can be reviewed and analysed. The reviewer may be a therapist, caregiver or clinician, checking the user's data and deciding on an appropriate action. Agents are being developed which can process and act upon the data generated by these systems in much the same way as a human expert would. These agent approaches allow more efficient utilisation of increasingly expensive human intervention and are becoming integrated into the ambient living environment and smart homes.

One such smart home is the Intelligent Sweet Home, developed at the Korea Advanced Institute of Science and Technology (KAIST), Korea. It focuses on human-friendly technical solutions for motion/mobility assistance, health monitoring, and advanced human–machine interfaces that provide easy control of both assistive devices and home-installed appliances (Lee et al., 2007). The smart house behaves in accordance with the user's commands, their intentions, and current health status. This environment and others like it (Chen et al., 2012) (Wan et al., 2013), represents a classic example of the implementation of ambient smart technology within a living environment. The

CASALA project in Dundalk IT, Ireland (http://www.casala.ie/) exhibits the investment which is now taking place in AAL research within the European Union.

AAL is a user-centred paradigm with sharp focus on the primary user. It is also a framework in which medical professionals, therapists, caregivers and other stakeholders can monitor and assess the living quality of the user in order to maintain or improve it (Cook et al., 2009). This approach promotes independence in otherwise potentially dependent user groups such as older adults, disabled people and those with injuries or chronic diseases. Provided the sensors are suitably discrete, the user will be generally unaware of their presence. Sensors can collect data on many aspects of the person's activities. Accelerometers embedded in clothing, switches embedded in beds, walls and seats and video monitoring can gather data. This data can then be transmitted remotely to a computer in order to extract meaningful information. Based on this data, remote algorithms can create a model of the patient's movement, compare this against a database of risk situations, calculate if the patient is at risk and then recommend appropriate intervention. This means the patient can live safely independently in their own home for longer, a model closely related to that of connected health, telehealth and telemedicine (O'Neill et al., 2012) (Bogan et al., 2010).

REHABILITATION IN AAL ENVIRONMENTS

AAL is extending beyond the monitoring applications listed above into the area of personalised rehabilitation. Telerehabilitation, or e-rehabilitation, is a well-established method whereby therapy is applied to a patient over a communication network, most commonly over videophones and teleconferencing units and more recently, webcams. The visual display that these technologies provide can be used in the following manners:

- The patient may be remotely observed doing their exercises by a therapist (Chinthammit et al., 2014).
- Exercise routines may be displayed on a monitor remotely from a clinic that the patient can follow in their own home (Casey et al., 2013).
- The patient may engage with an interactive display or interface (Durfee et al., 2005).

The last example is a particularly persuasive example of the utility of the AAL framework. In the context of a rehabilitation application, through the use of an appropriate interface, the patient may perform their exercises without real-time therapist interaction, perhaps within a gaming paradigm (Fern'ndez-Baena et al., 2012), in a virtual reality environment or while interacting with an assistive robotic agent (Merians et al., 2011). Accurate smart sensors can capture the patient's movement, actuators can assist with movement and smart computing can provide a quantitative measurement of progress in interactive displays, allowing the patient to monitor their own progress and take control of their own rehabilitation (Chang et al., 2012). Periodic progress updates can be accessed remotely by medical professionals.

The transformational technological advances in the last ten years have opened up many opportunities for the creation of rehabilitation solutions that facilitate remote environments. Through more efficient algorithms, smarter sensors, cloud data and pervasive computing; personalised rehabilitation is truly becoming part of the AAL framework and the benefits are clear. However this paradigm shift also presents its own specific constraints and drawbacks. In the following sections we will outline the benefits and challenges of AAL rehabilitation in this context.

Benefits of Personalised Rehabilitation within AAL Environments

Cost

The cost of traditional rehab sessions following an incident is high, both to the patient and the healthcare system (Huang et al., 2013). Allowing the patient to perform their exercises remotely at home may radically reduce this cost. Additionally, as technology develops, advanced solutions get cheaper and more easily reproducible (Chang et al., 2011) (Egglestone et al., 2009).

Motivation

Carrying out rehabilitation programmes in an unsupervised and remote environment can challenge the motivation of the patient. The exercises required can be dull and repetitive in nature. However the interactive aspects of AAL can overcome these challenges (Middleton and Ward, 2012) (Chang et al., 2012).

Performance Metrics

Traditionally, a patient's progress or status is captured through behavioural measures performed by a rehabilitation therapist. These measures often require the therapist exercise judgement based on an observation of behaviour that is not otherwise objectively measured. There are time, place and expertise constraints on this type of assessment. In other words, the patient must perform the required behavioural test in the presence of a suitably experienced and trained therapist at a specific time. The use of sensor technology in a connected health paradigm can ease these constraints. Using pervasive methods such as sensors that output acceleration, force, displacement or vital sign data can give a very accurate, repeatable, objective measurement which decouples the therapist from direct involvement if necessary. If the patient is following a virtual exercise regime these measurements can then be fed to exercise algorithms which will increase or decrease the difficulty accordingly (Bower et al., 2013) (Metcalf et al., 2013) in much the same way as a therapist.

Challenges of Personalised Rehabilitation within AAL Environments

Safety, Robustness, and Usability

Any kind of medical device used unsupervised in the home must reach a high standard of user centred design (Harte et al. 2013). Patients and therapists may be relying on a system not only for information on progress but also on alerts when something goes wrong during therapy. If a system fails to alert the appropriate body of a critical situation it could have very serious consequences. User frustration is another very important element in recovery and not one to be ignored (Middleton and Ward, 2012). If systems are wireless their battery life must be taken into consideration and a robust charging system must be in place. It must be noted that this technology may be used by groups who have limited experience in computing and mobile technology (Aloulou et al., 2013).

Culture and Policy

Cultural perception to AAL may vary. In Japan for example, robotics is accepted as a solution to many problems (Kakiuchi et al., 2013)(Tanaka, 2014). In the US and Europe, many people may be less willing to put their rehabilitation in the hands of a robot. They might prefer the personal interaction with a therapist and be reluctant to embrace an electronic approach (Lee and Sabanović, 2014).

The older generation in particular may oppose technology, in favour of traditional personal approaches. Since nearly three-quarters of all strokes occur in people aged over 65, this technophobia barrier is worth addressing. As well as this, lack of cohesive frameworks and policy may obstruct concentrated progress (Memon et al., 2014).

Invisibility

By its own definition pervasive and ambient systems must blend seamlessly into the background, otherwise they lose their appeal as a non-intrusive technology. The patient should not be aware of their presence. Therefore, clunky sensors, noisy devices and cumbersome robots do not follow the ambient model. Sensors should be discretely embedded in clothing, mattresses, chairs, desks, floors and walls and provide assistance only when needed (Nehmer et al., 2006).

Human Computer Interaction (HCI)

The patient may have to interact directly with a computing system, especially if they are performing specific rehabilitation exercises. The patient may have limited capacity to use, for example, a keyboard or mouse (Hertzum and Hornbæk, 2010), so more intuitive and direct interaction is required. AAL devices must have an intuitive HCI, allowing the patient to communicate via voice or gestures.

Data Storage, Networking, and Presentation

The huge quantity of data gathered, even from low complexity AAL systems, offers its own set of challenges: There are hardware challenges in terms of data storage. There are networking challenges in terms of sensor compatibility and communication protocols (Cavallo et al., 2009). There are software challenges in terms of accurately processing the data in order to give a useful output, such as progress of the user. The human expert must also be able to read and interpret the data (Mulvenna et al., 2011).

The benefits we have outlined of the AAL approach to rehabilitation cannot be ignored. The benefits of the conventional telerehabilitation model have been well explored and clearly presented in previous reviews (Hailey et al., 2011) and we feel that more ambient and user centred rehabilitation using the hidden technologies already mentioned is the next epoch in personalised rehabilitation. Likewise the challenges presented are not academic or easily overcome. However, in the following sections we will review some of the recently developed technologies which have looked to address the aforementioned challenges.

The Evolution of Personalised AAL Rehabilitation

In the following three sections we will review the latest developments in three main areas of AAL rehabilitation. Firstly we will have a look at motion capture technology. This refers to the use of sensors to capture the movements of the user's body. Using the patient's captured movement as an input, serious games have been developed, which will be further explored in our second section. These games are designed to provide interest and motivation to the patient, by using fun, appealing themes, rather than repetitive motion exercises. They require the patient to interact with the game, perhaps using movement of an affected limb, and track progress, adjusting the difficulty as necessary (Madeira et al., 2011). Finally, we will take a look at the latest robotic developments. Robotic agents can provide actuated support and assistance to limbs during rehabilitation. This support enacted within a home-based gaming paradigm or with virtual reality interfaces can lead to extremely effective rehabilitation outcomes.

In an effort to find the most relevant trends in these three areas we carried out a structured search using two well-known research databases,

Scopus and PubMed. We sought to only include journal articles and review papers, except where a conference paper was deemed to have a significant impact on the field of work as assessed by the authors. We also sought to restrict the search to papers published from 2010 onwards to provide the most current assessment of technological developments. We used various combinations of the listed keywords, ambient assisted living, rehabilitation, telerehabilitation, e-rehabilitation, gaming, serious games, motion capture, robot, robotics and robot therapy. In Table 1 we present the search terms used in various combinations and the number of search results each database returned.

From these search terms, and several other papers the authors had previous knowledge of, a total of 53 papers were reviewed to provide content to the following sections.

MOTION TRACKING

There are a number of sensors employed for rehabilitative motion tracking. The sensor may be a physical device attached to the patient's affected limb, or a wireless hands-free sensor that monitors movement via a camera and interprets the data. Furthermore, the wireless sensors may be marker or markerless. A marker-based system tracks physical markers attached to the patient's body. A markerless system is completely hands-free, meaning the patient has no physical interaction with the interface. The latter is desirable and is the most ambient-oriented approach. In an ambient system, the patient must feel that the movements they are making in their exercises are intuitive and the equipment used is discrete (Cavallo et al., 2009). From the examples below though, we will see that the markerless approach suffers from some challenges.

Rehabilitation systems have been taking advantage of motion gaming technology for years. Systems have been developed using the accelerometer-based Nintendo Wii remote as a motion

Table 1. Shows the various search combinations of the listed keywords and the corresponding entries

Search	Search Term	Operator	Pubmed	Scopus
1	Ambient Assisted Living	AND	8	10
	Rehabilitation			
2	Ambient Assisted Living	AND	11	2
	Telerehabilitation	OR		
	E-Rehabilitation			
3	Ambient Assisted Living	AND	1	0
	Rehabilitation			
	Gaming			
4	Ambient Assisted Living	OR	16	3
	Telerehabilitation	AND		
	Gaming			
5	Ambient Assisted Living	AND	4	1
	Rehabilitation			
	Virtual Reality			
6	Ambient Assisted Living	OR	9	4
	Telerehabilitation	AND		
	Gaming	OR		
	Serious Games			
	Motion Capture			
7	Ambient Assisted Living	AND	1	1
	Robot			
	Rehabilitation			
8	Ambient Assisted Living	OR	12	12
	Telerehabilitation	AND		
	Robotics	OR		
	Robot			
	Robot Therapy			

tracker (Saposnik et al., 2010). The Wiimote can be attached to a patient's affected limb, while the infrared sensor attached to the Wii monitors the movement. Similarly, work has been done with the PlayStation EyeToy (Neil et al., 2013), a webcam developed specifically for use with PS games. Also used was the PlayStation Move - a device that uses inertial sensors and a webcam to provide movement-based feedback (Parry et al., 2013).

Other systems have also been employed for motion tracking. Lockery et al employed a Magnetic Motion Tracker (MMT), specifically the miniBIRD 500 (Lockery et al., 2011). They attached it to various objects, which the patient would move to interact with a custom-designed game. The tracker uses a small, short range sensor and provides 6 degrees of freedom with a sample rate of 100Hz. Huber et al employed the 5DT 5

Ultra Glove, which has one optical sensor per finger. The movement of the patient's hand, in this case geared towards children with cerebral palsy, controls movement in a custom-built PS3 game (Huber et al., 2008). This convergence of game technology (software and hardware), the Internet, and rehabilitation science forms the second-generation virtual rehabilitation framework. This reduced-cost and patient/therapist familiarity facilitates adoption in clinical practice. Unlike precursor systems aimed at providing hand training for post-stroke adults in a clinical setting, the experimental system described by Huber et al was developed for in-home tele-rehabilitation on a game console for children and adults with chronic hemiplegia after stroke or other focal brain injury. Significant improvements in Activities of Daily Living function followed three months of training at home on the system.

All of the technologies mentioned above require the patient to interact with a physical device or interface. This may prove cumbersome and detract from the exercise. It is necessary in an AAL environment to make the interface devices as discrete and simple as possible. Many researchers have been taking advantage of Microsoft's Xbox Kinect and its markerless tracking abilities. We will discuss some high performing examples below.

The Kinect (http://www.xbox.com/en-IE/Kinect) uses an infrared depth sensor and RGB camera to track 25 joints of up to 6 people at a time. The Kinect has been validated against gold standard systems with positive results. Fern'ndez-Baena et al performed a comprehensive comparison of the Kinect's accuracy against MediaLab, a marker tracking device (Fern'ndez-Baena et al., 2012). They concluded that the Kinect has a mean error of up to 8.98 degrees when measuring joint rotation.

Chiang et al. also performed a validation on the Kinect and found it granted 80% accuracy. They claim this had a lot to do with confusion based on the patient's wheelchairs but still concluded that

the Kinect was a good quality tool for providing quantitative measurement of movement (Chang et al., 2011). They demonstrated the system on cerebral palsy suffers with positive outcomes reported for rehabilitation. Subsequently, Metcalf et al validated the Kinect as a tool for measuring finger kinematics, and then used it as a grip classification tool for stroke rehabilitation. Their validation against the marker-based Vicon system found the Kinect had 78% accuracy (Metcalf et al., 2013).

Benefits of the Kinect have been weighed up against the accuracy with claims that this level of accuracy may be sufficient for many rehabilitation applications and the cost, portability and markerless capabilities of the Kinect are significant advantages (Fern'ndez-Baena et al., 2012). It is also worth noting that subsequent to these validation tests, Microsoft have released a newer version of the Kinect that yields higher accuracy and are set to release a Version 2 in summer 2014.

The object of using the Kinect as a rehabilitation tool is that it can be programmed to record data from the patient's affected limb. Metcalf et al had their patients perform a series of hand grip motions. The Kinect tracked the movement of the hand and saved the data. This data was then analysed in post-processing and a model was created of the patient's performance and ability (Metcalf et al., 2013). Similarly Fern'ndez-Baena et al monitored the joint rotation of the patient (Fern'ndez-Baena et al., 2012).

The Kinect is a huge step forwards for ambient assisted rehabilitation. It provides a cheap intuitive markerless tracking system that can be used in clinics and in a patient's home. An additional benefit is that it provides a gesture-based usable interface for rehabilitation games. This has big implications for the adoption of AAL rehabilitation technology by user groups who may have avoided the use of computing devices due to overwhelming interfaces or cumbersome ergonomics.

SERIOUS GAMES

Serious games are computer games that serve a specific purpose. This may be education, industrial or corporate training or for medical purposes. Serious games have been also designed for use in rehabilitation (Levac et al., 2012).

Motivation is an important issue in movement-based rehabilitation. Traditional rehab games are, by necessity for the purpose of rewriting neural pathways and retraining weakened muscles, repetitive motions. However, this may become tedious for the user causing them to lose interest, possibly leading to a reduction in further compliance with rehabilitation programmes (Madeira et al., 2011) (Metcalf et al., 2013). When designing a movement-based rehabilitation game there is a fine line between challenge and frustration. The game must adapt its difficulty according to the progress of the patient but if it becomes too difficult the patient may become frustrated and lose interest. This could have a negative impact on their recovery (Middleton and Ward, 2012).

As discussed in the previous section, there are a number of marker and markerless movement tracking devices that may be used as input to the game. The movement data can be saved and transmitted elsewhere for processing or analysis by a therapist. Ideally the game will then take the movement data of the patient and use it to adjust the difficulty in real time, though this can also be done in post-processing and used in the next session (Lockery et al., 2011).

The following are examples of serious games developed specifically for movement-based rehabilitation. They use a variety of input devices and report positive results:

Huber et al created a serious game for children with hemiplegia (Huber et al., 2008). Their objective was to increase hand function in those affected by hemiplegia using an enjoyable activity, rather than the more traditional approach of restraint. In the latter case, the patient's higher functioning limb is restrained, forcing them to use their affected limb. Since their system is aimed at children, they propose that motivation, rather than restraint, may be more appealing. The games were designed using the Playstation 3 (PS3) software development kit (SDK) which allows access to a Linux based system on the PS3 device. The SDK is limited however, as the games cannot access the full processing power of the PS3.

Three games were designed. The first targeted range of motion in the fingers, requesting that the patient "clean" dirt off the screen to reveal an aesthetically pleasing image. The second was a finger velocity training game in which patients had to make a fist or open their hand as much as possible. Figure 1 shows how on-screen butterflies move in response to the gestures, making the exercise more entertaining to perform. The third game targeted the same range of motion as the butterfly game, but used a UFO theme instead, as shown in Figure 2 (a).

Fern'ndez-Baena et al developed a game called Rehabtimals that uses the Kinect as its controller (Fern'ndez-Baena et al., 2012). Screens from the game are shown in Figure 2 (b). The theme of the game is that as you recover an animal grows up. The patient must perform certain tasks to advance the game. In this study, they focused on joint rotation monitoring and rehabilitation.

Madeira et al designed a game aimed at aphasia rehabilitation, as shown in screen captures in Figure 3. Specifically, they targeted semantic categorisation and auditory and reading comprehension. Their system turned a wheelchair into a pervasive smart device using RFID for movement tracking and an Android tablet PC embedded into the chair (Madeira et al., 2011). The use of physiological signals as an indicator of patient enjoyment is highlighted and they aim to use this data to personalise the games, thus making them more motivational. Their games adapt according to the patient's progress, which is vital for maintaining the challenge/frustration ratio. Their game play scenarios involve "catching" objects and completing a circuit using wheelchair movement.

Figure 1. Glove interacting with Butterfly Game
Copyright Rutgers Tele-Rehabilitation Institute. Reprinted by permission.

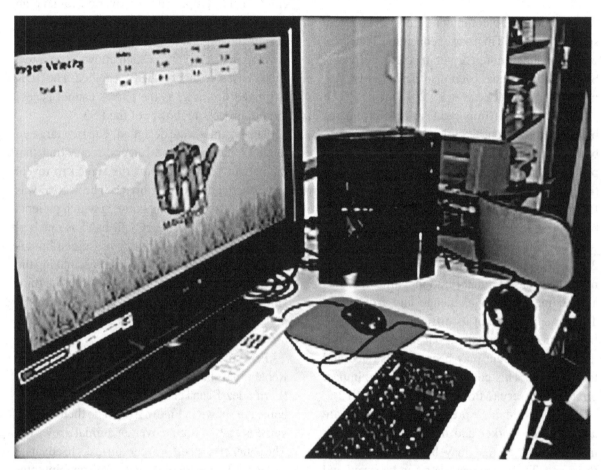

Figure 2. (a) UFO version of game ; (b) Screen Captures from Rehabtimals
Rutgers Tele-Rehabilitation Institute. Reprinted by permission.
Fern'ndez-Baena et al., 2012.

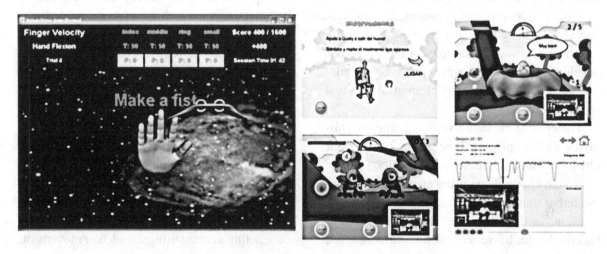

Figure 3. Screen capture from therapeutic serious game
Madeira et al., 2011.

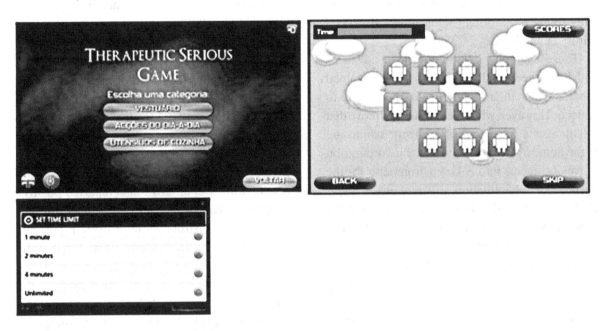

The location of the wheelchair is superimposed on a virtual map, available on the tablet. This virtual reality context has proved motivational and enjoyable. The system's costs were brought down by using the Android development system.

Chang et al. created a game in Unity3D that allows a user to "pick up" an object and drag it across the screen (Chang et al., 2012). In this scenario, the Kinect tracks the user's progress and will project a blue line if they are performing well. If the patient is deviating, a red line will appear with arrows guiding them back on track. This game is a good example of real-time feedback.

All of these examples show the efforts that have been made in creating serious games for the purpose of rehabilitation in AAL environments. The main problems encountered in these systems are the same as those which hindered the deployment of motion capture systems discussed in the previous section; that is accuracy. However the increasing accuracy of the sensors in these systems can only lead to further improvement. The

fact that most of these systems can be employed using commonly available home computers system highlights the main benefit of AAL based rehabilitation systems

ROBOTICS IN AAL ENVIRONMENTS

While gaming systems can be ambiently inserted into the average home, the seamless integration of robotic agents in ambient intelligence spaces has always been considered a major challenge for ubiquitous environments and AAL. The use of robotics in the home to provide assistance to the elderly and infirm is not a new endeavour. The need for robotic automation technology solutions in the home to help people in their daily activities has been addressed in different projects worldwide. A concrete application of these concepts is the human-friendly assistive home environment, developed at KAIST, South Korea (Lee et al., 2007). Other projects have used a mobile robot for ensuring assistive services dedicated to activities of daily living as well as providing health and daily living monitoring (Sakagami et al., 2002) (Gross et al., 2011).

These examples exhibit the huge advances which have been made in the application of trained robotic agents in providing quality healthcare to patients. However, while these examples prove that robotic agents can provide assistance or monitoring in the home in an ambient way, the incorporation of robotic agents into AAL environments for the purpose of rehabilitation still remains a major challenge. As well as this, we must consider the user safety challenges in the domain of AAL. The consideration becomes even more acute where the use of robotic agents is concerned. Devices like this used unsupervised in the home could cause discomfort, provide incorrect therapy or even cause serious injury to the user. We must also consider the user attitudes to interacting with a robotic agent, particularly among older adults (Zsiga et al., 2013). In this section we will discuss the most recent advances in ambient robotic rehabilitation and review them in terms of technology, safety, effectiveness, and user experience.

Robotic Rehabilitation in the Home

When we consider a robotic agent as an assistive agent, it can be used to enhance, complement or substitute a human function (Mohammed et al., 2012) but if we are to remain in the constraints of rehabilitation we will consider robotic agents that are used to improve human function in a therapeutic fashion, such as would be the case for a stroke patient.

Home robot rehabilitation systems are not new and indeed much research has been dedicated to the area in the last ten years and their effectiveness is well established (Ivlev et al., 2005) (Amirabdollahian et al., 2007) (Brochard et al., 2010)). It has been shown that the effect of robot-mediated

therapy can lead to more beneficial outcomes than the same duration of non-functional exercises (Coote et al., 2008).

The ArmAssist, developed by Tecnalia, is a system for at home telerehabilitation of post-stroke arm impairments. It consists of a wireless mobile base module, a global position and orientation detection mat, a PC with display monitor, and a tele-rehabilitation software platform (Jung et al., 2013). This system is in the early stages of development but tests have showed promising results. Linder et al. 2013 also reported positive results (increase in Fugl Meyer Scores) in their case study of a stroke sufferer using a portable robotic device and a Home Exercise Programme (Linder et al., 2013a). They demonstrated that wearable robotics deliver effective rehab in the home. The results prompted the design of a clinical trial (Linder et al., 2013b) . A haptic pantograph system described by Palsbo et al. showed that controlled robotic haptic feedback could be used to improve handwriting function (Palsbo et al., 2011). This desk mounted device incorporated into a computer interface assisted the user in 3-dimensional handwriting movements, with positive results being reported in a trial aimed at improving hand writing function in children.

Incorporation of Robotic Agents into Virtual Reality

Other systems have tried to improve the motivation fatigue suffered by home users by incorporating robotic agents with monitor based virtual reality interfaces, making for a more vivid and interactive experience for the user (Yang et al., 2011). A similar system was employed by Merians et al who used a glove-like exoskeleton with built in actuators to provide assistance to the user while their hand movements were tracked by smart sensors and emulated in a virtual reality screen interface (Merians et al., 2011). These enhanced interfaces encourage positive change in neural pathways, while the assistance provided from the robotic agents allow the user to carry out more complex movements than they would otherwise be able to perform, unassisted. Advancing even more into the domain of VR, Perez Marcos et al. used a headset to allow the user to 'take ownership of their virtual body.' This allows patients to enact body movements they may otherwise be unable to carry out, thereby stimulating and rebuilding critical neural pathways, while haptic robotics provide assistance to user's limb movements. In general, there is evidence for the effectiveness of these approaches for the rehabilitation of upper limbs in patients with stroke (Saposnik et al., 2011).

The Challenging Move towards Ambient Wearable Robots

The systems outlined above have proved effective for the purpose but are not quite compliant with the 'hidden' aspects of the AAL model. However a new generation of wearable robot devices have made an appearance which can provide effective assistance in an ambient manner (Mohammed et al., 2012). One such system described by Hassani et al employs an actuated orthosis to provide both active and passive support to an affected limb within an assist-as-needed paradigm (Hassani et al., 2014). Operating in two modes, the device, which resembles an exoskeleton, can either deliver all required effort or can respond to the effort exerted by the user. The sensors can adjust the actuators to the needs of the wearer within their own rehabilitation programme. This device is very discreet and can even be worn under clothing. The ever advancing technology will increase the viability of wearable robotics but perhaps a paradigm shift is needed to move away from the conventional idea of a robot as a clunky, metallic, mechanical device. In a review of developments in wearable robots for ankle rehabilitation, Jamwal et al. commented on recent systems that 'it was observed that most of them are

undesirably inspired by industrial robot designs'. This suggests that many systems do not fit into the AAL model (Jamwal et al., 2013). Seamlessly integrating the movement of the wearable device into the complex and multi-planar movement of human joints in real life environments has traditionally been the major challenge for such systems (Dellon and Matsuoka, 2007) and these challenges remain apparent (Mohammed et al., 2012). Safety is another notable concern with increasing attention being paid to the subtle and sensitive relationship between powerful actuated joints and comparably frail human joints (Claros et al., 2013)(O'Neill et al., 2013).

DISCUSSION AND CONCLUSION

AAL is no longer restricted only to a mere assistance domain. The increase in power and complexity of discreet sensors means that AAL can seamlessly be applied to movement-based rehabilitation. The ability of sensors to provide quantitative measurements is a big leap forward in therapy progress measurement. No longer do therapists and patients have to judge their improvements based on behavioural observations and human subjectivity alone.

As bandwidth and data-storage increases, and the physical size of devices diminish, transfer of this movement data is easier than ever. Patients can practice their rehabilitation exercises in their own home, monitored by compact, unobtrusive sensors, and have their progressed sent wirelessly for monitoring and analysis. This lessens the burden on the patient and the therapist. This data can also be analysed in real-time, thus providing feedback for the patient so they can adjust their movements.

Telerehabilitation, e-rehabilitation and AAL rehabilitation all refer to means by which the patient can perform their rehabilitation therapy at home. They may be monitored remotely by a camera feed to a therapist, or they may be following a video or computer game routine on a screen. Some solutions use a combination of both, with the most advanced solutions decreasing the need for a real-time therapist, allowing the patient to take control of their own rehabilitation in their personal environment. As we witness the progression we notice the more advanced the solution, the more ambient it becomes.

Sensors and the computer interfaces to which they provide feedback have advanced to the point where the patient may have no physical interaction with a device in order to complete their exercise programmes. Markerless tracking means the patient can perform their exercises unhindered by clunky intrusive devices.

A natural progression from the motion tracking devices is their use in serious games developed specifically for movement-based rehabilitation. Serious games address the issue of motivation that has plagued traditional rehab therapy. A well-designed rehabilitation game has a pleasing environment, a suitably difficult but enjoyable activity to perform in order to advance, and an adaption algorithm that will increase or decrease the difficulty according to the patient's performance.

Pervasive computing in a rehabilitation context still has some issues to address. Technophobia may cause reluctance in people, particularly older adults, to embrace electronic and computerised methods. In spite of the greater cost, they may prefer more traditional personal approaches. Some sensor technologies are not at a truly ambient stage yet, requiring physical sensors that the patient may find detracts from their experience. As the technology gets smaller and more accurate, it also gets more expensive. Markerless technologies are still far from 100% accuracy, though researchers claim in most cases, 80% accuracy is sufficient.

We observed that may robotics based solutions suffer from similar challenges. While the effectiveness of robotics is clear and well established, their design has not yet reached a point where they can be seamlessly integrated into an AAL environment. Like the motion capture and serious games solution, these challenges will be overcome with the advent of more discrete materials, sensors and interfaces.

Further to this, we found that many of the systems we reviewed are confined to a limited set of features and standards and technologies are used in a limited and isolated manner with no concentrated framework in place.

AAL rehabilitation is already addressing many issues surrounding traditional rehabilitation and with technology getting smaller, cheaper and more powerful, it can only improve. We find that potential is huge and the shift in demographics towards a more aging population demands this advance in technology. Coupled with this, the increasing demand for more discrete and ambient technologies means that the AAL paradigm is the next epoch of development for personalised rehabilitation.

REFERENCES

Adami, A. M., Pavel, M., Hayes, T. L., & Singer, C. M. (2010). Detection of movement in bed using unobtrusive load cell sensors. *IEEE Transactions on Information Technology in Biomedicine*, *14*(2), 481–490. doi:10.1109/TITB.2008.2010701 PMID:19171523

Aloulou, H., Mokhtari, M., Tiberghien, T., Biswas, J., Phua, C., Lin, J. H. K., & Yap, P. (2013). Deployment of assistive living technology in a nursing home environment: Methods and lessons learned. *BMC Medical Informatics and Decision Making*, *13*(1), 42. doi:10.1186/1472-6947-13-42 PMID:23565984

Amirabdollahian, F., Loureiro, R., Gradwell, E., Collin, C., Harwin, W., & Johnson, G. (2007). Multivariate analysis of the Fugl-Meyer outcome measures assessing the effectiveness of GENTLE/S robot-mediated stroke therapy. *Journal of Neuroengineering and Rehabilitation*, *4*(1), 4. doi:10.1186/1743-0003-4-4 PMID:17309791

Bogan, D., Spence, J., & Donnelly, P. (2010). *Connected Health: An All Island Review in Ireland (Informative Review No. 19th April 2010)*. Bio Business.

Bower, C., Taheri, H., & Wolbrecht, E. (2013). Adaptive control with state-dependent modeling of patient impairment for robotic movement therapy. In *Proceedings of 2013 IEEE International Conference on Rehabilitation Robotics* (ICORR). IEEE. doi:10.1109/ICORR.2013.6650460

Brochard, S., Robertson, J., Médée, B., & Rémy-Néris, O. (2010). What's new in new technologies for upper extremity rehabilitation? *Current Opinion in Neurology*, *23*(6), 683–687. doi:10.1097/WCO.0b013e32833f61ce PMID:20852420

Casey, M., Hayes, P. S., Heaney, D., Dowie, L., Ólaighin, G., & Matero, M. et al. (2013). Implementing transnational telemedicine solutions: A connected health project in rural and remote areas of six Northern Periphery countries Series on European collaborative projects. *The European Journal of General Practice*, *19*(1), 52–58. doi:10.3109/13814788.2012.761440 PMID:23432039

Cavallo, F., Aquilano, M., Odetti, L., Arvati, M., & Carrozza, M. C. (2009). A first step toward a pervasive and smart ZigBee sensor system for assistance and rehabilitation. In *Proceedings of 2009 IEEE International Conference on Rehabilitation Robotics, ICORR 2009*. IEEE. doi:10.1109/ICORR.2009.5209471

Chang, C.-Y., Lange, B., Zhang, M., Koenig, S., Requejo, P., Somboon, N., et al. (2012). Towards pervasive physical rehabilitation using Microsoft Kinect. In *Proceedings of 2012 6th International Conference on Pervasive Computing Technologies for Healthcare (PervasiveHealth)*. Academic Press.

Chang, Y.-J., Chen, S.-F., & Huang, J.-D. (2011). A Kinect-based system for physical rehabilitation: A pilot study for young adults with motor disabilities. *Research in Developmental Disabilities*, *32*(6), 2566–2570. doi:10.1016/j.ridd.2011.07.002 PMID:21784612

Chen, L., Nugent, C. D., & Wang, H. (2012). A Knowledge-Driven Approach to Activity Recognition in Smart Homes. *IEEE Transactions on Knowledge and Data Engineering*, *24*(6), 961–974. doi:10.1109/TKDE.2011.51

Chinthammit, W., Merritt, T., Pedersen, S., Williams, A., Visentin, D., Rowe, R., & Furness, T. (2014). Ghostman: Augmented Reality Application for Telerehabilitation and Remote Instruction of a Novel Motor Skill. *BioMed Research International*, *2014*, e646347. doi:10.1155/2014/646347 PMID:24829910

Claros, M., Soto, R., Rodriguez, J. J., Cantu, C., & Contreras-Vidal, J. L. (2013). Novel compliant actuator for wearable robotics applications. In *Proceedings of Annual International Conference of the IEEE Engineering in Medicine and Biology Society*. IEEE. doi:10.1109/EMBC.2013.6610135

Cook, D. J., Augusto, J. C., & Jakkula, V. R. (2009). Ambient intelligence: Technologies, applications, and opportunities. *Pervasive and Mobile Computing*, *5*(4), 277–298. doi:10.1016/j.pmcj.2009.04.001

Coote, S., Murphy, B., Harwin, W., & Stokes, E. (2008). The effect of the GENTLE/s robot-mediated therapy system on arm function after stroke. *Clinical Rehabilitation*, *22*(5), 395–405. doi:10.1177/0269215507085060 PMID:18441036

Dellon, B., & Matsuoka, Y. (2007). Prosthetics, exoskeletons, and rehabilitation [Grand Challenges of Robotics]. *IEEE Robotics & Automation Magazine, 14*(1), 30–34. doi:10.1109/MRA.2007.339622

Durfee, W. K., Weinstein, S. A., Carey, J. R., Bhatt, E., & Nagpal, A. (2005). Home stroke telerehabilitation system to train recovery of hand function. In *Proceedings of the 2005 IEEE 9th International Conference on Rehabilitation Robotics*. IEEE. doi:10.1109/ICORR.2005.1501118

Egglestone, S. R., Axelrod, L., Nind, T., Turk, R., Wilkinson, A., Burridge, J., et al. (2009). A design framework for a home-based stroke rehabilitation system: Identifying the key components. In *Proceedings of 3rd International Conference on Pervasive Computing Technologies for Healthcare*. Academic Press. doi:10.4108/ICST.PERVASIVEHEALTH2009.6049

Fern'ndez-Baena, A., Susin, A., & Lligadas, X. (2012). Biomechanical Validation of Upper-Body and Lower-Body Joint Movements of Kinect Motion Capture Data for Rehabilitation Treatments. In *Proceedings of 2012 4th International Conference on Intelligent Networking and Collaborative Systems*. Academic Press. doi:10.1109/iNCoS.2012.66

Fleck, S., & Straßer, W. (2008). Smart camera based monitoring system and its application to assisted living. *Proceedings of the IEEE, 96*(10), 1698–1714. doi:10.1109/JPROC.2008.928765

Gross, H., Schroeter, C., Mueller, S., Volkhardt, M., Einhorn, E., Bley, A., et al. (2011). Progress in developing a socially assistive mobile home robot companion for the elderly with mild cognitive impairment. In *Proceedings of 2011 IEEE/RSJ International Conference on Intelligent Robots and Systems (IROS)*. IEEE. doi:10.1109/IROS.2011.6094770

Hailey, D., Roine, R., Ohinmaa, A., & Dennett, L. (2011). Evidence of benefit from telerehabilitation in routine care: A systematic review. *Journal of Telemedicine and Telecare, 17*(6), 281–287. doi:10.1258/jtt.2011.101208 PMID:21844172

Harms, H., Amft, O., Roggen, D., & Tröster, G. (2009). Rapid prototyping of smart garments for activity-aware applications. *Journal of Ambient Intelligence and Smart Environments, 1*, 87–101. doi:10.3233/AIS-2009-0015

Hassani, W., Mohammed, S., Rifaï, H., & Amirat, Y. (2014). Powered orthosis for lower limb movements assistance and rehabilitation. *Control Engineering Practice, 26*, 245–253. doi:10.1016/j.conengprac.2014.02.002

Hertzum, M., & Hornbæk, K. (2010). How Age Affects Pointing With Mouse and Touchpad: A Comparison of Young, Adult, and Elderly Users. *International Journal of Human-Computer Interaction, 26*(7), 703–734. doi:10.1080/10447318.2010.487198

Huang, Y.-C., Hu, C.-J., Lee, T.-H., Yang, J.-T., Weng, H.-H., Lin, L. C., & Lai, S.-L. (2013). The Impact Factors on the Cost and Length of Stay among Acute Ischemic Stroke. *Journal of Stroke and Cerebrovascular Diseases, 22*(7), e152–e158. doi:10.1016/j.jstrokecerebrovasdis.2012.10.014 PMID:23253537

Huber, M., Rabin, B., Docan, C., Burdea, G., Nwosu, M. E., AbdelBaky, M., & Golomb, M. R. (2008). PlayStation 3-based tele-rehabilitation for children with hemiplegia. In Proceedings of Virtual Rehabilitation. Academic Press. doi:10.1109/ICVR.2008.4625145

Institute of Public Health Ireland. (2012). *Stroke Briefing*. Retrieved from www.publichealth.ie

Ivlev, O., Martens, C., & Graeser, A. (2005). Rehabilitation Robots FRIEND-I and FRIEND-II with the dexterous lightweight manipulator. *Technology and Disability*, *17*, 111–123.

Jamwal, P. K., Hussain, S., & Xie, S. Q. (2013). Review on design and control aspects of ankle rehabilitation robots. *Disability and Rehabilitation. Assistive Technology*, 1–9. doi:10.3109/17483107.2013.866986 PMID:24320195

Jung, J. H., Valencia, D. B., Rodríguez-de-Pablo, C., Keller, T., & Perry, J. C. (2013). Development of a powered mobile module for the ArmAssist home-based telerehabilitation platform. In *Proceedings of IEEE International Conference on Rehabilitation Robotics*. IEEE. doi:10.1109/ICORR.2013.6650424

Kakiuchi, Y., Nozawa, S., Yamazaki, K., Okada, K., & Inaba, M. (2013). Assistive system research for creative life management on robotics and home economics. In *Proceedings of 2013 IEEE Workshop on Advanced Robotics and Its Social Impacts (ARSO)*. IEEE. doi:10.1109/ARSO.2013.6705521

Lee, H. R., & Sabanović, S. (2014). Culturally Variable Preferences for Robot Design and Use in South Korea, Turkey, and the United States. In *Proceedings of the 2014 ACM/IEEE International Conference on Human-Robot Interaction, HRI '14*. ACM. doi:10.1145/2559636.2559676

Lee, J.-J., Seo, K.-H., Oh, C., & Bien, Z. Z. (2007). Development of a future Intelligent Sweet Home for the disabled. *Artificial Life and Robotics*, *11*(1), 8–12. doi:10.1007/s10015-006-0417-5

Leone, A., Diraco, G., & Siciliano, P. (2011). Detecting falls with 3D range camera in ambient assisted living applications: A preliminary study. *Medical Engineering & Physics*, *33*(6), 770–781. doi:10.1016/j.medengphy.2011.02.001 PMID:21382737

Levac, D., Rivard, L., & Missiuna, C. (2012). Defining the active ingredients of interactive computer play interventions for children with neuromotor impairments: A scoping review. *Research in Developmental Disabilities*, *33*(1), 214–223. doi:10.1016/j.ridd.2011.09.007 PMID:22093667

Linder, S. M., Reiss, A., Buchanan, S., Sahu, K., Rosenfeldt, A. B., & Clark, C. et al. (2013). Incorporating robotic-assisted telerehabilitation in a home program to improve arm function following stroke. *Journal of Neurologic Physical Therapy; JNPT*, *37*(3), 125–132. doi:10.1097/NPT.0b013e31829fa808 PMID:23872687

Linder, S. M., Rosenfeldt, A. B., Reiss, A., Buchanan, S., Sahu, K., & Bay, C. R. et al. (2013). The home stroke rehabilitation and monitoring system trial: A randomized controlled trial. *International Journal of Stroke Rehabilitation*, *8*(1), 46–53. doi:10.1111/j.1747-4949.2012.00971.x PMID:23280269

Lockery, D., Peters, J. F., Ramanna, S., Shay, B. L., & Szturm, T. (2011). Store-and-Feedforward Adaptive Gaming System for Hand-Finger Motion Tracking in Telerehabilitation. *IEEE Transactions on Information Technology in Biomedicine*, *15*(3), 467–473. doi:10.1109/TITB.2011.2125976 PMID:21536526

Lombardi, A., Ferri, M., Rescio, G., Grassi, M., & Malcovati, P. (2009). Wearable wireless accelerometer with embedded fall-detection logic for multi-sensor ambient assisted living applications. In *Proceedings of IEEE Sensors*. IEEE. doi:10.1109/ICSENS.2009.5398327

Madeira, R. N., Correia, N., Guerra, M., Postolache, O., Dias, A. C., & Postolache, G. (2011). Designing personalized therapeutic serious games for a pervasive assistive environment. In *Proceedings of 2011 IEEE 1st International Conference on Serious Games and Applications for Health (SeGAH)*. IEEE. doi:10.1109/SeGAH.2011.6165465

Memon, M., Wagner, S. R., Pedersen, C. F., Beevi, F. H. A., & Hansen, F. O. (2014). Ambient Assisted Living Healthcare Frameworks, Platforms, Standards, and Quality Attributes. *Sensors (Basel, Switzerland)*, *14*(3), 4312–4341. doi:10.3390/s140304312 PMID:24599192

Merians, A. S., Fluet, G. G., Qiu, Q., Saleh, S., Lafond, I., Davidow, A., & Adamovich, S. V. (2011). Robotically facilitated virtual rehabilitation of arm transport integrated with finger movement in persons with hemiparesis. *Journal of Neuroengineering and Rehabilitation*, *8*(1), 27. doi:10.1186/1743-0003-8-27 PMID:21575185

Metcalf, C. D., Robinson, R., Malpass, A. J., Bogle, T. P., Dell, T. A., Harris, C., & Demain, S. H. (2013). Markerless motion capture and measurement of hand kinematics: Validation and application to home-based upper limb rehabilitation. *IEEE Transactions on Bio-Medical Engineering*, *60*(8), 2184–2192. doi:10.1109/TBME.2013.2250286 PMID:23475333

Middleton, A. M., & Ward, T. E. (2012). The Pursuit of Flow in the Design of Rehabilitation Systems for Ambient Assisted Living: A Review of Current Knowledge. *International Journal of Ambient Computing and Intelligence*, *4*(1), 54–65. doi:10.4018/jaci.2012010105

Mohammed, S., Amirat, Y., & Rifai, H. (2012). Lower-Limb Movement Assistance through Wearable Robots: State of the Art and Challenges. *Advanced Robotics*, *26*(1-2), 1–22. doi:10.1163/016918611X607356

Mulvenna, M., Carswell, W., McCullagh, P., Augusto, J., Zheng, H., & Jeffers, P. et al. (2011). Visualization of data for ambient assisted living services. *IEEE Communications Magazine*, *49*(1), 110–117. doi:10.1109/MCOM.2011.5681023

Nehmer, J., Becker, M., Karshmer, A., & Lamm, R. (2006). Living assistance systems - An ambient intelligence approach. In *Proceedings - International Conference on Software Engineering*. Academic Press.

Neil, A., Ens, S., Pelletier, R., Jarus, T., & Rand, D. (2013). Sony PlayStation EyeToy elicits higher levels of movement than the Nintendo Wii: Implications for stroke rehabilitation. *European Journal of Physical and Rehabilitation Medicine*, *49*, 13–21. PMID:23172403

O'Neill, G., Patel, H., & Artemiadis, P. (2013). An intrinsically safe mechanism for physically coupling humans with robots. In *Proceedings of IEEE International Conference on Rehabilitation Robotics*. IEEE. doi:10.1109/ICORR.2013.6650510

O'Neill, S. A., Nugent, C. D., Donnelly, M. P., McCullagh, P., & McLaughlin, J. (2012). Evaluation of connected health technology. *Technology and Health Care*, *20*, 151–167. PMID:22735731

Oskoui, M., Coutinho, F., Dykeman, J., Jetté, N., & Pringsheim, T. (2013). An update on the prevalence of cerebral palsy: A systematic review and meta-analysis. *Developmental Medicine and Child Neurology*, *55*(6), 509–519. doi:10.1111/dmcn.12080 PMID:23346889

Palsbo, S. E., Marr, D., Streng, T., Bay, B. K., & Norblad, A. W. (2011). Towards a modified consumer haptic device for robotic-assisted fine-motor repetitive motion training. *Disability and Rehabilitation. Assistive Technology, 6*(6), 546–551. doi:10.3109/17483107.2010.532287 PMID:21091135

Parry, I., Carbullido, C., Kawada, J., Bagley, A., Sen, S., Greenhalgh, D., & Palmieri, T. (2013). Keeping up with video game technology: Objective analysis of Xbox Kinect™ and PlayStation 3 Move™ for use in burn rehabilitation. *Burns*. doi:10.1016/j.burns.2013.11.005

Pollack, M. E., Brown, L., Colbry, D., McCarthy, C. E., Orosz, C., & Peintner, B. et al. (2003). Autominder: An intelligent cognitive orthotic system for people with memory impairment. *Robotics and Autonomous Systems, 44*(3-4), 273–282. doi:10.1016/S0921-8890(03)00077-0

Sakagami, Y., Watanabe, R., Aoyama, C., Matsunaga, S., Higaki, N., & Fujimura, K. (2002). The intelligent ASIMO: system overview and integration. In *Proceedings of IEEE/RSJ International Conference on Intelligent Robots and Systems.* IEEE. doi:10.1109/IRDS.2002.1041641

Saposnik, G., & Levin, M.Outcome Research Canada. (2011). Virtual reality in stroke rehabilitation: A meta-analysis and implications for clinicians. *Stroke, 42*(5), 1380–1386. doi:10.1161/STROKEAHA.110.605451 PMID:21474804

Saposnik, G., Teasell, R., Mamdani, M., Hall, J., McIlroy, W., & Cheung, D. et al. (2010). Effectiveness of Virtual Reality Using Wii Gaming Technology in Stroke Rehabilitation A Pilot Randomized Clinical Trial and Proof of Principle. *Stroke, 41*(7), 1477–1484. doi:10.1161/STROKEAHA.110.584979 PMID:20508185

Tanaka, F. (2014). Robotics for Supporting Childhood Education. In Y. Sankai, K. Suzuki, & Y. Hasegawa (Eds.), *Cybernics* (pp. 185–195). Springer Japan. doi:10.1007/978-4-431-54159-2_10

US Centre for Disease Control and Prevention. (2010). *Stroke Statistics: Internet Stroke Center.* Author.

Wan, J., O'Grady, M. J., & O'Hare, G. M. P. (2013). Bootstrapping Activity Modeling for Ambient Assisted Living. In D. Zeng, C. C. Yang, V. S. Tseng, C. Xing, H. Chen, F.-Y. Wang, & X. Zheng (Eds.), *Smart Health* (LNCS), (pp. 96–106). Springer Berlin Heidelberg. doi:10.1007/978-3-642-39844-5_12

Yang, S., Peng, S., Song, A., Li, J., (2011). An one to many telerehabilitation training robot system based on virtual reality. *Gaojishu Tongxin/ Chinese High Technology Letters, 21,* 191–195. doi:10.3772/j.issn.1002-0470.2011.02.014

Zsiga, K., Edelmayer, G., Rumeau, P., Péter, O., Tóth, A., & Fazekas, G. (2013). Home care robot for socially supporting the elderly: Focus group studies in three European countries to screen user attitudes and requirements. *International Journal of Rehabilitation Research. Internationale Zeitschrift fur Rehabilitationsforschung. Revue Internationale de Recherches de Readaptation, 36*(4), 375–378. doi:10.1097/MRR.0b013e3283643d26 PMID:24189106

KEY TERMS AND DEFINITIONS

Ambient Assisted Living: Technology framework designed to unobtrusively assist the user and allow them to accomplish goals in their day-to-day activities.

e-Rehabilitation/Telerehabilitation: Delivery of rehabilitation services using digital communication mediums, such as the Internet.

Motion Capture: Recording the movement of people or objects.

Neurorehabilitation: Rehabilitation process resulting from a neurological injury, such as stroke.

Pervasive Computing: The presence of computing in day-to-day life particularly through the use of ambient and embedded technologies.

Rehabilitation: Aided recovery from an ailment, in this context dealing with movement-based impairments.

Robotic Agents: In this context, the use of interactive robotics in the field of rehabilitation.

Serious Games: Video games used for purposes other than pure entertainment, such as education or rehabilitation.

Virtual Reality: Computer simulated environment that gives an impression of reality to the user.

Wearable Sensors: Sensors that can be attached to a person or person's clothing that monitor various aspects of their movement or behaviour.

Chapter 5
Developing Team Work in IT Education to Foster Student Engagement

Nigel McKelvey
University of Ulster, UK

Kevin Curran
University of Ulster, UK

ABSTRACT

Teamwork is an important aspect that should be provided by both employers and employees. This chapter proposes relating this ethos to an educational environment in order to foster encouragement among students. Students demonstrating professionalism can provide important discussion points that can help the class environment run more efficiently. When issues arise in a class, students learn not to hesitate in speaking up. Many co-workers fail to work as a team because people do not voice their opinions on certain matters. Learning how to voice that opinion can aid students/employees in progressing an assignment without hindering any other processes. This chapter outlines how to incorporate teamwork into IT educational environments in order to encourage students to engage more with the process. It also gathers information based on student, staff, and industry surveys and strives to highlight the importance of teamwork as a skill essential for IT graduates.

INTRODUCTION

One of the most fundamental aspects of computer lab exercises is that students engage with the process of learning new technologies. These new technological skills help aid students in their goal to work in teams. By becoming active members of teams, students learn how to design, plan and build challenging projects and assignments (Fruchter R, 2001). Working together means the group can reach an understanding of the requirements in a much more efficient and coherent manner. The process of communication means that each group member will learn what part they play in the team and as a result can encourage each other to identify and nurture individual skills (Fruchter R, 2001).

Ever changing technologies are forcing the preservation of competitiveness and as a result are

DOI: 10.4018/978-1-4666-7284-0.ch005

Copyright © 2015, IGI Global. Copying or distributing in print or electronic forms without written permission of IGI Global is prohibited.

forcing higher educational institutions and business analysts to cooperate more effectively. According to their educational, scientific, knowledge-maker and generative characteristics, universities and colleges receive and play a more active role in the development of the economy (Marosi I & Bencsik A, 2010) . This in turn implies that colleges and universities need to play a greater role in preparing their graduates for life in industry.

It is important that no single team member takes full responsibility for every task. Everybody must play their part and the knowledge spread among the group (Lerner S, et al. 2009). By doing this, students can engage with the process of 'learning to learn'. Allowing students to determine roles is a crucial part of the learning process which will inevitably lead to greater efficiency in subsequent tasks. It is essential that the promotion of team work activities gets incorporated into the curriculum of an IT related discipline. Lecturers and facilitators often disagree about the direction colleges and universities should take when it comes to delivering modules that incorporate team activities. The majority of teamwork training within IT disciplines focuses in areas of case studies but more emphasis should be placed on developing team strategies to deal with code design and implementation which is more akin to a work environment. Generally all teams are different in terms of membership, group dynamics, and goals yet they go through similar processes as they develop from an immature team into one that is mature and productive (Lerner S, et al. 2009).

How effective a team's work is depends entirely on the internal group processes. In other words, the manner in which conflicts are managed, the amount of trust between members, and the use of an appropriate leadership style, etc (Lerner S, et al. 2009). It is important to note that team members need to be trained in how to work together and taught to understand the professional role and responsibility of each person. There is no "I" in TEAM!

BACKGROUND

In their paper "*What is the Curriculum Development Process?*" Clarke and Stow state that the term curriculum is: "a written plan which drives instruction. It delineates the skills and concepts taught and evaluated to enhance student achievement. Composed of a content area philosophy, strands with definitions, program goals, aligned scope and sequence, learner outcomes, and assessment tools, it is intentionally designed to meet district, state, and national standards." (Clarke N & Stow S, 2006)

Often the issue with developing a curriculum for a module within an IT discipline is that technology is constantly evolving. As a result, a module can become quickly outdated and below standard. Students deserve a module that will teach them about technologies and concepts that are current and relevant to their future careers. Incorporating reflective practice as teaching professionals can greatly help with this common issue. Misguided or redundant concepts can be removed or updated incrementally. This in turn goes some way to developing a curriculum that satisfies the requirements. This review should provide some insights into how developing a curriculum for IT can be problematic and also present some thoughts on how this might be addressed.

It is imperative that teachers and facilitators strategically align programme learning outcomes with module learning outcomes so that students can acquire the technological skills required by both educational establishments as well as by society itself (Fox-Turnbull W & Snape P, 2011). The responsibility for this curriculum falls on the facilitators and governing bodies of particular schools/colleges. With this responsibility comes accountability for the academic well-being of individuals and groups of people (Allen A & Mintrom M, 2010). It is evident that planning a successful educational framework within IT requires certain elements to be addressed effectively. Three strands identified are: technological practice, knowledge and nature (Eames C & Milne L, 2011). With regard to technological practice within an IT discipline, this entails students reviewing relevant case study material and/or implementing this knowledge through practical classes using the relevant software development tools. The technological knowledge itself should be generic and broad. So the students can have knowledge in as many different areas of their discipline as possible. Students should be encouraged to research and develop in areas that are not necessarily taught directly in the curriculum. Finally, the nature strand refers to the students' abilities to relate technology to and differentiate technology from human life (Eames C & Milne L, 2011). This in turn provides students with invaluable skills before entering the workforce such as team work.

Utilising tools such as Articulate can help enhance the learning environment. Articulate embeds itself into PowerPoint and allows a lecturer to develop quizzes, surveys and assessments as well as delivering video, audio and other types of media in a structured environment. The product is ideally suited to users of Blackboard because the interactive material runs within Blackboard. Using environments such as this helps to focus students and encourage interactivity within teams. One of the most common weaknesses identified among lecturing staff is an unwillingness to embrace change, whether that takes the form of adopting a new teaching methodology or adopting some new technologies as teaching aids. Perhaps students should be more actively involved in determining how a module gets delivered.

It is becoming increasingly more desirable to use some new teaching methodologies in order to better promote student motivation and attention. The methodology adopted will be dictated by many factors, including the group size, available time, student characteristics, lecturers' interpretation of a syllabus, etc. (Lacuesta R & Palacios G, 2009) Experience tends to show lecturers that most

students are somewhat reluctant to engage in the process of Team-Work in an educational setting. As a result the process is often disregarded as an educational tool. However informal discussions with 2 local IT related companies have shown that the ability to work in a team is invaluable when it comes to employing a graduate.

Eighty percent of potential employers felt that possessing the ability to work in a team was 'Very Important'. A survey of 28 students (at Letterkenny Institute of Technology) identified several interesting facts. One aspect related to the group process that most concerns students and teachers is the opportunist or parasite behavior of some group members. This problem arises most often in groups composed of four or more people or when the group works outside class hours. One of the ways of preventing this parasite behavior of the students is for the groups to lay down working rules or that the students sign internal contracts (Marin-Garcia J & Mauri J, 2007). When asked the question "Is Team-Work difficult?" the response was surprising.

As a result of the findings it became clear that students found working in teams difficult and awkward. Team work is not something new and therefore the transition from working as a team on a football pitch for example should not be so difficult to translate.

Rather startlingly, 58% of those surveyed had never worked as part of a team in an educational environment. This statistic is an obvious cause for concern and something that should be addressed. In contrast, students obviously felt that working in a team within a college or university was extremely important.

The necessity to adjust the level of participation of the students in the process of learning is increasing. A way to obtain this objective is by redesigning the manner in which the students partake in class. Active learning shifts the focus of content structuring from the teacher to the learner. By being actively involved in the shaping of the content, the learners gain a far better understanding of the information than they would otherwise have (Marin-Garcia J et al, 2009).

It is becoming apparent that industries whose primary focus is on knowledge and technology, are paving the way for economic recovery (Fruchter R, 2001a). Our location globally and the level of the graduates that we produce is now both an institutional and a national strategic issue. Existing in such a competitive environment is making any discrepancies in module learning outcomes more apparent. Lots of more recent institutions were established to focus on local and regional needs, and develop and help "retain an educated manpower in the area" (Fruchter R, 2001a). The Letterkenny Institute of Technology (LYIT) has a significant amount of mature students (over 23 years of age) – a figure of over 30%. These students are incredibly focused and deserve modules that will empower and encourage them to succeed.

For some institutes however, their role was originally viewed as "teaching only" but with a specific commitment to relevant knowledge and applied learning. Some were allowed to undertake limited research activity, but often with an emphasis (only) on development and consultancy. Over time, and commensurate with the global significance of the knowledge society, the commitment to providing "economically useful skills with industrial relevance" and ensuring that "academic activities are aligned with the economic development of their region" has become inextricably bound to offering advanced qualifications and growing research capacity (Fruchter R, 2001a). For this reason alone it is paramount that colleges and universities aim to produce the best possible caliber of student—capable of transferring a skill set easily to the workplace from an educational environment. While all team members should have a clear understanding about the team's goals and vision, many team members, due to poor communication within the team or lack of communication skills, are not aware of team objectives (Nejati

M et al, 2010). Evidence suggests that software development in an Agile educational setting could be beneficial.

AGILE

Within industry teams collocate because it enhances their ability to communicate. Working in the same room is core to all the agile methodologies (Miller A, 2008). Communication represents a significant part of the effort involved in delivering software, so opening up gateways to communication could increase a team's overall efficiency (Miller A, 2008). Many agile teams are distributed but almost all agile teams would sit together in a single room with the customer representative or product owner to maximize communication. It is therefore vital to integrate employees who can easily work in a team. More often companies are casting their net wider when looking to hire high quality employees (Miller A, 2008).

Agile Development has proven to be effective at improving the performance of many software development teams. Their productivity has increased and become more predictable and their defect rates have fallen (Grenning J, 2007). Many development processes attempt to take the human element out of software development, but agile's main focus is about leveraging the people and their interactions. It can be concluded that good people, working in teams who build successful software products. This point is often misconstrued to say that processes do not matter. Processes and discipline do matter, but people matter more (Grenning J, 2007).

Agile teaching is what lecturers often do in seminars and practical classes, where the environment makes it easier to have closer interaction with individual students. It is aimed at eliciting and addressing specific questions that students have, which as a result compliments a more rigid delivery of material in a conventional classroom environment (Razmov V. & Anderson R.J., 2006). However, not all courses are characterized by inflexibility of structure in the larger classroom. In many project-based courses and software development modules, the emphasis is away from content coverage in lectures, and instead falls heavily on student learning experiences in the process of working on projects or individual software artifacts (Razmov V. & Anderson R.J., 2006). This in turn marks a shift in what instructors can spend class time on, allowing them considerably more time and freedom to engage with the energy of the class – adjusting to student needs and providing advice on the pressing problems students are facing (Razmov V. & Anderson R.J., 2006). Teaching agile methodology can be challenging, but it is a worthwhile task as it enriches students' software development experience (Lu B & DeClue T. 2011). The skills these students learn will be invaluable in the workplace. Agile development can also focus a student in a particular area and as a result can increase skills levels quite significantly. Engaging with the process is paramount though – encouraging a student to do that will lie primarily with the lecturer, especially in the early stages.

Instructors must expect to encounter all personality types in their classrooms. Appealing to each personality type does not necessitate a complete rewrite of a teaching approach, but can help make the class more engaging and memorable for the students (Layman L et al. 2007). The responsibilities of the facilitator are not necessarily the group's leader although this is perfectly acceptable. It is better to think of the facilitator as the person who keeps the group focused on productivity. Therefore the facilitator should focus the team on the task, get participation from all team members, keep the team to its agreed-upon time frame (both short term and long term), suggest alternative procedures when the team is stalled, help team members confront problems and finally, summarize and clarify the team's decisions.

Many courses inherently favor introverts because of the focus on individual study and performance and as a result can isolate extraverts who tend to find their energy by working in groups. Finding an approach that will encourage both personality types is essential when incorporating Team-Work into the curriculum. This is particularly prevalent for computing disciplines. As a lecturer in this discipline, I often find that some of the most intelligent and capable students are quiet and introverted. Working as a software developer or as a project manager will entail working with other people and liaising with people daily. Therefore, incorporating activities that will help instill suitable traits in these graduates is essential.

For the facilitator it might be useful to put a label on the various common issues, which in turn might help to develop a curriculum that can address such issues quickly. (Breslow L, 2005) devised the following:

- **Hogging:** Talking too much.
- **Flogging:** Beating a dead horse.
- **Frogging:** Jumping from topic to topic.
- **Bogging:** Getting stuck on an issue.
- **Dead Buffaloes:** Tiptoeing around a contentious issue.

By labeling such activity, it might be easier to address the issues as they arise—which in itself is a learning exercise in team-work for the group.

PROFESSIONAL AND PERSONAL REFLECTION

In order to achieve a curriculum that will incorporate team activities correctly, it is essential to reflect on current modules so they can be altered correctly. Gauging how other professionals reflect on their day to day work provided some interesting statistics. 15 colleagues at LYIT were asked a series of questions about their reflective practice.

Obviously almost 94% of those surveyed teach in IT related disciplines which make the figures more relevant to subject area.

Reassuringly 94% stated that they do reflect regularly on their teaching. For the one person who did not, hopefully the survey itself might inspire them, as the merits greatly outweigh not partaking in the process.

When asked which areas they reflect most on, it was interesting to see that lectures and laboratory exercises came out on top with only 4% stating that they reflected on in-class discussions. Some of the discussions in class are in themselves a form of reflection. Nuggets of information can be gathered from inter-student conversations or student-lecturer conversations that might inspire a redraft of a particular topic or exercise. Again only 10% reflected on the feedback that they give students. How lecturers relay grades and critiques can have a significant impact on students' confidence and willingness to participate. Reflecting with a goal of making feedback a positive exercise every time, can go a long way in encouraging a student to improve and strive to achieve higher grades.

When teaching professionals discover that they do not or no longer reflect, it is important to work out what factors are involved. The question was asked as to which stumbling blocks prevent reflection. The overwhelming majority (54%) cited time constraints as the number one factor preventing them from carrying out active reflection. PPEs (or Programmatic Reviews) were second with 21%. When timetabling lecturing staff, it might be worth noting, that time should be provided to allow proper module reflection. Meetings and reviews are of course important but they really shouldn't detract from an instructor's ability to carry out their duties professionally and effectively. Facilitating reflection should be considered by management when allocating modules to individuals. Without honing modules, students will inevitably suffer as content will obviously be below par on occasions.

Student engagement is essential if graduates are to be of a certain caliber, therefore reflecting

on one's work goes some way to achieving this goal. Like others lecturers, I believe that reflection should not be a solitary process. The process should include students, colleagues and others (such as industry experts). Without sharing the information, reflection can become a less effective tool. I also believe that we reflect all the time and it is not whether we reflect but how effectively we reflect. What is the aim of reflection? Is it to improve the learning environment? On a practical level, I make use of critical note taking regarding areas that need improvement and portfolios/lab books for each student to monitor their success in certain sections which helps me to keep track of which teaching methodologies they react well to. Of course the students themselves have reacted well this semester to my obvious monitoring of activities. They seemed to genuinely appreciate the fact that I was critiquing my own work in order to give them a better learning experience and that I was willing to change elements as we went along. If we are to incorporate more team activities in our curriculum, then it is essential that the students are encouraged to get involved and give their ideas. After all, it is the students themselves that are doing the work, so they should have activities that they enjoy.

From personal experience, I noted in my diary that we can't assume that the students have previous knowledge in a particular area. Implementing change should be part and parcel of the job as opposed to a chore. Final year students commented to me in my Programming for Security module, that they would like to see more learning options provided by staff. Examples include, lectures, practicals, tutorials, public directory access to notes, VLE/BlackBoard, Articulate, Podcasts, etc. As time wasn't on my side this semester, I decided to change a piece of continuous assessment for this group in order to try and achieve some of the goals they wanted. Therefore, rather than producing a laboratory book, I asked them to surmise the module (including lectures and practicals) into a podcast. The podcast meant that they learnt new skills and by creating the podcast itself, they carried out revision without even being aware. What was produced could then be posted online and a link added to their Curriculum Vitae, as a means of show-casing their knowledge and skills.

Afterwards, the students commented on the fact that they had learned a lot and found the new assessment method extremely worthwhile and beneficial. Every semester, I look at my notes/handouts and decide if any of the topics would benefit from a Guest Speaker. As I lecture in a Computing Department, it is important that the students get to meet industry representatives. Lots of my content is quite new and therefore topical. Around October time, I noticed the fourth year digital forensic students becoming a little disillusioned. In order to foster encouragement, I organized Guest Speakers (who work in their field of expertise) to come in a talk to all forensic students (from all years). With around 100 digital forensic students together in one room listening to the possibility of working in a very interesting area with a few of them guaranteed to be employed before the end of the academic year, this gave them the drive they needed in order to keep studying and working together.

Again, the students (some of them not my own), commented and emailed me thanking me for providing them with this level of encouragement—proving that sometimes a simple gesture can have a significant impact.

Reflecting on my module content and making note of the fact that I noticed student attitudes becoming negative, meant that I was able to implement a change that helped turn things around without significantly impacting on my workload.

In contrast to my final year students, I also take first year students for Personal and Professional Development. Here the aim is to get the students interacting and getting to know each other through group activities. I noted in my diary early on in the semester that there were quite a few students in the class with very quiet personalities. It became clear that the proposed approach for the module may not be appropriate in order to include these students. As a result, I devised two new activities that would help the quieter students mingle with the more social students. It appeared to be effective as the "quieter" ones were equally as vocal as their counterparts by the end of the semester. Although it could also be argued that the more introverted students were encouraged by their more social colleagues. Team-work was a major player in this process and reflection was the catalyst for the module changes to be implemented.

One final entry in my diary referred to another group of final year students where I teach Governance for IT Enhancement. It was evident early in the semester that the students were finding the subject extremely theoretical and it became obvious that I needed to inject something more relevant for them. As a result, I divided the students into two groups – the board of directors and IT consultants. The 'board' needed to work together to establish their roles and how one depended on the other. The 'consultants' needed to work out the hardware and software requirements for the company, compile a presentation and present their findings to the 'board'. The 'board' then had to evaluate the findings and make decisions on whether or not they could progress (given their roles). After initial opposition to the task, the students later commented on how much they had learned and suddenly realized how much effort each team had to put in and where they could have done better. I also made note of some interesting observations with regard to student participation. In order to address the potential issue, I requested that the students compile one group report on the task and each individual also had to submit a mini-report outlining their contribution and what they had learned. When this task was made known to the students, suddenly participation improved greatly.

FUTURE RESEARCH DIRECTIONS

One of the most important aspects in today's organizations is Team-Work as it can increase work performance and result in better outcomes. For any team to be successful, there are key factors which should be addressed, including team members, their attitudes, etc. The research findings show that both desire and require Team-Work to be built into their current curriculum in IT. This is mainly because teamwork should be learned and can be enhanced through education and a proper working environment. Third level education should be concerned with giving its students the ability to learn as opposed to being taught every aspect of every subject. Industry also requires its employees to attain certain standards as undergraduates which will allow them to transfer their skills in to a team environment effortlessly. Colleges and Universities need to align with industry on a much larger scale in order to develop appropriate course content with particular reference to software development.

Larrivee's (Larrivee B, 2008) reference to 'surface' reflection is an important observation. Facilitators often reflect on their work as a means to an end or as a box that needs to be ticked. Reflection should be much deeper than that—plus the value of reflection should be obvious. Without reflection lessons, notes, exams, methodologies would become stagnant and outdated. Setting aside time with classes to ask them how they are coping and if they would to address any issues differently encourages students to be more forthcoming. Being a reflective professional implies that an obvious solution should not be overlooked in favour of a highfalutin approach which often does not address the issue(s) at hand. In a computing department, it is important to students at the end of every semester to fill out a QA questionnaire—in which they should be asked specific questions about courses and their content. It gives students an opportunity to give their opinions which often contain essential pieces of information that can be used for reflection. With the advancements in technology, it is now more possible than ever to gain information/reflection from others' work via online blogs. Lecturers should make use of these blogs in order to gain better insight into latest technologies/trends and to incorporate this into lesson plans. Kolb's (Kolb D, 1984) model for reflection is accurate, as reflection is certainly an ongoing task that has value and is necessary for teaching to be kept current and informative.

CONCLUSION

Some common weaknesses in teaching include an unwillingness to change, an over reliance on technology, being out of touch with latest techniques, padding out modules with irrelevant material and over assessment. Reflecting on these issues enables a facilitator to better prepare a curriculum in which the student is encouraged to engage with the process. Reflecting about the positive experiences with students allows lecturers to incorporate more of the good aspects into daily activities. As well as equipping the students with subject content to do well in exams, facilitators should ensure that the students have learned something more, for example, respect, working in a team, conflict resolution, becoming confident decision makers and problem solvers and simply making good choices and striving to be the best that they can possibly be. Howard Gardner (Gardner H, 1983) introduces the notion of Multiple Intelligences (MI). Different learners learn in different ways so to that extent there is merit in the theory. Teaching professionals must embrace these diversities and be prepared to adopt modules/lessons/practicals/assessments accordingly. Being in a position to swap and change the lesson content may not always be practical or possible but it certainly is something to consider. It is interesting to note that one student made the observation in the survey "I genuinely believe learning about human psychology can also be extremely helpful in understanding how people work together."

These Multiple Intelligences (MIs) provide a good focus for reflection. Understanding these MI could potentially help to enhance teaching practices and obviously help the students overall. Making use of the entire learning environment in order to keep the students interested—whether that's in class, around the campus, virtually or making use of industry—is extremely important. This might go some way to acknowledging these MIs.

They create environments which maximise opportunities to learn, in which pupils are well managed and motivated to learn. (Gardner H, 1983).

As professionals lecturers should strive to achieve this and often do meet the MIs of students incidentally. Students often comment on how introducing a new learning environment instantly revives a topic and often helps them to understand a topic/issue that they previously simply didn't comprehend. By doing so, teaching staff are automatically encouraging students to partake in activities. An effective teacher should remember that while they may have prepared for the class—during the class itself, it is the students that are doing the work—therefore, facilitators should allow them to take ownership of that. It is important to state that colleges and universities have to develop a curriculum for IT which will facilitate their marketability as well as their functionality in the educational and industrial markets. (Tomas M & Castro D, 2011). Using and incorporating Virtual Learning Environments (VLE) into a curriculum can help catapult a previously mundane module into the 21st Century. Within this "virtual reality", both the facilitator and the students can partake in a variety of curricular and extra-curricular activities (Lawless-Reljic S, 2011). This modern inclusion is a must moving forward when developing a curriculum for IT that is to foster and encourage team work.

REFERENCES

Allen, A., & Mintrom, M. (2010). Responsibility and School Governance. *Educational Policy*, *24*(3), 439–464. doi:10.1177/0895904808330172

Binkley, S. (2007). *The Importance of Teamwork in the Workplace*. Retrieved from http://www.associatedcontent.com/article/317564/the_importance_of_teamwork_in_the_workplace.html?cat=31

Breslow, L. (2005). How to Create a High Functioning Team. In *MIT, Guidelines for "Management Communication for Undergraduates"* (15.279). Sloan School of Management, MIT. Retrieved from http://web.mit.edu/tll/teaching-materials/teamwork/index-teamwork.html

Clarke, N., & Stow, S. (2006). *What is the Curriculum Development Process?* Retrieved from http://www.curriculumalignmentassociates.com/What%20is%20the%20Curriculum%20Development%20Process.pdf

Eames, C., & Milne, L. (2011). Teacher responses to a planning framework for junior technology classes learning outside the classroom. *Education: An International Journal*, *16*(2), 33–44.

Fox-Turnbull, W., & Snape, P. (2011). Technology teacher education through a constructivist approach. Education: An International Journal, 16(2), 45-56.

Fruchter, R. (2001). Dimensions of Teamwork Education. *International Journal of Engineering Education*, *17*(4), 34–42.

Fruchter, R. (2001a). Higher Education Management and Policy. *Journal of the Programme on Institutional Management in Higher Education*, *17*(2). Retrieved from http://www.oecd.org/dataoecd/53/61/42348396.pdf

Gardner, H. (1983). *Frames of mind: The theory of multiple intelligences*. New York: Basic Books.

Grenning, J. (2007). *Agile Embedded Software Development*. Paper presented at the Embedded Systems Conference. San Jose, CA. Retrieved from http://www.renaissancesoftware.net/files/articles/ESC-349Paper_Grenning-v1r2.pdf

Kolb, D. (1984). *Experiential Learning: Experience as the Source of Learning and Development*. Prentice-Hall.

Lacuesta, R., & Palacios, G. (2009). A preliminary Approach to ECTS Estimate within the Framework of Electrical and Electronic Engineering Based on Experience. *Mount Sinai Journal of Medicine*, *76*(1), 318–329. Retrieved from http://fie-conference.org/fie2009/papers/1183.pdf http://www.uwoanesthesia.ca/documents/teamwork_anesthesia.pdf

Larrivee, B. (2008). Development of a tool to assess teachers' level of reflective practice. *Reflective Practice*, *9*(3), 341–360. doi:10.1080/14623940802207451

Lawless-Reljic, S. (2011). The Effects of instructor-Avatar Immediacy in Second Life, an Immersive and Interactive 3D Virtual Environment. *eleed*, *7*. Retrieved from http://eleed.campussource.de/archive/7/3074

Layman, L., et al. (2007). Personality Types, Learning Styles, and an Agile Approach to Software Engineering Education. In *Proceedings of the 37th SIGCSE Technical Symposium on Computer Science Education* (Vol. 14, pp. 428-432). Academic Press. Retrieved from http://lucas.ezzoterik.com/papers/LCW06.pdf

Lerner, S. et al. (2009). Teaching Teamwork in Medical Education. *The International Journal of Learning*. *Journal of Medicine*, *76*(4), 20–32.

Lu, B., & DeClue, T. (2011). *Teaching Agile Methodology In A Software Engineering Capstone Course*. Department of Computer and Information Sciences, Southwest Baptist University. Retrieved from http://db.grinnell.edu/ccsc/ccsc-cp2011/Program/viewAcceptedProposal.pdf?sessionType=paper&sessionNumber=13

Marin-Garcia, J., et al. (2009). Enhancing motivation and satisfaction of students: analysis of quantitative data in three subjects of Industrial Engineering. *WSEAS Transactions on Advances in Engineering Education*, *6*(1), 32-44. Retrieved from http://www.wseas.us/e-library/transactions/education/2009/28-854.pdf

Marin-Garcia, J., & Mauri, J. (2007). Teamwork with University Engineering Students. Group Process Assessment Tool. In *Proceedings of the 3rd WSEAS/IASME International Conference on Educational Technologies*. Retrieved from http://personales.gan.upv.es/jlloret/pdf/edute2007-2.pdf

Marosi, I., & Bencsik, A. (2010). Teamwork in Higher Education: Teamwork as Chance of Success. *The International Journal of Learning*, *16*(5), 167–174. Retrieved from http://ijl.cgpublisher.com/product/pub.30/prod.2156

Miller, A. (2008). Distributed Agile Development at Microsoft patterns & practices. *MSDN white paper*. Retrieved from http://download.microsoft.com/download/4/4/a/44a2cebd-63fb-4379-898d-9cf24822c6cc/distributed_agile_development_at_microsoft_patterns_and_practices.pdf

Nejati, M. (2010). Teamwork Approach: An Investigation on Iranian Teamwork Attitudes. *Canadian Social Science*, *6*(3), 104–113. Retrieved from http://cscanada.net/index.php/css/article/view/1058/1077

Razmov, V., & Anderson, R. J. (2006). Experiences with Agile Teaching in Project-Based Courses. In *Proceedings of Annual Conference of the American Society for Engineering Education (ASEE)*. ASEE. Retrieved from http://www.cs.washington.edu/research/edtech/publications/RA06-ASEE_AgileTeaching.pdf

Tomas, M., & Castro, D. (2011). Multidimensional Framework for the Analysis of Innovations at Universities in Catalonia. *Educational Policy*, *19*(27), 48-60.

KEY TERMS AND DEFINITIONS

Agile Development: Methodology which is proving to be effective at improving the performance of many software development teams. Their productivity has increased and become more predictable and their defect rates have fallen. Many development processes attempt to take the human element out of software development, but AGILE's main focus is about leveraging the people and their interactions. It can be concluded that good people, working in teams who build successful software products.

Agile Teaching: An approach by lecturers in seminars and practical classes, where the environment makes it easier to have closer interaction with individual students. It is aimed at eliciting and addressing specific questions that students have, which as a result compliments a more rigid delivery of material in a conventional classroom environment.

Articulate: A tool to enhance the learning environment by embedding itself into PowerPoint and allows a lecturer to develop quizzes, surveys and assessments as well as delivering video, audio and other types of media in a structured environment. The product is ideally suited to users of Blackboard because the interactive material runs within Blackboard.

Curriculum: A written plan which drives instruction. It delineates the skills and concepts taught and evaluated to enhance student achievement. Composed of a content area philosophy, strands with definitions, program goals, aligned scope and sequence, learner outcomes, and assessment tools, it is intentionally designed to meet district, state, and national standards.

Educational Technology: Also termed instructional technology, information and communication technology(ICT) in education, EdTech, and learning technology, is the study and ethical practice of facilitating learning and improving performance by creating, using and managing appropriate technological processes and resource.

E-Learning (or eLearning): The use of electronic media, educational technology, and information and communication technologies (ICT) in education. E-learning includes numerous types of media that deliver text, audio, images, animation, and streaming video, and includes technology applications and processes such as audio or video tape, satellite TV underlying many e-learning processes.

Teamwork: Work done by several associates with each doing a part but all subordinating personal prominence to the efficiency of the whole. In a business setting accounting techniques may be used to provide financial measures of the benefits of teamwork which are useful for justifying the concept.

Chapter 6
Common Problems Faced When Developing Applications for Mobile Devices

Kevin Curran
University of Ulster, UK

Sean Carlin
University of Ulster, UK

Joseph McMahon
University of Ulster, UK

ABSTRACT

Mobile application development is relatively new and has seen growth of late. With this rapid expansion, there are growing pains within industry, as the usual time given to the evolution of an industry to learn from past mistakes has been significantly shortened and is even going on within the currently saturated market. Because of this, inexperienced developers are attempting to design applications based on what is of yet a shady set of design principals. This is providing problems during the development process and can be seen to be stifling innovation, as many developers have yet to get a grasp on the shift between traditional software engineering and what it means to implicate these designs on a mobile device. This chapter analyses these difficulties in depth, as well as attempting to draw solutions to these problems based on development in the context of the characteristics of mobile devices.

INTRODUCTION

Mobile Computing is currently growing and has no plans of slowing down in the near future. Gartner states that worldwide sales of mobile devices to end users totaled 428.7 million units in the second quarter of 2011, a 16.5 percent increase from the second quarter of 2010 (Pettey & Goasduff, 2011). This growth is attracting more and more developers to move away from traditional applications and web development. Many of these developers are now focused on developing applications for mobile devices. A mobile device is a generic term used to refer to a variety of devices that allow people

DOI: 10.4018/978-1-4666-7284-0.ch006

Copyright © 2015, IGI Global. Copying or distributing in print or electronic forms without written permission of IGI Global is prohibited.

to access data and information from where ever they are. This includes cell phones and portable devices (Hakoama & Hakoyama, 2011). A mobile device is a very broad term in the fact that it can refer to laptops, net books, smart phones and the most recent form of mobile technology known as tablets. When a person discusses mobile devices today, they are generally referring to a smart phone or tablet. Developers whether they are new to mobile development or seasoned veterans, run into many problems and are required to make tough calculated decisions based on number of factors affecting the deployment/ accessibility of their mobile application.

A large portion of Smartphone sales are driven by the availability of apps, and as the demand for apps increases, so grows the demand for app developers and quality applications. The fast pace at which the technology is being incorporated into mobiles and the pace at which it is developing brings with it its own problems. Since mobile application development is a relatively new field in computing and is also becoming a very profitable and enterprising market, several changes in the development process have to be taken onboard in order to create a successful product, such as how the application is going to perform from device to device, something that rarely had to be considered with developing software for desktop computers. While Smartphones now usually come pre-installed with applications which carry out a wide range of functionality specific to that operating system and device, utilizing the specific hardware in that circumstance, custom applications can also be downloaded onto the device and will vary in usefulness depending on their compatibility with that device's hardware and software. Developers must recognise what customers want from their devices, and make their product stand out in what is becoming a very over-saturated market, which in itself is one of the biggest challenges faced when developing mobile applications. As the number of technologies around us increase and start to pervade our

everyday routines, our methods of interacting with these technologies is also changing. We are seeing an increase in the number of wireless networks in public areas, as well as technologies that are interacting with each other wirelessly or over the internet and the mobile phone market has evolved naturally to incorporate and interact with these technologies. Social networking has emerged as one of the biggest trends in recent years, and has revolutionised the way in which people communicate with each other. This has converged with the evolution of mobile technology, providing users with the convenience of having access to the wider world at their fingertips. This is a perfect example of how the functionality of mobile devices has evolved to meet user's needs and has created a large demand from the users of mobile devices for more and more applications which incorporate these technologies. As the speed of mobile devices and the constant development of new technologies become available, more devices are being released with different sets of features to provide for a range of user needs. This has created a very fragmented development community, as the wide range of platforms and devices available mean that development cannot be too focused on a single set-up if it is to reach a wide audience or make money. Applications have been developed for many different tasks. Originally conceived as software to increase efficiency and productivity, such as personal planners on devices such as PDAs, as the hardware evolved and the widespread use of mobile devices continued, so did the variety of apps becoming available, with these mobile devices offering alternative platforms for casual gaming, offering businesses a portable way of communicating data and information to each other, as well as extensive use in the medical and educational fields. The portability and increasing capabilities of Smartphones and PDAs intrigued developers into incorporating media which we normally associate with desktop computers into the handhelds, providing users another avenue to access their emails, social networks, maps etc.

while not at the desk, as well as seeing many innovations using the location based technologies of the mobile devices.

So far, amongst the development community, no widely agreed on development model has been presented and thus the methods used in mobile application development are ultimately unwieldy as of yet. In this chapter, the problems faced when developing applications for mobile devices will be highlighted and evaluated, with a critical analysis given to any techniques which may be working in this field and any techniques which are benefitting or may be employed in the future. Developers have to deal with a slight paradigm shift in the development process. One of such main differences and challenges is the fact that the traditional PC development process doesn't translate very well to development on mobile platforms. Because of the wide range of mobile platforms and hardware available, portability between various technologies is a major issue in mobile app development, as each user may have a different mobile device which may function differently. This is not usually an issue with developing applications for computers, as development is usually very platform specific, therefore it would only have to be developed with that platforms functionality and specs in mind, with testing being able to be automated. Because of the vast amount of platforms out there, some of the developers of these platforms have released development guidelines based on developing on their specific devices. While this may be useful for developing applications to those specific platforms specifications, there are very little agreed on guidelines for developing over many platforms. With tools available to making cross-platform coding easier, there still lies the problem of incompatibilities that may crop up in the field. This means that a lot of mobile application development relies solely on the developer if they are to make the product compatible over different devices. This is the main issue when it comes to developing applications for mobile

devices, as portability between devices has to be taken into account in the coding process. Due to the large amount of operating systems available, their respective IDE's used when developing them also have their own coding languages and specific criteria for being loaded onto a mobile device. This is a problem for developers, as a wide knowledge and code based knowledge is needed if an application is to be deployed on several platforms. This chapter provides some insight into many common problems developers must face and overcome to develop an application for mobile devices.

BACKGROUND

The developer must consider the various physical limitations they are faced with when developing a mobile application such as:

- **Resource Limitations:** Mobile devices have a fraction of resources available to them in comparison to today's modern computers. Every mobile device designed and developed has a difference in physical resources to the previous or next. The current mobile devices have less ram available for applications and their processors are much smaller and slower in relation to modern desktop computers. This creates a large problem for developers as they are required to be much more economical with their resources and thorough in their planning in order to create a high performance application which works on multiple devices with varying resources.

- **Screen Size Limitations:** Developers must be creative and find a more visually friendly way of displaying information as they have smaller screens averaging between 2.5 – 4.0 inches with a multitude of screen resolutions. This can be a daunting task and is not feasible to test every screen size and resolution, which is why the developer must be completely up to date with the industries best practices and standards.

- **Power Limitations:** Inefficient mobile applications tend to consume a lot of battery life due to the waste of resources through unreleased ram and processes. With mobile devices being battery powered they only have a limited power supply until they are required to be plugged in and recharged, some mobile devices having as little as one days battery life. This puts the developer under pressure to make the application as efficient as possible in order to keep battery life consumption to a minimum while maximizing the applications performance.

- **Multiple Form Factors:** Mobile devices come in a variety of shapes, sizes and hardware configurations. Some have physical keyboards or virtual keyboards; some have touch screens; some have high resolutions others have low; some can be large and clunky or small and slim; some have cameras. A visual representation of different types of form factors of mobile devices can be seen in Figure 1. This kind of variety in form factors and hardware configurations is a very real problem for developers and can be a large factor affecting the usability of an application on a mobile device.

The fact that Smartphones are also mobile, incorporating various location based technologies, brings along a whole new set of design challenges as well. There are multiple dimensions of mobility that have to be considered during the mobile development process (B'Far, 2005). These dimensions are location awareness, network connectivity quality of service, limited device capabilities (storage and CPU), limited power supply, support for a wide variety of user interfaces, platform proliferation, and active transactions. These dimensions in relation to the development process mean that developers will have to take a different approach to the design of their applications, and begs a new set of design principals. This is a challenge as some of these dimensions may present many limitations on the intended functionality of the application, whilst some present completely new opportunities, opening a whole new range of technologies which can be implemented into, but may complicate the plan of the project. This also strongly affects the testing of the application.

Testing is a major process in the development lifecycle, and it has to be thoroughly executed if the final product is to function as intended in the field. In developing for mobile devices, testing is more difficult as there are many more variables to consider, as well as a lack of proper test cases by which to run the applications against. Because of the inherent variations in mobile devices, there

Figure 1. Showing an example of different form factors of mobile devices

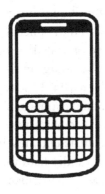 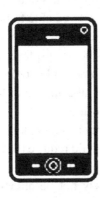  

is a range of different functionality and capabilities with each device and operating system, as well as the characteristics of being mobile as described earlier. This means that field testing would be impossible on every device, because there are simply too many different devices, so the scope of testing would have to be narrowed and specialized. This requires extra planning and time on the developer's part, which can put a lot of stress on the project. Emulators can be used to simulate a lot of the applications functionality over a variety of devices without having to physically have those devices at hand. This can only test the application to a certain extent though, as the emulator may not cover a lot of different models, as well as new ones constantly being released and a different emulator would have to be used for each different operating system. Emulators would only go so far in testing, as it would not be able to simulate a live environment as well as having the application running on a device. Things that vary in real life situations, such as signal strength, battery life remaining, and memory available would usually be overlooked, and many of the test cases may not be specific enough to cover many of these facets, possibly causing problems when the software is deployed in the field. Automation is a technique widely used for testing in the development industry. By formalizing the approach to testing by using software to carry out a set of test cases on the product, testing can be sped up and can determine whether the product functions as expected. When it comes to developing mobile applications, the number of variables that have to be taken into account, such as the constraints of the mobile platform itself, make pinning down test cases, and as a result, automation difficult, meaning that the developer will have to carry out most of these manually, costing time and resources (Kumar, 2007).

The portability of the application between hardware and operating systems will be one of the main factors that will complicate the process when it comes to mobile app development. In-consistencies between functionality of devices mean that the scope of a project will have to be very defined if it is to work on a wide range of devices. Factors that will have to be taken into account are the device's display, memory and the buttons, touch capabilities and sensors on the device. Because of these inherent inconsistencies of mobile devices in general, portability between platforms will have to be meticulously planned beforehand, and may involve lots of re-coding and re-development during the course of the project, with many problems that may crop up during the development phase which could not have been predicted beforehand, and could cause significant setbacks in the project due to incompatibility of the software between platforms. Aspects such as screen size and resolution are one of the main variations between models of mobile devices. If an application cannot stretch to fit the size of a screen, or the screen can't display some of the colours or match the resolutions, errors may crop up or crash the application altogether, which means precise coding will have to be incorporated into the application in order to detect the device's specifications and format the display as to show it correctly on the device's screen. Many devices also have the capability of turning the device to create a landscape view of the screen. Again, this will change the resolution of the screen. This is not a problem commonly associated with traditional software development and with the constant proliferation of mobile devices means that this is a challenge for developers to be able to predict and plan what methods they are going to use to be able to port their application over various device's displays, as well as if the application is being displayed as landscape or scaled down. Some applications may also be very large in size, or take up a lot of RAM in order to run. This may be due to the complexity of the application, or if it incorporates elements such as 3D graphics, which would require the device to be sufficiently fast in order to run it. This means that older hardware may not be able to keep up with the demands of the app, causing crashes. This is difficult to predict and test for on the developer's part, as there can be differences between a device's total RAM/CPU and the devices available RAM/CPU, depending on how many applications are running on the background amongst other factors. Unlike traditional desktop software development, where this is not usually a constraint, mobile devices are still lacking in the area of computational power, which will mean having to code for any situations in which a lack of memory or any other factors may impede the application's normal running, costing more time on the developers part. Many mobile devices these days contain several sensors in order to detect light levels, orientation etc. This means that applications geared towards making use of these functions will have to be very specific in scope, with a lot of research done on the developer's part as to which devices contain the appropriate technology and which devices and operating systems they will be targeting. All these factors combined will provide a big challenge on the developer's part, as much coding which could prepare the application for situations, such as dealing with a hardware or software incompat-

ibility may also slow it down, or consume more resources if the application's code becomes too bloated with exception handling, taking longer to process at runtime.

OPERATING SYSTEM CONSIDERATIONS

Mobile applications cannot be built without an operating system to run on therefore one of the most fundamental requirements for a developer building an application for a mobile device is to choose which operating systems they support. A key factor in influencing which operating system to develop their application for is how many people can access their application. Figure 2 displays the market shares of today's current mobile operating systems (Pettey & Goasduff, 2011).

The higher the user base that can access the application usually materializes to more profit/downloads for the application developer. Judging by the results above this is currently Android, which holds a 43% of the worldwide market share in mobile devices. This is an important factor

Figure 2. Mobile device operating systems market share % August 2011

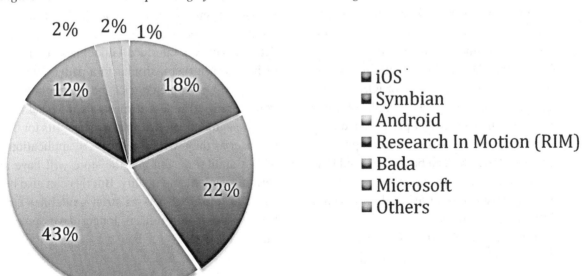

for the developer but it is not the only factor, the developer must think of other implications when choosing an operating system such as:

- **Privileges:** If the developer wishes to access the hardware of the mobile device and manipulate it to do exactly what they require, they will need root permissions. This is not a feature all operating system providers (namely apple) offer for their mobile devices, developers will not be able to access low-number network ports on iOS, for example, or do anything else that would typically require root or administrative access on a desktop computer (Mark, Nutting & LaMarche, 2011). This is a serious limitation when it comes to the developer's creativity and originality in their application. In contrast the more open android operating system developed by Google boasts "each application's process, data storage, and files are private unless explicitly shared with other applications via a full permission-based security mechanism" and allows developers to access any of the devices hardware components (Meier, 2010).

- **Developer Costs and Prerequisites:** When a developer chooses to write an application there will always need to be an investment of time, but in some cases money is also mandatory. An example of this is developing an application for iOS, the developer must register with apple as a developer, which costs £99 per year and they must also own a Macintosh computer to use the SDK. This can be an issue and hindrance for developers if they do not want to pay a yearly licensing fee or do not own a Macintosh computer.

- **Publishing Application Process:** Many of the mobile devices operating system

providers offer application stores or market places for developers to publish and monetize their applications. These application stores allow the end users to purchase, download and run the application on their mobile device. Some of the popular application stores and market places today are Apples app store, Google's android marketplace, Microsoft's windows phone market place, Nokia's ovi store and Blackberry's app world. The application stores have their own advantages and disadvantages for the developer. The application stores vary in strictness and standards, for example Google's android market place has no approval process for application distribution (Meier, 2010). This caters for the developers because there are no real standards and they have complete control of how they wish their application to look, feel and function. Having no approval process can cause an inconsistency in application quality and leave the store bundled with poor and insecure applications to the annoyance of the common users who use the applications.

On the other hand Apples app store includes a robust user inter- face tool that enables developers to use prebuilt components, supported with detailed Human Interface Guidelines (or HIG) of how to use them, similar to a pattern library (Fling, 2009). Apple is strict and the application will be refused unless it meets their visual and resource guidelines. This has real benefits for the end user as they will have access to applications with a similar design and the store will have a certain standard and quality. But this can also be an issue for developers as strict guidelines can lead to application refusal, longer development times and costs.

WEB BASED, NATIVE, OR HYBRID APPLICATION DEVELOPMENT

Developers have to understand their target markets and what functionality of the mobile device they will need to access. Central to every development platform is its software development kit (SDK), which enables third party developers to deliver applications running on the plat-form (Holzer & Ondrus, 2009). To use the most core functionality of the mobile device such as the camera, SMS or phone, a native application must be built using an SDK, which supports the mobile device and operating system. Native applications can utilize the full power of the mobile device but can cut revenue for the developer as the application may not work on a different device running a different operating system, an example of this is developing an application using the android SDK and not being able to run the application on a windows phone, blackberry or iPhone without developing a standalone native application for each of these devices. If a developer decides to create an application that does not require the use of GPS, camera, accelerometer, access to file system or any core functionalities of the device then the developer can develop a web-based application. The combination of familiar web technologies with minimal native code enables you to develop your application once and deploy to a variety of mobile devices (Jacobs, 2011). Mobile web applications run through the mobile devices browser enabling it to run on a variety of devices and operating systems. This can free up a lot of development time and testing but the developer has to sacrifice the core functionalities of the mobile device and the device must also be constantly connected to the Internet.

The alternative to the native and web-based applications mentioned above is that developers may choose to develop a hybrid application, this is now possible due to some "cross-platform development tools, such as RhoMobile's Rhodes and the open source PhoneGap, which can be used to create native applications on various brands of Smartphones. Along the same lines, Netbiscuits, Appcelerator, Kyte, and other companies provides tools and frameworks to support the creation of mobile web and hybrid sites using their SDK or one of the previously mentioned environments" (Wasserman, 2008). This allows the developer to create small-medium sized applications that will be cross platform, this approach is generally adopted by developers who need to create an application on multiple platforms as fast as possible. It does require the developer to adhere to many core software development principles such as abstraction and the developer has to plan and design their application thoroughly.

PLANNING AND MANAGEMENT

When developing a mobile application it is no different than developing a traditional computer application in the fact that the developer has to meticulous in their planning. The developer must plan for the worst and hope for the best as anything can happen during the development process and it is important that the developer has some sort of contingency plan. This way the developer will be prepared for over running deadlines or underestimating how much the project would cost etc. Documentation is key when developing any kind of application as it will allow one developer to pick up where another has left off, it also allows more developers to join the project and get up to speed quickly which limits the risk of project failure. Planning the development of the mobile device's application is essential for its success.

A common problem when developing mobile applications is deciding how the application will make profit to give the developer a return in their investment. The developer is faced with a variety of business models and revenues streams and it can be difficult to assess each and choose the correct one for the application. It is important that the developer understands each revenue stream and business model described below and chooses to use the best models that compliment their application.

- **Paid Applications:** The developer would set a standard price for their application on the application store and the user would pay the one off fee that gives them unlimited access to the applications functionality. This is the most basic type of revenue stream for developers often the company which owns the store where the application is published will usually take a 30% cut of the apps revenue.

- **Subscription and Pay-Per-Issue Applications:** This is a model where the developer can get constant revenue by supplying the user with new issues or content on a regular bases. The user pays a monthly fee or for the new issue of content, this does however require the developer to constantly update their application with fresh content to justify the constant bills on the users.

- **Free Applications with Advertising/ Affiliate Marketing:** The developer could make a return on their investment by making the application free to download and use in-app advertising or affiliate marketing to produce revenue. Affiliate Marketing is marketing products or services for other companies in exchange for a commission (Volk, 2010). This marketing technique is massive in the web as a revenue stream and is quickly being introduced to today's mobile device applications. In-app advertising and affiliate marketing operates very similarly to the pay per click model of the web; this has been modified for the current mobile markets as a pay per action model. Developers must not ignore these revenues streams, especially if their application is free.

SECURITY CONCERNS

One of the major problems when developing a mobile application is how to make the application secure (Lowe, 2011; Kumar, 2007). The fact that mobile technology is relatively new and beginning to incorporate technologies and protocols from desktop computing, such as operating systems, IP addresses and their ability to send and download software and execute code means that it is open to all the vulnerabilities seen on desktop computers, and possibly many more. Due to the fact that mobile technology is mobile as well, opens the devices and its users up for a whole new range of possible compromise, due to the fact that mobile devices often contain location based functionality, spyware can take a lot more information from the devices than could traditionally be attained from computers. Viruses of completely new classes are also popping up, using SMS and Bluetooth connections as a whole new avenue to spread from device. Preventing these issues from affecting the application or what information the app has stored on the device will be problematic for the developer from a technical standpoint. As viruses are constantly evolving, with new methods of attack being constantly created, it is important that the application is kept as simple as possible, so that every possible area in which it can be attacked can be barricaded. This may require a lot of time on the developer's part, and could warrant the deployment of later patches post-release if the device is at significant risk due to the application. It will also be the developer's responsibility to ensure that their application does not look or act suspicious to the user, as this could cause the application to get a bad reputation and harm the applications success.

Developers must be transparent with the end users and explain why they need access to certain permissions on the mobile device. It is also the developer's responsibility to use self-signed certificates, which developers can generate without anyone else's assistance or permission. One reason for code signing is to allow developers to update their application without creating complicated interfaces and permissions (Burns, 2008). Without self signed certificates the application could come from anyone, so it is important that the developers sign the application as their own, this will build confidence with the users and distributors (Onias-Kukkonen, 2003). When downloading an application, that platforms app market will often contain some information about the application, as well as what the application has access to, as can be seen in Figure 3.

While it is clearly defined what the application has access to, this can be often off-putting and daunting for first time users. For example, say if a simple application such as a calculator wants access to the device's GPS services, it can be quite unclear as to why this is needed exactly, and can feel like it is impeding on the user's privacy causing them to possibly avoid the app altogether,

Figure 3. Application permissions in Android

which can hurt application development. One way around this is to use the 'least privilege model', functioning on the least amount of privileges that are needed, for example if the app does not need access to the camera, it should not grant itself access to the camera, as this could impede on the processing speed or the running of other applications (Dwivedi et al., 2010), which will also give the user a more succinct overview of what the application is doing, so it may not seem as suspicious. Getting the application signed is also highly recommended and can reassure the user that the application and code are coming from a trusted source.

A lot of user information is handled by is connected to or stored physically on the mobile device, therefore if the device is stolen, the third party can possibly gain access to this information, which could be worth more than the device or possibly put the user at harm. This calls for a radical rethinking in the way that we handle our personal and sensitive information on mobile devices. One method to tackle this is not to store any of this information locally on the device. If information is stored on the device, it is usually only a matter of time before access can be gained to it through hacking or other methods. If the information can be stored remotely, the owner of the device will have more control over who can access this data. This will mean that future applications will have to be designed with the assumption that physical access to the device and the data contained on it is possible to third parties, with access to the information done over a remote server or a computer cloud. This may in turn though, inconvenience a genuine user, who will have to bypass security protocols when they want to access their own information. User identification technology is emerging increasingly in mobile devices, with some devices being able to identify user by fingerprint or facial recognition, which may go a long way in authenticating the user more quickly. Tools such as 'Zap it' by iAnywhere also present intriguing solutions to the aforementioned problem. This software allows the content on a phone to be erased remotely if certain criteria are not fulfilled, such as the user not signing in to the server in a set window of time, which would be useful in the case of a stolen device. Also the developer can implement more short term measures to ensure every possible level of protection for the user's information, such as sanitizing inputs so that exploits of the app cannot occur, as well as ensuring any information that does need to be stored locally is encrypted.

In certain operating systems the developers must use initiative and truly understand the fundamentals of the languages they are using. For example developers must be weary of creating buffer overflows by accident or by someone exploiting their code when using languages such as C/ Objective C. Developers must be concerned when allowing their applications to communicate to servers. All data transmitted to and from the server should be securely encrypted using SSL certificates especially when the data is of a sensitive nature such as medical and financial records. Once a developer publishes an application the application is never truly finished as bugs surface and loopholes become apparent, this is an inherent problem for developers when creating applications. Developers have to patch their applications and inform the users that their current version is out of date to keep their application secure.

As mobile devices continue to bring together various forms of media and technology into one device, their users' information for these various applications is also stored on the device, or accessed from the internet via the device. This poses a security risk, with either the loss of the device containing some unsecured or unencrypted personal information potentially being stolen or even gaps in the code of an application which handles sensitive information being hacked and stolen. When developing an application that handles or stores personal user information or other sensitive information, it is important on the developer's part to decide how to handle this information in

the safest possible way. From simple things such as displaying a "*" to hide the characters on the screen when a password is entered by the user, to encrypting any passwords or important information that is stored on the device, it is vital that the user feels that their details are secure, in order for the application to function successfully. The main problem with developing with this in mind is that, because the concept of carrying out transactions or storing important information using mobile devices is relatively new, and they can be used for such a range of different media, with users usually using their mobile device to converge all of their data, such as email, social network profiles, notes, messages, pictures, videos etc. into one, a single device can contain access, restricted or not, to a lot of that person's information. If someone gets a hold of the physical device it is only a matter of time before the security constraints are broke, and whatever data contained on the device accessed. This will pose a challenge to the developer, as it will mean adjusting their design principles around how information is going to be handled and protected on the system – this can range from using a dedicated server to cloud computing in order to allow the user to access their information, or to allow the system to verify the user (Dwivedi et al., 2010). While it is up to the user's discretion and common sense what information they choose to use their mobile device to handle, it is also the developer's responsibility, if the user is using their application, to ensure that their content is protected. Due to the need for applications to have access to various parts of a device's functionality or software APIs, security breaches, such as an application being given access to a sensitive area of the device's operating system can cause damage to the actual system. One of the problems faced by the developer's in this case are having the resources to implement a more secure system for their application, such as a remote server to store information, simply at times due to the cost of the hardware involved. Time and experience is also essential, and it will be difficult for the developer to completely test the application for any gaps or exploits in its security, as many different problems may crop up in the live environment which they may not be able to test for using an emulator, or in a controlled environment using an actual physical device. An inexperienced developer may also be developing an application that will store user information on the device, but due to their lack of familiarity with developing for the mobile platform, or even general security protocols, may leave gaps in their code, or application (for example – an SQL injection), which could be exploited by hackers.

USER INTERFACE

Usability is a key and often overlooked factor in the design of User Interfaces (UI). The design of the UI in mobile devices is especially important and, while it may not be immediately the first thing the user is interested in when looking for an app to carry out a task, it subconsciously affects their enjoyment of using the app and determines whether or not they will return to using it. Because of this, usability is an area which is only really now being highlighted when it comes to mobile application development. Mobile devices have very small screens, especially in comparison to desktop computer, therefore the typical information and content displayed on a desktop's monitor would be unable to fit onto a mobile devices screen and still be presentable, as the screen would be cluttered and some things would not format or fit on the screen at all. This calls for a radical re-imagining of the way we display this information on the smaller display as well as choosing what content would not be suitable for this smaller platform and how to substitute for this. This is one of the biggest difficulties facing the developer when it comes to user interface design.

We can see from Figure 4, while they may be from different applications and have different functionality; they both have a distinct UI. On the

Figure 4. UI design examples

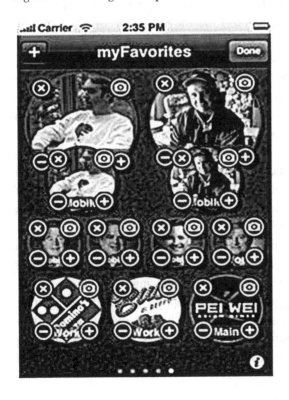
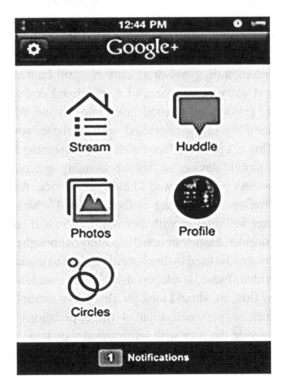

left the UI is cluttered, with too many buttons on the screen, which may cause the user to incorrectly touch the wrong button due to the screens small size and how close together the icons are. It also gives no indication as to what the icons mean, which could be confusing to a first time user. On the right is a very simple, clearly defined set of buttons, with indications of what they are and attractive icons. There is also very little chance of the user hitting the incorrect button, as they are very large and clearly defined. These two apps when contrasted show how much of a difference good UI design can go in improving the usability of an application. For the user, this will affect their interaction with the product greatly, as this will provide their dialogue with the application, and as a developer, it will be a challenge to provide both an attractive and functional UI that carries out exactly what the user wants the application to do without any distractions or over-complication of the process.

Of course, designing a successful application for mobile devices goes beyond simply what you can fit onto the screen, the user's interaction with the device a whole has to be considered. The design principles commonly associated with traditional interaction with software has to be re-thought. We usually take for granted the common drag-and-drop, cursor, scroll bars and text entry mechanisms of a traditional desktop for granted and generally associate software with naturally being interacted with in these ways. This is a problem faced with when designing for a mobile device, as this functionality generally doesn't port over well to a mobile device. As a developer, designing methods around which a user will interact with their application will take considerable planning and ingenuity. Although users may be used to direct manipulation to interact with software, developers shouldn't be constrained by this, but should look for alternative methods, such as personalisation of the applications to provide the user with information they need, or prompts based on that users preferences or meta-

information (Onias-Kukkonen, 2003). Developing like this is ultimately challenging, but a method that is increasingly popping up and becoming almost characteristic of mobile development in these early stages.

FUTURE RESEARCH DIRECTIONS

Mobile devices are becoming more prevalent as our main source of information and applications are becoming the gateway to which we can access it. This trend will continue into the near future, which will drive developers to follow and create numerous applications for these mobile devices. With every application created the developers will face the barrage of problems, issues and choices. These should not be ignored but taken into consideration when developing an application for a mobile device thus improving the overall quality, security and accessibility of the application. The mobile device industry is very much fragmented, which leaves developers making many difficult decisions in order to maximize their applications success and availability. The large corporations that control the market places do not agree on many standards and protocols, which is making the divide within the mobile device ecosystem larger. Security is becoming the main concern for the large mobile device providers as more and more people are using mobile devices this is becoming a new market for hackers and cyber criminals. Many developers leave their applications vulnerable and many do not patch their application, which puts the users of the application at great risk of malicious intent. One of the main aspects that is cropping up amongst the mobile apps community is personalisation and user centeredness. This can be achieved by analysing the user's behaviour and preferences and identifying areas where the applications can prompt the user with a suggestion based on these, or by automatically providing information that they may want and minimizing text entry (e.g. drop down boxes). This kind of approach, as mentioned earlier, is strongly becoming characteristic of mobile applications, and this can help bypass several of the limitations of the device and its UI if implemented correctly in the development stages. This design approach should be strongly emphasised in future application development as it will lead to more functional, user friendly applications. As apps are implicitly characteristic of compactness, ease of use, speed and functionality, it is important that the final product is able to deliver on these ideals if it is to be successful. It is important to the user that the application carries out exactly what is asked of it, with the minimum of fuss, and even just one annoying bug that impairs the app's functionality, even slightly, could turn the user off the product completely, seeking an application which does it better. This is why testing is crucial and any bugs which may visibly affect the running of the core functionality should be top-priority and stamped out immediately. By prioritizing bugs or potential problems by risk, based on what the developer imagines could go wrong with the application in the field, the developer can work towards trying to ensure that many of the main problems which may affect the running of the application, or the users enjoyment of the application, are avoided by writing test cases for these risks and testing for them, or tightening up the coding around these areas using error-handling code and other techniques. By carrying out a risk analysis during testing, the functionality of the final product can come out very stable, and as such the core functionality will be much less bug-prone, as the core functionality usually crops up as a high-priority risk, for which test cases can be built around and any problems resolved, as to ensure the user a silky smooth experience with the application. This kind of testing should be especially implemented into development for mobile applications, as the many problems associated with developing for the platform could be eased if the developer can

draw up some, even if rough, test cases for possible failures on the field, and prevent these from happening on the field.

Larger companies can spend money on specific, specialised testing done by humans, such as hiring a company to do their testing for them, improving the quality of final product and its appeal to users. On the flipside indie developers can spend more time on their product, as they are not usually restrained by time restrictions and can more openly discuss with their user base about what their feedback is on the application during its development and use this to improve their applications. With independently developed apps, the developer can usually develop a more unique or inspired product which may find a niche in the market, as the fact that they are developing an app may have come from inspiration of what is needed in the market, rather than a more business focused, productivity driven application. In either situation though, it is important to keep the scope of the project very focused, and not get distracted by complicating the design with any unnecessary functions or UI elements. This simplification of the plans means that the core functionality will receive more attention during development and should lead to a more polished and streamlined product. Unnecessary features will also need more time to develop and test and may cause compatibility issues.

Simplification of the project plans will also mean that the hardware requirements of the application will be lessened, and in the case of a resource costly application, will enable it to run on older or less capable devices. This streamlining should also apply to the User Interface. As the UI will provide the dialogue between the applications functions and the user's needs, it is important that the user can tell the application exactly what to do, and the app being able to produce results quickly and conveniently. This means that good UI design is tantamount to a successful app. For an app to thrive, the developer needs to know his target audience. In UI terms this boils down to what devices people are using and how best to make use of what hardware there is on these devices. Of the input methods concerned with mobile devices, the main ones that have to be considered when deciding how the user will interact with the application are the buttons. Hard buttons and soft buttons, as well as any shortcuts these may enable should function similarly to that device's native functions. This design prospect will require more time and effort in research but will ultimately increase usability of the app and increase user's enjoyment of using it (Dumaresq & Villenueve, 2010).

Uploading an application to an app market is a big step in the development cycle of an application, and it is up to the developer to take charge of how the application will be advertised after it is uploaded. As well as constraints placed on what can be uploaded to an app store, based on the platform, the developer will have to include screenshots and information about the application itself to give users a snapshot of what the app does and how it functions. This is a very important stage in selling the product to its intended audience, as there may be thousands of other apps like it, it is important that the functionality is concisely described and the actual software itself stand up to the description. Research into the applications intended audience, as well as preferred platform will ensure that the project id more focused and will be more likely to reach its intended audience. There are tools available such as Google analytics, which have APIs that can be imbedded into the app to measure various things such as where the app is popular, downloads, average usage time etc. can be used for research for future apps, descriptions for apps based on how they are used, giving information that can give an idea of what can be implemented into patched, or even run in a controlled test environment with a selection of users to see what functionality is being used, and what can be trimmed out of the final product.

CONCLUSION

Through critical analysis of the difficulties faced when developing mobile applications, it becomes apparent that much of the problem is our limited understanding of how to translate our traditional techniques of software development over to this platform and how this reciprocates through many different facets of application design. Some recommendations can be drawn from this conclusion. Firstly security seems to be constantly overlooked, especially in lower budget applications. Security should not be optional but mandatory and an application should be analyzed or open to a series of standard tests by some sort of body to ensure it is acceptable for the common user. With the mobile market being so vast and having so much potential it is very easily getting out of hand, all mobile applications should adhere to some sort of general standards, which again would be monitored by a committee and would create a stepping-stone towards unifying many of the fragmentation present today. User Interface design principles should be available as a resource for developers but should not be enforced, enforcing can hamper creativity and the originality of the application developer. Hopefully in the near future we will see many of these problems that developers are experiencing when creating applications for mobile devices being addressed. Allowing more robust applications to be created quicker, to a higher standard and making them more accessible therefore improving the experience for both the developers and end users.

REFERENCES

B'far, R. (2005). *Mobile computing principles: designing and developing mobile applications.* Cambridge, UK: Cambridge University Press.

Burns, J. (2008) Developing Secure Mobile Applications For Android. iSec Partners.

Dumaresq, T., & Villenueve, M. (2010). *Test Strategies for Smartphones and Mobile Devices.* Mississauga, Canada: Macadamian Technologies.

Dwivedi, H., Clark, C., & Thiel, D. (2010). *Mobile Application Security.* New York: McGraw-Hill.

Fling, B. (2009). *Mobile Design and Development.* Cambridge, MA: O'Reilly Publishers.

Hakoama, M., & Hakoyama, S. (2011). The impact of cell phone use on social networking and development among college students. *The American Association of Behavioral and Social Sciences Journal, 15*(1), 58–66.

Holzer, A., & Ondrus, J. (2009). Trends in Mobile Application Development. In C. Hesselman, C. Giannelli, O. Akan, P. Bellavista, J. Cao, F. Dressler, D. Ferrari, et al. (Eds.), Mobile Wireless Middleware, Operating Systems, and Applications – Workshops, (Vol. 12, pp. 55-64). Springer Berlin Heidelberg.

Jacobs, M. (2011). *Living on the Edge of Mobile Development.* Retrieved from http://java.sys-con.com/node/1719019

Kumar Jha, A. (2007). *A Risk Catalog for Mobile Applications.* BookSurge Pub.

Lowe, A. (2011). *Hacking on the rise – all around.* Retrieved from http://hexus.net/business/news/general-business/32399-hacking-rise-around/

Mark, D., Nutting, J., & LaMarche, J. (2011). *Beginning iPhone 4 Development Exploring the iOS SDK.* Apress Pub.

Meier, R. (2010). *Professional Android 2 Application Development.* Wiley Publishing Inc.

Onias Kukkonen, H. (2003). *Developing successful mobile applications.* Stanford University.

Pettey, C., & Goasduff, L. (2011). *Gartner Says Sales of Mobile Devices in Second Quarter of 2011 Grew 16.5 Percent Year-on-Year; Smartphone Sales Grew 74 Percent.* Retrieved from http://www.gartner.com/it/page.jsp?id=1764714

Volk, J. (2010). *Make Money Online With Affiliate Marketing.* Retrieved from www.jonathanvolk.com/4Xel2Sf9mj/jvolkaffiliateguide.pdf

Wasserman, A. (2010). *Software Engineering Issues for Mobile Application Development.* ACM Digital Library.

KEY TERMS AND DEFINITIONS

HTML5: HTML5 is a core technology markup language of the Internet used for structuring and presenting content for the World Wide Web. It is the fifth revision of the HTML standard (created in 1990) and, as of December 2012, is a candidate recommendation of the World Wide Web Consortium (W3C).

Human Computer Interaction (HCI): Human–computer interaction (HCI) involves the study, planning, design and uses of the interaction between people (users) and computers. It is often regarded as the intersection of computer science, behavioral sciences, design, media studies, and several other fields of study.

JavaScript: JavaScript (is a dynamic computer programming language. It is most commonly used as part of web browsers, whose implementations allow client-side scripts to interact with the user, control the browser, communicate asynchronously, and alter the document content that is displayed.

Location-Based Service (LBS): A Location-Based Service (LBS) is an information or entertainment service, accessible with mobile devices through the mobile network and utilizing the ability to make use of the geographical position of the mobile device.

Mobile Application Development: The process by which application software is developed for low-power handheld devices, such as personal digital assistants, enterprise digital assistants or mobile phones.

Protocol: An agreed-upon set of rules that facilitates the exchange information between two computers or devices. A protocol includes formatting rules that specify how data is packaged into messages. It also may include conventions like message acknowledgement or data compression to support reliable and/or high-performance network communication.

Standard Generalized Markup Language (SGML): An international standard in markup languages, a basis for HTML and a precursor to XML. SGML is both a language and an ISO standard for describing information embedded within a document.

Universal Resource Identifier (URI): The string (often starting with http) comprises a name or address that can be used to refer to a resource. It is a fundamental component of the World Wide Web.

Usability: This focuses on the creating of the system making sure it is useable. Using the user's experiences and the factors involved this helps to create a better view into the development of technology, and help provide and maintain a better experience for the user with future technologies.

W3C Consortium: The World Wide Web Consortium (W3C) is the main international standards organization for the World Wide Web (abbreviated WWW or W3).

Web Service: A Web Service is a software component that is described via WSDL and is capable of being accessed via standard network protocols such as but not limited to SOAP over HTTP. It has an interface described in a machine-processable format (specifically WSDL).

Chapter 7
Human Behaviour Recognition in Ambient Intelligent Environments

Hans W. Guesgen
Massey University, New Zealand

Stephen Marsland
Massey University, New Zealand

ABSTRACT

The recognition of human behaviour from sensor observations is an important area of research in smart homes and ambient intelligence. In this chapter, the authors introduce the idea of spatio-temporal footprints, which are local patterns in space and time that should be similar across repeated occurrences of the same behaviour. They discuss the spatial and temporal mapping requirements of these footprints, together with how they may be used. As possible formalisms for implementing spatio-temporal footprints, the authors discuss and evaluate probability theory, fuzzy sets, and the Dempster-Shafer theory.

INTRODUCTION

A common task that an ambient intelligence system could be required to perform is recognising human behaviour from observations in the environment; this can be useful for a variety of applications from monitoring the activities of elderly patients to identifying appropriate lighting and heating conditions (Cook, 2006; Mozer, 2005). The observations on which such recognition is based can range from direct observations made by video cameras to indirect observations detected by sensors. Although video cameras give a more complete picture, and hence might lend themselves more easily to recognising behaviours (with a consequent increase in the amount of computational processing required), it is often behaviour recognition based on sensors that is the preferred option, since the latter is less obtrusive and therefore more easily accepted in applications such as smart homes.

There is a significant body of research on behaviour recognition based on sensor data, which ranges from logic-based approaches to probabilistic machine learning approaches (Augusto & Nugent, 2004; Chua, Marsland, & Guesgen,

DOI: 10.4018/978-1-4666-7284-0.ch007

Copyright © 2015, IGI Global. Copying or distributing in print or electronic forms without written permission of IGI Global is prohibited.

2009; Duong, Bui, Phung, & Venkatesh, 2005; Gopalratnam & Cook, 2004; Rivera-Illingworth, Callaghan, & Hagras, 2007; Tapia, Intille, & Larson, 2004). Although the reported successes are promising, it has become clear that all approaches fall short of being perfect. Due to the limited information that is in the sensor data, noise, and the inherently complexity of human behaviours, it is often impossible to determine the correct behaviour from the sensor data alone, in particular if behaviours are overlapping or are being executed by more than one person.

Several researchers have realised that additional information can be useful to boost the behaviour recognition process (Aztiria, Augusto, Izaguirre, & Cook, 2008; Jakkula & Cook, 2008; Tavenard, Salah, & Pauwels, 2007). In this article, we focus on how spatio-temporal information, enriched with context information, can be used for this purpose. When a particular activity occurs, like preparing breakfast, it leaves a 'footprint' in space-time, i.e., a particular pattern of sensor observations in some set of locations over some period of time. The activity starts at some specific time and in some specific location, goes on for a specific duration in some specific area, and terminates at a specific time at some specific location. Since footprints differ from behaviour to behaviour—but often relatively little between different instances of the same behaviour—we can use these to inform the behaviour recognition process: if something is happening at 07:00 in the kitchen, it is more likely to be preparing breakfast than taking a shower. We can also use them to detect abnormal behaviour: if the inhabitant of the smart home uses the shower at 03:00 (when usually this is not a footprint that is seen), then this can be interpreted as abnormal.

Figure 1 shows an example of a possible set of footprints over three days, with a linear time axis that repeats each day, and a single space axis that could identify rooms, or similar (this is discussed in more detail in the next section). It can be seen

that some behaviours repeat more-or-less identically over the three days, while others only occur once. The challenge with such representation of behaviour as footprints is to identify and recognise the various behaviours that are represented.

The rest of this article investigates the role of spatio-temporal footprints in more detail. We start with a discussion of what space-time means in the context of smart homes, arguing that there is more than one space-time (or more precisely, representation of space-time). We then look at how behaviours leave footprints in space-time and explore invariants in these footprints, with the goal of classifying different forms of invariants and looking into how the footprints are distributed in space-time and what influences this distribution. Finally we discuss the advantages and disadvantage of using fuzzy sets, respectively the Dempster-Shafer theory, instead of probability theory to capture the idea of spatio-temporal footprints.

SPACE-TIME

When reasoning about time, we usually associate a time axis with the data. The time axis might use a calendar as reference system and absolute dates/ times to refer to points on the axis. Or it might use some artificial start point as zero time, such as the time when the smart home became operational, and some counter to advance time along the time axis. In the latter case, we would not be able to refer back to times before the birth of the smart home, while the first case would provide an infinite extension of time into both the past and the future.

As we will see later when discussing footprint invariants, it may sometimes be advantageous to view the time axis as a circular reoccurrence of time points. For example, if we are only interested in when behaviours occur during the day, then we might want to abstract from years, months, and

Figure 1. An example of space-time with footprints

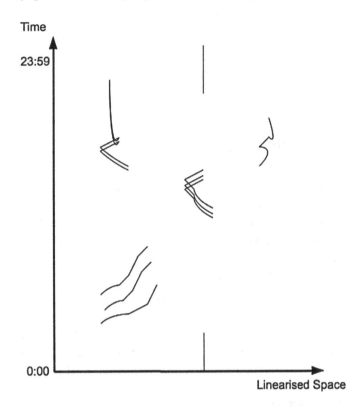

days, which would leave us with references to times of the day. At the end of the day, we would 'warp' time and start at the beginning of the time axis again.

Independently of whether we use linear or circular time, we still have to decide whether we view time as continuous or discrete. For example, when referring to 13:00, do we really mean this exact point on a continuous time axis? If this is the case, then a behaviour that occurs one millisecond after this time point would not match 13:00, unless we allow for 'fuzzy' matches. On the other hand, if we view it as a discrete time stamp, surrounded by, say, 12:55 and 13:05, then it would make sense to associate the behaviour with 13:00 rather than 12:55 or 13:05. This can be thought of as temporal 'resolution'.

Similar considerations can be made when referring to space. Although space is more complex than time (partially because we can move freely in

space, but not in time), it has many similarities to time. In the simplest case, it has the same dimensionality, for example if we can move only along a predefined trajectory (Mukerjee & Joe, 1990). The trajectory can be viewed as continuous, in which case we would associate the distance from the origin with locations on the spatial axis, or it can be discrete, in which case we need a way to associate distances with reference points on the spatial axis.

As with time, we can envision different representations of space. Not only can we extend the dimensionality of space to two or three, we can also move away from a canonical Euclidean space to a more abstract space. For example, we can use the rooms of the smart home to define space points, or the areas covered by the sensors of the smart home. Given some knowledge of the physical locations of sensors, the house can infer that when sensor events occur, the house inhabitant must be in the physical vicinity of that sensor (obviously, there are exceptions to this for certain sensors such as thermometers and for remote-controlled or time-controlled devices). The spatial pattern could then be some mapping between sensor locations, which could be based on the underlying physical layout of the house, but does not have to be.

The importance of this is that different resolutions can make recognition of particular footprints easier or more difficult. As the resolution becomes finer, footprints that appear to be exactly aligned start to separate, meaning that identifying them as examples of the same behaviour can require a clustering algorithm. Breakfast might not occur exactly at 08:00 each day, but it is likely that it happens at times that we associate with morning. Or reading a book might always occur in the lounge, but sometimes while sitting on the sofa and sometimes while lying back in an easy chair.

FOOTPRINT IDENTIFICATION

Each activity leaves a footprint in space-time (see Figure 1). If it is possible to determine mappings between footprints for the different instances of the same behaviour occurring in the smart home, then we can use that information to improve the behaviour recognition process. This section discusses what type of mappings we might usefully want to identify. There are effectively three different things that we might want to detect (where the first two are positive—examples of the same pattern—while the final one is negative):

- The same (or very similar) pattern occurring at the same time and place,
- The same (or very similar) pattern occurring at different times and/or places, and
- Different patterns occurring at the same time and place as another.

As an example of the first of these, consider the case that breakfast always takes place in the kitchen at 08:00. Then the mapping between this footprint on different days is simply the identity, as it leaves the same footprint in space-time each time it occurs. Of course, this assumes that we have chosen a suitable representation for space-time (e.g., one that only looks at the time of the day in a discrete way and uses the rooms of the smart home as spatial entities). It is unlikely that we observe this invariant very often, as it would require very rigid patterns of behaviour and a relatively abstract form of space-time.

The next type of transformation is that where we match patterns despite shifts in space-time. Here we can distinguish among three different types of shift:

- Shifts on the time axis only,
- Shifts on the space axes, and
- Shifts on all axes.

For example, the afternoon tea break might occur at different times but always in the lounge (time-only shift), while the afternoon nap might occur always at the same time but either in the bedroom or in the lounge (space-only). An example of a (coupled) shift in space-time would be breakfast at the weekend: while breakfast during the week happens at 08:00 in the kitchen, it might be shifted to 10:00 in the dining room on Saturday and Sunday.

The particular footprint that identifies a behaviour is caused by some set of sensors being activated in time. While we want some robustness to minor variation in the footprint, we need to be careful that just because two footprints occur in the same place and time, they are not necessarily the same event. To continue the breakfast analogy, a person working at home could go into the kitchen at 10:00 to make a cup of tea. This is not an example of them having a second breakfast (the weekend one), but a different behaviour that happens to occur at the same time and place.

There is one example of footprint change that we might need to be particularly careful about, which is the deformation of footprints in space-time. This again might be restricted to particular axes such as time, or might include all axes. We start the discussion of this by restricting ourselves to the time axis. The projection of a footprint onto the time axis is a time interval, consisting of a start point and an end point. We can restrict the deformation of the time interval to one of its boundaries, either the start or the end point, but not both. An example would be breakfast that always starts at 08:00 but might last between 10 and 20 minutes, or doing the dishes after dinner might start at any time, but always finishes in time to be ready for the soap opera on TV at 18:00. If we do not restrict ourselves to one of the boundaries, we obtain a deformation which (more or less) keeps the centre of the interval invariant. For example, taking a shower might always occur at around 20:00, starting about 10 minutes before that time and ending about 10 minutes after that time.

This same effect can be seen for space. In this case, we have to consider boundaries of regions in (usually) multi-dimensional space rather than start and end points of time intervals, which means that instead of considering two classes of deformation (one boundary vs. two boundaries), we have to consider an infinite number of classes. One way to achieve this is by determining the percentage of the boundary that stays the same and associating the behaviours with a finite set of classes that are given by a range of percentages. For example, we might want to distinguish just between those deformations that change more than 50% of the boundary and those that keep at least 50% of the boundary invariant.

It should be noted that our discussion of footprint invariants is closely related to the discussion around neighbourhood graphs in (Freksa, 1992), where Freksa introduces three forms of neighbourhood graphs for Allen's temporal logic (Allen, 1983). The graphs are based on shifts and two forms of deformations of time interval, in a way

closely related to the one outlined above. Similar discussions can be found around the region connection calculus, which is used for reasoning about spatial relations (Randell, Cui, & Cohn, 1992).

Thus, we are lead to consider two related methods of footprint identification: identifying the same footprint occurring in different places in space-time, and distinguishing between different footprints that occur at the same place in space-time.

FOOTPRINT PROBABILITY DISTRIBUTIONS

The examples of the previous sections indicate that footprints are not necessarily distributed evenly in space-time. A straightforward way to find the distribution of footprints is to empirically approximate for each behaviour the probability of a footprint occurring at a particular location (or within a particular cluster) in space-time. This does not require any extra knowledge about the behaviour or about particular regions in space-time, but it does require enough data to approximate the probabilities within reasonable error margins.

As an alternative to this approach, we can analyse the regions occupied by a particular behaviour in space-time in order to find the distributions of the corresponding footprints. Breakfast on weekends as opposed to weekdays is an example for that, as illustrated previously. Obviously, the footprints are not distributed evenly over the two clusters, but have a higher density in the weekday breakfast cluster than in the weekend breakfast cluster. We know that there are five weekdays per week, but only two weekend days (for the average working person). Assuming that the breakfast behaviour occurs exactly once per day, we conclude that the probability of a breakfast footprint being in the weekend cluster of breakfast footprints is 2/7, whereas the probability of it being in the weekday one is 5/7. Taking this approach a step further, we can then compute conditional probabilities, which give us further insides into where a footprint is located in space-time. For example, if we know that a behaviour occurred on a weekday, then the conditional probability of it being in the weekday cluster is 1 (and 0 for the weekend cluster). We will discuss this approach further in the next section.

In general, this leads to an approach where context information is taken into consideration when behaviours are related to space-time footprints. In the example above, the context is of a spatio-temporal nature, but this does not have to be the case, as it can make sense to utilise other types of context information as well, such as:

- **Linked Behaviours:** If a person has already had breakfast then they are unlikely to be having a second one, and if they have just had a shower they are unlikely to be having a bath. This kind of data can help to separate out the different footprints that might be recognised at the current time.
- **Environmental Information:** If it is cold outside and not all rooms of the home are heated properly, then the footprints of certain behaviours might shift in space-time along the spatial axes. Rather than taking a meal in the dining room, the inhabitant might choose to have it in the lounge where there is a fireplace.
- **Personal Information:** If the inhabitant is sick, he or she might choose to go to bed earlier than usual. This most likely has an effect on the footprints of events happening towards the end of the day, which would shift along the temporal axis.
- **Socio-Economic Information:** If there is a recession, the inhabitant might choose to save costs and therefore might decide to use the heating less. As a consequence, the footprint of that behaviour would be deformed.

Although in principle there is no limit to how much context information we use to get a better understanding of the relationship between behaviours and their space-time footprints, it is not practical to use context information excessively. Each bit of information requires us to explicitly model the correlation between the information and its impact on the behaviour–footprint relation, which requires a significant amount of world knowledge or data. In other words, we trade off the need for sufficient training data against the need for explicit modelling. In the next sections, we discuss the pros and cons of some formalisms that can be used to model spatio-temporal footprints.

FROM PROBABILITIES TO FUZZY SETS

Although behaviours often take place in particular contexts, there is usually no one-to-one relationship between a behaviour and the context it occurs in. Rather, given a certain behaviour, context information is determined according to some probability distribution. If B is a behaviour (e.g., making breakfast) and C some context information (e.g., in the kitchen), then $P(C|B)$ is the probability that C is true if B occurs (e.g., the behaviour takes place in the kitchen if we know that the behaviour is making breakfast).

Given the conditional probabilities $P(C|B)$, we can calculate conditional probabilities $P(B|C)$ using Bayes' rule. This assumes that we know the conditional probability for each context and behaviour. Moreover, we not only need $P(B|C)$ but also $P(B|C_1,...,C_n)$, since context information is usually correlated. Assuming that we have knowledge of all the necessary conditional probabilities is unrealistic.

Another potential problem of probability theory is that probabilities have to add up to one. In cases where we have perfect information or where we approximate probabilities through empirical studies, this is not a problem. However, when we do not have complete knowledge (e.g., in cases where we consult people about their beliefs in behaviours occurring in particular contexts), this may lead to counterintuitive results. For example, if we do not have any information that a behaviour normally occurs in the kitchen, we cannot assign a probability of 0 to P(B|C), since this would imply that P(¬B|C) equals 1, which would mean that the behaviour happens outside the kitchen (if it happens at all).

The Dempster-Shafer theory (Dempster, 1967; Shafer, 1976) offers a way out of this dilemma. It uses the concepts of belief (Bel) and plausibility (Pl) instead of probability to formulate uncertainty, where classical probability lies between belief and plausibility:

$$Bel(B|C) \leq P(B|C) \leq Pl(B|C)$$

Although this solves the problem of evidence not adding up to 1, it still leaves us with the problem of assigning appropriate basic probabilities to all subsets of the frame of discernment, which might not be possible in real-world scenarios. A qualitative approach helps to mitigate this problem. We introduce such an approach in the next section, but before that we take a detour and discuss a simpler framework, which is not as rigorous from the mathematical point of view, but which provides a simple and robust way to deal with context information. This approach is based on fuzzy sets.

Unlike traditional sets, fuzzy sets allow their elements to belong to the set with a certain degree. Rather than deciding whether an element d does or does not belong to a set A of a domain D, we determine for each element of D the degree with which it belongs to the fuzzy set $\tilde{A}$. In other words, a fuzzy subset $\tilde{A}$ of a domain D is a set of ordered pairs, $(d, \mu_{\tilde{A}}(d))$, where $d \in D$ and $\mu_{\tilde{A}}: D \rightarrow [0, 1]$ is the membership function of $\tilde{A}$. The membership function replaces the characteristic function of a classical subset $A \subset D$.

Rather than asking the question of what is the probability of a certain behaviour occurring in a particular context, we now pose the question as follows. Given some context information C, to which degree is a particular behaviour a C-behaviour? For example, if C is the day of the week, then we can ask for the degree of the behaviour to be a Monday behaviour, Tuesday behaviour, and so on. In terms of fuzzy sets, we define D as the set of the seven days of the week and $\mu_{\tilde{A}}$ as the membership function that determines to which degree the behaviour occurs on a particular day. For example, we might want to define a fuzzy set that reflects the degree to which a restaurant visit falls on a particular day. The membership function of such a fuzzy set is shown graphically in Figure 2. Unlike probabilities, the membership grades do not need to add up to one.

In the example above, the context information is still crisp information, despite the fact that it is used in a fuzzy set: for any restaurant visit, we can determine precisely on which day of the week it occurs. Other context information might not be precise, but rather conveys some vague information. For example, if we know that a behaviour occurs near the kitchen, we usually do not know exactly how many metres away from the kitchen the behaviour occurs. In this case, we can represent the context information itself as a fuzzy set, as illustrated in Figure 3.

Similarly, we can define a fuzzy set that expresses distances by rounding them to the closest half metre – something we as humans often do when we perceive distances, although not necessarily always on the same scale (see Figure 4).

As the examples have shown, fuzzy sets can be used for associating behaviours with context information and for representing imprecise context information. Fuzzy set theory also provides us with a means to convert fuzzy sets back to crisp sets, which is achieved with the notion of an α-level set. Let $\tilde{A}$ be a fuzzy subset in D, then the (crisp)

Figure 2. Graphical representation of a membership function that determines the degree to which a restaurant visit falls on a particular day of the week

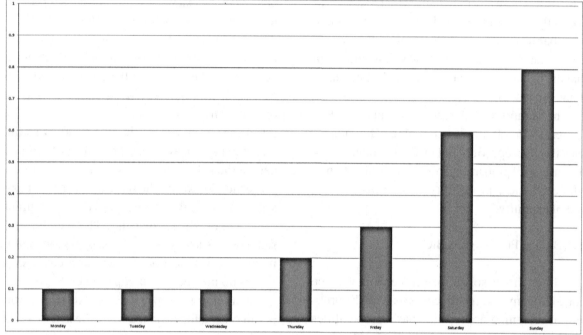

set of elements that belong to the fuzzy set Ã with a membership grade of at least α is called the α-level set of Ã:

$$A_\alpha = \{d \in D \mid \mu_{\tilde{A}}(d) \geq \alpha\}$$

If the membership grade is strictly greater than α, then the set is referred to as a strong α-level set.

To reason about fuzzy sets, we adopt one of the schemes for combining fuzzy sets that was originally proposed by Zadeh (1965). Given two fuzzy sets $\tilde{A}_1$ and $\tilde{A}_2$ with membership functions

Figure 3. A fuzzy set that maps distances to the qualitative values very near, near, far, and very far

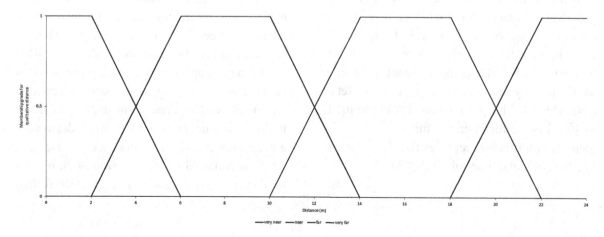

Figure 4. A fuzzy set that approximates distances with a granularity of half a metre

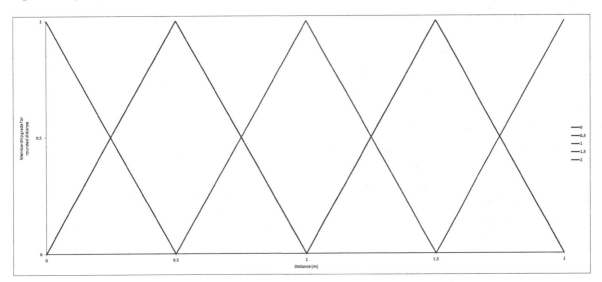

$\mu_{\tilde{A}1}(d)$ and $\mu_{\tilde{A}2}(d)$, respectively, then the membership function of the intersection $\tilde{A}_3 = \tilde{A}_1 \cap \tilde{A}_2$ is pointwise defined by:

$$\mu_{\tilde{A}3}(d) = \min\{\mu_{\tilde{A}1}(d), \mu_{\tilde{A}2}(d)\}$$

Analogously, the membership function of the union $\tilde{A}_3 = \tilde{A}_1 \cup \tilde{A}_2$ is pointwise defined by:

$$\mu_{\tilde{A}3}(d) = \max\{\mu_{\tilde{A}1}(d), \mu_{\tilde{A}2}(d)\}$$

The membership grade for the complement of a fuzzy set $\tilde{A}$, denoted as $\neg\tilde{A}$, is defined in the same way as the complement in probability theory:

$$\mu_{\neg\tilde{A}}(d) = 1 - \mu_{\tilde{A}}(d)$$

Zadeh (1965) stresses that the min/max combination scheme is not the only scheme for defining intersection and union of fuzzy sets, and that it depends on the context which scheme is the most appropriate. While some of the schemes are based on empirical investigations, others are the result of theoretical considerations (Dubois & Prade, 1980; Klir & Folger, 1988). However, (Nguyen,

Kreinovich, & Tolbert, 1993) proved that the min/max operations are the most robust operations for combining fuzzy sets, where robustness is defined in terms of how much impact uncertainty in the input has on the error in the output.

Regardless of which combination scheme is used, determining the fuzzy sets themselves is not a trivial exercise. There have been proposals to learn the fuzzy sets, mainly in the area of fuzzy control (Berenji & Khedkar, 1992; Nauck & Kruse, 1993; Van Cleave & Rattan, 2000). Adopting these approaches for human behaviour recognition and context-awareness is a possibility, but it would require a large amount of data. For that reason, explicit modelling seems to be the best option. However, this requires a good understanding of when and where particular behaviours occur, and that depends to a large extent on who exhibits the behaviours.

QUALITATIVE DEMPSTER-SHAFER THEORY

Before discussing a qualitative version of the Dempster-Shafer theory, we briefly review the main concepts of the theory, which uses the notions of belief (Bel) and plausibility (Pl) instead of probability to formulate uncertainty. Belief and plausibility are defined in the Dempster-Shafer theory on the basis of a mass assignment function, which assigns basic probabilities to any set that is a member of the power set of the universe U (which is also called the frame of discernment or set of hypotheses):

$$m: 2^U \rightarrow [0,1]$$

The only restrictions are that all mass assignments add up to 1 and that the mass assignment of the empty set is 0:

$$\sum_{X \subseteq U} m(X) = 1, \, m(\varnothing) = 0$$

Any subset X of U for which $m(X) \neq 0$ is called a focal element.

Using the mass assignment function, the belief and plausibility in any set of hypotheses is then defined as follows:

$$Bel(X) = \sum_{Y \subseteq X} m(Y), \, Pl(X) = \sum_{Y \cap X \neq \varnothing} m(Y)$$

It can be shown that the following holds for these two measures:

$$Bel(X) = 1 - Pl(\neg X), Pl(X) = 1 - Bel(\neg X), Bel(X) \leq Pl(X)$$

$$Bel(X) + Bel(\neg X) \leq 1, Pl(X) + Pl(\neg X) \geq 1$$

For $X \subseteq Y$: $Bel(X) \leq Bel(Y), Pl(X) \leq Pl(Y)$

If we have two mass assignment functions, we can combine these using the following rule:

$$[m_1 \oplus m_2](X) = \frac{\sum_{V \cap W = X} m_1(V) \cdot m_2(W)}{1 - \sum_{V \cap W = \varnothing} m_1(V) \cdot m_2(W)}$$

for $X \neq \varnothing$

$$[m_1 \oplus m_2](\varnothing) = 0$$

This assumes that the weight of conflict is not equal to 1, which means:

$$\sum_{V \cap W = \varnothing} m_1(V) \times m_2(W) \neq 1$$

To illustrate this framework, consider the following example (which has been adapted from (Parsons, 1994)). For the sake of simplicity, we assume that there are only three possible behaviours: having breakfast (B_b), eating dinner (B_d), and cleaning up dishes (B_c), which means that $U = \{B_b, B_c, B_d\}$. We know that one of these behaviours just took place, but our behaviour recognition system was not able to tell us which one it was, which means that we need to take additional evidence into consideration in the form of context information. Let us assume that spatial information tells us with 80% certainty that the behaviour was either having breakfast or washing dishes, since the behaviour was observed in the kitchen and 80% of the kitchen events are either having breakfast or washing dishes. This would suggest that we assign 0.8 as basic probability to the set $\{B_b, B_c\}$, which means that $m_s(\{B_b, B_c\}) = 0.8$. Since we have no other information, we assign the remaining probability to the whole frame of discernment:

$$m_s(\{B_b, B_c, B_d\}) = 0.2$$

Now assume that temporal information suggests with 60% certainty that the behaviour was either eating dinner or washing dishes, since the behaviour took place in the evening and 60% of evening events are either eating dinner or washing dishes. This means that we assign a probability of 0.6 to the set $\{B_c, B_d\}$ and the rest to the frame of discernment:

$$m_t(\{B_c, B_d\}) = 0.6 \quad m_t(\{B_b, B_c, B_d\}) = 0.4$$

Combining the spatial and temporal evidence results in the mass assignment that is shown in Table 1, where m_c denotes the combined mass assignment function.

Applying the definition of belief then results in the following:

- $Bel(\{B_b\}) = 0$
- $Bel(\{B_c\}) = 0.48$
- $Bel(\{B_d\}) = 0$
- $Bel(\{B_b, B_c\}) = 0.8$
- $Bel(\{B_b, B_d\}) = 0$
- $Bel(\{B_c, B_d\}) = 0.6$
- $Bel(\{B_b, B_c, B_d\}) = 1.$

Similar calculations can be made to determine the plausibility of the hypotheses:

- $Pl(\{B_b\}) = 0.4$
- $Pl(\{B_c\}) = 1$
- $Pl(\{B_d\}) = 0.2$
- $Pl(\{B_b, B_c\}) = 1$
- $Pl(\{B_b, B_d\}) = 0.52$

- $Pl(\{B_c, B_d\}) = 1$
- $Pl(\{B_b, B_c, B_d\}) = 1.$

Since $\{B_c\}$ is the only singleton hypothesis with a belief greater than 0, it makes sense to favour this hypothesis. It would not make any difference if we slightly changed the numerical values (e.g., assign a mass of 0.75 instead of 0.8 or 0.65 instead of 0.6). This raises the question whether we can replace the numerical values altogether by something that can be obtained more easily. Pearons (1994) suggested using qualitative values instead.

Let us assume that we are sure the behaviour could have been breakfast or dinner, but we cannot say for sure that it was either of them. This suggests that $m(\{B_b, B_d\})$ lies between 0 and 1, but would neither be 0 nor 1. We denote this value as qualitative value +; in fact, we use + instead of any positive numerical value. Adding two qualitative values results in +, as long as at least one of the values to be added is +. Multiplying two qualitative values results in + only if both of the values are +. In all other cases, the result of either operation is 0.

Applying this idea to the example of spatial and temporal context, we get the combined mass assignment shown in Table 2.

From this we can then combine a qualitative belief for each hypothesis:

- $Bel(\{B_b\}) = 0$
- $Bel(\{B_c\}) = +$
- $Bel(\{B_d\}) = 0$

Table 1. Combining mass assignment functions for the context example

⊕	$m_s(\{B_b, B_c\})$ $= 0.8$	$m_s(\{B_b, B_c, B_d\})$ $= 0.2$
Mass Assignment Functions		
$m_t(\{B_c, B_d\}) = 0.6$	$m_c(\{B_c\}) = 0.48$	$m_c(\{B_c, B_d\}) = 0.12$
$m_t(\{B_b, B_c, B_d\})$ $= 0.4$	$m_c(\{B_b, B_c\}) =$ 0.32	$m_c(\{B_b, B_c, B_d\}) =$ 0.08

Table 2. Combining mass assignment functions for the context example

⊕	$m_s(\{B_b, B_c\})$ $= +$	$m_s(\{B_b, B_c, B_d\})$ $= +$
Mass Assignment Functions		
$m_t(\{B_c, B_d\}) = +$	$m_c(\{B_c\}) = +$	$m_c(\{B_c, B_d\}) = +$
$m_t(\{B_b, B_c, B_d\})$ $= +$	$m_c(\{B_b, B_c\})$ $= +$	$m_c(\{B_b, B_c, B_d\})$ $= +$

- $Bel(\{B_b, B_c\}) = +$
- $Bel(\{B_b, B_d\}) = 0$
- $Bel(\{B_c, B_d\}) = +$
- $Bel(\{B_b, B_c, B_d\}) = +.$

As before, the only singleton hypothesis in $\{B_c\}$, and therefore this is the preferred hypothesis, unless we are inclined to consider more than one behaviour, like $\{B_b, B_c\}$ for instance. Of course, there are cases where the decision is not straight-forward and where qualitative beliefs convey less information than numerical ones. This occurs if the numerical values are significantly different. For example, if the belief in hypothesis X is 0.9 and the belief in Y is 0.1, we would prefer X over Y. However, this distinction disappears when we map numerical values to qualitative values.

There is still the question of how to obtain the mass assignments, either numerically or quali-tatively. One way is to base them on empirical studies. Given a particular context, whenever that context occurs we increment a counter for the set of behaviours happening in this context. For ex-ample, each evening we memorise the behaviours occurring on that evening. If the only behaviour is eating dinner, then the counter for $\{B_d\}$ is in-cremented by 1; if the only behaviour is washing dishes, then the one for $\{B_c\}$ is incremented; if both behaviours occur, then the counter for $\{B_c, B_d\}$ is incremented. In case we are only interested in a qualitative mass assignment, we use truth values instead of counters. Initially each subset of the frame of discernment is assigned false, but this is changed to true if the subset is observed in a particular context. Once we are finished with our empirical study, we normalise the counters such that their sum equals 1 (which, of course, is only necessary if we have used numerical values). The normalised counters then become the mass assignment for the particular context.

CONCLUSION

We have presented a representation of behaviours as patterns of activity in space-time, where each behaviour is represented as a trajectory of sensor events over some relatively short time window. It is hoped that by representing the behaviours in this way, individual behaviours will be more clearly recognised despite translation in space, time, or both. Additionally, it may give a useful pictorial representation of events that enables a carer to analyse the actions of a person and identify abnormal events once the smart home has raised an alarm.

Some of the challenges of recognising and using such footprints are caused by the natural variability between different instances of the same behaviour. We have discussed this in the context of things taking slightly more or less time, and the location changing, but it is also the case for dif-ferent orderings of the actions within a behaviour. The extent to which this is a problem will have to be examined once we are able to use real data to examine the footprint pattern.

As far as the implementation of spatio-temporal footprints is concerned, we discussed a number of approaches, all of which enable us to represent uncertainty. The first one is probability theory, which provides us with a rigorous mathematical model but which poses problem from the practical point of view. We then considered fuzzy sets and looked at the advantages and disadvantage that they will bring them. Finally we discussed the Dempster-Shafer theory as an option, including the use of qualitative values rather than numerical values as mass assignments.

It is impossible to draw a conclusion which of the methods is the preferred one. Even when restricting the development of a behaviour recog-nition system to a particular cultural background and perhaps even to a particular generation of people, it is difficult to argue that behaviours are uniform and that therefore a one-fits-all solution is possible. This means that we need to adapt the system to each person. If we have sufficient knowledge about this person, we might be able to explicitly model the person's behaviours and tie them in with context information. In this case, fuzzy sets might be the appropriate approach, in particular if we have some guarantee of robustness (through the appropriate choice of combination schemes) so that any mistakes that we make do not have a significant impact on the correctness of the system.

The question, of course, then is whether such a scenario is realistic. If we aim at an out-of-the-box system that is easily available from retailers, then the expectation most likely will be that such a system can be set up easily and without a large amount of pre-knowledge. Ideally, the system should learn and adapt automatically to the behaviours of a particular person. A probabilistic approach, either in its naïve form or in the form of the Dempster-Shafer theory, seems to be the obvious choice in this case. However, such an approach requires a large amount of data which we first have to acquire.

REFERENCES

Allen, J. (1983). Maintaining knowledge about temporal intervals. *Communications of the ACM, 26*, 832–843.

Augusto, J., & Nugent, C. (2004). The use of temporal reasoning and management of complex events in smart homes. In *Proceedings of the 16th European Conference on Artificial Intelligence* (pp. 778–782). Amsterdam, The Netherlands: IOS Press.

Aztiria, A., Augusto, J., Izaguirre, A., & Cook, D. (2008). Learning accurate temporal relations from user actions in intelligent environments. In *Proceedings of the 3rd Symposium of Ubiquitous Computing and Ambient Intelligence* (pp. 274–283). Berlin, Germany: Springer.

Berenji, H., & Khedkar, P. (1992). Learning and tuning fuzzy logic controllers through reinforcements. *IEEE Transactions on Neural Networks, 3*(5), 724–740. PMID:18276471

Chua, S.-L., Marsland, S., & Guesgen, H. W. (2009). *Spatio- temporal and context reasoning in smart homes*. Paper presented at the COSIT-09 Workshop on Spatial and Temporal Reasoning for Ambient Intelligence Systems. Aber Wrac'h, France.

Cook, D. (2006). Health monitoring and assistance to support aging in place. *Journal of Universal Computer Science, 12*(1), 15–29.

Dempster, A. (1967). Upper and lower probabilities induced by a multivalued mapping. *Annals of Mathematical Statistics, 38*(2), 325–339.

Dubois, D., & Prade, H. (1980). *Fuzzy Sets and Systems: Theory and Applications*. London: Academic Press.

Duong, T., Bui, H., Phung, D., & Venkatesh, S. (2005). Activity recognition and abnormality detection with the switching hidden semi-Markov model. In *Proceedings of IEEE Computer Society Conference on Computer Vision and Pattern Recognition* (pp. 838–845). Los Alamitos, CA: IEEE Computer Society.

Freksa, C. (1992). Temporal reasoning based on semi-intervals. *Artificial Intelligence, 54*, 199–227.

Gopalratnam, K., & Cook, D. (2004). Active LeZi: An incremental parsing algorithm for sequential prediction. *International Journal of Artificial Intelligence Tools, 14*(1–2), 917–930.

Jakkula, V., & Cook, D. (2008). Anomaly detection using temporal data mining in a smart home environment. *Methods of Information in Medicine, 47*(1), 70–75. PMID:18213431

Kiecolt-Glaser, J., & Glaser, R. (1999). Chronic stress and mortality among older adults. *Journal of the American Medical Association, 282*, 2259–2260. PMID:10605979

Klir, G., & Folger, T. (1988). *Fuzzy Sets, Uncertainty, and Information*. Englewood Cliffs, NJ: Prentice Hall.

Mozer, M. (2005). Lessons from an adaptive house. In D. Cook & R. Das (Eds.), *Smart Environments: Technologies, Protocols, and Applications* (pp. 273–294). Hoboken, NJ: Wiley.

Mukerjee, A., & Joe, G. (1990). A qualitative model for space. In *Proceedings of the 8th National Conference on Artificial Intelligence* (pp. 721–727). Palo Alto, CA: AAAI Press.

Nauck, D., & Kruse, R. (1993). A fuzzy neural network learning fuzzy control rules and membership functions by fuzzy error backpropagation. In *Proceedings of the IEEE International Conference on Neural Networks* (pp. 1022–1027). Los Alamitos, CA: IEEE Computer Society.

Nguyen, H., Kreinovich, V., & Tolbert, D. (1993). On robustness of fuzzy logics. In *Proceedings of the IEEE International Conference on Fuzzy Systems* (pp. 543–547). Los Alamitos, CA: IEEE Computer Society.

Parsons, S. (1994). Some qualitative approaches to applying the Dempster-Shafer theory. *Information and Decision Technologies, 19*, 321–337.

Randell, D., Cui, Z., & Cohn, A. (1992). A spatial logic based on regions and connection. In *Proceedings of the 3rd International Conference on Principles of Knowledge Representation and Reasoning* (pp. 165–176). San Francisco, CA: Morgan Kaufmann.

Rivera-Illingworth, F., Callaghan, V., & Hagras, H. (2010). Detection of normal and novel behaviours in ubiquitous domestic environments. *The Computer Journal, 53*(2), 142–151.

Shafer, G. (1976). *A Mathematical Theory of Evidence*. Princeton, NJ: Princeton University Press.

Tapia, E., Intille, S., & Larson, K. (2004). Activity recognition in the home using simple and ubiquitous sensors. In D. Hutchison, T. Kanade, J. Kittler, J. M. Kleinberg, A. Kobsa, F. Mattern, ... G. Weikum (Eds.), *Pervasive Computing: 2nd International Conference, PERVASIVE 2004* (LNCS) (Vol. 3001, pp. 158–175). Berlin, Germany: Springer.

Tavenard, R., Salah, A., & Pauwels, E. (2007). Searching for temporal patterns in AmI sensor data. In B. Schiele, A. K. Dey, H. Gellersen, M. Tscheligi, R. Wichert, E. Aerts, & A. Buchmann (Eds.), *Ambient Intelligence: European Conference, AmI 2007* (LNCS) (Vol. 4794, pp. 53–62). Berlin, Germany: Springer.

Van Cleave, D., & Rattan, K. (2000). Tuning of fuzzy logic controller using neural network. In *Proceedings of the IEEE National Conference Aerospace and Electronics* (pp. 305–312). Los Alamitos, CA: IEEE Computer Society.

KEY TERMS AND DEFINITIONS

Ambient Intelligence: Ubiquitous computer system networked with intelligent embedded devices that can sense the environment and react appropriately to it.

Behaviour Recognition: The process of determining which activity is performed in a smart home. Usually based on information produced by sensors or video cameras.

Context Awareness: Taking context information such as time, location, temperature, etc. into consideration in the reasoning process.

Dempster-Shafer Theory: Formalism for modelling belief based on the concepts of frame of discernment and mass assignment.

Fuzzy Sets: Extension of set theory based on the concept of degree of membership.

Qualitative Reasoning: Deductive process that uses linguistic values rather than numeric values.

Spatio-Temporal Footprints: Trail left in the abstract space defined by the three dimensions of physical space and the one dimension of time by activities occurring in a smart home.

Chapter 8
Ambient Intelligence in the Bedroom

Dorien Van Deun
KU Leuven, Belgium

Bart Haex
KU Leuven, Belgium & IMEC, Belgium

Tim Willemen
KU Leuven, Belgium & iMinds Research Institute, Belgium

Sabine Van Huffel
KU Leuven, Belgium & iMinds Research Institute, Belgium

Vincent Verhaert
KU Leuven, Belgium

Jos Vander Sloten
KU Leuven, Belgium

ABSTRACT

Over the past years, ambient intelligence has infiltrated our lives through various home applications, enabled by the decreasing size and cost of computing technology. While in transport or industry, its presence has become second nature; some areas, such as our bedroom, have remained fairly untouched. Since our bedroom hosts the beginning and end of our daily activities, it needs to assist us in the recovery and preparation of daily activities. Therefore, it holds an enormous opportunity for AI applications, which do exactly what is needed: sensibly assist the user, learn his preferences, and react to his/her mood and needs. This chapter outlines the different ways of assisting the user in his/her intelligent bedroom: ways to monitor health, improve both physical and mental recovery during the night by automatically optimising the environment, as well as automate a number of tedious tasks that reoccur at every start and end of the day.

WAYS TO MONITOR HEALTH

Since we spent almost a third of our lives in bed, it presents an enormous opportunity for general health monitoring. During the past decade, numerous methods and techniques have been developed to record vital body parameters such as respiratory and cardiac activity from within or around our bed. Some methods directly measure electrical activity of the heart, while others focus on the mechanical activity of both heart and lungs. The main idea is however to perform all measurements off-body, e.g. without attaching sensors directly to the skin. This will make sure that subjects are not disturbed

DOI: 10.4018/978-1-4666-7284-0.ch008

Copyright © 2015, IGI Global. Copying or distributing in print or electronic forms without written permission of IGI Global is prohibited.

before and during their sleep, both physically and mentally. Physical disturbance can occur due to skin irritation on places where sensors were attached, or the presence of wires connecting the sensors to a registration or transmitting device. Mental disturbance on the other hand can be due to the person being aware that he or she is being measured, or to the nuisance of attaching the sensors before being able to go to sleep.

Once heart and breathing rate are acquired, heart and breathing rate variability analysis (i.e. temporal changes in heart and breathing rate analysed in both time and frequency domain (Cardiology Task Force, 1996)) can lead to information regarding cardiac health, stress and sleep quality. The latter two are based on research that links the variability within heart and breathing rate to the sympathetic and parasympathetic variations within the autonomic nervous system (Somers, Dyken, Mark, & Abboud, 1993). Based on this link, differences in stress level of a person can be perceived (Hall et al., 2004), his/her sleep pattern can be analysed (Willemen et al., 2013) and possible sleep disorders can be detected (Stein & Pu, 2012).

In this subchapter on health monitoring, we will first discuss how respiratory and cardiac activity can be registered off-body from within or around our bed, after which we will go into more detail on the relevant information that can be extracted from these signals and how this information can be used.

Off-Body Registration of Respiratory and Cardiac Activity

Mechanical activity of heart and lungs leads to subtle body motions. Respiration causes obvious thorax and abdominal movement, whereas the pulsation of blood with every heart beat gives a small but detectable oscillation of the body due to conservation of momentum,

$$\vec{p}_{t_1} = \vec{p}_{t_2}$$

$$t_1 : \vec{p}_{t_1} = \vec{0}$$

$$t_2 : \vec{p}_{t_2} = m_{blood}\vec{v}_{blood} + m_{body}\vec{v}_{body}$$

With $\vec{p}$ the momentum at timestep 1 and 2 (t_1 and t_2), m the mass and $\vec{v}$ the velocity. The registration of the latter is formerly called a ballistocardiogram (BCG) (Braunstein, 1953).

This movement is different from the movement we can feel when placing our hand on our

Figure 1. Off-body detection of electrical activity from the heart (Peltokangas et al., 2012; Devot et al., 2007).

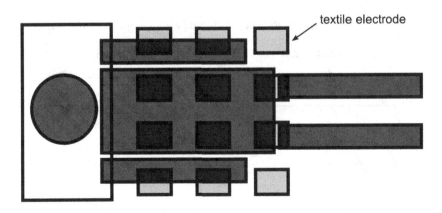

chest, the so-called seismocardiogram, which is a direct result of the contraction of the heart. The ballistocardiogram reflects purely the movement of the blood. To better understand its principle, we can compare it to the recoil when firing a gun (Figure 2). When someone shoots a bullet out of a gun, due to conservation of momentum the gun will experience a recoil opposite to the direction of the bullet.

In the case of the ballistocardiogram, the blood would be the bullet, and the human body would be the gun. At Every heartbeat, blood is ejected from the heart through the aorta, first moving a bit upwards, after which it moves down towards our digestive system and our legs. Due to these movements, our body will experience a consecutive down- and upward recoil with every heartbeat, after which the oscillation is absorbed (e.g. within the mattress material). Figure 3 shows an exemplary fragment of a registered ballistocardiogram that lasts eight seconds, in this case measured with a pressure sensor connected to a volume of air which was placed underneath the thorax of the subject. On top the combined respiration and heart beat signal is shown, whereas below the band filtered individual signals are presented, containing about two and a half respiration cycles and seven heart beats.

Existing methods that are able to measure this mechanical activity can be divided into several categories. A first category uses Doppler radar aimed at the chest area (Guohua, Jiangi, Yu, & Xijing, 2007). A second category uses load cells inside the four bed legs, detecting changes in the centre of mass of the bed plus sleeper (Brink, Müller, & Schierz, 2006), or accelerometers in one or more of the bed legs to detect repetitive vibrations coming from this mechanical activity (Nukaya, Shino, Kurihara, Watanabe, & Tanaka, 2012). A third category uses sensor pads placed below, within or on top of the mattress, positioned at the chest area. These sensor pads work either electronically (capacitive, piezoresistive, piezoelectric) (Alihanka, Vaahtoranta, & Saarikivi, 1981), mechanically (pressure variations in a fluid, accelerometers) (Shin et al., 2010; Heise et al., 2010) or optically (reflective changes due to bending of optical fibers) (Brüser, Kerekes, & Leonhardt, 2012). A last category places the same kind of sensor pads underneath, within or upon the pillow (Zhu et al., 2006). Figure 4 visualizes the most commonly used method (third category), with a sensor pad placed underneath the chest area.

Numerous algorithms of different complexity have been developed for extracting the heart rhythm from the BCG signal. A first category uses characteristic features of the general BCG complex shape to determine the heart beat locations, either using thresholds or using machine-learning mechanics such as clustering (Brüser, Stadlthanner, de Waele, & Leonhardt, 2011; Rosales, Skubic, Heise, Devaney, & Schaumburg, 2012; Heise et al., 2013). Sometimes these features are first enlarged by applying a differentiation or

Figure 2. Recoil of a gun, comparable to the recoil the body experiences in the ballistocardiogram

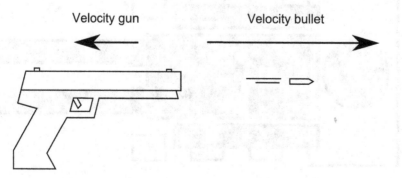

Figure 3. Example eight-second fragment of a registered ballistocardiogram

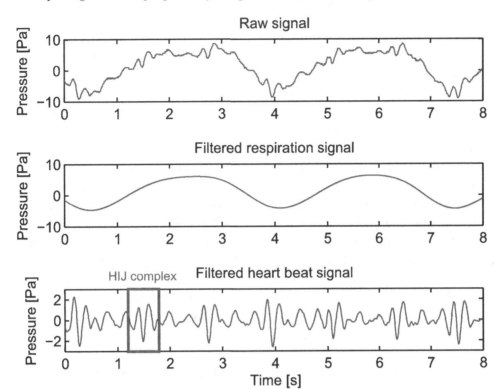

Figure 4. Off-body detection of mechanical activity from the heart
(Alihanka et al., 1981; Shin et al., 2010; Heise et al., 2010; Bruser et al., 2012).

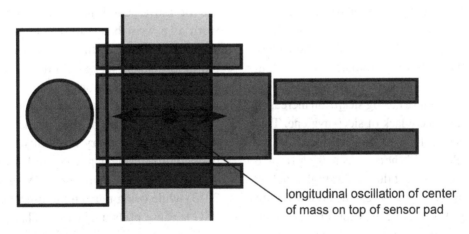

squaring filter (Mack, Patrie, Suratt, Felder, & Alwan, 2009; Kortelainen & Virkkala, 2007). A second category tries to determine the heart beat locations via correlation to either a BCG complex template constructed from a training set (Jansen, Larson, & Shankar, 1991), or to the previously detected heart beat cycle (Friedrich, Aubert, Führ, & Brauers, 2010; Brüser et al., 2011). Multiple algorithms have also been combined for improved robustness (Sprager & Zazula, 2012; Brüser et al., 2011; Friedrich et al., 2010; Brüser, Winter, & Leonhardt, 2013).

Although currently existing algorithms are able to successfully segment almost all individual heart beat cycles, they still experience difficulties in localizing the exact positions of the heart beat locations. This exact detection is important for heart rate variability analysis where the exact variations in time difference between the sequential heart beats are crucial. The main reason for these difficulties is the large variations in BCG complex shape, not only between registration methods, sleeping postures (due to differences in contact surface) and subjects (due to differences in cardiac strength, rhythm and exterior anatomical differences), but also over the respiration cycle (due to changes in cardiac filling of the left and right ventricle). Nevertheless, given the large surge of interest in BCG research during the last decade, and the current state of the art, these difficulties will most probably be overcome in the coming years.

EXTRACTION OF RELEVANT INFORMATION

Demographics show that nowadays up to 24% of the population is faced with regular sleep problems (National Sleep Foundation, 2012), due to e.g. insomnia (the inability to initiate and maintain sleep), obstructive sleep apnoea syndrome (OSAS; upper airway collapse during sleep), an increased stress level or a mere lack of sleep hygiene. This percentage seems to be raising every decade, inversely correlated with the ever decreasing average amount of sleep we get due to our highly active lifestyles (on average we sleep one hour less than 100 years ago). Therefore, it is not surprising that the importance of sleep is being emphasized more and more every year, next to the other important health pillars of healthy food and sufficient activity. Given the general trend of people becoming more proactive in following up on their own and their family member's health status, people want to follow up quality of sleep as well.

Sleep can roughly be divided into two main states, labelled Rapid-Eye-Movement (REM) and Non-REM (NREM (N1-N2-N3)) sleep, which alternate in cycles of about 90 minutes (Rechtschaffen & Kales, 1968). Figure 5 shows an example of a hypnogram from a healthy sleeper, with five alternating sleep cycles of NREM sleep and REM sleep. NREM sleep, especially deep sleep (N3), is more prominent during the first hours of sleep and is essential towards physical recovery (Haex, 2004; Ada & Oswald, 1984). REM sleep, linked to dreaming and more prominent during the last hours of sleep, acts towards the recovery of our mental state (Meerlo, Mistlberger, Jacobs, Heller, & McGinty, 2009).

Polysomnography (PSG) (Iber, Ancoli-Israel, Chesson, & Quan, 2007) is currently the gold standard in detailed sleep analysis. It requires however extensive amounts of on-body sensors (electroencephalogram for brain activity, electro-oculogram for eye activity, electromyogram for muscular activity, etc.), making the method costly and disturbing, and thus ruling out long-term monitoring. Actigraphy (ACT) (Morgenthaler et al., 2007) on the other hand, which makes solely use of movement information (accelerometer worn as a wrist band) to differentiate between Wake and Sleep, is both cheap and user-friendly, but unfortunately lacks both detail (such as the REM-NREM distinction) and accuracy (Paquet, Kwainska, & Carrier, 2007; Bulckaert et al., 2010). For this reason, sleep quality estimation using cardio-respiratory variability analysis suits perfectly to fill the gap between PSG and ACT, since it still has decent accuracy (Willemen et al., 2013) while being much more user friendly than PSG because of its unobtrusive character.

Deep sleep (N3) is characterized by a low variation in heart and breathing rate, while higher variation indicates light sleep (N1) or REM sleep. Furthermore, sudden raises in heart rate indicate periods of awakenings. This is certainly the case when followed by a period with a higher variability in inspiration and expiration lengths, since this

Figure 5. Example of a healthy hypnogram with 5 alternating cycles of NREM sleep (N1-N2-N3) and REM sleep

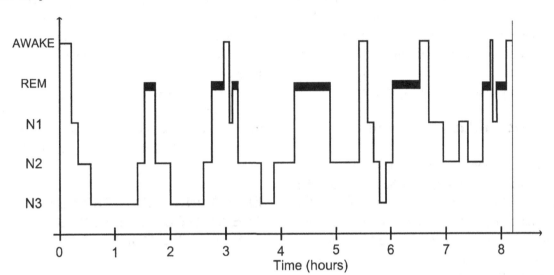

reflects a more conscious control of our breathing. During sleep, we breathe unconsciously, leading to more regular breathing intervals. Longer periods of immobility also point towards deep sleep (N3), whereas periods with large movement activity point towards wake and periods with repeating small movement activity (so-called twitches) points towards REM sleep (Willemen et al., 2013).

When we cut in our sleep time, we mainly reduce the amount of REM sleep we get since it is more prominent during the last hours of sleep. This thus reduces our mental recovery window. Increased amounts of stress, mood disorders and cognitive dysfunction are all linked to this reduction in REM sleep (Meerlo et al., 2009). When increased amounts of REM sleep are perceived towards the beginning of the night, it is a clear sign for a present or upcoming depression. When for older persons significant changes in sleep pattern are measured (mainly with regard to when they go to bed and when they get up again), it is often a sign of upcoming dementia or Alzheimer's disease (Moe, Vitiello, Larsen, & Prinz, 1995). Highly irregular breathing and moments of absent breathing could point towards a sleep disorder like

Obstructive Sleep Apnoea, which has an incidence rate that increases with age (Lee, Nagubadi Kryger, & Mokhlesi, 2008) and can have a serious impact on cardiovascular health.

Besides purely monitoring our sleep quality on a day-by-day basis to look for imminent disease, depression or possible sleep disorder, the monitoring system can also give recommendations on whether and how we have to reduce our stress level when we go to bed (detected in our heart rate variability pattern), or how to improve our sleep hygiene for obtaining better sleep (for example by drinking less caffeine and alcohol, or by making time for 30 minutes of relaxation before going to bed to be able to fall asleep more rapidly). Most of us are not aware that some of our activities or customs can have a significant impact on our sleep. By logging our activities and customs next to the day-by-day monitoring of our sleep, we can learn which ones affect our sleep in a negative way and should thus be avoided to improve our overall sleep quality. Information overload should however be prevented. We don't want to become so aware of our sleep, that it starts to have a detrimental effect. We all have experienced these situations where we truly want to fall asleep, but we fail to succeed in doing so because we are giving too much attention to it. The same principle applies here: obtaining the best quality of sleep should not become a competition. The system of monitoring, reporting and recommending should work in an empowering and not overpowering way.

Information-Based Adaptation

Besides reporting sleep quality to the user, information on sleep and sleep distribution can also be applied during the night itself. In order to influence and improve sleep quality, the bed and other bedroom properties could be adapted continuously to best fit our current sleep status. We do not need a 70 or 80 dB alarm to wake us up, for example, if we would already be lying awake in our bed; some soft music, and (gradually) turning on the lights would have the same effect. On the other hand, if we are still in deep sleep, and we definitely need to wake up at a particular time, increasing the volume higher than the standard 70 dB might help those of us who tend to sleep firmly. Further on, in the evening, a colder room (but warmer bed sheets) will get us all comfortable in bed, while in the morning a warmer room (but colder bed sheets) could help us to get from underneath our blankets more easily (which will be described in more detail in the next subchapter).

When we want to put on some light during the evening or night, it is often better to have a lower intensity of light than during the day to prevent significant suppression of the hormone melatonin which is produced during darkness and helps to regulate and promote sleep (McIntyre et al., 1989). In the morning, this depends on whether we want to wake up quickly or slowly, (probably depending on whether we need to go to work). Also the colour spectrum of the light can be adapted to our mood (Küller, Ballal, Laike, Mikellides, & Tonello, 2006). If we are stressed in the morning (measured through heart rate variability monitor-

ing from within our bed), some extra green and blue might help us relax. If we are just tired, some red and violet might give us the adrenaline boost we need to get ourselves going. If in the evening we arrive laughing to our bedroom, some yellow might improve our mood even more.

This active adaptation of our bedroom is a topic that, amongst others, will be further discussed in the next section, which focuses on how to improve our physical and mental recovery during the night.

IMPROVING RECOVERY DURING THE NIGHT BY OPTIMISING SLEEP CONDITIONS

Both physical and mental recovery occur during sleep, which can be seen as a muscle and brain relaxation state. While mental processing occurs during REM-sleep, physical recovery of our body is mainly situated during deep sleep (N3), also called slow wave sleep (SWS). To optimize physical recovery the bedding system plays a central role as it functions as a support to the human body. At present, more and more research is focusing on filling the knowledge gap related to the impact of the sleep surface on general sleep quality and other sleep related factors such as sleep architecture and body movements. For example, it has proven that applying ergonomic design principles can affect actual sleep (Van Deun et al., 2012). The same applies for bedroom and bed temperature. Since sleep occurs during the circadian phase of decreased heat production and increased heat loss (Van Someren, 2006), the major sleep period occurs during the decrease of core body temperature (CBT) in the circadian rhythm. Moreover, the ease of falling asleep is related to skin temperature at the extremities, such as hands and feet, and can be optimised to reduce sleep onset time or nightly awakenings. (Marotte & Timbal, 1982; Van Someren, 2006).

This subchapter will focus on optimization of body support and temperature during sleep, which are both subject-dependent and therefore require feedback control loops to be able to be used in (future) bedroom environments.

Body Support Optimization

Ideally, the body is supported in a way that allows the muscles to relax and intervertebral discs to recover from daily activities in which the spine is nearly continuous loaded (Nachemson & Elfström, 1970; Leblanc, Harlan, Schneider, Wendt, & Hedrick, 1994). From an ergonomic point of view, such optimal support during sleep refers to aligning the spine towards its reference shape, which is comparable to the shape while standing but with a slightly flattened lumbar lordosis due to the changed working axis of gravity (Dolan, Adams, & Hutton, 1988). The shape can be referenced to as the S-shape that would appear in a condition of weightlessness. Bed properties that provide this optimal support are both posture- and person-dependent. For instance, in most subjects lateral, frontal and posterior body contours differ, which results in a different spinal alignment when changing sleep posture (Gracovetsky, 1987; Verhaert et al., 2011; Haex, 2004).

To account for these variable conditions, a new approach in the development of state-of-the-art bedding systems consists of monitoring movement and sleep posture changes based on mattress indentation data (Verhaert et al., 2011). In addition, the combination of mattress indentation

measurements with personalized digital human models (Van Deun et al., 2013) allows estimating spinal alignment during sleep in an unobtrusive way (Verhaert et al., 2011b). this methodology was applied by Verhaert et al. (2013) to control mechanical bed properties (stiffness) of a sleep system during the night. Furthermore, follow-up studies by Van Deun et al. explored the influence of such an *active bedding system* (designed to continuously optimize spinal alignment) on objective and subjective sleep parameters. Overnight experiments in a dedicated sleep laboratory were performed in order to look at sleep macrostructure, body movements and subjective sleep parameters. The following paragraphs will dive deeper into the different aspects that are needed in state-of-the-art bedding systems to continuously and automatically optimize body support.

Mattress Indentation Measurements

The ability to instrument the bedding system has raised interest in studying body movement or monitoring sleep postures (Lu, Tamura, & Togawa, 1999; Adami, Pavel, Hayes, & Singer, 2010; Harada, Mori, Nishida, Yoshimi, & Sato, 1999; Brink, Müller, & Schierz, 2006; Hoque, Dickerson, & Stankovic, 2010). Mattress indentation measurements provide useful information to assess movements and sleep postures. Examples of a lateral (left) and supine (right) sleep posture are presented in Figure 6. Moreover, since mattress indentation provides direct information on how the mattress surface is deformed, these measure-

Figure 6. Example of mattress indentation measurements for right lateral (left) a supine (right) sleep postures

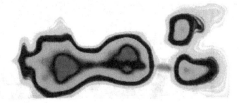

ments offer valuable insight in the deformation of the body (once the body itself is characterized in terms of shape and weight distribution, which is discussed further on). As opposed to pressure mapping, indentation measurements provide more appropriate information to assess spinal alignment during the night because of the direct link to body indentation. As an example, a person having wide and heavy shoulders will sink deep into the mattress when lying in a lateral sleep posture. A pressure recording of that person can be difficult to interpret because the measured pressure heavily depends on the soft tissue around his/her shoulder. More soft tissue better distributes pressure and would thus result in lower peak pressure.

According to Verhaert et al. (2012) movements and postures can be easily detected using mattress indentation measurements integrated in a bedding system. Sensitivity for posture recognition (supine, left lateral, right lateral and prone postures) varies between 83.6% and 95.9%. Movement detection shows a sensitivity of 91.2% in this study. Also so-called intermediate sleep postures have been recently studied. These postures show a combina-

tion of lateral and prone or supine sleep positions. An example is a subject lying in a lateral sleep posture according to his hip orientation while his shoulders are turned towards the mattress, and thus rather resemble a prone posture (Figure 7). Such in-between postures cause spinal torsion and thus should be avoided. Due to large interpersonal differences, they are more difficult to identify using static classification methods.

Digital Human Modelling

Human avatars, here defined as human mesh models having an underlying skeleton to enable posing of the mesh, are commonly used in modelling purposes such as modelling work space environments. The use of a *customized* human model (e.g. Figure 8) is of large importance in individualizing sleep ergonomics. It can be used to quantify body support (Verhaert et al., 2012), which is depending on a subject's anthropometric characteristics. In modelling sleep ergonomics, the need for a personalized human avatar is twofold. First of all, it can be used to classify a the

Figure 7. Example of an intermediate sleep posture in which the subject is lying in a right lateral posture with it shoulders turned towards the mattress

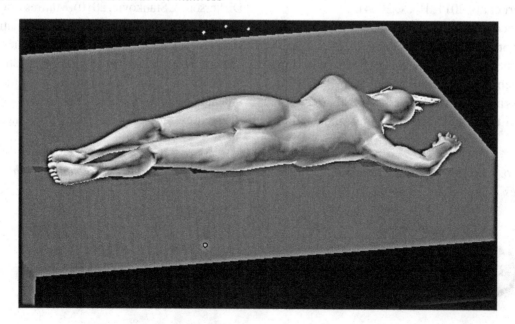

sleep posture or even track it during the night, for example by means of a particle filter which can be used when static posture recognition algorithms fail in recognizing so-called intermediate postures. This fail is mainly due to the fact that most recognition algorithms do not incorporate individualized anthropometric information. Secondly, when looking at body support – or specifically spinal alignment –, a digital human model is necessary to assess the spine shape of a person when lying on a sleep system in a specific posture. Therefore, only a customized human avatar can be used that takes into account the person-specific anthropometrics (such as sagittal and coronal body shapes, length and preferably also weight distribution) in order to calculate the shape of the spine.

Anthropometric information on the human body can be derived both manually (using caliper and tape) and automatically. Automatic methods include information from camera images such as contour information (Van Deun et al., 2013) and

depth and colour information (e.g. from Microsoft Kinect (Wijckmans et al., 2013)). Also 3D full body scanners can be used to generate complete 3D information but such scanners are much more expensive compared to camera information. More recently, mattress indentation measurements are used to generate customized human avatars. As opposed to camera images or body scanners, mattress indentation measurements also provide information on the weight distribution of the body since heavy body parts will sink deeper into the mattress. Therefore, these measurements are preferably used for digital human modelling in sleep ergonomics.

Most of the presented techniques will use a 3D base model (mesh model) of the human body that is adapted to the measured information, resulting in a customized model. Adaptation of the mesh can be performed by morphing, a technique in which vertices are repositioned along a (linear) deformation path between two extreme target positions,

Figure 8. Example of a digital human model that can be customized (www.blender.org).

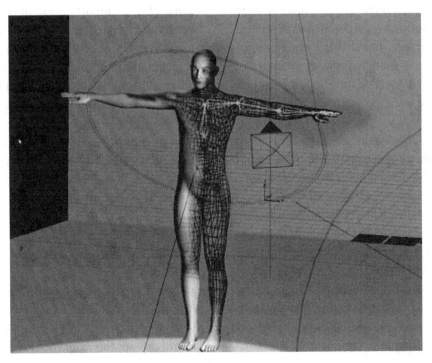

called morph targets (Volz, Blum, Hberling, & Khakzar, 2007; Klette & Zunic, 2004).

In order to use the human model for spine shape estimation, body weight needs to be distributed to the different body parts in accordance to mattress indentation measurements.

Smart Control of Spinal Alignment

The combination of mattress indentation measurements with customized information on the human body allows for estimating the shape of the spine unobtrusively, as shown by Verhaert et al. (2012). When incorporated into the bedding system, this allows for continuous follow-up of the spine shape during the night.

We can go one step further by introducing active components into the bedding system resulting in a so-called active or smart bedding system. Actuators are used to control the stiffness of the bedding system in different comfort zones as to create a non-homogeneous stiffness distribution. The necessary stiffness distribution is depending on both the person's anthropometric characteristics and the sleep posture in which he or she is lying. As a consequence, a smart bed also has a posture recognition algorithm incorporated, as described before. Furthermore, unobtrusive evaluation of the spine shape is used as input to a controller to regulate the stiffness of the comfort zones. A schematic representation of this control loop is presented in Figure 9.

A reference shape of the spine is used as input and refers to the optimal shape the spine would have in an unloaded condition. The reference shape is comparable to the spine shape while standing, however with a flattened lordosis since no gravity is working in the longitudinal direction when sleeping. Based on the difference between the reference and the estimated spine shape, a controller alters the stiffness in the different comfort zones of the bed resulting in a change in mattress indentation measurements and spinal alignment. This loop is continued until spinal alignment is similar to the optimal (reference) condition. Every time the sleeper changes posture, the stiffness distribution is optimized.

The Effect of Smart Body Support on Sleep, Sleep-Related Parameters, and Recovery

Overnight experiments have been performed to evaluate the effect of an optimized body support–provided by a smart bed–on both objective and subjective sleep parameters using polysomnographic recordings and questionnaires respectively. Van Deun et al. (2012) used the previously described bedding system during overnight sleep experiments in a dedicated sleep laboratory. Subjective results show a significant positive effect on both sleep and daytime quality after sleeping on an active bedding system. On the other hand, movement and sleep posture information–as retrieved from mattress indentation measurements–show no significant difference when the bedding system was not altering its stiffness distribution. Objective measurements on sleep parameters retrieved from a polysomnographic recording have shown that optimal body support during the night increases the amount of deep sleep, also called slow wave sleep (SWS). Since SWS is essential for physical recuperation (Shapiro, Bortz, Mitchell, Bartel, & Jooste, 1981) during the night, sleeping on a smart bed that provides optimal body support will result in a positive restorative effect on your body. This allows to (physically) recover from daily activities during the night. Mental recovery, on the other hand, mostly occurs during REM-sleep, which was not significantly altered.

Smart Control of Neck Extension in OSA Patients

For specific groups of people, such as patients suffering from obstructive sleep apnoea (OSA) syndrome, body support control or temperature control are not the prior focus to improve sleep.

Figure 9. Schematic representation of a control loop that optimizes spinal alignment by controlling stiffness actuators in different comfort zones.
Adopted from Verhaert et al. (2013).

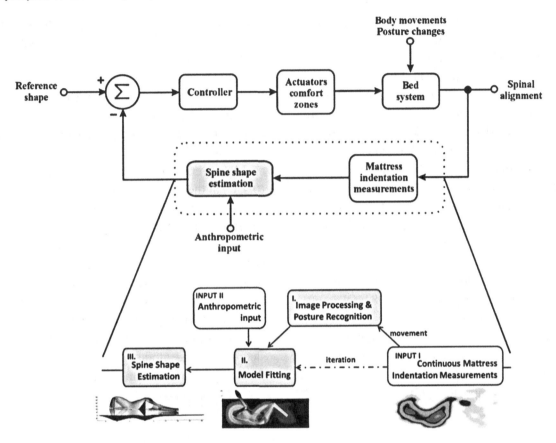

In 80% of the cases OSA is associated with more and longer apnoea's or hypopnea's in a supine sleep posture. The same relation applies to snoring. Therefore, sleep optimization (and improved recovery associated with it) during the night can be achieved by controlling the cervical position when sleeping in a supine posture. For example, it has been proven by Choi, Goldman, Koyal, & Clarck (2000) and Jan, Marchall, & Douglas (1994) that the resistance of the upper airway is reduced when the head is extended. As mentioned before, bedding systems exist that can detect the supine sleep posture and, when necessary, alter the stiffness distribution. Such systems can be used in OSA sufferers or snorers to increase head or neck extension by increasing the stiffness at the shoulders and upper body regions in order to enable a better air flow.

Temperature Optimization

Bedroom and bed temperature play a key role in optimising sleep by influencing sleep onset latency, nightly awakenings and sleep depth. Sleep onset closely follows the maximal rate of decline in Core Body Temperature (CBT) and maximal heat loss during the evening (Figure 10). This decline triggers sleep initiation and may facilitate entries into deeper sleep stages (Murphy & Campbell, 1997). The probability to wake up, on the other hand, increases during the early morning rise in CBT (Figure 10). As opposed to CBT, temperature of the skin extremities shows an inverse rhythm, i.e. skin temperature peaks during the habitual sleep period (Marotte & Timbal, 1982, Van Someren, 2006). Skin temperatures at the extremities such as hands and feet increase (e.g. prior to sleep onset) because of peripheral vasodilation, ending up cooling down your core body (Magnussen, 1939; Kleitman, Ramsaroop, & Engelmann, 1948). Under normal conditions the nocturnal increase of skin temperature is further amplified by postural change (Tikuisis & Ducharme, 1996; Kräuchi, Cajochen, & Wirz-Justice, 1997) or a warm microclimate resulting from insulated bedding (Goldsmith & Hampton, 1986; Muzet, Libert, & Candas, 1984; Okamoto, Mizuno, & Okudaira, 1997).

In general it is suggested that a rapid decline in CBT increases the likelihood of sleep initiation and may facilitate entries into deeper sleep stages (Murphy & Campbell, 1997).

The Effect of Skin Temperature on Sleep and Recovery

The above findings have already been used and studied in attempts to improve sleep and sleep onset by steering the skin temperature. For example, warming skin temperature in a direct or indirect manner prior to sleep has been shown to speed up sleep, resulting in a decreased sleep onset time as confirmed by Kräuchi, Cajochen, Werth, & Wirz-Justice (1999) and Gradisar & Lack (2004).

Moreover, mildly increased skin temperature (0.4°C) at the extremities was shown to increase the time spent in deep sleep (slow wave sleep) by Raymann, Roy, Swab, & Van Someren (2008). However, one should be careful with warming because a too warm skin during sleep initiation might induce arousals and elevation of the core body temperature (Raymann & Van Someren, 2007a; 2007b). This elevation of CBT, in turn, can lead to more nocturnal awakenings and decreased sleep. The same applies when the CBT is too low (below the thermoneutral zone).

Figure 10. Body temperature and its relation to sleep in adults; normal sleep occurs between 23:00h and 07:00h.

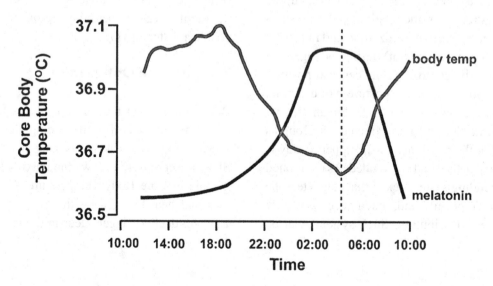

Based on the aforementioned evidence it is thus of utmost importance to limit thermal manipulations to the proximal and distal skin area, i.e. the area normally covered by bedding, without interfering with core body temperature and without interfering with normal room temperature. The magnitude, body location and timing of the skin temperature manipulation are also of large importance for its application to improve sleep. Results of a study by Raymann et al. (2008) indicated that a thermal sleep treatment should aim at individualized and time-of night-dependent control of skin temperature within the small range of reported skin and bed temperature microclimates during sleep (Goldsmith & Hampton, 1968; Muzet et al., 1984; Okamoto et al., 1997). Ideally, bed microclimate temperature should be kept, on average, above 33.5 and 33.2 °C for young adults and elderly (without sleep complaints) respectively. It is not advised to simply apply heating blankets, which warm up both the skin and core body. Moreover, the warming then occurs without knowledge about the actual body temperatures, which may become high and adversely affect sleep (Fletcher et al., 1999) such as by activating heat stress responses.

The Effect of Room Temperature on Sleep

Finally, when speaking of room temperature optimisation, the ideal case consists of starting the night with a slightly lower room temperature (e.g. around 18°C) which enables the core body to lower temperature by losing heat. During actual sleep, room temperature could be slightly increased in order to minimize any thermoregulatory efforts to maintain a stable body temperature during the night. This optimal temperature range is called the thermal neutral zone, in which the body's heat production is in equilibrium with the rate of heat loss to the environment. A normal range for a sleeper varies between 18°C and 22°C. If the room temperature becomes too hot or too cold, you are more likely to wake up during the night. Furthermore, the comfort level of the room temperature can specifically affect REM sleep since it is generally more vulnerable to temperature-related disturbance (Muzet, Ehrhart, Candas, Libert, & Vogt, 1983). The ideal room temperature is subject-dependent, as was the optimal skin temperature, but also the amount of insulation plays a central role. As an example, worse sleep has been reported with a bedroom air temperature of 30°C, as compared to 18 and 23°C (Freedman & Roehrs, 2006). REM sleep is then decreased, as did deep sleep (slow wave sleep) but to a lower extent.

Smart Control of Temperature

For bedroom applications at home, a system can be developed that is integrated in the bedding system itself which measures skin temperature and/or humidity as well as room temperature and controls the bed microclimate and bedroom temperature in feedback control loops (such as described before for body support). Unobtrusive temperature sensors, such as for example iButton devices, can be integrated in the blankets. The use of iButtons for temperature monitoring have been validated for home monitoring purposes by van Marken Lichtenbeld et al. (2006). Also the mattress can be equipped with temperature and humidity sensors. In the case where skin temperature should be increased, the sleep microclimate can be optimised by heat insulation (such as additional cloths or bedding) or warming up the bed using an electrical blanket. In the latter it is important to switch off heating during actual sleep to prevent interference with core body temperature. Another way is to use body heating such as a warm bad or a sauna prior to bedtime. Early morning awakenings, on the other hand, can only be tackled using an electrical blanket having a delayed start. Lowering the microclimate temperature can be achieved by systems that use a temperature controlled fluid or air flow integrated in a blanket or in the bedding system itself. Bedroom temperature can be more easily controlled using an air conditioning installation or the like.

AUTOMATING TEDIOUS TASKS WHICH REOCCUR EVERY DAY

Everyone will recognize that moment when you just crawled underneath the warm blankets of your bed, and it suddenly hits you that you forgot to turn off the lights in the kitchen, still have the manual override of the central heating on or forgot to lock the door. Or you just think you forgot. What if a central computer would know that everyone is up in his bed, and would just do this automatically for you so you never have to worry about this anymore? And this is just the beginning. We can all come up with numerous tedious tasks we lose time on every single day. It would be so much better if the central heating would turn on half an hour before our alarm clock would go off, that a warm bath would already be waiting in the bathroom, and a hot coffee with toast would be ready in the kitchen when we get downstairs.

While we don't mind technology aiding us in trying to find balance in our lives, we still like to believe we are in control of everything happening around us, at least in our own home. Some decisions should not be made without us being aware. After all, most people don't like or even fear the prospect of being controlled by technology. Especially when we take into account that more complex systems are also more vulnerable to malfunction.

On the other hand, it is also important for ambient technology not to work disruptively. If it decides to interact with us, it should try to do so in a way which is seamlessly interwoven with our lives. It should be aware of the context of the situation before reporting, and not interrupting our present activity. Since we spend most of the time in our bedroom sleeping, we don't want to be awoken every time our ambient intelligent bedroom decides to, for example, increase the

heating or change the back support from within the mattress. This is one of the main differences with other applications of ambient intelligence, namely the fact that we are not conscious.

Therefore, to solve this problem, and help people get comfortable with this unconscious interference, every decision the system makes should be nicely fitted into a report which is viewable for the user at any time. This way, people can build up their trust within the system, and truly experience how their intelligent bedroom transforms them into a healthier person.

CONCLUSION

In this book chapter, an overview was given on the current status of ambient intelligence for bedroom applications and its perspective to the future. We tried to give insight in the possibilities of ambient intelligence in the bedroom, as well as the current status of the technology and algorithms making it all possible. A focus was given on different aspects ranging from monitoring sleep and general health in our bedroom, towards automatically controlling body support and temperature during sleep. The combination of both health monitoring and environmental control in an intelligent and efficient way can prove of great benefit for all of us. Moreover, upcoming and state-of-the-art technology will enable a rapid growth of these applications in our future bedrooms.

The majority of this chapter was focused on research performed within our biomechanics division and we hope that it will lead to numerous useful applications.

ACKNOWLEDGMENT

Research supported by IWT SBO EASI-sleep, Research Council KUL: GOA MaNet, PFV/10/002 (OPTEC), several PhD/postdoc & fellow grants; iMinds: SBO dotatie 2013, ICON: NXT_Sleep,

Belgian Federal Science Policy Office: IUAP P7/19 (DYSCO, 2012-2017; ERC Advanced Grant: BIOTENSORS (n 39804).

REFERENCES

Adam, K., & Oswald, I. (1984). Sleep helps healing. *British Medical Journal, 289*, 1400–1401. PMID:6437572

Adami, A. M., Pavel, M., Hayes, T. L., & Singer, C. M. (2010). Detection of movement in bed using unobtrusive load cell sensors. *IEEE Transactions on Information Technology in Biomedicine, 14*(2), 481–490. PMID:19171523

Alihanka, J., Vaahtoranta, K., & Saarikivi, I. (1981). A new method for long-term monitoring of the ballistocardiogram, heart rate, and respiration. *The American Journal of Physiology, 240*(5), 384–392. PMID:7235054

Braunstein, J. (1953). The Ballistocardiogram: A Dynamic Record of the Heart. Springfield, IL: Springfield.

Brink, M., Müller, C. H., & Schierz, C. (2006). Contact-free measurement of heart rate, respiration rate, and body movements during sleep. *Behavior Research Methods, 38*(3), 511–521. PMID:17186762

Brüser, C., Kerekes, A., Winter, S., & Leonhardt, S. (2012). Multi-channel optical sensor-array for measuring ballistocardiograms and respiratory activity in bed. In *Proceedings of the 34th Annual Conference of the IEEE Engineering in Medicine and Biology Society (EMBS)*, (pp. 5042-5045). EMBS.

Brüser, C., Stadlthanner, K., de Waele, S., & Leonhardt, S. (2011). Adaptive beat-to-beat heart rate estimation in ballistocardiograms. *IEEE Transactions on Information Technology in Biomedicine, 15*(5), 778–786. PMID:21421447

Brüser, C., Winter, S., & Leonhardt, S. (2013). Robust inter-beat interval estimation in cardiac vibration signals. *Physiological Measurement, 34*(2), 123–138. PMID:23343518

Bulckaert, A., Exadaktylos, V., De Bruyne, G., Haex, B., De Valck, E., & Wuyts, J. et al. (2010). Heart rate based nighttime awakening detection. *European Journal of Applied Physiology, 109*, 317–322. PMID:20094892

Choi, J. K., Goldman, M., Koyal, S., & Clark, G. (2000). Effect of jaw and head position on airway resistance in obstructive sleep apnea. *Sleep and Breathing, 4*, 163–168. PMID:11894202

Devot, S., Bianchi, A. M., Naujokat, E., Mendez, M. O., Brauers, A., & Cerutti, S. (2007). Sleep Monitoring Through a Textile Recording System. In *Proceedings of the 29th Annual International Conference of the IEEE Engineering in Medicine and Biology Society (EMBS)*, (pp. 2560-2563). EMBS.

Dolan, P., Adams, M. A., & Hutton, W. C. (1988). Commonly adopted postures and their effect on the lumbar spine. *Spine, 13*, 197–201. PMID:3406840

Freedman, R. R., & Roehrs, T. A. (2006). Effects of REM sleep and ambient temperature on hot flash-induces sleep disturbance. *Menopause (New York, N.Y.), 13*, 576–583. PMID:16837879

Friedrich, D., Aubert, X. L., Führ, H., & Brauers, A. (2010). Heart rate estimation on a beat-to-beat basis via ballistocardiography – a hybrid approach. In *Proceedings of the 32nd Annual International Conference of the IEEE Engineering in Medicine and Biology Society (EMBS)*, (pp. 4048-4051). EMBS.

Goldsmith, R., & Hampton, I. F. (1968). Nocturnal microclimate of man. *The Journal of Physiology, 194*, 32P–33P. PMID:5639779

Gracovetsky, S. A. (1987). The Resting Spine – A conceptual Approach to the Avoidance of Spinal Reinjury During Rest. *Physical Therapy*, *67*, 549–553. PMID:2951749

Gradisar, M., & Lack, L. (2004). Relationships between the circadian rhythms of finger temperature, core temperature, sleep latency, and subjective sleepiness. *Journal of Biological Rhythms*, *19*(2), 157–163. PMID:15038855

Guohua, L., Jianqi, W., Yu, Y., & Xijing, J. (2007). Study of the Ballistocardiogram signal in life detection system based on radar. In *Proceedings of the 29th Annual International Conference of the IEEE Engineering in Medicine and Biology Society (EMBS)*, (pp. 2191-2194). EMBS.

Haex, B. (2004). *Back and Bed: Ergonomic Aspects of Sleeping*. Boca Raton, FL: CRC Press.

Hall, M., Vasko, R., Buysse, D., Ombao, H., Chen, Q., & Cashmere, J. D. et al. (2004). Acute stress affects heart rate variability during sleep. *Psychosomatic Medicine*, *66*(1), 56–62. PMID:14747638

Harada, T., Mori, T., Nishida, Y., Yoshimi, T., & Sato, T. (1999) Body parts positions and posture estimation system based on pressure distribution image. In *Proc. IEEE Int. Conf. Robot. Autom*, (pp. 968-975). IEEE.

Heise, D., Rosales, L., Sheahen, M., Su, B., & Skubic, M. (2013). Non-invasive measurement of heartbeat with a hydraulic bed sensor: Progress, challenges and opportunities. In *Proceedings of the 2013 IEEE International Instrumentation and Measurement Technology Conference (I2MTC)*, (pp. 397-402). IEEE.

Hoque, E., Dickerson, R. F., & Stankovic, J. A. (2010). *Monitoring body positions and movements during sleep using WISPs*. Paper presented at the WH '10 Wireless Health 2010. New York, NY.

Iber, C., Ancoli-Israel, S., Chesson, A. L., & Quan, S. F. (2007). *The AASM Manual for the Scoring of Sleep and Associated Events*. Westchester, IL: American Academy of Sleep Medicine.

Jan, M. A., Marchall, I., & Douglas, N. J. (1994). Effect of posture on upper airway dimensions in normal human. *American Journal of Respiratory and Critical Care Medicine*, *149*, 1285–1288. PMID:8111573

Jansen, B. H., Larson, B. H., & Shankar, K. (1991). Monitoring of the ballistocardiogram with the static charge sensitive bed. *IEEE Transactions on Bio-Medical Engineering*, *38*(8), 748–751. PMID:1937507

Kleitman, N., Ramsaroop, A., & Engelmann, T. G. (1948). Variations in skin temperatures of the feet and hands at the onset of sleep. *Federation Proceedings*, *7*, 66. PMID:18857960

Klette, R., & Zunic, J. (2004). Geometric algebra for pose estimation and surface morphing in human motion estimation. In Proceedings of IWCIA 2004, (LNCS), (vol. 3322, pp. 583-596). Berlin: Springer.

Kortelainen, J. M., & Virkkala, J. (2007). FFT averaging of multichannel BCG signals from bed mattress sensor to improve estimation of heart beat interval. In *Proceedings of the 29th Annual International Conference of the IEEE Engineering in Medicine and Biology Society (EMBS)*, (pp. 6685-6688). IEEE.

Kräuchi, K., Cajochen, C., Werth, E., & Wirz-Justice, A. (1999). Physiology: Warm feet promote the rapid onset of sleep. *Nature*, *401*, 36–37. PMID:10485703

Kräuchi, K., Cajochen, C., & Wirz-Justice, A. (1997). A relationship between heat loss and sleepiness: Effects of postural change and melatonin administration. *Journal of Applied Physiology (Bethesda, Md.)*, *83*, 134–139. PMID:9216955

Küller, R., Ballal, S., Laike, T., Mikellides, B., & Tonello, G. (2006). The impact of light and colour on psychological mood: A cross-cultural study of indoor work environments. *Ergonomics*, *49*(14), 1496–1507. PMID:17050390

LeBlanc, A. D., Harlan, J. E., Schneider, V. S., Wendt, R. E., & Hedrick, T. D. (1994). Changes in intervertebral disc cross-sectional area with bed rest and space flight. *Spine*, *19*, 812–817. PMID:8202800

Lee, W., Naqubadi, S., Kryger, M. H., & Mokhlesi, B. (2008, June). Epidemiology of obstructive sleep apnea: A population-based perspective. *Expert Review of Respiratory Medicine*, *2*(3), 349–364. PMID:19690624

Lu, L., Tamura, T., & Togawa, T. (1999). Detection of body movements during sleep by monitoring of bed temperature. Physiol. Meas., 137-148.

Mack, D. C., Patrie, J. T., Suratt, P. M., Felder, R. A., & Alwan, M. (2009). Development and preliminary validation of heart rate and breathing rate detection using a passive, ballistocardiography-based sleep monitoring system. *IEEE Transactions on Information Technology in Biomedicine*, *13*(1), 111–120. PMID:19129030

Magnussen, G. (1939). Vasomotorische Veränderingen in den Extremitäten im Verhältnis zu Schlaf und Schlafbereitschaft Acta. *Psychiatria et Neurologia*, *14*, 39–54.

Marotte, H., & Timbal, J. (1982). Circadian rhythm of temperature in man. Comparative study with two experimental protocols. *Chronobiologica*, *8*, 87–100.

McIntyre, I. M., Norman, T. R., Burrows, G. D., & Armstrong, S. M. (1989). Human melatonin suppression by light is intensity dependent. *Journal of Pineal Research*, *6*(2), 149–156. PMID:2915324

Meerlo, P., Mistlberger, R. E., Jacobs, B. L., Heller, H. C., & McGinty, D. (2009). New neurons in the adult brain: The role of sleep and consequence of sleep loss. *Sleep Medicine Reviews*, *13*, 187–194. PMID:18848476

Moe, K.E., Vitiello, M.V., Larsen, L.H., & Prinz, P.N. (1995). Sleep/wake patterns in Alzheimer's disease: relationships with cognition and function. *Journal of Sleep Research*, *4*, 15-20.

Morgenthaler, T., Alessi, C., Friedman, L., Owens, J., Kapur, V., & Boehlecke, B. et al. (2007). Practice Parameters for the Use of Actigraphy in the Assessment of Sleep and Sleep Disorders: An Update for 2007. *Sleep*, *30*, 519–529. PMID:17520797

Murphy, P. J., & Campbell, S. S. (1997). Nighttime drop in body temperature: A physiological trigger for sleep onset? *Sleep*, *20*(7), 505–511. PMID:9322266

Muzet, A., Ehrhart, J., Candas, V., Libert, J. P., & Vogt, J. J. (1983). Rem Sleep and Ambient Temperature in Man. *The International Journal of Neuroscience*, *18*, 117–125. PMID:6840976

Muzet, A., Libert, J. P., & Candas, V. (1984). Ambient temperature and human sleep. *Experientia*, *40*, 425–429. PMID:6723903

Nachemson, A., & Elfström, G. (1970). Intravital dynamic pressure measurements in lumbar discs. A study of common movements, maneuvers, and exercises. *Scandinavian Journal of Rehabilitation Medicine*, *1*, 1–40. PMID:4257209

Nukaya, S., Shino, T., Kurihara, Y., Watanabe, K., & Tanaka, H. (2012). Noninvasive bed sensing of human biosignals via piezoceramic devices sandwiched between the floor and bed. *IEEE Sensors Journal*, *12*(3), 431–438.

Okamoto, K., Mizuno, K., & Okudaira, N. (1997). The effects of a newly designed air mattress upon sleep and bed climate. *Applied Human Science*, *16*, 161–166. PMID:9343865

Paquet, J., Kwainska, A., & Carrier, J., (2007). *Wake detection capacity of actigraphy during sleep*. Academic Press.

Peltokangas, M., Verho, J., & Vehkaoja, A. (2012). Night-time EKG and HRV monitoring with bed sheet integrated textile electrodes. *IEEE Transactions on Information Technology in Biomedicine*, *16*(5), 935–942. PMID:22829424

Raymann, R. J. E. M., Swaab, D. F., & Van Someren, E. J. W. (2008). Skin deep: Enhanced sleep depth by cutaneous temperature manipulation. *Brain*, *131*, 500–513. doi:10.1093/brain/awm315 PMID:18192289

Raymann, R. J. E. M., Swaab, D. F., & Van Someren, E. J. W. (2007b). Skin temperature and sleep-onset latency: Changes with age and insomnia. *Physiology & Behavior*, *90*, 257–266. PMID:17070562

Raymann, R. J. E. M., & Van Someren, E. J. W. (2007a). Time-on-task impairment of psychomotor vigilance is affected by mild skin warming and changes with aging and insomnia. *Sleep*, *30*, 96–103. PMID:17310870

Rechtschaffen, A., & Kales, A. (1968). A manual of standardized terminology, techniques and scoring system for sleep stages of human subjects. In *National Institutes of Health Publications No. 204*. Washington, DC: U.S. Government Printing Office.

Rosales, L., Skubic, M., Heise, D., Devaney, M. J., & Schaumburg, M. (2012). Heartbeat detection from a hydraulic bed sensor using a clustering approach. In *Proceedings of the 34th Annual Conference of the IEEE Engineering in Medicine and Biology Society (EMBS)*, (pp. 2383-2387). EMBS.

Shapiro, C. M., Bortz, R., Mitchell, D., Bartel, P., & Jooste, P. (1981). Slow-wave sleep: A recovery period after exercise. *Science*, *214*(4526), 1253–1254. doi:10.1126/science.7302594 PMID:7302594

Shin, J. H., Chee, Y. J., Jeong, D. U., & Park, K. S. (2010). Nonconstrained sleep monitoring system and algorithms using air-mattress with balancing tube method. *IEEE Transactions on Information Technology in Biomedicine*, *14*(1), 147–156. PMID:19846378

Somers, V. K., Dyken, M. E., Mark, A. L., & Abboud, F. M. (1993). Sympathetic-nerve activity during sleep in normal subjects. *The New England Journal of Medicine*, *328*, 303–307. PMID:8419815

Sprager, S., & Zazula, D. (2012). Heartbeat and respiration detection from optical interferometric signals by using a multimethod approach. *IEEE Transactions on Bio-Medical Engineering*, *59*(10), 2922–2929. PMID:22907961

Stein, P. K., & Pu, Y. (2012). Heart rate variability, sleep and sleep disorders. *Sleep Medicine Reviews*, *16*(1), 47–66. PMID:21658979

Task Force of the European Society of Cardiology and the North American Society of Pacing and Electrophysiology. (1996, March). Heart rate variability: Standards of measurement, physiological interpretation and clinical use. *Circulation*, *93*(5), 1043–1065. PMID:8598068

The National Sleep Foundation. (2012). *What makes a good night's sleep*. Available: http://www.sleepfoundation.org

Tikuisis, P., & Ducharme, M. B. (1996). The effect of postural changes on body temperatures and heat balance. *European Journal of Applied Physiology*, *72*, 451–459. PMID:8925816

Van Deun, D., Verhaert, V., Willemen, T., Buys, K., Haex, B., & Vander Sloten, J. (2013). Automatic modeling of customized human avatars using contour information. In *Proceedings of the International Digital Human Modeling Symposium* (pp. 1-6). Academic Press.

Van Deun, D., Verhaert, V., Willemen, T., Wuyts, J., Verbraecken, J., & Exadaktylos, V. et al. (2012). Biomechanics-based active control of bedding support properties and its influence on sleep. *Work (Reading, Mass.), 41*(Suppl. 1), 1274–1280. PMID:22316894

Van Marken Lichtenbelt, W. D., Daanen, H. A., Wouters, L., Fronczek, R., Raymann, R. J., & Severens, N. M. et al. (2006). Evaluation of wireless determination of skin temperature using iButtons. *Physiology & Behavior, 88*, 489–447. PMID:16797616

Van Someren, E. J. W. (2006). Mechanisms and functios of coupling between sleep and temperature rhythms. *Brain Research, 153*, 309–324. PMID:16876583

Verhaert, V. et al. (2011b). The use of a generic human model to personalize bed design. In *Proceedings of 1st International Symposium on Digital Human Modeling*. Accepted for publication.

Verhaert, V., Druyts, H., Van Deun, D., Exadaktylos, V., Verbraecken, J., & Vandekerckhove, M. et al. (2012). Estimating spine shape in lateral sleep positions using silhouette-derived body shape models. *International Journal of Industrial Ergonomics, 42*(5), 489–498.

Verhaert, V., Haex, B., De Wilde, T., Berckmans, D., Vandekerckhove, M., Verbraecken, J., & Vander Sloten, J. (2011). Unobtrusive assessment of motor patterns during sleep based on mattress indentation measurements. *IEEE Transactions on Information Technology in Biomedicine, 15*(5), 787–794. PMID:21435985

Verhaert, V., Van Deun, D., Verbraecken, J., Vandekerckhove, M., Exadaktylos, V., Haex, B., & Vander Sloten, J. (2013). Smart control of spinal alignment through active adjustment of mechanical bed properties during sleep. *Journal of Ambient Intelligence and Smart Environments, 5*(4), 369–380.

Volz, A., Blum, R., Hberling, S., & Khakzar, K. (2007). Automatic, body measurements based generation of individual avatars using highly adjustable linear transformation. In *Proceedings of Digital Human Modelling*, (pp. 453-459). ICDHM.

Wijckmans, J., Van Deun, D., Buys, K., Vander Sloten, J., & Bruyninckx, H. (2013). Parametric Modeling of the Human Body Using Kinect Measurements. In *Proceedings on 4th International Conference and Exhibition on 3D Body Scanning Technologies* (pp. 117-126). Long Beach, CA: Academic Press.

Willemen, T., Van Deun, D., Verhaert, V., Vandekerckhove, M., Exadaktylos, V., & Verbraecken, J. et al. (2013). *An evaluation of cardio-respiratory and movement features with respect to sleep stage classification. IEEE Journal of Biomedical and Health Informatics.*

Zhu, X., Chen, W., Nemoto, T., Kanemitsu, Y., Kitamura, K., Yamakoshi, K., & Wei, D. (2006). Real-time monitoring of respiration rhythm and pulse rate during sleep. *IEEE Transactions on Bio-Medical Engineering, 53*(12), 2553–2563. PMID:17153213

KEY TERMS AND DEFINITIONS

Autonomic Nervous System (ANS): The part of our nervous system which regulates (mostly unconsciously) the functioning of our organs. Variations within the ANS, also occurring over different states of sleep, are known to be reflected in our heart rhythm, breathing rhythm and body temperature.

Ballistocardiography (BCG): The practice of registering the mechanical activity of the heart, originating from the pulsation of blood with every heart beat which shifts the blood's center of mass. The ballistocardiogram can be measured from within the bedding system.

Bedding System: A bedding or sleep system is the system on which we sleep. It generally comprises a bed base, a mattress and/or a pillow.

Core Body Temperature (CBT): The temperature of the body core, including the brain and the inner organs (such as liver, heart, etc.). Normal CBT is regulated around 37°C in humans.

Distal Skin Temperature: Temperature at distal skin regions, such as hands and feet. These regions can easily lose body heat to the environment when necessary. Distal skin temperature variations are three times larger than those of the core body temperature.

Mattress Indentation: The vertical displacement of the mattress surface, which is normally indented due to a subject's weight. Measurements of mattress indentation can be used, amongst others, to monitor sleep posture and spinal alignment.

Proximal Skin Temperature: Body temperature at proximal skin regions such as thigh, stomach, forehead, etc. Changes in proximal skin temperature show similar variations as the CBT.

Sleep Quality: A subjective evaluation of how a subject perceived his sleep. It is a number between 1 (ultimately bad) and 10 (extremely good) that is assessed through questionnaires half an hour after waking up.

Sleep: A state of the brain, associated with muscle relaxation and inhibition of environmental stimuli. Normal sleep comprises different brain states, ranging from light sleep (called N1) to deep sleep (or slow wave sleep) and REM sleep.

Chapter 9
Holophonor:
Designing the Visual Music Instruments of the Future

Jonathan Weinel
Glyndŵr University, UK

Richard Picking
Glyndŵr University, UK

Stuart Cunningham
Glyndŵr University, UK

Lyall Williams
Glyndŵr University, UK

ABSTRACT

This chapter considers the technological feasibility of the Holophonor, a fictional audio-visual instrument from the science fiction cartoon Futurama. Through an extended discussion of the progression of visual music towards interactive models, it was proposed that the Holophonor is an example of an ideal visual music instrument and could be constructed in the near future. This chapter recapitulates the key features of the fictional instrument. An evaluation of the technological feasibility of building a real-world version of the Holophonor is then given, with reference to existing technologies. In particular, it is proposed that the Holophonor's ability to respond to the emotional state of the performer may be facilitated by drawing on approaches from HCI and affective computing. Following this, a possible architecture for the Holophonor is proposed.

INTRODUCTION

This chapter considers the technological feasibility of the Holophonor': a fictional musical instrument of the 31ˢᵗ Century that was featured in the science-fiction TV series *Futurama* (Groening et al., 2001; Groening et al., 2003). The Holophonor resembles an Oboe, and when played produces holographic images that respond to the mood of the performer. The visual images produced can be compared with Disney's et al.'s *Fantasia* (1940), and associated with the artistic field of visual music, in which synesthetic animated visuals follow a musical structure. As discussed in our previous chapter *Holophonor: On the Future Technology of Visual Music*, the Holophonor can in many ways be considered as an example of the ideal visual music instrument. At once classically musical and capable of creating performances of a high artistic quality, the Holophonor can be

DOI: 10.4018/978-1-4666-7284-0.ch009

Copyright © 2015, IGI Global. Copying or distributing in print or electronic forms without written permission of IGI Global is prohibited.

picked up and played by anyone. While instantly accessible, a great deal of practice is required in order to become proficient and deliver virtuoso performances. Many features of the Holophonor are already demonstrated by existing visual music, and the wider sphere of associated audio-visual artworks and technologies. Nonetheless, there are currently no examples that combine these into a single, convenient, Holophonor-like instrument. We shall therefore proceed by discussing the technical feasibility of each of the main features of the Holophonor, allowing us to consider how these features could be implemented, and which areas require further research. Utilising existing approaches, a possible architecture is then proposed based around available technologies. Through the course of this discussion we will significantly draw upon approaches from the fields of HCI and affective computing, which we propose may provide solutions to some of the more futuristic aspects of the Holophonor design, such as ability for visual animations to respond to the mood of the performer.

TECHNOLOGICAL FEASIBILITY

In this section, the feasibility of the Holophonor is considered, based on an analysis of existing technologies and those in development or in early stages of research. This enables us to consider how a Holophonor-like device could be developed, and identify areas where further research may be required. Table 1 recapitulates the key features of the Holophonor.

The feasibility of these features will be considered in turn and where possible, they will be connected with existing technologies. In addition to technologies for creating sounds and visual projections, the nature of the Holophonor is such that it touches upon the integration of technologies with human emotion. This section therefore considers how proposed features of the Holophonor may be achieved using the approaches of affective computing. We also consider the HCI knowledge that exists, and the knowledge that needs to exist, to make the Holophonor successful.

Table 1. Key features of the Holophonor

Holophonor Feature	Description
Sounds	The Holophonor appears to be a reed instrument similar to an Oboe. The performer blows into the instrument and presses keys to produce a sound. The sounds produced encompass a range of traditional orchestral sounds and synthetic electroacoustic sounds.
Visuals	When melodies are performed on the Holophonor, visual images are produced. These are representational in quality, but can include surrealist or dream-like elements, similar to *Fantasia* (Disney et al., 1940). Morph transitions can occur between visual scenes.
Projection	Visual images are holographically projected in the space of performance. The projection is able to rescale to fit the size of the venue. In some instances, images can escape beyond the venue.
Emotionality	The sounds and visual images respond to the emotion of the performer. It is necessary for the performer to feel certain emotions in order to perform successfully with the instrument.
Portability	The device is portable and can be transported in an instrument case and played anywhere, similar to existing horns and reed instruments.
Accessibility	Anyone can attempt to play the Holophonor, but full mastery requires a lot practice. Virtuoso performance is possible.

Sounds

The sounds the Holophonor produces can be created using acoustic technologies, computer-based sound or a combination of these. Acoustic sound can be achieved using traditional reed-instrument design. Sound can be amplified if required using an in-built small-capsule condenser microphone. Additional digital signal processing could be applied using the acoustic signal as an input. Various effects such as reverberation, delay or spectral processes could be added.

Computer-based sound could be achieved using typical methods broadly associated with the field of electroacoustic music (Manning, 2002). For example, these could include various types of sound synthesis; additive, subtractive, FM, wavetable, granular or concatenative methods. Alternatively or additionally, triggering of pre-recorded sound samples may be used. Additional DSP could also be applied to these sounds.

The control of any computer-based sounds or DSP could occur digitally using digital MIDI or OSC signals from the reed and/or keys on the instrument, or through registering the emotion of the performer (further discussion below). Additional accelerometers, potentiometers or keys may provide further control over DSP processing or combined digital sounds. Various similar examples already exist, such as Kyle Evans' modified didgeridoo (Evans, 2009). Analysis of various low-level and high-level audio features (Mitrovic, Zeppelzauer & Breiteneder, 2010) may be used to provide control signals that affect additional digital sound processes. Any of these control signals could also be used to affect the visual material.

Visuals

The Holophonor projects visual material based on the performer's emotion and imagination. An idealised realisation of this might involve the automatic, real-time generation of animated materials based on the performer's imagination. Automatically generating these visuals based on brain activity might be possible through the use of brain-computer interfaces (BCI) for creative purposes (for example, Miranda, 2008), however further research is needed. We may also consider alternative methods for generating and controlling these visual images.

Digital animation techniques in both 2D and 3D are readily available, and would be appropriate means to generate the type of visuals produced by the Holophonor. While the Holophonor produces representational material, these materials contain non-realistic and imaginative elements, so computer animation may provide a suitable approach. Real-time rendering of visual material such as this is possible using existing technology. For example, video game engines and higher-specification computer graphics cards enable the real-time manipulation of 2D and 3D graphics, with increasing levels of sophistication. Video game engines such as *Unity3D* (Unity Technologies, 2013), or other visual tools such as Processing (Reas & Fry, 2001) could provide ways for real-time animations to be created for an instrument like the Holophonor.

It is likely that some pre-design of these materials may be required. This could be undertaken by the performer, or other collaborators. Animated sequences with scope for real-time variation could be stored in a library that is accessed according to the performance. This will be discussed in further detail later in the chapter.

Morphing transitions could occur between animated scenes by interpolating vector co-ordinates between animated scenes, or using other typical video transitions.

Projection

In order to provide the projection facilities of the Holophonor, various available technologies may be considered. There are some existing examples of holographic artworks (Gringrich, Renaud &

Emets, 2013), however we may also consider more typical 2D and 3D projection methods as possibilities, or immersive projection environments such as the previously discussed full-dome or CAVE systems.

Full-dome projection may provide a suitably immersive environment for Holophonor performances. Projection in a dome can be enhanced by the use of increasingly high pixel count display and projection systems, such as those that go beyond the currently emerging Ultra High Definition (UHD) 4k standard (Furuya, 2009). 8k full-dome projection, such as Sky Skan's *definiti* (2013) 8k system is already to be found within high-end, large capacity spaces, such as planetariums, but the acceleration of technology miniaturisation and affordability approximately in line with Moore's Law (1965) suggests that this is to be within reach of the consumer in the short-term future. It is the holographic element of the Holophonor that may be the main delay in its realisation in the medium to long term. It is also worth investigating projection systems that extend the projection area of existing full-dome, which provides a projection space that is hemispherical. More immersive projection for the Holophonor would ideally incorporate a full spherical projection, though difficulties naturally occur in projecting below the user or onto a floor.

Analogue holography is the traditional method to capture and generate holographic images. However, it requires highly controlled facilities to capture images, and it is expensive to manufacture high-quality holographic images. The elaborate and expensive equipment required when capturing images naturally led to the development of digital holography (Schnars & Jueptner, 2005). Although holographic imaging can produce moving sequences on printed materials, true holographic projections (of the type indicated by the Holophonor) are likely to be a long way into the future. Digital holograms often suffer from pixelation, breaking suspension of disbelief, and both analogue and digital holograms require accurate

positioning of a local light source to produce the synonymous depth and movement effects. This said then, alternative optical illusions such as Pepper's Ghost or Tomography might be solutions and have already been presented as such in several live music performance scenarios (Geere, 2010; BBC, 2012). It is therefore feasible to see a system evolving from these technologies that becomes adaptable to projection within an immersive environment, such as a full-dome.

Emotionality

The music and visuals produced by the Holophonor reflect the mood of the performer. Arguably this is already a feature of many musical instruments; in the hands of a skilled performer, many instruments are considered to achieve sophisticated expressions of mood. However it is also possible to consider the use of affective computing approaches, in order to automatically extract user emotion and translate it into digital signals. These signals could then be used to manipulate aspects of the graphics or sound. This may be considered particularly useful for generating the visual materials of the Holophonor, since the generation of animations that correspond to music and mood in real-time presents a substantial challenge.

In terms of performance, music and sound interaction, there is a body of existing knowledge on the topics of affective interaction with music and networked musical performance. For example, Janssen, van den Broek, and Westerink (2012) describe the development of an affective computing system that sets out to describe and model a relationship between mood and music. In particular, their work looks to enhance or achieve a desired emotional state, rather than produce a reflection as such. In this way, their work may be regarded as actively trying to induce an emotional response, rather than passively react or augment a current emotion, although this is acknowledged by Janssen *et al.* Their work to date involves participants listening to musical choices and tracking how sensor data responds, developing an intelligent model, using Kernel Density Estimates, based on this data, and evaluating the model in a series of scenarios. In terms of predicting the anticipated result, given a particular musical selection, their models were shown to be valid. As such, the argument may be made that if the processes are present to induce emotion, then there is a clear model that links emotional features to musical content. Limitations of the work, acknowledged by the authors, are primarily around the use of a single physiological measure (skin temperature) combined with subjective responses, and a small number of participants, though the study ran across a reasonable length of time.

In terms of integrating affective sensor data with sound, Winters and Wanderley (2013) describe a scenario in which the continuous sonification of emotion is considered. Whilst music may not always be a continuous sound, it is proposed that the perception of a musical performance, from the perspective of both performer and audience, is one of a continuous experience, for the finite period in which it exists. Their work particularly examines how concepts of emotional mapping, such as Russell's arousal/valence paradigm (1980), might be mapped to acoustic parameters. In particular, they report upon additional work where musical variations of a natural sound are manipulated. Broadly, their model controls volume and tempo parameters in response to arousal and harmonic and pitch factors are varied according to valence.

There is also a growing body of work by computer musicians exploring the use of biofeedback technology in the creation of sonic art (Ortiz et al. 2010). Devices such as Electroencephalography (EEG) headsets, Galvanic Skin Response (GSR) and Electrocardiograph (ECG) sensors can be used to provide data sources that reflect aspects of the user's condition. In our own *Psych Dome* project (Weinel et al., 2013), we begin to explore the use of dry sensor consumer-grade EEG as a means to provide automated control over an audio-visual

artwork using brainwaves, though much further work would be needed for this system to reflect the mood of the performer.

In principle approaches such as those discussed can be used to manipulate both the visual and sonic elements of a Holophonor instrument. The main challenges in this area are in effectively extracting data regarding emotion, and then finding suitable approaches for mapping it to trigger or affect sonic and visual materials. Further research in this area may enable us to achieve the described feature of the Holophonor, where visual material in particular relates to the emotion of the performer.

Portability

Portability of the main aspects of the Holophonor can be achieved. The instrument can be constructed as a typical horn-sized instrument. Available computational power is sufficient to provide the necessary digital processes in a small, portable device. Since amplified performances are commonplace, the use of mains electricity is unlikely to cause significant inconveniences, though it is likely that battery power may also be possible.

The main difficulty in achieving portability for the Holophonor is in providing the necessary projection facilities and biofeedback in a convenient manner. Some external equipment is likely to be required for creating immersive visual projections. Similarly, for any computer sounds, high quality monitoring may be required. Biofeedback is also likely to be an inconvenience. GSR and pulse sensors could be mounted on the device itself, which would be more convenient than (for example) medical grade EEG, which require contact fluids to be applied to the head, and a lengthy configuration process.

Accessibility

Futurama proposes that the Holophonor is incredibly difficult to play. On this particular point, we may wish to deviate slightly from the suggested design. In recent years, sonic artists and computer music researchers have succeeded in creating a wide variety of unique performance approaches and tools that have filled concerts with many interesting sounds and images. While these have contributed to computer music discourses both through associated articles and the works themselves, a consistent problem has been the inaccessibility of this type of artistic practice for wider spheres of non-specialists. With the exception of some community-based projects and workshops, published mobile apps, etcetera, the type of unique live computer music performances created with Max/MSP, Arduino, live instrument processing and/or laptops, tends to remain inaccessible for most people outside the field. Often those tools that are freely shared would be not easily be understood or used by others. The designers often lack the time and support to fully test applications for bugs and compatibility, or investigate their usability. Where schematics for devices or modifications have been made freely available as open source, they still require significant effort and expertise beyond that possessed by the average person unfamiliar with the field. We do not expect children learning pianos or guitars to be able to build the instrument before they play it, yet somehow it has become the norm for computer musicians to have to build their own instruments.

In the future we should hope to see widened accessibility of such real-time computer-based performance systems for all ages and backgrounds. Indeed, Rajmil Fischman makes an argument for this in his article *Back to the Parlour* (2011). For Fischman, gestural control methods may provide the most intuitive and accessible way for non-specialists to interact with computer-based musical instruments. We may also consider the automatic recognition of emotion through affective technologies, and usability testing as possible pathways to achieve more accessible devices. The proposed benefit of widened access to such instruments is to make computer music accessible as a means of performance for both amateurs and professionals, and to facilitate its use as a social activity for pleasure and for fun. A possible benefit is that collaborative, creative activity prepares us for co-operative work elsewhere in life, but moreover is enjoyable and culturally enriching. Collaboration could take place in local spaces, or across computer networks, on a potentially global scale.

While these instruments should be accessible in the first instance, they should also retain enough scope for learning and nuanced performance that virtuosity can eventually be obtained by some. Indeed one of the benefits of making the instrument available for a wider range of performers is that they may be able to dedicate themselves to performing new visual music with it in ways we cannot imagine. More effort can be spent on performing rather than instrument building. Though, perhaps scope will remain for customisation, modification and programming for those who wish to do so; the novice user may select preset patches that define the sounds and visual material that can be created, while the advanced user writes their own. Such modification may give scope for unique ways of combining audio and visual material.

Discussion

In general we see that the essential ingredients for the Holophonor are already in existence. In fact, we also already see some Holophonor-like examples (i.e. self-contained, interactive audio-visual instruments) that have been created, such as Grainstick (Leslie et al. 2010). There are some features of the Holophonor that may require further research to realise in the manner shown in *Futurama*, yet the fundamental system can be achieved with existing technology. Holophonor-like devices could be created now, adopting a range of synesthetic approaches to combine audio and video. The main requirement would be to bring together various aspects of those practices discussed in this piece, such that they can be performed by an individual on a single, portable device.

PROPOSED ARCHITECTURE

In the previous section we began to outline how various technologies could be interfaces in order to produce a Holophonor-like instrument. Some of the areas discussed would benefit from further research to improve effectiveness or convenience. Nonetheless, we find that most of the principle requirements are sufficient to develop a Holophonor-like instrument (where some adaptations are made to improve the feasibility of the building one with existing technologies). In this section we continue our discussion by reviewing the networking and data storage requirements of a Holophonor-like instrument, and propose a possible architecture.

Networking

Collaborative musical performance environments that allow (near) real-time interaction are not a new development. Early Internet-enabling technologies, particularly digital networking services such as ISDN, allowed musicians to compose and play together collaboratively despite being remote from one another (Liu et al. 1995; Jung et al. 2000; Kurtisi, Gu & Wolf 2006). Laterally, this drive has continued, with examples of projects such as BlockJam (Newton-Dunn Nakano & Gibson, 2003), which utilises physical devices with embedded software that can be networked; JamSpace a LAN based collaborative environment (Gurevich, 2006); the DIAMOUSES system of Alexandraki and Akoumianakis (2010) incorporates visual as well as audio streaming to support collaboration; recently, Fields (2012) reports upon a long-term case study of utilising networked music collaboration and the impacts not only on the practice of producing music but an analysis of the technology and changing creative practice.

Data Storage

Fundamentally, the Holophonor relies upon technologies that require data storage. Data communications and data storage requirements are largely all available at the time of writing, since the spread of optical and high speed wireless services has largely become commonplace. Similarly, data storage is relatively cheap and the advent of cloud storage permits easy of sharing of data to multiple parties.

Architecture

We now consider how the Holophonor could be built by considering its architectural properties. Although the Holophonor as depicted is a form of horn instrument, we propose that the user should be able to perform their music with a range of devices or interfaces to support accessibility and flexibility. The architecture is depicted in Figure 1 and is explained in further detail.

1. The user will interact with the Holophonor user interface in whatever way they wish, perhaps via a traditional musical instrument 'device' (instrument or human voice), or alternatively via more novel channels (e.g. gestures). Accessibility is critical, as a wider population as possible should be supported, facilitating usability for a range of abilities, ages, and prior musical performance experience.

2. Bio-sensors will enable aspects of mood and emotion to be sensed (for example EEG, heart rate, GSR, pupil dilation).

3. Real-time data from the user interface and bio-sensors will be processed by the context engine. The context engine is the central intelligence of the Holophonor. It will be responsible for interpreting the user data, for using this data to retrieve past experiences from the Holophonor database, and

Figure 1. Proposed holophonor architecture

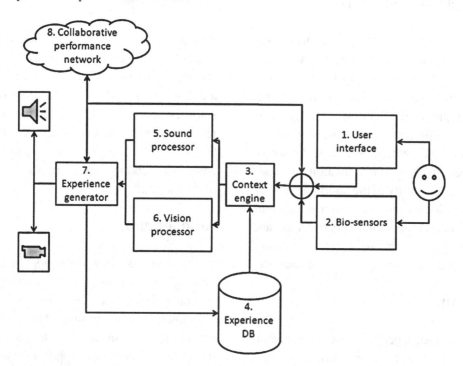

for sending packets of audio and visual data to the relevant media processors. The input to the context engine could be analogue audio signals or a digitized signal, such as MIDI. Clearly, a digital signal will be faster and easier to process. There will also be a requirement for the context engine to perform pattern recognition of musical motifs (as a form of multimedia database query explained in 4. below). This will again be easier to process with a MIDI signal, but there is also scope to research the feasibility of interpreting real-time analogue signals using intelligent and/or statistical approaches (e.g. neural networks, Bayesian classification, Gaussian mixtures).

4.   The experience database will store personalised representations that will be used to generate the user experience whilst playing the Holophonor. On initial training of the system, images, sounds etc. will be tagged

according to the user's views. For example, pictures of loved ones could be tagged with attributes such as 'love' and 'happy', whereas videos of adventure experiences could be tagged as 'joy', 'heart-racing'. Media objects in the database could also be tagged with musical motifs. For example, a certain pattern of notes could represent an individual person or thing. The experience database could be potentially very large, and hence could be (using current technology) situated as a cloud service (e.g. on social media such as Instagram). The database will also store previous Holophonor sessions (if desired by the user) so that future performances can generate similar and consistent experiences.

5.   The sound processor will essentially be responsible for taking the music data performed by the user, combined with any supporting sounds generated as a result of the context engine's experience database query.

6. The vision processor will work in a similar way. Combinations of real images from the database along with more abstract patterns (directly from the musical performance) will be prepared here for projection.

7. The experience generator will take the projected sound and vision performance and copy it into the experience database for possible permanent storage (if the user chooses to save it). It will also realise the performance for the user by interaction with the audio/visual system (using technology typical of today's game engines). Finally, quantifiable elements of the real-time experience as it is witnessed by the user (e.g. stroboscopic frequencies, musical beats per minute), will be fed back to the context engine to enable it to preserve the dynamics and stability of the overall performance.

8. The collaborative performance network will synchronize individual performances across a range of collaborative musicians when performing a piece together. Each individual performance will be merged into a holistic view, using visualisation techniques such as fish-eye views to personalise the individual experience.

CONCLUSION

In a previous chapter of ours titled, *Holophonor: On The Future Technology of Visual Music*, an extended discussion of visual music and associated works was provided. We have outlined the progression of visual music towards interactive systems that enable live control of synesthetic audio-visual material. This encompasses both academic strands of research and a large amount of work by artists in the popular sphere, all of which must be seen as valuable contributions. It was proposed that the Holophonor can in many ways be viewed as the ideal visual music performance instrument.

Many of the principle features of the Holophonor can be seen in existing practices and technologies of visual music, HCI and affective computing. Yet these have yet to be brought together into a single, accessible package. In this chapter we have identified the main features of the Holophonor and discussed their technological feasibility in relation to available technologies. In particular, we have also proposed that key features such as 'emotionality' may be provided by utilising biofeedback technologies and the approaches of affective computing. While our design inevitably adapts some aspects of the Holophonor from the portrayal given in *Futurama,* we have been able to retain most of the principle features in our proposed architecture.

Perhaps then, the main challenge is to enable a convergence of the existing technologies and approaches that have been used, to bring them together into discrete, accessible devices for a wider audience. This might be best accomplished through partnerships between the video games industry, academic research and VJs. As difficult as such arrangements can be to establish, the potential benefits for a truly accessible visual music instrument with unrestricted potential for expression and virtuosity, must be huge. As we enter into increasingly digital and globalised societies, such instruments could provide the methods of collaborative creative activity that have yet to be effectively realised through digital mediums. We can conceive of these performances between people in both real and virtual locations.

Beyond this, visual music at its core is really about playfulness with the universe we live in. In exploring patterns and links between audio and visual material, we make similar leaps to those when early man created cave paintings. One medium is connected with another; colours elicit sounds and ideas. We find and share new patterns of thinking and understanding through this, and we are able to enrich the spaces where we create this. Our world still consists of many caves, and cave networks. We can fill these with the harmony of colours, lights and sounds; the music of the spheres.

REFERENCES

Alexandraki, C., & Akoumianakis, D. (2010). Exploring new perspectives in network music performance: The diamouses framework. *Computer Music Journal*, *34*(2), 66–83.

BBC. (2012). Holograms won't replace live music performances. *Newsbeat*. Retrieved November 17, 2013 from: http://www.bbc.co.uk/newsbeat/18511859

Disney, W. (Producer), Sharpsteen, B. (Producer), Ferguson, N. (Director), Algar, J. (Director), Armstrong, S. (Director), Beebe, F. (Director),… Sharpsteen, B. (Director). (1940). *Fantasia* [Motion picture]. USA: Walt Disney Pictures.

Evans, K. (2009). *Electronically Modified Didgeridoo Kyle Evans* [Video]. Retrieved August 28, 2013 from: http://www.youtube.com/watch?v=d1VB1vA-UsI

Fields, K. (2012). Syneme: Live. *Organised Sound*, *17*(01), 86–95.

Fischman, R. (2011). Back to the Parlour. *Sonic Ideas/Ideas Sonicas*, *3*(2).

Furuya, M., Sterling, R., Bleha, W., & Inoue, Y. (2009). D-ILA® Full Resolution 8K Projector. In *Proceedings of SMPTE Conferences*, (pp. 1-9). Society of Motion Picture and Television Engineers.

Geere, D. (2010). 'Neurosonics Live' brings holograms to live music. *Wired*. Retrieved November 17, 2013 from: http://www.wired.co.uk/news/archive/2010-03/03/neurosonics-live-brings-holograms-to-live-music

Gringrich, O., Reaud, A., & Emets, E. (2013). KIMA – A Holographic Telepresence Environment Based on Cymatic Principles. *Leonardo*, *46*(4).

Groening, M. (Writer), Cohen, D.X. (Writer), Kaplan, E. (Writer), & Avanzino, P. (Director). (2001). Parasites Lost [Television series episode]. In Cohen, D. (Executive producer), & Groening, M. (Executive producer) Futurama. USA: 20th Century Fox Television.

Groening, M. (Writer), Cohen, D.X. (Writer), Keeler, K. (Writer), & Haaland, B. (Director). (2001). The Devil's Hands are Idle Playthings [Television series episode]. In Cohen, D. (Executive producer), & Groening, M (Executive producer) Futurama. USA: 20th Century Fox Television.

Gurevich, M. (2006). JamSpace: designing a collaborative networked music space for novices. In *Proceedings of the 2006 conference on New interfaces for musical expression*, (pp. 118-123). IRCAM—Centre Pompidou.

Janssen, J. H., van den Broek, E. L., & Westerink, J. H. (2012). Tune in to your emotions: A robust personalized affective music player. *User Modeling and User-Adapted Interaction*, *22*(3), 255–279.

Jung, B., Hwang, J., Lee, S., Kim, G. J., & Kim, H. (2000). Incorporating co-presence in distributed virtual music environment. In *Proceedings of the ACM Symposium on Virtual Reality Software and Technology*, (pp. 206-211). ACM.

Kurtisi, Z., Gu, X., & Wolf, L. (2006). Enabling network-centric music performance in wide-area networks. *Communications of the ACM*, *49*(11), 52–54.

Leslie, G., Schwarz, D., Warusfel, O., Bevilacqua, F., Zamborlin, B., Jodlowski, P., & Schnell, N. (2010). Grainstick: A Collaborative, Interactive Sound Installation. In *Proceedings of the International Computer Music Conference (ICMC) 2010*. Retrieved August 28, 2013 from: http://articles.ircam.fr/textes/Leslie10a/index.pdf

Liu, J. G., Liu, J. C., Chen, Y. G., & Yuang, M. C. (1995). DMTS: A distributed multimedia teleworking system. In *Proceedings of Local Computer Networks*, (pp. 326-335). IEEE.

Manning, P. (2002). *Electronic & Computer Music*. Oxford University Press.

Miranda, E., Durrant, S., & Anders, T. (2008). Toward Brain-Computer Music Interfaces: Progress and Challenges. In *Proceedings of the International Symposium on Applied Sciences in Biomedical and Communication Technologies (ISABEL2008)*. Aalborg, Denmark: ISABEL.

Mitrovic, D., Zeppelzauer, M., & Breitender, C. (2010). Features for Content-Based Audio Retrieval. *Advances in Computers: Improving the Web, 78*.

Moore, G.E. (1965, April 19). Cramming more components onto integrated circuits. *Electronics, 38*(8).

Newton-Dunn, H., Nakano, H., & Gibson, J. (2003, May). Block jam: a tangible interface for interactive music. In *Proceedings of the 2003 conference on New interfaces for musical expression*, (pp. 170-177). National University of Singapore.

Ortiz, M., Coghlan, N., Jaimovich, J., & Knapp, B. (2010). *Biosignal-drive Art: Beyond biofeedback. Sonic Ideas/Ideas Sonicas, 3(2)*.

Reas, C., & Fry, C. (2013). *Processing* [Programming language]. Academic Press.

Russell, J. A. (1980). A circumplex model of affect. *Journal of Personality and Social Psychology, 39*(6), 1161–1178.

Schnars, U., & Jueptner, W. (2005). *Digital holography*. Springer Berlin Heidelberg.

Sky-Skan. (2013). *Definiti Theaters Powered by DigitalSky 2 | Sky-Skan*. Retrieved November 16, 2013 from: http://www.skyskan.com/definiti

Unity Technologies. (2013). *Unity3D* [video game engine]. Author.

Weinel, J., Cunningham, S., Roberts, N., Roberts, S., & Griffiths, D. (2013). *Psych Dome* [Video installation]. Retrieved August 27 2013 from: https://vimeo.com/78153713

Winters, R. M., & Wanderley, M. M. (2013). Sonification of Emotion: Strategies for Continuous Display of Arousal and Valence. In *Proceedings of the 3rd International Conference on Music & Emotion (ICME3)*. University of Jyväskylä, Department of Music.

KEY TERMS AND DEFINITIONS

Affective Computing: Describes computer systems which recognise or exhibit properties of human emotion.

CAVE: A CAVE (Cave Automatic Virtual Environment) is a virtual reality environment in which immersion is enhanced through projection on multiple walls, often in combination with stereoscopic technology.

Electroacoustic Music: A type of 20th Century art music composed for concerts utilising loudspeakers.

Full-Dome: An immersive environment within a dome shaped structure, which uses a parabolic mirror to project on to the inside of the dome ceiling.

Holophonor: A fictional audio-visual instrument from the TV show *Futurama*. The instrument is similar to an oboe, and projects holographic visual images that correspond to the musical performance when played.

Visual Music: A type of artistic practice that involves the arrangement of visual material into music-like structures.

VJ Performance: A type of multimedia performance usually found in nightclubs, in which a VJ (visual jockey) combines video loops or computer graphics to accompany music.

Chapter 10
Smart Home Energy Management

David Lillis
University College Dublin, Ireland

Conor Muldoon
University College Dublin, Ireland

Tadhg O'Sullivan
University College Dublin, Ireland

Michael J. O'Grady
University College Dublin, Ireland

Thomas Holz
University College Dublin, Ireland

Gregory M. P. O'Hare
University College Dublin, Ireland

ABSTRACT

Autonomically managing energy within the home is a formidable challenge, as any solution needs to interoperate with a decidedly heterogeneous network of sensors and appliances, not just in terms of technologies and protocols but also by managing smart as well as "dumb" appliances. Furthermore, as studies have shown that simply providing energy usage feedback to homeowners is inadequate in realising long-term behavioural change, autonomic energy management has the potential to deliver concrete and lasting energy savings without the need for user interventions. However, this necessitates that such interventions be performed in an intelligent and context-aware fashion, all the while taking into account system as well as user constraints and preferences. Thus, this chapter proposes the augmentation of home area networks with autonomic computing capabilities. Such networks seek to support opportunistic decision-making pertaining to the effective energy management within the home by seamlessly integrating a range of off-the-shelf sensor technologies with a software infrastructure for deliberation, activation, and visualisation.

INTRODUCTION

The home area network (HAN) market is set to reach $3 billion by 2014, with 30 million households containing nearly 50 million smart home and energy management devices (On World, 2010). However, this opportunity can only be availed of

if real and tangible energy savings are achieved. In fact, over 80% of household owners are willing to pay for energy management services if they achieve savings of 30% or more (ON World, 2010).

Achieving savings of such a magnitude is a challenging problem. As numerous studies have shown, merely displaying energy consumption

DOI: 10.4018/978-1-4666-7284-0.ch010

Copyright © 2015, IGI Global. Copying or distributing in print or electronic forms without written permission of IGI Global is prohibited.

leads only to minimal savings (e.g. McKerracher & Torriti, 2012). Incentives, usually in the form of monetary savings, can have some effect on usage (Faruqui et al., 2009; Lui et al., 2010), but this may still not lead to lasting behavioural change, with users regressing to old consumption patterns over the course of several months (Hazas et al., 2011; Kluckner et al., 2013). Autonomically and intelligently managing energy consumption in the home, on the other hand, has the potential to deliver energy savings that are completely independent of occupant behaviour and, as such, are not susceptible to the weaknesses outlined above.

To enable autonomic energy management, there is a need for a pervasive sensing and networking configuration within the home. This configuration, referred to as an Autonomic Home Area Network Infrastructure (AUTHENTIC), must be capable of supporting opportunistic decision-making pertaining to residential energy management by seamlessly and effortlessly integrating several key enabling technologies. These include HAN technologies, physical sensing devices and a mechanism for sensing contextual data outside the home. Going forward, it will also be essential to provide a mechanism for integration with the smart grid.

The aim of this chapter is to present the design and implementation of the AUTHENTIC architecture. It first describes the overall system architecture, along with brief discussions of its constituent modules and their functionalities. Following this, particular focus is paid to the SIXTH middleware, which is a fundamental component of the system, acting as a conduit for sensor data and actuation commands so as to become the central hub of the overall architecture. The reasoning module of the system is based on the multi-agent paradigm and is discussed in detail in the next section. The effectiveness of the system is then illustrated via a simple use case scenario. A summary of related approaches to the problem is then outlined, before finally presenting conclusions and some ideas for further work.

SYSTEM ARCHITECTURE

The AUTHENTIC system follows a component-based software engineering approach adhering to the OSGi framework and is made up of five different modules (see also Figure 1):

- The communications module, which provides a unified interface to all sensors and actuators in the HAN;
- The semantic module, which infers situational context from low-level sensor data;
- The deductive module, which realises intelligent decision-making using the SIXTH middleware together with a multi-agent systems approach;
- The appliance scheduling module, which employs a constraint-based reasoning engine to schedule appliances based on different user preferences;
- The AUTHENTIC graphical user interface (GUI), which allows the occupant to interact with all facets of the system.

The following sections provide an overview over each of these modules, before a more in-depth look is taken at some of the enabling technologies of the deductive component, which is the focus of this paper.

Communications Module

The purpose of the communications module is to hide the inherent heterogeneity of the HAN infrastructure and to provide a unified interface to the other components of the architecture. It uses the publish/subscribe pattern to allow components to register their interest in device messages. When devices (such as appliances, actuators or sensors) are added to the network, or already existing devices sense or actuate, the communications module triggers an event message that is translated into a system-wide common format (JSON) and sent to subscribed components. All requests (e.g. com-

Figure 1. AUTHENTIC system architecture

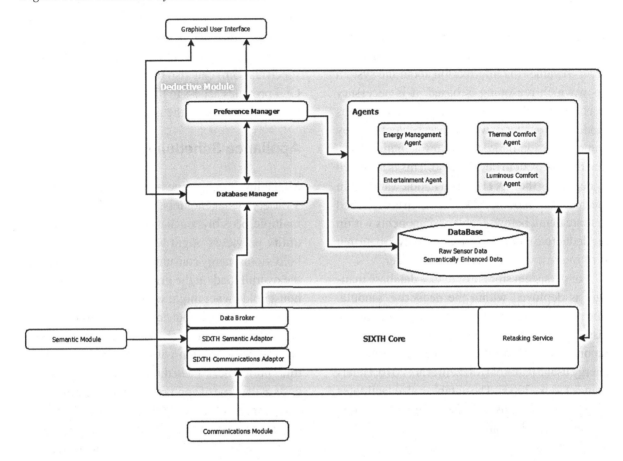

mand and get/set state variables) issued to devices within the HAN are similarly translated from JSON into the native format and protocol of the target device. The module currently supports communication via WiFi, Bluetooth, ZigBee, 6LoWPAN and X10. The use of JSON as a common message format means that this communications module can operate in a distributed fashion, for example in situations where remote monitoring of the HAN is desired.

Semantic Module

The semantic reasoning module aims to infer contextual information by classifying low-level sensor data gathered from the communications layer and to transform said information into a machine-readable format to be used by the deductive module. The Web Ontology Language (OWL) (McGuinness & Van Harmelen, 2004) is used to automate logical reasoning in order to infer new contextual knowledge from the information gathered. Examples of context inference include whether a room is occupied (e.g. based on data from a passive infrared sensor) or what activity an inhabitant is currently engaged in (e.g. that the inhabitant is making tea based on the kettle being switched on). Once an inference has been made, it is then passed on to the semantic adaptor in the deductive module.

Deductive Module

The deductive module is primarily concerned with decision-making and data management. In order to gather the information about the system upon which reasoning is based, it is necessary to connect to the semantic and communications modules, the latter of which necessitates two-way communication in order to allow actuation commands to be sent to devices also. This is achieved by deploying the SIXTH sensor middleware within the deductive module. SIXTH, which is described in more detail below, enables components within the deductive module to subscribe only to data that is of interest via the SIXTH data broker.

For persistent storage of data, a database manager is deployed within the deductive module. The recorded data is currently used for providing historical usage accounts (e.g. for energy usage reports) but can in future enable the learning of energy usage patterns (Ruzzelli et al., 2010; Heierman & Cook, 2003). The database also facilitates the storage of persistent user preferences, which are set and made available via a preference manager component.

The key decision-making component within the architecture is a multi-agent system based on Agent Factory Micro Edition (AFME) (Muldoon et al., 2006; O'Hare et al., 2012b). Agents are responsible for particular aspects of home management (e.g. adjusting heating or light settings) and do so by combining data received through the SIXTH middleware with user preferences that are set via the user interface. The multi-agent reasoning aspect of the architecture is described in more detail below.

Graphical User Interface

The AUTHENTIC graphical user interface is an application (currently developed for Android smartphones and tablets) that allows users to interact with all aspects of the HAN. Through the GUI, users can set or alter their preferences, such

as temperature levels or light levels. Current and historical data associated with devices within the HAN (e.g. the current energy usage of a specific appliance or the overall energy used within a specific room) can also be reviewed. Finally, the GUI provides access to the appliance scheduling feature described in the next section.

Appliance Scheduling

Managing energy usage within the home involves a variety of stakeholders, each of which can have multiple, possibly conflicting, goals. For example, utility providers might want to reduce a household's total energy consumption in order to balance the overall load on the grid. On the other hand, a household owner might want to minimise overall energy cost but without compromising comfort in the home. Appliance scheduling aims to optimise how devices function within the HAN based on time preferences (scheduling windows), energy costs at the time of appliance usage and the energy consumption of schedulable appliances. Users are provided, through the GUI, with detailed schedules for all appliances with the option of overriding the schedules at their own discretion. The primary purpose of said schedules is to ensure that appliances operate in an efficient manner with regard to energy usage and cost while staying within the constraints set by the user.

SIXTH Middleware

SIXTH is a Java-based sensor middleware that is capable of sourcing data from a variety of sources (O'Hare et al., 2012a). This incorporates both physical sensing apparatus and also other programmatically-accessible data sources (accessed via cyber-sensors). SIXTH features an adaptor abstraction that allows sources to be accessed in a consistent manner. Applications running on SIXTH can access this data in a source-agnostic fashion, while also gaining the ability to actuate sensing devices through a retasking service. This allows devices to be enabled or disabled, or for their behaviour to be changed (e.g. to change the sensing frequency).

For the purposes of the AUTHENTIC architecture, a number of adaptors were developed in order to interact with the various architectural components of the system (as outlined in Figure 1). These include: a communications adaptor (to interact with physical devices) and a semantic adaptor (to gain semantically-enhanced data from the semantic module). Both adaptors are outlined in the following sections.

Communications Adaptor

The communications adaptor acts as the gateway between the SIXTH middleware and the communications module. This adaptor allows sensor and status data to be injected into the architecture in a consistent manner. It also allows devices to be actuated through a uniform interface that is agnostic of device type or the underlying communications protocols used. This is done through the SIXTH retasking service. In a typical SIXTH deployment (e.g. those envisaged in Carr et al., 2012; O'Grady et al., 2013), a separate SIXTH adaptor is developed for each type of device desired. However, the architecture illustrated in Figure 1 is intended to demonstrate that the additional features of SIXTH (e.g. the data broker, described below) are equally applicable when some existing effort has been invested in developing a module that is capable of interacting with devices.

In the present architecture, the communications module exposes a number of APIs relating to HAN devices and sensors using a variety of communications protocols. In addition to allowing agents and other components to invoke these APIs, the communications adaptor also adds a level of abstraction to facilitate the reasoning process. For example, one commonly-used home automation device is a dimmer switch. Dimmer switches based on the X10 protocol are typically one-way devices, in that they can receive actuation commands but do not report on their own status. An additional challenge is that commands are available to increase or reduce the light intensity level by a set delta amount, rather than setting the light to a particular level (using *bright* and *dim* commands respectively). Thus in order to set lights to a specific desired level, it is necessary to record the current light level in software, since the device cannot report its current level. The communications adaptor provides an abstraction that allows agents (or other applications) to change light levels to specific values, translating these to the appropriate *bright* or *dim* commands, based on previously recorded light levels, to pass to the communications module.

Semantic Adaptor

The semantic adaptor offers a service similar to the communications adaptor, feeding data from the semantic layer through the SIXTH middleware. This also allows the agents and other applications to gain access to semantic data by registering their interest with the data broker. Unlike the communications adaptor, this is a one-way process, since no additional configuration or retasking of the semantic module is required.

Data Broker

The data broker is the conduit through which data is routed through the SIXTH middleware. All data from the communications and semantic adaptors are sent via the SIXTH core to the data broker for further dissemination. The task of the data broker is to forward only relevant data to interested parties, rather than flooding the system with superfluous and irrelevant data notifications.

Rather than subscribing to a type of message, SIXTH supports the registration of queries with the data broker through a simple Java interface. The registration of a query is associated with the component that created it, so that data received by the data broker that is a match to any registered queries is forwarded to the component associated with a particular query. There is no restriction to the number of queries that an individual component may register.

For example, a heating agent may register a query whereby it receives a notification only if a room's temperature falls below (or exceeds) a threshold temperature, in which case it can switch the heating on (or off). Under the simpler publish/subscribe mechanism, the agent would get constant updates from the room's temperature sensor rather than only when it is actually relevant to the agent's decision-making process.

This approach ensures the extensibility of the SIXTH middleware, allowing a diverse range of applications to be deployed on the HAN. Within the architecture outlined in Figure 1, the database manager registers to receive all data flowing through the system so that it can be recorded. Agents within the deliberative module can register to receive only data that is relevant to their particular tasks. Further applications that reside outside the architecture itself are facilitated in the same way.

Database Manager

A MySQL database is used to store information relevant to the HAN. This includes descriptions of all devices and appliances in the network, any data associated with said devices and appliances (e.g. location, sensor readings, state), semantic information and user preferences set through the GUI. The database manager is an OSGi service that acts as a database front-end for a number of components within the HAN that require database access.

One of the more interesting features of the database manager from a user's perspective is the ability to provide dynamic real-time and historical data from devices within the HAN. Users can specify devices they wish to monitor and the relevant information is extracted from the HAN database (e.g. device type, measurement type,

measured value and measurement timestamp). This is then displayed in a dynamic (in the case of real-time data) or static graph, as illustrated in Figure 2. Through the AUTHENTIC GUI, users can also request an energy report, which is also provided by the database manager. It presents the user with the energy usage and cost of devices within the system between time periods specified by the user. Both of these features allow users to better understand how energy is being used within their home environment and better manage both their energy consumption and energy cost (Eßer, Kamper, Franke, Möst, & Rentz, 2007).

Multi-Agent Reasoning

The multi-agent reasoning functionality with the HAN has been implemented using the Agent Factory Micro Edition (AFME) agent platform. AFME is a minimised-footprint intelligent agent platform based on the Agent Factory agent development framework (Collier et al. 2003), but designed for use with the Java Micro Edition (JME) Constrained Limited Device Configuration (CLDC). Although, primarily intended for highly constrained devices, applications developed for JME CLDC can also be used on desktop machines running Java Standard or Enterprise Edition. The agents developed for the HAN, at present, are deployed on the HAN Gateway, but it is envisaged that some of these will in future be deployed directly on the sensor or actuation devices to enable inter-device collaboration.

AFME is concerned with the development of computationally reflective agents. Computational reflection is a technique that enables a system to maintain meta-information about itself and to use this information to determine its behaviour. In the agent community parlance, this meta-information is commonly referred to as an agent's belief set or an agent's model of the world. Many intelligent agent platforms, including AFME, draw from folk psychological concepts, such as those identified by the philosopher Daniel Dennett (Dennett,

Figure 2. Dynamic sensor graphing

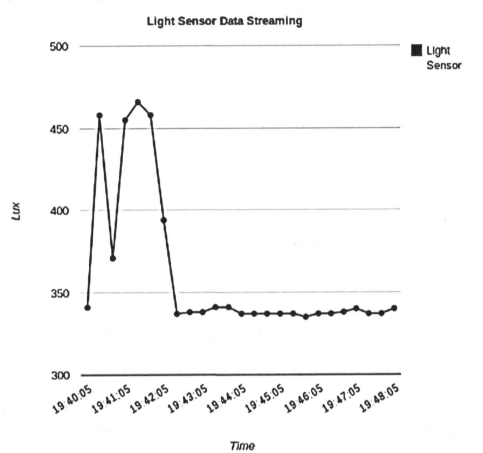

With the design stance, we assume that the entity in question has been designed for a particular purpose and our predictions are based on the idea that the entity will behave as designed. When someone turns on an electric fan, they predict that it will behave in a certain manner i.e. the fan will cool down the room. They do not need to know anything about the physical constitution of the fan to make the prediction. Predictions made from the design stance are based on two assumptions that the entity is designed for the purpose that the user thinks it to be designed for and that it will perform as designed without malfunctioning. This does not mean that the design stance is always used for entities that have been designed. The physical stance could be used to predict what would happen to the fan if it were knocked onto the floor or if it malfunctioned, but in most cases there is no need to go to a lower level of granularity.

1987). Specifically, those types of agent platforms employ the notion of the intentional stance as a tool for modelling complex systems through the attribution of mental attitudes, such as beliefs and goals, to agents so as to explain and predict behaviour. According to Dennett, there are three different strategies we use when confronted with an object or system, namely the physical stance, the design stance, and the intentional stance.

To predict the behaviour of an entity according to the physical stance, we use information about its physical constitution along with information about the laws of physics. The physical stance, for example, is employed when we predict the path of a ball in flight.

We can often improve our predictions of the design stance by adopting the intentional stance. When making predictions from this stance, we interpret the behaviour of an entity by treating it as a rational agent whose behaviour is governed by mental attitudes. The intentional stance is adopted where it is useful to do so. This is often the case in situations whereby we do not fully understand the design of the system, for example, when considering living organisms. It is less useful when we do understand the inner workings of a particular system. Suppose, for instance, we apply the intentional stance to a doorbell, i.e. we imagine that it is a rational agent that reasons about its beliefs and desires and intends to alert us when someone is at the door. This is not particularly useful because we can understand the functionality of a doorbell in simpler physical or mechanical terms. In contrast, suppose we wish to explain or predict the behaviour of a person or complex computer system. In such cases, it is necessary to form a higher level of abstraction if we do not fully understand their inner workings or design. The intentional stance can be applied to anything, but it is more practical to use when it leads to simpler descriptions than would otherwise be available.

The behaviour of agents in AFME is represented using declarative antecedent-consequence rules that determine the conditions under which commitments are adopted and actions are performed. To facilitate this, the conditions are matched against belief sets (meta-information maintained by agents) at periodic points throughout execution.

The HAN multi-agent architecture comprises a set of agents, a set of actuators, a set of perceptors, and the HAN service, which is a class that enables agents to interact with the SIXTH middleware. At present, within the HAN, there are six agents: the Luminosity Comfort Agent, the Thermal Comfort Agent, the Security Agent, the Entertainment Agent, the Energy Management Agent, and the Schedule Agent. The Thermal Comfort Agent

ensures that temperature levels in the room match the user preferences. The Luminosity Comfort Agent acts in a similar manner, but with regard to light. The Security Agent informs the user when a security event is triggered, while the Entertainment Agent controls the application behaviour when the user is sitting down and watching television. The Energy Management Agent proactively heats water in anticipation of user behaviour, while the Schedule Agent informs the user when water has been wasted and asks the user to change their scheduling preferences.

Perceptors were developed to enable agents to receive information in relation to sensor data, user preferences, deductions arising from the semantic module, and the user's schedule. This information is obtained through the AUTHENTIC service, which is a SIXTH receiver that registers with the SIXTH data broker and preference manager when the application begins to operate. Actuators were developed to enable agents to send commands to control devices in the HAN. The actuators also use the AUTHENTIC service in delivering this functionality. In particular, the actuators make use of the SIXTH retasking service.

Use Case Scenario

In order to demonstrate the functionality of the HAN, the system was deployed in a physical environment and a use case scenario was envisioned to illustrate the effectiveness of the HAN system in regards to internal stimuli. A number of appliances, sensors and actuators were deployed in room (see Figure 3) in order to simulate a living room.

When an individual enters the room, the passive infrared (PIR) sensor fires and an occupancy message is sent to the deductive module. The middleware then retrieves the user-set light and temperature levels from the preference manager. The lights in the room are turned on and set to the preferred level. If the current temperature of the room is below the user's preferred level, the heat-

Figure 3. Sensors involved in the use case scenario: (1) HAN, (2) PIR sensor, (3) temperature & luminescence sensor, (4) radiator, (5) smart TV with smart plug, (6) couch with pressure sensor, (7) lamp with dimmer switch and (8) window with contact sensor

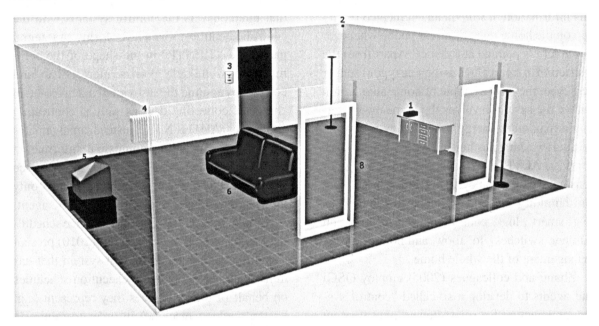

ing is also turned on until the room temperature reaches said level. If the heating is turned on, the user is notified of this through the GUI.

If the user sits on the couch, the pressure sensor sends a message through the communications module and the smart TV is turned on. At the same time, the lights in the room are dimmed to the user's preferred level for this activity. If the user stands, the smart TV turns off and the lights return to their previous luminescence levels.

When the window in the room is opened or closed, the contact sensor fires and sends a stated changed message through the communications module to the deductive module. If the state of the sensor is open then the user is notified through the GUI that the window has been opened.

RELATED WORK

Current HAN automation research is often limited to one type of technology, most often ZigBee or WiFi (e.g. Gill et al., 2009; Han & Lim, 2010), or power line communication (Cook et al., 2006, Son et al., 2010). However, as Parikh and colleagues (2010, see also Güngör et al. 2011) note, different technologies offer different benefits and drawbacks. Therefore, heterogeneity must be assumed to be inherent to any HAN, which is why AUTHENTIC was deliberately designed to handle a multitude of technologies, protocols and data formats by abstracting from these details and providing a unified interface to higher-level services.

Furthermore, most research on home energy management is focused on providing feedback about energy usage to consumers rather than proactively managing energy consumption. Jahn and colleagues (2010), for example, developed a smart home system on top of the OSGi-based Hydra middleware (Eisenhauer et al., 2010). Similar to the communications module in AUTHENTIC, Hydra provides a unified interface to heterogeneous networks of embedded devices irrespective of communication protocol. The developed system harnesses smart plugs to measure energy consumption on a per-device basis and displays this information *in situ* via an augmented reality app on the home owner's smart phone whenever its camera is pointed at a device. Apart from the restriction to smart plugs as the sole type of sensor deployed, the only example of home automation within the system involves the home owner setting a maximum energy price, below which the (virtual) washing machine is switched on. In stark contrast, AUTHENTIC incorporates a range of sensors (e.g. occupancy, temperature, luminosity and humidity sensors) and controllable devices (e.g. smart plugs, controllable thermostats and dimmer switches) to allow autonomic energy management of the whole home.

Zhang and colleagues (2005) employ OSGi and agents to develop a so-called "control system architecture for smart homes", but treat an individual home as the smallest unit of interest within the wider smart grid rather than actually specifying the internal operation an individual smart home. Further, Zhang and colleagues assert that "[t]he Home Gateway should be designed to have a high availability and deliver services with a specified level of determinism. These requirements necessitate remote management and monitoring Home Gateway services and home devices." AUTHENTIC, instead, puts full control of the internal HAN management in the hands of the user. All data remains local and all autonomic decision-making is carried out in line with user-specified preferences and constraints. We believe this degree of user control to be vital in alleviating legitimate privacy concerns and engender trust within the user (Lui et al., 2010; Krishnamurti et al., 2011).

Zhao and colleagues (2010) present a conceptual framework for energy management in both residential and commercial buildings, which also takes a multi-agent approach. However, while their proposed framework shows obvious parallels to the AUTHENTIC architecture, it also takes only

a very high-level approach to the problem, for example by assuming "[a]n underlying layer of communication infrastructure [...] to be in place that interconnects the control systems with the controlled entities." This layer forms an integral part of AUTHENTIC in the shape of the communications module. Furthermore, Zhao and colleagues assume the individual agents to be in charge of collecting data as well as controlling appliances. AUTHENTIC, instead, amalgamates all the data, including contextual information provided by the semantic module, in one place (the SIXTH data broker) and then disperses only information directly relevant to a specific agent.

Similar to AUTHENTIC's appliance scheduling facility, Abras and colleagues (2010) present a multi-agent home automation system that has individual agents negotiate execution schedules on behalf of the appliances they represent (e.g. heater, washing machine) in order to minimise overall energy consumption. Agents take into account predicted power consumption as well as user comfort and are mapped one to one onto an appliance. By contrast, scheduling of appliances in AUTHENTIC is handled by a constraint-based reasoning system, whereas agents, rather than controlling access to a singular appliance, deliver services that include potentially multiple appliances and, more importantly, are based on intelligent decisions borne out of sensor data gathered from within and outside the home. This approach also allows for the easy integration of additional services not related to energy management but still dependent on the HAN infrastructure (e.g. security, assisted living and entertainment).

Closest to the spirit of AUTHENTIC is probably MavHome (Cook et al., 2006), an agent-based smart home. MavHome exhibits a similar architecture to AUTHENTIC, with a decision layer (the equivalent of the deductive module), an information layer (semantic module), a communication layer (communications module) and a physical layer (home entities). However, rather than constituting an overall architecture for the system, every agent in MavHome is realised as an entity consisting of these four layers. The physical layer, corresponding to the perceptors and actuators in an AFME agent, represents physical sensors and appliances as well as potentially other agents. The communications layer is responsible for connecting the agent's higher levels to the physical layers, while the information layer generates contextual knowledge from raw sensor data. The decision layer, finally, selects which actions to perform based on this knowledge.

Separating these layers into distinct individual modules, rather than instantiating them on every agent deployed in the system, allows agents in AUTHENTIC to gather information from multiple sensor sources in a centralised fashion through the SIXTH data broker and its query interface, thereby minimising the amount of information each agent has to process. Furthermore, abstracting communication technologies through a dedicated module implies that adding a new protocol involves only an update to the one module rather than every single agent. Likewise, devices added to the system, as well as inferences added to the semantic module, are automatically available to all agents, ensuring AUTHENTIC's extensibility.

In summary, while the constituent technologies and approaches of the AUTHENTIC system might have been evident in the prior literature, this project has succeeded in delivering a complete and integrated solution that is uniquely adapted to the delivering autonomic intelligent energy control in a smart home environment.

CONCLUSION

Achieving effective energy management within the home is an objective shared by home occupants and government agencies alike. How best to meet this objective is still open to question, however. The approach proposed in this chapter advocates the augmentation of HAN technologies with a physical sensing infrastructure. Such an infrastructure is low-cost, as it harnesses off-the shelf components and can avail itself of, and co-exist, with a pre-existing HAN. Though smart grid technologies are in their infancy in terms of consumer adoption, harnessing any services enabled by such grids is essential going forward.

Many challenges must be overcome before homeowners will adopt such technologies at mass scale. These are not confined solely to system issues; rather those of privacy, security and trust must also be addressed. Introducing systems, such as those envisaged by AUTHENTIC, radically challenge perceptions and expectations of how energy management is delivered and experienced within the home. Should these be perceived in a negative fashion, adoption will be slower and insufficient. Many efforts to date have been technology-centric. If effective energy management within homes is to be realised, a more human-centric approach must be enabled, and delivered.

FUTURE WORK

One of the primary aims of the AUTHENTIC project going forward is to enable integration with the smart grid, for example, to allow agents to intelligently negotiate tariffs with utility providers in order to feed micro-generated power into the grid, or to adapt HAN-internal consumption to enable utility providers to balance load and reduce peak usage over a large number of customers (Niyato et al., 2011; Lui et al., 2010).

With future plans of integrating machine learning technologies into the current system, the HAN will not only be able to react via a set of preconceived rules but also to learn based on users' activities (Ruzzelli et al., 2010; Heierman & Cook, 2003). It is hoped that this added layer of intelligence will be of great benefit to future users of the system.

Within the AUTHENTIC project, the HAN is viewed as a key enabling technology that should be able to accommodate the coexistence of multiple applications. These may consist of a variety of services, for example, ambient assisted living (Korhonen et al., 2013), home security and home entertainment (Messer et al., 2006), alongside the presented energy management functions.

AUTHENTIC thus seeks to future-proof such requirements within its design by framing it within the key drivers of cost, ease of deployment, ease of use, adherence to standards and the need for it to be an ambient technology offering.

ACKNOWLEDGMENT

The support of Enterprise Ireland under grant TC20121002A is gratefully acknowledged. In addition this work is supported by Science Foundation Ireland under grant 07/CE/11147.

REFERENCES

Abras, S., Ploix, S., Pesty, S., & Jacomino, M. (2008). *A multi-agent home automation system for power management. In Informatics in Control Automation and Robotics* (pp. 59–68). Springer.

Carr, D., O'Grady, M. J., O'Hare, G. M., & Collier, R. (2013). *SIXTH: A Middleware for Supporting Ubiquitous Sensing in Personal Health Monitoring. In Wireless Mobile Communication and Healthcare* (pp. 421–428). Springer.

Choi, T.-S., Ko, K.-R., Park, S.-C., Jang, Y.-S., Yoon, Y.-T., & Im, S.-K. (2009). *Analysis of energy savings using smart metering system and IHD (in-home display).* Paper presented at the Transmission & Distribution Conference & Exposition: Asia and Pacific. New York, NY.

Collier, R., O'Hare, G., Lowen, T., & Rooney, C. (2003). *Beyond prototyping in the factory of agents. In Multi-Agent Systems and Applications III* (pp. 383–393). Springer.

Cook, D. J., Youngblood, M., & Das, S. K. (2006). *A multi-agent approach to controlling a smart environment. In Designing smart homes* (pp. 165–182). Springer.

Dennett, D. C. (1987). *The intentional stance.* The MIT Press.

Eisenhauer, M., Rosengren, P., & Antolin, P. (2010). *Hydra: A development platform for integrating wireless devices and sensors into ambient intelligence systems. In The Internet of Things* (pp. 367–373). Springer.

Eßer, A., Kamper, A., Franke, M., Möst, D., & Rentz, O. (2007). *Scheduling of electrical household appliances with price signals. In Operations Research Proceedings 2006* (pp. 253–258). Springer.

Faruqui, A., Sergici, S., & Sharif, A. (2010). The impact of informational feedback on energy consumption—A survey of the experimental evidence. *Energy, 35*(4), 1598–1608.

Gill, K., Yang, S.-H., Yao, F., & Lu, X. (2009). A ZigBee-based home automation system. *IEEE Transactions on* Consumer Electronics, *55*(2), 422–430.

Gungor, V. C., Sahin, D., Kocak, T., Ergut, S., Buccella, C., Cecati, C., & Hancke, G. P. (2011). Smart grid technologies: communication technologies and standards. *IEEE Transactions on Industrial Informatics, 7*(4), 529-539.

Han, D.-M., & Lim, J.-H. (2010). Smart home energy management system using IEEE 802.15. 4 and ZigBee. *IEEE Transactions on* Consumer Electronics, *56*(3), 1403–1410.

Hazas, M., Friday, A., & Scott, J. (2011). Look back before leaping forward: Four decades of domestic energy inquiry. *IEEE Pervasive Computing, 10*(1), 13–19.

Heierman, E. O., III, & Cook, D. J. (2003). *Improving home automation by discovering regularly occurring device usage patterns*. Paper presented at the Data Mining, 2003. Washington, DC.

Hussain, S., Schaffner, S., & Moseychuck, D. (2009). *Applications of wireless sensor networks and RFID in a smart home environment*. Paper presented at the Communication Networks and Services Research Conference. New York, NY.

Jahn, M., Jentsch, M., Prause, C. R., Pramudianto, F., Al-Akkad, A., & Reiners, R. (2010). *The energy aware smart home*. Paper presented at the Future Information Technology (FutureTech). New York, NY.

JSON. (n.d.). *JavaScript Object Notation*. Retrieved from http://www.json.org/

Kluckner, P. M., Weiss, A., Schrammel, J., & Tscheligi, M. (2013). *Exploring Persuasion in the Home: Results of a Long-Term Study on Energy Consumption Behavior. In Ambient Intelligence* (pp. 150–165). Springer.

Korhonen, I., Parkka, J., & Van Gils, M. (2003). Health monitoring in the home of the future. *IEEE Engineering in Medicine and Biology Magazine, 22*(3), 66–73. PMID:12845821

Krishnamurti, T., Schwartz, D., Davis, A., Fischhoff, B., de Bruin, W. B., Lave, L., & Wang, J. (2012). Preparing for smart grid technologies: A behavioral decision research approach to understanding consumer expectations about smart meters. *Energy Policy, 41*, 790–797.

Lui, T. J., Stirling, W., & Marcy, H. O. (2010). Get smart. *IEEE Power and Energy Magazine, 8*(3), 66–78.

McGuinness, D. L., & Van Harmelen, F. (2004). OWL web ontology language overview. *W3C Recommendation, 10*(2004-03), 10.

McKerracher, C., & Torriti, J. (2012). Energy consumption feedback in perspective: integrating Australian data to meta-analyses on in-home displays. *Energy Efficiency*, 1-19.

Messer, A., Kunjithapatham, A., Sheshagiri, M., Song, H., Kumar, P., Nguyen, P., & Yi, K. H. (2006). *InterPlay: A middleware for seamless device integration and task orchestration in a networked home*. Paper presented at the Pervasive Computing and Communications, 2006. Washington, DC.

Muldoon, C., O'Hare, G. M., Collier, R., & O'Grady, M. J. (2006). *Agent factory micro edition: A framework for ambient applications. In Computational Science–ICCS 2006* (pp. 727–734). Springer.

Niyato, D., Xiao, L., & Wang, P. (2011). Machine-to-machine communications for home energy management system in smart grid. *IEEE Communications Magazine, 49*(4), 53–59.

O'Grady, M. J., Murdoch, O., Kroon, B., Lillis, D., Carr, D., Collier, R. W., & O'Hare, G. M. (2013). *Pervasive Sensing: Addressing the Heterogeneity Problem*. Paper presented at the Journal of Physics: Conference Series. New York, NY.

O'Hare, G. M. P., Collier, R. W., Dragone, M., O'Grady, M. J., Muldoon, C., & Montoya, A. D. J. (2012b). Embedding Agents within Ambient Intelligent Applications. In T. Bosse (Ed.), *Agents and Ambient Intelligence* (pp. 119–135). IOS Press.

O'Hare, G. M. P., Muldoon, C., O'Grady, M. J., Collier, R. W., Murdoch, O., & Carr, D. (2012a). Sensor web interaction. *International Journal of Artificial Intelligence Tools, 21*(02).

Parikh, P. P., Kanabar, M. G., & Sidhu, T. S. (2010). *Opportunities and challenges of wireless communication technologies for smart grid applications*. Paper presented at the Power and Energy Society General Meeting. New York, NY.

Ruzzelli, A. G., Nicolas, C., Schoofs, A., & O'Hare, G. M. (2010). *Real-time recognition and profiling of appliances through a single electricity sensor.* Paper presented at the Sensor Mesh and Ad Hoc Communications and Networks (SECON). Washington, DC.

Son, Y.-S., Pulkkinen, T., Moon, K.-D., & Kim, C. (2010). Home energy management system based on power line communication. *IEEE Transactions on* Consumer Electronics, *56*(3), 1380–1386.

World, O. N. (2010). *The Smart Energy Home Market to Reach $3 Billion in 2014.* Retrieved from http://www.onworld.com/news/newssmart-energy.htm

Zhang, H., Wang, F.-Y., & Ai, Y. (2005). *An OSGi and agent based control system architecture for smart home.* Paper presented at the Networking, Sensing and Control, 2005. Washington, DC.

Zhao, P., Simões, M. G., & Suryanarayanan, S. (2010). *A conceptual scheme for cyber-physical systems based energy management in building structures.* Paper presented at the 9th IEEE/IAS International Conference on Industry Applications (INDUSCON). Washington, DC.

KEY TERMS AND DEFINITIONS

Agent: A software component that exhibits autonomy and social ability, while being reactive to changes in its environment and pro-active in achieving its goals.

Autonomic Computing: The ability of a computer system to manage its own low-level function without the requirement for user interaction.

Home Area Network: A local area network intended to facilitate communication between diverse digital devices within a home.

Open Service Gateway initiative (OSGi): A modular component system for the Java programming language that allows individual software components to be loaded and unloaded at runtime.

Semantic Reasoning: The inference of logical consequences from a set of asserted facts or axioms.

SIXTH: A sensor middleware built upon the OSGi framework that provides a unified interface for the deployment of heterogeneous sensors within a system.

Smart Grid: An energy supply grid that is capable of leveraging digital communication technologies in order to react to real-time changes in energy usage patterns.

Chapter 11
Application Mobility:
Concept and Design

Dan Johansson
Luleå University of Technology, Sweden

Mikael Wiberg
Umeå University, Sweden

ABSTRACT

Mobility has become an omnipresent part of our modern IT society. Alongside the general taxonomy of mobile users, terminals, sessions, and services, there are also more specialized forms of mobility. Context-Awareness Supported Application Mobility (CASAM) or "Application Mobility" is one such form that is explored in this chapter. CASAM builds on the idea of using context to move an application between different devices during its execution in order to provide relevant information and/or services. The authors use a concept-driven approach to advance mobile systems research, integrating it with a more traditional user-centric method and a case study, further exploring the concept of CASAM. To empirically situate our design work they conducted an empirical study of a home care service group serving the Swedish municipality of Skellefteå, followed by an exercise in matching the properties of the CASAM concept in relation to problems within current workflow.

1. INTRODUCTION

In the mid 90s, Leonard Kleinrock (1996) presented his classic paper entitled "Nomadicity: Anytime, anywhere in a disconnected world". In his paper, Kleinrock argued that although users were now IT nomads (using IT and computer based services at different places, pausing or shutting down in between), systems were not fully nomadically-enabled. The assumption of us being always connected was wrong. Instead, being

disconnected was a common mode, and moving from your desk to a conference room in the very same building required a nomadic mode, as the IT environment could be completely different in the two locations.

Indeed, much has happened since Kleinrock wrote his article. Mobile IT usage has become an omnipresent part of our modern society (Beale, 2009; Kaikkonen, 2009; Koblentz, 2009). Recent statistics show that the number of Internet users exceeds two and a half billion, and that there are

DOI: 10.4018/978-1-4666-7284-0.ch011

Copyright © 2015, IGI Global. Copying or distributing in print or electronic forms without written permission of IGI Global is prohibited.

more than two billion active mobile-broadband subscriptions throughout the world (ITU, 2014). Mobile users act within a space of flows (Castells, 2000), transcending the well-known space of physical places. In the space of flows, both information and technology roam through time and space, more or less unaffected by physical boundaries. Concepts like cloud computing present opportunities to use thin clients to access data and services, execute programs via the Internet and store data in virtual folders. Mobile IT is indeed an important part of the often brought up vision of ubiquitous computing, described as unobtrusive services and applications that are always accessible (Mark Weiser, 1993, 1994).

In the light of this, one could say that IT users have gone from being simply nomadic to being truly mobile, able to access and use the same services constantly, regardless of current place or device. This assumption has many flaws though. Despite the increase in mobile devices used along with new communication technologies (3G, 4G, WiMax, new highly improved versions of WiFi etc.) and an abundance of web and cloud services, society still lacks the ability to use IT anywhere, anytime. An Internet connection might be missing or broken, trust issues can prevent a user from consuming different services (such as virtual storage) and the metaphor of the cloud might not be intuitive to all users. There are still areas within mobile computing that are not fully explored; areas that might contain concepts that help complement the ambition of systems that fully support mobile IT usage. One such concept could well be Context-Awareness Supported Application Mobility. Taking this as a point of departure, the purpose of this paper is to conceptually advance "application mobility" – the ability for an application to migrate between different applications during its execution – towards design, i.e. to explore the concept in search for solutions that increase mobility.

Purpose and Disposition

The purpose of our research is to conceptually advance application mobility towards design. In more specific terms that means to elaborate and examine the concept of CASAM, testing the viability of the concept by defining it, manifesting it within a prototype, exposing it to real users, and relating it to state of the art research within the field of mobile systems, according to the method of concept-driven design research (see section 3).

In outlining the paper we first present a literature study of related technologies and projects (section 2), followed by a description of the concept-oriented method guiding our research (section 3). In section 4 we apply the phases of the concept-driven research method to explore, critique and express the notion of CASAM. Following the method of concept-driven design research we then examine CASAM through an external design critique (section 5), followed by a discussion of CASAM as mobile IT support for home care groups (section 6) before concluding the paper in section 7.

2. RELATED WORK ON CONTEXT-AWARENESS SUPPORTED APPLICATION MOBILITY

The basic notion of "mobility" has been applied on different aspects of the IT usage context, e.g. terminal mobility, session mobility (mobility of information and media streams), service mobility or personal mobility (ITU, 2002). Applications can also be mobile. In 1995, Bharat and Cardelli presented migratory applications as:

… a new genre of user interface applications that can migrate from one machine to another, taking their user interface and application contexts with them, and continue from where they left off.

Such applications are not tied to one user or one machine, and can roam freely over the network, rendering service to a community of users, gathering human input and interacting with people. (p. 133)

Migratory, or mobile, applications thus resemble mobile agents, but the latter are typically non-interactive and function as silent agents on the user's or client's behalf. Mobile applications are not restricted to certain types of programs, and they also always have user interfaces and keep all of their states when migrating (Bharat & Cardelli, 1995). The border between intelligent agents and migratable applications is sometimes blurry.

There are also other, similar migration technologies, but they all differ from application mobility in one or several decisive ways. Migratable interfaces allow some degree of mobility; this is often called partial migration (Bandelloni & Paternò, 2004) and is characterized by moving parts of a graphical user interface (or "display content part") to a new device, e.g. a large computer screen, while keeping control functionality on the original host device. While only parts of the application are migrated, there is still a need to adapt the graphical user interface at runtime. This is often orchestrated by a centralized control device, in one of three ways: either in a one to one fashion, where parts of an interface is mirrored by another device; or in a one to many fashion, e.g. migration to a dual screen; or many to one, where several control units migrate parts of their interfaces onto a common host, e.g. to create an ad hoc surface for cooperation. The goal of partial migration is often to exploit the better input and especially output capabilities of other available devices.

Code mobility is when migrating code from one device to another (Fuggetta, Picco, & Vigna, 1998). Neither application states nor other related information is transferred; only the byte code. Thus this migration type differs from application mobility. Strong code mobility is an extension of

this technology, where sequential flows of computation are migrated. Execution states are migrated along with the byte code, thus becoming strongly related to application mobility.

Some technologies do not include migration, but rather the cloning (Bharat and Cardelli, 1995) of an application, creating dual (or multiple) copies. These instances of the original application might or might not be standalone applications.

Application Mobility

There are several dimensions to take into account when classifying systems providing application mobility. Yu, Ma, Cao and Lu (2013) e.g. list the entity dimension, the spatial dimension, and the temporal dimension, respectively corresponding to the questions of "what", "when", and "where". True application mobility is achieved when migrating both code and applications states (Cabri, Leonardi, & Quitadamo, 2006), and in their definition Bharat and Cardelli (1995) add related information to what has to be migrated. Koponen, Gurtov and Nikander (2005) define application mobility as when moving an application between hosts during its execution.

Migration can be either sender initiated, when the user or the system actively sends the application to a new host device, or receiver initiated, when the application is instead fetched onto the new host (Cui, Nahrstedt, & Xu, 2004). Regardless of migration type, the application first has to be paused, then moved (using a wired or, in mobile scenarios, preferably wireless communication technology) and finally made to continue its execution on the new device, thus being completely removed from the original host. Zhou et al (2007) name these stages suspension, migration and resumption.

The question of where the migration takes place can be answered by examining networks and devices (Yu et al, 2013). For example, an application can be migrated between devices connected to the same subnet, where the network operator might have full control over the infrastructure, being able to configure routers and open firewalls to help transferring the application. However, an application can also be migrated from a subnet to another network connected to the Internet, or between devices with different network interfaces, e.g. cellular networks with different operators (Johansson, Andersson, & Åhlund, 2013). There is also a multitude of potential host devices, heterogeneous in their nature. Devices can have different input and output capabilities, varying network interfaces, come from various vendors and execute on diverse operating systems. New devices such as smartphones, tablets and portable gaming consoles, and also the ever increasing amount of computers being embedded into everyday things building the Internet of things (Coetzee & Eksteen, 2011) poses new challenges to the design of application mobility, not least when it comes to addressing, portability, and resource binding (Yu et al, 2013).

Context-Awareness

When transferring an application between different devices during its execution, one has accordingly achieved application mobility. Application mobility always exists within a *context*. Here we use Dey and Abowd's definition, describing context as,

… any information that can be used to characterize the situation of an entity. An entity is a person, place or object that is considered relevant to the interaction between a user and an application, including the user and applications themselves. (1999, pp. 3–4).

Making a system capable of sensing its context and then act according to its own reasoning upon the data describing the situation, is making it context-aware (Loke, 2007).

Sensing is achieved through direct input to the system from the user or other systems. However, dedicated sensors are often used to capture context data. These sensors can be placed in mobile devices (Hinckley, Pierce, Sinclair, & Horvitz, 2000), e.g. touch sensors, proximity sensors, and tilt sensors. Location data can be captured using techniques like RFID (Ahson & Ilyas, 2008) and GPS (Huang & Tsai, 2008). Some sensors are really simple, delivering binary on-off mechanisms, while other provide analogous scale, and some even capture the whole meaning of a situation, e.g. delivers information about if a room is used for a meeting (Kummerfeld, Quigley, Johnson, & Hexel, 2003).

Albeit being a powerful calculator, the computer has limited capabilities in terms of reasoning compared to the human brain (Loke, 2007). By applying different algorithms and logic models to gathered context data, the context-aware system can mimic "thinking" and draw conclusions. Among the methods we find physical mathematical models, feature-based inference techniques, and cognitive-based models. One example is the hidden Markov model (Rabiner, 1989), which can be used to determine hidden parameters from sensor data. E.g. if it is known that Alice is more keen on using the Internet during rainy days, the hidden Markov model can use information about Alice's current position and network usage to draw conclusions about the weather conditions at a certain location. Cognitive-based models often include fuzzy logic (Mendel, 1995), combining numerical data and linguistic knowledge, being a versatile tool when dealing with both objective and subjective knowledge within the context model. The reasoning is often inexact, producing approximations and degrees of possibilities rather than exact answers.

Having sensed and though, the context-aware system then acts, proposing a decision to the system (Loke, 2007).

Defining "Context-Awareness Supported Application Mobility"

Combining Dey and Abowd's (1999) definitions of Context-Awareness with state of the art definitions of application mobility (e.g. Koponen, Gurtov, & Nikander, 2005), the concept of Context-Awareness Supported Application Mobility (henceforth referred to through the acronym CASAM) could be described as when using context to move an application between different devices during its execution, to provide relevant information and/ or services, where relevancy depends on the user's task.

3. METHOD-CONCEPT-DRIVEN DESIGN RESEARCH

There are different methodologies to choose between when designing IT. User-centered approaches, along with participatory design, activity theory, contextual design, and to some extent ethnographic methods, are all examples of empirically oriented approaches, very common in contemporary IT design. A fundamental element of these empirical approaches is that IT design must be derived from thorough analysis of an existing situation. In making a systematic and complete investigation of users and their context, the IT design will emerge somewhat automatically, as the natural answer to the consideration of all variables of the problem. Empirical approaches have certainly proven successful when designing IT artifacts for existing cases and concrete situations.

However, designing IT can also have an impact on constructing theories. Building upon theories of futuristic use scenarios and reasoning grounded in theory (discussed by Karl Weick, 1989), Stolterman and Wiberg (2010) present a complementary design approach, labeled concept-driven design research.

In concept-driven design research the striving for new knowledge is structured in seven basic phases consisting of:

1. Concept generation,
2. Concept exploration,
3. Internal concept critique,
4. Design of artifacts,
5. External design critique,
6. Concept revisited, and finally,
7. Concept contextualization.

Through the process of concept generation new possible concepts are formulated based on earlier theoretical work in the field. This generation of new concepts is typically a process not possible to prescribe: it may be done by working with associations, metaphors, conflicting or opposing theoretical concepts, theories from other design fields, and historical or other paradigmatic examples. The second process is called concept exploration. In this process the researcher works hands-on with materials, creating models and prototypes and experimenting with unusual materials, forms and content in the exploration of new design spaces. The aim with this process is to explore the design spaces given a formulated guiding concept.

In the third process, called internal concept critique, the strength of the chosen concept is examined before moving on to a more formalized design. In this phase it is, according to Stolterman and Wiberg (2010), important to relate the design and its underlying concepts to the established theoretical foundation. The success of this phase relies on the identification and establishment of:

1. The uniqueness of the chosen core concepts,
2. To what extent the concepts relate to existing theory, and
3. How well these concepts can be clearly expressed in a concrete design.

Having established the conceptual ground the fourth process, design of artifacts, involves the carving out and expressing of a concrete artifact as a manifested composition that incorporates the concept design as a "whole". This means that the development of the actual manifestation becomes part of the design process and of the theoretical development. This is where concept-driven design research relates theoretical development with the skilled craft of making artifacts that manifest the full meaning of a theoretical concept (Stolterman & Wiberg 2010).

The fifth process called external design critique is about tests and evaluations. In most approaches, testing includes a question of user acceptance (as is the case in usability testing from the perspective of user-centered design). In concept-driven design research, testing means instead that the conceptual design is exposed to a public and critiqued as a composition. It is an evaluation of the idea, the concept and the inherent theoretical principles that the design manifests.

Based on the results from the tests and evaluations, the sixth process, concept revisited, is about revising and refining the concept that has guided the design. In this sense the evaluation in phase 5 serves as a basis for theory development in this process.

Finally, the last part of this method called concept contextualization is about relating and valuing this new concept against the current body of concepts and theory in the field, to positioning it against similar concepts, and showing how it contributes to previous work.

In our research project, as presented in this paper, we have set out to follow the basic steps of this method with particular focus on the concept of CASAM–Context-Awareness Supported Application Mobility, and how it can be conceptually advanced towards design through a process including concept definitions, concept interpretations, concept implementation in the form of a working prototype, and finally refined and further related to the current body of research within this field.

A possible result is the emergence of a strong concept (Höök & Löwgren, 2012), or at least a seed for such a conceptual construct. Strong concepts can be found in the intermediate design knowledge, in-between mere instances (prototypes, products, concretized ideas), and full-scale theories. Strong concepts carry the core design ideas, not neces-

sarily tied to a certain use situation or application domain. They are interactive in nature and can mediate a use practice and behavior over time.

4. CONCEPT EXPLORATION, CRITIQUE, AND EXPRESSION

The concept of CASAM has been studied by several research groups, often from a strictly technical point of view. Projects like Roam (Chu et al, 2004), Sparkle (Siu et al, 2004), Gaia (Ranganathan, Shankar, & Campbell, 2005), Desktop Migration System (Hwang, Park, & Chung, 2006), MDAgent (Zhou et al 2007), SAMProc (Schmidt, Kapitza, & Hauck, 2007), MSP (Hojgaard-Hansen, Nguyen, & Schwefel, 2010), and DPartner (Zhang, Huang, Zhang, Liu, & Mei, 2012) all resulted in centralized solutions, often with a middleware taking care of communication and controlling migration, in most cases using centralized code loading. Centralized architectures rely on stable network connections to function satisfactory. These systems become very Internet-dependent, which can be seen as a weakness when it comes to supporting mobile technologies in contexts where network quality differs or connections sometimes go down.

Johansson and Andersson (2012) explore application mobility from a web technology perspective, analyzing the ability of the emerging HTML5 standard along with related frameworks to support application mobility. The proposed architecture allows for offline work and usage in heterogeneous environments, but is however partially centralized in its nature. Realization (and subsequent empirical evaluation) of the architecture through prototyping is still in progress.

The Hydra project (Satoh, 2005) was based upon a decentralized solution, which had a multicast setup, RFID supported location awareness and possible separation of input, output and logic on different devices. These papers do not reveal any occurrences of case studies being conducted, nor have real users evaluated the prototypes.

Instead evaluations focus on the measurement of suspension, migration and resumption times in laboratory environments. Also, few comparisons with competing or complementing technologies and paradigms are made. Concept discussions in a wider perspective are left out for the benefit of a more technical focus.

A recent architectural proposal for supporting application mobility was presented by Johansson, Åhlund and Åhlund (2011). This architecture contains several novel features building on peer-to-peer technology to handle application identification and context management, taking advantage of the overlay network topology for managing nodes and spreading context data over distributed hash tables. By adding Mobile IP to the architecture, usage is not restricted to local networks, and applications can be migrated to any authorized device connected to the network, regardless of location. Thus, the architecture supports full mobility in a global scope, while it still maintains a decentralized structure.

All these projects and resulting prototypes have a common factor in that they show that application mobility can be achieved, and that there are several different methods possible when designing for application mobility.

CASAM vs. Cloud-Based Virtualization and Migration Services

This section headline is provocative as it puts CASAM head to head with the cloud paradigm. Still, we find it important to clarify the differences between these two ways of supporting mobility; they both have their specific strengths and weaknesses. CASAM will not replace cloud-based application frameworks, rather co-exist and complement other existing mobile technologies.

"The cloud" is a metaphor for the Internet, and cloud computing is essentially about virtualizing software, platforms, infrastructure and/or hardware, presenting abstractions to the user. Through a single point of access, the user can execute programs, store and retrieve files and make use of different networks. Rimal, Choi, and Lumb (2009) make a good compilation of the pros and cons of cloud computing. The single point of entry creates easy access to services. The clients can be thin, as applications can be run and used through normal web browsers, while in reality being executed on external servers. The same applies to all files and data, which can be put in external repositories and fetched onto a thin client whenever needed. This however creates a dependency of a good and reliable connection; offline usage of cloud services is very limited and sometimes impossible. The user also becomes dependent on one or more service providers. If a service provider cannot deliver (flagrant examples of major outages are listed in Rimal et al, 2009), the user's ability to create workarounds is minimized; as the central idea of cloud computing is about abstractions, system transparency is often narrowed down to a minimum. Another challenge for cloud services is security and trust. Users cannot control where data is stored, neither can they monitor the status of firewalls, supposedly secure connections and other important factors of keeping data safe. Furthermore, users cannot control who is accessing their data, when and in what purpose. Kotz, Avancha and Baxi (2009) formulate an explicit research question for the larger scientific community to address, when making inquiries about how mobile hardware and software architectures should be designed to help protect user privacy. Kovachev and Klamma (2012) also point out cost model issues as challenging when designing for application mobility within the cloud. E.g. how to balance available resources between user goals, system constraints, and device profiles. A concrete example of application mobility through cloud-based virtualization is the Internet Suspend/ Resume (Satyanarayanan, Kozuch, Helfrich, & O'Hallaron, 2005), where the complete machine is suspended and the resumed at another device, using a virtual machine and a distributed file system. Migrating a complete computing environment is of course very demanding in terms of resources (e.g. bandwith) compared to the migration of specific applications.

CASAM, compared to cloud-based virtualization service solutions, is more complex to the single user. Services are not abstracted in the same manner as with cloud-based application frameworks or migration services; we need to install programs, monitor their functionality by ourselves and bring or fetch applications, rather that just make use of a single point of access for all services. The clients must be thicker; strong enough to process code, fast enough to handle memory and have the ability to store the actual applications locally. On the other hand, the importance of reliable Internet connections is vastly reduced. CASAM could in fact be carried out within a local area network or, in critical cases, through near field communication. Also, a CASAM user does not have to rely upon service providers as the application runs on the local device. When it comes to security, the application moves with the user (or at least according to the user's will). This means that it will not be accessible though entry points other than the ones that the user chooses, most often the single device currently executing the application. The user can also control firewalls and which networks and communication channels to use in broader extent than if relying on cloud services.

Manifesting the Concept

Our first concrete manifestation of the expressed concept of CASAM is a middleware providing seamless application mobility, while being context-aware and deployed in a decentralized manner. The middleware is called A2M, specified in Åhlund et al (2009). In short, the system consists of three major components: the migration manager, the application adapter, and the GUI adapter.

The migration manager is the core component, acting as device discoverer and server component (lowering the risk of application loss)

through multicasting. A context collector module is responsible for the gathering and storing of context information. In the prototype we draw on user location based on RFID sensor technology to determine user presence. Also embedded within the migration manager component is a mobile application manager module. It allows the component to control migration between devices through TCP sockets. Using Java Reflection, a migrated application can resume its execution on the new device without the destination host having knowledge of the application prior to the migration. The migration manager must be installed on all presumptive host devices.

The application adapter sees to that the migrated application adapts to the capabilities and restraints of its new device. It is responsible for keeping the execution states so that the application can continue to execute where it left off when suspended.

Finally, the GUI adapter modifies the graphical user interface of the application, so it will suit the new host device.

Videoconference Application

The fundamental task of the A2M system is to migrate applications between devices. To allow the A2M to carry out its intended task, we built a videoconference application using Flash and Java. The videoconference application allows two users to communicate through both video and audio in real time. The application also provides a chat window for sending asynchronous text messages.

5. EXTERNAL DESIGN CRITIQUE

To further explore a feasible realization and implementation based on the concept of CASAM, we wanted to identify a potential user group which could offer us insights from an outside perspective, to situate empirically our concept exploration in practice. For this we needed a suitable research site with a mobile user group. To qualify, the user group had to be mobile in the sense that we, among their tasks, could find information to be carried between and/or needed in different contexts of their work. We found such a group in an organization called "the Mobile Team", a mobile home care service group.

During a two-day field study, we examined the typical workflow within the Mobile Team. The field study was designed following the directions of the contextual inquiry method (Beyer & Holtzblatt, 1998), emphasizing observation in combination with non-formal interviews and conversation during the work situation. Throughout the study the interviewer must interfere as little as possible with the work of the interviewee, preserving a normal work context. Broad and plentiful data gathering for in-depth post analysis is an essential part of the method.

The Mobile Team

In the Swedish municipality of Skellefteå, around 700 people are employed within the home care service sector. Just over 20 of these people, all certified nursing assistants (CNAs), form a group called the Mobile Team. The team assists the regular home care service in caring for patients that have just been dismissed from hospital, or who need tending at the last stages of life. The CNAs in the Mobile Team work day and night in shifts. The team is (as stated in team name) mobile; every shift consists of seven simultaneous cars, operating within a 20 km radius with a shared office as base.

Group organization is flat; the employees take turns in shouldering the role as planner, deciding how to organize and divide the work for the upcoming two weeks. The work schedule must be updated every morning, as new patients are added, old patients no longer need care, and reorganization if circumstances change, such as if an employee becomes ill. If the planner cannot fill

the schedule, he/she compiles available resources and offers these to all the 32 substitute coordinators within the municipal home care service in Skellefteå. These resources can then be booked and used by other home care service areas. When the advertisement of these free resources is finished, the planner heads out in the field, attending to the same work as everybody else in the group, while still remaining in the role as planner. A certain amount of planning and scheduling continues constantly, as certain events can occur with short notice. This scheduling must be made ad hoc, putting high demands on the planner.

The current level of IT support is low. There are two stationary computers in the shared office. The computers are used for emailing and for compiling the text documents, containing available resources. All scheduling is made manually, with pen and paper. Communication between employees is carried out face to face in the office, through notes in a dedicated folder placed on the desk in the common office, or via mobile phone. Logs concerning the care of the specific patients being treated are placed in the residences of the patients, so that the patients, their relatives and the responsible CNAs can catch up on what kind of care has been given. Often a patient is treated by two or more CNAs during the typical two to three weeks of care by the Mobile Team.

Typical Workflow within the Mobile Team

Every morning, for approximately two hours, the planner schedules care efforts for the upcoming two weeks. Free time slots in the schedule are identified, summarized in a text document and e-mailed to the 32 substitute coordinators within the municipal home care service. The substitute coordinators can at any time return with requests of booking available resources, and the schedule is then updated accordingly. At the same time, the text document containing free time slots must be updated, so that a time is not offered twice, causing double booking. Comparing the schedule with the list of available time slots is experienced as a messy and time-consuming task.

A paper copy of the schedule for the day is placed on the desk in the shared office. The planner carries the original schedule throughout the day, updating the schedule ad hoc if needed. This might cause a disturbance if the planner is busy tending a patient, as there is no possibility to update the copy when in the field.

At the beginning of a shift, when employees arrive at the shared office, they read the schedule to find out which patients to visit. Sometimes they also read the personal file about the patient, stored within the office. Then a key to the assigned car is received, and the CNAs start their work in the field, visiting the patients in their homes. Addresses might be hard to find, especially if the patient lives in the countryside. Arriving at the patient's residence, the CNA reads the patient's log. Finding this log might also be hard, as patients, their relatives and/or the responsible CNAs does not always remember to put it in the same place every time after reading it. The CNA checks the medication list, medicates the patient and might also do some cleaning and/or cooking, depending on the needs of the patient. Comments about the

work are written down in the log by the CNA. As the log is kept within the patient's home, these comments can be read by both CNAs, patients and relatives, and thus the log can be used for asynchronous communication between the parties.

During the day, most often the CNA will return to the shared office for lunch and/or coffee breaks. When the shift is over (or during the day if the office is visited earlier), notes can be left in the diary folder so that other members of the Mobile Team can read about special events. As this information is written on paper in a chronological manner, historical notes can be hard to find. Also, every CNA is responsible for recording time spent and type of care given for every patient. Sometimes this can be hard to remember.

Concept Evaluation

To evaluate the CASAM concept, a workshop was organized where scientists, developers and personnel from the Mobile Team would participate. The workshop consisted of three phases: 1) concept presentation and field study summary, 2) test of the A2M system that acted as a manifestation of the CASAM concept and 3) focus group. Attending the workshop were five CNAs from the Mobile Team, all with different attitudes towards

Table 1. Identified problems

Set of Tasks	Identified Problem(s)
Scheduling	• The schedule is bound to physical locations. • The copy of the schedule cannot be updated from afar. • Changes in the schedule are made with a pen, disallowing rearrangement without first deleting entries. • Hard to match free time slots in the schedule with the list submitted to substitute coordinators. • Possible disturbance to the patient if scheduling ad hoc in the field.
Going to the patient	• The patient's address might be difficult to find.
The care situation	• The patient's log can be difficult to locate.
Communication with other team members	• Information in the diary folder is not sorted by subject. • Older pieces of information in the diary folder might be hard to find.
Debriefing	• Time reports are sometimes forgotten. • Sometimes hard to remember carried out work. • Often time consuming.

new technology and IT usage (a deliberate choice to capture a wider range of opinions); one of the developers of the A2M system; and two senior computer scientists. The workshop was hosted and chaired by the first author of this chapter.

Concept Presentation and Field Study Summary

First of all, the concept of CASAM was presented to the workshop participants. Some participants had prior experience of the technology, but for most participants the subject was new. The notions of application mobility, context, and Context-Awareness was explained and demonstrated. A summary of the field study was also presented. During the presentations, the CNAs could ask questions and make comments. The problems identified during the field study were confirmed by the attending CNAs.

Testing the A2M

To further demonstrate the CASAM concept and give the workshop attendees a chance to experience CASAM hands on, a user test session was carried out. The A2M system, acting as concept manifestation, was installed on two laptops and used in combination with our own-developed videoconference application. The workshop attendees took turns in communicating with each other via the laptops. After a while, one of the users switched to a new device (a mini PC), at the same time automatically migrating the application so that he or she could continue the videoconference from that device.

Focus Group Study

After being introduced to the concept of CASAM, in line with the concept-driven design research method, a focus group was conducted with the purpose of evaluating the concept and informing the design ideas. The focus group was deliberately open ended, with as little steering as possible from the workshop host. Many opinions about the prototype and the concept, as well as possible applications were raised and discussed. Among the most important and/or interesting was that the prototype usage was experienced as intuitive with the location connected to an RFID tag, and that migration was considered seamless despite migration times of between five to nine seconds. There was a belief that a CASAM based work support would save time (no need for login, up-start, manual resuming of applications etc.) and simplify the current workflow. Worries about security were expressed, but mobile devices could be protected with card reader technology, already adopted within the organization. As for artifact design, it should be easy to understand, but the system should also be able to understand the user. Integrating the design with mobile phones was considered important, and a discussion about GPS navigation support was also had. Regarding modalities, video did not emerge as a prioritized means of communication.

6. TOWARDS DESIGN: CASAM AS IT SUPPORT FOR MOBILE HOME CARE GROUPS

An often adapted approach to implementation of IT support within the health care area is digitalization and centralized storage (Avison & Young, 2007; Thompson & Dean, 2009). This could benefit home care groups such as the Mobile Team in some extent. Digitalizing scheduling, maps, journals, diaries etc. and storing them within the cloud would in the ideal case allow the CNAs access to important data in the field. However, this solution does not stem from the CASAM concept, and, as powerful it may be, it also has some major drawbacks. In addition to the need for centralized security solutions and the increase in Internet dependency, the mismatch between these kinds of solutions and the work practices they should support is often put forth as a criticism (Avison & Young, 2007).

Following the method of concept-driven design research (Stolterman & Wiberg, 2010) and leaning on the results of the focus group, we have created a specification of an IT artifact (i.e. artifact using IT as the basic element in its fundamental structures and functionalities) that manifests our desired theoretical ideas of CASAM as, to not only conceptually advance "application mobility", but also as an attempt to move from concept exploration towards design. We call our design A-Maid (Application Mobility Aid) and as a design draft it will be further presented in the following section.

The artifact is comprised of several tiers. The first tier consists of network and hardware components (both mobile and stationary) providing the infrastructure needed for transferring applications. The second tier is the middleware, controlling the migration processes and maintaining a peer-to-peer overlay network, used to manage the devices and the context data. The top tier is the actual application. Figure 1 summarizes this design.

Regarding hardware, all CNAs will be equipped with mobile devices, in this particular case smartphones with interfaces for 3G, WiFi and short-range communication technologies (NFC and/or Bluetooth). GPS functionality is also offered. The smartphones fill two purposes within the A-Maid system: they serve as communication tools, as well as means of using and carrying the application.

Figure 1. The A-Maid artifact

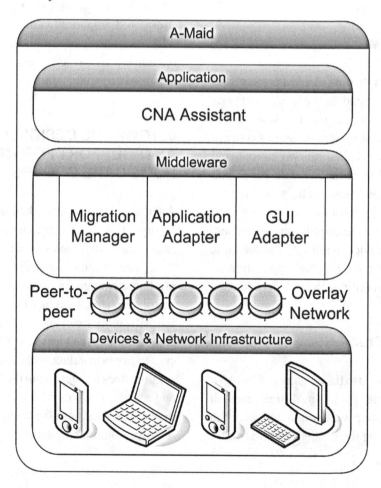

The CNA responsible for planning also brings a laptop, giving better input and output modalities compared to the smartphones. All patients also have thin clients stationed in their homes. The most important features of the thin clients are big screens (compared to the smartphones'), small local storage and the possibility to communicate with the smartphones via NFC or WiFi. No Internet connection is needed.

As a basis for communication we make use of the technology within the Peer-to-peer (P2P) paradigm (Buford, Yu, & Lua, 2009). We create an overlay network consisting of the smartphones, laptop, thin clients and stationary PC nodes, which can be distributed geographically throughout the area in which the Mobile Team operates. Full technical details about the proposed P2P architecture are provided in Johansson, Åhlund and Åhlund (2011), and in Johansson, Andersson, and Åhlund (2013). The middleware linking application and infrastructure must be capable of handling all the important communication between the two tiers. It contains a Migration Manager, providing interfaces for the application when it comes to connectivity, context handling and migration control. The Migration Manager is installed on all nodes that form the A-Maid net. It also contains an Application Adapter, which embeds the application and sees to that the application adapts according to the specifications received from the system. Finally, a GUI Adapter helps with changing graphical user interfaces, adapting these to the requirements and modalities supported by the device onto which the application will migrate. Much of this is already implemented within the A2M middleware (Åhlund et al, 2009) used during the workshop test session.

The context-aware mobile application is to be seen as a secretary or assistant to the CNA. It contains a calendar tool, a map tool and a journal-editing tool. The calendar tool answers up to the problems connected to scheduling. By swapping the paper schedule with a digital version, bound to the calendar tool, the schedule is taken from the space of physical places to the space of flows (as defined by Castells, 2000). This makes the schedule available to the CNAs in the field and enables new types of editing, not bound to a physical place or the use of a pencil. The planner can edit the schedule by running the application on the laptop, and then either push the schedule data onto other CNAs mobile devices through tunneling (if connected to the Internet) or synchronizing the data when back at the shared office. The possible disturbance of the patient when rescheduling in the field is kept to a minimum when this can be done without making phone calls back and forth. The map tool makes use of the GPS in the smartphones, but can also be used when offline, letting the CNA navigate against maps downloaded beforehand while at the shared office. The most explicit use of CASAM is shown in the journal-editing tool. The tool never leaves the CNA, nor does the data; like a digitalized version of a small word processor, the tool follows him or her everywhere, and the data is stored locally.

From the conceptual exploration as reported in this paper we have identified three major advantages of using CASAM to complement solutions of digitalization and central storage:

1. Introducing an application that supports current workflow rather that substituting it with a new data flow where the data is separated from the context makes the IT usage more intuitive for the CNA.
2. Security is prioritized as important data follows the user (actually the data follows the application, which in turn follows the user). There is never a need to send or store sensitive data in the cloud.
3. A-Maid is non-Internet dependent. All that is needed to carry out the migration of the application is a local network, based on radio technology, NFC or Bluetooth.

While these advantages points at specific advantages of using CASAM as a guiding concept for this particular design, we simultaneously see how this exemplifies and validates the concept-driven design research method as a fruitful approach to the problem at hand. CASAM clearly has the potential to grow into a strong concept.

7. CONCLUSION

The purpose of this paper was to conceptually advance "application mobility" towards design. In more detail: examining the concept of Context-Awareness supported application mobility (CASAM), testing the viability of the concept by defining it, manifesting it within a prototype, exposing it to real users and relating it to state of the art research and technology within the field of mobile systems. This, in accordance with the method of concept-driven design research.

In this endeavor CASAM was defined through identifying and describing the different parts of the concept, being application mobility, context and Context-Awareness. It was then compared to the concept of cloud computing, pointing out the strengths and drawbacks of this kind of IT usage depending on the chosen technology. A literature study was conducted to compare the concept to related projects and techniques. CASAM was concretely manifested in a prototype called A2M.

The most important contribution from this work was the exploration of the concept through identification and survey of a real work case, consisting of a field study and a workshop, allowing us to expose our concept to a public and through a focus group inform the subsequent creation of a specification of an artifact that manifests our desired conceptual ideas of CASAM. The artifact, A-maid, is a digital CNA assistant characterized by supporting current workflow, prioritizing security and being non-Internet dependent.

To summarize, this work has shown how a mobile IT concept can be formulated, explored and validated through a concept-driven design research approach; how user participation and concept manifestation can help for evaluating the concept; and finally and for this particular case, how IT artifacts derived and developed from and for the concept of CASAM can be used to support the work of home care service groups. Our focus has been on recognizing and making use of a mobility concept, rather than being about using mobile technology to overcome problems connected to mobile contexts. Therefore, we see our results operating at both a practical level as well as on the level of the conceptual. It is our belief that CASAM has the potential to grow into a strong concept.

ACKNOWLEDGMENT

This book chapter has been compiled as part of the Mobile and Open Service Access project (MOSA, 2010) and the Nordic Interaction and Mobility Research Platform (NIMO, 2014), which are both supported by EU structural funds. Parts of the text were previously published in International Journal of Ambient Computing and Intelligence (Johansson & Wiberg, 2012).

The authors would like to thank the CNAs of the Mobile Team for participating. The authors would also like to thank Emma Karlsson for her very useful contribution during the field study, and Karl Andersson for much appreciated help and assistance during research and project planning. Our thanks also go to Sarah Fahlesson for valuable comments on our manuscript.

REFERENCES

Åhlund, A., Mitra, K., Johansson, D., Åhlund, C., & Zaslavsky, A. (2009). Context-aware application mobility support in pervasive computing environments. In *Proceedings of the 6th International Conference on Mobile Technology, Applications & Systems* (pp. 21:1–21:4). New York: ACM.

Ahson, S., & Ilyas, M. (2008). *Rfid handbook: applications, technology, security, and privacy.* Boca Raton, FL: CRC Press. doi:10.1201/9781420055009

Avison, D., & Young, T. (2007, June). Time to rethink health care and ict? *Communications of the ACM,50*(6),69–74.doi:10.1145/1247001.1247008

Bandelloni, R., & Paternò, F. (2004). Flexible interface migration. In *Proceedings of the 9th International Conference on Intelligent User Interfaces* (pp. 148–155). New York: ACM.

Beale, R. (2009). What does mobile mean? *International Journal of Mobile Human Computer Interaction, 1*(3), 1–8. doi:10.4018/jmhci.2009070101

Beyer, H., & Holtzblatt, K. (1998). *Contextual design: defining customer-centered systems.* San Francisco, CA: Morgan Kaufmann Publishers Inc.

Bharat, K. A., & Cardelli, L. (1995). Migratory applications. In *Proceedings of the 8th Annual ACM Symposium on User Interface and Software Technology* (pp. 132–142). New York, NY: ACM.

Cabri, G., Leonardi, L., & Quitadamo, R. (2006). Enabling java mobile computing on the ibm jikes research virtual machine. In *Proceedings of the 4th International Symposium on Principles and Practice of Programming in Java* (pp. 62–71). New York, NY: ACM. doi:10.1145/1168054.1168064

Castells, M. (2000). The information age: Economy, society and culture: The rise of the network society (2nd ed., vol. 1). Malden, MA: Blackwell.

Chu, H.-H., Song, H., Wong, C., Kurakake, S., & Katagiri, M. (2004). Roam, a seamless application framework. *Journal of Systems and Software, 69*(3), 209–226. doi:10.1016/S0164-1212(03)00052-9

Coetzee, L., & Eksteen, J. (2011). The internet of things - Promise for the future? An introduction. In *Proceedings of 1st-Africa Conference, 2011* (pp. 1–9). IEEE.

Cui, Y., Nahrstedt, K., & Xu, D. (2004). Seamless user-level handoff in ubiquitous multimedia service delivery. *Multimedia Tools and Applications, 22*(2), 137–170. doi:10.1023/B:MTAP.0000011932.28891.a0

Dey, A. K., & Abowd, G. D. (1999). *Towards a better understanding of context and context-awareness* (Tech. Rep. No. GIT-GVU-99-22). College of Computing, Georgia Institute of Technology.

Fuggetta, A., Picco, G. P., & Vigna, G. (1998). Understanding code mobility. *IEEE Transactions on Software Engineering, 24*(5), 342–361. doi:10.1109/32.685258

Hinckley, K., Pierce, J., Sinclair, M., & Horvitz, E. (2000). Sensing techniques for mobile interaction. In *Proceedings of the 13th Annual ACM Symposium on User Interface Software and Technology* (pp. 91–100). New York, NY: ACM. doi:10.1145/354401.354417

Hojgaard-Hansen, K., Nguyen, H. C., & Schwefel, H. (2011). Session mobility solution for client-based application migration scenarios. In *Proceedings of the Eighth International Conference on Wireless On-Demand Network Systems and Services* (pp. 76–83). IEEE.

Höök, K., & Löwgren, J. (2012). Strong concepts: Intermediate-level knowledge in interaction design research. *ACM Trans. Comput.-Hum. Interact., 19*(3), 23:1–23:18.

Huang, J.-Y., & Tsai, C.-H. (2008). Improve gps positioning accuracy with context awareness. In *Proceedings of Ubi-Media Computing,* (pp. 94–99). IEEE.

Hwang, T., Park, H., & Chung, J. W. (2006). Desktop migration system based on dynamic linking of application specific libraries. In *Proceedings of Advanced Communication Technology,* (Vol. 3, pp. 1586–1588). ICACT.

ITU. (2002, March). *Itu-t recommendation h.510, mobility and collaboration procedures: mobility for h-series multimedia systems and services.* Retrieved from http://www.itu.int/rec/dologin\pub.asp?lang=e\&id=T-REC-H.510-200203-I!!PDF-E\&type=items

ITU. (2014, September). *ICT statistics.* Retrieved from http://www.itu.int/itu-d/statistics/

Johansson, D., Åhlund, A., & Åhlund, C. (2011). A mip-p2p based architecture for application mobility. In *Proceedings of the 10th International Conference on Mobile and Ubiquitous Multimedia* (pp. 85–93). New York: ACM. doi:10.1145/2107596.2107606

Johansson, D., & Andersson, K. (2012). Web-based adaptive application mobility. In *Proceedings of the 1st IEEE International Conference on Cloud Networking* (p. 87-94). IEEE.

Johansson, D., Andersson, K., & Åhlund, C. (2013). Supporting user mobility with peer-to-peer-based application mobility in heterogeneous networks. In *Proceedings of the 38th IEEE Conference on Local Computer Networks Workshops (LCN Workshops)* (p. 150-153). IEEE. doi:10.1109/LCNW.2013.6758512

Johansson, D., & Wiberg, M. (2012). Conceptually advancing "application mobility" towards design: Applying a concept-driven approach to the design of mobile it for home care service groups. *International Journal of Ambient Computing and Intelligence, 4*(3), 20–32. doi:10.4018/jaci.2012070102

Kaikkonen, A. (2009). Mobile internet: Past, present, and the future. *International Journal of Mobile Human Computer Interaction, 1*(3), 29–45. doi:10.4018/jmhci.2009070104

Kleinrock, L. (1996). Nomadicity: Anytime, anywhere in a disconnected world. *Mobile Networks and Applications, 1*(4), 351–357.

Koblentz, E. (2009). How it started: Mobile internet devices of the previous millennium. *International Journal of Mobile Human Computer Interaction, 1*(4), 1–3. doi:10.4018/jmhci.2009062601

Koegel Buford, J. F., Yu, H. H., & Lua, E. K. (2009). P2P networking and applications. Amsterdam: Elsevier/Morgan Kaufmann.

Koponen, T., Gurtov, A., & Nikander, P. (2005). Application mobility with hip. In *Proc. of ICT'05.* IEEE.

Kotz, D., Avancha, S., & Baxi, A. (2009). A privacy framework for mobile health and home-care systems. In *Proceedings of the First ACM Workshop on Security and Privacy in Medical and Home-Care Systems* (pp. 1–12). New York: ACM. doi:10.1145/1655084.1655086

Kovachev, D., & Klamma, R. (2012). Beyond the client-server architectures: A survey of mobile cloud techniques. In *Communications in China Workshops (ICCC),* (pp. 20–25). IEEE. doi:10.1109/ICCCW.2012.6316468

Kummerfeld, B., Quigley, A., Johnson, C., & Hexel, R. (2003). Merino: Towards an intelligent environment architecture for multi-granularity context description. In Proc. User Modeling for Ubiquitous Computing (pp. 1–7). Academic Press.

Loke, S. (2007). *Context-aware pervasive systems: Architectures for a new breed of applications.* Boca Raton, FL: Auerbach Publications.

Mendel, J. (1995). Fuzzy logic systems for engineering: A tutorial. *Proceedings of the IEEE, 83*(3), 345–377. doi:10.1109/5.364485

MOSA. (2010, January). *Mobile and open service access*. Retrieved from http://www.mosaproject.org/

NIMO. (2014, September). *Nordic interaction and mobility research platform*. Retrieved from http://nimoproject.org/

Rabiner, L. (1989). A tutorial on hidden markov models and selected applications in speech recognition. *Proceedings of the IEEE, 77*(2), 257–286. doi:10.1109/5.18626

Ranganathan, A., Shankar, C., & Campbell, R. (2005). Application polymorphism for autonomic ubiquitous computing. *Multiagent Grid Syst., 1*(2), 109–129.

Rimal, B., Choi, E., & Lumb, I. (2009). A taxonomy and survey of cloud computing systems. In *Proceedings of Inc, IMS and IDC, 2009* (pp. 44–51). IEEE. doi:10.1109/NCM.2009.218

Satoh, I. (2005). Self-deployment of distributed applications. In N. Guelfi, G. Reggio, & A. Romanovsky (Eds.), Scientific engineering of distributed java applications (Vol. 3409, p. 48-57). Springer Berlin/Heidelberg.

Satyanarayanan, M., Kozuch, M. A., Helfrich, C. J., & O'Hallaron, D. R. (2005). Towards seamless mobility on pervasive hardware. *Pervasive and Mobile Computing, 1*(2), 157–189. doi:10.1016/j.pmcj.2005.03.005

Schmidt, H., Kapitza, R., & Hauck, F. J. (2007). Mobile-process-based ubiquitous computing platform: a blueprint. *In Proceedings of the 1st Workshop on Middleware-Application Interaction: In Conjunction with Euro-Sys 2007* (pp. 25–30). New York, NY: ACM.

Siu, P., Belaramani, N., Wang, C., & Lau, F. (2004). Context-aware state management for ubiquitous applications. In L. Yang, M. Guo, G. Gao, & N. Jha (Eds.), *Embedded and ubiquitous computing* (Vol. 3207, pp. 776–785). Springer Berlin Heidelberg. doi:10.1007/978-3-540-30121-9_74

Stolterman, E., & Wiberg, M. (2010). Concept-driven interaction design research. *Human-Computer Interaction, 25*(2), 95–118. doi:10.1080/07370020903586696

Thompson, S. M., & Dean, M. D. (2009). Advancing information technology in health care. *Communications of the ACM, 52*(6), 118–121. doi:10.1145/1516046.1516077

Weick, K. E. (1989). Theory construction as disciplined imagination. *Academy of Management Review, 14*(4), 516–531.

Weiser, M. (1993). Hot topics-ubiquitous computing. *Computer, 26*(10), 71–72. doi:10.1109/2.237456

Weiser, M. (1994). The world is not a desktop. *Interaction, 1*(1), 7–8. doi:10.1145/174800.174801

Zhang, Y., Huang, G., Zhang, W., Liu, X., & Mei, H. (2012). Towards module-based automatic partitioning of java applications. *Frontiers of Computer Science, 6*(6), 725–740.

Zhou, Y., Cao, J., Raychoudhury, V., Siebert, J., & Lu, J. (2007). A middleware support for agent-based application mobility in pervasive environments. In *Proceedings of the 32nd International Conference on Distributed Computing Systems Workshops* (p. 9). Los Alamitos, CA: IEEE Computer Society. doi:10.1109/ICDCSW.2007.12

KEY TERMS AND DEFINITIONS

Application Mobility: The process of migrating applications between different host devices during application execution.

Cloud Computing: Virtualizing software, platforms, infrastructure and/or hardware, using the network (typically the Internet) as a mediator for this service delivery.

Concept-Driven Design Research: The design and creation of a concept and an artifact that manifests desired theoretical ideas as a compositional whole.

Context: Information that characterizes the situation of an entity.

Context-Awareness Supported Application Mobility (CASAM): Using context to move an application between different devices during its execution, to provide relevant information and/or services, where relevancy depends on the user's task.

Context-Awareness: A system's capability of sensing its context and, consequently, act according to its own reasoning about the context.

IT Artifact: A manmade thing (which may or may not be abstract), using IT as the basic element in its fundamental structures and functionalities.

Chapter 12
CAFCLA:
A Framework to Design, Develop, and Deploy AmI-Based Collaborative Learning Applications

Óscar García
University of Salamanca, Spain

Dante I. Tapia
University of Salamanca, Spain

Ricardo S. Alonso
University of Salamanca, Spain

Juan M. Corchado
University of Salamanca, Spain

ABSTRACT

Ambient Intelligence (AmI) promotes the integration of Information and Communication Technologies (ICT) in daily life in order to ease the execution of everyday tasks. In this sense, education becomes a field where AmI can improve the learning process by means of context-aware technologies. However, it is necessary to develop new tools that can be adapted to a wide range of technologies and application scenarios. Here is where Agent Technology can demonstrate its potential. This chapter presents CAFCLA, a multi-agent framework that allows developing learning applications based on the pedagogical CSCL (Computer-Supported Collaborative Learning) approach and the Ambient Intelligence paradigm. CAFCLA integrates different context-aware technologies so that learning applications designed, developed, and deployed upon it are dynamic, adaptive, and easy to use by users such as students and teachers.

1. INTRODUCTION

In recent years there has been a technological explosion that has flooded our society with a wide range of different devices (García, Tapia, Alonso, Rodríguez, & Corchado, 2011). Moreover, the processing and storage capacity of these devices, their user interfaces or their communication skills are improved day by day. Thanks to these advances, we are currently surrounded by technology that has changed our habits and customs (Jorrín-Abellán & Stake, 2009). All this has caused the apparition of new fields such as Ambient Intelligence, whose main objective is to simplify the use of technology to improve people's quality of life (Tapia, Abraham, Corchado, & Alonso, 2009).

Education is one of the areas in which Ambient Intelligence presents a greater potential as it pro-

DOI: 10.4018/978-1-4666-7284-0.ch012

Copyright © 2015, IGI Global. Copying or distributing in print or electronic forms without written permission of IGI Global is prohibited.

vides new ways of interaction and communication between individuals and technological systems (Scardamalia, Bereiter, McLean, Swallow, & Woodruff, 1989). The usage of Information and Communication Technologies (ICT) has been present in educational innovations over recent years (Scardamalia, Bereiter, McLean, Swallow, & Woodruff, 1989), modernizing the traditional transmission of contents through electronic presentations, email or more complex learning platforms such as Moodle or LAMS and fostering collaboration between students (Collaborative Learning) (Gómez-Sánchez et al., 2009). Beside the use of those general-purpose tools in education, other tools that make more specific use of technology have appeared. This applies to those that make use of Context-awareness information and ubiquitous computing and communication, fundamental parts of Ambient Intelligence (Traynor, Xie, & Curran, 2010).

Mobile Learning has become the umbrella under which new ways of learning have emerged, including areas such as Mobile Computer Supported Collaborative Learning (MCSCL), based on traditional CSCL, Context-aware Pervasive Learning or, more recently, Location-Based Learning (Roschelle, 2003). There are several approaches proposed by the scientific community in these research areas which share a common element: the use of mobile devices and wireless communications (Roschelle, 2003).

The inclusion of context-awareness in educational scenarios and processes refers to Context-aware Learning (Laine & Joy, 2009), a particular area of application of Context-aware Computing (Dey, 2001). Moreover, the ability to characterize and customize the context that surrounds a learning situation at a certain time and place provides flexibility in the educational process. This way, learning does not only occur in classrooms, but also in a museum, park or any other place (Bruce, 2009), obtaining ubiquitous learning spaces. Thus, there is an extensive literature that addresses the problem of this kind of learning, highlighting

those works that attempt to solve contextual information acquisition and providing data to users (Chen et al., 2007; Martín et al., 2010). The use and integration of different technologies and the approach to specific learning activities characterize these solutions. However, the complexity of understanding and use of the technology and solutions in the aforementioned works does not allow a wide use of them. In addition, the use of intelligent management techniques is another lack in the reviewed works. In this sense, the ability to operate in a distributed way, predict, adapt and anticipate the users' actions provides a dynamic personalization of the learning process that benefits and improves the acquisition of knowledge by students (Traynor, Xie, & Curran, 2010).

This paper presents a conceptual multi-agent framework aimed at designing, developing and deploying AmI-based educational scenarios. Teachers are able to characterize the context where the learning activity will occur through the creation of a world model in which locate data collectors (e.g., sensors), identify and characterize areas of interest (e.g., paintings in a museum), etc. Moreover, the collaboration between students and the customization of the information available is also provided and can be integrated in the activity design. The framework is supported by a multi-agent architecture that provides intelligence to the learning process by helping to manage the activity, all the communications involved, the context-awareness and the collaboration between students and teachers. In addition, developers and technicians benefit from the Application Programming Interface and the formal schemas provided by CAFCLA.

The following section describes the background and problem description related to the presented approach. Then, the main characteristics of CAFCLA are described: what kinds of activities are covered, how the context of the activity can be defined, who the users are, which activities are implemented by the framework, and how the multi-agent architecture and the context-aware technologies involved are. Later, the framework functioning is described. Finally, the conclusions and future work are depicted.

2. MOTIVATION

A growing interest in educational software, commonly known as e-learning, has appeared over recent years (Gómez-Sánchez et al., 2009). Among the wide range of existing educational software are CSCL (Computer Supported Collaborative Learning) applications (Dillenbourg, 1999). A collaborative learning system consists of a set of tools that facilitate the implementation, development and deployment of learning activities. Those activities allow different ways of interaction between the involved participants that activate learning mechanisms (Koschmann, 1996). CSCL has become an important research field within education that attracts different interests, from the purely educational to those focused on improving human-computer interaction (Gómez-Sánchez et al., 2009).

Mobile devices provide important benefits to education: mobility, communication skills including collection and provision of contextual information, as well as precise location anytime. Mobile Learning is defined as "the processes of coming to know through conversations across multiple contexts amongst people and personal interactive technologies" (Sharples, Taylor, & Vavoula, 2010). This definition implies two important ideas: first of them is that technology can be involved into the learning process; the second idea suggests that mobile learning emphasizes the communication between the involved people and their interaction with the context (Glahn & Börner, 2010). Based on the ability to interconnect devices we can assert that they can be useful to foster collaboration among students, that is, they can act as a tool that supports CSCL (Koschmann, 1996).

The use of mobile devices into a CSCL system is known as Mobile CSCL (MCSCL) (Zurita,

Baloain, & Baytelman, 2008). The analysis of the literature allows us to identify several contributions that describe MCSCL-based systems. Among them we can find modifications of traditional learning management systems that are able to adapt usual utilities from e-learning platforms taking into account the mobile devices' requirements and specifications through their integration into Web Services (Trifonova & Ronchetti, 2006). Beyond adaptation of traditional e-learning platforms, multiple applications specifically developed to support CSCL using mobile devices have been described (Zurita, Baloain, & Baytelman, 2008). Such applications provide an easier way to improve ubiquitous collaboration or foster face-to-face activities (Zurita, Baloain, & Baytelman, 2008).

MCSCL systems are usually designed with a client-server architecture in which all participants join the same network. The introduction of MANETs (Mobile Ad-hoc NETworks) into collaborative learning environments with mobile devices is intended to relax this operational model (Vasiliou & Economides, 2007). Moreover, MANETs allow learners to work outside the classroom to enhance collaborative learning both indoor (e.g., museums) or outdoor (e.g., parks) spaces that present any didactic interest (Neyem, Ochoa, Pino, & Guerrero, 2005). New mobile devices are equipped with features that facilitate the acquisition of contextual information and location. Contextual information includes any data that can be used to characterize a person, place or object that is considered relevant to the interaction between users, between user and applications or systems, or even between systems and applications (Tapia, Abraham, Corchado, & Alonso, 2009). In addition to the relevant information that context provides, it is important to consider other parameters that relevantly affect this type of information, such as identification, time and location (Traynor, Xie, & Curran, 2010). The information exchange taking place between technology and users, in order to contextualize an environment in which learning takes place, and customize the content of the learning activity can be understood as collaboration. Thus, Context-aware Learning must take into account the interactions between people and the different technological components of the system in all its combinations.

2.1. Providing Context-Aware in Learning

Providing contextual information and fostering collaboration between students benefit the learning process (García, Tapia, Alonso, Rodríguez, & Corchado, 2011). Moreover the combination of Collaborative and Context-aware Learning naturally leads to thinking about ubiquitous learning spaces, characterized by "providing intuitive ways for identifying right collaborators, right contents and right services in the right place at the right time based on learners surrounding context such as where and when the learners are (time and space), what the learning resources and services available for the learners, and who are the learning collaborators that match the learners' needs" (Hwang, Yang, Tsai, & Yang, 2009).

A better understanding of environment through technology allows educators to customize the content provided to students. Similarly, technology facilitates the interaction with the environment and between students. This should be reached in a way as transparent and ubiquitous as possible. The technologies used for the collection of contextual information and for the communication between different devices are the cornerstone of the different works presented here. Literature about Context-aware Learning proposals has been deeply reviewed in this work. Some of the most representative works are classified in this paper, following technological criteria related to communications and data collection.

A first approach to provide contextual information is "tagging the context". Even though RFID (Radio Frequency IDentification) is the most spread technology (Blöckner, Danti, Forrai, Broll, & De Luca, 2009), there are other technologies

such as NFC (Near Field Communication) or QR Codes (Quick Response Codes) (Tan et al., 2009) which are growing fast. As can be seen in the usage of Active RFID, both location and context-awareness are closely related: knowing precisely location of objects and people allows determining what is surrounding them and, consequently, characterizing the context in which they are involved. GPS (Global Positioning System) is the most used technology to provide location in Context-aware Learning (Driver et al., 2008; Padovitz et al., 2008). This location system provides a high accuracy level and is currently implemented in a wide range of smart phones and mobile devices. In those cases, the mobile device provides a position to the system. Those solutions are used in different scenarios such as route planning (Padovitz, Loke, & Zaslavsky, 2008) or student's scheduler management (Driver & Clarke, 2008). However, most of those works do not implement a specific case of use, but propose a general purpose model in which GPS technology is included to facilitate the provision of contextual data.

Furthermore, GPS technology does not work indoors because of the direct vision necessary between satellites and devices. However, indoor environments are very common in learning: museums, laboratories or the school are places where activities that require mobility can be developed. Trying to cover this lack, different location systems based on Active RFID (Blöckner, Danti, Forrai, Broll, & De Luca, 2009) or Wi-Fi (Martín, Peire, & Castro, 2010) are used. Both cases the performance of systems is similar: student's position is determined by the access point which is providing coverage in each moment. This type of approach has significant limitations when developing context-aware learning activities: the location accuracy is too poor. This situation presents an important problem when areas where context information is different are close (e.g., two paintings in a museum).

Changing the way of contextualizing the environment where the learning activity occurs, some tendencies propose the use of sensor networks (Martín, Peire, & Castro, 2010). A sensor is an electrical or mechanic device that measures a certain physical magnitude. In this case environmental characterizations are reduced to those data provided by the sensors (Chen, Yu, & Chen, 2007). In order to make the learning process more transparent to students, ad-hoc networks are considered to collect and transport data from sensors to remote points (Chen, Yu, & Chen, 2007). These networks facilitate the connection between devices anytime and anywhere without a previous infrastructure.

The review of the literature evidences some lacks in the Context-aware Learning systems proposed until now. Even some works try to combine different technologies to cover as much situations as possible (Martín, Peire, & Castro, 2010), most of them only cover specific learning situations, as those where tagging context with RFID/NFC (Tan et al., 2009) is necessary or those where learning occurs outdoors (Padovitz, Loke, & Zaslavsky, 2008). The combination of both situations is only addressed by M2learn (Martín, Peire, & Castro, 2010). However, this solution does not provide a precise and efficient location systems or the possibility to integrate wireless sensor networks, except for RFID systems.

2.2. AmI to Raise Collaboration, Management, and Usability

None of the solutions mentioned before takes into account Ambient Intelligence guidelines. The proposed solutions focus their work on the architectural description, framework developers or end-user applications whose designers have not taken into account how complex will be them for educators or students. Some aspects such as designing intuitive and attractive interfaces or abstracting end users from the complexity of technology, issues on which Ambient Intelligence pays special attention, are not taken into account.

Thus, if these aspects are excluded from each solution's design process, the final result may be rejected by students and educators. For this reason, the design process must take into account, from the beginning, the opinion of all the interested parties (Gómez-Sánchez et al., 2009), that is, educators, designers and developers. This way is easier to accomplish with Ambient Intelligent issues related to user interfaces and usability of final applications.

Moreover, the works analyzed in this review do not include mechanisms for data or communication management. Ambient Intelligence emphasizes the transparency of technologies for users. In addition, technology is used to ease ordinary tasks or improve activities and the quality of life (Traynor, Xie, & Curran, 2010). In this sense, systems that combine different technologies do not facilitate mechanisms to change between them (e.g., different communication protocols) attending to the needs of a situation. Similarly, data have to be managed in an intelligent and efficient way. Most of the literature reviewed does not include this issue, using only standard data repositories that only consider persistency and consistency (García, Tapia, Alonso, Rodríguez, & Corchado, 2011). Functionalities like data redundancy to solve network failures help to make the system dynamic and benefit data accessibility with independence of the place and the moment.

In this sense, multi-agent systems are used in learning and collaborative learning applications for different purposes. Multi-agent architectures are commonly designed to adapt contextual information in context-aware learning systems (Yaghmaie & Bahreininejad, 2011), manage the performance of learning activities (Lu, Chang, Kinshuk, Huang, & Chen, 2011) or deploy mobile devices (Macarro, Pedrero, & Fraile, 2009). Although collaboration between agents is considered by those works, collaboration between students is not properly taken into account when these multi-agent systems are designed.

Even though it is well known that collaboration benefits the learning process (García, Tapia, Alonso, Rodríguez, & Corchado, 2011), collaboration between students is an issue not considered by many proposals (Chen, Yu, & Chen, 2007). Including mobile devices and wireless communication protocols in any learning design that requires mobility (as discussed in this paper) is nowadays necessary. Mobile devices easily connect each other so including collaboration between students is an easy task, increasing the variety of activities and improving the learning process.

Furthermore, this work is developed following Ambient Intelligence guidelines, such as personalization of the provided context or transparency and ease of use for teachers and users. Moreover, the inclusion of reasoning mechanisms facilitate the personalization of data provision or the communication management of these kinds of complex systems (García, Tapia, Alonso, Rodríguez, & Corchado, 2011).

3. FRAMEWORK OVERVIEW

CAFCLA (Context-Aware Framework for Collaborative Learning Applications) is a multi-agent framework focused on the design, development and deployment of collaborative learning applications that make use of contextual information. CAFCLA involves multiple users and characterizes each one according to their role in the design, development, deployment and implementation of a learning activity. Moreover, CAFCLA takes into consideration all aspects surrounding the whole learning process design. These aspects include the objectives or goals that students must reach, the contents of the learning activity, the teaching resources available, the physical or virtual spaces selected or the assessment and activity monitoring. All these aspects do not only involve the teacher, but there is also a technical component that must be undertaken by staff that sometimes do not present an education profile. More specifically, three different roles can be identified in the process of design and development of activities considered in this work.

First, there are the teachers (educational profile) who are responsible for the conceptual and contextual design of the activity. They guide the development of the activity and the content of it. Second, there are the software developers that design and develop the end user application and implement all the necessary infrastructure to carry out the activity (software oriented technical profile). Third, the process requires the participation of technical staff to deploy the hardware infrastructure needed for the activity (hardware oriented technical profile).

As any learning process needs students, this role is included into CAFCLA. Thus, there are four types of users defined in CAFCLA: teachers, developers, technicians and students. Each of them has different profiles and skills to access and manage the different functionalities of the framework. A brief description of each user's functions is depicted here:

- **Teacher:** Responsible for designing the activity that will be deployed using CAFCLA. Some of the task that teachers carry out includes defining which students participate in the activity, what kind of activity is carried out, which collaborations between students are allowed, which areas and objects of interest are described in the activity, which are the objectives of the activity and which is the data that the system will store to be provided during the activity.
- **Developer:** Makes use of all the tools provided by CAFCLA (analysis and design, programming, etc.) to develop the application that students will use, according to the activity designed by teachers.

- **Technician:** Responsible for deploying the technology infrastructure needed to carry out the activity developed using CAFCLA, following the premises and recommendations set by the framework.

- **Student:** The participant who finally conducts the activity designed by the teacher. They can access the resources offered by the application through different devices selected for that purpose. In addition, they are able to collaborate between them to achieve the objectives of the activity. Their performance follows the rules set by the teacher at all times.

Once CAFCLA users have been defined, the way in which contextual information is organized is described. According to AmI premises, CAF-CLA emphasizes on technological transparency and ease of use for both students and teachers. Contextual information is closely related to the environment where the activity takes place, so any place or item can provide relevant information to be used in the learning process. Thus, teachers are able to describe any place or item relevant to the activity regardless of size and location. In order to better structure contextual information, three description levels have been defined, so that the information can be provided with the granularity required by the activity.

- **Scenario:** The whole scenario where the activity takes place. It represents the physical space where the activity will be deployed. To better illustrate the explanation a botanical garden has been chosen to deploy a collaborative learning activity. This scenario consists of an outdoor enclosure where different species of trees, shrubs and flowers grow. Furthermore, in the center of the enclosure there is a greenhouse where multiple flower species grow (Figure 1). In this case the scenario is the botanical garden and it could be divided into two sub-environments: the first one that includes all the study to be performed

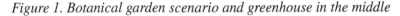

Figure 1. Botanical garden scenario and greenhouse in the middle

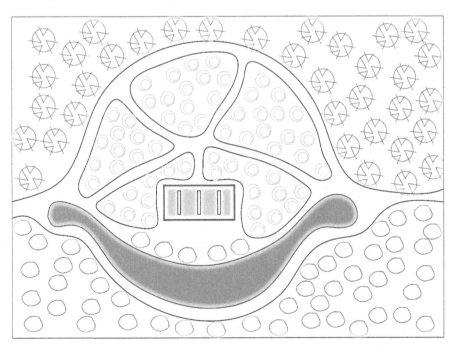

in the greenhouse (indoor plants), and the second, which would cover the rest of the botanical garden, including all the growth area of outdoor plants.

- **Area of Interest:** Different areas that determine spaces in which a relevant part of the activity will take place. These areas include a physical space where one or several goals of the activity should be reached. The teacher is responsible for identifying, locating and making relevant contextual characterization into them. The areas of interest provide contextual information to the students in the way that the design made by the teacher shows. Continuing the example of the botanical garden, in the external environment three different species of trees grow: pine, oak and poplar. In this case the teacher can create four areas of interest: three individual areas covering spaces where trees grow (marked in Figure 2 in brown for pines, pink for oaks, and green for poplars) and a fourth area which is the

greenhouse. For each of them, the teacher defines the physical space that it delimits. It also includes a description of each area, based on the design of the activity, that is given to students.

- **Object of Interest:** in the same way that the environments in which the scenario is divided in different areas of interest, within these areas can be included several specific objects that are interesting to the learning activity. Teachers follow the same procedure as in previous cases, since they are responsible for identifying, locating and characterizing these objects. In the example of the botanical garden there may be multiple objects of interest within each of the areas of interest. For example, in the greenhouse grow a wide variety of flowers, and each kind may be an object of interest so teachers are able to identify, place and characterize each one into the greenhouse (Figure 3).

Figure 2. Areas of interest into the botanical garden scenario

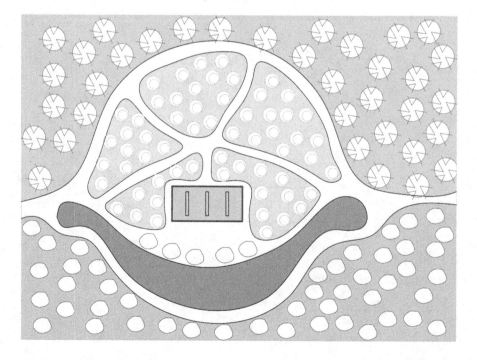

The activities that can be deployed using CAFCLA is another important part of the framework implementation. Different collaborative activities have been evaluated to be integrated by CAFCLA and three of them have been selected: "Treasure Hunting", "Collaborative WebQuest" and "Jigsaw". Different criteria have been taken into account to choose these activities. First of all, these activities can be deployed anywhere and anytime. Secondly, collaboration is possible to be included in all of them. Thirdly, the activities allow teachers to create a learning process that can be monitored and modified at all times. Fourthly, the participants of these activities can be divided into different groups. And finally, all of them can include different routes or physical paths to be followed by the students. However, CAFCLA is an open framework that is able to integrate any other activities that teachers may consider in the future.

Depending on the chosen collaborative activity, the teacher can add the necessary data to complete the learning process. More specifically, the requirements to be considered for each of the activities that are included are described as follows.

First activity implemented is a Treasure Hunt. In this activity the teacher can create working groups that are assigned to the corresponding students and determines which devices are used by each student's group. Students that form a group are able to collaborate with each other at all times. Furthermore, the teacher can define different routes that students must follow to uncover clues and collect information. After setting the scenario, the areas of interest and the objects of interest, the teacher defines each route on the map, and indentifies which are the clues given to each group. Routes do not have to be composed of one only path, but may include branches that allow the division of tasks between the different students that are part of the group. The teacher can assign a path or more to a particular group and also may indicate which tracks are key, so that the students are required to complete a milestone to continue receiving information. Finally, the teacher defines a challenge or final question that must be completed or answered with the information received on each track, such as a questionnaire, a document or a presentation to be made.

Collaborative WebQuest is the second activity implemented. The process of defining and describing the scenario, the areas and the objects of interest, the users and the groups of students is common to all the activities. In this activity the teacher is able to design a battery of questions to be answered in each area of interest. Questions can be presented to be answered in a written way or as a test which offers different response options. These questionnaires can be tailored to each users' level and several can be defined for the same area

Figure 3. Objects into the "Greenhouse" area of interest

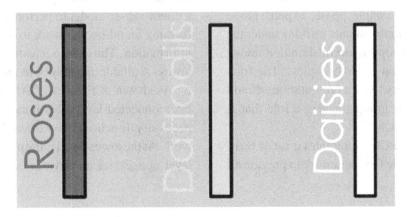

or object of interest. In addition, the teacher can create a final questionnaire to be performed at a particular location (e.g., the classroom) which summarizes all questions regarding the questionnaires that have been made in the activity. Likewise, the teacher has the capacity to define different working groups formed by the number of students it may consider, assigning devices that each group or student uses. Likewise, the teacher indicates the questionnaires that each group must respond. The onset of the activity is performed for each group in the particular zone determined by the teacher through a first task in explanation of the activity.

The last implemented activity is a Jigsaw. As in the previous activities, the process of defining and describing the scenario, the areas and the objects of interest, the users and the groups of students is the first step to be completed. In this activity the teacher divides the activity into different subjects to study individually and then in different groups. First, the teacher assigns each student a specific topic in which will be "expert". Later, two different types of groups are formed: on the one hand by students who have been assigned with different topics (each group will consist of an expert in each of the different themes described) and on the other hand by "expert" students in the same topic. Similarly, the teacher determines which of the areas of interest that have been created belongs to each of the assigned topics. For the proper operation of the activity, the teacher indicates what documents will be generated at each of its stages: single phase, experts phase (collaboration among students working under the same topic) and group phase (collaboration among students working on different topics). The final result of the activity (e.g., a presentation) should be exposed by the group's leader, a role that is assigned by the teacher.

Moreover, CAFCLA integrates a set of technologies that enable the framework to provide all the functionalities that each level requires. Among them are wireless sensor networks, positioning systems and real-time wireless communication protocols that facilitate the transmission and reception of information between users and the environment. For managing the information, communication and collaboration in an intelligent way, CAFCLA also integrates a multi-agent system. From a technical devices standpoint, the teacher may decide to use different communication devices (e.g., smartphones, laptops, tablet PC, etc.) and associate each one to the students. The assignment can be one to one, one to many (i.e., a device assigned to several students to work in team with one machine) or many to one (i.e., a student can work with several devices based on the needs of the moment). Next section explores these technological features of the framework.

4. FRAMEWORK DESCRIPTION

CAFCLA is a framework aimed at designing, developing and deploying AmI-based educational scenarios, focusing on collaborative and context-aware activities. The framework integrates a set of wireless context-aware technologies and communication protocols (e.g., GPS, ZigBee, Wi-Fi, or GPRS/UMTS). Those technologies allow establishing collaborative activities based on Ambient Intelligence among students and teachers. In this sense, communication models vary dynamically depending on the activity; for example, following a client-server model to perform a data query or forming an ad-hoc network to gather contextual information. Thus, the contextual information is always available and may be modified every time.

As shown in Figure 4, CAFCLA has several interconnected layers that joined provide all the necessary functionalities offered by the framework. At the lowest level is the physical layer. This layer consists of all devices (such as tablet PC, smart-phones, laptops, etc.), sensors or any other physical element involved in the system. Above the physical layer the communication layer is placed. This layer includes all the communication protocols currently integrated in the framework: 3G/GPRS, Wi-Fi and ZigBee. Over the communication layer appears the context-aware layer. This layer integrates GPS, a ZigBee based real time locating system and different ZigBee based wireless sensor networks. Thus, the framework can provide contextual information at anytime and anywhere. The management layer is designed so that the context-aware layer and the communication layer can operate in an efficient, predictable and distributed way. This layer integrates a multi-agent system that provides with intelligence to the framework. As is discussed in more detail in the next section, the different actors manage available communications, the background data needed by the students or the proper schedule of learning activities. Finally, the application layer includes the API (Application Programming Interface) offered by CAFCLA to develop services or applications that make use of the remaining layers and will be used by educators to design, develop and deploy the learning activity that students will carry out.

Figure 5 shows how the communication takes place between the different components of CAFCLA. Any application developed with CAFCLA uses the API provided by the framework. Multiple choices of design, programming and implementation are offered by the framework to make the process easy and fast, as well as hide the technological complexity associated. This API provides all the functionality offered by the multi-agent system and context-aware technologies integrated into the framework. Moreover, the system also integrates a distributed database where developed data and services or applications are stored.

From now on, this paper defines the functionalities provided by the multi-agent architecture designed and the context-aware technologies involved, both integrated into CAFCLA.

Figure 4. CAFCLA layers diagram

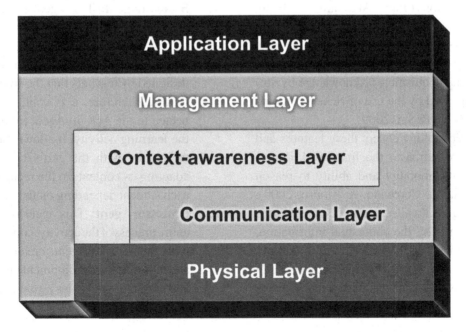

Figure 5. CAFCLA communication schema

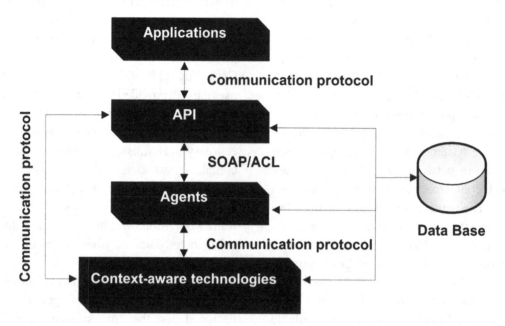

4.1. CAFCLA Multi-Agent Architecture

Ambient Intelligence guidelines require consideration into the design process of framework different features such as distributed way operation, adaptability or the ability to predict and anticipate the users' decisions (Tapia, Abraham, Corchado, & Alonso, 2009). These requirements, along with context-sensitive technologies, facilitate the dynamic customization of the learning process. Therefore, the acquisition of knowledge by students is improved by the use of richer scenarios (Li, Feng, Zhou, & Shi, 2009).

Agent Technology covers these features and provides information to the framework due to its pro-activity, mobility and ability to reason (Tapia, Abraham, Corchado, & Alonso, 2009). The multi-agent architecture is responsible for the management of the contextual information, the communications and the learning activity process. The system's functions include planning and reasoning mechanisms. These mechanisms

are integrated into deliberative agents BDI (belief-desire-intention) (Tapia, Bajo, Sánchez, & Corchado, 2008). Figure 6 shows the different deliberative agents based on the BDI model included in CAFCLA. The role of each of them is as follows:

1. **StudentAgent:** This agent stores the student's profile and all the information related to the activity process concerning a particular user. Its operation depends on a learning plan designed by teachers that the student has to follow. Therefore, it is continuously connected to the ActivityAgent to further plan the learning activity. It allows the students to interact with the end-user application adapting its contents to the requirements of each student depending on the device used.
2. **ProfessorAgent:** This agent monitors the entire process of the activity: communicating with the ActivityAgent, creates, modifies and monitors the development of an activity, and creates or modifies a role of a student.

Figure 6. CAFCLA agents schema

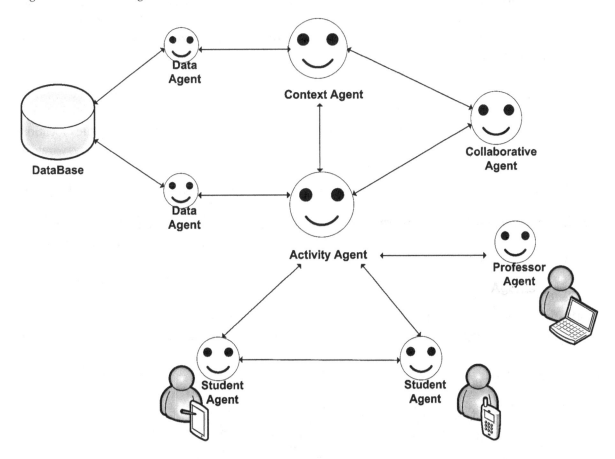

It can be considered as an interface agent that provides the interaction between the teacher and the system to perform all the tasks mentioned before.

3. **ActivityAgent:** This agent coordinates and manages the whole activity. It receives all the information from the ProfessorAgent (profiles, contextual data, collaborations, etc.). As it communicates with the ContextAgent, it decides which information is provided to each student at a particular time and learning activity model.

4. **ContextAgent:** This agent is responsible for controlling all the information gathered by the sensor network. It also interacts with the DataAgent to update data from any physical service implemented by the sensor network and monitors the users location. The agent is responsible for coordinating and monitoring the wireless sensor network that collects environmental data and the Real Time Locating System that determines the position of each student within the scenario.

5. **DataAgent:** This agent maintains the integrity of data during the learning process. It decides what data should be stored at all times in order to have full availability during the activity process. It relates to the ActivityAgent which indicates what information should be stored or asks for a specific information. Moreover, this agent collects information from the Context-Agent, related to the position of the student or the wireless sensor network.

6. **CollaborativeAgent:** This agent monitors the entire process of the activity communicating with the ActivityAgent and with the ContextAgent. With the information received from the ContextAgent it can know where each student is at all times. The CollaborativeAgent combines this data with the available collaborations that gets from the ActivityAgent to suggest on real time new collaborations that can take place in the activity.

4.2. Context-Aware Technologies

Contextual information is useful in the educational process, facilitating the acquisition of new knowledge and training. The use of contextual information allows a better understanding of the environment surrounding the learning and student in a given time. With this knowledge, the information received by the students can be dynamically optimized, customized and adapted to their needs and requirements.

In order to provide contextual information for a wide range of learning scenarios, CAFCLA integrates three different context-aware technologies. More specifically, CAFCLA integrates location capabilities and a platform to deploy wireless sensor networks.

As shown in Figure 7, the main purpose of integrating these technologies is to cover the widest range of possible learning situations. Thus, the contextualization of any object or place will be facilitated by an outside location and / or a representative indoor plan of the place or places where the learning activity is taking place. Thus, the system knows when and what information should be provided to students based on knowledge of

Figure 7. CAFCLA working schema

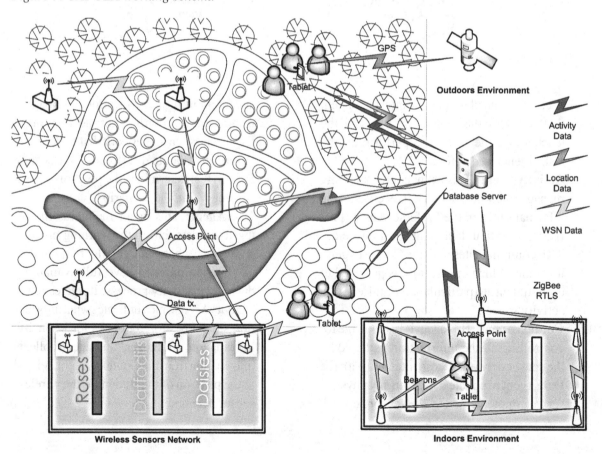

their positions. Moreover, some contextualization can involve physical measurements, so CAFCLA offers the deployment of wireless sensor networks.

The functionalities of each of the context sensitive technologies integrated into the framework are described in the next sections.

4.2.1. Wireless Sensor Networks

The integration of a platform to deploy sensor networks in the framework is useful to cover situations in which the contextualization of an environment requires the collection of physical quantities.

CAFCLA integrates the n-Core platform (Nebusens, 2013), which allows the integration of multiple sensors (e.g., temperature, humidity or pressure). The sensors form a mesh network through which data are sent to the access point that sends information to the CAFCLA data server. There, information is stored and processed. Moreover, the sensors can be connected with other ZigBee devices (e.g., a laptop or Tablet PC) and share the data they collect through an ad-hoc connection established in that moment for that purpose. In this case, educators must decide the location of each sensor, the data type and how often data have to be collected and sent to CAFCLA data server. So CAFCLA records where each sensor is placed and implements the protocol to communicate with other sensors, users or data server.

Students will be able to receive data from sensors as they approach them by forming an ad-hoc network. Furthermore, the system is aware of which student has approached, so that the information provided can be customized or filtered.

4.2.2. Outdoor Real Time Locating System

The outdoor location system, specifically the GPS positioning system, is fully integrated into a wide range of mobile devices. For this reason, it is easy to integrate this technology into learning activities. This functionality requires a GPS device and maps platform like Google Maps or OpenStreetMap. CAFCLA integrates all the necessary logical background that may be available on the system and hides all the complexity inherent to the use of this technology to educators.

When designing an activity, teachers draw an area on the map. There, all the contextual information related to the area is placed, including different versions of information that are used in different activities or by different users. The system is capable of associating an area to one or more descriptions, so that personalization is easy to achieve. During the development of the activity, students use an integrated GPS device that transmits its position continuously. When the student enters into a characterized area or approaches an object of interest, he or she receives contextual information according to the design of the activity.

4.2.3. Indoor Real Time Locating System

CAFCLA also provides an indoor Real Time Locating System. The main reason to include this technology is the technical failure of the GPS system to determine the position of users indoors. The Real Time Locating System is based on n-Core Polaris (Nebusens, 2013), a system that uses the ZigBee wireless communication protocol and that determines the position of users with up to 1 meter accuracy.

The n-Core platform facilitates the localization process. The area where the tracking system is deployed is equipped with a set of beacons called n-Core Sirius D. These beacons are able to communicate and send information about the location of a student to the network access point. Each student has a ZigBee device called n-Core Sirius B that communicates with the beacons closest to his position. Beacons collect different types of signals sent by mobile devices and send them to the access point. The access point sends all information to the activity server where a location engine calculates the position of the student.

Teachers include any kind of information related to any area and students can receive the same way as it is done with the GPS tracking system. Thus, the complexity for educators is reduced and they only have to worry about what information is included in the system regardless of where they perform contextualization.

5. CAFCLA FUNCTIONING

To illustrate how CAFCLA works, this section describes the design process of an activity on the teacher's side. The same example scenario in which the activity takes place in previous sections, the botanical garden, has been chosen.

The implemented activity is a Collaborative WebQuest. Students must answer different questions by identifying different trees and flowers in the botanical garden. They should also collect information about temperature and humidity in different parts of the park, in order to relate each

plant to certain specific physical conditions. In addition, students must work together to identify all plants. For this, different groups of students have access to different parts of the total set of information. Once the scenario is described, CAFCLA guides teachers on the design of the learning activity by following different steps.

In the first step, the teacher defines a collaborative activity to be designed and developed from a given list. Then, the teacher must complete a general description of the activity that all students will see. This description can be regarded as an available statement of the activity to be developed by the students. It indicates what the objectives of the activity are and which resources are available to carry it out.

After choosing the type of activity, the teacher has to include the students who will participate in it (see Figures 8 and 9). This activity will be performance by 18 students divided into six groups of three people each one. Each group has assigned with a Tablet PC and a ZigBee tag to be located.

After inclusion of the participants in the activity, the teacher can contextualize the scenario, the areas of interest and the objects of interest,

Figure 8. Adding users with CAFCLA

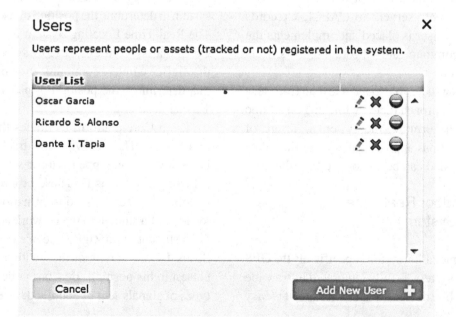

Figure 9. Registration form for a new user

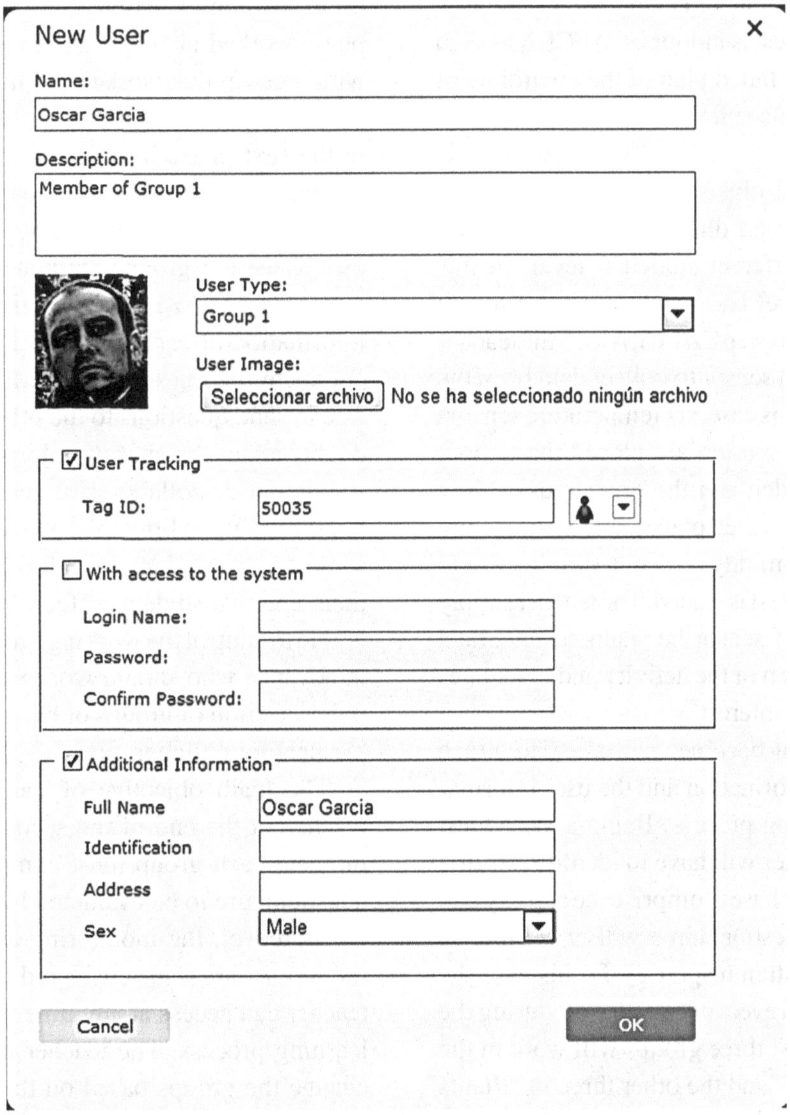

so that each one offers and provides personalized information to each student. The scenario of the activity designed is the botanical garden. Then, it is divided into two areas of interest which are "Outdoor Plants" and "Indoor Plants". At the same time, each area of interest is divided into three objects of interest. "Outdoor Plants" contains the objects of interest: "Pines", "Oaks" and "Poplars". Meanwhile, the area of interest "Indoor Plants"

consists of the next objects of interest: "Roses", "Daffodils" and "Daisies".

To make a success of contextualization, the teacher includes a plan of the scenario, in this case a map of the botanical garden. Then, he creates the two areas of interest to provide personalized information. In this case the teacher identifies the outdoor environment as "Outdoors Plants" area of interest and the greenhouse where flowers grow as "Indoors Plants" area of interest (see Figure 10).

To accomplish this task, the teacher determines if the working environment is indoors or outdoors. If the area of interest is indoors, CAFCLA asks to provide a more detailed plan of the environment and also asks to place it within the main map of the activity.

Each area and object is characterized by a distinctive name and different descriptions according to the different students' level. In this case the same level has been considered for all students. In the next step CAFCLA asks the teacher whether to place a sensor to collect data from the environment. In this case, six temperature sensors and six humidity sensors are placed throughout the botanical garden and the greenhouse. More specifically the teacher places one temperature sensor and one humidity sensor in the area where each object of interest is placed. The teacher simply selects the type of sensor he wants to integrate, places it on the plan of the activity and associates it to the object of interest.

At this point it becomes necessary to attach the contextual information and the user information to the learning process. Being a WebQuest activity, the teacher will have to identify, on first place, how many phases comprise the activity and what types of questionnaires will arise in each phase (test or written response). In this case the teacher designs an event of two phases: during the first phase the first three groups will work in the "Outdoors Plants" and the other three in "Plants Indoors". Each group receives information only from the objects of interest that are included into the area of interest assigned for this phase. The test will consist of questions specific to each object of interest that students receive upon entering the area occupied by each. The teacher must include this test and characterize them with the phase they will be provided and the groups that can receive the test.

Similarly, the teacher defines the second phase of the activity. In this case there will be a collabora-tion between groups from different areas of interest to share information. A group that in the first phase worked in "Outdoors Plants" collaborates with a group that worked in "Indoor Plants". So that, they share the answers of the tests completed in the first phase in order to complete a global writing questionnaire. The teacher must match these collaborations according to his criteria. In this phase the groups circulate freely throughout the scenario and they will receive generic information of each object of interest as help to complete the questionnaire. Moreover, they are free to send questions to the other group to solve doubts about the sharing information. From the standpoint of collaborative activity, the teacher has the ability to limit the collaborations between students, restricting the information offered to them and that students offer each other. Thus he is able to control the working groups, establishing in advance who should work with whom by the only selection of groups or by selecting potential partners for collaboration.

The main objective of the activity will be reached at the end of the second phase. At this moment each group must complete the writing questionnaire to be evaluated by the teacher.

Moreover, the monitoring and evaluation of the activity are also considered in CAFCLA. The teacher can access at any time to the state of the learning process. The teacher has the ability to change the groups based on the progress of the activity and even to modify the questionnaires or planning according to specific needs of the moment. In addition, the teacher can see, in retrospect, how the activity was performed, receiving information communication between students, reporting or responding to questionnaires, how they have carried out the routes or the rate of participation of each student in the full group activity.

Once the teacher has included all the information of the activity, CAFCLA facilitates the development process by using the application

Figure 10. (a) Defining "Indoors Plants" area of interest with CAFCLA; (b) areas of interest in the example activity

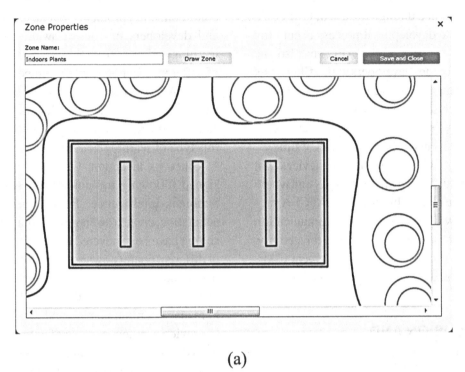

(a)

(b)

programming interface it offers. This API includes all the programming tools needed to develop applications designed through the use of CAFCLA. In addition, the development process is not only facilitated by the use of the API, but also the framework provides developers with a filtered set of programming functions and design diagrams to be used in each section. Thus, the developers can program the system according to the specification made by the teacher in a short period of time.

Finally, CAFCLA identifies the devices that are necessary to implement the activity and where they need to be placed. In addition, CAFCLA suggests the network topology and communication protocols that must be integrated in the activity. Furthermore, proposes how to implement CAFCLA storage and data management systems.

6. CONCLUSION AND FUTURE WORK

The use of Information and Communication Technology in the different areas has increased in recent years thanks to the emergence in society of mobile devices, easy access to currently existing technology and the many features they present, such as communication protocols and context-aware technologies. However, it is difficult to develop applications to squeeze all the potential offered by technology, especially when the main objective is the development of technological applications that are transparent to users, as is suggested by the paradigm of Ambient Intelligence

For this reason, and centered in the field of education, CAFCLA has been designed with the objective to design and develop a set of tools that provide a basis for designing, developing and implementing Ambient intelligence based collaborative learning activities that use contextual information. CAFCLA is a framework that integrates different context-aware technologies, such as Real Time Locating Systems, and several communication protocols that abstract educators and developers of context-aware collaborative learning activities from the complexity of the use of different technologies simultaneously. In this case, CAFCLA focuses on provide a set of tools and methods to teachers, developers and technical staff in order to easily design, develop and deploy this type of learning activities.

Since its inception, CAFCLA has been designed following the guidelines established by Ambient Intelligence. Requirements such as adaptation, context awareness, anticipation or reasoning have been covered by the implementation of different context-aware technologies that allow the framework to be able to cover a wide range of learning scenarios. Moreover, it is necessary to manage communication and data intelligently to provide a system capable of anticipating situations through reasoning mechanisms. Multi-agent systems are presented as an appropriate technology to support these functions. Therefore, CAFCLA integrates a multi-agent system composed of different agents responsible for the coordination and management of different parts of the system depending on their roles. Moreover, CAFCLA presents an innovative way to design and develop learning activities, taking into account all staff involved in the process, facilitating the tasks each one is responsible.

Future work includes the design, development and deployment of a specific use case where all the features of CAFCLA are implemented. This work will be developed by different teachers and developers in order to compare the results reached by all of them and evaluate the framework in different real scenarios. So that, all the features implemented by CAFCLA will be evaluated and improved thanks to the feedback of final users.

REFERENCES

Blöckner, M., Danti, S., Forrai, J., Broll, G., & De Luca, A. (2009). Please touch the exhibits!: using NFC-based interaction for exploring a museum. In *Proceedings of the 11th International Conference on Human-Computer Interaction with Mobile Devices and Services* (pp. 71:1–71:2). New York, NY: ACM. doi:10.1145/1613858.1613943

Bruce, B. C. (2009). Ubiquitous learning, ubiquitous computing, and lived experience. In W. Cope & M. Kalantzis (Eds.), *Ubiquitous learning* (pp. 21–30). Champaign, IL: University of Illinois Press.

Chen, T.-S., Yu, G.-J., & Chen, H.-J. (2007). A framework of mobile context management for supporting context-aware environments in mobile ad hoc networks. In *Proceedings of the 2007 International Conference on Wireless Communications and Mobile Computing* (pp. 647–652). Academic Press. doi:10.1145/1280940.1281078

Dey, A. K. (2001). Understanding and Using Context. *Personal and Ubiquitous Computing*, *5*(1), 4–7. doi:10.1007/s007790170019

Dillenbourg, P. (1999). What do you mean by "Collaborative Learning"? In *Collaborative Learning. Cognitive and Computational Approaches* (pp. 1–19). Oxford, UK: Elsevier Science Ltd.

Driver, C., & Clarke, S. (2008). An application framework for mobile, context-aware trails. *Pervasive and Mobile Computing*, *4*(5), 719–736. doi:10.1016/j.pmcj.2008.04.009

García, Ó., Tapia, D. I., Alonso, R. S., Rodríguez, S., & Corchado, J. M. (2011). Ambient intelligence and collaborative e-learning: A new definition model. *Journal of Ambient Intelligence and Humanized Computing*.

Glahn, C., & Börner, D. (2010). Mobile informal learning. In A report from the STELLAR Alpine Rendez-Vous workshop series (pp. 28–31). Nottingham, UK: Academic Press.

Gómez-Sánchez, E., Bote-Lorenzo, M. L., Jorrín-Abellán, I. M., Vega-Gorgojo, G., Asensio-Pérez, J. I., & Dimitriadis, Y. A. (2009). Conceptual framework for design, technological support and evaluation of collaborative learning. *International Journal of Engineering Education*, *25*(3), 557–568.

Hwang, G.-J., Yang, T.-C., Tsai, C.-C., & Yang, S. J. H. (2009). A context-aware ubiquitous learning environment for conducting complex science experiments. *Computers & Education*, *53*(2), 402–413. doi:10.1016/j.compedu.2009.02.016

Jorrín-Abellán, I. M., & Stake, R. E. (2009). *Does Ubiquitous Learning Call for Ubiquitous Forms of Formal Evaluation?: An Evaluand oriented Responsive Evaluation Model. In Ubiquitous Learning: An International Journal* (p. 1). Melbourne, Australia: Common Ground Publisher.

Koschmann, T. (1996). *CSCL : theory and practice of an emerging paradigm*. Mahwah, NJ: Lawrence Erlbaum.

Laine, T. H., & Joy, M. S. (2009). Survey on Context-Aware Pervasive Learning Environments. *International Journal of Interactive Mobile Technologies*, *3*(1), 70–76.

Li, X., Feng, L., Zhou, L., & Shi, Y. (2009). Learning in an Ambient Intelligent World: Enabling Technologies and Practices. *IEEE Transactions on Knowledge and Data Engineering*, *21*(6), 910–924.

Lu, C., Chang, M., Kinshuk, Huang, E., & Chen, C.-W. (2011). Architecture and collaborations among agents in mobile educational game. In *Proceedings of 2011 IEEE International Conference on Pervasive Computing and Communications Workshops (PERCOM Workshops)* (pp. 556–560). IEEE. doi:10.1109/PERCOMW.2011.5766951

Macarro, A., Pedrero, A., & Fraile, J. A. (2009). Multiagent-Based Educational Environment for Dependents. In J. Cabestany, F. Sandoval, A. Prieto, & J. M. Corchado (Eds.), *Bio-Inspired Systems: Computational and Ambient Intelligence* (pp. 602–609). Springer Berlin Heidelberg.

Martín, S., Peire, J., & Castro, M. (2010). M2Learn: Towards a homogeneous vision of advanced mobile learning development. In Proceedings of Education Engineering (EDUCON), (pp. 569–574). IEEE.

Nebusens. (2013). *n-Core®: A Faster and Easier Way to Create Wireless Sensor Networks*. Retrieved from http://www.nebusens.com

Neyem, A., Ochoa, S. F., Pino, J. A., & Guerrero, L. A. (2005). Sharing Information Resources in Mobile Ad-hoc Networks. In *Proceedings of 11th Workshop on Groupware, CRIWG05*, (pp. 351–358). CRIWG. doi:10.1007/11560296_28

Padovitz, A., Loke, S., & Zaslavsky, A. (2008). The ECORA framework: A hybrid architecture for context-oriented pervasive computing. *Pervasive and Mobile Computing*, 4(2), 182–215. doi:10.1016/j.pmcj.2007.10.002

Roschelle, J. (2003). Unlocking the learning value of wireless mobile devices. *Journal of Computer Assisted Learning*, 19(3), 260–272. doi:10.1046/j.0266-4909.2003.00028.x

Scardamalia, M., Bereiter, C., McLean, R. S., Swallow, J., & Woodruff, E. (1989). Computer-Supported Intentional Learning Environments. *Journal of Educational Computing Research*, 5(1), 51–68.

Sharples, M., Taylor, J., & Vavoula, G. (2010). A Theory of Learning for the Mobile Age. In B. Bachmair (Ed.), *Medienbildung in neuen Kulturräumen* (pp. 87–99). Wiesbaden: VS Verlag für Sozialwissenschaften. doi:10.1007/978-3-531-92133-4_6

Tan, Q., Kinshuk, Kuo, Y.-H., Jeng, Y.-L., Wu, P.-H., Huang, Y.-M., … Chang, M. (2009). Location-Based Adaptive Mobile Learning Research Framework and Topics. In *Proceedings of International Conference on Computational Science and Engineering,* (Vol. 1, pp. 140–147). IEEE. doi:10.1109/CSE.2009.96

Tapia, D. I., Abraham, A., Corchado, J. M., & Alonso, R. S. (2009). Agents and ambient intelligence: Case studies. *Journal of Ambient Intelligence and Humanized Computing*, 1(2), 85–93. doi:10.1007/s12652-009-0006-2

Tapia, D. I., Bajo, J., Sánchez, J. M., & Corchado, J. M. (2008). An Ambient Intelligence Based Multi-Agent Architecture. In *Developing Ambient Intelligence* (pp. 68–78). Paris: Springer Paris. doi:10.1007/978-2-287-78544-3_7

Traynor, D., Xie, E., & Curran, K. (2010). Context-Awareness in Ambient Intelligence. *International Journal of Ambient Computing and Intelligence*, 2(1), 13–23. doi:10.4018/jaci.2010010102

Trifonova, A., & Ronchetti, M. (2006). Hoarding content for mobile learning. *International Journal of Mobile Communications*, 4(4), 459–476. doi:10.1504/IJMC.2006.008952

Vasiliou, A., & Economides, A. A. (2007). Mobile collaborative learning using multicast manets. *International Journal of Mobile Communications*, 5(4), 423–444. doi:10.1504/IJMC.2007.012789

Yaghmaie, M., & Bahreininejad, A. (2011). A context-aware adaptive learning system using agents. *Expert Systems with Applications*, 38(4), 3280–3286. doi:10.1016/j.eswa.2010.08.113

Zurita, G., Baloain, N., & Baytelman, F. (2008). Using Mobile Devices to Foster Social Interactions in the Classroom. In *Proceedings of Computer Supported Cooperative Work in Design*. CSCW. doi:10.1109/CSCWD.2008.4537123

KEY TERMS AND DEFINITIONS

Adaptive Learning: Educational method in which contents are adapted, using computers or other interactive devices, to students' needs.

Agent Technology: Artificial intelligence software that learns and automate processes.

Ambient Intelligence: Considered as a vision of the future in which electronic environment will be sensitive and responsible to people's needs.

Computer Supported Collaborative Learning: Pedagogical vision in which interaction between students through computers or interactive devices is the base of the learning.

Context-Aware Learning: Educational method in which contents are adapted to the environment in which the learning process is taking place.

Location-Based Learning: Educational method in which contents are adapted the location in which the learning process is taking place.

Ubiquitous Computing: Computer science branch wherein computing devices are everywhere.

Chapter 13

Contemporary Gold Rush or Scientific Advancement:
A Review of Social Network Analysis Approaches and Their Impact

Darren Quinn
University of Ulster, UK

Liming Chen
De Montfort University, UK

Maurice Mulvenna
University of Ulster, UK

ABSTRACT

Following the expansion and mass adoption of Online Social Networks, the impact upon the domain of Social Network Analysis has been a rapid evolution in terms of approach, developing sophisticated methods to capture and understand individual and community interactions. This chapter provides a comprehensive review, examining state-of-the-art Social Network Analysis research and practices, highlighting key trends within the domain. In section 1, the authors examine the growing awareness concerning data as a marketable and scientific commodity. Section 2 reviews the context of Online Social Networking, highlighting key approaches for analysing Online Social Networks. In section 3, they consider modelling motivations of networks, discussing models in line with tie formation approaches. Section 4 outlines data collection approaches along with common structural properties observed in related literature. The authors discuss future directions and emerging approaches, notably semantic social networks and social interaction analysis before conclusions are provided.

1. INTRODUCTION

In recent times the influence and value of data have been brought into sharp focus within both the public domain and the scientific community. Reports such as that of the hacking of Adobe systems in October 2013, where the data of more than 38 million users were acquired[15], including encrypted passwords, names, debit and credit card numbers have now become a frequent incident, following on from a succession of high profile security breaches against targeted organisations.

DOI: 10.4018/978-1-4666-7284-0.ch013

Copyright © 2015, IGI Global. Copying or distributing in print or electronic forms without written permission of IGI Global is prohibited.

Commercially, the value of data is also being realised with the flotation of major Online Social Networking sites. In May 2012 the New York Stock Exchange (NYSE) valued Facebook at $104bn[16] and more recently in November 2013 the flotation of Twitter valued the company at $18bn. To further underline the current focus on data, technology's industry leaders are eager to understand its users behavioural patterns and interactions, and are highly sensitive to potential gains, describing it as the "the new oil"[17]. With such riches readily associated to user data, it creates the feel of a modern day gold rush for those aiming to comprehend and exploit data for both scientific and commercial advantage. However, understanding data and the behavioural patterns of users has evolved rapidly, particularly over the last decade within its scientific domain of Social Network Analysis (SNA).

The role of SNA is summarised as being to disclose how individuals and communities interact. As online technology evolved, advancements have meant that interactions which would have traditionally occurred face-to-face, now occur more frequently though Online Social Networks, facilitated by an array of social based platforms such as Twitter[1], Facebook[2] and Instgram[3] etc. User adoption has exploded and in less than ten years

Facebook amassed 1.19 billion users (Facebook Statistics, 2013) epitomising the rapid growth and adoption levels. Subsequently, interactions now occur on an unprecedented scale, with users generating billions of interactions on a daily basis in the form of tweets, instant messages and the sharing of photos etc. As such, exciting opportunities have arisen within SNA whereby communications can now be observed across the globe between all demographics.

However, the resulting challenge for SNA has been a rapid evolution in approach, in terms of how user interactions are captured and understood; interpreting the new insights gained from an expansion in the volume and mode of social interactions. Scientifically the domain has advanced significantly, particularly over the last decade, in-line with online and mobile technology. Increased interest in SNA is evidenced through the rising number of published articles on SNA. As illustrated in Figure 1, an explosion in domain popularity can be clearly observed from 2005 onwards where the number of articles began and has continued to rise year on year. This rise coincides directly with the commercialisation and mass adoption of social computing, with popularised social networking sites such as Facebook and Bebo[4] which emerged in 2004 and 2005 respectively.

Figure 1. Trending of published social network articles from 1995 to 2012

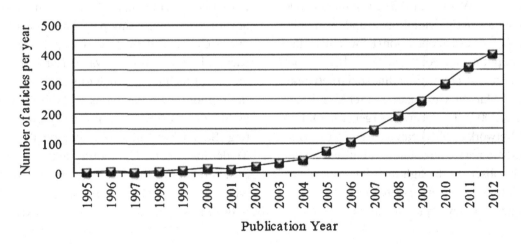

1.1. Context for Social Networking

The World Wide Web has brought change to a point where it would now be difficult to imagine an unconnected world without online networks. The latest internet penetration statistics disclose that, in June 2012, 63% of Europe's 821 million population were internet users (Internet World Stats, 2013). Nevertheless, online social networking is arguably one of most innovative applications to emerge from the Web. Their social and economic impact for individuals and business is described as 'profound', rendering a new global footprint (Charron, Favier, & Li, 2006). Their usage has evolved from initially being a communication tool, towards a content sharing and social platform. Subsequently, a diverse range of sites emerged, ranging from generic social networking sites to content sharing networks such as Youtube[5] and Flickr[6], or for specific demographics such as ageing users, with sites such as Eons[7]and Sagazone[8] were developed.

As such, research of online social networks, commonly referred to as SNA, gained increasing attention. SNA intends to model and analyse the interdependent relationships and hidden patterns that make up a social network structure, e.g., friendships, kinships beliefs or interests. Social networks have been studied extensively in multiple disciplines with works in communication (Wasserman & Faust, 1994), anthropology (Barnes, 1972) and sociology (Wellman, 1983). Examples include its application in Epidemiology to understand the spread of disease in a population (Klovdahl, 1985), or in Computing Science to understand the impact of community structures in online social networks (Mislove, Marcon, Gummadi, Druschel, & Bhattacharjee, 2007). The recent emergence of Online Social Networks (OSN) can be viewed as being the contemporary equivalent of traditional social networks observed through the social science of anthropology. As such, research of online SNA is only a recent development, still in its infancy.

OSN have many unique characteristics differentiating them from traditional social networks in terms of formation, evolution and analysis approaches. Firstly, OSN form and evolve in a bottom-up way with individuals driving, shaping and controlling the networks. Secondly, an individual or group's social network is no longer location restricted, allowing users access to social networks which may previously have been restricted by a location or demographic. An enhanced network reach is providing users with greater exposure and visibility to relatable communities and information. Thirdly, OSN allow for more controlled, directed communications and contact to draw information from specific domains of interest. In addition, contact frequency and information disclosure are self-imposed, allowing a user to perform in an observational or contributory role. Given the unique features of OSN, SNA requires a new wave of approaches and methods, differing from approaches traditionally applied in social sciences to gain insights and discover intrinsic regularities. Currently there are a whole raft of SNA approaches being developed, ranging from network modelling, community formation and semantic analysis (Erétéo, Gandon, Corby, & Buffa, 2009b; Kumpula, Onnela, Saramäki, Kaski, & Kertész, 2007; Pfeil & Zaphiris, 2007).

As discussed, SNA has the potential to be applied to a broad range of areas. The intention of this chapter is to review the area of SNA, focusing particularly on the impact OSN have made on the area of SNA, discussing past, present and future approaches and their potential applications. As such, a literature review was performed using a variety of techniques, including searches within the bibliographic databases of Web of Science and Google Scholar with key terms and phrases (e.g. Social Network Analysis, Social Network Modelling, Social Computing and Community Structure). A further filtering process followed whereby all literature was assessed for suitability within the scope. All relevant literature was classified for inclusion within distinct sub categories and discussed within the appropriate section headings. The remit is not to discuss areas in specific detail, as has already been achieved in a number of related works and studies, but to provide a general insight into common approaches within this broad area. The aim will be to review the current state of the art of SNA, identifying trends, approaches and technologies of SNA and potential future directions. It will discuss the fundamental areas and related works associated with SNA. The remainder of the discussion is organised as follows. Section 2 discusses the trend of social networking sites, their application and trends in related research. Section 3 investigates the motivations of why social networks should be modelled. A range of network models and their impact on a network structure are examined. As key network concepts, tie formation and network evolution are reviewed. Section 4 discusses traditional and contemporary data collection approaches, elaborating on common structural properties in understanding the user role in a network and social network metrics. Section 5 discusses potential future directions of semantics in online network modelling and analysis. Section 6 provides a summary on the key issues within SNA.

2. BACKGROUND AND CONTEXT FOR SOCIAL NETWORK ANALYSIS

Online social networking has been designed with two primary purposes;

1. To enable the sharing and interaction of data, and
2. To support the social activities of users.

Trends can be seen to have been driven by the advancements in technology, with many of today's popular sites developed after the emergence of web 2.0. As a term coined by (DiNucci, 1999), Web 2.0 provided users with a generation of sites which facilitated interactive information sharing, enabling users to become active authors and contributors of content. As an archetypal web 2.0 site, Flickr was developed as a photo management site allowing users to apply semantic meaning through the 'tagging' of images, a process whereby metadata is applied to provide context to flat data. With such capabilities, social networking sites now provide an increasingly enriched and personalised user experience, a key feature which helped fuel the explosion in popularity, to the stage whereby their impact is an accepted 'phenomenon' (Cooke & Buckley, 2008; Kwai Fun, 2008; Parameswaran & Whinston, 2007). In a short time social networking established itself as a recognised paradigm for communication and interaction. As an example of research carried out in online social networks and their diverse application(s), Facebook has been demonstrated for its use in the sharing of experiences, diagnosis and management of disease (Farmer, A.D., BrucknerHolt, C.E.M., Cook, M.J. & Hearing, S.D., 2009). Social networking as a communication and interaction tool is providing connections for isolated individuals or groups wishing to share experiences, events and emotions. The large scale uptake and popularity of such technologies has already generated data sets that are being exploited by both research and industry for the analysis and observation of social networking.

As user popularity increases in online social networks, so has the associated research interest in a range of disciplines, investigating issues relating to members profiles (Pfeil & Zaphiris, 2007; Thelwall, 2008), information revelation and privacy (Gross, Acquisti, & Heinz III, 2005), community structures (Lewis, Kaufman, Gonzalez, Wimmer, & Christakis, 2008; Porter, Onnela, & Mucha, 2009; Traud, Kelsic, Mucha, & Porter, 2008), social networking patterns (Pfeil & Zaphiris, 2009; Pfeil, Arjan, & Zaphiris, 2009; Zaphiris & Sarwar, 2006) and social network modelling (Hunter, Goodreau, & Handcock, 2008; Kumpula et al., 2007).

In terms of user volume, studies by Chau *et al.* (2007), Mislove *et al.* (2007) and Wilson *et al.* (2009) are noteworthy collecting over 10 million profiles. Mislove *et al.* (2007), at the time was the largest analysis of online social networks, containing over 11.3 million users and 328 million links. In this work four popular online social networking sites of YouTube, Flickr, LiveJournal[9] and Orkut[10] were analysed. The large scale measurement and analysis of structural properties within online social networks confirmed the in-degree and out-degree of users is likely to be equal, and that such online networks contain a heavily connected nucleus of high-degree users; a core connecting to small groups of strongly clustered, low-degree users at the fringes of the network.

In more recent times, the direction of social network analysis has begun to shift with a greater focus on discovering how individual users engage. Wilson *et al.* (2009) carried out a large scale study on Facebook, analysing in excess of 10 million user profiles and wall posts, investigating user interaction patterns across large user groups. Wilson's study differed, in that it moved away from previous works which had carried out static analysis of network ties, to an approach which aimed to assess social interaction dynamics on top of static ties, including interaction patterns, evolution, types and weights. Discrete interactions have also been investigated at the micro level (D. Quinn, Chen, & Mulvenna, 2011a; D. Quinn, Chen, & Mulvenna, 2011b), determining precisely how particular demographic groups interact within online social networking platforms. Within this work it contrasted behavioural patterns of disparate age groups, these being younger and older users. Results acquired through a process of profile extraction and analysis established a precise profile for each user and subsequently for each cohort, determining connectivity, length of engagement, application usage, engagement frequency classification and profile maintenance frequency. In the work of Abdulrahman *et al.* (2013) Online Social Network Retrieval System (OSNRS) were extended based on a Multi Agent System (MAS) enabled user profiles to be monitored continuously through the employment of an API integrating directly with the OSN provider, overcoming previous issues of user profile changes. With this work, it further demonstrates the complexity of approaches when extracting social network data employing algorithms, API's and MAS alongside text mining capabilities with results understanding the dynamic behaviour of OSN users. In the work of Psallidas et al. (2013) the issue of cross social media content is explored through the development of a distributed crawler, harnessing information from multiple OSN's. The model applied 'Soc-Web' which essentially connects aggregated social networks through a flexible API. Results acquired assorted qualitative and quantitative performance criteria, including freshness of facts, scalability, quality of fetched data from each OSN and network robustness. Further examples of diverse works in social network data analysis include a topic crawler developed to detect drug community in Russian segments of Livejournal.com by Yakushev *et al.* (2013) employing a crawler approach, or the work of Blackburn (2013) proposing an architecture for collecting longitudinal social data architecture. This work applied a general framework for large scale observational studies of dynamic social networks with the ability to capture and aggregate data from multiple sources, making them available for analysis in real time

3. SOCIAL NETWORK MODELLING

An online social network can simply be viewed as a structure of individuals, groups or organisations and their respective connections. The individual (group or organisation) within the network is represented as a 'node', and the connections between nodes are represented and termed as 'ties'. Nodes will traditionally form ties through interdependencies such as kinship, friendship or belief etc. and will in most instances be reflective of the sites purpose. For example, the social networking service LinkedIn[11] is designed to link professionals and the interdependencies between nodes are created on the basis of a professional acquaintance (i.e. industry related). The foundations of any network are built upon a network model and the subsequent tie formation approach, and as such models are the means by which we gain a greater understanding of how networks form and evolve, and enable us to specify the structure of interaction (Toivonen et al., 2009). As discussed by Robins et al. (2007) the modelling of social network structures is driven through five primary motivations (Table 1). Network models and tie formation approaches are discussed for their influence in online social networks.

3.1. Models

A host of social network models exists, within the context of online social networks. These models can be classified into three major categories, namely Network Evolution Models (NEM), Network Attribute Models (NAM) and Exponential Random Graph Models (ERGM). Some researchers like Toivonen et al. (2009) further classified the three categories within eight network models. In their work social network models were defined in three categorises, however focus was on NEM and NAM. ERGM (also referred to as P* models) were included within this work for comparison purposes only, and will not be discussed within the context of this survey. As a model ERGM is

Table 1. Social network modelling motivations

Motivating Reasons for Modelling Social Networks
• Social behaviour is complex. • Modelling social network structure enables an ability to make inferences about the substructures in a network. • To assess the nature of clustering (community structures) in the network. • They are useful for complex structures. • Assessment of local and global processes.

noted as not addressing the network evolution process, a key element when considering dense community structure. NEM's (growing or dynamical) are defined as the addition of links being dependent on the network structure. NAM's (also referred to as spatial models) are defined by the generation of new links being dependent only on nodal attributes (e.g. interest or hobbies). As being representative of the many large scale social networks the formation of community structures is of importance within the overall context of the survey, and it is with this criterion that appropriate models and related literature are further discussed.

Toivonen *et al.* (2006) presented a model for social networks based on an undirected growing network. The results produced highly connected vertices as a platform for studying sociodynamic phenomena. The approaches used were random attachment, and implicit preferential attachment. The model produced network results that resemble real world social networks, where they retained assortative degree correlations, high clustering, short average path lengths, broad degree distributions and prominent community structures.

In their investigation on the influence of weights, and the formation of community structures, Kumpala *et al.* (2007) produced highly dense community structures through the application of network weights, weights which were based on a coupling in the network structure and interaction strengths. These results are compatible with Granovetter (1973) '*The Strength of Weak Ties*' hypothesis which states that within a social network, weak ties play a key role in network diffusion. As a network model, community structures emerged only when the strengthening / probability of the assigned weight were at the desired level, taking full account of interaction strength. Fundamentally new ties would only be created preferably through strong ties, and every interaction created thereafter was designed as part of the network model to strengthen the ties.

3.2. Tie Formation Approaches

Network formation and subsequent evolution occurs as nodes form ties, to communicate and share information across the network. Evolution comes about as nodes are added to a network, and ties are established between nodes within the network (e.g. node A joins network and connects to B and C). Attribute databases retain a user's profile, where comparison functions determine a similarity value to other network users. As an example, Facebook uses algorithms to compare and contrast similarity of users. Those nodes deemed to be of a designated probability / weight are then displayed and returned to the user as potential new network tie formations as, 'Friend recommendations'. The concept of evolution in a social network model is of crucial importance when considering how it defines and affects a networks topology. The two principal network evolution methods Triadic closure and Homophily are discussed below.

Triadic Closure, also referred to as cyclic closure (Kumpula et al., 2007), (Figure 2a), was established by Simmel (1950), and subsequently popularised by Granovetter (1973) 'Strength of Weak Ties' article. In this instance, tie formation occurs based on the tendency of two friends of an individual to become acquainted. For example, node A is friends with Node B. Node A is also friends with Node C. Triadic closure therefore states that nodes B and C may also become ac-

quainted. Due to its nature such networks, evolve in an outward fashion until the network model is satisfied and this can be through node number constraints within a network.

Homophily (Figure 2b) is tie formation occurring based on the tendency for like to interact with like, and associated with the phrase 'Birds of a feather flock together' (McPherson, Smith-Lovin, & Cook, 2001). Homophily, in a social network context identifies nodes sharing common characteristics, which have been expressed through their nodal attributes. Two random nodes completely unknown to each other within a network structure can be introduced with a high probability factor due to the similarity of their stated node attributes. For example, node A is male, aged 27, likes soccer, fishing and walking. Node B also likes the same. Homophily therefore states node A and B may become acquainted due to the strength of their similarities. As a concept, it is primarily associated with weighted networks. As an approach, it is employed to structure network ties of various types, most commonly associated with friendship, interest, age, gender, work and marriage etc.

The key difference between the aforementioned approaches is that homophily connections can be established throughout the wider network, whereas triadic closure connections are restricted to within the range of their own sub network. Facebook's 'Find friends' application tool is an example of a homophily based network, as people connect

Figure 2. (a) Triadic closure (b) homophily

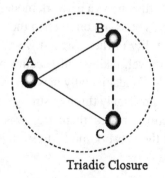

Triadic Closure

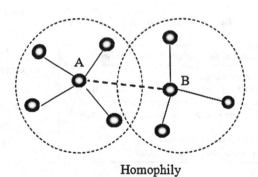

Homophily

throughout the wider social network with like-minded people sharing similar attributes. As each social network has its designated design and function the appropriateness or suitability of the network formation approach is situation dependent.

4. SOCIAL NETWORK ANALYSIS

SNA can quantify and qualify a social network by analysing and visualising a network, its structure and properties. Analysis usually involves data collection and analysis of relevant structural properties, network metric specification, both of which are described below.

4.1. Data Collection

Data collection methods for SNA have changed considerably over the past two decades. Traditionally data were collected using field observation, simulated experiments and the most used methods of interview and questionnaires (Table 2). Krackhardt and Stern (1988) collected data on the friendships among members of a university class, as part of a study simulating corporations. They applied questionnaires to rate friendships based on a five point scale for their respective class members. Coleman *et al.* (1966) is a further example of the approach of questionnaires being applied when researching the diffusion of a medical innovation among physicians.

Data collected using such approaches would normally have been stored in physical media and analysed manually. As such these methods required huge amounts of human resources, i.e., researchers to collect and analyse data and subjects to provide information. The process required for traditional data collection is time-consuming, cost-expensive, and context and region dependent, i.e., the results only reflect the patterns or trends of a specific sampling regions or population. This has led to the situation in which data collection became a bottleneck of SNA.

Online social network structures may contain millions of nodes, and the application of traditional data collection methods would in this instance be inefficient and uneconomical both in terms of cost and labour. With the advance and prevalence of Web technologies and online social networking sites, the landscape of SNA has completely changed. Firstly, data acquisition becomes easy as online social networks contain huge user numbers without subject to various constraints of traditional ways, e.g., region and sampling population. Secondly, data collection can be done automatically using crawlers. This gives rise to a number of contemporary approaches (Table 2). These new approaches enable for the remote observation of online social network activity, providing a much less intrusive means of assessing social network structures and dependencies.

Contemporary approaches are now applied as an extremely efficient method for data collection. Facebook API's (Application Programming Interface) are an example of contemporary data collection, whereby software communicates with a remote application over the web through a succession of calls, operated by a web service to

Table 2. Examples of data collection approaches

Traditional Data Collection	Contemporary Data Collection
• Observation • Experiments • Interviews • Archival Records (Diaries) • Questionnaires	• API (Application Programming Interface) • MAS (Multi Agent Systems • Plug-ins • Web Crawlers • Online Interviews • Online Questionnaires

provide the network data required. Increasingly the Web is being viewed as an information sharing system, and online social network data collection is now an accepted contemporary solution to the traditional data collection methods. User privacy restricts access to large portions of network data and innovative approaches such as browser plug-in, API's, and web crawlers are routinely applied in contemporary SNA.

Mislove *et al.* (2007) carried out a large scale measurement (11.3 million users, 328 million links) and analysis of online social networks to identify common structural properties. They employed API's and data crawling algorithms as a method of data collection. Common algorithms for crawling graphs included the use of breadth-first (BFS) and depth-first search (DFS). The data collection component accesses through an API with either a BFS or DFS applied dependent upon individual platform restrictions. The methodology employed is known as statistical sampling, where coverage is approximated, dependent on the number of reachable links.

Data collection undertaken by Wilson *et al.* (2009) overcame Facebook network restrictions through regional network crawls, where access was unauthenticated and opens to all users. A multi-threaded crawler was applied through python, acquiring over 10 million users in less than 24 hours. Similar to the approach of Mislove *et al.* (2007), they employed a testing method of repeating crawls for error measurement, achieving a differential of 0.1% for potential missing networks links. As can be seen from existing works, modern approaches provide a means to accurately assess large scale online social networks and their structural properties, overcoming challenges of time, cost, and regional restrictions.

4.2. Structural Properties

Structural properties are measures and metrics that can be used to characterise a social network model. They were proposed and studied by New-

man (2003) in the influential research on complex networks and has been used extensively for SNA in the plethora of following research (Caverlee & Webb, 2008; Erétéo, Gandon, Corby, & Buffa, 2009b; Lewis et al., 2008; Mislove et al., 2007; Traud et al., 2008). By analysing structural properties we can answer questions such as; how compact is a network? Or, how important is a particular node? Due to limited space, we will only cover the prominent properties of Geodesic, Clustering, Cliques and Centrality to give a general understanding to commonly applied analysis.

Geodesic is concerned with the path length between nodes and is the shortest path between two nodes (Wasserman & Faust, 1994). The distance between two nodes is defined as the length of the geodesic and the average length of geodesic paths provides a measurement used in analysis to describe a networks compactness. As such, Geodesic is applied to determine a measurement of closeness/connectivity in networks.

Clustering is best understood when considering the formation of a community within a social network. It is visualised in network analysis with approaches such as scatter graphs, or through connected graphs such as a dendrogram to give an intuitive representation of dense node formations. With the application of a connected graph as an analysis approach it is important to realise that all points within a network will eventually fuse into a single cluster, and that the number and size of clusters to be identified is dependent upon the cut-off threshold.

Cliques within a network are defined as 'pockets of high density' (Scott, 2000). In both a sociological and online context, social relations may in some instances be further divided into cohesive subgroups, producing what is referred to as a clique. Cliques both in the real world and within online social networks are identifiable as groups within groups, with nodes within a subgroup sharing a sub set of values or interests. Cliques in a network are nodes interacting at higher rates in the network, and provide a measure in SNA of community structure (Scott, 2000; Wasserman & Faust, 1994). Cliques form and become recognised as being such within a social network when interactions have been deemed to have reached a desired level of intensity or assessed according to their connectedness.

Centrality is a fundamental social network property, and associated as being the node that is most popular within their particular network sub group. Bavelas (1950) whose primary interests lay in communication networks is acknowledged as an early pioneer in defining the properties of centrality. Nodes of high centrality are extensively involved in relationships with others, a network measurement that assesses the level of influence and connectedness of a node in a network. Related concepts such as betweenness (Freeman, 1979), degree and closeness are extensively used in network analysis (Hanneman & Riddle, 2005; Newman, 2003; Wasserman & Faust, 1994). Closeness centrality is the sum of geodesic distances to all other nodes and the inverse measurement of centrality. Betweenness centrality is the number of times that a node lies along the shortest path between two others nodes. Degree centrality is a count of the number of ties to other nodes in the network and therefore provides a measurement for the level of importance of a particular node in a network.

More recently metrics are being developed to give real meaning to the individual and their discrete personal behaviours within large scale online social networks. In particular Quinn *et al.* (2013) developed a series of ten social networking metrics for Facebook users, interaction analysis metrics detailing behavioural elements such as how long a user has been active, the total number and type of activities or defining the number of activities a user is likely to perform on their days of engagement. Such measures perform a variety of functions. Initially they allow SNA to understand discrete users, however more fundamentally it will allow observations on various demographic

groups, providing a platform for the next wave in social network analysis to understand how OSN impact real world issues such as quality of life.

5. FUTURE DIRECTIONS

While SNA has made substantial progress, existing research has mainly focused on static link analysis, investigating a networks structural property. More recently the direction of research in SNA has begun to change with a range of new directions being explored, some of which are discussed below.

Interest is increasing in exploiting the ability of semantic technology to model social networks, networks which contain ties enriched with meaning, and the subsequent data produced. As semantics are defined as being 'the study of meaning in language'' (Crystal, 2011), the semantic web is the rational extension in an online context. Semantic technology enables inferencing and logic to be applied, driven by intelligent agents capable of identifying related information and executing tasks automatically. Since Berners-Lee provided his view which envisioned "The semantic web will facilitate the development of automated methods for helping users to understand the content produced by those in other scientific disciplines" (Berners-Lee & Hendler, 2001) the semantic web has come a long way. The impact for online social networks is that technologies are now capable of detecting relationships between objects, enabling an extremely personalised user experience through inferencing and logic. As online social networks have grown in volume and complexity (Golbeck, 2007), there is an increasing interest into the structural and social relationships that are involved on the semantic web (Erétéo, Gandon, Corby, & Buffa, 2009a; Gruber, 2008; Pfeil & Zaphiris, 2007; Pfeil & Zaphiris, 2009). Semantic technologies have been explored for data modelling, content generation, activity representation, and also for their application in analysing interaction patterns (D. Chen, Yang, & Wactlar, 2004). Their diverse nature has also seen them investigated as a modelling and representation approach, within ambient assisted living (L. Chen & Nugent, 2009; L. Chen, Nugent, Mulvenna, Finlay, & Hong, 2009; Klein, Schmidt, & Lauer, 2007; Latfi, Lefebvre, & Descheneaux, 2007).

As a framework operating within the semantic web, ontologies are a track gaining increasing attention. As a commonly cited definition, an ontology is "an explicit specification of the conceptualisation of a domain" (Guarino, 1998). In reality this means that ontologies can be viewed as a set of general reasoning controls operating within the semantic web. With regard to network modelling, ontologies have demonstrated ability to model and manage the social relations of both generic and specific network domains. Models are designed to exploit the power of semantics to support inferencing, reasoning and logic. This is with particular regard to a social networks relational data and user ties (is a friend of, is a relation of, has affiliation to etc), with the semantic web and social network models now being used to support each other. Semantic modelling using ontology's has been studied and a number of models have been developed such as SIOC[12] (Semantically-Interlinked Online Communities), SKOS[13] (Simple Knowledge Organization System) and FOAF[14] (Friend of a Friend). Network modelling using FOAF is of particular interest due to the relational ties between users in a network. FOAF is designed to represent information about people, and in particular their social connections with three core aspects described; personal information, membership in groups and social connections. FOAF is a subject of research interest, with examples of works including the linking of social networks with FOAF (Golbeck & Rothstein, 2008), or more recently for video recommendation (Li, Zhang, & Sun, 2010).

Semantic social network analysis such as that in the work of Ereteo et al. (2009a) demonstrates an enhanced ability to exploit social network data through semantic analysis, enhancing the analysis of online social networks. Research in such areas is aimed at gaining a greater understanding into the influence of relations in a network.

When considering the representation of social links through the use of semantic technology, they can be seen to provide rich mechanisms for describing social links. Analysis of social metrics in terms of semantic structures and specifically the typed relationship allow investigations at a deeper level, to gain an enhanced understanding not just of the relationships within networks, but also begin to understand the interactions which occur within these networks and their substructures. Interaction analysis is viewed as an interesting future direction, an approach which can allow a greater understanding to be achieved in determining the impact the social network has for the individual user, allowing for an assessment of key issues such as contact quality. Wilson et al. (2009) questioned "are social links valid indicators of real user interaction?" in their investigation of user interaction in social networks. They proposed interaction graphs within this work as a new mode of semantic analysis to quantify user interactions. The findings suggest that social network based sites should be designed with interaction graphs in mind, a method which would better reflect real user activity rather than that of social linkage alone. Interaction analysis of the behavioural differences in Facebook by Quinn *et al* (2011a & 2011b) further contributed to the area, demonstrating the approaches ability to understand the use of social network features for each individual user, across young and old age groups. As an approach it involved the investigation of each individual's wall activity, an approach which took full account of a user's interaction history.

6. CONCLUSION

It has been shown that as the internet has grown, so has the development of online social networks.

Technologies such as Web2.0, and the increasing use of semantic functionalities changed the user role, with users empowered with authoring capabilities, enabling an enriched personalised experience. User control fuelled adoption rates, to the point where their ensuing social and economic impact is an acknowledged phenomenon. Social networking sites are now an accepted communication tool, connecting users with access throughout the globe for a diverse range of purposes.

Social network models are managing and structuring connections that not too long ago would have remained anonymous. Models have demonstrated their ability in the formation of dense community structures, echoing those of real life, through the use of weighted networks as one example. An enhanced understanding of online social networks is being facilitated through the discipline of SNA, with contemporary data collection methods such as API's defining the structural properties of large scale complex networks. Analysis is now providing an understanding to how user networks form, and evolve. However, more recently the interactions which occur across the networks ties are beginning to be understood in greater detail.

The emergence of online social networks has evolved social network analysis rapidly over the past two decades. Traditional approaches are no longer appropriate for the analysis of large scale online social networks. API's, crawlers and MAS as just some approaches that have been applied in a host of recent literature, used successfully to discover hidden patterns. Structural properties such as clustering and centrality are providing metrics to help understand the complexities that are now being routinely uncovered in related research across a range of areas.

Online social networks present opportunities for a variety of domains to discover and understand the communications of users. While still at infancy, existing limited work on semantic modelling and analysis in this survey highlights the potential to exploit semantic technologies in SNA. However, what is of particular interest is the opportunity that may lie within interaction analysis as a new approach, extending traditional social network analysis through the application and observation of semantically enriched technologies, research that may provide a greater understanding of the individual. It can be viewed that we are now at the point where we know all about online networks and their dynamic properties. However, works such as Quinn (2013) are evidence that we are now beginning to understand the individual user. Although we know users adopted technology in their billions, such work is revealing the cyber physical impact disclosing how the merging of the online world affects the real world, answering questions such as; do such networks positively affect real world communications, if so to what extent? Or can Quality of Life be enhanced through such technologies. Such work employing combined qualitative and quantitative approaches bring to together interactions and real life impact. With the increasing array of online networks it is hoped collaboration can be increased between network providers and research institutes, creating opportunities to understand this phenomenon and their potential. However, in summation to the question as to whether Online Social Networks are indeed a contemporary gold rush or scientific advancement, evidence in this work has shown that both perspectives are true. Networks have rapidly become hugely profitable global organisations, much in demand by investors with almost all lines of business engaging. Nevertheless, science has also rapidly evolved and advanced significantly, understanding user interactions and behaviours, from all demographics on a scale never observed before. As both worlds intersect issues concerning data privacy and security are required to be addressed to ensure the trust of those network users upon which networks are built, with an aim of establishing long-term relationships.

REFERENCES

Abdulrahman, R., Neagu, D., Holton, D., Ridley, M., & Lan, Y. (2013). *Data extraction from online social networks using application programming interface in a multi agent system approach. Transactions on Computational Collective Intelligence, 11,* 88–118.

Barnes, J. A. (1972). Social networks. *Addison-Wesley Module in Anthropology, 26,* 1-29.

Bavelas, A. (1950). Communication patterns in task-oriented groups. *The Journal of the Acoustical Society of America, 22,* 725–730.

Berners-Lee, T., & Hendler, J. (2001). Scientific publishing on the semantic web. *Nature, 410*(6832), 1023–1024. doi:10.1038/35074206 PMID:11323639

Blackburn, J., & Iamnitchi, A. (2013). An architecture for collecting longitudinal social data. In *Proceedings of Communications Workshops (ICC),* (pp. 184-188). ICC.

Caverlee, J., & Webb, S. (2008). A large-scale study of MySpace: Observations and implications for online social networks. In *Proceedings of ICWSM.* ICWSM.

Charron, C., Favier, J., & Li, C. (2006). *Social computing.* Forrester Research. Retrieved from http://www.cisco.com/web/offer/socialcomputing/SocialComputingBigIdea.pdf

Chau, D. H., Pandit, S., Wang, S., & Faloutsos, C. (2007). Parallel crawling for online social networks. In *Proceedings of the 16th International Conference on World Wide Web,* (pp. 1283-1284). Academic Press. doi:10.1145/1242572.1242809

Chen, D., Yang, J., & Wactlar, H. D. (2004). Towards automatic analysis of social interaction patterns in a nursing home environment from video. In *Proceedings of the 6th ACM SIGMM International Workshop on Multimedia Information Retrieval,* (pp. 283-290). ACM. doi:10.1145/1026711.1026757

Chen, L., & Nugent, C. (2009). Ontology-based activity recognition in intelligent pervasive environments. *International Journal of Web Information Systems, 5*(4), 410–430. doi:10.1108/17440080911006199

Chen, L., Nugent, C., Mulvenna, M., Finlay, D., & Hong, X. (2009). Semantic smart homes: Towards knowledge rich assisted living environments. *Intelligent Patient Management, 189,* 279–296. doi:10.1007/978-3-642-00179-6_17

Coleman, J. S., Katz, E., Menzel, H., & Columbia University. Bureau of Applied Social Research. (1966). *Medical innovation: A diffusion study.* Bobbs-Merrill Company.

Cooke, M., & Buckley, N. (2008). Web 2.0, social networks and the future of market research. *International Journal of Market Research, 50*(2), 267.

Crystal, D. (2011). Dictionary of linguistics and phonetics (6th ed.). Oxford, UK: Wiley-Blackwell.

DiNucci, D. (1999). Fragmented future. *Print, 53*(4), 32–33.

Erétéo, G., Gandon, F., Corby, O., & Buffa, M. (2009a). Semantic social network analysis. *ArXiv:0904.3701.*

Erétéo, G., Gandon, F., Corby, O., & Buffa, M. (2009b). Semantic social network analysis. *Cornell University Library,* (arXiv:0904.3701)

Facebook Statistics. (2013). *Facebook statistics 2013.* Retrieved June 11, 2013 from http://newsroom.fb.com/content/default.aspx?NewsAreaId=22

Farmer, A. D., Bruckner Holt, C. E. M., Cook, M. J., & Hearing, S. D. (2009). Social networking sites: A novel portal for communication. *Postgraduate Medical Journal, 85*(1007), 455–459. doi:10.1136/pgmj.2008.074674 PMID:19734511

Freeman, L. C. (1979). Centrality in social networks conceptual clarification. *Social Networks, 1*(3), 215–239. doi:10.1016/0378-8733(78)90021-7

Golbeck, J. (2007). The dynamics of web-based social networks: Membership, relationships, and change. *First Monday, 12*(11). doi:10.5210/fm.v12i11.2023

Golbeck, J., & Rothstein, M. (2008). Linking social networks on the web with foaf: A semantic web case study. AAAI, 1138–1143.

Granovetter, M. S. (1973). The strength of weak ties. *Ajs, 78*(6), 1360.

Gross, R., Acquisti, A., & Heinz, H. J. III. (2005). Information revelation and privacy in online social networks. In *Proceedings of the 2005 ACM Workshop on Privacy in the Electronic Society*. ACM. doi:10.1145/1102199.1102214

Gruber, T. (2008). Collective knowledge systems: Where the social web meets the semantic web. *Web Semantics: Science, Services, and Agents on the World Wide Web, 6*(1), 4–13. doi:10.1016/j.websem.2007.11.011

Guarino, N. (1998). *Formal ontology in information systems*. Amsterdam: IOS Press.

Hanneman, R. A., & Riddle, M. (2005). *Introduction to Social Network Methods*. Riverside, CA: University of California.

Hunter, D. R., Goodreau, S. M., & Handcock, M. S. (2008). Goodness of fit of social network models. *Journal of the American Statistical Association, 103*(481), 248–258. doi:10.1198/016214507000000446

Internet World Stats. (2013). *Internet users in Europe*. Retrieved May 16, 2012 from http://www.internetworldstats.com/stats4.htm

Klein, M., Schmidt, A., & Lauer, R. (2007). Ontology-centred design of an ambient middleware for assisted living: The case of soprano. In *Proceedings of Towards Ambient Intelligence: Methods for Cooperating Ensembles in Ubiquitous Environments (AIM-CU), 30th Annual German Conference on Artificial Intelligence (KI 2007)*. Academic Press.

Klovdahl, A. S. (1985). Social networks and the spread of infectious diseases: The AIDS example. *Social Science & Medicine, 21*(11), 1203–1216. doi:10.2307/2786835

Krackhardt, D., & Stern, R. N. (1988). Informal networks and organizational crises: An experimental simulation. *Social Psychology Quarterly, 51*(2), 123–140. doi:10.2307/2786835

Kumpula, J. M., Onnela, J. P., Saramäki, J., Kaski, K., & Kertész, J. (2007). Emergence of communities in weighted networks. *Physical Review Letters, 99*(22), 228701. doi:10.1103/PhysRevLett.99.228701 PMID:18233339

Kwai Fun, I. (2008). Weblogging: A study of social computing and its impact on organizations. *Decision Support Systems, 45*(2), 242–250. doi:10.1016/j.dss.2007.02.004

Latfi, F., Lefebvre, B., & Descheneaux, C. (2007). Ontology-based management of the telehealth smart home, dedicated to elderly in loss of cognitive autonomy. In *Proceedings of the OWLED 2007 Workshop on OWL: Experiences and Directions*. OWLED.

Lewis, K., Kaufman, J., Gonzalez, M., Wimmer, A., & Christakis, N. (2008). Tastes, ties, and time: A new social network dataset using facebook.com. *Social Networks, 30*(4), 330–342.

Li, S., Zhang, Y., & Sun, H. (2010). Mashup FOAF for video recommendation LightWeight prototype. In *Proceedings of Web Information Systems and Applications Conference (WISA)*, (pp. 190-193). WISA. doi:10.1109/WISA.2010.49

McPherson, M., Smith-Lovin, L., & Cook, J. M. (2001). Birds of a feather: Homophily in social networks. *Annual Review of Sociology*, 27(1), 415–444. doi:10.1146/annurev.soc.27.1.415

Mislove, A., Marcon, M., Gummadi, K. P., Druschel, P., & Bhattacharjee, B. (2007). Measurement and analysis of online social networks. In *Proceedings of the 7th ACM SIGCOMM Conference on Internet Measurement*. ACM. doi:10.1145/1298306.1298311

Newman, M. E. J. (2003). The structure and function of complex networks. *SIAM Review*, 45(2), 167–256. doi:10.1137/S003614450342480

Parameswaran, M., & Whinston, A. B. (2007). Research issues in social computing. *Journal of the Association for Information Systems*, 8(6), 336–350.

Pfeil, U., Arjan, R., & Zaphiris, P. (2009). Age differences in online social networking-A study of user profiles and the social capital divide among teenagers and older users in MySpace. *Computers in Human Behavior*, 25(3), 643–654. doi:10.1016/j.chb.2008.08.015

Pfeil, U., & Zaphiris, P. (2007). Patterns of empathy in online communication. In *Proceedings of the SIGCHI Conference on Human Factors in Computing Systems*, (pp. 919-928). ACM. doi:10.1145/1240624.1240763

Pfeil, U., & Zaphiris, P. (2009). Investigating social network patterns within an empathic online community for older people. *Computers in Human Behavior*, 25(5), 1139–1155. doi:10.1016/j.chb.2009.05.001

Porter, M. A., Onnela, J. P., & Mucha, P. J. (2009). Communities in networks. *Notices of the American Mathematical Society*, 56(9), 1082–1097.

Psallidas, F., Ntoulas, A., & Delis, A. (2013). Soc web: Efficient monitoring of social network activities. In *Proceedings of the 14th International Conference on Web information systems Engineering–WISE 2013* (pp. 118-136) Nanjing, China: Springer. doi:10.1007/978-3-642-41154-0_9

Quinn, D. (2013). *Analysis of how young and older people interact using online social networks*. (PhD Dissertation). University of Ulster, Ulster, UK.

Quinn, D., Chen, L., & Mulvenna, M. (2011a). Does age make a difference in the behaviour of online social network users? In *Proceedings of Internet of Things (iThings/CPSCom), 2011 International Conference on and 4th International Conference on Cyber, Physical and Social Computing*, (pp. 266-272). Academic Press.

Quinn, D., Chen, L., & Mulvenna, M. (2011b). An examination of the behaviour of young and older users of facebook. In *Proceedings of 4th International Conference on eHealth*, (pp. 9-16). Academic Press.

Robins, G., Pattison, P., Kalish, Y., & Lusher, D. (2007). An introduction to exponential random graph (p*) models for social networks. *Social Networks*, 29(2), 173–191. doi:10.1016/j.socnet.2006.08.002

Scott, J. (2000). Social network analysis: A handbook (2nd ed.). London: Sage Publications.

Simmel, G. (1950). The sociology of georg simmel. (K. H. Wolff, Trans.). Simon and Schuster.

Thelwall, M. (2008). Social networks, gender, and friending: An analysis of MySpace member profiles. *Journal of the American Society for Information Science and Technology*, 59(8), 1321–1330. doi:10.1002/asi.20835

Toivonen, R., Kovanen, L., Kivelä, M., Onnela, J. P., Saramäki, J., & Kaski, K. (2009). A comparative study of social network models: Network evolution models and nodal attribute models. *Social Networks*, *31*(4), 240–254. doi:10.1016/j.socnet.2009.06.004

Toivonen, R., Onnela, J. P., Saramäki, J., Hyvönen, J., & Kaski, K. (2006). A model for social networks. *Physica A*: *Statistical and Theoretical Physics*, *371*(2), 851–860. doi:10.1016/j.physa.2006.03.050

Traud, A. L., Kelsic, E. D., Mucha, P. J., & Porter, M. A. (2008). Community structure in online collegiate social networks. *ArXiv, 809*

Wasserman, S., & Faust, K. (1994). *Social network analysis methods and applications*. Cambridge, UK: Cambridge University Press. doi:10.1017/CBO9780511815478

Wellman, B. (1983). Network analysis: Some basic principles. *Sociological Theory*, *1*, 155–200. doi:10.2307/202050

Wilson, C., Boe, B., Sala, A., Puttaswamy, K. P. N., & Zhao, B. Y. (2009). User interactions in social networks and their implications. In *Proceedings of the 4th ACM European Conference on Computer Systems*, (pp. 205-218.) ACM. doi:10.1145/1519065.1519089

Yakushev, A. V., Boukhanovsky, A. V., & Sloot, P. M. (2013). Topic crawler for social networks monitoring. *Knowledge Engineering and the Semantic Web, 394*, 214-227.

Zaphiris, P., & Sarwar, R. (2006). Trends, similarities, and differences in the usage of teen and senior public online newsgroups. *ACM Transactions on Computer-Human Interaction (Tochi)*, *13*(3), 422. doi:10.1145/1183456.1183461

KEY TERMS AND DEFINITIONS

Facebook: A popular free social networking website that allows registered users to create profiles, upload photos and video, send messages and keep in touch with friends, family and colleagues.

Interaction Analysis: This is a research procedure used to investigate and measure the behaviour of communities. It involves the use of a system of categories to record and analyse the different ways in which individuals interact in terms of mode and frequency.

Online Social Networks: Websites where one connects with those sharing personal or professional interests, place of origin, education at a particular school, etc.

Quality of Life: A highly subjective measure of happiness that is an important component of many financial decisions. Factors that play a role in quality of life vary according to personal preferences, but they often include financial security, job satisfaction, family life, health and safety.

Semantics: A branch of linguistics and logic concerned with meaning. The two main areas are logical semantics, concerned with matters such as sense and reference and presupposition and implication, and lexical semantics, concerned with the analysis of word meanings and relations between them.

Social Computing: An area of computer science that is concerned with the intersection of social behaviour and computational systems. It has become an important concept for use in business. It is used in two ways as detailed below. Social computing is the collaborative and interactive aspect of online behaviour.

Social Interaction Analysis: An extension of Interaction which specifically deals with evaluating how social an individual, providing a detailed examination of the elements or structure of social engagement carried out in Online Social Networks.

Social Network Analysis: The use of network theory to analyse social networks. Social network analysis views social relationships in terms of network theory, consisting of nodes, representing individual actors within the network, and ties which represent relationships between the individuals, such as friendship, kinship, organizations and sexual relationships.

Social Networking: The use of dedicated websites / services and applications to interact with other users, or to find people with similar interests to one's own E.g. Facebook, LinkedIn or Twitter.

ENDNOTES

1. www.twitter.com.
2. www.facebook.com.
3. www.instagram.com.
4. www.bebo.com.
5. www.youtube.com.
6. www.flickr.com.
7. www.eons.com.
8. www.sagazone.co.uk.
9. www.livejournal.com.
10. www.orkut.com.
11. www.linkedin.com.
12. www.sioc-project.org.
13. www.w3.org/TR/skos-reference.
14. www.foaf-project.org.
15. http://nakedsecurity.sophos.com/2013/10/30/adobe-breach-thirteen-times-worse-than-thought-38-million-users-affected/.
16. http://www.bbc.co.uk/news/business-18105608.
17. http://www.prnewswire.com/news-releases/the-united-nations-of-digital--technology-231137551.html.

Chapter 14
Current Trends in Interoperability, Scalability, and Security of Pervasive Healthcare Systems

Albert Brugués
University of Applied Sciences Western Switzerland (HES-SO), Switzerland & Universitat Politècnica de Catalunya – BarcelonaTech (UPC), Spain

Josep Pegueroles
Universitat Politècnica de Catalunya – BarcelonaTech (UPC), Spain

Stefano Bromuri
University of Applied Sciences Western Switzerland (HES-SO), Switzerland

Michael Schumacher
University of Applied Sciences Western Switzerland (HES-SO), Switzerland

ABSTRACT

The development of pervasive healthcare systems consists of applying ubiquitous computing in the healthcare context. The systems developed in this research field have the goals of offering better healthcare services, promoting the well-being of the people, and assisting healthcare professionals in their tasks. The aim of the chapter is to give an overview of the main research efforts in the area of pervasive healthcare systems and to identify which are the main research challenges in this topic of research. Furthermore, the authors review the current state of the art for these kinds of systems with respect to some of the research challenges identified. In particular, the authors focus on contributions done regarding interoperability, scalability, and security of these systems.

INTRODUCTION

Pervasive healthcare is an emerging scientific discipline that involves the use of the ubiquitous computing technology (pervasive computing) in the healthcare environment (Arnrich et al.,

2010). As defined by Varshney (Varshney, 2007) pervasive healthcare is the "healthcare to anyone, anytime, and anywhere by removing locational, time and other restrains while increasing both the coverage and the quality of healthcare".

DOI: 10.4018/978-1-4666-7284-0.ch014

Copyright © 2015, IGI Global. Copying or distributing in print or electronic forms without written permission of IGI Global is prohibited.

The health challenges of the OECD countries are a motivation for doing research on the pervasive healthcare discipline. These challenges can be summarized as the following:

- There is a huge increase of the ratio between elderly and young people.
- Healthcare costs and the chronic diseases are increasing as people grew older.
- Current lifestyles (e.g. smoking, obesity, and inactivity) are contributing to the prevalence of chronic diseases.
- The constantly expansion of the scope of medicine contributes to increase both, the healthcare costs and the average life expectancy.
- There is an increasing lack of clinical professionals due to retirement and small number of medical and nursing students.

Moreover, research on pervasive healthcare is also motivated by the Europe 2020 program, a 10-year strategy proposed by the European Commission on 2010 for advancement of the economy of the European Union (EU). An integral part of Europe 2020 is to promote good health, and to do so there are four among the seven flagship initiatives of Europe 2020 relevant to the healthcare domain, which are the following:

- **Innovation Union:** Aims to maximize EU's capacity for innovation. In the healthcare domain the goal is to make Europe a world-leader in developing ways to promote active and healthy aging.
- **Digital Agenda for Europe:** Focused on developing and using digital applications. There are four key actions related with health:

    ◦ Give Europeans secure online access to their medical health data and achieve widespread telemedicine deployment.
    ◦ Propose a recommendation to define a minimum common set of data.
    ◦ Foster EU-wide standards, interoperability testing and certification of eHealth.
    ◦ Reinforce the Ambient Assisted Living Joint Programme.

- **Agenda for New Skills and Jobs:** Focuses on highlight the economic role of mental health and the health of the workforce. This should improve working conditions and workplaces that prioritize the health and well-being of their employees.
- **European Platform against Poverty:** Aims to ensure economic and social cohesion. The European Commission will contribute by boosting efforts on health promotion and prevention with a focus in reducing health inequality.

The pervasive healthcare discipline tries to find new solutions and approaches to mitigate these challenges. To achieve this goal pervasive healthcare tries to modify the healthcare service delivery model in the Western countries, by moving it from a centralized approach focused on doctors to a decentralized one based on the patients (Arnrich et al., 2010). In other words, it tries to move from a reactive model in which people go to hospital because they are ill, to a pro-active and preventive model where people are active participants in their own well-being, and thus providing a more personalized healthcare. This personalization involves the use of technologies that can move the patient treatment and care from hospitalization to home. It also involves a continuous monitoring of vital signs (e.g. blood sampling, blood pressure, etc.) done automatically by the patient, rather than the periodic sample done inside the hospitals.

APPLICATION ENVIRONMENTS

Research in pervasive healthcare is focused on different topics that can be classified by their environment of application. Hence we have these four main environments:

1. Body sensor networks focused on monitoring vital signs and activities of the patient;
2. Ambient assisted living (AAL) technologies to help people live more independent;
3. Pervasive computing for hospitals help the medical staff to coordinate their work; and
4. Persuasive technologies to encourage people to have a healthier live.

Body Sensor Networks

The focus of the body sensor networks applications is to move the sampling technologies from the labs to the hands of the patient. To do so, one of the main goals is to design and develop reliable and non-intrusive wearable sensors that do not disturb the daily activities of the patient, and as well sensors with more powerful communication and processing mechanisms.

Typical applications consist of a common architecture with three different layers: Body Area Network (BAN), gateways, and remote monitoring system. The remote monitoring system is usually a server hosted at the hospital side which collects, stores, and eventually analyzes health-related information. The gateway acts as a relay node between the BAN and the remote monitoring system, while the BAN consists of a set of sensors deployed on the body of the patient. The goal of the BAN can be:

- The monitoring of vital signs (Xu et al., 2010) such as the electrocardiogram (ECG), the heart rate, the oxygen saturation (SpO2), the blood pressure, among others.
- The detection of the activities of daily life (ADL) such as walking, standing, sitting, reading, eating, or lying, when combining sensor networks with machine learning approaches (Aziz et al., 2011).

On both cases the aim is to produce safety, assistance and early warnings to the patient. This help can be extended by informing both the users' emergency contacts (Liang et al., 2012) and the doctor in charge of the patient (Bromuri et al., 2011) when a dangerous situation is detected. Body sensor networks can also be used to mitigate diseases on an early stage in order to prevent them from occurring (Peng et al., 2011).

Body sensor networks applications have specific challenges such as the transmission of vital signs over limited and variable capacity wireless networks. The monitoring system should operate autonomously, and it must be taken into account that when the number of patients using the system grows it can increase significantly the amount of network traffic depending on the number of sensed vital signs, and their upload frequency. This increase of traffic can affect the reliability of message delivery to the remote monitoring system (Varshney, 2007).

Examples of applications applying body sensor networks include among others, a fall detection system based on a smartphone which uses an accelerometer worn on the waist (Abbate et al., 2012); a rehabilitation support system for the elderly using a set of sensors to track the movement, ECG and the breath rate of the patient (Pioggia et al., 2010); the detection of early signs of dementia based on the eye tracking performed with electrodes (Vidal et al., 2012); novel applications such as automatic dietary monitoring which can be done using different techniques based on sensors

(Amft & Tröster, 2009); and support applications based on agents to provide assistance in form of diagnostic advice (Mabry et al., 2003).

Ambient Assisted Living (AAL) Technologies

The goal of AAL technologies is to support the daily lives of people in general (e.g. elderly, ill, disabled), to help them to have an independent life with respect to wellness, health and safety. In contrast with body sensor networks in AAL technologies sensors are placed on the environment rather than on the body of the patient. This approach gives contextual information that can be used to complement the information provided by the body sensor networks (ElSayed et al., 2010).

When some kind of intelligence is added to the sensing environment, this is known as "Ambient Intelligence" (Cook et al., 2009). In these intelligent environments the tasks are not just to sense the current conditions of the patient, but analyzing them and deciding if a reaction is needed and which one (Baumgarten & Mulvenna, 2011). A subject of current research, in both body sensor networks and AAL technologies, is to determine how this intelligence is accomplished, where it is provided and how it is managed. To address the scalability of the system the raw data can be analyzed by the sensors themselves, rather than send it every time to a central server for further processing. This could lead to a shorter lifetime of the battery that can be compensated by the reduction in the amount of communications needed. On the other hand, it must be taken into account that in some applications the processing capabilities of the sensors might be not enough.

Some research efforts in AAL technologies are focused on the so-called "smart homes", where the sensing environment is the house of the patient. The smart homes are equipped with different sensing, interaction, and assistance facilities to provide the technology and measurement environment for an AAL scenario. These can include (Kleinberger et al., 2007): ambient sensors integrated in switches, blinds or power sockets; position tracking solutions (e.g. smart carpet equiped with Radio Frequency Identification (RFID)); intelligent household appliances (e.g. refrigerator that warn about spoiled food); an autonomous robot transportation platform; among others. All these technologies can be used to proactively assist people through early detection of problems, however the use of these assistive devices transfer the dependence from human side to machinery side which reduces social connections of assisted people (Sun et al., 2007).

Assisted living systems promise a huge potential for handicapped and elderly people, but they must meet these three requirements (Kleinberger et al., 2007):

- They have to be ambient and unobtrusive to reach high acceptance.
- They have to adapt themselves to changing personal situations or capabilities of the individual and the environment to fulfill individual needs.
- They have to provide their services in an accessible way to enhance usability.

Examples of AAL implementations include among others, in-home monitoring of healthy independent elders (Botia et al., 2012); monitoring falls in home of elderly (Yu et al., 2012); the eCAALYX system, a solution to reduce morbidity and mortality of elderly people suffering from comorbidity (Prescher et al., 2012); and several applications based on agents such as a home health system to identify chronic conditions from the patterns of symptoms (Cervantes et al., 2007); a smart home in which specific scenarios such as insomnia are detected by means of scenario recognizer agents (Rialle et al., 2003); and the NOCTURNAL system in which patients are monitored while sleeping using ambient sensors and agents (Carswell et al., 2011).

Pervasive Computing for Hospitals

The working environment of a hospital and the tasks performed on it are very different from the ones executed inside an office, therefore current computing technology fit very poorly on hospitals (J. E. Bardram, 2008). The goal of placing pervasive computing inside hospitals is to help clinicians to coordinate their work in an efficient manner. To do so these technologies must provide easy and secure access to data, without cumbersome login procedures, and fast navigation in the large datasets, and taking into account that physicians must have access to many applications in different locations (J.E. Bardram & Christensen, 2007).

The new kinds of pervasive computing technologies suited for hospitals are mostly used for:

1. The advanced management of health information (e.g., patient health records, pharmaceutical information, etc.) and

2. Provision of location and context-aware services (Doukas & Maglogiannis, 2008). This allows clinical personnel easy access to relevant clinical data in specific situations. For example, the use of location provision based on Bluetooth beacons in combination with mobile phone applications, can make easier the task of finding a surgeon that isn't currently in surgery and inform him about the new surgery (Hansen et al., 2006). The RFID technology in combination with agent technology can also be used to assist on the planification of the nurses work, which in turn helps them to gain time (Corchado et al., 2008).

Different projects have been carried out to introduce pervasive computing inside the hospitals. The Activity-Based Computing (ABC) project (Bardram & Christensen, 2007) proposes a framework based on activities. An activity is a collection of tasks, supporting multiple users as participants, and can be suspended and resumed

over time and space. The iHospital system (Hansen et al., 2006), a hospital scheduling and awareness system which incorporates location tracking, large interactive displays, and mobile phones. The infrastructure is based on the application *Aware-Media* that shows information about the work in different operating rooms, and the *AwarePhone* a program that provides an overview of people at work and the status of surgeries in the operating rooms. Other example is (Kuroda et al., 2012), in which two embedded systems are developed, an ubiquitous echograph and a networked digital camera by replacing the bus of the devices with the network of the Hospital Information System (HIS).

Persuasive Technologies

The idea of persuasive technologies is to use the technology to motivate desirable behaviors. Fogg was the originator of this field of research by coining the term "captology" (Fogg, 2003), an acronym for "Computers as Persuasive Technologies", which explores the overlap between persuasion in general and computing technology.

Persuasive technologies applied into the healthcare domain covers a gap left by the body sensor networks and AAL technologies, as some of the diseases that people suffer are caused by inappropriate lifestyles such as smoking, drinking, inactivity or stress. Thus, the monitoring of the patients is not enough. The goal of persuasive technologies in the healthcare domain is to shift the healthcare paradigm from managing illness to maintaining wellness by seeking to alter peoples' lifestyles (J. E. Bardram, 2008). These types of systems help users by motivating them towards the improvement of their health habits, and by enabling them to monitor and visualize their behaviors, reminding them to perform specific tasks, and recommending healthier behaviors or actions (Bardram et al., 2012).

A specific challenge for the designers of these technologies is the consideration of different users'

231

personality types, rather than design applications for general audience, to sustain user interest over time (Halko & Kientz, 2010).

Examples of already implemented persuasive systems include among others, mobile games designed to increase teenagers' physical activity (Arteaga et al., 2012); a personal digital assistant based on relational agents that encourage people to walk more (Bickmore et al., 2009); the MONARCA system, a persuasive system for bipolar patients based on Android (Bardram et al., 2012).

CHALLENGES FOR THE PERVASIVE HEALTHCARE

Pervasive healthcare has two main general challenges which are:

1. To provide better healthcare services to an increasing number of people; and
2. To reduce the long-term cost of the healthcare services (Varshney, 2007).

On the other hand, pervasive healthcare has specific technological challenges related with the following areas:

- **Interoperability:** Most of the existing implementations do not interoperate well (Baumgarten & Mulvenna, 2011), resulting in segmented solutions that are highly specific in nature, often known as the so called "closed" systems. These systems are not able to communicate with other components in order to support a collaborative behavior. A suitable way to achieve interoperability is using healthcare standards such as HL7 for messages, and/or SNOMED for ontology representation, among others.
- **Scalability:** In systems with an extremely large number of patients, regular physi-

ological data might have to be stored and analyzed. Such systems should be horizontally scalable, that is, the performance of the system must scale linearly when adding new patients (Kailas & Stefanidis, 2012).

- **Privacy and Security:** Among other things healthcare data should be available anytime anywhere, but only to authorized persons (Varshney, 2003). The devices must provide an authentication interface for the legal users of the pervasive system (Liu & Li, 2006). This is to avoid, for example, that insurance companies refuse coverage for people with poor health.
- **Mobility:** In the environments with a large amount of heterogeneous devices and a wide deployment scale, a crucial issue is to properly describe and discover available healthcare services taking into account the dynamic operational and environmental context interactions (Toninelli et al., 2009).
- **Formalization of Domain Knowledge:** In those implementations with clinical decision support the domain knowledge needs to be transformed for machine processing. In many cases, this knowledge can be difficult to formalize and depends mostly on the expertise of medical staff (Kleinberger et al., 2007).
- **Usability:** Pervasive healthcare systems should provide intuitive interfaces to encourage people their use. Those who are less familiar with technology are generally willing to use intelligent mobile devices if these devices allow them to live more independently (Varshney, 2007).
- **Legal and Regulatory Implications:** Legal frameworks already exist for protecting sensitive medical information, and therefore all the solutions are required to address these laws. Those legal frameworks are the "Health Insurance Portability and Accountability Act of 1996" (HIPAA) in

the USA, and the "Directive 95/46/EC on the protection of individuals with regard to the processing of personal data and on the free movement of such data" in Europe.

Other challenge for pervasive healthcare is how to evaluate the evidence for improvement in health. Bardram proposed a methodological approach named clinical proof-of-concept (Bardram, 2008). In this method a prototype of the system that works on its own, should be deployed in a real clinical environment, and be used by real users for a short but sufficient period of time, to collect evidence that the technology seems promising in addressing its specific goal. This evidence is qualitative in nature, involving observations, questionnaires, studies of perceived usefulness and usability.

STATE OF THE ART

In this section we review different research efforts that contributed to the state of the art of pervasive healthcare systems. We focus the review on contributions done into three of the research challenges identified in the previous section: interoperability, scalability and security.

Interoperability

The IEEE defines interoperability as "the ability of two or more systems or components to exchange information and to use the information that has been exchanged" (IEEE, 1991). The exchange of information is known as technical interoperability, whereas the ability to use the transferred information is known as semantic interoperability. Two independent systems are able to interoperate if they implement a specific interface for that purpose. However, the number of interfaces to implement grows approximately half the square of the number of systems able to interoperate.

$$I = \frac{N(N-1)}{2}$$

To perform an effective communication, both sender and receiver of information must share a common "framework" which allows their communication. This is the reason why the use of standards is so important to achieve interoperability, especially in the medical domain where there is a huge number of concepts, and a big number of systems, which must cooperate. Nowadays there are different available standards in the healthcare domain, which can be organized in different categories:

- **Messaging and Data Exchange Standards:** These standards allow the exchange of information between systems and organizations in a consistent way, because they contain specifications for the format, the data elements and their structure. Common examples in this group are the Health Level 7 (HL7) for the exchange, integration, sharing, and retrieval of electronic health information, Digital Imaging and Communications in Medicine (DICOM) for handling, storing, printing, and transmitting information in medical imaging, ISO/IEEE 11073 which enables communication between medical devices and with external computer systems.

- **Terminology Standards:** These standards are concerned with terms and they provide specific codes for clinical concepts. Examples in this group are Systemized Nomenclature of Medicine Clinical Terms (SNOMED CT) which provides a collection of clinical terms covering diseases, findings, procedures, microorganisms, substances, etc., International Classification of Diseases (ICD) provides a system of diagnostic codes for classifying diseases,

Logical Observation Identifiers Names and Codes (LOINC) a standard for identifying medical laboratory observations.

- **Document Standards:** These standards are intended to specify an architecture for the exchange of Electronic Health Records (EHR). This group includes the Clinical Document Architecture (CDA) a standard based on XML intended to specify the encoding, structure and semantics of clinical documents, and the CEN/ISO EN13606 a standard to define a rigorous information architecture for communicating part or all of the EHR of a single patient.

Moreover, there are different approaches to support the use of existing healthcare standards. An example is the Integrating the Healthcare Enterprise (IHE) initiative which provides a framework that defines specific implementations of established standards to achieve integration goals between different healthcare institutions. Other example is the Continua Health Alliance, an international nonprofit industry organization with more than 200 member companies, aiming to provide interoperable health devices and services.

Health Level 7 International is one of the most important organizations involved in the development of healthcare standards, with approximately 500 corporate members. The name "Level 7" is a reference to the seventh layer of the Open Systems Interconnection (OSI) communications model, which indicates that HL7 standards are focused on the application layer. A widely adopted standard of this organization is HL7 v2.x which defines electronic messages to support hospital workflows. The first version of this standard was released in 1989 and over the years it has refined to cover the requirements in different institutions and in different countries. The HL7's v2 philosophy is that newer versions of HL7 v2 should be backwards compatible with older versions of the standard. This means that new data elements and messages added to newer

versions are marked as optional elements, which in fact makes more difficult its implementation. The drawbacks found in HL7 v2 lead the development of the new HL7 v3 standard which was firstly released in 2005. HL7 v3 defines the Reference Information Model (RIM), an essential part of the HL7 v3 development methodology representing a large pictorial of the clinical data from which all messages are derived.

Another standard developed by the HL7 organization is the CDA R2 (Dolin et al., 2006). CDA is a document markup standard that specifies the structure and semantics of a clinical document for the purpose of exchange. A CDA document is a defined and complete information object that can include text, image, sounds, and other multimedia content. CDA documents are encoded in XML and they derive their machine processable information from the RIM. Every CDA document has a header and a body. The header identifies and classifies the document and provides information on authentication, the encounter, the patient, and the involved providers. The body contains the clinical report, organized into sections whose narrative content can be encoded using standard vocabularies. The CDA R2 model is richly expressive, enabling the formal representation of clinical statements (such as observations, medication administrations, reverse events, etc.) such that a computer can interpret them. On the other hand, CDA R2 offers a low bar for adoption, providing a mechanism for wrapping a non-XML document.

HL7 standards have been adopted in some research projects on pervasive healthcare. Mainly there are projects that implement HL7 messages for the communication between the different parts of the system, and systems that create a CDA report of the state of the patient. In (Lebak et al., 2004) the authors present a prototype of body sensor networks for home monitoring that utilizes HL7 messages and the IEEE 1073 standard, known as the Medical Information Bus (MIB). Their prototype has four major parts,

1. Base station, data logger, sensors and LabVIEW routines,
2. A local database,
3. An HL7 communication tool, and
4. Automated or doctor driven analysis and feedback.

Data collected by sensors are uploaded wirelessly using MIB via Bluetooth to a data logger worn by the patient. The data logger uploads the measurements, again using MIB via Bluetooth, to a base station running a LabVIEW program which stores the values to a local database. The HL7 communication module is a client/server application implemented using the Interfacewares' Chameleon software, which can send the information from the local database using HL7 messages to an external application situated in the hospital side. The novelty of this work is that physicians can remotely make changes to the monitoring system based on data, for example changing the sample rate of an ECG, closing the loop of the monitoring system. However, authors claim this as a potential add-on to the system.

A similar system is presented in (Lin et al., 2009) but using a mobile device and a telemedicine data center. The mobile device is in charge to gather physiological data information such as blood sugar, blood pressure, ECG, temperature and oxygen saturation in blood. While the telemedicine data center analyzes the data based on thresholds. The communication of the physiological data between both parts of the system is done using the encapsulated HL7 standard EHR. The originality of this system resides in the fact that the telemedicine data center can eventually trigger a conference with the mobile if an alert is detected.

Inside the hospitals there are also pervasive systems like MobileMed (Choi et al., 2006) using HL7 v2.x messages to send information. The goal of MobiMed is to allow to different healthcare institutions to access clinical results about patients. Each hospital has an HL7 Message Server (HMS), which is in charge to send the laboratory results to Central Clinical Database (CCDB) by generating each time the appropriate HL7 message. The information stored in the CCDB can be accessed by the physicians by means of a PDA, this way they can share patient clinical information with small time delays. The authors assume that the CCDB, as a central shared repository, would be managed by a government organization. This system introduces an original approach to share data between hospitals; however, the centralized CCDB represents a single point of failure of the system.

The CDA standard has been used as well in different research projects. In (Hansen et al., 2006) the authors report a Home Telecare System (HTS) consisting of a patient database and a report system. The database stores parameters extracted from raw signals of vital signs, whereas the report system takes the data from the database to perform analysis on it. The report system first converts the information to XML format which in turn is used to generate a CDA report, and then analyzes data with the trends path and the alerts path. Trends path performs statistical analysis of data like mean and standard deviation, while the alerts path is an expert system based on ripple-down rules which generate warnings and alerts. The combination of an analysis system with the generation of the CDA report is the novelty of this work.

A smart home healthcare system is presented in (Khan et al., 2012). In this system the data about different activities is collected through motion sensors, preprocessed using different algorithms (sensory based, video based, location tracking), and stored in XML format. Each activity includes information about type of activity, sensor information, name of the person, activity name, identification of the sensor location, and occurrence time of the activity. The originality of this work resides on the HL7 compliancy module, which generates a CDA document based on the activities. This CDA document can be then transmitted to all registered healthcare systems with the smart home.

Koutkias et al. (2010) propose a novel framework focused on medication treatment manager to provide safety with respect the medication by coping with Adverse Drug Events (ADEs). Their architecture is composed of two subsystems the patient site and the medical site. Patient site has a body area network with sensors measuring the blood pressure and the heart rate, and a Mobile Base Unit (MBU), which coordinates the sensor network and notifies the monitoring to the medical site. The medical site is in charge to store the sensed parameters at the patient site and to send to the MBU information related with the prescription such as treatment goals in terms of monitored signs, important ADEs that may occur, and ADE detection patterns. XML is used for the communications between both subsystems. From the medical site to the patient site the drug prescription information is encoded using an own schema, and in the reverse channel the reports of the monitoring are provided by using the CDA.

Research efforts had also been done on providing custom EHR. In (Kumar et al., 2010) the authors propose a standard data object structure based on XML to intermediate among hospitals. They define all the components of the document and provide the algorithms to generate and process them. However, this approach does not look suitable to provide global interoperability between institutions.

All the reviewed systems provide interoperability by sending HL7 messages or generating CDA documents. However, most of them are prototypes, which have not been evaluated with potential users, and none of them provides information about which HL7 messages have been used nor the structure of the generated CDA documents.

Scalability

Scalability is a concept which connotes the ability of a system to process growing volumes of work gracefully, and/or to be susceptible to enlargement, both due to accommodate an increasing number of elements or objects (Bondi, 2000). Therefore, scalability is a desirable attribute for any network, system or process. In the case of a server application there are few design principles that can be used to scale it up (Roe & Gonik, 2002):

- **Divide and Conquer:** The idea is to split the system into smaller subsystems that must deal with focused tasks. This approach includes also the replication of the system to process specific load coming from the same physical place.
- **Asynchrony:** This means that the system can schedule the tasks to do according to the available resources, rather than process the tasks in the same order that they arrive.
- **Encapsulation:** By applying this principle the systems' components are loosely coupled, so there is little or no dependence between them. Ideally the components should not wait for the work of the other components to perform their tasks.
- **Concurrency:** This principle helps to scalability by ensuring that the maximum possible work is active at all times, and activating new resources when they are needed.
- **Parsimony:** Means that the designer must design the application carefully, taking into account that each piece of code has a cost. If the designer is not economical on what he or she does the costs for the tasks to do can increase exponentially.

The scalability is not taken as a concern in most of the pervasive healthcare systems. In (Kailas & Stefanidis, 2012) the authors review several systems and they conclude that the foremost issue of these systems is the scalability. However, in the literature we can find few pervasive healthcare systems, which specifically address the scalability challenge.

The eCAALXY (Prescher et al., 2012) is a system designed for elder people suffering from comorbidity, to improve their quality of life and reduce morbidity and mortality of elders. The system is composed by three subsystems. First, the mobile monitoring system, which is a Smart Garment embedded with sensors and an Electronic Control Unit (ECU) controlling the sensors. Second, the home monitoring system composed by a Set-Top-Box (STB) which allows to use the television as an interactive tool to receive health education via videos, show the vital parameters, check the health agenda, and do videoconference with the doctors; a router which acts as a hub for the sensors to send the sensed data to the caretaker site; and an Intelligent Sensor System (ISS) composed by a set of sensors deployed in the home. Third, the caretaker site composed by a server responsible for patient management, data visualization, health agenda and observation pattern management. The authors report that due to the centralized communication architecture, the server on the caretaker side receives several dozen of messages per user each second. Thus, the system has low capability in scaling. To solve this issue the authors purpose, as future work, an improved version of the architecture including a middle-layer between the data-acquisition components and the caretaker server to achieve:

1. Decentralized data acquisition,
2. Early pipeline processing, and
3. Migration to well known technologies capable of handling high data rates.

Therefore, the authors purpose to scale up their system by applying the next three techniques:

1. Assign the same task to multiple elements,
2. Do an early processing of the information, and
3. Increase the computational power of the elements of the system.

The Artemis monitoring system (Blount et al., 2010) is designed to perform real-time analysis of data coming from sensors. According to the authors, the high-frequency analysis of the physiological data streams could lead to early detection of life-threatening conditions, and they apply it into an Intensive Care Unit (ICU) for neonates. One of the design goals of the system is to be able to scale with the number of data streams and patients connected to the system. In order to be able to interface with a great number of different medical devices, Artemis employs a set of hardware and software from Capsule Tech Inc. Data acquired from sensors are forwarded to a DataCaptor terminal unit which converts the data streams to IP data streams. Then these data are forward to a Capsule DataCaptor Interface server, which can support up to 500 simultaneously connected devices. The authors purpose the use of multiple servers to achieve scalability, although they claim that a single server is sufficient for the deployment of the system.

Lounis et al. (2012) propose an architecture in which a healthcare institution is able to manage data collected by wireless sensor networks. In order to be able to collect and access large amounts of data the architecture is based on cloud storage. The use of the cloud implies some security challenges. The first is to ensure the confidentiality of data stored on the cloud with a fine-grained access control. This challenge is addressed using Attribute Based Encryption (ABE). The second one is the management of data, which is addressed by using an external institution called Healthcare Authority, in charge to enforce the security polices of the healthcare institution. The use of the cloud provides scalability due to its virtually infinite storage capacity, so in this work the idea to achieve scalability is to offer much more space than the one that will be needed.

Aingeru (Tablado et al., 2004) is a tele assistance system for the elderly. Each monitored patient carries a Personal Digital Assistance (PDA) that is connected to sensors that sample physiological parameters. In the PDA there is an agent deployed in JADE that analyzes the data forwarded by the sensors. Two types of alarms can be activated from the PDA:

1. **Manual Activation:** When the patient feels bad can notify it, and
2. **Automatic Activation:** When the agent detects an anomalous situation an alarm is sent to the doctor.

In the hospital side there is a server that stores in a database all data sent by patients. The relevant contribution of this paper is the local analysis of data done in the PDA. This measure reduces the amount of data sent through the network and therefore minimizes the amount of work that the server side must perform. This is demonstrated in the evaluation of the system where the communication costs are measured, comparing the approach of making local data analysis with other approaches where data analysis is done externally. The idea to provide scalability is to analyze data before using the network interfaces.

The pervasive healthcare system proposed by ElHelw et al. (2009) is a solution for monitoring the activities of their users. This could be useful in measuring postoperative patient recovery. The system combines two types of sensors, wearable and ambient sensors. The wearable sensors are embedded in a device worn in the ear, whereas the ambient sensors are visual-based sensors. The system has a three-tier architecture. First, the sensing environment of the patient in which health data is captured and sent to a broker server through a gateway. Second, the data fusion and analysis layer composed by different distributed servers and brokers. The servers are in charge of performing different tasks such as acquisition, processing, storage and visualization of data, while the brokers provide communications between the servers. Third, the stakeholders interface, which allows to retrieve stored information or carry out specific data processing algorithms. The scalabil-

ity of the system is based on the loose coupling of the different heterogeneous components of the system.

Other approach to achieve scalability is the one proposed by Kilic et al. (Kilic et al., 2010). The infrastructure they provide, although is not a pervasive healthcare system, allows to exchange EHR between communities. Their proposition is to address the challenges not covered by the IHE Cross Community Access (XCA), a profile that defines a protocol to query and retrieve patient healthcare data across communities. One of these challenges is the scalability for which they propose to use a peer-to-peer (P2P) network. However, using a fully decentralized P2P network the search of the desired information may require flooding the network. Instead of that, the architecture is based on the superpeer model on which there are special peers called superpeers. The superpeers provide directory services for their connected peers, and use its directory of indexes to route requests. In this work the techniques applied to achieve scalability are the delegation and/or division of tasks.

In the reviewed systems the scalability challenge was taken into account from the design stage. Only in the eCAALXY (Prescher et al., 2012) the solutions are proposed after the evaluation of the system. All the systems offer different approaches to achieve scalability according to its specific application. However, most of the authors just claim their systems as scalable systems. Only in the Aingeru (Tablado et al., 2004) agent-based system the scalability is evaluated.

Privacy and Security

Pervasive healthcare systems allow the possibility of monitoring patients by collecting great amounts of different physiological values. When this information is analyzed the safety of the users is increased because it is possible to detect anomalous health conditions and even prevent diseases. However, the electronic nature of the data collected by these systems implies many security risks that did not exist before, when the patient data was stored on paper-based format. Therefore, to provide privacy and security on pervasive healthcare systems is an important · aspect to increase the users' acceptance of these systems (Acharya, 2010). By privacy meaning that data can only be accessed by the authorized entities who have the rights to do so, and security meaning that data is securely stored and transmitted (Li et al., 2010).

In pervasive healthcare systems there is a trade-off between the privacy/security of the system and the safety and utility that is provides to the patients (Moncrieff et al., 2009). On one hand, doctors and patients will not adopt a system that does not provide any kind of privacy and security. On the other hand, a system providing the maximum level of privacy would not provide any safety and utility to the patients. In (Halperin et al., 2008) the following safety and utility goals have been identified for Implantable Medical Devices (IMDs). Some of these goals can also be applied to pervasive healthcare systems:

- **Accessibility to Medical Data:** Only the appropriate entities must have access to the medical data.
- **Accuracy of Measurements:** The sensors used to monitor the physiological parameters must be accurate, as these data is used for the monitoring and treatment of the patient.
- **Traceability and Identification of Medical Devices:** Must have mechanisms that allow it to make its presence clear to authorized entities, whenever it is necessary.
- **Maintenance and Reconfigurability:** Authorized personnel may alter the sensors' configuration, either locally or remotely.

- **Resources Efficiency:** That is, extend the sensors' battery life, through minimization of power consumption.

On the other hand, the privacy and security goals that must fulfill the pervasive healthcare systems are not different from the traditional computing systems. These goals are the following:

- **Authentication:** Refers to methods and mechanisms, which allow to an entity proof to another entity that is the one claimed.
- **Authorization:** The access control to data is defined with a set of policy rules to prevent disclosure of data to not allowed entities.
- **Data Integrity:** The assurance that in a data transmission the received data is as it was sent, so it has not been modified between the two entities.
- **Data Confidentiality:** The protection of data from unauthorized disclosure while it is stored or transmitted.
- **Availability:** Consist on preventing denial-of-service attacks, or jamming the communications.

In the particular case of body sensor network applications the following components need to be secured:

- **Body Area Network (BAN):** This layer is the one that captures the physiological values of the patient. The BAN is conformed by a Wireless Sensor Network (WSN) deployed on the patients' body. When securing WSN several considerations must be taken into account (Li et al., 2010). On one hand, the limited resources of sensors limits the types of security algorithms that can be used, so a trade-off exists between the additional computation and the achieved level of protection. On the other hand, an attacker may place faked sensors to masquerade authentic ones, inject false data, or capture the real one if there is a lack of authentication.

- **Gateway:** The gateway is a handheld device used by the patient, such as a smartphone or a PDA. This device collects and aggregates the physiological values measured by the BAN, and forwards the data to the remote monitoring system. The physical security of this device is important as it may store sensitive health information, and thus can be subject to a privacy leakage if misused. To solve this issue the device must provide correct authentication to the real user of the system.

- **Remote Monitoring System:** In this layer there is usually a server located at the hospital site, which stores and analyzes the health data. Storing data in a secure manner is important to protect patient privacy. The threats to avoid are the intentional alteration of medical data, and the disclosure of these data to third parties such as insurance companies. Only the authorized doctors and health personnel should have access to this information. One of the common techniques used for access control in healthcare systems is Role-Based Access Control (RBAC) (Ferraiolo & Kuhn, 1992), in which access control policies are defined according to users' roles. However, in the healthcare domain emergency situations might arise. To handle properly these emergency situations a model called Critically Aware Access Control (CAAC) is presented in (Gupta et al., 2006).

In the literature we can find different approaches to actively address the privacy and security of pervasive healthcare systems. These approaches are based on different strategies such as the use of

security layers, the use of physiological values for key agreement, distributed queries for distributed databases, and self protecting entities of data.

Garcia-Morchon et al. (2009) propose a security framework for wireless sensor networks based on layers. They define the security mechanisms for 3 different layers:

1. **The Medical Sensor Network (MSN):** A wireless sensor network used at a specific location, and operated by a given organization,
2. **The Patient Area Network (PAN):** A set of wireless medical sensors associated to a user which are used to monitor the health conditions, and
3. **The Back-End Services:** Allows a user carrying a PAN to move across MSNs operated by different organizations.

The MSN security layer is based on a central authority used for the registration of the medical sensors and actuators, or monitoring devices carried by doctors. In this security layer, when two devices need a key agreement to provide confidentiality in their communications they exchange their identities to generate the key. The pairwise key is used then for entity authentication by means of e.g. a challenge-response mechanism. The PAN security layer is a patient-centered layer to control the PAN security while interacting with the MSNs. It is based on an entity called Personal Security Manager Star, which allows the handling the security relationships between the PAN members. Finally, the back-end security layer is based on public-key cryptography by means of digital certificates. Each user of the healthcare system owns a physical card in which there is stored the certificate, which can be used to secure communications between a PAN and back-end services.

The Physiological Signals Based Key Agreement (PSKA) (Venkatasubramanian et al., 2010) is a protocol to secure communications between the sensors of a BAN. The novelty of this method is the use of physiological values to address the problem of key distribution between the sensors of the BAN. The idea behind the PSKA is that the human body is dynamic and complex, and the physiological state of a subject is quite unique at a given time. The key agreement process in PSKA works as follows, the sender sensor computes a feature vector obtained from the physiological signal, and generates a polynomial whose coefficients are the random symmetric key. Then the key is hidden based on the fuzzy vault scheme, that is, the values of the feature vector are projected over the polynomial and mixed with random generated points, named chaff points. The hidden key is sent to the receiver sensor that uses its own feature vector to obtain the symmetric key using the Lagrangian interpolation, after compensating the differences between its feature vector and the one used by the sender. The hiding of the legitimate points among much larger number of chaff points difficult the job of identifying them, and the security of the PSKA scheme relies on the difficulty of polynomial reconstruction without knowing which are the legitimate points.

Siegenthaler & Birman (2009) propose an architecture to protect patients' privacy in the context of distributed databases. In their architecture distributed data can be queried as if resided in a centralized database, by broke the query into pieces each one to be executed at a different data owner. The process to answer a query is divided in two phases, a global search followed by the query execution. In the global search the patients' global unique identifier is transformed into a set of data handles, each of which is a reference to a record stored at some data owner. Then the query execution proceeds, and as each query is run by different entities, no entity can combine the final results of the query. The architecture relies on the use of a trusted third party in order to collect the results from the different entities and return the final result to whom it issued the original query.

To protect patients' health data privacy Salih et al. (Salih et al., 2011) propose a novel mecha-nism known as Active Bundles (ABs). An AB is a self protecting entity of data generated in the monitoring devices, which has 3 main components:

1. **Sensitive Data:** Contains the physiological data, information about the patient and the healthcare provider and identification of the devices that data comes from,
2. **Metadata:** Includes the privacy policy used to determine access rights for the sensitive data, and
3. **Virtual Machine:** The program that enforces the privacy policy.

The access to data is protected with 4 different mechanisms: apoptosis, integrity check, enforcing privacy policies, and evaporation. The drawback of the AB is that needs a trusted third party in order to obtain the trust level of the visited host.

A similar approach to protect health data is presented in (Fragopoulos et al., 2009). This framemork is based on the use of the MPEG-21 Intellectual Property Management and Protection (IPMP) components to provide self-security to the health data. The MPEG-21 is a standard proposed for its use in the multimedia world including a part called IPMP which provides mechanisms to protect the digital content. The scenario of application is based on body sensor networks, in which the gateway collects and aggregates the values sent by the sensors of the BAN, and additionally do the necessary operations to encapsulate the data into an MPEG-21 container before send it to the remote monitoring system. The encapsulated medical data consists on three different items, each one with its own license of usage, which grants access to file contents to a specific user. The architecture assumes that patient, doctors, and other medical staff have a prearranged set of public-private keys, so the contents can be encrypted with the public key of the entity for which the data is transmitted.

The reviewed systems propose security solu-tions that can be applied on the different layers of pervasive healthcare systems. The security layers of Garcia-Morchon et al. (2009) provide security to the BAN of the patient, while the PSKA algorithm propose a solution for the key distribution between the sensors of the BAN. The privacy of patients' information stored on the remote monitoring system can be enforced with the method of distributed queries. Finally, the healthcare information collected by the gateway can be secured using the self-protecting entities of information.

CONCLUSION

In this chapter, we presented an overview of pervasive healthcare systems. We started by analyzing the motivations for doing research on this field, based on the health challenges of the OECD countries and the European Union. We classified the different systems that can be found in the literature according to where the technology is placed, and we identified the main challenges related with the development of those systems. We then presented a review of different solutions addressing the challenges of interoperability, scalability, and security. We aim that the reader will find in this chapter a snapshot of the current trends in research related with pervasive healthcare systems.

REFERENCES

Abbate, S., Avvenuti, M., Bonatesta, F., Cola, G., Corsini, P., & Vecchio, A. (2012). A Smartphone-based Fall Detection System. *Pervasive and Mobile Computing*, 8(6), 883–899. doi:10.1016/j. pmcj.2012.08.003

Acharya, D. (2010). Security in Pervasive Health Care Networks: Current R&D and Future Challenges. In *Proceedings of Mobile Data Management (MDM)*, (pp. 305–306). Academic Press. doi:10.1109/MDM.2010.38

Amft, O., & Tröster, G. (2009). On-Body Sensing Solutions for Automatic Dietary Monitoring. *IEEE Pervasive Computing*, 8(2), 62–70. doi:10.1109/ MPRV.2009.32

Arnrich, B., Mayora, O., Bardram, J., & Tröster, G. (2010). Pervasive Healthcare Paving the Way for a Pervasive, User-centered and Preventive Healthcare Model. *Methods of Information in Medicine*, 49(1), 67–73. doi:10.3414/ME09-02-0044 PMID:20011810

Arteaga, S. M., González, V. M., Kurniawan, S., & Benavides, R. A. (2012). Mobile Games and Design Requirements to Increase Teenagers' Physical Activity. *Pervasive and Mobile Computing*, 8(6), 900–908. doi:10.1016/j.pmcj.2012.08.002

Aziz, O., Atallah, L., Lo, B. P. L., Gray, E., Athanasiou, T., Darzi, A., & Yang, G.-Z. (2011). Ear-worn Body Sensor Network Device: An Objective Tool for Functional Postoperative Home Recovery Monitoring. *Journal of the American Medical Informatics Association*, 18(2), 156–159. doi:10.1136/jamia.2010.005173 PMID:21252051

Bardram, J. E. (2008). Pervasive Healthcare as a Scientific Discipline. *Methods of Information in Medicine*, 47(3), 178–185. doi:10.3414/ME9107 PMID:18473081

Bardram, J. E., & Christensen, H. B. (2007). Pervasive Computing Support for Hospitals: An overview of the Activity-Based Computing Project. *IEEE Pervasive Computing*, 6(1), 44–51. doi:10.1109/MPRV.2007.19

Bardram, J. E., Frost, M., Szántó, K., & Marcu, G. (2012). The MONARCA Self-assessment System: A Persuasive Personal Monitoring System for Bipolar Patients. In IHI (pp. 21–30). Academic Press. doi:10.1145/2110363.2110370

Baumgarten, M., & Mulvenna, M. D. (2011). Cognitive Sensor Networks: Towards Self-adapting Ambient Intelligence for Pervasive Healthcare. In PervasiveHealth (pp. 366–369). Academic Press.

Bickmore, T. W., Mauer, D., & Brown, T. (2009). Context Awareness in a Handheld Exercise Agent. *Pervasive and Mobile Computing, 5*(3), 226–235. doi:10.1016/j.pmcj.2008.05.004 PMID:20161031

Blount, M., Ebling, M. R., Eklund, J. M., James, A. G., McGregor, C., & Percival, N. et al. (2010). Real-Time Analysis for Intensive Care: Development and Deployment of the Artemis Analytic System. *IEEE Engineering in Medicine and Biology Magazine, 29*(2), 110–118. doi:10.1109/MEMB.2010.936454 PMID:20659848

Bondi, A. B. (2000). Characteristics of Scalability and Their Impact on Performance. In *Proceedings of the 2nd international workshop on Software and performance* (pp. 195–203). New York: ACM. doi:10.1145/350391.350432

Botia, J. A., Villa, A., & Palma, J. (2012). Ambient Assisted Living System for in-home Monitoring of Healthy Independent Elders. *Expert Systems with Applications, 39*(9), 8136–8148. doi:10.1016/j.eswa.2012.01.153

Bromuri, S., Schumacher, M. I., Stathis, K., & Ruiz, J. (2011). Monitoring Gestational Diabetes Mellitus with Cognitive Agents and Agent Environments. In *Proceedings of Web Intelligence and Intelligent Agent Technology (WI-IAT)*, (Vol. 2, pp. 409–414). WI-IAT. doi:10.1109/WI-IAT.2011.37

Carswell, W., Augusto, J., Mulvenna, M., Wallace, J., Martin, S., & McCullagh, P. J. … Jeffers, W. P. (2011). The NOCTURNAL Ambient Assisted Living System. In *Proceedings of Pervasive Computing Technologies for Healthcare (PervasiveHealth)*, (pp. 208–209). Academic Press.

Cervantes, L., Lee, Y.-S., Yang, H., Ko, S., & Lee, J. (2007). Agent-Based Intelligent Decision Support for the Home Healthcare Environment. In M. Szczuka, D. Howard, D. Ślęzak, H. Kim, T. Kim, I. Ko, … P. A. Sloot (Eds.), Advances in Hybrid Information Technology (Vol. 4413, pp. 414–424). Springer Berlin Heidelberg. Retrieved from doi:10.1007/978-3-540-77368-9_41

Choi, J., Yoo, S., Park, H., & Chun, J. (2006). MobileMed: A PDA-Based Mobile Clinical Information System. *IEEE Transactions on* Information Technology in Biomedicine, *10*(3), 627–635. doi:10.1109/TITB.2006.874201

Cook, D. J., Augusto, J. C., & Jakkula, V. R. (2009). Ambient Intelligence: Technologies, Applications, and Opportunities. *Pervasive and Mobile Computing, 5*(4), 277–298. doi:10.1016/j.pmcj.2009.04.001

Corchado, J. M., Bajo, J., de Paz, Y., & Tapia, D. I. (2008). Intelligent Environment for Monitoring Alzheimer Patients, Agent Technology for Health Care. *Decision Support Systems, 44*(2), 382–396. doi:10.1016/j.dss.2007.04.008

Dolin, R. H., Alschuler, L., Boyer, S., Beebe, C., Behlen, F. M., Biron, P. V., & Shvo, A. S. (2006). HL7 Clinical Document Architecture, Release 2. *Journal of the American Medical Informatics Association, 13*(1), 30–39. doi:10.1197/jamia.M1888 PMID:16221939

Doukas, C., & Maglogiannis, I. (2008). Intelligent Pervasive Healthcare Systems. In M. Sordo, S. Vaidya, & L. Jain (Eds.), *Advanced Computational Intelligence Paradigms in Healthcare - 3* (Vol. 107, pp. 95–115). Springer Berlin Heidelberg. Retrieved from; doi:10.1007/978-3-540-77662-8_5

ElHelw, M., Pansiot, J., McIlwraith, D., Ali, R., Lo, B., & Atallah, L. (2009). An Integrated Multi-sensing Framework for Pervasive Healthcare Monitoring. In *Pervasive Computing Technologies for Healthcare*, (pp. 1–7). Academic Press. doi:10.4108/ICST.PERVASIVEHEALTH2009.6038

ElSayed, M., Alsebai, A., Salaheldin, A., El Gayar, N., & ElHelw, M. (2010). Ambient and Wearable Sensing for Gait Classification in Pervasive Healthcare Environments. In *Proceedings of e-Health Networking Applications and Services (Healthcom)*, (pp. 240–245). IEEE. doi:10.1109/HEALTH.2010.5556563

Ferraiolo, D., & Kuhn, R. (1992). Role-Based Access Control. In *Proceedings of 15th NIST-NCSC National Computer Security Conference* (pp. 554–563). NIST-NCSC.

Fogg, B. J. (2003). *Persuasive Technology: Using Computers to Change What We Think and Do.* Academic Press.

Fragopoulos, A., Gialelis, J., & Serpanos, D. (2009). Security Framework for Pervasive Healthcare Architectures Utilizing MPEG-21 IPMP Components. *International Journal of Telemedicine and Applications*, 2009. PMID:19132095

Garcia-Morchon, O., Falck, T., Heer, T., & Wehrle, K. (2009). Security for Pervasive Medical Sensor Networks. In Proceedings of Mobile and Ubiquitous Systems: Networking Services, MobiQuitous, (pp. 1–10). Academic Press. doi:10.4108/ICST.MOBIQUITOUS2009.6832

Gupta, S. K. S., Mukherjee, T., & Venkatasubramanian, K. (2006). Criticality Aware Access Control Model for Pervasive Applications. In *Proceedings of Pervasive Computing and Communications*. IEEE. doi:10.1109/PERCOM.2006.19

Halko, S., & Kientz, J. A. (2010). Personality and Persuasive Technology: An Exploratory Study on Health-promoting Mobile Applications. In *Proceedings of the 5th International Conference on Persuasive Technology* (pp. 150–161). Berlin: Springer-Verlag. doi:10.1007/978-3-642-13226-1_16

Halperin, D., Kohno, T., Heydt-Benjamin, T. S., Fu, K., & Maisel, W. H. (2008). Security and Privacy for Implantable Medical Devices. *IEEE Pervasive Computing*, 7(1), 30–39. doi:10.1109/MPRV.2008.16

Hansen, T. R., Bardram, J. E., & Soegaard, M. (2006). Moving Out of the Lab: Deploying Pervasive Technologies in a Hospital. *IEEE Pervasive Computing*, 5(3), 24–31. doi:10.1109/MPRV.2006.53

IEEE. (1991). IEEE Standard Computer Dictionary. A Compilation of IEEE Standard Computer Glossaries. *IEEE Std, 610.* doi:10.1109/IEEESTD.1991.106963

Kailas, A., & Stefanidis, D. (2012). On Medical Informatics for Pervasive and Ubiquitous Computing in eHealth. In *Proceedings of e-Health Networking, Applications and Services (Healthcom),* (pp. 111–118). IEEE. doi:10.1109/HealthCom.2012.6379372

Khan, W. A., Hussain, M., Khattak, A. M., Afzal, M., Amin, B., & Lee, S. (2012). Integration of HL7 Compliant Smart Home Healthcare System and HMIS. In M. Donnelly, C. Paggetti, C. Nugent, & M. Mokhtari (Eds.), *Impact Analysis of Solutions for Chronic Disease Prevention and Management* (Vol. 7251, pp. 230–233). Springer Berlin Heidelberg. doi:10.1007/978-3-642-30779-9_32

Kilic, O., Dogac, A., & Eichelberg, M. (2010). Providing Interoperability of eHealth Communities Through Peer-to-Peer Networks. *IEEE Transactions on* Information Technology in Biomedicine, *14*(3), 846–853. doi:10.1109/TITB.2010.2041029

Kleinberger, T., Becker, M., Ras, E., Holzinger, A., & Müller, P. (2007). Ambient Intelligence in Assisted Living: Enable Elderly People to Handle Future Interfaces. In C. Stephanidis (Ed.), *Universal Access in Human-Computer Interaction. Ambient Interaction* (Vol. 4555, pp. 103–112). Springer Berlin Heidelberg. doi:10.1007/978-3-540-73281-5_11

Koutkias, V., Chouvarda, I., Triantafyllidis, A., Malousi, A., Giaglis, G. D., & Maglaveras, N. (2010). A Personalized Framework for Medication Treatment Management in Chronic Care. *IEEE Transactions on Information Technology in Biomedicine*, *14*(2), 464–472. doi:10.1109/TITB.2009.2036367 PMID:20007042

Kuroda, T., Sasaki, H., Suenaga, T., Masuda, Y., Yasumuro, Y., & Hori, K. et al. (2012). Embedded Ubiquitous Services on Hospital Information Systems. *IEEE Transactions on* Information Technology in Biomedicine, *16*(6), 1216–1223. doi:10.1109/TITB.2012.2210434

Lebak, J. W., Yao, J., & Warren, S. (2004). HL7-Compliant Healthcare Information System for Home Monitoring. In *Proceedings of Engineering in Medicine and Biology Society,* (Vol. 2, pp. 3338–3341). IEEE. doi:10.1109/IEMBS.2004.1403938

Li, M., Lou, W., & Ren, K. (2010). Data Security and Privacy in Wireless Body Area Networks. *IEEE Wireless Communications*, *17*(1), 51–58. doi:10.1109/MWC.2010.5416350

Liang, X., Barua, M., Chen, L., Lu, R., Shen, X., Li, X., & Luo, H. Y. (2012). Enabling Pervasive Healthcare Through Continuous Remote Health Monitoring. *IEEE Wireless Communications*, *19*(6), 10–18. doi:10.1109/MWC.2012.6393513

Lin, S.-C., Chiang, Y.-L., Lin, H.-C., Hsu, J., & Wang, J.-F. (2009). Design and Implementation of a HL7-based Physiological Monitoring System for Mobile Consumer Devices. In *Proceedings of Consumer Electronics,* (pp. 1–2). ICCE. doi:10.1109/ICCE.2009.5012233

Liu, Y., & Li, F. (2006). PCA: A Reference Architecture for Pervasive Computing. In *Pervasive Computing and Applications,* (pp. 99 –103). Academic Press. doi:10.1109/SPCA.2006.297550

Lounis, A., Hadjidj, A., Bouabdallah, A., & Challal, Y. (2012). Secure and Scalable Cloud-Based Architecture for e-Health Wireless Sensor Networks. In *Proceedings of Computer Communications and Networks (ICCCN),* (pp. 1–7). ICCCN. doi:10.1109/ICCCN.2012.6289252

Mabry, S. L., Schneringer, T., Etters, T., & Edwards, N. (2003). *Intelligent Agents for Patient Monitoring and Diagnostics* (pp. 257–262). SAC. doi:10.1145/952576.952585

Moncrieff, S., Venkatesh, S., & West, G. (2009). A Framework for the Design of Privacy Preserving Pervasive Healthcare. In *Proceedings of Multimedia and Expo,* (pp. 1696–1699). IEEE. doi:10.1109/ICME.2009.5202847

Peng, H., Hu, B., Liu, Q., Dong, Q., Zhao, Q., & Moore, P. (2011). User-centered Depression Prevention: An EEG Approach to Pervasive Healthcare. In *Proceedings of Pervasive Computing Technologies for Healthcare (PervasiveHealth),* (pp. 325–330). Academic Press.

Pioggia, G., Tartarisco, G., Valenza, G., Ricci, G., Volpi, L., Siciliano, G., & Bonfiglio, S. (2010). A Pervasive Activity Management and Rehabilitation Support System for the Elderly. In Proceedings of PerCom Workshops (pp. 813–816). PerCom. doi:10.1109/PERCOMW.2010.5470548

Prescher, S., Bourke, A. K., Koehler, F., Martins, A., Sereno Ferreira, H., Boldt Sousa, T. . . . Nelson, J. (2012). Ubiquitous Ambient Assisted Living Solution to Promote Safer Independent Living in Older Adults Suffering From Co-morbidity. In *Proceedings of Engineering in Medicine and Biology Society (EMBC),* (pp. 5118–5121). IEEE. doi:10.1109/EMBC.2012.6347145

Rialle, V., Lamy, J.-B., Noury, N., & Bajolle, L. (2003). Telemonitoring of Patients at Home: A Software Agent Approach. *Computer Methods and Programs in Biomedicine*, *72*(3), 257–268. doi:10.1016/S0169-2607(02)00161-X PMID:14554139

Roe, C., & Gonik, S. (2002). Server-side Design Principles for Scalable Internet Systems. *Software, IEEE*, *19*(2), 34–41. doi:10.1109/52.991330

Salih, R. M., Othmane, L. B., & Lilien, L. (2011). Privacy Protection in Pervasive Healthcare Monitoring Systems with Active Bundles. In *Proceedings of Parallel and Distributed Processing with Applications Workshops (ISPAW),* (pp. 311–315). IEEE. doi:10.1109/ISPAW.2011.60

Siegenthaler, M., & Birman, K. (2009). Privacy Enforcement for Distributed Healthcare Queries. In *Proceedings of Pervasive Computing Technologies for Healthcare,* (pp. 1–6). Academic Press. doi:10.4108/ICST.PERVASIVE-HEALTH2009.6016

Sun, H., De Florio, V., Gui, N., & Blondia, C. (2007). Promises and Challenges of Ambient Assisted Living Systems. In *Proceedings of Information Technology: New Generations,* (pp. 1201–1207). ITGN. doi:10.1109/ITNG.2009.169

Sunil Kumar, C., Guru Rao, C. V., & Govardhan, A. (2010). A Framework for Interoperable Healthcare Information Systems. In *Proceedings of Computer Information Systems and Industrial Management Applications (CISIM),* (pp. 604–608). CISIM. doi:10.1109/CISIM.2010.5643522

Tablado, A., Illarramendi, A., Bagüés, M. I., Bermúdez, J., & Goñi, A. (2004). Aingeru: an Innovating System for Tele Assistance of Elderly People. In Proceedings of TELECARE (pp. 27–36). Academic Press.

Toninelli, A., Montanari, R., & Corradi, A. (2009). Enabling Secure Service Discovery in Mobile Healthcare Enterprise Networks. *IEEE Wireless Communications, 16*(3), 24–32. doi:10.1109/MWC.2009.5109461

Varshney, U. (2003). Pervasive Healthcare. *IEEE Computer, 36*(12), 138–140. doi:10.1109/MC.2003.1250897

Varshney, U. (2007). Pervasive Healthcare and Wireless Health Monitoring. *Mobile Networks and Applications, 12*(2-3), 113–127. doi:10.1007/s11036-007-0017-1

Venkatasubramanian, K. K., Banerjee, A., & Gupta, S. K. S. (2010). PSKA: Usable and Secure Key Agreement Scheme for Body Area Networks. *IEEE Transactions on* Information Technology in Biomedicine, *14*(1), 60–68. doi:10.1109/TITB.2009.2037617

Vidal, M., Turner, J., Bulling, A., & Gellersen, H. (2012). Wearable Eye Tracking for Mental Health Monitoring. *Computer Communications, 35*(11), 1306–1311. doi:10.1016/j.comcom.2011.11.002

Xu, L., Guo, D., Tay, F. E. H., & Xing, S. (2010). A wearable vital signs monitoring system for pervasive healthcare. In *Proceedings of Sustainable Utilization and Development in Engineering and Technology (STUDENT),* (pp. 86–89). IEEE. doi:10.1109/STUDENT.2010.5687003

Yu, M., Rhuma, A., Naqvi, S. M., Wang, L., & Chambers, J. (2012). A Posture Recognition-Based Fall Detection System for Monitoring an Elderly Person in a Smart Home Environment. *IEEE Transactions on* Information Technology in Biomedicine, *16*(6), 1274–1286. doi:10.1109/TITB.2012.2214786

KEY TERMS AND DEFINITIONS

Ambient Assisted Living (AAL): Housing that provides facilities to disabled or elderly people to improve their daily lives.

Body Area Network (BAN): Set of sensors deployed on the body of a patient to monitor its physiological parameters.

Clinical Document Architecture (CDA): XML based standard that specifies the encoding, structure and semantics of clinical documents with the purpose of their exchange.

Computer Security: Protections applied to computing systems and the data they can store and transmit over the Internet.

Health Level 7 (HL7): Set of standards on the application layer (layer 7 of the OSI model) for the exchange of medical data between health information systems.

Interoperability: Ability of making two or more different systems to exchange information and use that information.

Pervasive Healthcare: Use of the ubiquitous computing technologies in the medical domain to improve the quality of healthcare services and patient's wellbeing.

Scalability: Ability of a system to process a growing volume of information without decreasing substantially its performance.

Chapter 15
Holophonor:
On the Future Technology of Visual Music

Jonathan Weinel
Glyndŵr University, UK

Richard Picking
Glyndŵr University, UK

Stuart Cunningham
Glyndŵr University, UK

Lyall Williams
Glyndŵr University, UK

ABSTRACT

This chapter discusses the progression of visual music and related audio-visual artworks through the 20th Century and considers the next steps for this field of research. The principles of visual music are described, with reference to the films of early pioneers such as John Whitney. A further exploration of the wider spectrum of subsequent work in various audio-visual art forms is then given. These include visualisations, light synthesizers, VJ performances, digital audio-visual artworks, projection mapping artworks, and interactive visual music artworks. Through consideration of visual music as a continuum of related work, the authors consider the Holophonor, a fictional audio-visual instrument, as an example of the ideal visual music instrument of the future. They conclude by proposing that a device such as the Holophonor could be constructed in the near future by utilising inter-disciplinary approaches from the fields of HCI and affective computing.

INTRODUCTION

The Holophonor is a musical instrument of the 31st Century; it is best described as a combination of an Oboe and a Holographic Projector.

The notes played by its user triggers the projector to show holographic images that relate to the mood of the notes. Due to its complicated nature, it requires a great amount of skill to play. According to Leela, only a few people possess the skill to play the instrument - and they are not very good at it. – Holophonor: Futurama Wiki (n.d.).

The Holophonor is a fictional audio-visual performance instrument, as seen in the science fiction TV show *Futurama* (Groening et al., 2001; Groening et al., 2003), created by Matt Groening. It is an example of the type of new instrument that could result from research or commercial developments in the fields of visual music or interactive audio-visual artworks. In many ways, the Holophonor

DOI: 10.4018/978-1-4666-7284-0.ch015

Copyright © 2015, IGI Global. Copying or distributing in print or electronic forms without written permission of IGI Global is prohibited.

is the ideal visual music instrument: it operates in real-time, is classically musical, responds expressively to the performer, is portable and creates spectacular, unique visuals that integrate perfectly with the music. As such, the Holophonor provides an excellent lens through which to identify some of the challenges that we might seek to address in order to create the visual music instruments of the future.

This chapter commences with a contextual review of visual music, and the increasingly large sphere of associated audio-visual art, including light synths, visualisations, light shows, VJ performances, music videos, electroacoustic audio-visual compositions, projection-mapped artworks and real-time audio-visual installations. This provides a necessary background to the field in which inventions like the Holophonor would be situated. The main features of the Holophonor are reviewed, establishing the creative and computing challenges for research in this area.

VISUAL MUSIC

There is geometry in the humming of the strings, there is music in the spacing of the spheres. – Pythagoras (569-475 B.C.).

'Visual music' as a 20th Century art form consists of moving visual images or animations, which are organised in a way that the composer considers to be musical. Works may include an original musical soundtrack, or may use an existing piece of music to provide a soundtrack. Others may not use a soundtrack at all, but are considered musical through the structure and arrangement of visual materials. Notable pioneers, as archived by the Centre for Visual Music (2013) include John Whitney, Oskar Fischinger, Jordan Belson, Mary Ellen Bute and Charles Dockum. The work of direct animation (a process where materials are applied directly to film without the use of a camera) film-makers such as Len Lye, Norman McLaren, Harry Smith and Stan Brakhage may also be associated with the visual music label. In a broader context, visual music can be seen as part of the avant-garde artistic practices and experimental film making movements of the early 20th Century (Russett & Starr, 1976).

The origins of visual music date back to the early colour organ inventions (Moritz, 1997) and the paintings of artists such as Kandinsky or Klee, which explore correspondences between music, colours and forms (Collopy, 2000, p.357). While composers have devised various methods to create such correspondences, works are sometimes associated with the phenomenon of synaesthesia: the blurring of senses. For synaesthetes, colours may be perceived to have a sound (and vice versa), smells may be perceived to have a taste, and other sensory correspondences may be experienced. Visual music in essence, realises this phenomena through film, for audiences who do not need to be synaesthetes, and in accordance with the artistic design of a composer (who also may not necessarily be a synaesthete). Perhaps because psychedelic drugs such as LSD heighten the sensory experience and produce synesthetic perception (Julien, 2000, p.347), visual music has also on occasion become associated with psychedelic culture; a link that will become apparent through the course of this chapter.

Visual music compositions usually use abstract (rather than representational) images such as geometric forms and shapes. Compositions such as John Whitney's *Catalogue* (1961) or *Matrix III* (1972) recall the investigations of the great mathematician Pythagoras, who demonstrated the geometric relationship between harmonic notes in music. For Pythagoras, music expressed the beauty of the underlying mathematical principles of the universe, which could also be experienced through the movement of planets and in other areas of nature. In this sense, music is in essence geometry and movement, and visual music compositions such as Whitney's are able to explore this through harmony of animated visual forms as well as sound. Visual music as practiced by composers such as Jordan Belson can also be seen as film of the 'inner eye' (Wees, 1992). From this point of view, the abstract visual images are a reflection of the type of internal visual experience that might be perceived in dreams or hallucinations.

While abstract visual imagery and geometric forms are a typical feature of classic visual music, this chapter will adopt a more flexible definition of the term which also encompasses representational visual material. Certainly we may conceive of visual music that includes representational images, Disney's *Fantasia* (Disney et al., 1940) being perhaps the most famous example. While *Fantasia* demonstrates a representational approach, it can certainly be seen as synesthetic, and the fantastical (or nightmarish) content certainly situates it alongside other works of visual music that address internal experience. Of the works of visual music we will discuss in this chapter, *Fantasia* is perhaps the most similar example to the Holophonor.

THE WIDER SPECTRUM

Visual music now occupies a space within an area of artworks which includes other audio-visual artworks, such as visualisations, light synthesizers, VJ performances, music videos, video music, 3D projection artworks, hacked and circuit-bent TVs and visual devices, laser shows, light shows and audio-visual (or music themed) video games. The pioneers of visual music can be seen as a vital precursor to some (but not necessarily all) of this work. Over the late 20th Century (post 1980 especially) and beyond, the area has rapidly expanded to encompass a wide range of related practices such as those mentioned. This section discusses key developments in these related areas, and the approaches used. This is necessary to situate visual music in a modern context, and to identify associated technologies or developments that may be of relevance to visual music devices

of the future such as the Holophonor. This section does not provide an exhaustive history, but rather a tour of relevant areas with illustrative examples.

Visualisations and Light Synths

Visual synthesizers and associated devices date back to the 1960s and 1970s (Audiovisualizers Inc., 2013). The technology ranges from specialised one-off devices capable of visual synthesis, to mass-produced devices for either professional use (such as visual effects) or home use. For example, in 1976 Atari released the Atari Video Music, an analogue device that could be connected to a home hi-fi system, producing coloured diamond shapes that respond to the amplitude of the audio input (Sonmisonmi, 2007). Devices like this foreshadow subsequent light synthesizers for home computers, such as those Jeff Minter designed for Atari ST and Commodore Amiga computers during the 1980s. Minter also produced the *Virtual Light Machine* (VLM) for the Atari Jaguar video games console (Minter, 1990). More recently Minter's *Neon* provides the light visualizer for the Xbox 360 (Minter, 2005). *Neon* is another example of a visualizer that can be used with user-selected music, as commonly found in other media players and games consoles. Minter also produced a feature length visualisation movie *Merak* (Wagner & Minter, 2005) in collaboration with composer Adrian Wagner, which draws upon progressive/psychedelic rock influences and Douglas Trumbull's 'Stargate' sequence (Trumbull, 1968) from *2001: A Space Odyssey* (Kubrick, 1968). Of relevance here is also *DeepWave* (Wagner & Carroll, 2001), which explored the generation of visualisations in 3D, utilising analysis of frequency and amplitude of up to 8 audio inputs.

While visualisations have the flexibility to operate with any audio as the source input, Dannenberg (2005, p.28) draws our attention toward the limitations of the approach used. Visualisations usually rely primarily on the use of low-level audio features[1] such as amplitude, which then provide a basis for colourful patterns derived from the waveform. For Dannenberg, this approach is less interesting than those works that find relationships between higher-level features such as musical structure or conceptual meaning. These higher-level features are typically harder to extract; particularly where subjective composition or design is required to form the relationships. Audio feature extraction is likely to remain a useful means to form audio-visual correspondences, and by examining higher-level features we may be able to develop more sophisticated automated or semi-automated visualisations. However following Dannenberg's argument these should probably be incorporated selectively by a composer, or with interactive features as in Minter's light synths.

Liquid Light Shows and VJ Performances

The area of VJ performance arguably grows out of the psychedelic light shows and multimedia performances of the 1960s. During the late 60s and 70s, visual artists such as the Joshua Light Show (Signore, 2007), Mark Boyle and Joan Hills (Robinson, 2007) created 'liquid light shows' for psychedelic rock bands of the time. These shows typically involved live manipulation of oils under projection lamps, and in the case of Boyle and Hills shows with the Soft Machine, chemical reactions. These produced the spontaneously changing and colour projections readily associated with performances of the psychedelic era. As noted previously, the synesthetic properties of hallucinogens such as LSD, which were popular among the counter culture of the time, may have been among the factors that increased the appreciation for these psychedelic light shows for some audiences. Around the same time, Andy Warhol's 'Exploding Plastic Inevitable' multimedia performances with The Velvet Underground and Nico also combined film projection with music and dance.

While many of these performances were transient events, there are clear parallels with visual music films. In particular these practices use materials such as oil, which, as a result of their properties, produce finely detailed variations. Similar aesthetics are found in some of the direct animation films, such as Harry Smith's *Early Abstractions* (1946-57). These 'organic' (as I shall term them) aesthetics, which incorporate natural, micro variation, become less common in audio-visual arts once computer graphics and digital techniques become popular. Efforts have certainly been made to incorporate organic or life-like variations; notably in the evolutionary art of researchers such as William Latham and Karl Sims (Lambert, Latham & Leymarie, 2013), or the work of software artist Scott Draves (2013b). Nonetheless, much of computer graphics through the 1980s and 1990s tended to assume a synthetic aesthetic which remains discernable from 'real-world' forms or 'natural' materials like paint.

Multimedia performances can be seen to continue through the stage and light shows of popular music through the 70s and 80s. In the late 80s and 90s, widespread availability of home computing systems and advances in computer graphics saw an explosion of their presence in audio-visual mediums. Of particular interest for our discussion are the developments around this time that are associated with the rave or electronic dance music scenes of this period. Examples such as Humanoid's *Stakker Humanoid* (McLean, Scott, & Dougans, 1988) music video demonstrate the renewed computer graphics-driven psychedelic visualisations of the acid house scene. The rave movement can be seen as a psychedelic revival of sorts, with 1988 dubbed the 'The Second Summer of Love' (Reynolds, 2008, p.46). In the UK around this time, the drug Ecstasy (MDMA) in particular, and electronic dance music were used as technologies through which young people could experience hedonistic rapture. As the movement spread, 1960s counter culture advocate Timothy Leary resurfaced to proclaim that the computer technology and virtual reality was the medium through which humanity would find evolutionary transcendence (Leary et al., 1994), while Terrance McKenna also spoke as an advocate for the evolution of consciousness through psychedelic drugs and rave music (McKenna & The Shamen, 1992). In this cultural climate, rave parties saw an appetite amongst audiences for immersive laser light shows, computer graphics and 'cyberdelic' symbolism. These are readily captured by popular music videos of the time such as the Prodigy's *One Love* (Howlett & Hyperbolic Systems, 1993), which show regular young men (dance music at this time assumes a similar stance to punk music, where the performers are not presented as particularly separate or other from their audience) experiencing rapturous dance that returns them to notions of tribal unity and spiritual fulfilment; a notion explicitly discussed by McKenna.

Computer graphics at this time can be viewed as the visual counterpart to techno music. Projected at raves, computer graphics enable an additional sensory experience that contributes to the ecstatic sensory overload sought by ravers. Beyond this, the surface aesthetic of the computer graphics (as opposed to the content represented) also becomes a meaningful symbol for the movement. The futuristic look of technology is sought in rave imagery, just as the sound of technology is sought in the aesthetics of techno music (Trowell, 2001). Amidst the rave scene, computer graphics projections were used where possible, and we see examples of VJ mixing: the visual equivalent to a DJ performance, but using visual materials such as short animated 3D loops instead of records. Studio !K7's *X-Mix* series gives an example of 90s VJ mixing and aesthetics (1993-1998), combined with DJ mixes by top house music DJs of the time such as Paul Van Dyk and Laurent Garnier.

Today VJ mixing encompasses a broad range of practices in both live and composed settings. The pioneers of visual music retain some direct relevance for VJ culture; for example, VJ Chaotic (an active VJ and Visual Music composer) cites John Whitney and his book *Digital Harmony: On The Complementarity of Music and Visual Art*

(1981) as his main inspiration (K. Scott aka. VJ Chaotic, personal communication July 7, 2013). VJ Chaotic utilises his own bespoke 3D software *Harmony* (Scott, 2013) to create visual music. A wide range of other software is also available and commonly used for VJ performances. The spectrum runs from purpose-built mixing and video loop performance software such as *Resolume* (Koning et al. 2013) and *VDMX* (VIDBOX, 2013), to programming environments like *Max/MSP/Jitter* (Cycling '74, 2013), *Processing* (Reas & Fry, 2001) or *vvvv* (VVVV Group, 2013). Live mixing and real-time manipulation of visuals using a computer is currently more viable than ever before due to increases in the power of portable computers, however in many cases the rendering processes sought have also increased in computational demand. This often necessitates some form of pre-rendering, usually by the composer, unless royalty-free loops have been purchased, or some other mode of distributed computing is utilised (as in Scott Draves' *Electric Sheep,* 2013a).

While modern works tend to have distinct digital aesthetics, those earlier practices involving oils or direct animation techniques can be incorporated by digitizing the materials or using live camera feeds. For example, at Glyndŵr University digitized direct animation on 8mm film is an approach used by Weinel's visual music composition *Mezcal Animations* (2013). *Mezcal Animations* represents a more traditional approach to visual music, but once works of this type have been digitized, they can be reprocessed and used as source material in other software such as *VDMX*.

Music Videos, Video Music, and Electroacoustic Audio-Visual Compositions

Music video, as popularised by MTV during the 1980s presents popular music with an associated video for television audiences. The aesthetic considerations usually differ from those of visual music, since music videos typically represent highly stylised versions of live performances, augmented by camera techniques, lighting, sets, costumes and other theatrical narrative elements. Consequently the majority of music videos have only passing relevance to a discussion of visual music, though some (such as those previously identified) may provide examples of approaches for visual accompaniments to music where representational visual material is sought. In some cases music videos may also assume compositional forms that are also fundamentally similar to visual music. The video for Autechre's *Gantz Graf* (Rutterford & Autechre, 2002) is an example, which uses computer graphics to forge abstract geometry that corresponds with the music. Alex Rutterford, author of the video, cites visual patterns of hallucination seen under LSD as the inspiration for the work, which is designed using a mixture of audio feature extraction and (more predominantly) compositional design (Rutterford & Kilroy, 2002).

Elsewhere, large-scale works of audio-visual film have been devised. Of note is Jochem Paap (known to techno listeners as Speedy J) and Scott Pagano's full-length film *Umfeld* (Paap & Pagano, 2007). Consisting of mostly abstract 3D geometry and digital manipulations of photography (images of industrial surfaces, rust etc.), the piece is presented in 5.1 surround sound.

In the area of electroacoustic audio-visual composition[2], a range of approaches have been demonstrated by artists using various combinations of film, animation and computer graphics. For example Diego Garro's *Patah* (2010) demonstrates correspondences between visual material and spectromorphology (Smalley, 1986). Weinel's piece, *Tiny Jungle* (2011b) uses altered states of consciousness as a basis for the design of sonic and visual material (Weinel, 2011a). Most fixed electroacoustic audio-visual compositions make use of combinations of digital camera work, 3D, particle effects, visual compositing software or programming environments such as Jitter. Composers such as Diego Garro have found fractal generating software such as *Artmatic* (Wenger,

2012) and *Mandelbulb3D* (Jesse, 2013), a package that enables 3D animated fractals to be produced. Digitizations of analogue material have also yielded impressive results, such as Paul O'Donoghue's *Chasing Waves* (2010), constructed using analogue hardware at the Experimental Television Centre in New York.

Projection Artworks and Immersive Environments

While projection mapping (or video mapping) dates back to the 1960s (Jones & Sohdi, 2012), it has seen significant growth as an art form over the last decade. This has been used to project on buildings, enabling interesting animations that create illusions of perspective. This method has been used for arts installations, though is most typically used for celebrations, advertisements and other promotional purposes (Roberts, 2012). The illusory quality of projection mapping can be seen as a way in which to induce experiences analogous to hallucination for audiences, who are excited by their disbelief as buildings appear to dissolve, change shape etc. The hallucinatory potential of using digital technology to animate otherwise static objects is more explicitly sought by artists who use projections and LED sculptures as part of the ultraviolet décor for psychedelic trance festivals (3Delica, 2013; Trip Hackers, 2013). These synesthetic artworks can also be considered as a type of visual music.

Stereoscopic 3D has been around for a long time in various forms, but more recently has become commonplace in cinemas and available for living rooms via 3D TV. A few pieces were devised in stereoscopic 3D by the early pioneer (Mortiz, 1999). More recent examples exist, such as Parralaxis work (2010).

Immersive projection can also be achieved using CAVE (Cave Automatic Virtual Environment) or 'Full-Dome' projection environments. These immersive environments facilitate visual projection that surrounds the viewer, usually by either using multiple projectors (CAVE), or by reflecting projections onto contoured surfaces using parabolic mirrors (Full-Dome). Mario Di Maggio's 'Dome Club' in Birmingham uses Full-Dome for experiences that can be viewed as part of visual music culture. For example, the upcoming Dome Club shows combine classic Pink Floyd albums with immersive visualisations (McEuen, 2013).

In our recent work at Glyndŵr University, *Psych Dome* (Weinel et al. 2013) was an interactive visual music artwork that was presented in a Full-Dome. *Psych Dome* used the NeuroSky MindWave: a consumer-grade electroencephalograph (EEG) headset as a control device. Signals from the EEG headset were used to affect various sound and graphical parameters of the artwork. Aesthetically the work was based upon visual music and altered states of consciousness principles.

Laser light shows also deserve a brief mention in this category of other presentation and projection methods. Systems such as Pangolin (2013) enable 3D images and sophisticated compositions reminiscent of John Whitney's work to be created using lasers (LaserimageSweden, 2009). An audiovisual instrument has even been devised using lasers: the *Laser Harp* (Hobley, 2008).

Circuit Bending and Hardware Hacks

'Circuit bending' is the term coined by Reed Ghazala to describe the practice of hardware hacking and modification for the purposes of creating interesting sonic results (Wilson, 2012). The process is often used on devices which are cheaply available, or which may otherwise have become obsolete technology. While circuit bending is most commonly applied to various sound-making devices: children's 'speak and spell' toys, keyboards etc., there are also examples where these practices extend to the visual domain. For example, James Connolly and Kyle Evans' 'Cracked Ray Tube' projects modify TV screens to produce interesting visual patterns with associated sounds (Connolly & Evans, 2013). Karl Klomp (2011) also modifies

hardware such as video mixers in order to produce interesting visual results. Some examples such as these are able to use sound as an input to affect the visual results, and therefore could be considered as a form of 'glitch' (Cascone, 2002) visual music.

Music Video Games

Music-based video games have existed as a niche market for some time. The popularity of *PaRappa the Rapper* (NanaOn-Sha, 1996) on the PlayStation during the mid 1990s substantially boosted the market, with various other audio-based games following in its success. Around this time, some titles exploited the connection between video games and rave culture, a connection that Sony actively supported at points through their marketing approach toward young adults (Poole, 2004, p.7). This strategy even included creating a promotional lounge at the Ministry of Sound nightclub in London (Kushner, 2012, p.28). This link was manifested in various PlayStation titles; through the techno soundtracks of games like *Wipeout* (Psygnosis, 1995), music-making titles like *Music 2000* (Jester Interactive, 1999), or *Fluid* (Opus, 1998): an ambient techno orientated game where the player controls a dolphin and creates remixes. It was also reciprocated, as rave audiences adopted the Playstation as a post-clubbing device, and dance producers sometimes sampled the games in their music (Reynolds, 2008, p.124).

While explicitly rave-orientated titles were (and remain) a niche in video games, the connection was also seen in a minority of subsequent titles on various systems, such as *Rez* (United Game Artists, 2001) and more recently its prequel *Child of Eden* (Q Entertainment, 2011). These are essentially action games that involve shooting enemies, however they utilise a musical twist in that the player's weapon is synchronised with the music, and triggers musical sounds (such as drum or keyboard 'hits'). Aesthetically the titles exploit the association between rave culture and futuristic computer graphics impressions discussed previously. In doing so, the visual material falls somewhere between representations of futuristic machines, luminescent organic life forms (evoking the ultraviolet decor of psychedelic trance festivals) and abstract geometry that recalls visual music pioneers such as John Whitney. The music consists of electronic dance and trance music by established producers. Since musical control is limited the games do not particularly satisfy a description of 'audio-visual instruments', but do show a possible method of integrating music with representational and abstract visual material. Critically as video games they are also real-time, so it is possible for us to conceive of games such as these being adapted to provide increased musical or visual control for the player.

In the past decade *Guitar Hero* (Harmonix, 2005) is notable as one of the most commercially successful audio-game titles. *Guitar Hero* follows a familiar system used by many other music-related video games, where the player must complete a pattern in synchronisation with the music. Though there are obvious parallels with the performance of scored music, these type of games are of less interest to my discussion than those that enable a greater level of creative control. *Guitar Hero* offers very limited scope for individual choice concerning the timing or arrangement of notes: the game rewards machine-like precision, and punishes improvisation or other deviation from the 'score'.

Of more interest to my discussion are those titles such as *Electroplankton* (2006), *Thicket* (Interval Studios, 2010) or the forthcoming *SoundSelf* (Arnott, 2013), which enable greater levels of creative choice from the player to construct audio-visual experiences. These titles give the player open control over the audio-visual experience, albeit mediated by the design of the software. In this sense they are fundamentally similar to computer-based audio-visual musical instruments. *SoundSelf* generates visualisations from the player's voice, the sound of which is also augmented using digital signal processing. This

premise is technically similar to other interactive visualisations discussed, however, seen in the recent resurgence of indie gaming (the project is independent and crowd-funded), titles such as this could pave the way for further audio-visual games or instruments for a wider audience.

Real-Time Visual Music Performances

Lastly, we may also consider the real-time visual music performances that are presented in concerts and events such as *Seeing Sound* (Bath Spa University, 2013). *Seeing Sound* is a biannual conference on visual music, which in 2013 focused on real-time visual music performance, and included a programme of real-time concerts alongside screenings of new and classic works of fixed-media visual music. Amongst the real-time performances: Ryo Ikeshiro's *Construction in Kneading*, a live audiovisualisation based on Mandelbox fractal (Ikeshiro, 2013); Max Hattler and Matthias Kispert's *Feeding You*, a neo-psychedelic anti-retail piece which visually and sonically warps a variety of corporate brandings (Hattler & Kispert, 2013) and *Hidden Fields / Danceroom Spectroscopy*, a live performance that combines real-time visual music with dance, using methods form computational physics as a design principle for the visuals (Glowacki et al., 2013).

DISCUSSION

As with much of art and music in general in the late 20th Century and early 21st Century, we have seen a significant expansion and diversification of practices broadly related to visual music and audio-visual art. Several emergent areas of visual music culture have been identified, and from these examples have been provided, and approaches discussed. Across these we find many different methods for creating synesthetic combinations and audio and visual material, with valuable contributions from both academic research and work in the popular sphere. Almost all these works rely on some form of projection. The examples given emerge from different areas of culture, but under a less ridged definition of the 'visual music' term, can be seen as part of a visual music continuum. The general trend of this continuum seems to point towards interactive audio-visual artworks, with computer audio and graphics.

HOLOPHONOR

We may argue that the Holophonor is in many ways the ideal visual music instrument. In a single, portable instrument it offers many of the features that visual music performers seem to strive for. It is highly expressive and adaptable, providing audio-visual material that is perfectly integrated, synesthetic and immersive. Performed materials respond closely to the emotions of the performer. While some learning is required, virtuoso performances of a high artistic quality are possible. The Holophonor may therefore be a useful example, in considering the challenges and next steps when designing the visual music instruments of the future.

Among the visual music examples discussed in this chapter, many demonstrate individual features or capabilities that would make up a Holophonor-like device, but none combine all of these features in a single, portable and expressive device. The sounds of the Holophonor can be achieved using established approaches of musical composition and performance. Visual material of the type should can be mixed and combined with sound using existing technology. While holographic projection as shown in *Futurama* may not yet be possible, highly immersive projection can be achieved using high-definition screens or domes (for example). The ability of the Holophonor to respond to the emotions of the user could be facilitated through the use of biofeedback technologies and approaches from affective computing

(Picard, 2000). Computing technologies are now also small and powerful enough to facilitate the digital requirements of a Holophonor-like device in a portable package.

Perhaps the main challenge for visual music research then, is to converge existing technologies into a single, portable package that anyone can pick up, learn and play. Music video games offer this level of accessibility, but do not seem to facilitate truly original or adaptable performances of a high artistic quality. Conversely, many of the real-time visual music examples discussed demonstrate high artistic quality, yet lack accessibility for a general audience. Many of the current performers are experts in artistic and computer programming fields (or comprise teams of experts); this seems to be a necessity for realising interactive visual music performances of high technical and artistic quality. Yet this level of required expertise reduces the potential for most regular people to enjoy actually playing and performing visual music. Arguably this also shifts the emphasis away from performing with an instrument, and on to building and designing it. What the Holophonor seems to offer that current systems do not, is an 'off-the-shelf' convenience; one could walk into a shop, try out and buy a Holophonor, just as one might do with a guitar or trumpet. As Fischman discusses then (2011), it is this accessibility coupled with the potential for adaptability and virtuoso performance that is one of the main challenges for research in this field.

CONCLUSION

Through the course of this chapter we have discussed visual music and the wider spectrum of associated audio-visual artistic practices and technologies. It should be apparent that there are clear links and parallels between these different areas, and that work in this area should be informed by the knowledge and practices that have emerged from both academic and popular spheres.

The continuum of visual music as discussed here undoubtedly points towards real-time performance instruments. Yet current examples do not provide the convenience and accessibility of traditional acoustic musical instruments. In this context the Holophonor is useful as a fictional representation of a kind of ideal visual music instrument, and enables us to recognise some of the challenges which research in this area might seek to address. While most of the key features of the Holophonor can be found in the various examples given, we do not find them all in one place. Hence it seems that a convergence of approaches is needed, combined with research that addresses issues of accessibility. We may then be able to provide the visual music instruments of the future, which enable anyone (even Fry) to create and enjoy the 'music of the spheres', not just specialists.

REFERENCES

Arnott, R. (2013). *Soundself by Robin Arnott – Kickstater*. Retrieved November 19, 2013 from: http://www.kickstarter.com/projects/soundself/soundself

Audiovisualizers Inc. (2013). *Video Synthesizers Homage Page*. Retrieved August 28, 2013 from: http://www.audiovisualizers.com/toolshak/vsynths.htm

Bath Spa University. (2013). *Seeing Sound 2013*. Retrieved December 10, 2013 from: http://www.seeingsound.co.uk/seeing-sound-2013/

Cascone, K. (2002). The Aesthetics of Failure: Post Digital Tendencies in Contemporary Computer Music. *Computer Music Journal, 24*(4).

Centre for Visual Music. (2013). *Centre for Visual Music*. Retrieved July 11, 2013 from: http://www.centerforvisualmusic.org/

Collopy, F. (2000). Color, Form, and Motion: Dimensions of a Musical Art of Light. *Leonardo, 33*(5), 355–360. doi:10.1162/002409400552829

Connolly, C., & Evans, K. (2013). *Cracked Ray Tube*. Retrieved August 28, 2013 from: http://crackedraytube.com/

Cycling '74. (2013). *Max/MSP/Jitter* [Programming language]. Author.

Danneberg, R. (2005). Interactive Visual Music: A Personal Perspective. *Computer Music Journal, 29*(4).

3. Delica. (2013). *3Delica* [Facebook group]. Retrieved November 19, 2013 from: https://www.facebook.com/3Delica

Disney, W. (Producer), Sharpsteen, B. (Producer), Ferguson, N. (Director), Algar, J. (Director), Armstrong, S. (Director), Beebe, F. (Director),… Sharpsteen, B. (Director). (1940). *Fantasia* [Motion picture]. USA: Walt Disney Pictures.

Draves, S. (2013a). *Electric Sheep*. Retrieved August 27, 2013 from: http://www.electricsheep.org/

Draves, S. (2013b). *Scott Draves: Software Artist*. Retrieved August 27, 2013 from: http://scottdraves.com/

Q Entertainment. (2011). *Child of Eden* [Video game]. PlayStation 3.

Fischman, R. (2011). Back to the Parlour. *Sonic Ideas/Ideas Sonicas, 3*(2).

Garro, D. (2010). *Patah* [Video]. Retrieved August 27, 2013 from: https://vimeo.com/14112798

Glowacki, D., Tew, P., Mitchell, T., Hyde, J., Kriefman, L., Asano, M.… Thomas, L.M. (2013). Hidden Fields / Danceroom Spectroscopy [Multimedia performance]. Performed at Seeing Sound 2013, Bath Spa University, November 23, 2013.

Groening, M. (Writer), Cohen, D.X. (Writer), Kaplan, E. (Writer), & Avanzino, P. (Director). (2001). Parasites Lost [Television series episode]. In Cohen, D. (Executive producer), & Groening, M (Executive producer) Futurama. USA: 20th Century Fox Television.

Groening, M. (Writer), Cohen, D.X. (Writer), Keeler, K. (Writer), & Haaland, B. (Director). (2001). The Devil's Hands are Idle Playthings [Television series episode]. In Cohen, D. (Executive producer), & Groening, M (Executive producer) Futurama. USA: 20th Century Fox Television.

Harmonix. (2005). *Guitar Hero* [video game]. Author.

Hattler, M., & Kispert, M. (2013). Feeding You [Audio-visual performance]. Performed at Seeing Sound 2013, Bath Spa University, November 24, 2013.

Hobley, S. (2008). *Laser Harp Fully Functional* [Video]. Retrieved August 28, 2013 from: http://www.youtube.com/watch?v=sLVXmsbVwUs

Holophonor: Futurama Wiki. (n.d.). Retrieved August 28, 2013 from the Futurama Wiki: http://futurama.wikia.com/wiki/Holophonor

Howlett, L. (Music), & Hyperbolic Systems (Video artist). (1993). *Prodigy: One Love* [Video]. Retrieved August 27, 2013 from: http://www.youtube.com/watch?v=-noCS_dtZMg

Ikeshiro, R. (2013). Construction in Kneading [Audio-visual performance]. Performed at Seeing Sound 2013, Bath Spa University, November 24, 2013.

Indieszero. (2005). *Electroplankton* [Video game]. Nintendo DS.

Interval Studios. (2010). *Thicket* [Mobile application]. iOS. Retrieved August 28, 2013 from: http://www.youtube.com/watch?v=I8XklLnZ7rs

Jesse. (2012). *Mandelbulb3D* [Software]. PC. Retrieved August 28, 2013 from: http://www.fractalforums.com/mandelbulb-3d/

Jester Interactive. (1999). *Music 2000* [Video game]. PlayStation.

Jones, B., & Sohdi, R. (2012). *The Illustrated History of Projection Mapping.* Retrieved August 28, 2013 from: http://www.projection-mapping.org/index.php/intro/160-the-history-of-projection-mapping

Julien, R. M. (2001). *A Primer of Drug Action.* New York: Worth Publishers.

Klomp, K. (2011). *Karl Klomp.* Retrieved November 13, 2013 from: http://karlklomp.nl

Koning, E., Ploeg, B., Walther, T., Berio, D., Jong, J., & Vink, M. (2013). *Resolume* [VJ software]. Mac & PC.

Kubrick, S. (Producer & Director). (1968). *2001: A Space Odyssey* [Motion picture]. USA: Metro-Goldwyn-Mayer (MGM).

Kushner, D. (2012). *Jacked: The Outlaw Story of Grand Theft Auto.* John Wiley & Sons.

Lambert, N., Latham, W., & Leymarie, F. F. (2013). The Emergence and Growth of Evolutionary Art 1980-1993. *Leonardo, 46*(4), 367–375. doi:10.1162/LEON_a_00608

LaserimageSweden. (2009). *Lasershow using Pangolin.* Retrieved August 28, 2013 from: http://www.youtube.com/watch?v=i5Va8yyJFGA

Leary, T., Horowitz, M., Marshall, V., Ferris, C., Keller, V., Haring, K. …Horowitz, C. (1994). Chaos & Cyber Culture. Ronin Publishing.

Manning, P. (2002). *Electronic & Computer Music.* Oxford University Press.

McEuen, A. (2013). *Pink Floyd 360: Dark Side Of The Moon* [Video]. Starlight Productions. Presented at Dome Club [Audio-visual event series], January 24, 2013, The Old Custard Factory, Birmingham.

McKenna. T., & The Shamen (1992). *Narration from Re:Evolution*. Retrieved September 2, 2013 from: http://deoxy.org/t_re-evo.htm

McLean, M. (Video artist), Scott, C. (Video artist), & Dougans, B. (Music). (1988). *Humanoid: Stakker Humanoid* [Video]. Retrieved August 27, 2013 from: http://www.youtube.com/watch?v=hxEoU-oE0j4

Minter, J. (1990). *Virtual Light Machine* [Software]. Atari Jaguar. Retrieved August 28, 2013 from: http://www.youtube.com/watch?v=8CrQOk7TseY

Minter, J. (2005). *Neon* [Software]. X-Box 360.

Mitrovic, D., Zeppelzauer, M., & Breitender, C. (2010). Features for Content-Based Audio Retrieval. *Advances in Computers: Improving the Web, 78.*

Moritz, W. (1997). The Dream of Colour Music and the Machines that Made it Possible. *Animation World Magazine, 2*(1). Retrieved August 27, 2013 from: http://www.awn.com/mag/issue2.1/articles/moritz2.1.html

Mortiz, W. (1999). *Stereoscopic abstract films* [PDF document]. Retrieved August 28, 2013 from: http://www.centerforvisualmusic.org/WMlecstereo.pdf

NanaOn-Sha. (1996). *PaRappa the Rapper* [Video game]. PlayStation.

O'Donoghue, P. (2010). *Chasing Waves* [Video]. Retrieved August 27, 2013 from: https://vimeo.com/10314195

Opus. (1998). *Fluid* [Video game]. Playstation.

Paap, J. (Musical composer), & Pagano, S. (Video artist). (2007). *Umfeld* [Video]. Retrieved August 27, 2013 from: http://www.youtube.com/watch?v=_e_h9pyQwH4

Pangolin. (2013). *Laser light show software from Pangolin Laser Systems*. Retrieved August 28, 2013 from: http://www.pangolin.com/

Parallaxis. (2010). *Parallaxis 3D audio-visual liveact // Track: Spiral* [Video]. Retrieved August 28, 2013 from: https://vimeo.com/11987591

Picard, R. (2000). *Affective Computing*. MIT Press.

Poole, S. (2004). *Trigger Happy: Videogames and Entertainment Revolution*. Arcade Publishing.

Psygnosis. (1995). *Wipeout* [Video game]. PlayStation.

Reas, C., & Fry, C. (2013). *Processing* [Programming language].

Reynolds, S. (2008). *Energy Flash: A Journey Through Rave Music and Dance Culture*. Picador.

Roberts, P. (2012). *10 projection mapping demos that will blow your mind!* [Web log comment]. Retrieved August 28, 2013 from: http://www.creativebloq.com/video/projection-mapping-912849

Robsinson, J. (2007, April 14). Tripping the Lights. *The Guardian*. Retrieved August 27, 2013 from: http://www.theguardian.com/artanddesign/2007/apr/14/art.culture/print

Russett, R., & Starr, C. (1976). *Experimental Animation: Origins of a New Art*. New York: Da Capo Press Inc.

Rutterford, A. (Video artist), & Autechre (Music). (2002). *Autechre: Gantz Graf* [Video]. Retrieved August 27, 2013 from: http://www.youtube.com/watch?v=nfwD05XA2YQ

Rutterford, A., & Kilroy, N. (2002). *Alex Rutterford on the creation of the Gantz Graf Video* [Web log comment]. Retrieved August 28, 2013 from: http://warp.net/records/autechre/alex-rutterford-on-the-creation-of-the-gantz-graf-video

Scott, K. (2013). *Harmony* [Software]. Not publically available. Retrieved August 28, 2013 from: http://www.digitalchaotics.com/harmony/

Signore, J. D. (2007, April 2). Joshua White: The Joshua Light Show. *Gothamist*. Retrieved August 27, 2013 from: http://gothamist.com/2007/04/02/interview_joshu.php

Smalley, D. (1986). Spectro-morphology and Structuring Processes. In S. Emmerson (Ed.), *The Language of Electroacoustic Music* (pp. 61–93). London: Macmillan.

Smith, H. (1946-1957). *Early Abstractions* [Video]. Retrieved August 27, 2013 from: http://www.youtube.com/watch?v=-wYJ51nSXRQ

Sonmisonmi. (2007). *Atari video music* [Video]. Retrieved August 28, 2013 from: http://www.youtube.com/watch?v=-NWwtZCpC2M

Studio! K7. (Record Label). (1993-1998). *X-Mix* [Video series]. Retrieved August 27, 2013, from http://www.youtube.com/watch?v=izelmqskjaA&list=PLEA51AB0E440929B2

Trip Hackers. (2013). *Trip Hackers* [Facebook Group]. Retrieved November 19, 2013 from: https://www.facebook.com/TRIPHACKERS.RU?fref=ts

Trowell, I. (2001). Auto Synthesis. *Organised Sound, 6*(3).

Trumbull, D. (1968). Creating Special Effects for 2001: A Space Odyssey. *American Cinematographer, 49*(6). Retrieved August 27, 2013 from: http://www.visual-memory.co.uk/sk/2001a/page3.html

United Game Artists. (2001). *Rez* [Video game]. Dreamcast.

VIDVOX, LLC. (2013). *VDMX5* [Software]. Mac. Retrieved August 28, 2013 from: http://vidvox.net

VVVV Group. (2013). *VVVV* [Programming language]. PC.

Wagner, A. (Music), & Minter, J. (Video artist). (2005). *Merak* (Motion picture). DVD version of VHS PAL release, 1988. UK: Media Quest Production. Retrieved August 27, 2013 from: http://www.adrianwagner.com/awmerak.html

Wagner, M., & Carroll, S. (2001). DeepWave: Visualizing Music with VRML. In *Proceedings of the Seventh International Conference on Virtual Systems and Multimedia* (VSMM'01). doi:10.1109/VSMM.2001.969717

Wees, W. C. (1992). Making Films for the Inner Eye: Jordan Belson, James Whitney, Paul Sharits. In *Light Moving in Time: Studies in the Visual Aesthetics of Avant-garde Film*. University of California Press.

Weinel, J. (2011a). Tiny Jungle: Psychedelic Techniques in Audio-Visual Composition. In *Proceedings of the International Computer Music Conference 2011*. Retrieved August 27, 2013 from: http://www.jonweinel.com/wp-content/uploads/2011/08/JW_ICMC2011-Tiny_Jungle.pdf

Weinel, J. (2011b). *Tiny Jungle* [Video]. Retrieved August 27, 2013 from: https://vimeo.com/13719729

Weinel, J. (2013). *Mezcal Animations #1-3* [Video]. Retrieved August 27, 2013 from: http://vimeo.com/69790818

Weinel, J., Cunningham, S., Roberts, N., Roberts, S., & Griffiths, D. (2013). *Psych Dome* [Video installation]. Retrieved August 27 2013 from: https://vimeo.com/78153713

Wenger, E. (2012). *ArtMatic* [Software]. Mac. Retrieved August 28, 2013 from: http://uisoftware.com

Whitney, J. (1961). *Catalogue* [Video]. Retrieved August 27, 2013 from: http://www.youtube.com/watch?v=TbV7loKp69s

Whitney, J. (1972). *Matrix III* [Video]. Retrieved August 27, 2013 from: http://www.youtube.com/watch?v=ZrKgyY5aDvA

Whitney, J. (1981). *Digital Harmony: On The Complementarity of Music and Visual Art.* McGraw-Hill Inc.

Wilson, D. (2012). *Circitified: Circuit Bending Workshop* [Lecture slides online]. Retrieved November 19, 2013 from: http://www.slideshare.net/circitfied/circuit-bending-workshop

KEY TERMS AND DEFINITIONS

Acid House: A type of electronic dance music originating in Chicago during the 1980s, which typically features baselines constructed with the Roland TB-303 synthesizer.

Affective Computing: Describes computer systems which recognise or exhibit properties of human emotion.

CAVE: A CAVE (Cave Automatic Virtual Environment) is a virtual reality environment in which immersion is enhanced through projection on multiple walls, often in combination with stereoscopic technology.

Electroacoustic Audio-Visual Composition: A variation of electroacoustic music that combines electroacoustic music with video.

Electroacoustic Music: A type of 20th Century art music composed for concerts utilising loudspeakers.

Holophonor: A fictional audio-visual instrument from the TV show *Futurama*. The instrument is similar to an oboe, and projects holographic visual images that correspond to the musical performance when played.

Projection Mapping: A method of projection in which projected images are 'mapped' on to irregularly shaped objects such as buildings in order to manipulate their appearance.

Spectromorphology: An approach to sound materials and musical structure established by Denis Smalley, which focuses on the spectrum of available pitches and their shaping in time.

Visual Music: A type of artistic practice that involves the arrangement of visual material into music-like structures.

VJ Performance: A type of multimedia performance usually found in nightclubs, in which a VJ (visual jockey) combines video loops or computer graphics to accompany music.

ENDNOTES

1   For a detailed explanation of audio features, see Mitrovic, Zeppelzauer & Breiteneder (2010). 'Low-level' refers to objective measurements such as amplitude, while 'high level' refers to features such as time signature or genre that require interpretation in accordance with a musical or cultural system.

2   Use of the term 'electroacoustic' here refers to 'electroacoustic music': the art music tradition of creating music for loudspeakers using tape, electronic equipment and computers (Manning, 2002). 'Electroacoustic audio-visual composition' is a branch of electroacoustic music which includes a video component.

Chapter 16
Smart Displays in Ambient Intelligence Environments

Fernando Reinaldo Ribeiro
Algoritmi Research Centre, University of Minho, Portugal

Rui José
Algoritmi Research Centre, University of Minho, Portugal

ABSTRACT

A public display that is able to present the right information at the right time is a very compelling concept. However, realising or even approaching this ability to autonomously select appropriate content based on some interpretation of the surrounding social context represents a major challenge. This chapter provides an overview of the key challenges involved and an exploration of some of the main alternatives available. It also describes a novel content adaptation framework that defines the key building blocks for supporting autonomous selection of the Web sources for presentation on public displays. This framework is based on a place model that combines content suggestions expressed by multiple place visitors with those expressed by the place owner. Evaluation results have shown that a place tag cloud can provide a valuable approach to this issue and that people recognize and understand the sensitivity of the system to their demands.

1. INTRODUCTION

In Ambient Intelligence scenarios, the environment can perceive and react to people, sense on-going Human activities and proactively respond to them. Public digital displays have always been part of this vision (the "boards" (Weiser, 1993)), and their increasingly ubiquitous presence in our socio-digital landscape has been opening new opportunities for their use as important building blocks for many types of Ambient Intelligence multimedia environments. However, most public displays today are mere distribution points for pre-defined and centrally created content. They assume passive users and they are completely unaware of the Human activities taking place at that same location. Consequently, they are not very valued by their potential users and their content is often perceived as too institutional or dull (Huang, Koster, & Borchers, 2009).

Ambient Intelligence, social media and the ubiquitous presence of interaction devices rep-

DOI: 10.4018/978-1-4666-7284-0.ch016

Copyright © 2015, IGI Global. Copying or distributing in print or electronic forms without written permission of IGI Global is prohibited.

resent huge opportunities to move towards new display concepts that are able to act as situated artefacts. These displays would no longer be isolated from the people and the data around them. Instead, they would be smart displays capable of dynamically aligning their behaviour with their usage circumstances. This smart behaviour may include the ability to dynamically integrate content from the web and select sources according to their relevance to the social context around the display. The number and diversity of content sources on the Internet offers the potential to guarantee a continuously updated stream of relevant content for the displays. The potential is so vast that we can safely say that content would no longer be a scarce resource and that proper selection would indeed become the key problem. Mobile technology, on the other hand, may offer the potential to implement multiple forms of automated personalization, or adaptation, of the displays.

This chapter explores the concept of smart displays in Ambient Intelligence environments. This generic concept has been explored from many different perspectives and through the development of many types of reactive displays that sense and adapt in some way to their surrounding circumstances. These various systems entail a very broad range of design approaches and assumptions, highlighting the diversity of ways in which the notion of smart display can be approached. We will start by presenting an overview of the design space, framing our work within this broader concept of smart displays. We will then take a closer look at the more specific concept of an adaptive display as a display that is able o select content that is tailored to the preferences or goals of the individuals or groups visiting the place where the display is set. This would make each display system unique and closely related with the specific place where it is installed, providing the ground for highly situated displays that reflect the expectations, interests and practices associated with the people in a particular place. As part of our work on this topic, we have developed an adaptive

display system that autonomously selects from web sources the content deemed more relevant according to a dynamic place model that is sensitive to the people around the display. Regardless of specific technical options, e.g. the use of tag clouds or the use of Bluetooth names to express tags, the overall system provides a general framework for the key building blocks that an adaptive display should be able to support, and will thus be used as a reference system to describe how to approach this particular problem.

2. APPROACHES FOR ADAPTIVE CONTENT ON PUBLIC DISPLAYS

The idea of a public display that is able to present the right information to the right users, at the right time and in the right way is obviously very compelling. However, realising it, or even approaching it in some way, is extremely challenging because of the complex issues involved, such as obtaining information about preferences in a non-obtrusive and privacy-preserving way, the need to combine the various preference expressions of the people in that place, and the complexities involved with making meaningful inferences about relevance based on the information available. The first major challenge however is to properly characterize the problem and its key assumptions, as a very broad range of approaches have been followed to explore different views of this problem domain. To clarify the overall design space for adaptive content on public displays, we will start with an overview of the overall scheduling principles that determine how content is selected and we will analyse how previous work has explored the different possibilities offered by that design space.

2.1. Content Scheduling for Public Displays

The process of determining which content to show on public displays is normally termed content scheduling. The overall scheduling process may be seen as spawning two major phases, specification and execution, and possibly involving three types of entities: Display Owners, System, and Viewers.

Specification is the phase where the schedule is being designed to correspond to an envisioned display concept. A display owner is expected to have a major role in this phase as the designer of some intended user experience. The existence of this intention is what separates the public display from a simple desktop system where the user could simply access the entire range of services without any system-defined boundaries. This process occurs outside the real display context and therefore the specification must either ignore that context by making a full specification in advance or leave some open decision points that will be resolved in execution time. Execution is the phase where immediate decisions must be made to select what to display next. Scheduling may enable multiple types of dynamic decisions to occur at this phase that may take into account the execution context or explicit indication from owners or users. Figure

1 represents this range of possibilities and how the different entities can have some role in each of these two phases.

The specification of the schedule by the display owner is where the most fundamental decisions about the intended display concept are normally made. In traditional Digital Signage systems, this is actually where all the decision are made, as the schedule, both content and the way it will be presented, is fully specified in-advance by display owners, leaving no space for smart content selection or user requests. However, smart displays may explore a dynamic scheduling model in which the specification defines policies that determine the high-level behaviour of the system, but not exactly what it will do. In the end, the effective behaviour exhibited by the system will result from the combination between those policies and the stimuli received from the environment. When considering how to approach this goal, we have explored two major alternatives: modelling this problem as a context-awareness problem and modelling it as a recommendation problem.

Figure 1. Design space for scheduling decisions

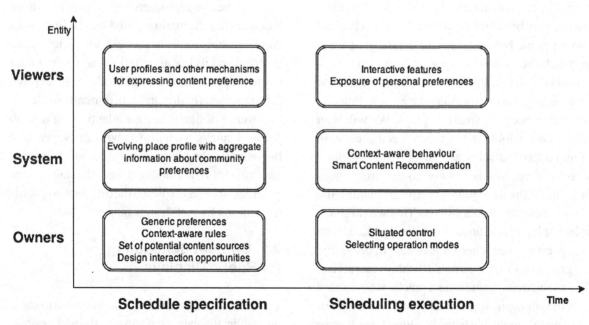

2.2. Adaptive Scheduling as Context-Aware Content Selection

To approach adaptive scheduling as a context-awareness problem, the scheduler should be able to access data about the display context and make scheduling decisions that reflect rational choices about what is most appropriate for each particular context. This requires some type of knowledge that associates context states with specific content

A first possibility is to embed into the scheduling process a number of behaviour rules that represent the empirical knowledge of how the system should select content according to the continuously changing context around the display. For example, we may want to say that a particular piece of content should be scheduled for presentation when the local temperature is above a certain threshold, or that another item should not be shown twice in the presence of any particular Bluetooth device, or that yet another item should only be shown when there is no one being detected in the immediate physical proximity of the display. However, specifying meaningful rules that can apply to generic usage situations can be extremely difficult. Even though it seems intuitive to think that certain situations can affect what is the most appropriate content to be presented in a particular context, it is not trivial to explicitly translate, based only on empirical knowledge, subtle interpretations of context into formal and generic specifications that will rule the display behaviour in multiple real-world contexts. Smartness seems to be a rather vague concept that for most cases does not map directly into just one predefined type of reaction.

Considering these challenges, an alternative is to enable the display system to learn a particular notion of smart behaviour, by training the system to generate new domain knowledge.

In a supervised learning process, there would be a training stage, in which a set of training cases of the expected behaviour would be generated, an inference stage, in which new rules would be inferred, and then a dissemination stage, in which those rules would become domain knowledge ready to be embedded into scheduling processes. It is unclear, however, how much of the generated knowledge would be generic enough to be applied to multiple displays. Each display will have its own context and content items and, moreover, these will be evolving with time.

In a process of unsupervised learning, the scheduler would be able to learn with the experience gained from the operation at a particular place and seamlessly adapt to the specific characteristics of that environment. However, this would require a generic feedback mechanism whereby users could express their opinion on the scheduling decisions, or more specifically about the relevance of what is being shown. This learning process could lead to two complimentary types of result: information about the global popularity of individual items; and information about the effect of context in content popularity. To explore the potential of this approach, we conducted a user study to assess what type of context variables could possibly affect people's perception about content relevance (F. R. Ribeiro & José, 2007). The results have shown that particular content items were systematically rated more relevant, regardless of any context changes. We have not found any statistical significance whatsoever in any of the associations between the relevance of a particular item and any of the context variables. People seemed to associate the relevance of content much more with the place in which it was being presented rather than with any of the forms of context being sensed.

These first experiments have revealed important limitations in the notion of context-aware adaptation in public displays. The difficulties in expressing or inferring meaningful associations between context variables and content items mean that the scope of situation in which those approaches can be effective will not be as broad as is often suggested. While not claiming to have extensively explored all the alternatives, it seems clear that context-awareness would only be efficient in cases where we have a very direct association between a particular context state and a specific system reaction, normally something in the form of a trigger. These conclusions are aligned with previous findings that suggest that context-aware systems should promote a tight integration between sensing and action instead of decomposing them as separate parts of the same process (Leahu, Sengers, & Mateas, 2008) or that the relevance of the sensor readings corresponding to context variables cannot be established a priori outside the specific situation of use in which it is being generated (Dourish, 2004).

2.3. Adaptive Scheduling as a Recommender System

Approaching adaptive scheduling as a recommendation problem may be formulated as follows: Given a set of preferences implicitly or explicitly expressed by the people around a display, how can they be combined with the characteristics of the place to enable the system to select from web sources the most appropriate content to be displayed in that context. By framing the issue of adaptive scheduling as a recommendation problem, we can potentially benefit from the wealth of well-known solutions that already exist for that problem. However, the specific scenario of recommending content from web sources for presentation on a public display raises new challenges that break some of the assumptions we often find in recommendation algorithms and that may limit their applicability. This section summarises the main differences between both problem domains.

Limited Set of Preference Indications

Unlike other media, attention and engagement are far from being a given with public displays. In most cases, the system is autonomously selecting what to presented next and people are very limited in their ability to influence the display decisions. This happens, not just because of technical limitations resulting from the lack of a mouse and keyboard, but essentially because the display is public and not under the control of any single user. Most public displays are thus conceived with the single goal of being seen by the people in their vicinity, without considering any other forms of interaction. Even in the few cases in which there is some interaction support, the richness of those interactions, and consequently, the richness of the digital footprints they generate, is much more limited than in the more traditional scenarios of recommender systems, such as the web. Public displays can thus be used without generating any relevant information about how they are used, much less about the users' interests or preferences. Without such information, it is not feasible to implement recommendation techniques that depend very heavily on implicit or explicit expressions of interest.

Profiles for Place-Based Adaptation

While most recommendation systems target individual recommendations, public displays must be designed for shared and communal use in public and semi-public settings. Therefore, instead of a user profile, recommendations for public display should be based on some sort of place profile that combines the preferences of the person managing the display, who we call the place owner, with the preferences of the multiple people that may be in the vicinity of the display.

A place owner who installs a public display will have specific expectations regarding the way in which the display is going to contribute to the creation of a particular concept of place. An effective profile model must acknowledge this role of public displays and provide the place owner with some control over the nature and scope of the recommendations. If the selected content is not aligned with the place values, practices or commercial strategies, its public presentation may become a source of embarrassment.

Place visitors, on the other hand, are the main consumers of the content presented on the display and for that reason they must also play an active role in guiding the display behaviour. Since public displays will typically have multiple simultaneous users, the adaptation process will need to consider the best strategy for dealing with the potentially very varied interests expressed by those people. This generates a trade-off between the selection based on a profile combing the multiple interests of the multiple persons present and the selection based the use of each individual profile, one at the time (Alt et al., 2009). The first is a balanced approach, but faces the risk of not really matching anyone's specific interests. The second approach can be targeted for each individual, but it raises additional privacy issues and may conflict with the idea of public displays as a place-making tool.

Select, Not Just Recommend

Most recommender systems assume some type of collaborative process or mixed-initiative model. The system may suggest multiple data items from various sources and present them in the form of short summaries with links for further details, but the user is then expected to assess the multiple relevance cues provided and select which content may be of interest. For example, when browsing a video sharing web site, new video suggestions are normally presented after a video is finished. This gives users the possibility to explore the video collection in a more serendipitous way, but they are also free to ignore the suggestion and follow their own path. In Internet radio systems, the system autonomously selects the next music, but the user can easily override selections by skipping to a next song. The implicit assumption is that the system responsibility is mainly to facilitate a selection process that is ultimately controlled by the user.

In a public display, none of these possibilities is naturally available. Since there is normally no intermediate stage between content being sug-gested and being presented, the selections of the system will be shown without necessarily being evaluated by a Human, and possibly without any immediate mechanisms for skipping it. Further-more, given that people will not normally have the possibility to control presentation, content will normally be shown in its full extent. This raises considerably higher risks of presenting irrelevant or even inappropriate content and substantially raises the responsibility of the system in being able to only recommend appropriate items.

Dynamic and Open Content Sources

A common assumption in content selection for public displays is the existence of some predefined list of content alternatives from which content should be selected. This allows a strict control over the type of content that can be presented on the display, but it would fail to address our initial motivation of benefiting from the wealth of content and information sources on the web. To really take advantage of the potential of web information, the display system should allow display users to freely express their interests and be able to dynamically select anywhere from the Internet the most adequate sources.

The focus on dynamic content from web sources also means that the relevance of the respective content is likely to face considerable oscillations. The same source may at a given moment have rich and recently updated information and at some other moment strongly deprecated or even non existing information. The notion of relevant source may thus change very quickly, not just because of changes in the display context, but also because of changes in the content itself. As a consequence, the adaptation processes at the various selection levels must all be very dynamic and frequently re-evaluate their selection decisions. Moreover, previous feedback on a particular source may itself become deprecated very quickly, given that the respective content may have changed considerably.

Presentation Cycles

In a recommender system, content is presented once and after that the system assumes the user is no longer interested in the same content. In a public display, the same content may be presented multiple times because it will most likely be seen by different people at different times. A recommendation system for public displays needs to take into account the existence of presentation cycles in which it becomes acceptable to show the same content again, if it remains relevant. The calculation of relevance may thus have to balance the inherent relevance of a content item with the effect on that relevance of previous presentations of that same content item.

3. RELATED WORK

In this section, we analyse the main approaches for adaptive content on public displays that have been explored in previous work. We also look into recommender systems and the use of tag clouds for interaction and profile representation.

3.1. Scheduling in Situated Displays

For most system, the scheduling process is a based on a fixed schedule that cycles through pre-defined content, but several adaptive scheduling alternatives have been explored that introduce sensibility of the display to some type of external variable. Proactive displays (McCarthy, McDonald, Soroczak, Nguyen, & Rashid, 2004; McDonald, McCarthy, Soroczak, Nguyen, & Rashid, 2008) select content that is scheduled on-the-fly according to the interests of users within the direct vicinity of the display. It recognizes specific presences and display information from associated profiles. Similarly, Groupcast (McCarthy, Costa, & Liongosari, 2001) uses identification and user profiles to present information about the interests

of people in the vicinity of the display. Context-aware informative display (Zhu, Zhang, Zhang, & Lim, 2007) and context sensitive public display for adaptive multi-user information visualization (Morales-Aranda & Mayora-Ibarra, 2007) also aim to provide people with relevant content in an opportune and personalized way. Dynamo (Izadi, Brignull, Rodden, Rogers, & Underwood, 2003) or BlueBoard (Russell, 2003) are examples of systems that give users direct control of the display and thus content selection is directly handled by users rather than by the system. The BlueScreen (Payne, David, Jennings, & Sharifi, 2006) selects and displays adverts in response to users detected in the audience. It utilizes Bluetooth-enable devices as proxies for identifying users and utilizes history information of past users' exposure to certain sets of adverts. Advertisements are preferentially shown to those users that have not seen them yet. Muller et al. (Müller, Kruger, & Kuflik, 2007) describes a mechanism to adapt advertisements on digital signage to the interests of the audience. He proposes a system that uses a naïve Bayes classifier to estimate the probability that a user is interested in a certain advertisement. It uses adverts keywords, users' history, time, location and voucher collection information as feedback to determine the best advert to display. Tacita is a system to allow mobile users to express personalisation preferences to nearby public displays (Kubitza, Clinch, Davies, & Langheinrich, 2012). A mobile client discovers nearby displays, determines the set of applications available, and triggers personalisation. Instant Places (José, Pinto, Silva, & Melro, 2013) enables people to express their content preferences in the form of pins that are recognised when the user checks-in to a display using a mobile client. The displays will then preferably select the content sources associated with those pins.

Even though some of these systems are able to support unassisted and adaptive scheduling, they employ customized scheduling algorithms, mostly based on individual profiles. In our work, we assume that we have no a priori knowledge about users' profiles, and use a place specification as the basis for autonomous content selection.

3.2. Adaptive Engagement

A number of audience behaviour frameworks have been proposed to model the various phases of engagement with public displays as a series of sequential steps that users need to go through to move from being simple passers-by to being engaged users. Adaptive engagement defines different audience situations that can be sensed by the display and specific ways in which the behaviour of the display should adapt to the audience, more specifically their distance or their attention to the display.

The Hello.Wall (Streitz et al. 2003b) is an ambient display is designed around an audience behaviour model that considers three levels of interactivity corresponding to three zones: Ambient, Notification and Cell interaction zones. The display aims to maximise engagement by exhibiting an appropriate behaviour for each engagement phase. The interactive public ambient display (Vogel and Balakrishnan 2004) detects the audience's body posture and adjust behaviour according to a four-phase interaction model based on proximity and attention that may be seen as a refinement of the three phases of the Hello.Wall model. The Peddler Interaction Framework (Wang, Boring, & Greenberg, 2012) extends the Audience Funnel Framework (Michelis & Müller, 2011) to incorporate continuous proxemic measures such as distance and orientation, attention states, such as digression and loss of interest, and the passerby's interaction history. The goal is to adjust the display behaviour is a way that maximises the ability to attract Attention, maintain Interest, create Desire, and lead customers to Action. Even though these

systems are clear examples of adaptive displays, their focus is attracting and maintaining user attention. They do not address the autonomous selection of content based on the current context around the display.

3.3. Recommender Systems

Approaches to recommender systems deal mainly with two types of entities: users and items. The user entity is normally a user profile that is based on either manual user input of preferences or automatic user modelling i.e. deriving user preferences and providing recommendations on the basis of user's history of content consumption. The item entity is usually characterized with a set of metadata that is supplied by the source, but this information can also be extended with additional information that is inserted by users. These entities are the basis of all recommendation techniques that normally depend on extensive data about both. However, the specificities of how they are used differ between the three main recommendation techniques in use today: content-based recommendations, collaborative recommendations and hybrid approaches.

In content-based recommendation, the system suggests to the user the items that best fit the user profile. A set of attributes that characterize each item is used to determine appropriateness of the item for recommendation purposes. The user will be recommended items that are similar to the ones preferred in the past. A key limitation of these techniques is that the system cannot recommend items that are different from anything the user has seen before. This is particularly limiting in our case because the ability to find new content that is totally unrelated with what has already been presented is an important requirement.

Collaborative techniques, in their common form, are also difficult to apply. They make recommendations based on information of people with similar tastes and preferences, trying to predict the utility of items for a particular user based on the items previously rated by other users. Their main limitation is not being very good in dealing with new content items and also with frequently updated sources (Das, Datar, Garg, & Rajaram, 2007), making them unsuitable for our scenarios of selecting content feeds in a timely way. Moreover, the focus on a single display, the reduced number of users in our system and also the potentially very low rating density raise additional challenges to the application of collaborative recommendation techniques.

González et. al (González et al., 2006) present a system that extends traditional approaches to recommender systems. They analysed cross-disciplinary trends from the users' affective factors perspective in the next generation of ambient recommender systems. They combine a model of the user's emotional information with intelligent agents and machine learning to provide relevant recommendations in everyday life. This work also builds on previous work in recommendation systems and retrieval models for feed search (Arguello, Elsas, Callan, & Carbonell, 2008; Bihun et al., 2007; Seo & Croft, 2007).

The use of tag clouds for content recommendation has been described by Pessemier et.al (Pessemier, Deryckere, & Martens, 2009). Tag clouds are generated from user ratings to create a form of personal profile. These tag clouds are then used to recommend movies to that person. In our work, we also suggest the use of tag clouds for recommendation purposes, but in our case this corresponds to a place or situation profile, and not to the profile of a single individual. This related work demonstrates how tag cloud can indeed support many roles outside their original context. However, the use of tag clouds as a situated representation of place that drives the content selection on a public displays remains to the best of our knowledge a novel approach.

4. A FRAMEWORK FOR ADAPTIVE CONTENT ON PUBLIC DISPLAYS

As part of our work on this topic, we have developed an adaptive content scheduler for public displays that is able to select the information feeds deemed more relevant for the current social setting around the display (F. Ribeiro & José, 2013). Even though this scheduling system has been instantiated around specific technologies, such as content feeds and tag clouds, its fundamental principles should also apply to other instantiations of the problem domain and may thus constitute a more general framework to the issue of content recommendation for public displays. There are three main sub-systems in this architecture: a place sub-system representing a dynamic and evolving view of place that combines the place owner specifications with the contributions made by place visitors; a selector sub-system that takes keywords from the tag cloud in the place sub-system and retrieves relevant content for each of those tags using dynamic web sources as content providers; and a scheduler sub-system that considers the available content as well as the weight and presence level of the represented tags to select which content is going to be shown next. This layered design has evolved throughout multiple iterations and its final architecture is represented in Figure 2.

4.1. Place Sub-System

A place model combines the place-making role of a place owner with the ability to allow the multiple visitors to also exert some influence on the characteristics of place. In our model, a tag cloud was used as a shared and evolving view of the expressions of interest made by the place owner and the people around the display.

The place tag cloud is first created by the place owner. Place-making parameters allow a place owner to provide additional characterization and

Figure 2. System architecture

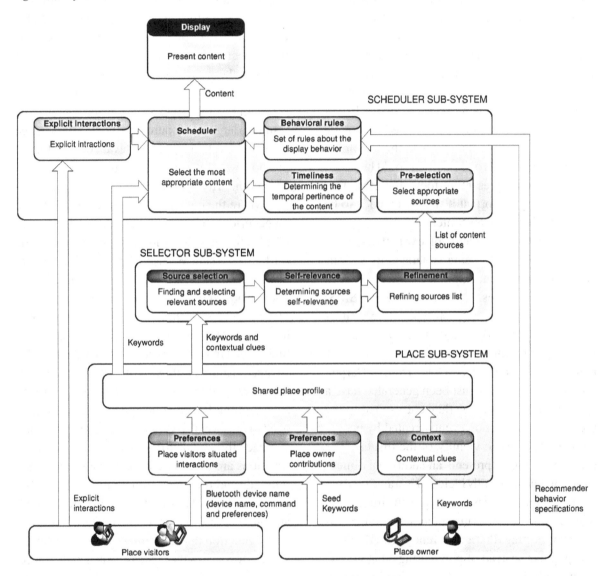

specify adaptation boundaries for a tag cloud. Even though the tag cloud is expected to emerge from interaction, these parameters provide a way for aligning the display behaviour with the general expectations of appropriateness of the display owner and its place-making objectives. The main part of these specifications is a set of keyword lists that enable some control of the tags in the tag cloud. The first is a blocked words list. This list may include words that are very common in a given language, but not very meaningful in a tag

cloud. Excluding these words is already a common procedure in traditional tag clouds, but in this case we may also want to use this to prevent abusive or offensive keywords from making it into the tag cloud. We also have a list of seed keywords that serve to initialise the tag cloud and maintain a number of place keywords when there are not enough keywords being generated. Seed tags are defined with a minimum popularity value that determines how visible they remain when other tags begin to emerge. A *SeedsOnly* parameter can be used to determine that a particular tag cloud will only accept seed words. This works as a white list that restrains the accepted words to those on the list and may be useful to promote aggregation around thematic tag clouds, e.g. a tag cloud with sport teams, emoticon symbols, or music styles. Finally, there is also a list of contextual keywords that can be used to provide additional context to the words in the tag cloud. For example, Sports and Football could be added to a tag cloud representing football teams. This is particularly important if the tag cloud is to be used for selecting web content.

The tag cloud will then evolve with the continuous stream of words being generated by various types of implicit and explicit interactions, such as Bluetooth names, Obex exchanges or SMS/MMS messages. In our prototype, place visitors could publish their own tags into the tag cloud, by including *tag* commands in their Bluetooth device name, as described in (José, Otero, Izadi, & Harper, 2008). Tags that have just been generated have a special meaning because they correspond to the presence or interaction events created by people who are now in the vicinity of the display. The presence of tags represents an additional dimension that is not normally included in traditional tag clouds, but may be key to interpret the immediate relevance of those tags in content selection, possibly favouring tags that are currently present, albeit less popular, instead of popular tags that no one is currently generating. The tag cloud resulting from combining the initial specification by the place-owner with the continuous stream of words originating from presence and interaction provides the evolving and dynamic representation of place that will be used as the basis for content selection.

4.2. Selector Sub-System

The selector sub-system is responsible for autonomously finding and selecting relevant content sources from the Internet. To fully benefit from the wealth of sources on the Internet, the selector

should be able to consider the generic relevance of a source, in the sense of popularity, and also its timeliness, in the sense of how up to date is the respective information.

Using keywords from the place tag cloud we recur to a feeds aggregator for searching sources according to the needs of the place model. The result is a large set of sources without any relevance criterion. We then apply a relevance algorithm to promote sources that rank higher in popularity. This popularity is independent of the usage context where the content is consumed and is based on generic measurements such as the percentage of all Internet users who visit a given site or the traffic to the site. We use Alexa search engine to obtain the traffic rank, a measure obtained from Alexa Toolbar users. Another important measure of feed relevance is the number of users subscribed to the feed. Higher values of subscriptions denote higher feed interest. Through the Newsgator API, we get the number of users that subscribe each of the sources. Because both traffic rank and feed subscriptions have distinct numeric domains they need to be normalized. We do that by defining acceptance thresholds for both measures. Sigmoid functions are used for characterizing acceptance intervals and provide a smooth interpolation between the limits of those intervals. Both traffic rank and number of subscribers are thus combined in a single function that determines the most relevant sources for each of the tags associated with a place.

4.3. Scheduler Sub-System

The scheduler sub-system decides which content to present next on the display. This decision involves two steps. The first is to select which of the tags in the place tag cloud will be used next for content presentation. For each tag, there is information about the respective popularity and whether or not it is currently present, i.e. someone who is now around the display is announcing that tag. Additionally, there is also a list of recently used tags. When selected for presentation, a tag is then placed on this list for a number of iterations to prevent it from being successively selected. The algorithm selects the most popular tag among those who are present and not in the waiting queue, or if none is present, the most popular tag not in the waiting queue.

The second step is the selection of which of the content feeds associated with the selected tag will be displayed next. This decision is based on a multi-criteria utility function that considers three parameters: timeliness, content structure and scheduling history. Timeliness represents the measure of the temporal pertinence of content, i.e. how recent are the last updates. Content structure is an empirical measure of the appropriateness of the content in the feeds for presentation on a public display. This is not related with the semantics or the quality of content, but only with the fact that, in certain cases, the structure of content can make it inadequate for presentation in a public display, either because it is link-intensive, because the text is too long, or for some other similar reason. For example, we analyse the length of the text, the content language, the number of links found in the text or the number of image links in the feeds. Scheduling history considers the previous presentation of similar content. The scheduler should be aware of the recently presented content and avoid presenting content that is very similar, even if supplied from distinct sources. This is very common with news sources, which may be showing very similar headlines. A combination of these parameters, jointly with the scheduler behaviour configuration, supports the scheduler decisions of what to present at each moment.

4.4. Evaluation

The evaluation of this adaptive content system comprised a set of smaller user studies and a final public deployment to assess its overall operation in a real-world scenario. This diverse set of evaluation approaches enabled us to progressively improve architectural designs and gain a broad understanding of the key issues involved.

The first study addressed relevance from the perspective of timeliness (F. R. Ribeiro & José, 2009b). The goal was to understand the key criteria for evaluating the timeliness of content across several types of dynamic sources and results have shown that the users' perception of timeliness was properly represented by the concept of timeliness as supported by the framework. The results suggest a reasonable match between our model and the users' perspectives on timeliness and also show that the model is able to make comparative calculations of timeliness for different types of dynamic source. The appropriateness and accuracy of the method for obtaining relevant sources based on simple keywords from the place model was evaluated in a second study (F. R. Ribeiro & José, 2009a, 2009b). The results have shown that keywords can be very effective in driving user-generated content, but they often need to be complemented with contextual information that disambiguates their semantics. The ability of the framework to autonomously select from web sources the content deemed more relevant according to a dynamic place model was also evaluated (F. Ribeiro & José, 2013). The place model was based on a tag cloud that combined content suggestions expressed by multiple place visitors with those expressed by the place owner. Results of this experiment indicate that people perceive the content autonomously selected from the tags as being relevant to the context where the display is situated. They also recognized and understand the sensitivity of the system to their demands and how their interactions influenced the display behaviour.

5. DISCUSSION AND CONCLUSION

This chapter has discussed the overall issue of how to support adaptive content selection for public displays. We have explored different adaptation strategies, particularly those based on context-awareness and content recommendation.

Our assessment of the context-aware approach suggests that context *per se* was not enough to support adaptive content selection, in part due to the limited context information available, but also largely because of the challenges involved in specifying or inferring generic context adaptation rules for matching context situations with the utility of particular content items. More context information, and possibly more work on rule formulation, could probably lead to better results, but our subsequent work with the tag clouds would also highlight how a more simple approach, albeit one people can reason about, may also have important advantages. We have also identified obvious similarities between content adaptation in public displays and recommendation systems. However, there are also clearly different assumptions in both problems that severely limit the direct application of existing recommendations techniques.

Based on these observations, we have developed and evaluated a novel content adaptation system for public displays that uses a shared and public place profile in the form of a place tag cloud to combine the multiple interests of the place owner and place visitors. Overall, the positive results obtained during the evaluation suggest that this is a viable approach to the problem of content adaptation for public displays. The results showed that place visitors recognize the sensitivity of the system to their demands and that a place tag cloud was able to provide an adequate representation of place.

Despite their simplicity, tag clouds have revealed to be a promising solution to our specific scenario. Their main advantage is their ability to dynamically integrate the preferences of both place owner and place visitors into a single representation, and thus generate a representation of the social environment as a whole instead of each individual interest at a time. Still, the use of tag clouds as place models is obviously a limited approach from the perspective of descriptive richness and we are not suggesting that they are an appropriate model for other place representation scenarios. However, their simplicity and their visual nature may have been an important element in the positive results obtained with our system. Through the use of the tag clouds, we have made a key part of the system model explicit and visible, allowing people to reason about it and actuate according to their goals. It also enabled people to perceive interactions being generated by other nearby users and observe the respective effect on the system. This ability to build an understanding of what was happening and interpret the system behaviour has been suggested in the interviews as something that may have contributed to increase user acceptance, even when the content shown was not perceived as the most appropriate option. We consider this to be an important finding, but it remains an interesting research topic to quantify this effect and be able to understand how does this ability to reason about what is happening in the subjective perception that people formulate about the system behaviour compares against other approaches potentially more effective and sophisticated, but less open to user inspection.

REFERENCES

Alt, F., Balz, M., Kristes, S., Shirazi, A. S., Mennenoh, J., Schmidt, A., et al. (2009). *Adaptive User Profiles in Pervasive Advertising Environments*. Paper presented at the European Conference on Ambient Intelligence. Salzburg, Austria. doi:10.1007/978-3-642-05408-2_32

Arguello, J., Elsas, J. L., Callan, J., & Carbonell, J. G. (2008, March 30-April 2). *Document Representation and Query Expansion Models for Blog Recommendation*. Paper presented at the International Conference on Weblogs and Social Media. Seattle, WA.

Bihun, A., Goldman, J., Khesin, A., Marur, V., Morales, E., & Reynar, J. (2007). *US Patent No. 20070061297A1*. US Patent & Trademark Office.

Das, A. S., Datar, M., Garg, A., & Rajaram, S. (2007). *Google news personalization: scalable online collaborative filtering*. Paper presented at the 16th international conference on World Wide Web. Banff, Canada doi:10.1145/1242572.1242610

Dourish, P. (2004). What we talk about when we talk about context. *Personal and Ubiquitous Computing*, *8*(1), 19–30. doi:10.1007/s00779-003-0253-8

González, G., Rosa, J. L. d. l., Dugdale, J., Pavard, B., Jed, M. E., Pallamin, N., ... Klann, M. (2006). *Towards Ambient Recommender Systems: Results of New Cross-disciplinary Trends*. Paper presented at the Workshop on Recommender Systems in European Conference on Artificial Intelligence on Recommender Systems. Riva del Garda, Italy.

Huang, E. M., Koster, A., & Borchers, J. (2009). *Overcoming Assumptions and Uncovering Practices: When Does the Public Really Look at Public Displays?* Paper presented at the 6th International Conference on Pervasive Computing. Sydney, Australia.

Izadi, S., Brignull, H., Rodden, T., Rogers, Y., & Underwood, M. (2003, November). *Dynamo: A public interactive surface supporting the cooperative sharing and exchange of media*. Paper presented at the Symposium on User Interface Software and Technology. Vancouver, Canada. doi:10.1145/964696.964714

José, R., Otero, N., Izadi, S., & Harper, R. (2008, October-December). Instant Places: Using Bluetooth for Situated Interaction in Public Displays. *IEEE Pervasive Computing*, *7*(4), 52–57. doi:10.1109/MPRV.2008.74

José, R., Pinto, H., Silva, B., & Melro, A. (2013). Pins and posters: Paradigms for content publication on situated displays. *IEEE Computer Graphics and Applications*, *33*(2), 64–72. doi:10.1109/MCG.2013.16 PMID:24807941

Kubitza, T., Clinch, S., Davies, N., & Langheinrich, M. (2012). Using mobile devices to personalize pervasive displays. *Mobile Computing and Communications Review*, *16*(4), 26–27. doi:10.1145/2436196.2436211

Leahu, L., Sengers, P., & Mateas, M. (2008, September 21-24). *Interactionist AI and the promise of ubicomp, or, how to put your box in the world without putting the world in your box*. Paper presented at the 10th International Conference on Ubiquitous Computing. Seoul, South Korea. doi:10.1145/1409635.1409654

McCarthy, J. F., Costa, T. J., & Liongosari, E. S. (2001). *UniCast, OutCast & GroupCast: Three Steps toward Ubiquitous Peripheral Displays*. Paper presented at the International Conference on Ubiquitous Computing. Atlanta, GA. doi:10.1007/3-540-45427-6_28

McCarthy, J. F., McDonald, D. W., Soroczak, S., Nguyen, D. H., & Rashid, A. M. (2004). *Augmenting the Social Space of an Academic Conference*. Paper presented at the CSCW. Chicago, IL.

McDonald, D. W., McCarthy, J. F., Soroczak, S., Nguyen, D. H., & Rashid, A. M. (2008). Proactive Displays: Supporting Awareness in Fluid Social Environments. *ACM Transactions on Computer-Human Interaction*, *14*(4), 1–31. doi:10.1145/1314683.1314684

Michelis, D., & Müller, J. (2011). The Audience Funnel: Observations of Gesture Based Interaction With Multiple Large Displays in a City Center. *International Journal of Human-Computer Interaction, 27*(6), 562–579. doi:10.1080/104473 18.2011.555299

Morales-Aranda, A. H., & Mayora-Ibarra, O. (2007, June 19 -25). *A Context Sensitive Public Display for Adaptive Multi-User Information Visualization* Paper presented at the Third International Conference on Autonomic and Autonomous Systems. Athens, Greece. doi:10.1109/CONIELECOMP.2007.40

Müller, J., Kruger, A., & Kuflik, T. (2007). *Maximizing the Utility of Situated Public Displays.* Paper presented at the Adjunct Proceedings of User Modeling. Corfu, Greece. doi:10.1007/978-3-540-73078-1_52

Payne, T., David, E., Jennings, N. R., & Sharifi, M. (2006). *Auction Mechanisms for Efficient Advertisement Selection on Public Displays.* Paper presented at the European Conference on Artificial Intelligence. Riva del Garda, Italy.

Pessemier, T. D., Deryckere, T., & Martens, L. (2009). *Context aware recommendations for user-generated content on a social network site.* Paper presented at the 7th European Interactive Television Conference. Leuven, Belgium.

Ribeiro, F., & José, R. (2013). Smart content selection for public displays in ambient intelligence environments. *International Journal of Ambient Computing and Intelligence, 5*(2), 35–55. doi:10.4018/jaci.2013040103

Ribeiro, F. R., & José, R. (2007). *Proactive Scheduling for Situated Displays.* Paper presented at the Workshop on Ambient Intelligence Technologies and Applications. Guimarães.

Ribeiro, F. R., & José, R. (2009a). Place-aware content selection from dynamic web sources for public displays. In *Proceedings of 5th International Conference on Signal-Image Technology & Internet-Based Systems* (pp. 302-309). Marrakech: IEEE Computer Society Press. doi:10.1109/SITIS.2009.56

Ribeiro, F. R., & José, R. (2009b). *Timeliness for dynamic source selection in situated public displays* Paper presented at the 5th Int. Conference on Web Information Systems and Technologies. Lisbon, Portugal.

Russell, D. M., & Sue, A. (2003). Large Interactive Public Displays: Use Patterns, Support Patterns, Community Patterns. In K. O'Hara, M. Perry, E. Churchill, & D. Russell (Eds.), *Public and Situated Displays* (Vol. 2, pp. 3–17). Dordrecht, The Netherlands: Springer Netherlands. doi:10.1007/978-94-017-2813-3_1

Seo, J., & Croft, W. B. (2007). *UMass at TREC 2007 Blog Distillation Task.* Paper presented at the Text Retrieval Conference. Gaithersburg, MD.

Wang, M., Boring, S., & Greenberg, S. (2012). *Proxemic peddler: a public advertising display that captures and preserves the attention of a passerby.* Paper presented at the 2012 International Symposium on Pervasive Displays. Porto, Portugal. doi:10.1145/2307798.2307801

Weiser, M. (1993). Some Computer Science Issues in Ubiquitous Computing. *Communications of the ACM, 36*(7), 75–84. doi:10.1145/159544.159617

Zhu, M., Zhang, D., Zhang, J., & Lim, B.Y. (2007). *Context-Aware Informative Display.* Paper presented at the International Conference on Multimedia and Expo. Beijing, China.

ADDITIONAL READING

Alt, F., Shirazi, A. S., Kubitza, T., & Schmidt, A. (2013). *Interaction techniques for creating and exchanging content with public displays*. Paper presented at the Proceedings of the SIGCHI Conference on Human Factors in Computing Systems, Paris, France. doi:10.1145/2470654.2466226

Cardoso, J., & José, R. (2009). A Framework for Context-Aware Adaptation in Public Displays. In R. Meersman, P. Herrero, & T. Dillon (Eds.), *On the Move to Meaningful Internet Systems: OTM 2009 Workshops* (Vol. 5872, pp. 118–127). Berlin: Springer Berlin Heidelberg. doi:10.1007/978-3-642-05290-3_21

Clinch, S., Davies, N., Kubitza, T., & Schmidt, A. (2012). *Designing application stores for public display networks*. Paper presented at the Proceedings of the 2012 International Symposium on Pervasive Displays, Porto, Portugal. doi:10.1145/2307798.2307808

Davies, N., Langheinrich, M., José, R., & Schmidt, A. (2012). Open Display Networks: A Communications Medium for the 21st Century. *Computer*, *45*(5), 58–64. doi:10.1109/MC.2012.114

Elhart, I., Langheinrich, M., Davies, N., & José, R. (2013, 18-22 March). *Key Challenges in Application and Content Scheduling for Open Pervasive Display Networks*. Paper presented at the 2013 IEEE International Conference on Pervasive Computing and Communications Workshops (PERCOM Workshops), San Diego. doi:10.1109/PerComW.2013.6529524

Konomi, Shin'ichi, Inoue, Sozo, Kobayashi, Takashi, Tsuchida, Masashi, & Kitsuregawa, Masaru. (2006). Supporting Colocated Interactions Using RFID and Social Network Displays. *IEEE Pervasive Computing, 5*(3), 48-56. doi: 10.1109/mprv.2006.60

Linden, T., Heikkinen, T., Ojala, T., Kukka, H., & Jurmu, M. (2010). *Web-based framework for spatiotemporal screen real estate management of interactive public displays*. Paper presented at the Proceedings of the 19th international conference on World wide web, Raleigh, North Carolina, USA. doi:10.1145/1772690.1772901

Müller, J., Alt, F., Schmidt, A., & Michelis, D. (2010, October 25–29). *Requirements and Design Space for Interactive Public Displays*. Paper presented at the International Conference on Multimedia Firenze, Italy. doi:10.1145/1873951.1874203

Müller, J., Exeler, J., Buzeck, M., & Krüger, A. (2009). ReflectiveSigns: Digital Signs That Adapt to Audience Attention. In H. Tokuda, M. Beigl, A. Friday, A. J. B. Brush, & Y. Tobe (Eds.), *Pervasive Computing* (Vol. 5538, pp. 17–24). London: Springer Berlin Heidelberg. doi:10.1007/978-3-642-01516-8_3

O'Hara, K., Lipson, M., Jansen, M., Unger, A., Jeffries, H., & Macer, P. (2004). *Jukola: democratic music choice in a public space*. Paper presented at the Proceedings of the 5th conference on Designing interactive systems: processes, practices, methods, and techniques, Cambridge, MA, USA. doi:10.1145/1013115.1013136

Storz, O., Friday, A., & Davies, N. (2006). Supporting content scheduling on situated public displays. *Computers & Graphics*, *30*(5), 681–691. doi:10.1016/j.cag.2006.07.002

KEY TERMS AND DEFINITIONS

Ambient Intelligence: Digital environments that proactively supports people in their everyday lives.

Context Awareness: Systems that sense their environment and adapt their behavior accordingly.

Interactive Systems: Systems that accept input from users and react to these inputs.

Recommender Systems: A system that is able to recommend new content that may be of interest to an entity, based on information about the preferences, past actions or properties of the entity.

Smart Displays: A display situated in a public place that is able to present the right information to the right users, at the right time and in the right way.

Ubiquitous Computing: A paradigm where the environment becomes intelligent by integrating information processing capabilities into everyday life objects and places.

User Generated Content: Content that is created by consumers or end-users.

Chapter 17
A Literacy and Numeracy E-Learning Mobile Application for Pre-Schoolers

Niall McCarroll
University of Ulster, UK

Kevin Curran
University of Ulster, UK

ABSTRACT

The Northern Ireland pre-school curriculum promotes educational development through enabling learning environments and active learning through play and exploration. Enabling learning environments are rich in books, pictures, signs, symbols, rhymes, and multimedia technology. Through play and exploration, children are engaged in activities that interest and preoccupy them. The resources that are used as a context for play have an important bearing on the depth of learning experienced by a child. According to the Early Years Foundation Stage, from age 40 months, a child's literacy and numeracy can develop rapidly with the support of a wide range of interesting materials, activities, media, and technologies (Department for Education, 2008). The aim of this project is to create the "SmartFun" literacy and numeracy E-Learning application. "SmartFun" is a fun, engaging environment to promote the early learning of letters and numbers for pre-school and primary one children.

INTRODUCTION

The Nursery Education Guidelines Curriculum is a comprehensive statutory framework that sets the standards for the learning, development and care of children from birth to five in Northern Ireland. The guidelines set values for the educational development of young children in settings outside of home, in an effort to promote educa-

tional progress and positive partnerships between parents and teaching professionals (NICC, 1998). Every child is a competent learner from birth and a nurturing environment plays a key role in supporting and extending children's development and learning. Children develop and learn in different ways and at different rates and all areas of learning and development are equally important and inter-connected (DENI, 1997). According to the

DOI: 10.4018/978-1-4666-7284-0.ch017

Copyright © 2015, IGI Global. Copying or distributing in print or electronic forms without written permission of IGI Global is prohibited.

pre-school curriculum in Northern Ireland, as set by the Department of Education (DENI) "There is no place at this stage for the introduction of formal schooling in the sense of an established body of knowledge to be acquired or a set of skills to be mastered" (NICC, 1989). The aim instead is to build upon children's learning experiences and development at home through a rich variety of play activities and other experiences.

The curriculum aims to develop learning associated with Personal, Social and Emotional Development, Physical Development, Creative/Aesthetic Development, Language Development, Early Mathematical Experiences, Early Experiences in Science and Technology and Knowledge and Appreciation of the Environment. In order to fully understand how these areas are approached within local schools, an interview with a pre-school teacher was conducted. This helped to identify a number of important parameters within the pre-school educational framework that had particular relevance when designing this early learning application, such as limitations on formal learning techniques (Eames & Milne, 2011)

While there is no formal schooling as such, a number of key developmental areas are identified—or early learning goals—including language development and numeracy, which the 'Smartfun' application aims to promote. In the rest of the UK the curriculum is weighted slightly more in favour of formal academic teaching regarding letters and numbers, but the objectives are essentially the same—to effectively teach children in a stimulating and challenging environment. The Early Years Foundation Stage (EYFS) recommends that all the goals for learning and development must be delivered through planned, purposeful play, with a balance of adult-led and child-initiated activities (Department for Education, 2008). "Language development" is one of the main areas of development within the Northern Ireland pre-school curriculum. The areas within language development focus on communication with others, attention and listening, enjoyment of books and writing/

mark making. The 'SmartFun' application aims to incorporate all four of these key skills on different levels, as well as impart basic information about letters and their function within words. It is essentially aimed at bridging the gap between pre-school and primary one age children, when children move from simply recognising letters and being aware of their use, to actually using letters to form words and sentences (Fox-Turnbull & Snape, 2011).

Mathematical development and basic numeracy are also important components of the curriculum (Edwards, 2009). The areas within mathematical development aim to support children in their understanding of numeracy, reasoning and problem solving and focus on counting reliably up to ten everyday objects., recognising numerals 1 to 10, using language such as 'greater', 'smaller', 'heavier' or 'lighter' to compare quantities, talking about, recognising and recreating simple patterns., using language such as 'circle' or 'bigger' to describe the shape and size of solids and flat shapes and using everyday words to describe position, such as, in front of, behind, above and below. While this application primarily concentrates on language development, 'SmartFun' also incorporates some numeracy tasks to demonstrate how it can be further developed to promote learning in other areas. The focus here will be on recognising numerals 1 through to 10, basic counting of objects and simple number matching activities.

Much emphasis is placed on the role of imaginative and creative activities which can help children to make sense of their experiences and 'transform' their knowledge, fostering cognitive development ((Rabah, 2005; Mano et al., 2006; Tomas & Castro, 2011). By creating colourful characters which children can interact with on-screen, the 'SmartFun' application aims to create a new learning environment through story-telling and animation. It should appeal to children on a familiar level through the stories, as well as appeal to their sense of curiosity by teaching new skills and technology via a tablet device. There is a strong focus on allowing children to learn without experiencing a sense of failure. That is why tools such as iPads and other new technology have such a useful place in the classroom, providing a novel and innovative way of teaching through play and interaction. All children learn more effectively through engaging activities, making interactive games the ideal vehicle for learning. The aim is to create a flexible learning environment – allowing the child to interact with technology, and also to engage in a range of different activities with a shared goal. DENI also recommends that children explore different media and respond to a variety of sensory experiences, which makes the use of the tablet devices ideal as new learning tools. Children can engage with the 'SmartFun' application on different levels—simple story telling, or identifying letters and numbers and interacting with the application. If they choose to engage with it their efforts are acknowledged and rewarded visually by the characters.

Teaching children to use simple learning applications such as this has a twofold effect: it enhances their ability to focus on tasks such as identifying letters, as well as using a new technology to complete them. On a practical level the 'Smartfun' environment is therefore also a way of not just enhancing children's learning experiences in language and numeracy, but also in the area of information technology. Primary schools are now being built with state of the art computer suites, and classrooms are being equipped with interactive whiteboards and other technology designed to support teaching. So learning to use tablet devices at nursery level is already familiarising children with the use of technology as another medium for learning and communication, making it a natural progression for them at a later stage. Having identified the key areas within pre-school education that would most benefit from an interactive learning tool, the challenge is to develop an application that is both effective and fun. But perhaps the bigger challenge is the creation of a programme that can

be easily manipulated and enjoyed by such young children, who, as we all know, are the most critical and demanding customers.

BACKGROUND

The goal of this learning application is to create a fun, engaging environment to promote the early learning of letters and numbers for pre-school to primary one children. Because the emphasis is on learning through play, the application had to be visually entertaining and appealing with bright colours and engaging animation. Keeping in mind the DENI recommendation that children should not be taught through formal learning techniques, the programme is very much child-led and fun. While encouraged to follow the letter and number shapes children can enjoy doodling on the screen, but they will also be praised for following the patterns and achieving the stipulated goals. It is hoped that through positive reinforcement they will learn without even being aware of it, about letters and numbers, and their functions.

Choice of Learning Medium

The aim was to produce a clean and simple user interface which would be easily navigated by young pre-school children with limited motor skills. In order to facilitate full interaction it was decided the best medium was the touch screen which meant children did not have to learn to control a mouse. Instead they can enjoy a completely tactile experience by controlling things with their own fingers, similar in many ways to finger painting or playing with a magna-doodle. According to mobile manufacturer Ericsson, studies indicate that soon 80% of people accessing the internet will do so from a mobile device, so it makes sense that children have early access to a technology that will be so prevalent in their lives in the future. And the touch screen aspect is a tactile way for children to engage with learning, just as in drawing or painting. The 2011 Horizon report reveals that the age at which children access their first mobile device is dropping, and with the popularity of tablets steadily growing, more and more children will be using them at home and in the classroom (New Media Consortium, 2011). The report highlights the fact that many people now have access to full length books on their mobile devices with software accessing literature, textbooks, children's books, novels, articles, and journals in a pocket sized format. This collection of features and their potential for enhancing learning experiences is what is of most interest to schools.

Thus it makes sense that these new educational tools are introduced at such an early stage, using simple applications in a fun environment. While the use of mobile phones is still taboo in a classroom situation, the use of tablets is much less so and could transform traditional lessons, according to the Horizon Report. These devices effectively "encompass many of the tools smartphones have to offer, while presenting an ever-expanding collection of tools for learning". While much has been made of the difficulty faced by children in manipulating buttons and keypads, and the limitations on usage, Shuler (2009) points out that "developments in touch screen and gestural input may significantly improve the way children interact with mobile devices".

Another reason for using such applications is their accessibility, they can be implemented as learning tools, not just in a classroom environment, but also at home. A child's first educators are its parents, and there is much emphasis on the role of the parent in pre-education. In fact the DENI curriculum describes parents as partners in children's education. By downloading learning applications such as 'SmartFun', parents are employing a useful tool that can be used to reinforce classroom based lessons, allowing them a more active role in their child's education. The fact that children are becoming exposed to technology at a younger age means that tablet devices are also being used

by increasing numbers of children at home. This fact is manifest in the launch of the Leapfrog Leappad tablet for children in 2011, which is so popular that manufacturers simply cannot keep up with demand. In fact it has sold out across Ireland in the run up to Christmas, indicating the levels of demand for toys that mimic adult technology (Irish Daily Mail online, 2011).

The screen resolution for the iPad in a landscape position is 1024 x 768 pixels and 1024 x 620 pixels for the Samsung Galaxy Tab. A design decision was made to fix absolute width and height for the interface of the 'SmartFun' application at 980 x 620 pixels to fit in with the dimensions of these tablet devices in the sideways orientation (Figure 1 (1)). Fixing absolute widths and heights goes against design best practice in terms of creating an application that can run on multiple screen resolutions—from mobile phones to large widescreen monitors. However, the decision was considered appropriate given that a sufficiently large workspace is required for young users to navigate with ease. The learning activities that the 'SmartFun' application supports would not be feasible on a smaller mobile device screen (Figure 1 (2)).

Interface and Character Design

Four characters were created—Amy Ant, Bonny Bee, Cosy Cat and Dizzy Dog. As well as using alliteration in their names to reinforce the learning of the letters, each character is visually composed of their letter to some extent. Again the first name is the upper case and the second name the lower case of their representative letter (Figure 2). It was important that the font itself also reflected the simplicity of the design, with easily recognisable letters and numbers scaled up for visual impact. The application prototype is restricted to the letters A, B, C and D to make development manageable within the time-frame of the project. A limited release of letters also makes sense commercially, as the initial batch could be released for free with further letters available to buy on demand.

Figure 1. Design decisions for the 'SmartFun' application: 1. the interface has a fixed width and height (980 x 621 pixels) creating an accommodating workspace for a child user; 2. the tablet touch screen makes it very easy for a child to manipulate on-screen elements.

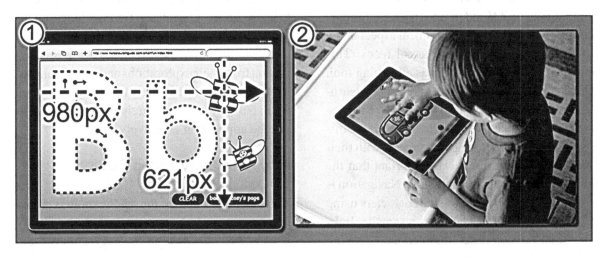

Figure 2. The SmartFun characters are bright and colourful and visually composed of the letters they represent.

The characters themselves are designed to appeal to children's sense of creativity and fun—bright colours and quirky designs, things they are familiar with on TV and in story books. This puts more emphasis on the entertainment aspect of the design, rather than the educational focus. This application is as much for fun as a learning tool, which is in keeping with the emphasis on learning through play at this level in schools. Keeping in mind the limited dexterity of children at this age, who are still gripping their pencils with their fists or palmer grasps, it was important that the interface was as simple as possible. Navigation is achieved simply by pressing the characters using Image Maps, removing buttons and smaller links which may overcomplicate the interface—keeping it simple and clean. This will allow the child as much control as possible without having to rely on an adult to help navigate through the application (Figure 3).

This ease of navigation is also in keeping with recommendations regarding Active Learning, which stresses that to be mentally or physically engaged in learning, children need to feel at ease, secure and confident.

Active learning occurs when children are keen to learn and are interested in finding things out for themselves, so by making the 'SmartFun' interface simple to use, children can gain a sense of satisfaction from their explorations and investigations. They can share the experience with adults if they wish, but they are not entirely reliant on them to use the application effectively.

Amy Ant's Story Telling Section

The story element of the application is a key feature as it is a link between the familiar—story books—and the new technology children are learning to use. Story telling plays a significant role in nursery learning, as stressed in DENI's curricular guidance document, which recommends that "Children should have access to a well stocked library of story and information books suited to their needs, interests, race and culture." It also states that "Children (should) enjoy and share books with each other and engage in role play"

Figure 3. Using image maps over the 'SmartFun' characters makes the application easy to navigate on a touch screen device.

(p.18). Using iPads or other tabled devices provides another opportunity for children to access stories and become aware of the written word. Teachers use simple stories to both entertain and educate, establishing links between home and school, as well as introducing new words and concepts to children, building both knowledge and experience. Each 'SmartFun' character has an associated story to provide a vehicle for introducing the letters in a number of different contexts and words, providing more opportunity for children to familiarise themselves with them visually. They also provide entertainment and reinforce the letter itself in a child's mind by providing an extra memory trigger—a name they are probably familiar with already, i.e. Amy Ant.

According to research carried out into the effects of vocabulary training by computer at nursery level, the audio and visual elements of 'living books'—books read on computer—provide extra motivation for children. Sergers and Verhoeven (2003) carried out research based on children who used living books for 300 minutes over a seven week period. At the end of this time they observed a significant learning gain on the combined variable of 'verbal abilities', these included pictorial and verbal memory, word knowledge, verbal fluency, and opposite analogies. This supports the use of audio and animated cues and rewards in basic literacy and numeracy applications, as simple but effective methods of reinforcing information in a child's mind (Figure 4). As Shuler (2009) highlights in her paper 'Pockets of Potential' mobile devices can actually make learning experiences more personalised, as they encourage one to one interaction between parent and child. 'There are significant opportunities for genuinely supporting differentiated, autonomous and individualised learning through mobile devices,' she argues.

Early Learning Goals

The Story telling section achieves a number of the DENI early learning goals for language and literacy:

Figure 4. The Story telling section provides a number of different ways for the child to interact. Pressing any of the 'A' words will sound out the letter 'A' and pressing the target food words - 'apple', 'avocado' or 'artichoke', will cause the pictures of the food to pop up in the air through animation of their associated <div> tags.

1. Letters:
   a. Linking sounds to letters.
   b. Naming and sounding letters of the alphabet.
   c. Hearing and saying sounds in words.
   d. Identifying and using knowledge of letters.
2. Reading:
   a. Developing an interest in books.
   b. Knowing that print conveys meaning.
   c. Showing an understanding of the elements of stories, such as main character, sequence of events and openings.

Cosy Cat's Letter Trace Section

In the Cosy Cat, or letter trace section, children will learn to trace out the capital and lower case versions of letters using the touch screen. This application will make use of the powerful new canvas element which has been introduced to HTML 5. By using their fingers to trace the shapes of the letters children can improve their dexterity and learn how to form the appropriate letter shapes. This level of engagement with the actual letters helps to reinforce their learning, rather than just relying on visual recognition (Figure 5).

As the letter guides are in the background with the canvas floating on top there are no strict guidelines for adhering to the trace guides. In theory the user can doodle on the entire canvas but the aim is for the parent to encourage the child to copy the letters by tracing the shapes with their fingers. The space is quite big so that younger children aren't too restricted in reproducing the letters, as children at this age generally like to draw things on a bigger scale.

One of the market leading products for letter tracing is 'Alphabet Fun' which is developed by Tapfuze (www.tapfuze.com). Alphabet Fun is aimed at slightly older children as it uses line rules for the child to trace within, whereas this application is more simplified for use by a younger less dextrous child. Alphabet Fun simply presents the letter and then provides a separate area for the child to redraw the letter shape. The 'SmartFun' application encourages the child to draw directly over the letter shape simplifying the interface for a younger user (Figure 6).

Figure 5. The child can draw anywhere on the canvas using their fingers but should be encouraged to trace the letters following the trace guides.

Both DENI and the Early Years framework stress the value of experimenting with mark-making in the interim stage before children learn to write, and the importance of children learning to associate meaning with the symbols produced. The letter trace section of the App is ideal for children trying to experiment with reproducing shapes and letters.

Early Learning Goals

The letter tracing section achieves a number of the DENI early learning goals for writing and literacy:

1. Letters:
    a. Identifying and using knowledge of letters.
2. Writing:
    a. Experimenting with mark-making, sometimes ascribing meaning to marks.
    b. Using some clearly identifiable letters to communicate meaning.

As the child builds a greater understanding of the relationship between the spoken and written word, their writing skills develop from making random marks and lines to writing basic recognisable letters.

Bonny Bee's Letter Match Section

The Bonny Bee section has a letter match function where the child can touch and drag an unsorted letter to the appropriate place in the sorted word. Each letter will sound upon being placed in the right location and a large cartoon version of the letter will also appear on screen to reinforce the letter in the child's mind. If the letter is moved to the wrong position it will be indicated through a gentle error sound. When the user matches all letters correctly there will be an animated response by the Bonny Bee with an associated 'applause' sound and the option to play again (Figure 7).

Another important aspect to note here is that the child is simply matching patterns, not specifically spelling words, which is in keeping with the DENI recommendation that children should not have to learn off letters at this stage in their development. But ultimately it is reinforcing the concept of

Figure 6. The Tapfuze Alphabet fun application is geared towards older more dexterous children with a focus on word formation as opposed to simple single letter training.

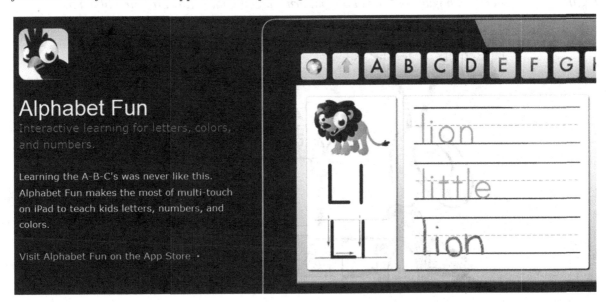

forming words by matching the letters and hearing the resulting sounds. The child doesn't even have to know the alphabet to be successful at the task because it is simply a matching exercise—so they are learning without realising they are learning.

Early Learning Goals

The Letter Matching section achieves a number of the DENI early learning goals for language and literacy:

1. Letters:

   a. Identifying and using knowledge of letters.
   b. Naming and sounding letters of the alphabet.
   c. Hearing and saying sounds in words.
   d. Linking sounds to letters.

Dizzy Dog's Number Section

A few simple numeracy tasks are introduced in Dizzy Dog's section to promote learning of the numbers one to ten. Number Match is a replication of the Letter Match game with numbers replacing letters and Number Trace again uses the canvas element to allow children to trace over number templates. As children are not expected to understand mathematical procedures at this level, the focus is on recognising and matching up the numbers in order, which can be easily achieved through the number match and number trace functions. In the Number Match game, numbers are presented out of order along the top of the screen and the child must identify and match them to the ones in sequence at the bottom of the screen. This teaches them to identify the correct number sequence, and by listening to the numbers being said aloud, to identify the numbers themselves (Figure 8).

The number trace function allows children to become familiar with the shapes of the numbers and to practice reproducing those shapes on the screen.

Early Learning Goals

The Number Match and Number Trace sections achieve a number of the DENI early learning goals for numeracy and writing:

Figure 7. The Letter Match game is more about pattern matching than direct training of letters.

1. Numbers as Labels for Counting:
   a. Saying number names in order from one to ten.
   b. Counting reliably up to ten everyday objects.
   c. Recognising numerals one through to ten.
   d. Ordering numbers up to ten.
2. Writing:
   a. Experimenting with mark-making, sometimes ascribing meaning to marks.
   b. Using some clearly identifiable numbers to communicate meaning.

IMPLEMENTATION

This section will present a detailed walkthrough of the 'SmartFun' application in use. The application was tested on a 31/2 year old girl with assistance from her mother. All relevant issues, including observed strengths and weaknesses, were recorded in order to assess the degree to which the prototype addresses the intended goals. Conclusions will be drawn and this information will be used as additional requirements for a second revision of the system that will address recorded implementation issues.

Screen Navigation

As the 'SmartFun' application is targeted towards young children in the three to five age group, navigation has to be made as simple as possible. Text and small button links were rejected in favour of large area image maps that can be easily pressed without any great level of accuracy. To create the feel of a cartoon or picture story book, the interfaces use bright colours and engaging graphics with minimal text (Figure 9).

The content structure is on three levels so that learning games are only two navigation clicks from the home page. Each section also has a visible button that allows back-tracking to the home page making navigation straightforward and obvious. There is always a concern about using large images in web pages when considering download times. All images were maintained at screen resolution (72 dpi) to ensure smaller file sizes. Even with this simple navigation system, assistance was needed from the test subject's parent when attempting to return to the home or sub-menu screens. given the very young age of the candidate, but this is not

Figure 8. The SmartFun number games: 1. The Number Match Game, 2. The Number Trace Game

surprising. It should be emphasised that this application is to be used as a teaching along tool for pre-schoolers and encourages as much interaction from the parent or teacher as possible, especially in the reading sections.

Amy Ant's Story Telling Section

In the interactive story telling section, the first step was the creation of colourful characters to represent each letter and examining how the use of alliteration would help to reinforce the role of the letters within simple words and sentences. According to the Early Years Foundation Stage Framework, children should explore and experiment with sounds, words and texts so the sound element became a key component of the programme. The EYFS framework emphasises the importance of linking sounds to written letters, and naming and sounding letters of the alphabet.

Each character has a story related to them, which is divided into segments each containing a small amount of text and images. Within the text, alliteration is used to continually emphasise the target letter that the character represents. In this section parents can read the story to their child,

and each time the child presses a word, it sounds out the letter, so they are always aware of the sound the letter will make within the word. There are also a few target words, such as 'Apple', 'Bee' or 'Cat', which are highlighted within the story. When the child presses a target word an associated image representing the word will be animated or an associated noise will be sounded. This promotes interaction and the child can clearly link the words with the animated characters or sounds.

The amount of interaction is up to the child, and parents can simply read the stories to begin with to familiarise the child with the characters, before moving on to linking in the letters. This is in keeping with the DENI recommendation that a child should know that print carries meaning and, in English, is read from left to right and top to bottom. It was found through testing this section that it is better to let an adult navigate through the pages and direct the child's attention to the various learning elements, which is in keeping with all parent led learning activities. The test subject found the story sections engaging, continually pressing the target words to listen to the associated letter sounds.

Figure 9. The colourful 'SmartFun' user interface creates the feel of a comic book with more emphasis on play than learning.

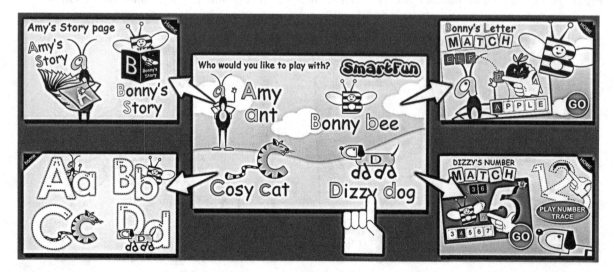

Letter Match and Number Match Sections

The Letter Match and Number Match games are implemented in code using a combination of jQuery functions and CSS styles to add drag and drop functionality to the set of letter or number boxes. Dragging and dropping is a very intuitive way for the child to interact with these matching games. Many matching games played at home or in a nursery environment involve dragging cards from one pile to another to form paired groups. The letter/number boxes are big enough to be easily grabbed by the user and a 'snap-to' function ensures that the child does not have to be precisely accurate when dropping the boxes over their matching pairs.

HCI guidelines are adhered to as constant feedback is given to the user in a number of different ways. When a random letter/number box is selected it switches from green to blue to indicate that it is active. When a letter/number box is dropped on its matching target the corresponding letter or number is sounded to the user, a large cartoon version of the letter or number is displayed, and the white target box turns green to indicate success. If an unsorted letter/number box is dropped over a mismatched target, the box will be returned to

the top unsorted pile and a gentle error noise will be sounded. After successful completion, when all cards have matched correctly a 'congratulations' message box appears showing Bonny Bee giving the thumbs up accompanied by an applause sound bite (Figure 11).

A random set of letters or numbers is generated every time each game loads by using the Math.random() function in JavaScript. This allows the child to match up a unique combination of letters or numbers each time the game is played keeping the experience fresh and challenging. An observation of the test subject's interaction with the Letter and Number Match games was that more instruction is initially needed to explain the purpose of the game. An initial design decision had been made that a graphic showing the movements of the hand with dotted lines was sufficient (Figure 11 (1)). On reflection, more clarity is needed as the purpose of the game is not entirely apparent from the beginning. This could be achieved by a small animation explaining the basic steps of the game or a helpful voiceover. The game was thoroughly enjoyed by the child, who requested to replay a number of the games a number of times. A particularly positive response was observed upon successful matching of all letters when the

Figure 10. Amy Ant's story telling section makes good use of alliteration to reinforce the role of letters within words.

'Bonny Bee' congratulations message pops up with the sound of applause.

Letter Trace and Number Trace Sections

The Letter and Number Trace sections make use of the powerful new HTML5 canvas element. The canvas element is used in conjunction with the JavaScript API for two-dimensional drawing of lines and fills with functionality very similar to Microsoft's MS Paint. The canvas tag defines a drawable region within a HTML document with height and width attributes. JavaScript code is then used to access the area defined by the canvas element allowing for dynamically generated graphics. In the 'SmartFun' application the canvas is floated above a background image of letter or number outlines that act as tracing guides for the child. The child should be encouraged to trace over the letters or numbers but also has the freedom to doodle over the entire canvas.

The Cosy Cat and Dizzy Dog Letter and Number Trace sections proved very popular with the test subject. Initially the child drew at random

enjoying the experience of making marks and lines on screen . With active encouragement from her parent she began to follow the trace guidelines and make recognisable letters and numbers as can be seen from the screen shots in Figure 12. It was noted however that the child attempted to fill in or scribble over the trace guides instead of tracing one complete line. An initial design decision had been made to keep the trace letters large and wide enough to accommodate the finger movements of less dextrous younger children. It is possible that the letters are too wide and, with a white background, appear to be a space to be coloured in as opposed to a line that has to be traced over.

There are a number of letter tracing products on the market today that incorporate a lot more additional functionality than the simple tracing functions of 'SmartFun'. Two products that are very popular and feature prominently in Apple's App store are Montessorium's 'Intro to letters' and GDIplus' 'iWriteWords'. Both these products have impressive interfaces and functionality but are equally quite restrictive and result driven. 'iWriteWords' displays numbered discs that dictate the order in which letter tracing should

Figure 11. Examples of the interaction and feedback with the letter and number match games: 1. when an unsorted letter/number box is selected it turns blue to indicate that it is active; 2. when an unsorted letter/number box is dropped on to its matching pair it turns green and sounds out the letter or number. 3. after successful completion a 'congratulations' message appears with the sound of applause.

be carried out (Figure 13 (2)). 'Intro to letters' displays arrow cues and restricts tracing within the confines of the letter outline (Figure 12 (1)). Both applications do not let the user move on to the next screen until the letter has been successfully traced. These products are probably more suited to older children who are being taught letter writing in the more formal framework of primary education.

Cross Browser Compatibility

At the time of project submission there are a number of unresolved cross browser compatibility issues that require further attention and workarounds in the next revision of this application. All of the application's functionality is fully realised in the Mozilla Firefox and Opera browsers with identical performance.

There are a number of issues with the 'Smart-Fun' functionality on Apple's Safari browser. The first obvious problem is that none of the sound effects work in any of the sections. This may be due to the use of .WAV files which are not readily supported by Apple. A workaround for this will involve using cross browser compatible sound files such as .MP3 files which will be sourced for all letter and number sounds for the next revi-sion. In the Letter and Number matching sections, the draggable letter/number boxes work to some extent. However, if you drag a letter/number over an incorrect target it sticks and cannot be moved. It was also noted that after successful matching of all letters or numbers no 'congratulations' message appears making it impossible to play again or move to the next game (Figure 14).

Tests on Internet Explorer 9 also show that the sound effects do not work on this platform. A more serious error was observed in the letter and number match games. In the IE9 platform the CSS styled letter and number boxes do not display on screen (Figure 15). Upon further research it has been discovered that IE9 only offers partial support to the new CSS3 drop shadow style effects that are used for the letter/number boxes. It is possible that these styling effects have resulted in the boxes not appearing. A stripped back version of the Letter and Number Match games will be created to test if this is the cause of the fault in the IE9 browser.

Touch-Screen Functionality

Work is continuing with efforts to port the 'Smart-Fun' application to a touch-screen tablet. There have been a number of issues with the integration of mouse events with finger touch and trace events.

Figure 12. Screen grabs from the tracing efforts of the child subject; at time of submission, work has been continuing to port 'SmartFun' onto a touch screen tablet. Experiments were carried out using the traditional mouse click method which will be less accurate than the results produced from finger tracing.

Figure 13. Two of the Apple App Store's most popular letter tracing apps: 1. Montessorium's 'Intro to letters' and 2. The GDIplus 'iWriteWords' app.

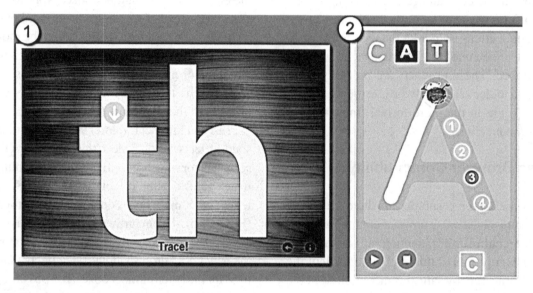

The interface has to work with both of these events which are handled differently in JavaScript. Testing of the 'SmartFun' application was carried out using the traditional mouse method which does not truly reflect the simplicity of its functionality. Work also continues on disabling elastic scrolling feature in iPad as it is important for the canvas to remain static with touch-move events.

W3 XHTML VALIDATION CHECKS

The W3 Consortium's validation service is used to check the validity of web documents coded in a number of languages including XHTML. Each page that was created for the 'SmartFun' application was tested by the validity checker implementing XHTML 1.0 Strict. Validation results yielded a number of errors on a few documents that were easily remedied. However, pages that use the canvas element still have a number of unresolved errors. The W3 XHTML validation service had issues with attributes assigned to the canvas such

as 'id', 'width' and 'height'. The same errors were observed even when testing switched from Strict to Transitional. Removing the direct width and height styling attributes from the canvas tag and placing them into a linked Cascading Style sheet caused unusual behaviour with the 'paint' trace being offset from the point of contact. These issues and potential remedies will be investigated further in the second revision of the application. All other documents successfully passed the XHTML 1.0 Strict validation test.

MobiReady Mobile Readiness Check

The mobiReady testing tool provided by the dot-Mobi resource centre evaluates mobile-readiness of web sites and applications using industry best practices and standards. As mentioned earlier, studies from Ericsson indicate that 80% of people accessing the internet will do so from a mobile device making it important to evaluate how accessible an application is on these types of devices. The 'SmartFun' home page was tested as

Figure 14. Problems on the Safari browser: 1. the success message does not appear after all letters have been successfully matched. The matched letter boxes remain the blue colour and do not switch to green to indicate success; 2. when an unsorted letter box is dragged over the incorrect target the box sticks and does not release back to the unsorted pack; 3. this is the successful implementation of the letter match game on Mozilla Firefox browser with a success message and all matched targets switched to green colour.

Figure 15. The screen on the left shows the Letter Match game displaying properly in the Mozilla Firefox browser. The screen on the right is Letter Match game displayed in the IE9 browser with all letters missing.

a representative page on the mobiReady validator and as can be seen from Figure 16, performed quite poorly.

There are a number of reasons why the 'Smart-Fun' application does not rate highly on the mobi-Ready test. Some issues are important for overall functionality and need to be addressed, whereas others are more unique to smaller mobile devices which are not the target medium of this application. The use of image maps is not supported on

some mobile devices. This design decision was intended to make it easy for young children to tap a touch screen and navigate without any great precision. This could be replicated using larger clickable images that can be positioned using div styles. Large images are used throughout this application and this has led to large download sizes for some of the pages. However, it is intended that this application be downloaded and run from an operating system as opposed to online. Regardless of this implementation decision, all efforts should be made to make file sizes as small as possible for efficient operation.

The mobiReady validator reported measure errors with the use of pixel or absolute widths, heights and positioning being detected in the style sheets. It suggests using relative measures such as percentages, 'em' and 'larger' to allow the mobile browser to 'decide' on flow of content . Absolute measures were used deliberately in this application. It is intended that the 'SmartFun' environment be presented on a tablet device in a landscape orientation to make use of both the touch screen capabilities and the dimensions that

are required for ease of use by a young pre-school child. The interface dimensions of 980 x 621 pixels is way beyond those of most mobile devices which average around 200 pixels. However, as stated above, a larger screen is needed for less dextrous smaller children. It was decided that there was no better way to present the information as the tracing and letter/number matching games would be impossible to implement on such small screens. When developing a web application, important consideration has to be given to the range of potential devices that will be accessing the service. Before launching a product such as 'SmartFun' commercially, it would be important

Figure 16. 'SmartFun' does not perform well on the mobiReady mobile-readiness test.

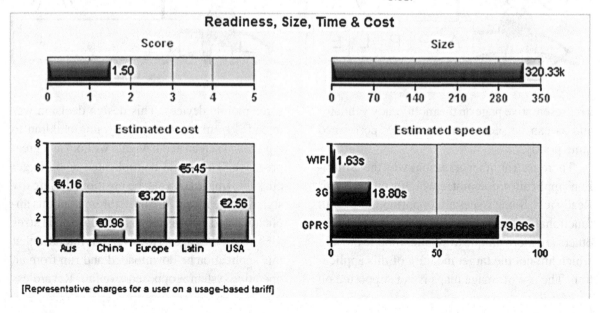

to stipulate in the marketing that this product is aimed towards very young children, and designed for tablet devices with larger screen dimensions.

CONCLUSION

As stated in 'Pockets of Potential' by Carly Shuler: 'Just as Sesame Street helped transform television into a revolutionary tool for learning among young children four decades ago, advances in mobile technologies are showing enormous untapped educational potential for today's generation.' (Shuler, 2009). The 'SmartFun' application is being developed within a burgeoning market for child education apps, however it has a number of unique selling points that sets it apart from the competition. Firstly it is targeted at the pre-school market with its very simplistic interface and functionality. Many of the alternative applications that are on the market, including 'Alphabet Fun', 'Intro to letters' and 'iWritewords' are geared towards slightly older children. These products are more restrictive in that they are slightly too regimented for a younger audience, demanding strict adherence to writing procedure. The child can't draw outside the letter outlines or number discs that have to be followed, which is unsuitable for young children who are experiencing letters for the first time. The Letter/Number Trace games in the 'SmartFun' application allow the child the freedom to make random marks or follow the guidelines if they choose, rather than focusing on accuracy. When the user is finished with that section they can move on and enjoy a different game rather than making the application results driven. It is simply a colourful and child friendly way to introduce basic letter and number skills to a child.

Compared to other products currently available 'SmartFun' offers much more with its engaging characters and colourful design. This makes the application much less like a learning environment and more like a comic or picture book with child-friendly appeal. SmartFun also deviates from the intensive letter practice focus of other packages, which is slightly too advanced for a very young audience with a more limited attention span. The addition of letter/number match and story-telling creates a more complete package, addressing a wider range of learning goals whilst maintaining interest. The story telling section extends the functionality of the application, adding an important new dimension by increasing interaction between the adult (parent or teacher) and the child.

The Letter Match game introduces the letters that the child has been tracing and places them into context with this simple yet highly interactive concept, which involves simply matching letters rather than identifying them. Low level numeracy tasks are also introduced in this application. The Tapfuze 'Alphabet Fun' has a small numeracy section which is effectively a number board covering the numerals 1-10. When the user presses the number it responds with a sound and an equivalent amount of animals are displayed. The SmartFun app takes this further through the use of Number Match and Number Trace games. 'SmartFun' is undoubtedly commercially viable, especially with its range of marketable, themed characters all with recognizable personalities and names. There is a major emphasis on the creation of new characters to compete with existing ranges such as Moshi Monsters which has generated a hugely profitable franchise machine. Obviously SmartFun is aimed towards the education arena and the application would be a perfect accompaniment to a classroom based book, or it could be simply integrated into a classroom based teaching programme.

The 'SmartFun' prototype is developed around the first four letters of the alphabet—Amy Ant, Bonny Bee, Cosy Cat and Dizzy Dog—in order to make the prototype development manageable. However, as highlighted earlier, commercially it would be possible to initially release this first set of characters for free to test the market. This seems to be a common business model on the Apple App store where, many developers release a small amount of functionality for free—to whet the appetite before charging for the complete package. Overall the SmartFun application ticks many of the boxes required to produce a successful educational application geared towards a pre-school market, whilst carving a niche for itself in a highly competitive industry. It's simplicity of design and play-based learning tasks are created in accordance with the overall pre-school curriculum objectives and it is easy to see how this application could be useful in an interactive learning environment. As the industry advances, children are beginning their journey into the realm of technology at an increasingly early age, and it is vital that their first experiences are fun and informative. SmartFun is an easy introduction to the world of interactive learning, where education and technology work together to enhance children's learning experiences.

REFERENCES

Department for Education. (2008). *Statutory Framework for the Early Years Foundation Stage: Setting the Standards for Learning, Development and Care for children from birth to five*. Retrieved from https://www.education.gov.uk/publications/eOrderingDownload/00267-2008BKT-EN.pdf

Department of Education for Northern Ireland (DENI). (1997). *Curricular Guidance for Pre-School Education*. Retrieved from http://www.deni.gov.uk/preschool_curricular-2.pdf

Eames, C., & Milne, L. (2011). Teacher responses to a planning framework for junior technology classes learning outside the classroom, Faculty of Education, University of Waikato, New Zealand. *Design and Technology Education: An International Journal, 26*(2).

Edwards, J. (2009). Cutting Through the fog of Cloud Security. *Computerworld*. Retrieved from http://www.computerworld.com/article/2550812/security0/cutting-through-the-fog-of-cloud-security.html

Fox-Turnbull, W., & Snape, P. (2011) Technology teacher education through a constructivist approach. Design and Technology Education: An International Journal, 16(2).

Mano, C. D., DuHadway, L., & Striegel, A. (2006). A Case for Instilling Security as a Core Programming Skill. In *Proceedings of Frontiers in Education Conference*, (vol. 4, pp. 13-18). doi:10.1109/FIE.2006.322347

New Media Consortium. (2011). *The Horizon Report 2011 edition*. Available from: http://www.nmc.org/horizon-project/horizon-reports/horizon-report-k-12-edition

Northern Ireland Council for Curriculum (NICC). (1989). *Nursery Education Guidelines - 'The Curriculum'*. Retrieved from http://www.deni.gov.uk/pre_school_guidance_pdf

Rabah, K. (2005). Secure Implementation of Message Digest, Authentication and Digital Signature. *Information Technology Journal, 4*(3), 204-221.

Segers, E., & Verhoeven, L. (2003). Effects of vocabulary training by computer in kindergarten. *Journal of Computer Assisted Learning, 19*(3), 557–566. doi:10.1046/j.0266-4909.2003.00058.x

Shuler, C. (2009). Pockets of potential: Using mobile technologies to promote children's learning. *Joan Ganz Cooney Centre*. Retrieved from http://www.joanganzcooneycenter.org/upload_kits/pockets_of_potential_1_.pdf

Tomas, M., & Castro, D. (2011) Multidimensional Framework for the Analysis of Innovations at Universities in Catalonia. *Educational Policy, 19*(2), 20-32.

KEY TERMS AND DEFINITIONS

Early Years Foundation Stage Framework (EYFS): The EYFS framework emphasises the importance of linking sounds to written letters, and naming and sounding letters of the alphabet.

HTML5: HTML5 is a core technology markup language of the Internet used for structuring and presenting content for the World Wide Web. It is the fifth revision of the HTML standard (created in 1990) and, as of December 2012, is a candidate recommendation of the World Wide Web Consortium (W3C).

Human Computer Interaction (HCI): Human-computer interaction (HCI) involves the study, planning, design and uses of the interaction between people (users) and computers. It is often regarded as the intersection of computer science, behavioral sciences, design, media studies, and several other fields of study.

Javascript: JavaScript (is a dynamic computer programming language. It is most commonly used as part of web browsers, whose implementations allow client-side scripts to interact with the user, control the browser, communicate asynchronously, and alter the document content that is displayed.

Leappad: LeapPad is a range of tablet computers developed for children. Various models of the LeapPad have been developed since 1999. The latest of the range is the LeapPad Explorer, which was released in 2011.

Mobiready: The mobiReady testing tool is provided by the dotMobi resource centre evaluates mobile-readiness of web sites and applications using industry best practices and standards.

Nursery Education Guidelines Curriculum: The Nursery Education Guidelines Curriculum is a comprehensive statutory framework that sets the standards for the learning, development, and care of children from birth to five in Northern Ireland.

W3C Consortium: The World Wide Web Consortium (W3C) is the main international standards organization for the World Wide Web (abbreviated WWW or W3).

Chapter 18
Light Therapy in Smart Healthcare Facilities for Older Adults:
An Overview

Joost van Hoof
Fontys University of Applied Sciences, The Netherlands & ISSO, The Netherlands

Björn Schrader
Lucerne University of Applied Sciences and Arts, Switzerland

Mariëlle P. J. Aarts
Eindhoven University of Technology, The Netherlands

Eveline J. M. Wouters
Fontys University of Applied Sciences, The Netherlands

Adriana C. Westerlaken
TNO, The Netherlands

Harold T. G. Weffers
Eindhoven University of Technology, The Netherlands

Myriam B. C. Aries
Eindhoven University of Technology, The Netherlands

ABSTRACT

Light therapy is applied as treatment for a variety of problems related to health and ageing, including dementia. Light therapy is administered via light boxes, light showers, and ambient bright light using ceiling-mounted luminaires. Long-term care facilities are currently installing dynamic lighting systems with the aim to improve the well-being of residents with dementia and to decrease behavioural symptoms. The aim of this chapter is to provide an overview of the application of ceiling-mounted dynamic lighting systems as a part of intelligent home automation systems found in healthcare facilities. Examples of such systems are provided and their implementation in practice is discussed. The available, though limited, knowledge has not yet been converted into widespread implementable lighting solutions, and the solutions available are often technologically unsophisticated and poorly evaluated from the perspective of end-users. New validated approaches to the design and application of ambient bright light are needed.

DOI: 10.4018/978-1-4666-7284-0.ch018

Copyright © 2015, IGI Global. Copying or distributing in print or electronic forms without written permission of IGI Global is prohibited.

1. INTRODUCTION

Light therapy is increasingly administered and studied as a non-pharmacological treatment for a variety of health-related problems including dementia. It is applied in a variety of ways, ranging from being exposed to daylight, to being exposed to light emitted from electric sources both at the own home and in institutional healthcare facilities (Aarts et al., 2014; Aries et al., 2013; Ellis et al., 2013; van Hoof et al., 2013). The systems used for light therapy include light boxes, light showers, and ambient bright light. Ambient bright light is one of the ways to administer light therapy by using electric lighting. It encompasses the increase of the general illuminance levels in buildings using special luminaires, light sources, and control technology for the luminaire. It does not include luminance or shading devices. Some ambient bright light solutions expose occupants to dynamic lighting scenarios that mimic the natural daylight cycle. Light therapy covers an area in medicine where medical sciences meet the realms of physics, engineering and technology (van Hoof et al., 2012). This article deals with therapy by electric light sources only.

Light therapy is an emerging therapy within the domain of dementia care. Dementia can be caused by a number of progressive disorders that affect memory, thinking, behavior, and the ability to perform everyday activities. Alzheimer's disease is the most common cause of dementia. Recent research indicates that the quality of life of people with dementia can be improved, and that dementia could be slowed down by treatments that reset the body's biological clock (and one's circadian rhythmicity), light therapy in particular. This kind of research started with the work by van Someren et al. (1997), who conducted a study on the effects of ambient bright light emitted from ceiling-mounted luminaires on rest-activity patterns. In a randomised controlled study by Riemersma-van der Lek et al. (2008), brighter daytime lighting was applied to improve the sleep of persons with dementia, and to slow down cognitive decline. A full overview of effects is given by van Hoof et al. (2010; 2013). At the same time, the scientific basis for ambient bright light, as seen from a medical perspective, is still weak. Forbes et al. (2009) concluded that due to the lack of randomised controlled studies, there are no clear beneficial outcomes of light therapy for older persons. Also, Shikder et al. (2012) concluded that the implementation of therapeutic aspects of lighting in buildings is still debatable due to insufficient relevant investigations and robustness of their findings. At the same time, many light therapy studies are methodologically flawed from an engineering perspective, too (van Hoof et al., 2012).

Still, the rationale for applying light therapy in dementia care is clear. Persons with dementia do not venture outdoors as much as healthy younger adults, due to mobility impairments. When institutionalised, going outside is no longer part of one's daily routine and mostly depends on time and effort of the family. Indoors, older persons are exposed to light levels that are not sufficient for proper vision, let alone yielding positive outcomes to circadian rhythmicity and mood (Sinoo et al., 2011; Aarts and Westerlaken, 2005; Aries et al., 2013). Using light as a care instrument does not only apply to people with dementia, it also applies to ageing in general.

Although the evidence regarding the positive impact of light on the well-being of especially older people and persons with dementia or other neurological diseases are hopeful but not convincingly and scientifically affirmed (Forbes et al., 2009; Brown et al., 2013), these insights are already being converted to implementable solutions. Applying light as an instrument for treatment has tremendous benefits. Ambient bright light is non-invasive, it is relatively cheap in its implementation and maintenance, and it has a high level of intuitive use creating a low threshold for acceptance. However, another complicating factor in the implementation of light therapy is that there is no conclusive evidence on which lighting conditions are most favourable to persons being exposed. The wider community also lacks a clear definition of what technicians and product developers call "healthy lighting", lighting that meets both human visual and non-visual demands without causing visual discomfort. It is also largely unknown how to design and install such healthy lighting systems, for instance, in relation to the emergence of new energy-friendly light sources as light emitting diodes (LED) (van Hoof et al., 2012). Therefore, this work focuses on the application and design of intelligent light therapies for older adults with dementia.

2. TECHNOLOGY: DESIGN AND IMPLEMENTATION

Dynamic ambient bright light systems are being developed and implemented for the use in geriatric care facilities (Figure 1). The Netherlands are frontrunner in this field, both from the perspective of research and implementation. The underlying assumption of such dynamic lighting systems is that human beings evolved in daylight conditions, which are highly dynamic and variable, and that the/a dynamic component further contributes to the positive effects of the lighting systems. Figure 2 shows the rationale behind a dynamic lighting protocol and the way it has been shaped in practice. As can be seen in the figure, both il-luminance and colour temperature are controlled through dedicated software, and both parameters vary throughout the day. In most projects, only the main luminaire in the living room is steered via a dynamic protocol. Almost all luminaires contain fluorescent light sources. In addition, the majority of research was carried out with fluorescent light sources although in the future new light source as LED (Light Emitting Diode) or OLED (Organic Light Emitting Diode) may be used.

The required illuminance levels of (dynamic) light therapy lighting systems are much higher than average, i.e., values of two to five times higher than normal conditions in healthcare facilities. Basically, all 'daylight mimicking systems" produce higher levels than currently achieved with electric lighting (which is actually based on visual performance). It is often said that il-luminance should exceed 1000 lx, but the exact threshold levels have not yet been determined in a combination of laboratory and field studies. In addition, the (correlated) colour temperature of the light is much higher, too. The colour temperature should exceed 5000 K, or even 6500 K, although no exact threshold values can be given due to a lack of research data. Values of fluorescent light sources used in office environments range from 2700 to 4000 K. In practice, both illuminance and colour temperature are controlled through dedicated software. As there is no validated set of algorithms which can be used in these lighting systems, including evidence regarding the relative

Figure 1. Examples of dynamic lighting installed in Dutch nursing homes: Amadea by Derungs, Biosun by Van Doorn, and Strato by Philips

Figure 2. Example of a protocol for dynamic lighting; the horizontal illuminance on the table level varies between 0 and 1500 lx (left axis). The colour temperature of the light varies between 0 and 6500 K (right axis). The so-called post lunch dip can be found in the first hour of the noon.

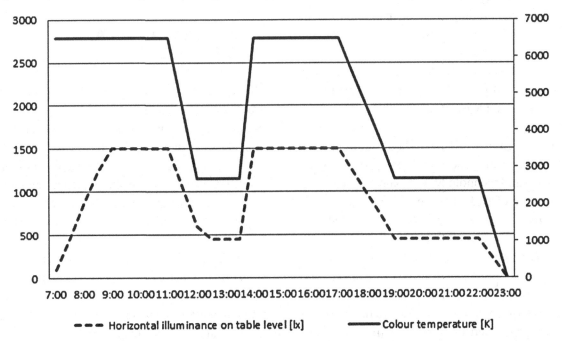

effects of static versus dynamic lighting protocols, there is still room for innovation and research (Figueiro, 2008; Barroso and den Brinker, 2013). In fact, there is no conclusive data that dynamic lighting protocols have better results than static lighting systems. The dynamic lighting protocols currently in use are also static compared to the daylight since they only change over the day, but not between days. Manufacturers and dealers of dynamic lighting systems claim that the lighting has a positive effect on the behaviour and the sleep-wake rhythm of people with dementia. The vast majority of scientific literature reports only about the results of experiments using static lighting systems (Aarts et al., 2014). When searching for the influence of dynamic lighting systems on (older) persons with dementia, only one scientific study was found (Spreeuwenberg et al., 2010). This was a longitudinal quasi-experimental study that lasted three months. The study was conducted in two living rooms for geriatric patients with dementia among 10 people in the control group and 10 in the light intervention group. The results show that the activity level in the intervention group decreased significantly, during night-time, as well as during daytime, compared to baseline. The ratio between day and night time activities remained the same. The research team concluded that more research is necessary before the results can be fully interpreted. The maximum correlated colour temperature of the lighting of the system was 4600 K. The maximum illuminance was 1200 lx.

In all the studies concerning light therapy, the exposure to daylight is often an ill-described aspect. We do, therefore, not fully understand the effects of the interactions between daylight and electric lighting. Daylight has a dynamic character, which is mimicked by dynamic lighting systems in a simplified manner. With new technologies, electric lighting can be supplemented to the available daylight, which also has positive effects on energy consumption. This requires that new lighting solutions are to be integrated within a framework of smart home control systems (including sensor-based networks, ambient-assisted living) and smart façade systems (measuring incoming daylight and its spectral composition), and, last but not least, a building that is optimised for daylight use.

New lighting solutions should combine all sources of daylight and novel lighting technologies such as LED technology. It should be noted that in the case of LED, the spectral composition of the light determines its use. The intricate balance between daylight and electric light sources calls for smart sensors in the dwelling and dedicated software to steer the lighting exposure of persons, and buildings that are suitable for daylight use. These sensors should also measure the presence of occupants, and the type of activity they are engaged in. The dip in lighting protocols (Figure 2) is related to the length of the lunch break. If this break takes longer, perhaps the dip in the protocol should be too. The protocol should ideally follow the care regime. Apart from manual controls, a sensor-based network can help achieve accounting for the regime. This also creates a more dynamic protocol that differs per day (real dynamic lighting).

In addition, light therapy also calls for an attractive design of the lighting equipment, especially when it is applied in an all-day living situation of people. General light therapy equipment (i.e., for acne treatment) can still be a light box. Indoor lighting conditions may be perceived as unfavourable from the perspective of personal preferences and taste, particularly with higher colour temperature lighting or light with a dedicated spectrum which accounts for the human circadian photoreception sensitivity that peaks at approximately 480 nm (following from the $C(\lambda)$ curve (Pechacek et al., 2008)). Sometimes, in order to improve the acceptance of such systems,

a smaller, more home-like luminaire is mounted below the dynamic luminaire.

3. IMPLEMENTATION AND FUTURE CHALLENGES

The effects of the dynamic electric lighting systems are often unclear, although the additional costs of these systems are significant. These issues are very relevant as budgets in long-term care are under extreme pressure due to political choices and prioritisation. Although the evidence regarding the positive impact of light on the well-being is hopeful but not convincingly and scientifically affirmed, these insights are already being converted to implementable solutions. Applying light therapy as an instrument for care has obvious benefits. It is non-invasive, non-pharmacological, it is cheap in implementation and maintenance, and it has a high level of intuitive use creating a low threshold for acceptance. As mentioned before, two additional incentives for the purchase of (dynamic) lighting solutions are:

1. That persons with dementia do not venture outdoors as much as healthy younger adults, due to mobility impairments, and
2. Inside their homes they are exposed to light levels which are insufficient.

Another complication factor is the lack of standardisation and documentation dealing with lighting for older people. These documents can serve as an underlying basis when conducting research and for product and service innovation. There is, however, a growing interest within the building community for the non-visual aspects of light (Webb, 2006). The European standard EN 12464-1 (2011) summarises recommendations of lighting of indoor work places. The standard specifies horizontal illuminances for health care facilities, such as waiting rooms, corridors, examination rooms, and spaces for diagnostics in hospitals. Nursing homes are not included in this standard, as the standard deals with work places (staff) and not any residential areas (nursing homes). The standard does not specifically include colour temperature for health care facilities in general, too. At the same time, we need to be critical. There is still a lot we do not know. To date, we do not know if dynamic systems have better outcomes than static lighting systems, and how such systems (should) interact with available daylight. We do know that vision can be improved by raising general illuminance levels and glare control; the non-visual benefits cannot be quantified yet. Therefore, the economic and well-being benefits of accounting for these parameters are not yet clear.

As long as there are many uncertainties, maybe we should suggest exposing our older citizens to plenty of daylight, for instance, by taking them out for a stroll. Instead of evidence-based practice, we see the results of market-based research: with care facilities buying new lighting technologies because of their supposed health benefits. One could argue that given the lack of negative side-effects, investing in lighting equipment is a sound option, and that science is always one step behind practice. Still, geriatric care facilities are not a place for reckless experimentation. The innovations in the realm of sensors and ambient intelligence in the home environment hold a promise that in the future the nursing home can administer the right amount of light to its residents, which allows them to enjoy the highest degree of quality of life, mainly though improving conditions for proper vision. Significant innovations and system improvements can be expected when dynamic lighting systems are integrated with self-learning sensors, motion detectors, sensors that recognise certain (behavioural) rhythms, learning, guiding, or probabilistic algorithms instead of the "static" one-day dynamic electric light protocol.

REFERENCES

Aarts, M. P. J., Aries, M. B. C., & Straathof, J., & van Hoof. J. (2014). (in press). Dynamic lighting systems in psychogeriatric care facilities in The Netherlands: A quantitative and qualitative analysis of the subjective responses of stakeholders and technology. *Indoor and Built Environment*. doi:10.1177/1420326X14532387

Aarts, M. P. J., & Westerlaken, A. C. (2005). Field study of visual and biological light conditions of independently-living elderly people. *Gerontechnology*, *4*(3), 141–152. doi:10.4017/gt.2005.04.03.004.00

Aries, M. B. C., Aarts, M. P. J., & van Hoof, J. (2014). (in press). Daylight and health: A review of the evidence and consequences for the built environment. *Lighting Research & Technology*. doi:10.1177/1477153513509258

Barroso, A., & den Brinker, B. (2013). Boosting circadian rhythms with lighting: A model driven approach. *Lighting Research & Technology*, *45*(2), 197–216. doi:10.1177/1477153512453667

Brown, C. A., Berry, R., Tan, M. C., Khoshia, A., Turlapati, L., & Swedlove, F. (2013). A critique of the evidence base for non-pharmacological sleep interventions for persons with dementia. *Dementia*, *12*(2), 210–237. doi:10.1177/1471301211426909 PMID:24336770

CEN / Comité Européen de Normalisation. (2011). *EN 12464-1. Light and lighting - Lighting of work places – Part 1: Indoor work places*. Brussels, Belgium: Comité Européen de Normalisation.

Ellis, E. V., Gonzalez, E. W., & McEachron, D. L. (2013). Chronobioengineering indoor lighting to enhance facilities for ageing and Alzheimer's disorder. *Intelligent Buildings International*, *5*(sup1), 48–60. doi:10.1080/17508975.2013.807764

Figueiro, M. G. (2008). A proposed 24 h lighting scheme for older adults. *Lighting Research & Technology*, *40*(2), 153–160. doi:10.1177/1477153507087299

Forbes, D., Culum, I., Lischka, A. R., Morgan, D. G., Peacock, S., Forbes, J., & Forbes, S. (2009). Light therapy for managing cognitive, sleep, behavioural, or psychiatric disturbances in dementia. *Cochrane Database of Systematic Reviews*, CD003946. PMID:19821317

Pechacek, C. S., Andersen, M., & Lockley, S. W. (2008). Preliminary method for prospective analysis of the circadian efficacy of (day)light with applications to healthcare architecture. *LEUKOS*, *5*(1), 1–26. doi:10.1080/15502724.2008.10747625

Riemersma-van der Lek, R. F., Swaab, D. F., Twisk, J., Hol, E. M., Hoogendijk, W. J. G., & van Someren, E. J. W. (2008). Effect of bright light and melatonin on cognitive and noncognitive function in elderly residents of group care facilities. A randomized controlled trial. *Journal of the American Medical Association*, *299*(22), 2642–2655. doi:10.1001/jama.299.22.2642 PMID:18544724

Shikder, S., Mourshed, M., & Price, A. (2012). Therapeutic lighting design for the elderly: A review. *Perspectives in Public Health*, *132*(6), 282–291. doi:10.1177/1757913911422288 PMID:23111083

Sinoo, M. M., van Hoof, J., & Kort, H. S. M. (2011). Lighting conditions for older adults in the nursing home. Assessment of environmental illuminances and colour temperature. *Building and Environment*, *46*(10), 1917–1927. doi:10.1016/j.buildenv.2011.03.013

Spreeuwenberg, M. D., Willems, C., Verheesen, H., Schols, J., & de Witte, L. (2010). Dynamic lighting as a tool to influence the day-night rhythm of clients with psychogeriatric disorders: A pilot study in a Dutch nursing home. *Journal of the American Geriatrics Society*, *58*(5), 981–982. doi:10.1111/j.1532-5415.2010.02825.x PMID:20722824

van Hoof, J., Aarts, M. P. J., Rense, C. G., & Schoutens, A. M. C. (2009). Ambient bright light in dementia: Effects on behavior and circadian rhythmicity. *Building and Environment*, *44*(1), 146–155. doi:10.1016/j.buildenv.2008.02.005

van Hoof, J., Kort, H. S. M., Duijnstee, M. S. H., Rutten, P. G. S., & Hensen, J. L. M. (2010). The indoor environment and the integrated building design of homes for older people with dementia. *Building and Environment*, *45*(5), 1244–1261. doi:10.1016/j.buildenv.2009.11.008

van Hoof, J., Schoutens, A. M. C., & Aarts, M. P. J. (2009). High colour temperature lighting for institutionalised older people with dementia. *Building and Environment*, *44*(9), 1959–1969. doi:10.1016/j.buildenv.2009.01.009

van Hoof, J., Westerlaken, A. C., Aarts, M. P. J., Wouters, E. J. M., Schoutens, A. M. C., Sinoo, M. M., & Aries, M. B. C. (2012). Light therapy: Methodological issues from an engineering perspective. *Health Care and Technology*, *20*, 11–23. PMID:22297710

van Hoof, J., Wouters, E. J. M., Schräder, B., Weffers, H. T. G., Aarts, M. P. J., Aries, M. B. C., & Westerlaken, A. C. (2013). Intelligent light therapy for older adults: Ambient assisted living. In A. Agah (Ed.), *Medical Applications of Artificial Intelligence* (pp. 341–351). Boca Raton, FL: CRC Press/Taylor & Francis Group. doi:10.1201/b15618-22 van Someren, E. J. W., Kessler, A., Mirmiran, M., & Swaab, D. F. (1997). Indirect bright light improves circadian rest-activity rhythm disturbances in demented patients. *Biological Psychiatry*, *41*(9), 955–963. doi:10.1016/S0006-3223(97)89928-3 PMID:9110101

Webb, A. R. (2006). Considerations for lighting in the built environment: Non-visual effects of light. *Energy and Building*, *38*(7), 721–727. doi:10.1016/j.enbuild.2006.03.004

KEY TERMS AND DEFINITIONS

Ambient Bright Light: Lighting providing an area with overall high illuminance levels exceeding 1000 lx.

Colour Temperature: Property of a light source, which corresponds to a temperature of an ideal black-body radiator that radiates light of comparable hue to that of the light source. It is stated in kelvins [K].

Illuminance: The total luminous flux incident on a surface, per unit area. It is stated in lux (lx) or lm/m^2.

Light Therapy: (Or phototherapy) Consists of exposure to daylight or to specific wavelengths of light. This light is administered for a prescribed amount of time and/or at specific times of day.

Light: Electromagnetic radiation visible to the human eye, having a wavelength in the range of 400 to 700 nm.

Luminaire: Electrical device used to create artificial light by use of an electric lamp. Also known as a light fixture or light fitting.

Chapter 19
Context–Aware Mobile and Wearable Device Interfaces

Claas Ahlrichs
University of Bremen, Germany

Hendrik Iben
University of Bremen, Germany

Michael Lawo
University of Bremen, Germany

ABSTRACT

In this chapter, recent research on context-aware mobile and wearable computing is described. Starting from the observation of recent developments on Smartphones and research done in wearable computing, the focus is on possibilities to unobtrusively support the use of mobile and wearable devices. There is the observation that size and form matters when dealing with these devices; multimodality concerning input and output is important and context information can be used to satisfy the requirement of unobtrusiveness. Here, Frameworks as middleware are a means to an end. Starting with an introduction on wearable computing, recent developments of Frameworks for context-aware user interface design are presented, motivating the need for future research on knowledge-based intuitive interaction design.

INTRODUCTION

Mobile devices in the form of Smartphones have become a part of our everyday life. We expect them to perform a variety of tasks that cover a much broader field than just making phone calls. Equipped with applications for many tasks, these small computer systems are meant to adapt to our needs and give us access to many functions that are relevant to our current situation. While many people find using these devices easy their interfaces are very different from what is present in typical desktop computing systems. Compared to normal desktop computing environments or notebooks, a mobile device has many limitations in terms of computing power, information density and input mechanisms. By using a different approach in the design of mobile applications these limitations can be overcome or mitigated. While the first mobile digital assistants still tried to re-

DOI: 10.4018/978-1-4666-7284-0.ch019

Copyright © 2015, IGI Global. Copying or distributing in print or electronic forms without written permission of IGI Global is prohibited.

semble small versions of desktop applications with windows, icons, menus and pointer metaphors, it became quickly clear that this approach did not really fit the circumstances. Nowadays application design reflects the state of mind of the user and incorporates dynamic sources of information. Location information, software generated data or sensors adapt the interface.

Devices will become more and more invisible and integrated into clothing of the user or worn by the user. While mobile applications still require a form of active use, future devices will provide a different kind of supporting functionality. To achieve this goal, the mobile interface paradigm has to be generalized into something different to mechanisms for information display and user input as used so far. For a wearable application interface the use of implicit information sources will be a central design aspect where the user's needs are anticipated and only a minimum of explicit input is required.

Before diving deeper into the topic, a short definition and history of wearable computing is needed to understand how the user interaction in this field demands changes to the traditional concept of assessing a user interface (UI).

Wearable computing describes body worn computing devices that provide useful information relevant to a physical real world task. Unlike mobile devices, the focus is on the task and the device should not unnecessarily distract from it. To fulfill this expectation the wearable device cannot depend on direct interaction with the wearer but needs to process information from the environment to infer the next helpful action to be taken. This relevant information is the context of a wearable computing application. There are many sources for contextual information: One can use sensors that measure physical properties like location, lighting conditions, the presence of digital markers to name a few. Other possibilities are known aspects of the work-flow and the resulting mental model of the user to take pro-active actions, software gener-

ated information from databases, current time, simulations, or implicit interaction by analyzing the actions of the wearer or co-workers.

The first wearable computing system, built with the intention of supporting a real world task, can be found in the experiments on Roulette wheel prediction by Thorp (Thorp, 1998) as early as 1955. While the core idea is quite simple, it shows some general needs of wearable applications. To predict the outcome of Roulette wheels, a shoe-integrated computer was used where timing information about the current game was input with the toes. The result of the computation was transmitted to another device[1] worn by a (potentially different) person and mediated by audible signals. Analyzing the needed information here can be quickly done. The computer system needs timing information that is abstracted by keeping track of the time when a button is pressed. The transmitted result is a single symbol that either specifies where to place the bet or not to bet at all. While the setup in this early experiment is technically very direct, it can be logically abstracted. On the one side is an action from the user such as pressing a button that is not used directly as a means of control but indirectly used to setup a timespan, very similar to the control scheme of a stop watch. On the other side, an abstract output symbol is computed that needs to be conveyed to the wearer. While this example is very simple, it shows one important property. Neither the actual physical source of the input, nor the actual physical representation of the output are important for the application and can be replaced by other means. This has actually been done with the Eudaemons' shoe (The Eudaemons' Shoe, 1998), a project directly related to the work of Thorp. In this project, instead of an audio output, a tactile feedback device was used to convey the computed symbol to the wearer.

This example provides a first hint at the differences to other uses of computer systems. A field that is very close to wearable computing but more known to the general public is mobile computing.

The main difference between the two fields is the form of interaction between the device and the user. Unlike with a wearable system, a mobile device is used to directly accomplish a certain task, such as looking up information or sending messages. There is however no clear separation between the domains of Wearable and mobile computing that can be based on the physical device alone. A wearable system can provide functionality that has a mobile computing character, as seen with the Google Glass. But a mobile device can exhibit also wearable characteristics as observed with the current trend of combining implicit tracking of body functions for health monitoring and sports.

In either case, some forms of output and input are required for a system suitable for the anticipated use. Unlike in a stationary setting, a device cannot expect to have the full attention of its user and needs to provide interfaces that allow quick interaction (Oulasvirta, Tamminen, Roto, & Kuorelahti, 2005). These limitations lead to reduced interfaces that only provide the needed information and do not necessarily show all available interaction mechanisms. An example for this kind of reduction is found in mobile applications, were information is displayed while control elements are hidden or only shown for a short amount of time. A common set of touch gestures is often used to navigate these applications. While they are not intuitive, the user can quickly learn utilizing them effectively.

While these reduced interfaces allow quick interaction, other challenges exist to make a device usable. As the conditions of use change over short times in a mobile setting, interfaces have to adapt to their surroundings. Simple examples are the automatic rotation of the display content to match the device orientation or the adjustment of brightness in reaction to ambient light. These adaptive interfaces make use of information from the environment to allow a better perception and reduce interaction. All non-functional aspects of an interface can be affected by the environment to provide a better experience to the user but care has to be taken to convey the nature of the change to the user avoiding confusion.

As a common pattern found in mobile and wearable application design adaptive user interfaces emerge. In contrast to classical user interface design, a developer or designer cannot dictate the layout of a specific interface but needs to design a model by which information is arranged according to the current situation. For mobile devices this often means to react to the current screen orientation, size and resolution. Additionally ambient light sensors can be used to change the brightness of a display. While this approach is of course very effective, it cannot be applied to the wearable computing domain. In its pure idea, the output medium is interchangeable: There could be a display on the wrist, a head mounted display (HMD), speech synthesis or just a small non-graphical display. Information can also be conveyed via audio or tactile elements (Hoggan & Brewster, 2007). To support all these and future mechanisms, the information has to be separated from its presentation in the interface. This is of course difficult as it is not clear, for example, how to convey a graph via a tactile output device. There are however some approaches to this that can be applied to suitable domains. The remaining part of this chapter will focus on relevant individual work and on selected results of projects in the field of adaptive interfaces.

WEARABLE COMPUTING

Thad Eugene Starner has been active in the wearable computing community since the early 1990s and continues to remain so. Over the previous two decades, Starner has focused on the application of wearable computers in everyday situations, worked on human-computer-interaction (HCI), evaluated numerous input and output modalities as well as physical aspects of wearables (e.g. size, weight, heat dissipation, energy consumption and harvesting). As part of his research and daily life, Starner has been wearing a wearable computer for many years and consequently gathered many firsthand experiences. As a result he is aware of social implications and aspects as well as on-body interaction in general. In his opinion, the ideal attributes of a wearable computer include persistence and constant access to (relevant) information. Furthermore, the wearable should relate to the wearer's context (i.e. sense and model it), adapt interaction methods (e.g. based on the wearer's context and environment) as well as augment / mediate interactions with the wearer's environment (Starner T., The challenges of wearable computing: Part 1, 2001). The reasons to use wearable computers are the mediation of interactions, aiding communication, providing context sensitive reminders and augmenting reality. The challenges on the other hand are power efficiency, heat dissipation, networking (e.g. off-body communications, interoperability, and communications with near-body objects), interface design and privacy (Starner T., The challenges of wearable computing: Part 2, 2001; Starner T., The challenges of wearable computing: Part 1, 2001).

"Ideally, wearable computing can be described as the pursuit of a style of interface as opposed to a manifestation in hardware." (Starner T., The challenges of wearable computing: Part 1, 2001) Starner sees the wearable computer as an intelligent agent or a stereotypical British butler rather than a plain information processor. Just like a real-world agent, a wearable should provide the required assistance in an unobtrusive manner at the right time. The attention, that is required to operate it, is another part of interaction with wearable devices (in general this is true for all sorts of devices, but for wearables in particular). Ideally, the least amount of attention and effort should be invested during interactions with wearable devices (or at least they should be short). Walking (as a primarily visual task) would likely conflict with reading a text document on a head mounted

display and could end tragically if crossing a busy intersection without paying the proper amount of attention to traffic. The concept of attention and dual tasks as well as their relationship to wearable computing is outlined by Starner (Starner T., 2002). Simple experiments yielded to the conclusion that humans can indeed master dual tasks, but it largely depends on the tasks at hand and how their interaction modalities stay in conflict (e.g. multiple visual tasks are likely to stay in conflict whereas a visual and auditory task are less likely to stay in conflict) as well as the people's experiences and practice. Nonetheless, a separation between primary and secondary task should be considered during interaction design in wearable computing. The "hot-wire" was introduced by Witt and colleagues (Witt H., Human-Computer Interfaces for Wearable Computers: A Systematic Approach to Development and Evaluation, 2007) to evaluate the conflict between primary and secondary tasks. This is also used to evaluate the effectiveness and appropriateness of different options for interrupting the user. The general idea behind these experiments is that the "hot-wire" game resembles an exemplary primary task (with sufficient complexity) while participants were asked to complete secondary tasks (e.g. solving math equations on an HMD using gestures for input).

As such, non-visual interfaces for wearable computers and mobile devices are important. Brewster et al. (Non-visual interfaces for wearable computers, 2000) have investigated the use of sound as a non-visual interface for wearable and mobile displays. They have shown that the addition of sound (to visual interfaces) can "improve usability and make [wearables] more effective in mobile environments" (Non-visual interfaces for wearable computers, 2000). Furthermore, the authors created a virtual auditory sphere (around the user's head). They then added head, hand and device gestures to control multiple streams of data. This type of interface can be seen as a supplementary interface which can be more effective in mobile environments where the user's visual attention is otherwise occupied. The auditory interface also enables the use of another sense and thus helps to overcome the problem of limited screen and interaction space on mobile / wearable devices (Brewster, Lumsden, Bell, Hall, & Tasker, 2003). The use of auditory and tactile interfaces can be utilized to portray information when other senses/ channels are impaired or overloaded. Crossan and colleagues found that foot taps can also be used for interaction with mobile and wearable device as long as the interactions are kept short (i.e. number of taps should be less or equal to five) (Crossan, Brewster, & Ng, 2010). Alternatively, the use of thermal feedback has been investigated (Wilson, Halvey, Brewster, & Hughes, 2011). This could potentially be employed in environments that are too loud for audio and/or too bumpy for haptic feedback.

Knowledge on human perception can be used for automatic information presentation across diverse modalities. Certain kind of information (e.g. alarms or textual output) can be transported from one modality to another (e.g. visual → auditory, visual → tactile, etc.). The concept of icons can be applied to all mentioned modalities. When referring to a graphical user interface (GUI), an icon is used to represent an action that is performed when clicked upon. Such actions range from executing an application to saving a document. However icons are also used to represent a state (e.g. weather forecast). Nonetheless, the same concept exists in tactile and auditory user interfaces (tactons (Brewster & Brown, Tactons: Structured Tactile Messages for Non-visual Information Display, 2004), earcons (Hoggan & Brewster, 2007) and musicons (McLachlan, McGee-Lennon, & Brewster, 2012)). They can just as well be used to represent an action or state.

The ease of access plays an important role for wearable devices. In this sense, the participants of a short survey regarding the use of mobile appointment scheduling (Starner, Snoeck, Wong, & McGuire, 2004) yielded to the finding that a large portion of the subjects switched to making notes on a scrap piece of paper rather than their preferred method (e.g. paper-based day-planer, PDA, memory). Starner at el. found that scrap paper is often used as a buffer which is later copied to a day-planer or PDA (Starner, Snoeck, Wong, & McGuire, 2004). Put quite plainly, if the relevant functionality (or information) is not readily and easily accessible through the wearable computer then it is not going to be used. This boils down to the previously outlined attributes of persistence and constant access.

The remembrance agent (RA) (Rhodes, 1997) is one possible application for wearable devices. It assists the wearer by augmenting human memory and provides context sensitive reminders. At the time of publication (1996), it was assumed that the computer mostly waited for the user (i.e. waiting for the next keystroke, network packet, the next mouse movement, etc.) and that this "wasted" CPU time could be used more efficiently. The RA runs continuously and displays a list of documents which might be relevant in the current context of the wearer. No interaction is required and as such the wear is free to choose whether the information is helpful or to simply ignore it. It provides a passive recommendation (passive in the sense that the user does not need to interact with the RA) rather than requiring inputs from the user (this is a problem if the user does not remember enough or does not even realize that he/she has forgotten something).

The recognition of American Sign Language (ASL) has been a major topic throughout Starner's career. One of the first implementations used optical sensors only. They were mounted on a baseball cap, facing down (Starner, Weaver, & Pentland, A Wearable Computer Based American Sign Language Recognizer, 1998). Later publications included different sensors like accelerometers (Brashear, Starner, Lukowicz, & Junker, 2003), the Microsoft Kinect (Zafrulla, Brashear, Starner, Hamilton, & Presti, 2011) and brain imaging (Mehta, Starner, Jackson, Babalola,

& James, 2010). The primary goal was to enable handicapped people to communicate more easily as well as lowering the burden of non-signers. The wearable could recognize and potentially translate ASL. The recognition of ASL provides reasonable complex gestures and merely presents a single application within the field of gesture recognition. Generalizing from this approach, gestures can also be used to interact with wearable devices (Starner T. E., 1999) instead of person-to-person communications. Another application is the use of gestures to control home automation scenarios (e.g. turn on/off light, control the television or stereo, etc.) or use the system for monitoring medical conditions (e.g. pathological tremors (Gandy, Starner, Auxier, & Ashbrook, 2000)).

For evaluation of various aspects of wearable computing devices, games like "Mind-Warping" (Starner, Leibe, Singletary, & Pair, 2000) have been developed. Games have been used to explore new hardware, metaphors, and modalities and study HCI of wearable computers (Starner, Leibe, Singletary, & Pair, 2000). They provide unique test scenarios in which users are generally more susceptible to innovations and less reluctant to come in contact with new devices. Even users who would otherwise not be interested in experimenting with prototypic systems may be more open to gaming scenarios than they would otherwise be.

In 2000, Lyons proposed a context-based document storage system (Lyons, Starner, & Harvel, A Context-Based Document System for Wearable Computers, 2000) to handle the flood of documents which can easily accumulate on a continuously running wearable system. Instead of using a hierarchical structure for storing files (i.e. like in today's desktop machines), the option to organize documents by their content is explored. The authors proposed to use time information in conjunction with context information of the user as well as attributes associated with the files.

The everyday use of wearable computers has been outlined by members of the "wearfolk" from the MIT wearable computing group (Starner, Rhodes, Weaver, & Pentland, 1999). There they recite and explore possible application domains as well as various social aspects of the continued use of wearable computers in public environments. Through the use of anecdotes they share their experiences.

Passive haptic learning can be used for the purpose of rehabilitation or learning the piano. In 2010, Huang et al. presented the Mobile Music Touch (MMT) (Huang, et al., 2010) which was designed to teach users to play piano melodies while they perform other tasks. Here fingerless gloves are combined with haptic actuators and a Bluetooth interface controlled by a mobile phone. The melodies to be learned are played repeatedly while the wearer performs other tasks. For each note of the passage, a vibrator on the corresponding finger in the gloves activates, indicating which finger has to be used to play the specific note. The authors showed that using the MMT system for 30 minutes (while performing a reading comprehension test) "was significantly more effective than a control condition where the passage was played repeatedly but the subjects' fingers were not vibrated" (Huang, et al., 2010). The authors also compared the use of active vs. passive training. It was found that participants with no prior piano experience are able to repeat randomly generated passages after having used the MMT system.

Additionally, Starner evaluated various physical aspects of wearable computers. This includes heat dissipation and energy consumption as well as energy harvesting. As part of his thesis, Starner proposed to use the unconventional method of thermal coupling with the wearer to further increase heat limits (Starner & Maguire, Heat Dissipation in Wearable Computers Aided by Thermal Coupling with the User, 1999; Starner T. E., 1999). Load bearing and placement of wearable computers need to be considered as well (Starner T. E., 1999). Regarding the source of energy, next to batteries and accumulators, ambient power (e.g. light or radio energy) or human powered (e.g. body heat, respiration, blood pressure, implants in shoes or the plain old pedal-based power generator) were deemed feasible (Starner T. E., Powerful Change Part 1: Batteries and Possible Alternatives for the Mobile Market, 2003; Starner T. E., 1999).

Lyons et al. proposed the use of dual-purpose speech (Lyons, et al., Augmenting Conversations Using Dual-purpose Speech, 2004). The recognition of socially acceptable speech/keywords can potentially enhance the usability of wearable computers. An envisioned application was a calendar that could automatically navigate to the referred day and make entries based on the wearer's conversation. Regarding dual purpose speech, every day phrases and keywords are used to instruct the wearable while the wearer is seamlessly talking to someone (e.g. making an appointment, taking notes, etc.). In doing so human memory and cognition can be augmented. The authors found that speech input (compared to a PDA control group) is more direct and reduces manual inputs (Lyons, Skeels, & Starner, Providing Support for Mobile Calendaring Conversations: A Wizard of Oz Evaluation of Dual-purpose Speech, 2005).

The use of various mobile displays in terms of their perceived ease of use and overall performance has been evaluated by Vadas et al. (Vadas, et al., 2006). Among the evaluated displays were: a MicroOptical SV-3 monocular head-mounted display, a Sony Libri´e electronic ink e-book display, and an OQO palmtop computer display. It was found that the HMD performed least well for a task in which users had to read a text and walk a preset path. A later study compared audio to hand-held displays (Vadas, Patel, Lyons, Starner, & Jacko, 2006) while participants walked a preset path. The authors found that audio displays were less demanding.

The level of dexterity and attention that is available while sitting in front of a desktop computer / laptop can simply not be assumed when using a wearable computer on-the-go (Starner T., Reading Your Mind: Interfaces for Wearable Computing, 2008). As such the interfaces need to be designed in

a way that they require as little attention as possible in order to minimize the negative effects on the wearer's primary task (e.g. walking, conversing, etc.). Not only how the interaction is performed is of importance but also where it is performed. This is especially true for on-body interactions. A study by Profita et al. (Profita, et al., 2013) showed that interactions on the forearm and wrist were socially acceptable. Rico and Brewster also evaluated the social acceptability of gesture for mobile interfaces. The authors found that "location and audience had a significant impact on a user's willingness to perform gestures" (Rico & Brewster, 2010).

Frameworks

As mentioned above, wearable computing requires multimodality concerning the input and output devices. Thus to allow the application developer to be independent of the specific hardware device and its restrictions frameworks are used as a wearable computing specific middleware. In the following we show a set of frameworks which are designed for the generation of wearable and mobile user interfaces. Their primary focus is such that they may reduce development efforts of user interfaces as they can be automatically generated or they can be reused on multiple devices.

WUI Toolkit

In 2005, Witt introduced "a toolkit for context-aware UI development for wearable computers" (Witt H., A Toolkit for Context-aware User Interface Development for Wearable Computers, 2005) called WUI toolkit. It was designed to meet requirements of wearable computing and aimed to ease development of wearable user interfaces (WUIs). The toolkit utilized reusable UI components and was based around a model-driven approach and supports self-adapting UIs without being limited to specific interaction devices or graphical UIs (Witt H., A Toolkit for Context-aware User Interface Development for Wearable Computers, 2005; Witt, Nicolai, & Kenn, 2007). The WUI toolkit has been used to create numerous applications and prototypes (Maurtua, Kirisci, Stiefmeier, Sbodio, & Witt, 2007; Kluge & Witt, 2007; Witt, Nicolai, & Kenn, Designing a Wearable User Interface for Hands-free Interaction in Maintenance Applications, 2006; Nicolai, Sindt, Witt, Reimerdes, & Kenn, 2006; Lawo, Herzog, & Witt, 2007).

Witt's toolkit was meant to allow application developers to build WUIs without the need of expert knowledge on creating UIs for wearables. It provided an easy alternative to creating specialized WUIs from scratch. An UI for an application is built on an abstract model that is independent of its concrete representation. No "concrete" UI components (e.g. text field, button, etc.) are used but instead an UI is created with abstract components (e.g. information, trigger, etc.). The additional layer of abstraction allows the rendering in diverse modalities instead of being limited to GUI or a single visual representation.

Furthermore the toolkit supports an automatic adaption of its rendered UI according to available contextual information. At run-time a device- and context-specific UI can be generated, which can then be used to optimize the rendering of the UI and maintain usability when context changes occur (e.g. adapting brightness levels and contrast or changing the interface representation when walking or sitting).

Huddle

HUDDLE was first introduced in 2004 (Nichols, et al., 2004) and it automatically generates task-based UIs for appliances in multi-device environments (e.g. home theater or presentation room). These systems of connected appliances are becoming increasingly difficult to use as the number of available services and devices grows. HUDDLE makes use of an XML-based language for describing functionalities of appliances in

those environments (e.g. televisions, DVD players, printers or microwave ovens). It has been used to generate graphical and speech interfaces on mobile phones, handhelds and desktop computers (Nichols, et al., 2004; Nichols & Myers, Creating a Lightweight User Interface Description Language: An Overview and Analysis of the Personal Universal Controller Project, 2009; Nichols, Rothrock, Chau, & Myers, 2006).

Users of those environments often find themselves in situations where they have to interact with multiple interfaces (e.g. use multiple remote controls) in order to perform a single task (e.g. watch a DVD movie). HUDDLE was designed to ease interaction with and support expandability as well as innovation of those systems (Nichols, Rothrock, Chau, & Myers, 2006). Automatic interface generation systems like HUDDLE allow adding further features to multi-device environments which would otherwise be difficult to implement by (human) designers.

Content flow is an important concept being applied in the design of HUDDLE, which is utilized to help users successfully perform their tasks. Content flows appear to be "closely related to user goals with multi-appliance systems" (Nichols, Rothrock, Chau, & Myers, 2006). They "can be described as the separate flows within each appliance combined with a wiring diagram" (Nichols, Rothrock, Chau, & Myers, 2006), which shows the connections between all appliances. Such a wiring diagram is the only system-specific piece of information required by the HUDDLE framework. Each appliance's functionality could be modeled by its manufacturer whereas the actual wiring is provided by the user, another application or some future wiring technology.

The framework is based on three main features that enable the creation of interfaces: a flow-based UI, a planner and aggregate interface generators. The flow-based UI allows users to specify the content flow between appliances. They choose the endpoints and optionally select a concrete path (if multiple of such routes exist). The planner (based on GraphPlan algorithm (Blum & Furst, 1995)) is used to configure appliances along the selected path, allowing the requested content flow. Finally, the aggregate interface generators are responsible for creating the actual UIs. They automatically generate a single coherent interface for multiple appliances by using ``knowledge of the appliance's functions and how these functions relate to the content flows'' (Nichols, Rothrock, Chau, & Myers, 2006).

SUPPLE

SUPPLE was first introduced in 2004 (Gajos & Weld, 2004) and it is intended as an alternative to creating UIs in a hand-crafted fashion. Instead UIs are automatically generated with respect to a person's device, abilities and preferences. The actual generation of UIs with SUPPLE is interpreted as an optimization problem (Gajos & Weld, 2004; Gajos, Weld, & Wobbrock, 2010). SUPPLE searches for a rendering, meets the device's constraints and minimizes the user efforts. In contrast to earlier work (Cardelli, 1988; Olsen, Jefferies, Nielsen, Moyes, & Fredrickson, 2000; Fogarty & Hudson, 2004) the SUPPLE system also picks individual UI elements for the final rendition. The rendition process is based on three inputs: a functional interface specification, a description of device capabilities and user traces.

The interface specification relies on describing what functionality should be exposed to the user rather than specifying the presentation of functionality. Hints on the representation and other properties can be added. The description of device capabilities contain a set of available UI widgets, a set of device-specific constraints and device-specific functions used to estimate the appropriateness of utilizing "particular widgets in particular contexts" (Gajos & Weld, 2004). UI widgets are used to give abstract UI elements a concrete representation. User traces are used for an automatic adaption of the UIs. They express usage patterns of a particular user, which in turn are used to adapt the UI. An interesting property of these traces is the fact that they are device-independent and can therefore be used to adopt the same UI on different devices; even on those that have not been used before by the user.

AbstractUI

The AbstractUI (AUI) framework has been introduced in 2011 (Ahlrichs, Lawo, & Iben, 2011) and can be considered as a complete remake of the WUI toolkit. As such it makes use of similar metaphors. It has been specifically designed to meet requirements of mobile and wearable devices. Reusable UI components and an abstract description are used in order to generate concrete representations. Application developers describe what is to be displayed rather than how an UI is displayed. While doing so, developers make use of several UI components and can interact with them just like they would with standard UI components of other toolkits and frameworks. Once an application is completed, it is passed to a renderer, which in turn takes care of the concrete representation. Furthermore, development efforts are reduced as the same application can be used on multiple devices. A context-aware representation of an AUI can be generated at run-time.

CONCLUSION AND OUTLOOK

Context aware interfaces are still in early stages of development. Current commercial systems feature user interfaces that adapt to rather obvious circumstances, such as device orientation or lighting conditions, but are still relying on explicit input from the user to perform a requested operation. Somewhat surprisingly we are still waiting for the Smartphone that *just knows* when to switch of audible alerts during a meeting or movie, although plenty of sensors are available. While our communication devices get smarter and smaller over time, the technological advances also allow the field of wearable computing to slowly reach a broader range of users. While first body worn devices that feature complex input and output mechanisms become available to customers their current use is still very similar to mobile devices. In the future these devices will be able to proactively change their behavior in anticipation of their user's wishes and carry out tasks for them without needing explicit commands. One of the challenges here is not just to find a new arrangement of existing mobile user interface structures but also to embrace the available information from the environment as part of user interaction. The thought of having devices act on their own is of course controversial for privacy and security reasons. In the end, a balance has to be found between convenience and control. This balance will have to adapt to the individual user, just as the interface has to adapt to changing circumstances.

REFERENCES

Ahlrichs, C., Lawo, M., & Iben, H. (2011). An Abstract User Interface Framework for Mobile and Wearable Devices. *International Journal of Ambient Computing and Intelligence, 3*(3), 28–35. doi:10.4018/jaci.2011070104

Blum, A., & Furst, M. L. (1995). Fast Planning Through Planning Graph Analysis. In Proceedings of the 14th International Joint Conference on Artificial Intelligence (Vol. 2, pp. 1636–1642). San Francisco, CA: Morgan Kaufmann Publishers Inc. Retrieved from http://dl.acm.org/citation.cfm?id=1643031.1643111

Brashear, H., Starner, T., Lukowicz, P., & Junker, H. (2003). Using Multiple Sensors for Mobile Sign Language Recognition. In *Proceedings of 2012 16th International Symposium on Wearable Computers*. Academic Press.

Brewster, S., & Brown, L. M. (2004). Tactons: Structured Tactile Messages for Non-visual Information Display. In Proceedings of the Fifth Conference on Australasian User Interface (Vol. 28, pp. 15–23). Darlinghurst, Australia: Australian Computer Society, Inc. Retrieved from http://dl.acm.org/citation.cfm?id=976310.976313

Brewster, S., Lumsden, J., Bell, M., Hall, M., & Tasker, S. (2003). Multimodal 'Eyes-free' Interaction Techniques for Wearable Devices. In Proceedings of the SIGCHI Conference on Human Factors in Computing Systems (pp. 473–480). New York: ACM. Retrieved from http://doi.acm.org/10.1145/642611.642694

Cardelli, L. (1988). *Building User Interfaces by Direct Manipulation. In Proceedings of the 1st Annual ACM SIGGRAPH Symposium on User Interface Software* (pp. 152–166). New York: ACM. doi:10.1145/62402.62428

Crossan, A., Brewster, S., & Ng, A. (2010). Foot Tapping for Mobile Interaction. In *Proceedings of the 24th BCS Interaction Specialist Group Conference* (pp. 418-422). Swinton, UK: British Computer Society. Retrieved from http://dl.acm.org/citation.cfm?id=2146303.2146366

Fogarty, J., & Hudson, S. E. (2004). *GADGET: A Toolkit for Optimization-based Approaches to Interface and Display Generation. In ACM SIGGRAPH 2004 Papers* (pp. 730–730). New York: ACM. doi:10.1145/1186562.1015789

Gajos, K., & Weld, D. S. (2004). *SUPPLE: Automatically Generating User Interfaces. In Proceedings of the 9th International Conference on Intelligent User Interfaces* (pp. 93–100). New York: ACM. doi:10.1145/964460.964461

Gajos, K. Z., Weld, D. S., & Wobbrock, J. O. (2010, August). Automatically Generating Personalized User Interfaces with Supple. *Artificial Intelligence, 174*(12-13), 910-950. doi:10.1016/j.artint.2010.05.005

Gandy, M., Starner, T., Auxier, J., & Ashbrook, D. (2000). The Gesture Pendant: A Self-illuminating, Wearable, Infrared Computer Vision System for Home Automation Control and Medical Monitoring. In *Proceedings of 2012 16th International Symposium on Wearable Computers*. Academic Press.

Hoggan, E., & Brewster, S. (2007). *Designing Audio and Tactile Crossmodal Icons for Mobile Devices. In Proceedings of the 9th International Conference on Multimodal Interfaces* (pp. 162–169). New York: ACM. http://doi.acm.org/10.1145/1322192.1322222

Huang, K., Starner, T., Do, E., Weiberg, G., Kohlsdorf, D., Ahlrichs, C., & Leibrandt, R. (2010). *Mobile Music Touch: Mobile Tactile Stimulation for Passive Learning. In Proceedings of the SIGCHI Conference on Human Factors in Computing Systems* (pp. 791–800). New York, NY: ACM. doi:10.1145/1753326.1753443

Kluge, E. M., & Witt, H. (2007, March). Developing Applications for Wearable Computers: A Process driven Example. In *Proceedings of Applied Wearable Computing (IFAWC),* (pp. 1-12). IFAWC.

Lawo, M., Herzog, O., & Witt, H. (2007). *An Industrial Case Study on Wearable Computing Applications. In Proceedings of the 9th International Conference on Human Computer Interaction with Mobile Devices and Services* (pp. 448–451). New York, NY: ACM. http://doi.acm.org/10.1145/1377999.1378052

Lyons, K., Skeels, C., & Starner, T. (2005). *Providing Support for Mobile Calendaring Conversations: A Wizard of Oz Evaluation of Dual-purpose Speech. In Proceedings of the 7th International Conference on Human Computer Interaction with Mobile Devices & Services* (pp. 243–246). New York, NY: ACM. doi:10.1145/1085777.1085821

Lyons, K., Skeels, C., Starner, T., Snoeck, C. M., Wong, B. A., & Ashbrook, D. (2004). *Augmenting Conversations Using Dual-purpose Speech. In Proceedings of the 17th Annual ACM Symposium on User Interface Software and Technology* (pp. 237–246). New York, NY: ACM. http://doi.acm.org/10.1145/1029632.1029674

Lyons, K., Starner, T., & Harvel, L. (2000). A Context-Based Document System for Wearable Computers. In *Proceedings of 2012 16th International Symposium on Wearable Computers*. Academic Press.

Maurtua, I., Kirisci, P. T., Stiefmeier, T., Sbodio, M. L., & Witt, H. (2007, March). A Wearable Computing Prototype for supporting training activities in Automotive Production. In *Proceedings of 4th International Forum on Applied Wearable Computing (IFAWC),* (pp. 1-12). IFAWC.

McLachlan, R., McGee-Lennon, M., & Brewster, S. (2012). *The sound of musicons: Investigating the design of musically derived audio cues.* Retrieved from http://hdl.handle.net/1853/44429

Mehta, N. A., Starner, T., Jackson, M. M., Babalola, K. O., & James, G. A. (2010). Recognizing Sign Language from Brain Imaging. In *Proceedings of the 2010 20th International Conference on Pattern Recognition* (pp. 3842-3845). Washington, DC: IEEE Computer Society. doi:10.1109/ICPR.2010.936

Nichols, J., & Myers, B. A. (2009, November). Creating a Lightweight User Interface Description Language: An Overview and Analysis of the Personal Universal Controller Project. *ACM Transactions on Computer-Human Interaction, 16*(4), 17:1-17:37. http://doi.acm.org/10.1145/1614390.1614392

Nichols, J., Myers, B. A., Litwack, K., Higgins, M., Hughes, J., & Harris, T. K. (2004). Describing Appliance User Interfaces Abstractly with XML. In *Proceedings of Workshop on Developing User Interfaces with XML: Advances on User Interface Description Languages*. Academic Press.

Nichols, J., Rothrock, B., Chau, D. H., & Myers, B. A. (2006). *Huddle: Automatically Generating Interfaces for Systems of Multiple Connected Appliances. In Proceedings of the 19th Annual ACM Symposium on User Interface Software and Technology* (pp. 279–288). New York, NY: ACM. doi:10.1145/1166253.1166298

Nicolai, T., Sindt, T., Witt, H., Reimerdes, J., & Kenn, H. (2006, March). Wearable Computing for Aircraft Maintenance: Simplifying the User Interface. In *Proceedings of 3rd International Forum on Applied Wearable Computing (IFAWC)*, (pp. 1-12). IFAWC.

Non-visual interfaces for wearable computers. (2000, January). *IET Conference Proceedings*, 6-6(1). Retrieved from http://digital-library.theiet.org/content/conferences/10.1049/ic_20000511

Olsen, J. D., Jefferies, S., Nielsen, T., Moyes, W., & Fredrickson, P. (2000). *Cross-modal Interaction Using XWeb. In Proceedings of the 13th Annual ACM Symposium on User Interface Software and Technology* (pp. 191–200). New York, NY: ACM. doi:10.1145/354401.354764

Oulasvirta, A., Tamminen, S., Roto, V., & Kuorelahti, J. (2005). *Interaction in 4-second Bursts: The Fragmented Nature of Attentional Resources in Mobile HCI. In Proceedings of the SIGCHI Conference on Human Factors in Computing Systems* (pp. 919–928). New York, NY: ACM. doi:10.1145/1054972.1055101

Profita, H. P., Clawson, J., Gilliland, S., Zeagler, C., Starner, T., Budd, J., & Do, E. Y.-L. (2013). *Don'T Mind Me Touching My Wrist: A Case Study of Interacting with On-body Technology in Public. In Proceedings of the 2013 International Symposium on Wearable Computers* (pp. 89–96). New York, NY: ACM. doi:10.1145/2493988.2494331

Rhodes, B. J. (1997). The wearable remembrance agent: a system for augmented memory. In *Proceedings of 2012 16th International Symposium on Wearable Computers*. Academic Press.

Rico, J., & Brewster, S. (2010). *Usable Gestures for Mobile Interfaces: Evaluating Social Acceptability. In Proceedings of the SIGCHI Conference on Human Factors in Computing Systems* (pp. 887–896). New York, NY: ACM. doi:10.1145/1753326.1753458

Starner, T. (2001a, July). The challenges of wearable computing: Part 1. *Micro, IEEE, 21*(4), 44–52. doi:10.1109/40.946681

Starner, T. (2001b, July). The challenges of wearable computing: Part 2. *Micro, IEEE, 21*(4), 54–67. doi:10.1109/40.946683

Starner, T. (2002, October). Attention, memory, and wearable interfaces. *Pervasive Computing, IEEE, 1*(4), 88–91. doi:10.1109/MPRV.2002.1158283

Starner, T. (2008). Reading Your Mind: Interfaces for Wearable Computing. In *Proceedings of International Symposium on Ubiquitous Virtual Reality*. Academic Press.

Starner, T., Leibe, B., Singletary, B., & Pair, J. (2000). *MIND-WARPING: Towards Creating a Compelling Collaborative Augmented Reality Game. In Proceedings of the 5th International Conference on Intelligent User Interfaces* (pp. 256–259). New York, NY: ACM. doi:10.1145/325737.325864

Starner, T., & Maguire, Y. (1999, March). Heat Dissipation in Wearable Computers Aided by Thermal Coupling with the User. *Mob. Netw. Appl., 4*(1), 3-13. 10.1023/A:1019113924178

Starner, T., Rhodes, B., Weaver, J., & Pentland, A. (1999). Everyday-use Wearable Computers. In *Proceedings of International Symposium on Wearable Computers*. Academic Press.

Starner, T., Weaver, J., & Pentland, A. (1998). *A Wearable Computer Based American Sign Language Recognizer. In Assistive Technology and Artificial Intelligence, Applications in Robotics, User Interfaces and Natural Language Processing* (pp. 84–96). London, UK: Springer-Verlag. http://dl.acm.org/citation.cfm?id=646629.696531

Starner, T. E. (1999). *Wearable Computing and Contextual Awareness*. Massachusetts Institute of Technology. Retrieved from http://hdl.handle.net/1721.1/9543

Starner, T. E. (2003). Powerful Change Part 1: Batteries and Possible Alternatives for the Mobile Market. *IEEE Pervasive Computing, 2*(4), 86–88. doi:10.1109/MPRV.2003.1251172

Starner, T. E., Snoeck, C. M., Wong, B. A., & McGuire, R. M. (2004). *Use of Mobile Appointment Scheduling Devices. In Proceedings of CHI '04 Extended Abstracts on Human Factors in Computing Systems* (pp. 1501–1504). New York, NY: ACM. http://doi.acm.org/10.1145/985921.986100

The Eudaemons' Shoe. (1998). *The Eudaemons' Shoe*. Retrieved from http://wearcam.org/historical/node3.html

Thorp, E. O. (1998). *The Invention of the First Wearable Computer. In Proceedings of the 2nd IEEE International Symposium on Wearable Computers* (p. 4). Washington, DC: IEEE Computer Society. http://dl.acm.org/citation.cfm?id=857199.858031

Vadas, K., Lyons, K. M., Ashbrook, D., Yi, J. S., Starner, T., & Jacko, J. A. (2006). *Reading on the go: An evaluation of three mobile display technologies*. Retrieved from http://hdl.handle.net/1853/13112

Vadas, K., Patel, N., Lyons, K., Starner, T., & Jacko, J. (2006). *Reading On-the-go: A Comparison of Audio and Hand-held Displays. In Proceedings of the 8th Conference on Human-computer Interaction with Mobile Devices and Services* (pp. 219–226). New York, NY: ACM. doi:10.1145/1152215.1152262

Wilson, G., Halvey, M., Brewster, S. A., & Hughes, S. A. (2011). *Some Like It Hot: Thermal Feedback for Mobile Devices. In Proceedings of the SIGCHI Conference on Human Factors in Computing Systems* (pp. 2555–2564). New York, NY: ACM. doi:10.1145/1978942.1979316

Witt, H. (2005). A Toolkit for Context-aware User Interface Development for Wearable Computers. In *Proceedings of Doctoral Colloquium at the 9th International Symposium on Wearable Computers (ISWC)*. ISWC.

Witt, H. (2007). *Human-Computer Interfaces for Wearable Computers: A Systematic Approach to Development and Evaluation*. (Ph.D. dissertation). Bremen.

Witt, H., Nicolai, T., & Kenn, H. (2006). Designing a Wearable User Interface for Hands-free Interaction in Maintenance Applications. In *Proceedings of IEEE International Conference on Pervasive Computing and Communications Workshops,* (pp. 652-655). IEEE. doi:10.1109/PERCOMW.2006.39

Witt, H., Nicolai, T., & Kenn, H. (2007, June). The WUI-Toolkit: A Model-Driven UI Development Framework for Wearable User Interfaces. In *Proceedings of 27th International Conference on Distributed Computing Systems Workshops, 2007* (pp. 43-43). ICDCSW. doi:10.1109/ICDCSW.2007.80

Zafrulla, Z., Brashear, H., Starner, T., Hamilton, H., & Presti, P. (2011). *American Sign Language Recognition with the Kinect. In Proceedings of the 13th International Conference on Multimodal Interfaces* (pp. 279–286). New York, NY: ACM. http://doi.acm.org/10.1145/2070481.2070532

KEY TERMS AND DEFINITIONS

Attention: When dealing with computer systems attention is a human resource that is split up between the interaction with the machine, the task and the real world. Computer systems can try to actively seek attention from the user through various means, e.g. sound, visual cues or dialogs.

Context Aware: A context aware system incorporates information from the environment into the interaction mechanisms. This enables the system to perform actions without explicit user interaction thus reducing the amount of needed interaction.

Human-Computer-Interaction: Human-computer-interaction (HCI) deals with the design challenges to create computer systems that are used by human operators. While it is often associated with the design of software user interfaces it also encompasses hardware aspects such as ergonomics.

Mobile Computing: The mobile computing paradigm describes the design concept of applications for mobile devices such as smartphones. In contrast to traditional computing the factors of divided attention, location based services and others have a strong impact.

Multimodal Interaction: The concept of multimodal interaction allows information to be interpreted in different modalities depending on the circumstances. Textual information for example can either be displayed graphically or spoken via speech synthesis. Also notifications to the user can occur via audio, by vibration or other means.

User Interface Generation: In traditional application design the user interface is explicitly modelled by an interface designer. When the interaction mechanisms (e.g. output devices) are not known beforehand a user interface can be generated algorithmically by estimating the best layout for the given circumstances.

Wearable Computer: A wearable computer is a computation device that is worn by the user. Either directly like a wristwatch or integrated into clothing. Wearable computers are potentially always interacting with the environment or the user to support a task in the real world.

Wearable Computing: The wearable computing paradigm describes the design concept of applications for wearable computing devices. It shares many similarities with mobile computing but differs in the interaction aspect. A wearable computing application always supports a task in the real world. The user of such an application is carrying out this task while the application monitors the environment to provide needed information without disturbing the user.

ENDNOTES

[1]   The receiver here is actually just an audio playback device.

Compilation of References

3Delica. (2013). *3Delica* [Facebook group]. Retrieved November 19, 2013 from: https://www.facebook.com/3Delica

Aarts, M. P. J., Aries, M. B. C., & Straathof, J., &_van Hoof. J. (. (2014). (in press). Dynamic lighting systems in psychogeriatric care facilities in The Netherlands: A quantitative and qualitative analysis of the subjective responses of stakeholders and technology. *Indoor and Built Environment*. doi:10.1177/1420326X14532387

Aarts, M. P. J., & Westerlaken, A. C. (2005). Field study of visual and biological light conditions of independently-living elderly people. *Gerontechnology (Valkenswaard)*, *4*(3), 141–152. doi:10.4017/gt.2005.04.03.004.00

Abbate, S., Avvenuti, M., Bonatesta, F., Cola, G., Corsini, P., & Vecchio, A. (2012). A Smartphone-based Fall Detection System. *Pervasive and Mobile Computing*, *8*(6), 883–899. doi:10.1016/j.pmcj.2012.08.003

Abdulrahman, R., Neagu, D., Holton, D., Ridley, M., & Lan, Y. (2013). *Data extraction from online social networks using application programming interface in a multi agent system approach. Transactions on Computational Collective Intelligence*, *11*, 88–118.

Abras, S., Ploix, S., Pesty, S., & Jacomino, M. (2008). *A multi-agent home automation system for power management. In Informatics in Control Automation and Robotics* (pp. 59–68). Springer.

Acharya, D. (2010). Security in Pervasive Health Care Networks: Current R&D and Future Challenges. In *Proceedings of Mobile Data Management (MDM)*, (pp. 305–306). Academic Press. doi:10.1109/MDM.2010.38

Ackerman, E. (2011, June 17). *Microsoft Releases Kinect SDK, Roboticists Cackle With Glee*. Retrieved from IEEE Spectrum - Automaton: http://spectrum.ieee.org/automaton/robotics/diy/microsoft-releases-kinect-sdk-roboticists-cackle-with-glee

Adami, A. M., Pavel, M., Hayes, T. L., & Singer, C. M. (2010). Detection of movement in bed using unobtrusive load cell sensors. *IEEE Transactions on Information Technology in Biomedicine*, *14*(2), 481–490. doi:10.1109/TITB.2008.2010701 PMID:19171523

Adam, K., & Oswald, I. (1984). Sleep helps healing. *British Medical Journal*, *289*, 1400–1401. PMID:6437572

Ahlrichs, C., Lawo, M., & Iben, H. (2011). An Abstract User Interface Framework for Mobile and Wearable Devices. *International Journal of Ambient Computing and Intelligence*, *3*(3), 28–35. doi:10.4018/jaci.2011070104

Åhlund, A., Mitra, K., Johansson, D., Åhlund, C., & Zaslavsky, A. (2009). Context-aware application mobility support in pervasive computing environments. In *Proceedings of the 6th International Conference on Mobile Technology, Applications & Systems* (pp. 21:1–21:4). New York: ACM.

Ahson, S., & Ilyas, M. (2008). *Rfid handbook: applications, technology, security, and privacy*. Boca Raton, FL: CRC Press. doi:10.1201/9781420055009

Akl, A., & Valaee, S. (2010). Accelerometer-based gesture recognition via dynamic-time warping, affinity propagation, & compressive sensing. In *Proceedings of International Conference on Acoustics, Speech and Singal Processing* (pp. 2270-2273). IEEE. doi:10.1109/ICASSP.2010.5495895

Alexandraki, C., & Akoumianakis, D. (2010). Exploring new perspectives in network music performance: The diamouses framework. *Computer Music Journal*, *34*(2), 66–83.

Alihanka, J., Vaahtoranta, K., & Saarikivi, I. (1981). A new method for long-term monitoring of the ballistocardiogram, heart rate, and respiration. *The American Journal of Physiology*, *240*(5), 384–392. PMID:7235054

Allen, A., & Mintrom, M. (2010). Responsibility and School Governance. *Educational Policy*, *24*(3), 439–464. doi:10.1177/0895904808330172

Allen, J. (1983). Maintaining knowledge about temporal intervals. *Communications of the ACM*, *26*, 832–843.

Aloulou, H., Mokhtari, M., Tiberghien, T., Biswas, J., Phua, C., Lin, J. H. K., & Yap, P. (2013). Deployment of assistive living technology in a nursing home environment: Methods and lessons learned. *BMC Medical Informatics and Decision Making*, *13*(1), 42. doi:10.1186/1472-6947-13-42 PMID:23565984

Alt, F., Balz, M., Kristes, S., Shirazi, A. S., Mennenoh, J., Schmidt, A., et al. (2009). *Adaptive User Profiles in Pervasive Advertising Environments*. Paper presented at the European Conference on Ambient Intelligence. Salzburg, Austria. doi:10.1007/978-3-642-05408-2_32

Amft, O., & Tröster, G. (2009). On-Body Sensing Solutions for Automatic Dietary Monitoring. *IEEE Pervasive Computing*, *8*(2), 62–70. doi:10.1109/MPRV.2009.32

Amirabdollahian, F., Loureiro, R., Gradwell, E., Collin, C., Harwin, W., & Johnson, G. (2007). Multivariate analysis of the Fugl-Meyer outcome measures assessing the effectiveness of GENTLE/S robot-mediated stroke therapy. *Journal of Neuroengineering and Rehabilitation*, *4*(1), 4. doi:10.1186/1743-0003-4-4 PMID:17309791

Arguello, J., Elsas, J. L., Callan, J., & Carbonell, J. G. (2008, March 30-April 2). *Document Representation and Query Expansion Models for Blog Recommendation*. Paper presented at the International Conference on Weblogs and Social Media. Seattle, WA.

Aries, M. B. C., Aarts, M. P. J., & van Hoof, J. (2014). (in press). Daylight and health: A review of the evidence and consequences for the built environment. *Lighting Research & Technology*. doi:10.1177/1477153513509258

Arnett, F., Edworthy, S., Bloch, D., Mcshane, D., Fries, F., Cooper, N., & Hunder, G. (1988). The American Rheumatism Association 1987 Revised Criteria for the Classification of Rheumatoid Arthritis. *Arthritis and Rheumatism*, *14*(2), 315–324. doi:10.1002/art.1780310302 PMID:3358796

Arnott, R. (2013). *Soundself by Robin Arnott – Kickstater*. Retrieved November 19, 2013 from: http://www.kickstarter.com/projects/soundself/soundself

Arnrich, B., Mayora, O., Bardram, J., & Tröster, G. (2010). Pervasive Healthcare Paving the Way for a Pervasive, User-centered and Preventive Healthcare Model. *Methods of Information in Medicine*, *49*(1), 67–73. doi:10.3414/ME09-02-0044 PMID:20011810

Arnstein, L., Grimm, R., Hung, C., Kang, J. H., LaMarca, A., & Look, G. et al. (2002). Systems Support for Ubiquitous Computing: A Case Study of Two Implementations of Labscape. In *Proceedings of the First International Conference on Pervasive Computing (Pervasive '02)*. Springer-Verlag.

Arteaga, S. M., González, V. M., Kurniawan, S., & Benavides, R. A. (2012). Mobile Games and Design Requirements to Increase Teenagers' Physical Activity. *Pervasive and Mobile Computing*, *8*(6), 900–908. doi:10.1016/j.pmcj.2012.08.002

Arthritis: Rheumatoid Arthritis. (2008). Retrieved December 08, 2011, from American Society for Surgery of the Hand: http://www.assh.org/Public/HandConditions/Pages/ArthritisRheumatoidArthritis.aspx

Ashton, L., & Myers, S. (2004). Serial Grip Testing- Its role In Assessment Of Wrisy And Hand Disability. *The Internet Journal of Surgery*, *5*(1), 32–44.

Audiovisualizers Inc. (2013). *Video Synthesizers Homage Page*. Retrieved August 28, 2013 from: http://www.audiovisualizers.com/toolshak/vsynths.htm

Augusto, J., & Nugent, C. (2004). The use of temporal reasoning and management of complex events in smart homes. In *Proceedings of the 16th European Conference on Artificial Intelligence* (pp. 778–782). Amsterdam, The Netherlands: IOS Press.

Avison, D., & Young, T. (2007, June). Time to rethink health care and ict? *Communications of the ACM, 50*(6), 69–74. doi:10.1145/1247001.1247008

Aziz, O., Atallah, L., Lo, B. P. L., Gray, E., Athanasiou, T., Darzi, A., & Yang, G.-Z. (2011). Ear-worn Body Sensor Network Device: An Objective Tool for Functional Postoperative Home Recovery Monitoring. *Journal of the American Medical Informatics Association, 18*(2), 156–159. doi:10.1136/jamia.2010.005173 PMID:21252051

Aztiria, A., Augusto, J., Izaguirre, A., & Cook, D. (2008). Learning accurate temporal relations from user actions in intelligent environments. In *Proceedings of the 3rd Symposium of Ubiquitous Computing and Ambient Intelligence* (pp. 274–283). Berlin, Germany: Springer.

B'far, R. (2005). *Mobile computing principles: designing and developing mobile applications.* Cambridge, UK: Cambridge University Press.

Bandelloni, R., & Paternò, F. (2004). Flexible interface migration. In *Proceedings of the 9th International Conference on Intelligent User Interfaces* (pp. 148–155). New York: ACM.

Bardram, J. E., Frost, M., Szántó, K., & Marcu, G. (2012). The MONARCA Self-assessment System: A Persuasive Personal Monitoring System for Bipolar Patients. In IHI (pp. 21–30). Academic Press. doi:10.1145/2110363.2110370

Bardram, J. E. (2008). Pervasive Healthcare as a Scientific Discipline. *Methods of Information in Medicine, 47*(3), 178–185. doi:10.3414/ME9107 PMID:18473081

Bardram, J. E., & Christensen, H. B. (2007). Pervasive Computing Support for Hospitals: An overview of the Activity-Based Computing Project. *IEEE Pervasive Computing, 6*(1), 44–51. doi:10.1109/MPRV.2007.19

Barnes, J. A. (1972). Social networks. *Addison-Wesley Module in Anthropology, 26*, 1-29.

Barroso, A., & den Brinker, B. (2013). Boosting circadian rhythms with lighting: A model driven approach. *Lighting Research & Technology, 45*(2), 197–216. doi:10.1177/1477153512453667

Basili, V., & Selby, R. (1987). Comparing the Effectiveness of Software Testing Strategies. *IEEE Transactions on Software Engineering, 21*(3), 1278–1296. doi:10.1109/TSE.1987.232881

Baskiyar, S. (2002). A real-time fault tolerant intra-body network. In *Proceedings of Local Computer Networks,* (pp. 235-240). IEEE.

Bath Spa University. (2013). *Seeing Sound 2013.* Retrieved December 10, 2013 from: http://www.seeingsound.co.uk/seeing-sound-2013/

Baumgarten, M., & Mulvenna, M. D. (2011). Cognitive Sensor Networks: Towards Self-adapting Ambient Intelligence for Pervasive Healthcare. In PervasiveHealth (pp. 366–369). Academic Press.

Bavelas, A. (1950). Communication patterns in task-oriented groups. *The Journal of the Acoustical Society of America, 22*, 725–730.

BBC. (2012). Holograms won't replace live music performances. *Newsbeat.* Retrieved November 17, 2013 from: http://www.bbc.co.uk/newsbeat/18511859

Beale, R. (2009). What does mobile mean? *International Journal of Mobile Human Computer Interaction, 1*(3), 1–8. doi:10.4018/jmhci.2009070101

Benlamri, R., & Docksteader, L. (2010). Morf: A mobile health-monitoring platform. *IT Professional, 12*(3), 18–25. doi:10.1109/MITP.2010.3

Berenji, H., & Khedkar, P. (1992). Learning and tuning fuzzy logic controllers through reinforcements. *IEEE Transactions on Neural Networks, 3*(5), 724–740. PMID:18276471

Berners-Lee, T., & Hendler, J. (2001). Scientific publishing on the semantic web. *Nature, 410*(6832), 1023–1024. doi:10.1038/35074206 PMID:11323639

Beyer, H., & Holtzblatt, K. (1998). *Contextual design: defining customer-centered systems.* San Francisco, CA: Morgan Kaufmann Publishers Inc.

Bharat, K. A., & Cardelli, L. (1995). Migratory applications. In *Proceedings of the 8th Annual ACM Symposium on User Interface and Software Technology* (pp. 132–142). New York, NY: ACM.

Bickmore, T. W., Mauer, D., & Brown, T. (2009). Context Awareness in a Handheld Exercise Agent. *Pervasive and Mobile Computing*, 5(3), 226–235. doi:10.1016/j.pmcj.2008.05.004 PMID:20161031

Bihun, A., Goldman, J., Khesin, A., Marur, V., Morales, E., & Reynar, J. (2007). *US Patent No. 20070061297 A1*. US Patent & Trademark Office.

Binkley, S. (2007). *The Importance of Teamwork in the Workplace*. Retrieved from http://www.associatedcontent.com/article/317564/the_importance_of_teamwork_in_the_workplace.html?cat=31

Blackburn, J., & Iamnitchi, A. (2013). An architecture for collecting longitudinal social data. In *Proceedings of Communications Workshops (ICC)*, (pp. 184-188). ICC.

Black, S., Kushner, I., & Samols, D. (2004). C-reactive Protein. *The Journal of Biological Chemistry*, 279(47), 48487–48490. doi:10.1074/jbc.R400025200 PMID:15337754

Blöckner, M., Danti, S., Forrai, J., Broll, G., & De Luca, A. (2009). Please touch the exhibits!: using NFC-based interaction for exploring a museum. In *Proceedings of the 11th International Conference on Human-Computer Interaction with Mobile Devices and Services* (pp. 71:1–71:2). New York, NY: ACM. doi:10.1145/1613858.1613943

Blount, M., Ebling, M. R., Eklund, J. M., James, A. G., McGregor, C., & Percival, N. et al. (2010). Real-Time Analysis for Intensive Care: Development and Deployment of the Artemis Analytic System. *IEEE Engineering in Medicine and Biology Magazine*, 29(2), 110–118. doi:10.1109/MEMB.2010.936454 PMID:20659848

Blum, A., & Furst, M. L. (1995). Fast Planning Through Planning Graph Analysis. In Proceedings of the 14th International Joint Conference on Artificial Intelligence (Vol. 2, pp. 1636–1642). San Francisco, CA: Morgan Kaufmann Publishers Inc. Retrieved from http://dl.acm.org/citation.cfm?id=1643031.1643111

Boehm, B. (1988). A Spiral Model for Software Development and Enhancement. *IEEE Computer*, 12(3), 61–72. doi:10.1109/2.59

Bogan, D., Spence, J., & Donnelly, P. (2010). *Connected Health: An All Island Review in Ireland (Informative Review No. 19th April 2010)*. Bio Business.

Bohn, J., Coroama, V., Langheinrich, M., Mattern, F., & Rohs, M. (2005). Social, economic, and ethical implications of ambient intelligence and ubiquitous computing. In Ambient Intelligence. Springer.

Bondi, A. B. (2000). Characteristics of Scalability and Their Impact on Performance. In *Proceedings of the 2nd international workshop on Software and performance* (pp. 195–203). New York: ACM. doi:10.1145/350391.350432

Botia, J. A., Villa, A., & Palma, J. (2012). Ambient Assisted Living System for in-home Monitoring of Healthy Independent Elders. *Expert Systems with Applications*, 39(9), 8136–8148. doi:10.1016/j.eswa.2012.01.153

Bower, C., Taheri, H., & Wolbrecht, E. (2013). Adaptive control with state-dependent modeling of patient impairment for robotic movement therapy. In *Proceedings of 2013 IEEE International Conference on Rehabilitation Robotics (ICORR)*. IEEE. doi:10.1109/ICORR.2013.6650460

Bradski, G., & Kaehler, A. (2008). *Learning OpenCV: Computer vision with the OpenCV library. Sebastapol*, CA: O'Reilly Media, Inc.

Brashear, H., Starner, T., Lukowicz, P., & Junker, H. (2003). Using Multiple Sensors for Mobile Sign Language Recognition. In *Proceedings of 2012 16th International Symposium on Wearable Computers*. Academic Press.

Braunstein, J. (1953). The Ballistocardiogram: A Dynamic Record of the Heart. Springfield, IL: Springfield.

Breslow, L. (2005). How to Create a High Functioning Team. In *MIT, Guidelines for "Management Communication for Undergraduates"* (15.279). Sloan School of Management, MIT. Retrieved from http://web.mit.edu/tll/teaching-materials/teamwork/index-teamwork.html

Brewster, S., & Brown, L. M. (2004). Tactons: Structured Tactile Messages for Non-visual Information Display. In Proceedings of the Fifth Conference on Australasian User Interface (Vol. 28, pp. 15–23). Darlinghurst, Australia: Australian Computer Society, Inc. Retrieved from http://dl.acm.org/citation.cfm?id=976310.976313

Brewster, S., Lumsden, J., Bell, M., Hall, M., & Tasker, S. (2003). Multimodal 'Eyes-free' Interaction Techniques for Wearable Devices. In Proceedings of the SIGCHI Conference on Human Factors in Computing Systems (pp. 473–480). New York: ACM. Retrieved from http://doi.acm.org/10.1145/642611.642694

Brink, M., Müller, C. H., & Schierz, C. (2006). Contact-free measurement of heart rate, respiration rate, and body movements during sleep. *Behavior Research Methods*, *38*(3), 511–521. PMID:17186762

Brochard, S., Robertson, J., Médée, B., & Rémy-Néris, O. (2010). What's new in new technologies for upper extremity rehabilitation? *Current Opinion in Neurology*, *23*(6), 683–687. doi:10.1097/WCO.0b013e32833f61ce PMID:20852420

Bromuri, S., Schumacher, M. I., Stathis, K., & Ruiz, J. (2011). Monitoring Gestational Diabetes Mellitus with Cognitive Agents and Agent Environments. In *Proceedings of Web Intelligence and Intelligent Agent Technology (WI-IAT)*, (Vol. 2, pp. 409–414). WI-IAT. doi:10.1109/WI-IAT.2011.37

Brown, C. A., Berry, R., Tan, M. C., Khoshia, A., Turlapati, L., & Swedlove, F. (2013). A critique of the evidence base for non-pharmacological sleep interventions for persons with dementia. *Dementia (London)*, *12*(2), 210–237. doi:10.1177/1471301211426909 PMID:24336770

Bruce, B. C. (2009). Ubiquitous learning, ubiquitous computing, and lived experience. In W. Cope & M. Kalantzis (Eds.), *Ubiquitous learning* (pp. 21–30). Champaign, IL: University of Illinois Press.

Brüser, C., Kerekes, A., Winter, S., & Leonhardt, S. (2012). Multi-channel optical sensor-array for measuring ballistocardiograms and respiratory activity in bed. In *Proceedings of the 34th Annual Conference of the IEEE Engineering in Medicine and Biology Society (EMBS)*, (pp. 5042-5045). EMBS.

Brüser, C., Stadlthanner, K., de Waele, S., & Leonhardt, S. (2011). Adaptive beat-to-beat heart rate estimation in ballistocardiograms. *IEEE Transactions on Information Technology in Biomedicine*, *15*(5), 778–786. PMID:21421447

Brüser, C., Winter, S., & Leonhardt, S. (2013). Robust inter-beat interval estimation in cardiac vibration signals. *Physiological Measurement*, *34*(2), 123–138. PMID:23343518

Bulckaert, A., Exadaktylos, V., De Bruyne, G., Haex, B., De Valck, E., & Wuyts, J. et al. (2010). Heart rate based nighttime awakening detection. *European Journal of Applied Physiology*, *109*, 317–322. PMID:20094892

Burns, J. (2008) Developing Secure Mobile Applications For Android. iSec Partners.

Cabri, G., Leonardi, L., & Quitadamo, R. (2006). Enabling java mobile computing on the ibm jikes research virtual machine. In *Proceedings of the 4th International Symposium on Principles and Practice of Programming in Java* (pp. 62–71). New York, NY: ACM. doi:10.1145/1168054.1168064

Cardelli, L. (1988). *Building User Interfaces by Direct Manipulation. In Proceedings of the 1st Annual ACM SIGGRAPH Symposium on User Interface Software* (pp. 152–166). New York: ACM. doi:10.1145/62402.62428

Carefusion. (2011). *Carefusion nicolet*. Retrieved 2011 from http://www.carefusion.com/medicalproducts/neurology/neurodiagnostic-monitoring/eeg/nicolet-ambulatorymonitor.aspx

Carmody, T. (2010, November 5). *How Facial Recognition Works in Xbox Kinect*. Retrieved from Wired: http://www.wired.com/gadgetlab/2010/11/how-facial-recognition-works-in-xbox-kinect/

Carr, D., O'Grady, M. J., O'Hare, G. M., & Collier, R. (2013). *SIXTH: A Middleware for Supporting Ubiquitous Sensing in Personal Health Monitoring. In Wireless Mobile Communication and Healthcare* (pp. 421–428). Springer.

Carswell, W., Augusto, J., Mulvenna, M., Wallace, J., Martin, S., & McCullagh, P. J. ... Jeffers, W. P. (2011). The NOCTURNAL Ambient Assisted Living System. In *Proceedings of Pervasive Computing Technologies for Healthcare (PervasiveHealth)*, (pp. 208–209). Academic Press.

Cascone, K. (2002). The Aesthetics of Failure: Post Digital Tendencies in Contemporary Computer Music. *Computer Music Journal, 24*(4).

Casey, M., Hayes, P. S., Heaney, D., Dowie, L., Ólaighin, G., & Matero, M. et al. (2013). Implementing transnational telemedicine solutions: A connected health project in rural and remote areas of six Northern Periphery countries Series on European collaborative projects. *The European Journal of General Practice, 19*(1), 52–58. doi:10.3109/13814788.2012.761440 PMID:23432039

Castells, M. (2000). The information age: Economy, society and culture: The rise of the network society (2nd ed., vol. 1). Malden, MA: Blackwell.

Cavallo, F., Aquilano, M., Odetti, L., Arvati, M., & Carrozza, M. C. (2009). A first step toward a pervasive and smart ZigBee sensor system for assistance and rehabilitation. In *Proceedings of 2009 IEEE International Conference on Rehabilitation Robotics, ICORR 2009.* IEEE. doi:10.1109/ICORR.2009.5209471

Caverlee, J., & Webb, S. (2008). A large-scale study of MySpace: Observations and implications for online social networks. In *Proceedings of ICWSM.* ICWSM.

CEN / Comité Européen de Normalisation. (2011). *EN 12464-1. Light and lighting - Lighting of work places – Part 1: Indoor work places.* Brussels, Belgium: Comité Européen de Normalisation.

Center for Technology and Aging. (2009). *Technologies for remote patient monitoring in older adults.* Center for Technology and Aging.

Centre for Visual Music. (2013). *Centre for Visual Music.* Retrieved July 11, 2013 from: http://www.centerforvisualmusic.org/

Cervantes, L., Lee, Y.-S., Yang, H., Ko, S., & Lee, J. (2007). Agent-Based Intelligent Decision Support for the Home Healthcare Environment. In M. Szczuka, D. Howard, D. Ślęzak, H. Kim, T. Kim, I. Ko, … P. A. Sloot (Eds.), Advances in Hybrid Information Technology (Vol. 4413, pp. 414–424). Springer Berlin Heidelberg. Retrieved from doi:10.1007/978-3-540-77368-9_41

Chaczko, Z., & Yeoh, L. (2007). *A Preliminary Investigation on Computer Vision for Telemedicine Systems using OpenCV.* Swinburne, Australia: 2010 Second International Conference on Machine Learning and Computing.

Chakraborty, S., Poolsappasit, N., & Ray, I. (2007). Reliable Delivery of Event Data from Sensors to Actuators in Pervasive Computing Environments. In *Proceedings of 21st Annual IFIP WG 11.3 Working Conference on Data and Applications Security (DBSec'07)* (LNCS), (vol. 4602, pp. 77-92). Redondo Beach, CA: Springer.

Chang, C.-Y., Lange, B., Zhang, M., Koenig, S., Requejo, P., Somboon, N., et al. (2012). Towards pervasive physical rehabilitation using Microsoft Kinect. In *Proceedings of 2012 6th International Conference on Pervasive Computing Technologies for Healthcare (PervasiveHealth).* Academic Press.

Chang, Y.-J., Chen, S.-F., & Huang, J.-D. (2011). A Kinect-based system for physical rehabilitation: A pilot study for young adults with motor disabilities. *Research in Developmental Disabilities, 32*(6), 2566–2570. doi:10.1016/j.ridd.2011.07.002 PMID:21784612

Charron, C., Favier, J., & Li, C. (2006). *Social computing.* Forrester Research. Retrieved from http://www.cisco.com/web/offer/socialcomputing/SocialComputingBigIdea.pdf

Chau, D. H., Pandit, S., Wang, S., & Faloutsos, C. (2007). Parallel crawling for online social networks. In *Proceedings of the 16th International Conference on World Wide Web,* (pp. 1283-1284). Academic Press. doi:10.1145/1242572.1242809

Chen, M., Gonzalez, S., Vasilakos, A., Cao, H., & Leung, V. C. (2011). Body area networks: A survey. *Mob. Netw. Appl., 16*, 171–193. doi: 10.1007/s11036-010-0260-8

Chen, T.-S., Yu, G.-J., & Chen, H.-J. (2007). A framework of mobile context management for supporting context-aware environments in mobile ad hoc networks. In *Proceedings of the 2007 International Conference on Wireless Communications and Mobile Computing* (pp. 647–652). Academic Press. doi:10.1145/1280940.1281078

Chen, Y., Cheng, T., & Hsu, S. (2009). Ultrasound in rheumatoid arthritis. *Formosan Journal of Rheumatology,* 1-7.

Chen, D., Yang, J., & Wactlar, H. D. (2004). Towards automatic analysis of social interaction patterns in a nursing home environment from video. In *Proceedings of the 6th ACM SIGMM International Workshop on Multimedia Information Retrieval*, (pp. 283-290). ACM. doi:10.1145/1026711.1026757

Chen, L., & Nugent, C. (2009). Ontology-based activity recognition in intelligent pervasive environments. *International Journal of Web Information Systems*, 5(4), 410–430. doi:10.1108/17440080911006199

Chen, L., Nugent, C. D., & Wang, H. (2012). A Knowledge-Driven Approach to Activity Recognition in Smart Homes. *IEEE Transactions on Knowledge and Data Engineering*, 24(6), 961–974. doi:10.1109/TKDE.2011.51

Chen, L., Nugent, C., Mulvenna, M., Finlay, D., & Hong, X. (2009). Semantic smart homes: Towards knowledge rich assisted living environments. *Intelligent Patient Management*, 189, 279–296. doi:10.1007/978-3-642-00179-6_17

Chetan, S., Ranganathan, A., & Campbell, R. (2005, Spring). Towards fault tolerance pervasive computing. *IEEE Technology and Society Magazine*, 24(1), 38–44. doi:10.1109/MTAS.2005.1407746

Chinthammit, W., Merritt, T., Pedersen, S., Williams, A., Visentin, D., Rowe, R., & Furness, T. (2014). Ghostman: Augmented Reality Application for Telerehabilitation and Remote Instruction of a Novel Motor Skill. *BioMed Research International*, 2014, e646347. doi:10.1155/2014/646347 PMID:24829910

Choi, T.-S., Ko, K.-R., Park, S.-C., Jang, Y.-S., Yoon, Y.-T., & Im, S.-K. (2009). *Analysis of energy savings using smart metering system and IHD (in-home display).* Paper presented at the Transmission & Distribution Conference & Exposition: Asia and Pacific. New York, NY.

Choi, J. K., Goldman, M., Koyal, S., & Clark, G. (2000). Effect of jaw and head position on airway resistance in obstructive sleep apnea. *Sleep and Breathing*, 4, 163–168. PMID:11894202

Choi, J., Yoo, S., Park, H., & Chun, J. (2006). MobileMed: A PDA-Based Mobile Clinical Information System. *IEEE Transactions on* Information Technology in Biomedicine, 10(3), 627–635. doi:10.1109/TITB.2006.874201

Chua, S.-L., Marsland, S., & Guesgen, H. W. (2009). *Spatio- temporal and context reasoning in smart homes.* Paper presented at the COSIT-09 Workshop on Spatial and Temporal Reasoning for Ambient Intelligence Systems. Aber Wrac'h, France.

Chu, H.-H., Song, H., Wong, C., Kurakake, S., & Katagiri, M. (2004). Roam, a seamless application framework. *Journal of Systems and Software*, 69(3), 209–226. doi:10.1016/S0164-1212(03)00052-9

Chung, L., Cesar, J., & Sampaio, J. (2009). On Non-Functional Requirements in Software Engineering. *Lecture Notes in Computer Science*, 28(3), 363–379. doi:10.1007/978-3-642-02463-4_19

Cinque, M., Cotroneo, D., Kalbarczyk, Z., & Iyer, R. (2007b). How do mobile phones fail? A failure data analysis of symbian os smart phones. In *Proceedings of Dependable Systems and Networks*, (pp. 585–594). IEEE.

Cinque, M., Coronato, A., & Testa, A. (2011). A Failure Modes and Effects Analysis of Mobile Health Monitoring Systems. In *Proceedings of the 2011 International Conference on Systems, Computing Sciences and Software Engineering (SCSS), part of the International Joint Conferences on Computer, Information, and Systems Sciences, and Engineering (CISSE 11). Academic Press.*

Cinque, M., Coronato, A., & Testa, A. (2012). Dependable Services for Mobile Health Monitoring Systems. *International Journal of Ambient Computing and Intelligence*, 4(1), 1–15. doi:10.4018/jaci.2012010101

Cinque, M., Cotroneo, D., Di Martinio, C., & Russo, S. (2007a). Modeling and Assessing the Dependability of Wireless Sensor Networks. In *Proceedings of the 26th IEEE International Symposium on Reliable Distributed Systems (SRDS '07).* IEEE Computer Society.

Clarke, N., & Stow, S. (2006). *What is the Curriculum Development Process?* Retrieved from http://www.curriculumalignmentassociates.com/What%20is%20the%20Curriculum%20Development%20Process.pdf

Claros, M., Soto, R., Rodriguez, J. J., Cantu, C., & Contreras-Vidal, J. L. (2013). Novel compliant actuator for wearable robotics applications. In *Proceedings of Annual International Conference of the IEEE Engineering in Medicine and Biology Society.* IEEE. doi:10.1109/EMBC.2013.6610135

Coetzee, L., & Eksteen, J. (2011). The internet of things - Promise for the future? An introduction. In *Proceedings of 1st-Africa Conference, 2011* (pp. 1–9). IEEE.

Coleman, J. S., Katz, E., Menzel, H., & Columbia University. Bureau of Applied Social Research. (1966). *Medical innovation: A diffusion study.* Bobbs-Merrill Company.

Collier, R., O'Hare, G., Lowen, T., & Rooney, C. (2003). *Beyond prototyping in the factory of agents. In Multi-Agent Systems and Applications III* (pp. 383–393). Springer.

Collopy, F. (2000). Color, Form, and Motion: Dimensions of a Musical Art of Light. *Leonardo*, *33*(5), 355–360. doi:10.1162/002409400552829

Condell, J., Curran, K., Quigley, T., Gardiner, P., McNeill, M., Winder, J., et al. (2012). Finger Movement Measurements in Arthritic Patients Using Wearable Sensor Enabled Gloves. *International Journal of Human Factors Modelling and Simulation, 2*(4), 276-292. DOI: 10.1504/IJHFMS.2011.045000

Condell, J., Curran, K., Quigley, T., Gardiner, P., McNeill, M., Winder, J., & Connolly, J. (2010). *Finger Movement Measurements in Arthritic Patients Using Wearable Sensor Enabled Gloves.* University of Ulster.

Conger, S. (2011). Software Development Life Cycles and Methodologies: Fixing the Old and Adopting the New. *International Journal of Information Technologies and Systems Approach*, *8*(3), 1–22. doi:10.4018/jitsa.2011010101

Connolly, C., & Evans, K. (2013). *Cracked Ray Tube.* Retrieved August 28, 2013 from: http://crackedraytube.com/

Cook, D. (2006). Health monitoring and assistance to support aging in place. *Journal of Universal Computer Science*, *12*(1), 15–29.

Cook, D. J., Augusto, J. C., & Jakkula, V. R. (2009). Ambient intelligence: Technologies, applications, and opportunities. *Pervasive and Mobile Computing*, *5*(4), 277–298. doi:10.1016/j.pmcj.2009.04.001

Cook, D. J., Youngblood, M., & Das, S. K. (2006). *A multi-agent approach to controlling a smart environment. In Designing smart homes* (pp. 165–182). Springer.

Cooke, M., & Buckley, N. (2008). Web 2.0, social networks and the future of market research. *International Journal of Market Research*, *50*(2), 267.

Coote, S., Murphy, B., Harwin, W., & Stokes, E. (2008). The effect of the GENTLE/s robot-mediated therapy system on arm function after stroke. *Clinical Rehabilitation*, *22*(5), 395–405. doi:10.1177/0269215507085060 PMID:18441036

Corchado, J. M., Bajo, J., de Paz, Y., & Tapia, D. I. (2008). Intelligent Environment for Monitoring Alzheimer Patients, Agent Technology for Health Care. *Decision Support Systems*, *44*(2), 382–396. doi:10.1016/j.dss.2007.04.008

Coronato, A., & De Pietro, G. (2010). Formal design of ambient intelligence applications. *Computer*, *43*(12), 60–68. doi:10.1109/MC.2010.335

Coronato, A., & De Pietro, G. (2011, July). Tools for the Rapid Prototyping of Provably Correct Ambient Intelligence Applications. *IEEE Transactions on Software Engineering*, 20.

Costantini, G., Saggio, G., & Todisco, M. (2010). A data glove based sensor interface to expressively control musical processes. In *Proceedings of International Conference on Sensor Device Technologies and Applications*, (pp. 217-220). Academic Press.

Crossan, A., Brewster, S., & Ng, A. (2010). Foot Tapping for Mobile Interaction. In *Proceedings of the 24th BCS Interaction Specialist Group Conference* (pp. 418-422). Swinton, UK: British Computer Society. Retrieved from http://dl.acm.org/citation.cfm?id=2146303.2146366

Crystal, D. (2011). Dictionary of linguistics and phonetics (6th ed.). Oxford, UK: Wiley-Blackwell.

Cui, Y., Nahrstedt, K., & Xu, D. (2004). Seamless user-level handoff in ubiquitous multimedia service delivery. *Multimedia Tools and Applications*, *22*(2), 137–170. doi:10.1023/B:MTAP.0000011932.28891.a0

Curiac, D., Volosencu, C., Pescaru, D., Jurca, L., & Doboli, A. (2009). A view upon redundancy in wireless sensor networks. In *Proceedings of the 8th WSEAS International Conference on Signal Processing, Robotics and Automation (ISPRA'09).* WSEAS.

Cycling '74. (2013). *Max/MSP/Jitter* [Programming language]. Author.

Danneberg, R. (2005). Interactive Visual Music: A Personal Perspective. *Computer Music Journal, 29*(4).

DAS Booklet - Quick reference guide for Healthcare Professionals. (2010, February). Retrieved December 08, 2011, from National Rheumatoid Arthritis Society: http://www.nras.org.uk/includes/documents/cm_docs/2010/d/das_quick_reference.pdf

Das, A. S., Datar, M., Garg, A., & Rajaram, S. (2007). *Google news personalization: scalable online collaborative filtering*. Paper presented at the 16th international conference on World Wide Web. Banff, Canada doi:10.1145/1242572.1242610

de Kraker, M., Selles, R., Molenaar, T., Schreuders, A., Hovius, S., & Stam, H. (2009). Palmar Abduction Measurements: Reliability and Introduction of Normative Data in Healthy Children. *The Journal of Hand Surgery, 8*(4), 1704–1708. doi:10.1016/j.jhsa.2009.06.011 PMID:19762165

Dellon, B., & Matsuoka, Y. (2007). Prosthetics, exoskeletons, and rehabilitation[Grand Challenges of Robotics]. *IEEE Robotics & Automation Magazine, 14*(1), 30–34. doi:10.1109/MRA.2007.339622

Dempster, A. (1967). Upper and lower probabilities induced by a multivalued mapping. *Annals of Mathematical Statistics, 38*(2), 325–339.

Dennett, D. C. (1987). *The intentional stance*. The MIT Press.

Department for Education. (2008). *Statutory Framework for the Early Years Foundation Stage: Setting the Standards for Learning, Development and Care for children from birth to five*. Retrieved from https://www.education.gov.uk/publications/eOrderingDownload/00267-2008BKT-EN.pdf

Department of Defense – USA (1980). *Us mil std 1629 1980: Procedure for performing a failure mode, effect and criticality analysis, method 102*. Author.

Department of Education for Northern Ireland (DENI). (1997). *Curricular Guidance for Pre-School Education*. Retrieved from http://www.deni.gov.uk/preschool_curricular-2.pdf

Devot, S., Bianchi, A. M., Naujokat, E., Mendez, M. O., Brauers, A., & Cerutti, S. (2007). Sleep Monitoring Through a Textile Recording System. In *Proceedings of the 29th Annual International Conference of the IEEE Engineering in Medicine and Biology Society (EMBS)*, (pp. 2560-2563). EMBS.

Dey, A. K., & Abowd, G. D. (1999). *Towards a better understanding of context and context-awareness* (Tech. Rep. No. GIT-GVU-99-22). College of Computing, Georgia Institute of Technology.

Dey, A. K. (2001). Understanding and Using Context. *Personal and Ubiquitous Computing, 5*(1), 4–7. doi:10.1007/s007790170019

Dicks, K. E. (2007). *Telemedicine 2.0 has arrived. Future Healthcare Magazine*.

Dillenbourg, P. (1999). What do you mean by "Collaborative Learning"? In *Collaborative Learning. Cognitive and Computational Approaches* (pp. 1–19). Oxford, UK: Elsevier Science Ltd.

DiNucci, D. (1999). Fragmented future. *Print, 53*(4), 32–33.

Dipietro, L., Sabatini, A., & Dario, P. (2008). A Survey of Glove-Based Systems and Their Applications. *IEEE Transactions on Systems, Man and Cybernetics. Part C, Applications and Reviews, 22*(4), 461–482. doi:10.1109/TSMCC.2008.923862

Disney, W. (Producer), Sharpsteen, B. (Producer), Ferguson, N. (Director), Algar, J. (Director), Armstrong, S. (Director), Beebe, F. (Director),…Sharpsteen, B. (Director). (1940). *Fantasia* [Motion picture]. USA: Walt Disney Pictures.

Dolan, P., Adams, M. A., & Hutton, W. C. (1988). Commonly adopted postures and their effect on the lumbar spine. *Spine, 13*, 197–201. PMID:3406840

Dolin, R. H., Alschuler, L., Boyer, S., Beebe, C., Behlen, F. M., Biron, P. V., & Shvo, A. S. (2006). HL7 Clinical Document Architecture, Release 2. *Journal of the American Medical Informatics Association, 13*(1), 30–39. doi:10.1197/jamia.M1888 PMID:16221939

Doukas, C., & Maglogiannis, I. (2008). Intelligent Pervasive Healthcare Systems. In M. Sordo, S. Vaidya, & L. Jain (Eds.), *Advanced Computational Intelligence Paradigms in Healthcare - 3* (Vol. 107, pp. 95–115). Springer Berlin Heidelberg. Retrieved from; doi:10.1007/978-3-540-77662-8_5

Dourish, P. (2004). What we talk about when we talk about context. *Personal and Ubiquitous Computing, 8*(1), 19–30. doi:10.1007/s00779-003-0253-8

Draves, S. (2013a). *Electric Sheep*. Retrieved August 27, 2013 from: http://www.electricsheep.org/

Draves, S. (2013b). *Scott Draves: Software Artist*. Retrieved August 27, 2013 from: http://scottdraves.com/

Driver, C., & Clarke, S. (2008). An application framework for mobile, context-aware trails. *Pervasive and Mobile Computing, 4*(5), 719–736. doi:10.1016/j.pmcj.2008.04.009

Dubois, D., & Prade, H. (1980). *Fuzzy Sets and Systems: Theory and Applications*. London: Academic Press.

Duman, H., Hagras, H., & Callaghan, V. (2010). A multi-society-based intelligent association discovery and selection for ambient intelligence environment. ACM Trans. Autonom. Adapt. Syst., 5(2).

Dumaresq, T., & Villenueve, M. (2010). *Test Strategies for Smartphones and Mobile Devices*. Mississauga, Canada: Macadamian Technologies.

Duong, T., Bui, H., Phung, D., & Venkatesh, S. (2005). Activity recognition and abnormality detection with the switching hidden semi-Markov model. In *Proceedings of IEEE Computer Society Conference on Computer Vision and Pattern Recognition* (pp. 838–845). Los Alamitos, CA: IEEE Computer Society.

Durfee, W. K., Weinstein, S. A., Carey, J. R., Bhatt, E., & Nagpal, A. (2005). Home stroke telerehabilitation system to train recovery of hand function. In *Proceedings of the 2005 IEEE 9th International Conference on Rehabilitation Robotics*. IEEE. doi:10.1109/ICORR.2005.1501118

Dwivedi, H., Clark, C., & Thiel, D. (2010). *Mobile Application Security*. New York: McGraw-Hill.

Eames, C., & Milne, L. (2011). Teacher responses to a planning framework for junior technology classes learning outside the classroom. *Education: An International Journal, 16*(2), 33–44.

Eberhardt, K., Malcus-Johnson, P., & Rydgren, L. (1991). The Occurence and Significance of Hand Deformities in Early Rheumatoid Arthritis. *British Journal of Rheumatology, 34*(5), 211–213. doi:10.1093/rheumatology/30.3.211 PMID:2049583

Edwards, J. (2009). Cutting Through the fog of Cloud Security. *Computerworld*. Retrieved from http://www.computerworld.com/article/2550812/security0/cutting-through-the-fog-of-cloud-security.html

Egglestone, S. R., Axelrod, L., Nind, T., Turk, R., Wilkinson, A., Burridge, J., et al. (2009). A design framework for a home-based stroke rehabilitation system: Identifying the key components. In *Proceedings of 3rd International Conference on Pervasive Computing Technologies for Healthcare*. Academic Press. doi:10.4108/ICST.PERVASIVEHEALTH2009.6049

Eisenhauer, M., Rosengren, P., & Antolin, P. (2010). *Hydra: A development platform for integrating wireless devices and sensors into ambient intelligence systems. In The Internet of Things* (pp. 367–373). Springer.

ElHelw, M., Pansiot, J., McIlwraith, D., Ali, R., Lo, B., & Atallah, L. (2009). An Integrated Multi-sensing Framework for Pervasive Healthcare Monitoring. In *Pervasive Computing Technologies for Healthcare,* (pp. 1–7). Academic Press. doi:10.4108/ICST.PERVASIVEHEALTH2009.6038

Ellis, E. V., Gonzalez, E. W., & McEachron, D. L. (2013). Chronobioengineering indoor lighting to enhance facilities for ageing and Alzheimer's disorder. *Intelligent Buildings International, 5*(sup1), 48–60. doi:10.1080/17508975.2013.807764

Ellis, K., & Barca, J. C. (2012). *Exploring Sensor Gloves for Teaching Children Sign Language*. Advances in Human-Computer Interactions.

ElSayed, M., Alsebai, A., Salaheldin, A., El Gayar, N., & ElHelw, M. (2010). Ambient and Wearable Sensing for Gait Classification in Pervasive Healthcare Environments. In *Proceedings of e-Health Networking Applications and Services (Healthcom)*, (pp. 240–245). IEEE. doi:10.1109/HEALTH.2010.5556563

Erétéo, G., Gandon, F., Corby, O., & Buffa, M. (2009b). Semantic social network analysis. *Cornell University Library,* (arXiv:0904.3701)

Eßer, A., Kamper, A., Franke, M., Möst, D., & Rentz, O. (2007). *Scheduling of electrical household appliances with price signals. In Operations Research Proceedings 2006* (pp. 253–258). Springer.

Evans, K. (2009). *Electronically Modified Didgeridoo Kyle Evans* [Video]. Retrieved August 28, 2013 from: http://www.youtube.com/watch?v=d1VB1vA-UsI

Facebook Statistics. (2013). *Facebook statistics 2013*. Retrieved June 11, 2013 from http://newsroom.fb.com/content/default.aspx?NewsAreaId=22

Farmer, A. D., Bruckner Holt, C. E. M., Cook, M. J., & Hearing, S. D. (2009). Social networking sites: A novel portal for communication. *Postgraduate Medical Journal, 85*(1007), 455–459. doi:10.1136/pgmj.2008.074674 PMID:19734511

Faruqui, A., Sergici, S., & Sharif, A. (2010). The impact of informational feedback on energy consumption—A survey of the experimental evidence. *Energy, 35*(4), 1598–1608.

Fees, E. (1987). A method for checking Jamar dynamometer calibration. *Journal of Hand Therapy, 16*(1), 28–32. doi:10.1016/S0894-1130(87)80009-1

Fern'ndez-Baena, A., Susin, A., & Lligadas, X. (2012). Biomechanical Validation of Upper-Body and Lower-Body Joint Movements of Kinect Motion Capture Data for Rehabilitation Treatments. In *Proceedings of 2012 4th International Conference on Intelligent Networking and Collaborative Systems*. Academic Press. doi:10.1109/iNCoS.2012.66

Ferraiolo, D., & Kuhn, R. (1992). Role-Based Access Control. In *Proceedings of 15th NIST-NCSC National Computer Security Conference* (pp. 554–563). NIST-NCSC.

Fess, E. (1995). Documentation: Essential elements of an upper extremity assessment battery. In J. Hunter, E. Mackin, & A. Calahan (Eds.), *Rehabilitation of the hand: Surgery and therapy* (4th ed., pp. 185–214). St. Louis, MO: Mosby.

Fields, K. (2012). Syneme: Live. *Organised Sound, 17*(01), 86–95.

Figueiro, M. G. (2008). A proposed 24 h lighting scheme for older adults. *Lighting Research & Technology, 40*(2), 153–160. doi:10.1177/1477153507087299

Fischman, R. (2011). Back to the Parlour. *Sonic Ideas/Ideas Sonicas, 3*(2).

Fleck, S., & Straßer, W. (2008). Smart camera based monitoring system and its application to assisted living. *Proceedings of the IEEE, 96*(10), 1698–1714. doi:10.1109/JPROC.2008.928765

Fling, B. (2009). *Mobile Design and Development*. Cambridge, MA: O'Reilly Publishers.

Fogarty, J., & Hudson, S. E. (2004). *GADGET: A Toolkit for Optimization-based Approaches to Interface and Display Generation. In ACM SIGGRAPH 2004 Papers* (pp. 730–730). New York: ACM. doi:10.1145/1186562.1015789

Fogg, B. J. (2003). *Persuasive Technology: Using Computers to Change What We Think and Do*. Academic Press.

Forbes, D., Culum, I., Lischka, A. R., Morgan, D. G., Peacock, S., Forbes, J., & Forbes, S. (2009). Light therapy for managing cognitive, sleep, behavioural, or psychiatric disturbances in dementia. *Cochrane Database of Systematic Reviews*, CD003946. PMID:19821317

Fox-Turnbull, W., & Snape, P. (2011) Technology teacher education through a constructivist approach. Design and Technology Education: An International Journal, 16(2).

Fragopoulos, A., Gialelis, J., & Serpanos, D. (2009). Security Framework for Pervasive Healthcare Architectures Utilizing MPEG-21 IPMP Components. *International Journal of Telemedicine and Applications*, 2009. PMID:19132095

Freedman, R. R., & Roehrs, T. A. (2006). Effects of REM sleep and ambient temperature on hot flash-induces sleep disturbance. *Menopause (New York, N.Y.)*, *13*, 576–583. PMID:16837879

Freeman, L. C. (1979). Centrality in social networks conceptual clarification. *Social Networks*, *1*(3), 215–239. doi:10.1016/0378-8733(78)90021-7

Freksa, C. (1992). Temporal reasoning based on semi-intervals. *Artificial Intelligence*, *54*, 199–227.

Friedrich, D., Aubert, X. L., Führ, H., & Brauers, A. (2010). Heart rate estimation on a beat-to-beat basis via ballistocardiography – a hybrid approach. In *Proceedings of the 32nd Annual International Conference of the IEEE Engineering in Medicine and Biology Society (EMBS)*, (pp. 4048-4051). EMBS.

Fries, J., Spitz, P., Kraines, R., & Holman, H. (1980). Measurement of patient outcome in arthritis. *Arthritis and Rheumatism*, *14*(3), 137–145. doi:10.1002/art.1780230202 PMID:7362664

Fruchter, R. (2001a). Higher Education Management and Policy. *Journal of the Programme on Institutional Management in Higher Education*, *17*(2). Retrieved from http://www.oecd.org/dataoecd/53/61/42348396.pdf

Fruchter, R. (2001). Dimensions of Teamwork Education. *International Journal of Engineering Education*, *17*(4), 34–42.

Fuggetta, A., Picco, G. P., & Vigna, G. (1998). Understanding code mobility. *IEEE Transactions on Software Engineering*, *24*(5), 342–361. doi:10.1109/32.685258

Furuya, M., Sterling, R., Bleha, W., & Inoue, Y. (2009). D-ILA® Full Resolution 8K Projector. In *Proceedings of SMPTE Conferences*, (pp. 1-9). Society of Motion Picture and Television Engineers.

Gajos, K. Z., Weld, D. S., & Wobbrock, J. O. (2010, August). Automatically Generating Personalized User Interfaces with Supple. *Artificial Intelligence*, *174*(12-13), 910-950. doi:10.1016/j.artint.2010.05.005

Gajos, K., & Weld, D. S. (2004). *SUPPLE: Automatically Generating User Interfaces. In Proceedings of the 9th International Conference on Intelligent User Interfaces* (pp. 93–100). New York: ACM. doi:10.1145/964460.964461

Gandy, M., Starner, T., Auxier, J., & Ashbrook, D. (2000). The Gesture Pendant: A Self-illuminating, Wearable, Infrared Computer Vision System for Home Automation Control and Medical Monitoring. In *Proceedings of 2012 16th International Symposium on Wearable Computers*. Academic Press.

García, Ó., Tapia, D. I., Alonso, R. S., Rodríguez, S., & Corchado, J. M. (2011). Ambient intelligence and collaborative e-learning: A new definition model. *Journal of Ambient Intelligence and Humanized Computing*.

Garcia-Morchon, O., Falck, T., Heer, T., & Wehrle, K. (2009). Security for Pervasive Medical Sensor Networks. In Proceedings of Mobile and Ubiquitous Systems: Networking Services, MobiQuitous, (pp. 1–10). Academic Press. doi:10.4108/ICST.MOBIQUITOUS2009.6832

Gardner, H. (1983). *Frames of mind: The theory of multiple intelligences*. New York: Basic Books.

Garro, D. (2010). *Patah* [Video]. Retrieved August 27, 2013 from: https://vimeo.com/14112798

Gartner. (2012). *Forecast: PC Installed Base, Worldwide, 2004-2012*. Gartner, Inc. Retrieved from http://www.gartner.com/newsroom/id/703807

Geere, D. (2010). 'Neurosonics Live' brings holograms to live music. *Wired*. Retrieved November 17, 2013 from: http://www.wired.co.uk/news/archive/2010-03/03/neurosonics-live-brings-holograms-to-live-music

Gelernter, D. (1985, January). Generative communication in Linda. *ACM Transactions on Programming Languages and Systems*, *7*(1), 80–112. doi:10.1145/2363.2433

Georgalis, Y., Grammenos, D., & Stephanidis, C. (2009). Middleware for Ambient Intelligence Environments: Reviewing Requirements and Communication Technologies. In *Proceedings of the 5th International on ConferenceUniversal Access in Human-Computer Interaction. Part II: Intelligent and Ubiquitous Interaction Environments (UAHCI '09)*. Springer-Verlag.

GigE Vision for 3D Medical Research. (2010, May 13). Retrieved from Allied Vision Technologies: http://www.alliedvisiontec.com/us/products/applications/application-case-study/article/gige-vision-for-3d-medical-research.html

Gill, K., Yang, S.-H., Yao, F., & Lu, X. (2009). A ZigBee-based home automation system. *IEEE Transactions on Consumer Electronics*, *55*(2), 422–430.

Gladstone, D. J., Danells, C. J., & Black, S. E. (2002). The fugl-meyer assessment of motor recovery after stroke: A critical review of its measurement properties. *Neurorehabilitation and Neural Repair*, *16*(3), 232–240. doi:10.1177/154596802401105171 PMID:12234086

Glahn, C., & Börner, D. (2010). Mobile informal learning. In A report from the STELLAR Alpine Rendez-Vous workshop series (pp. 28–31). Nottingham, UK: Academic Press.

Glowacki, D., Tew, P., Mitchell, T., Hyde, J., Kriefman, L., Asano, M. ... Thomas, L.M. (2013). Hidden Fields / Danceroom Spectroscopy [Multimedia performance]. Performed at Seeing Sound 2013, Bath Spa University, November 23, 2013.

Golbeck, J., & Rothstein, M. (2008). Linking social networks on the web with foaf: A semantic web case study. *AAAI*, 1138–1143.

Golbeck, J. (2007). The dynamics of web-based social networks: Membership, relationships, and change. *First Monday*, *12*(11). doi:10.5210/fm.v12i11.2023

Goldsmith, R., & Hampton, I. F. (1968). Nocturnal microclimate of man. *The Journal of Physiology*, *194*, 32P–33P. PMID:5639779

Gómez-Sánchez, E., Bote-Lorenzo, M. L., Jorrín-Abellán, I. M., Vega-Gorgojo, G., Asensio-Pérez, J. I., & Dimitriadis, Y. A. (2009). Conceptual framework for design, technological support and evaluation of collaborative learning. *International Journal of Engineering Education*, *25*(3), 557–568.

González, G., Rosa, J. L. d. l., Dugdale, J., Pavard, B., Jed, M. E., Pallamin, N., . . . Klann, M. (2006). *Towards Ambient Recommender Systems: Results of New Cross-disciplinary Trends*. Paper presented at the Workshop on Recommender Systems in European Conference on Artificial Intelligence on Recommender Systems. Riva del Garda, Italy.

Gopalratnam, K., & Cook, D. (2004). Active LeZi: An incremental parsing algorithm for sequential prediction. *International Journal of Artificial Intelligence Tools*, *14*(1–2), 917–930.

Gracovetsky, S. A. (1987). The Resting Spine – A conceptual Approach to the Avoidance of Spinal Reinjury During Rest. *Physical Therapy*, *67*, 549–553. PMID:2951749

Gradisar, M., & Lack, L. (2004). Relationships between the circadian rhythms of finger temperature, core temperature, sleep latency, and subjective sleepiness. *Journal of Biological Rhythms*, *19*(2), 157–163. PMID:15038855

Granovetter, M. S. (1973). The strength of weak ties. *Ajs*, *78*(6), 1360.

Grenning, J. (2007). *Agile Embedded Software Development*. Paper presented at the Embedded Systems Conference. San Jose, CA. Retrieved from http://www.renaissancesoftware.net/files/articles/ESC-349Paper_Grenning-v1r2.pdf

Gringrich, O., Reaud, A., & Emets, E. (2013). KIMA – A Holographic Telepresence Environment Based on Cymatic Principles. *Leonardo*, *46*(4).

Groening, M. (Writer), Cohen, D.X. (Writer), Kaplan, E. (Writer), & Avanzino, P. (Director). (2001). Parasites Lost [Television series episode]. In Cohen, D. (Executive producer), & Groening, M. (Executive producer) Futurama. USA: 20th Century Fox Television.

Groening, M. (Writer), Cohen, D.X. (Writer), Keeler, K. (Writer), & Haaland, B. (Director). (2001). The Devil's Hands are Idle Playthings [Television series episode]. In Cohen, D. (Executive producer), & Groening, M (Executive producer) Futurama. USA: 20th Century Fox Television.

Gross, H., Schroeter, C., Mueller, S., Volkhardt, M., Einhorn, E., Bley, A., et al. (2011). Progress in developing a socially assistive mobile home robot companion for the elderly with mild cognitive impairment. In *Proceedings of 2011 IEEE/RSJ International Conference on Intelligent Robots and Systems (IROS)*. IEEE. doi:10.1109/IROS.2011.6094770

Gross, R., Acquisti, A., & Heinz, H. J. III. (2005). Information revelation and privacy in online social networks. In *Proceedings of the 2005 ACM Workshop on Privacy in the Electronic Society*. ACM. doi:10.1145/1102199.1102214

Gruber, T. (2008). Collective knowledge systems: Where the social web meets the semantic web. *Web Semantics: Science, Services, and Agents on the World Wide Web*, *6*(1), 4–13. doi:10.1016/j.websem.2007.11.011

Guarino, N. (1998). *Formal ontology in information systems*. Amsterdam: IOS Press.

Gungor, V. C., Sahin, D., Kocak, T., Ergut, S., Buccella, C., Cecati, C., & Hancke, G. P. (2011). Smart grid technologies: communication technologies and standards. *IEEE Transactions on Industrial Informatics, 7*(4), 529-539.

Guo, S., & Song, Z. (2008). VR-based active rehabilitation system for upper limbs. In *Proceedings of IEEE International Conference on Automation and Logistics*, (pp. 1077-1082). IEEE. doi:10.1109/ICMA.2008.4798757

Guohua, L., Jianqi, W., Yu, Y., & Xijing, J. (2007). Study of the Ballistocardiogram signal in life detection system based on radar. In *Proceedings of the 29th Annual International Conference of the IEEE Engineering in Medicine and Biology Society (EMBS)*, (pp. 2191-2194). EMBS.

Gupta, S. K. S., Mukherjee, T., & Venkatasubramanian, K. (2006). Criticality Aware Access Control Model for Pervasive Applications. In *Proceedings of Pervasive Computing and Communications*. IEEE. doi:10.1109/PERCOM.2006.19

Gurevich, M. (2006). JamSpace: designing a collaborative networked music space for novices. In *Proceedings of the 2006 conference on New interfaces for musical expression*, (pp. 118-123). IRCAM—Centre Pompidou.

Haex, B. (2004). *Back and Bed: Ergonomic Aspects of Sleeping*. Boca Raton, FL: CRC Press.

Hailey, D., Roine, R., Ohinmaa, A., & Dennett, L. (2011). Evidence of benefit from telerehabilitation in routine care: A systematic review. *Journal of Telemedicine and Telecare*, *17*(6), 281–287. doi:10.1258/jtt.2011.101208 PMID:21844172

Hakoama, M., & Hakoyama, S. (2011). The impact of cell phone use on social networking and development among college students. *The American Association of Behavioral and Social Sciences Journal*, *15*(1), 58–66.

Halko, S., & Kientz, J. A. (2010). Personality and Persuasive Technology: An Exploratory Study on Health-promoting Mobile Applications. In *Proceedings of the 5th International Conference on Persuasive Technology* (pp. 150–161). Berlin: Springer-Verlag. doi:10.1007/978-3-642-13226-1_16

Hall, E. C. (1996). *Journey to the Moon: The History of the Apollo Guidance Computer*. American Institute of Aeronautics and Astronautics.

Hall, M., Vasko, R., Buysse, D., Ombao, H., Chen, Q., & Cashmere, J. D. et al. (2004). Acute stress affects heart rate variability during sleep. *Psychosomatic Medicine*, *66*(1), 56–62. PMID:14747638

Halperin, D., Kohno, T., Heydt-Benjamin, T. S., Fu, K., & Maisel, W. H. (2008). Security and Privacy for Implantable Medical Devices. *IEEE Pervasive Computing*, *7*(1), 30–39. doi:10.1109/MPRV.2008.16

Hamilton, A., Balnave, R., & Adams, R. (1994). Grip strength testing reliability. *Journal of Hand Therapy*, *7*(3), 163–170. doi:10.1016/S0894-1130(12)80058-5 PMID:7951708

Han, D.-M., & Lim, J.-H. (2010). Smart home energy management system using IEEE 802.15. 4 and ZigBee. *IEEE Transactions on* Consumer Electronics, *56*(3), 1403–1410.

Handout on Health: Rheumatoid Arthritis. (2009). Retrieved from National Institute of Arthritis and Musculoskeletal and Skin Diseases: http://www.niams.nih.gov/Health_Info/Rheumatic_Disease/default.asp

Hanna, S. (2009). Regulations and standards for wireless medical applications. In *Proc. of the 3rd Int. Symp. on Medical Information and Communication Technology.* Academic Press.

Hanneman, R. A., & Riddle, M. (2005). *Introduction to Social Network Methods.* Riverside, CA: University of California.

Hansen, T. R., Bardram, J. E., & Soegaard, M. (2006). Moving Out of the Lab: Deploying Pervasive Technologies in a Hospital. *IEEE Pervasive Computing, 5*(3), 24–31. doi:10.1109/MPRV.2006.53

Hanson, M., Powell, H., Barth, A., Ringgenberg, K., Calhoun, B., Aylor, J., & Lach, J. (2009). Body area sensor networks: Challenges and opportunities. *Computer, 42*(1), 58–65. doi:10.1109/MC.2009.5

Hao, Y., & Foster, R. (2008). Wireless body sensor networks for health-monitoring applications. *Physiological Measurement, 29*(11), R27–R56. doi:10.1088/0967-3334/29/11/R01 PMID:18843167

Harada, T., Mori, T., Nishida, Y., Yoshimi, T., & Sato, T. (1999) Body parts positions and posture estimation system based on pressure distribution image. In *Proc. IEEE Int. Conf. Robot. Autom,* (pp. 968-975). IEEE.

Harmonix. (2005). *Guitar Hero* [video game]. Author.

Harms, H., Amft, O., Roggen, D., & Tröster, G. (2009). Rapid prototyping of smart garments for activity-aware applications. *Journal of Ambient Intelligence and Smart Environments, 1*, 87–101. doi:10.3233/AIS-2009-0015

Hassani, W., Mohammed, S., Rifaï, H., & Amirat, Y. (2014). Powered orthosis for lower limb movements assistance and rehabilitation. *Control Engineering Practice, 26*, 245–253. doi:10.1016/j.conengprac.2014.02.002

Hattler, M., & Kispert, M. (2013). Feeding You [Audiovisual performance]. Performed at Seeing Sound 2013, Bath Spa University, November 24, 2013.

Hazas, M., Friday, A., & Scott, J. (2011). Look back before leaping forward: Four decades of domestic energy inquiry. *IEEE Pervasive Computing, 10*(1), 13–19.

Heierman, E. O., III, & Cook, D. J. (2003). *Improving home automation by discovering regularly occurring device usage patterns.* Paper presented at the Data Mining, 2003. Washington, DC.

Heise, D., Rosales, L., Sheahen, M., Su, B., & Skubic, M. (2013). Non-invasive measurement of heartbeat with a hydraulic bed sensor: Progress, challenges and opportunities. In *Proceedings of the 2013 IEEE International Instrumentation and Measurement Technology Conference (I2MTC),* (pp. 397-402). IEEE.

Hertzum, M., & Hornbæk, K. (2010). How Age Affects Pointing With Mouse and Touchpad: A Comparison of Young, Adult, and Elderly Users. *International Journal of Human-Computer Interaction, 26*(7), 703–734. doi:10.1080/10447318.2010.487198

Hinckley, K., Pierce, J., Sinclair, M., & Horvitz, E. (2000). Sensing techniques for mobile interaction. In *Proceedings of the 13th Annual ACM Symposium on User Interface Software and Technology* (pp. 91–100). New York, NY: ACM. doi:10.1145/354401.354417

Hobley, S. (2008). *Laser Harp Fully Functional* [Video]. Retrieved August 28, 2013 from: http://www.youtube.com/watch?v=sLVXmsbVwUs

Hoggan, E., & Brewster, S. (2007). *Designing Audio and Tactile Crossmodal Icons for Mobile Devices. In Proceedings of the 9th International Conference on Multimodal Interfaces* (pp. 162–169). New York: ACM. http://doi.acm.org/10.1145/1322192.1322222

Hojgaard-Hansen, K., Nguyen, H. C., & Schwefel, H. (2011). Session mobility solution for client-based application migration scenarios. In *Proceedings of the Eighth International Conference on Wireless On-Demand Network Systems and Services* (pp. 76–83). IEEE.

Holophonor: Futurama Wiki. (n.d.). Retrieved August 28, 2013 from the Futurama Wiki: http://futurama.wikia.com/wiki/Holophonor

Holzer, A., & Ondrus, J. (2009). Trends in Mobile Application Development. In C. Hesselman, C. Giannelli, O. Akan, P. Bellavista, J. Cao, F. Dressler, D. Ferrari, et al. (Eds.), Mobile Wireless Middleware, Operating Systems, and Applications – Workshops, (Vol. 12, pp. 55-64). Springer Berlin Heidelberg.

Höök, K., & Löwgren, J. (2012). Strong concepts: Intermediate-level knowledge in interaction design research. *ACM Trans. Comput.-Hum. Interact., 19*(3), 23:1–23:18.

Hoque, E., Dickerson, R. F., & Stankovic, J. A. (2010). *Monitoring body positions and movements during sleep using WISPs.* Paper presented at the WH '10 Wireless Health 2010. New York, NY.

Howlett, L. (Music), & Hyperbolic Systems (Video artist). (1993). *Prodigy: One Love* [Video]. Retrieved August 27, 2013 from: http://www.youtube.com/watch?v=-noCS_dtZMg

Huang, E. M., Koster, A., & Borchers, J. (2009). *Overcoming Assumptions and Uncovering Practices: When Does the Public Really Look at Public Displays?* Paper presented at the 6th International Conference on Pervasive Computing. Sydney, Australia.

Huang, J.-Y., & Tsai, C.-H. (2008). Improve gps positioning accuracy with context awareness. In *Proceedings of Ubi-Media Computing,* (pp. 94–99). IEEE.

Huang, K., Starner, T., Do, E., Weiberg, G., Kohlsdorf, D., Ahlrichs, C., & Leibrandt, R. (2010). *Mobile Music Touch: Mobile Tactile Stimulation for Passive Learning. In Proceedings of the SIGCHI Conference on Human Factors in Computing Systems* (pp. 791–800). New York, NY: ACM. doi:10.1145/1753326.1753443

Huang, Y.-C., Hu, C.-J., Lee, T.-H., Yang, J.-T., Weng, H.-H., Lin, L. C., & Lai, S.-L. (2013). The Impact Factors on the Cost and Length of Stay among Acute Ischemic Stroke. *Journal of Stroke and Cerebrovascular Diseases, 22*(7), e152–e158. doi:10.1016/j.jstrokecerebrovasdis.2012.10.014 PMID:23253537

Huber, M., Rabin, B., Docan, C., Burdea, G., Nwosu, M. E., AbdelBaky, M., & Golomb, M. R. (2008). PlayStation 3-based tele-rehabilitation for children with hemiplegia. In Proceedings of Virtual Rehabilitation. Academic Press. doi:10.1109/ICVR.2008.4625145

Hunter, D. R., Goodreau, S. M., & Handcock, M. S. (2008). Goodness of fit of social network models. *Journal of the American Statistical Association, 103*(481), 248–258. doi:10.1198/016214507000000446

Hussain, S., Schaffner, S., & Moseychuck, D. (2009). *Applications of wireless sensor networks and RFID in a smart home environment.* Paper presented at the Communication Networks and Services Research Conference. New York, NY.

Hwang, T., Park, H., & Chung, J. W. (2006). Desktop migration system based on dynamic linking of application specific libraries. In *Proceedings of Advanced Communication Technology,* (Vol. 3, pp. 1586–1588). ICACT.

Hwang, G.-J., Yang, T.-C., Tsai, C.-C., & Yang, S. J. H. (2009). A context-aware ubiquitous learning environment for conducting complex science experiments. *Computers & Education, 53*(2), 402–413. doi:10.1016/j.compedu.2009.02.016

Iber, C., Ancoli-Israel, S., Chesson, A. L., & Quan, S. F. (2007). *The AASM Manual for the Scoring of Sleep and Associated Events.* Westchester, IL: American Academy of Sleep Medicine.

IEEE. (1991). IEEE Standard Computer Dictionary. A Compilation of IEEE Standard Computer Glossaries. *IEEE Std, 610.* doi:10.1109/IEEESTD.1991.106963

Ikeshiro, R. (2013). Construction in Kneading [Audiovisual performance]. Performed at Seeing Sound 2013, Bath Spa University, November 24, 2013.

Indieszero. (2005). *Electroplankton* [Video game]. Nintendo DS.

Institute of Public Health Ireland. (2012). *Stroke Briefing.* Retrieved from www.publichealth.ie

Internet World Stats. (2013). *Internet users in Europe*. Retrieved May 16, 2012from http://www.internetworld-stats.com/stats4.htm

Interval Studios. (2010). *Thicket* [Mobile application]. iOS. Retrieved August 28, 2013 from: http://www.youtube.com/watch?v=I8XklLnZ7rs

ITU. (2002, March). *Itu-t recommendation h.510, mobility and collaboration procedures: mobility for h-series multimedia systems and services*. Retrieved from http://www.itu.int/rec/dologin\pub.asp?lang=e\&id=T-REC-H.510-200203-I!!PDF-E\&type=items

ITU. (2014, September). *ICT statistics*. Retrieved from http://www.itu.int/itu-d/statistics/

Ivlev, O., Martens, C., & Graeser, A. (2005). Rehabilitation Robots FRIEND-I and FRIEND-II with the dexterous lightweight manipulator. *Technology and Disability, 17*, 111–123.

Izadi, S., Brignull, H., Rodden, T., Rogers, Y., & Underwood, M. (2003, November). *Dynamo: A public interactive surface supporting the cooperative sharing and exchange of media*. Paper presented at the Symposium on User Interface Software and Technology. Vancouver, Canada. doi:10.1145/964696.964714

Jack, D., Boian, R. M. A., Burdea, G. C., & Poizner, H. (2001). Virtual reality - enhanced stroke rehabilitation. Transactions on Neural Systems and Rehabilation Engineering, 308-318.

Jacobs, M. (2011). *Living on the Edge of Mobile Development*. Retrieved from http://java.sys-con.com/node/1719019

Jahn, M., Jentsch, M., Prause, C. R., Pramudianto, F., Al-Akkad, A., & Reiners, R. (2010). *The energy aware smart home*. Paper presented at the Future Information Technology (FutureTech). New York, NY.

Jakkula, V., & Cook, D. (2008). Anomaly detection using temporal data mining in a smart home environment. *Methods of Information in Medicine, 47*(1), 70–75. PMID:18213431

James, C. B. H., Cook, R. & Konwinski, J. (2004). *Failure mode effects and criticality analysis (fmeca)*. Home ECG test kit.

Jamwal, P. K., Hussain, S., & Xie, S. Q. (2013). Review on design and control aspects of ankle rehabilitation robots. *Disability and Rehabilitation. Assistive Technology*, 1–9. doi:10.3109/17483107.2013.866986 PMID:24320195

Jan, M. A., Marchall, I., & Douglas, N. J. (1994). Effect of posture on upper airway dimensions in normal human. *American Journal of Respiratory and Critical Care Medicine, 149*, 1285–1288. PMID:8111573

Jansen, B. H., Larson, B. H., & Shankar, K. (1991). Monitoring of the ballistocardiogram with the static charge sensitive bed. *IEEE Transactions on Bio-Medical Engineering, 38*(8), 748–751. PMID:1937507

Janssen, J. H., van den Broek, E. L., & Westerink, J. H. (2012). Tune in to your emotions: A robust personalized affective music player. *User Modeling and User-Adapted Interaction, 22*(3), 255–279.

Jesse. (2012). *Mandelbulb3D* [Software]. PC. Retrieved August 28, 2013 from: http://www.fractalforums.com/mandelbulb-3d/

Jester Interactive. (1999). *Music 2000* [Video game]. PlayStation.

Johansson, D., Åhlund, A., & Åhlund, C. (2011). A mip-p2p based architecture for application mobility. In *Proceedings of the 10th International Conference on Mobile and Ubiquitous Multimedia* (pp. 85–93). New York: ACM. doi:10.1145/2107596.2107606

Johansson, D., & Andersson, K. (2012). Web-based adaptive application mobility. In *Proceedings of the 1st IEEE International Conference on Cloud Networking* (p. 87-94). IEEE.

Johansson, D., Andersson, K., & Åhlund, C. (2013). Supporting user mobility with peer-to-peer-based application mobility in heterogeneous networks. In *Proceedings of the 38th IEEE Conference on Local Computer Networks Workshops (LCN Workshops)* (p. 150-153). IEEE. doi:10.1109/LCNW.2013.6758512

Johansson, D., & Wiberg, M. (2012). Conceptually advancing "application mobility" towards design: Applying a concept-driven approach to the design of mobile it for home care service groups. *International Journal of Ambient Computing and Intelligence, 4*(3), 20–32. doi:10.4018/jaci.2012070102

Jones, B., & Sohdi, R. (2012). *The Illustrated History of Projection Mapping*. Retrieved August 28, 2013 from: http://www.projection-mapping.org/index.php/intro/160-the-history-of-projection-mapping

Jorrín-Abellán, I. M., & Stake, R. E. (2009). *Does Ubiquitous Learning Call for Ubiquitous Forms of Formal Evaluation?: An Evaluand oriented Responsive Evaluation Model. In Ubiquitous Learning: An International Journal* (p. 1). Melbourne, Australia: Common Ground Publisher.

José, R., Otero, N., Izadi, S., & Harper, R. (2008, October-December). Instant Places: Using Bluetooth for Situated Interaction in Public Displays. *IEEE Pervasive Computing*, *7*(4), 52–57. doi:10.1109/MPRV.2008.74

José, R., Pinto, H., Silva, B., & Melro, A. (2013). Pins and posters: Paradigms for content publication on situated displays. *IEEE Computer Graphics and Applications*, *33*(2), 64–72. doi:10.1109/MCG.2013.16 PMID:24807941

JSON. (n.d.). *JavaScript Object Notation*. Retrieved from http://www.json.org/

Julien, R. M. (2001). *A Primer of Drug Action*. New York: Worth Publishers.

Jung, J. H., Valencia, D. B., Rodríguez-de-Pablo, C., Keller, T., & Perry, J. C. (2013). Development of a powered mobile module for the ArmAssist home-based telerehabilitation platform. In *Proceedings of IEEE International Conference on Rehabilitation Robotics*. IEEE. doi:10.1109/ICORR.2013.6650424

Jung, B., Hwang, J., Lee, S., Kim, G. J., & Kim, H. (2000). Incorporating co-presence in distributed virtual music environment. In *Proceedings of the ACM Symposium on Virtual Reality Software and Technology*, (pp. 206-211). ACM.

Kaikkonen, A. (2009). Mobile internet: Past, present, and the future. *International Journal of Mobile Human Computer Interaction*, *1*(3), 29–45. doi:10.4018/jmhci.2009070104

Kailas, A., & Stefanidis, D. (2012). On Medical Informatics for Pervasive and Ubiquitous Computing in eHealth. In *Proceedings of e-Health Networking, Applications and Services (Healthcom)*, (pp. 111–118). IEEE. doi:10.1109/HealthCom.2012.6379372

Kakiuchi, Y., Nozawa, S., Yamazaki, K., Okada, K., & Inaba, M. (2013). Assistive system research for creative life management on robotics and home economics. In *Proceedings of 2013 IEEE Workshop on Advanced Robotics and Its Social Impacts (ARSO)*. IEEE. doi:10.1109/ARSO.2013.6705521

Kansal, A., Hsu, J., Zahedi, S., & Srivastava, M. B. (2007). Power management in energy harvesting sensor networks. *ACM Transactions on Embedded Computing Systems*, 6.

Kea, X., Saksena, P., & Holly, A. (2011). *The Determinants of Health Expenditure: A Country-Level Panel Data Analysis*. Geneva, Switzerland: World Health Organization.

Khan, W. A., Hussain, M., Khattak, A. M., Afzal, M., Amin, B., & Lee, S. (2012). Integration of HL7 Compliant Smart Home Healthcare System and HMIS. In M. Donnelly, C. Paggetti, C. Nugent, & M. Mokhtari (Eds.), *Impact Analysis of Solutions for Chronic Disease Prevention and Management* (Vol. 7251, pp. 230–233). Springer Berlin Heidelberg. doi:10.1007/978-3-642-30779-9_32

Kiecolt-Glaser, J., & Glaser, R. (1999). Chronic stress and mortality among older adults. *Journal of the American Medical Association*, *282*, 2259–2260. PMID:10605979

Kilic, O., Dogac, A., & Eichelberg, M. (2010). Providing Interoperability of eHealth Communities Through Peer-to-Peer Networks. *IEEE Transactions on* Information Technology in Biomedicine, *14*(3), 846–853. doi:10.1109/TITB.2010.2041029

Kinsella, K. H. W. (2009). *International Population Reports*. Washington, DC: U.S. Census Bureau.

Kleinberger, T., Becker, M., Ras, E., Holzinger, A., & Müller, P. (2007). Ambient Intelligence in Assisted Living: Enable Elderly People to Handle Future Interfaces. In C. Stephanidis (Ed.), *Universal Access in Human-Computer Interaction. Ambient Interaction* (Vol. 4555, pp. 103–112). Springer Berlin Heidelberg. doi:10.1007/978-3-540-73281-5_11

Klein, M., Schmidt, A., & Lauer, R. (2007). Ontology-centred design of an ambient middleware for assisted living: The case of soprano. In *Proceedings of Towards Ambient Intelligence: Methods for Cooperating Ensembles in Ubiquitous Environments (AIM-CU), 30th Annual German Conference on Artificial Intelligence (KI 2007)*. Academic Press.

Kleinrock, L. (1996). Nomadicity: Anytime, anywhere in a disconnected world. *Mobile Networks and Applications*, *1*(4), 351–357.

Kleitman, N., Ramsaroop, A., & Engelmann, T. G. (1948). Variations in skin temperatures of the feet and hands at the onset of sleep. *Federation Proceedings*, *7*, 66. PMID:18857960

Klette, R., & Zunic, J. (2004). Geometric algebra for pose estimation and surface morphing in human motion estimation. In Proceedings of IWCIA 2004, (LNCS), (vol. 3322, pp. 583-596). Berlin: Springer.

Klir, G., & Folger, T. (1988). *Fuzzy Sets, Uncertainty, and Information*. Englewood Cliffs, NJ: Prentice Hall.

Klomp, K. (2011). *Karl Klomp*. Retrieved November 13, 2013 from: http://karlklomp.nl

Klovdahl, A. S. (1985). Social networks and the spread of infectious diseases: The AIDS example. *Social Science & Medicine*, *21*(11), 1203–1216. doi:10.2307/2786835

Kluckner, P. M., Weiss, A., Schrammel, J., & Tscheligi, M. (2013). *Exploring Persuasion in the Home: Results of a Long-Term Study on Energy Consumption Behavior. In Ambient Intelligence* (pp. 150–165). Springer.

Kluge, E. M., & Witt, H. (2007, March). Developing Applications for Wearable Computers: A Process driven Example. In *Proceedings of Applied Wearable Computing (IFAWC)*, (pp. 1-12). IFAWC.

Koblentz, E. (2009). How it started: Mobile internet devices of the previous millennium. *International Journal of Mobile Human Computer Interaction*, *1*(4), 1–3. doi:10.4018/jmhci.2009062601

Koegel Buford, J. F., Yu, H. H., & Lua, E. K. (2009). P2P networking and applications. Amsterdam: Elsevier/Morgan Kaufmann.

Kolb, D. (1984). *Experiential Learning: Experience as the Source of Learning and Development*. Prentice-Hall.

Koning, E., Ploeg, B., Walther, T., Berio, D., Jong, J., & Vink, M. (2013). *Resolume* [VJ software]. Mac & PC.

Koponen, T., Gurtov, A., & Nikander, P. (2005). Application mobility with hip. In *Proc. of ICT'05*. IEEE.

Korhonen, I., Parkka, J., & Van Gils, M. (2003). Health monitoring in the home of the future. *IEEE Engineering in Medicine and Biology Magazine*, *22*(3), 66–73. PMID:12845821

Kortelainen, J. M., & Virkkala, J. (2007). FFT averaging of multichannel BCG signals from bed mattress sensor to improve estimation of heart beat interval. In *Proceedings of the 29th Annual International Conference of the IEEE Engineering in Medicine and Biology Society (EMBS)*, (pp. 6685-6688). IEEE.

Koschmann, T. (1996). *CSCL : theory and practice of an emerging paradigm*. Mahwah, NJ: Lawrence Erlbaum.

Kotz, D., Avancha, S., & Baxi, A. (2009). A privacy framework for mobile health and home-care systems. In *Proceedings of the First ACM Workshop on Security and Privacy in Medical and Home-Care Systems* (pp. 1–12). New York: ACM. doi:10.1145/1655084.1655086

Koutkias, V., Chouvarda, I., Triantafyllidis, A., Malousi, A., Giaglis, G. D., & Maglaveras, N. (2010). A Personalized Framework for Medication Treatment Management in Chronic Care. *IEEE Transactions on Information Technology in Biomedicine*, *14*(2), 464–472. doi:10.1109/TITB.2009.2036367 PMID:20007042

Kovachev, D., & Klamma, R. (2012). Beyond the client-server architectures: A survey of mobile cloud techniques. In *Communications in China Workshops (ICCC)*, (pp. 20–25). IEEE. doi:10.1109/ICCCW.2012.6316468

Kräuchi, K., Cajochen, C., Werth, E., & Wirz-Justice, A. (1999). Physiology: Warm feet promote the rapid onset of sleep. *Nature*, *401*, 36–37. PMID:10485703

Kräuchi, K., Cajochen, C., & Wirz-Justice, A. (1997). A relationship between heat loss and sleepiness: Effects of postural change and melatonin administration. *Journal of Applied Physiology (Bethesda, Md.)*, *83*, 134–139. PMID:9216955

Krishnamurti, T., Schwartz, D., Davis, A., Fischhoff, B., de Bruin, W. B., Lave, L., & Wang, J. (2012). Preparing for smart grid technologies: A behavioral decision research approach to understanding consumer expectations about smart meters. *Energy Policy*, *41*, 790–797.

Kubitza, T., Clinch, S., Davies, N., & Langheinrich, M. (2012). Using mobile devices to personalize pervasive displays. *Mobile Computing and Communications Review*, *16*(4), 26–27. doi:10.1145/2436196.2436211

Kubrick, S. (Producer & Director). (1968). *2001: A Space Odyssey* [Motion picture]. USA: Metro-Goldwyn-Mayer (MGM).

Küller, R., Ballal, S., Laike, T., Mikellides, B., & Tonello, G. (2006). The impact of light and colour on psychological mood: A cross-cultural study of indoor work environments. *Ergonomics*, *49*(14), 1496–1507. PMID:17050390

Kumar Jha, A. (2007). *A Risk Catalog for Mobile Applications*. BookSurge Pub.

Kummerfeld, B., Quigley, A., Johnson, C., & Hexel, R. (2003). Merino: Towards an intelligent environment architecture for multi-granularity context description. In Proc. User Modeling for Ubiquitous Computing (pp. 1–7). Academic Press.

Kumpula, J. M., Onnela, J. P., Saramäki, J., Kaski, K., & Kertész, J. (2007). Emergence of communities in weighted networks. *Physical Review Letters*, *99*(22), 228701. doi:10.1103/PhysRevLett.99.228701 PMID:18233339

Kuroda, T., Sasaki, H., Suenaga, T., Masuda, Y., Yasumuro, Y., & Hori, K. et al. (2012). Embedded Ubiquitous Services on Hospital Information Systems. *IEEE Transactions on* Information Technology in Biomedicine, *16*(6), 1216–1223. doi:10.1109/TITB.2012.2210434

Kurtisi, Z., Gu, X., & Wolf, L. (2006). Enabling network-centric music performance in wide-area networks. *Communications of the ACM*, *49*(11), 52–54.

Kushner, D. (2014). Virtual reality's moment. IEEE Spectrum, 51(1), 34-37.

Kushner, D. (2012). *Jacked: The Outlaw Story of Grand Theft Auto*. John Wiley & Sons.

Kwai Fun, I. (2008). Weblogging: A study of social computing and its impact on organizations. *Decision Support Systems*, *45*(2), 242–250. doi:10.1016/j.dss.2007.02.004

Lacuesta, R., & Palacios, G. (2009). A preliminary Approach to ECTS Estimate within the Framework of Electrical and Electronic Engineering Based on Experience. *Mount Sinai Journal of Medicine*, *76*(1), 318–329. Retrieved from http://fie-conference.org/fie2009/papers/1183.pdfhttp://www.uwoanesthesia.ca/documents/teamwork_anesthesia.pdf

Laine, T. H., & Joy, M. S. (2009). Survey on Context-Aware Pervasive Learning Environments. *International Journal of Interactive Mobile Technologies*, *3*(1), 70–76.

Lambert, N., Latham, W., & Leymarie, F. F. (2013). The Emergence and Growth of Evolutionary Art 1980-1993. *Leonardo*, *46*(4), 367–375. doi:10.1162/LEON_a_00608

Larrivee, B. (2008). Development of a tool to assess teachers' level of reflective practice. *Reflective Practice*, *9*(3), 341–360. doi:10.1080/14623940802207451

LaserimageSweden. (2009). *Lasershow using Pangolin*. Retrieved August 28, 2013 from: http://www.youtube.com/watch?v=i5Va8yyJFGA

Latfi, F., Lefebvre, B., & Descheneaux, C. (2007). Ontology-based management of the telehealth smart home, dedicated to elderly in loss of cognitive autonomy. In *Proceedings of the OWLED 2007 Workshop on OWL: Experiences and Directions*. OWLED.

Latino, R. J. & Flood, A. (2004). Optimizing fmea and rca efforts in healthcare. *Journal of Healthcare Risk Management*, *24*(3), 21–28. doi: .10.1002/jhrm.5600240305

Lawless-Reljic, S. (2011). The Effects of instructor-Avatar Immediacy in Second Life, an Immersive and Interactive 3D Virtual Environment. *eleed*, *7*. Retrieved from http://eleed.campussource.de/archive/7/3074

Lawo, M., Herzog, O., & Witt, H. (2007). *An Industrial Case Study on Wearable Computing Applications. In Proceedings of the 9th International Conference on Human Computer Interaction with Mobile Devices and Services* (pp. 448–451). New York, NY: ACM. http://doi.acm.org/10.1145/1377999.1378052

Layman, L., et al. (2007). Personality Types, Learning Styles, and an Agile Approach to Software Engineering Education. In *Proceedings of the 37th SIGCSE Technical Symposium on Computer Science Education* (Vol. 14, pp. 428-432). Academic Press. Retrieved from http://lucas.ezzoterik.com/papers/LCW06.pdf

Leahu, L., Sengers, P., & Mateas, M. (2008, September 21-24). *Interactionist AI and the promise of ubicomp, or, how to put your box in the world without putting the world in your box.* Paper presented at the 10th International Conference on Ubiquitous Computing. Seoul, South Korea. doi:10.1145/1409635.1409654

Leary, T., Horowitz, M., Marshall, V., Ferris, C., Keller, V., Haring, K. ...Horowitz, C. (1994). Chaos & Cyber Culture. Ronin Publishing.

Lebak, J. W., Yao, J., & Warren, S. (2004). HL7-Compliant Healthcare Information System for Home Monitoring. In *Proceedings of Engineering in Medicine and Biology Society,* (Vol. 2, pp. 3338–3341). IEEE. doi:10.1109/IEMBS.2004.1403938

LeBlanc, A. D., Harlan, J. E., Schneider, V. S., Wendt, R. E., & Hedrick, T. D. (1994). Changes in intervertebral disc cross-sectional area with bed rest and space flight. *Spine, 19,* 812–817. PMID:8202800

Lee, H. R., & Sabanović, S. (2014). Culturally Variable Preferences for Robot Design and Use in South Korea, Turkey, and the United States. In *Proceedings of the 2014 ACM/IEEE International Conference on Human-Robot Interaction, HRI '14.* ACM. doi:10.1145/2559636.2559676

Lee, J.-J., Seo, K.-H., Oh, C., & Bien, Z. Z. (2007). Development of a future Intelligent Sweet Home for the disabled. *Artificial Life and Robotics, 11*(1), 8–12. doi:10.1007/s10015-006-0417-5

Lee, W., Naqubadi, S., Kryger, M. H., & Mokhlesi, B. (2008, June). Epidemiology of obstructive sleep apnea: A population-based perspective. *Expert Review of Respiratory Medicine, 2*(3), 349–364. PMID:19690624

Leone, A., Diraco, G., & Siciliano, P. (2011). Detecting falls with 3D range camera in ambient assisted living applications: A preliminary study. *Medical Engineering & Physics, 33*(6), 770–781. doi:10.1016/j.medengphy.2011.02.001 PMID:21382737

Lerner, S. et al. (2009). Teaching Teamwork in Medical Education. *The International Journal of Learning. Journal of Medicine, 76*(4), 20–32.

Leslie, G., Schwarz, D., Warusfel, O., Bevilacqua, F., Zamborlin, B., Jodlowski, P., & Schnell, N. (2010). Grainstick: A Collaborative, Interactive Sound Installation. In *Proceedings of the International Computer Music Conference (ICMC) 2010.* Retrieved August 28, 2013 from: http://articles.ircam.fr/textes/Leslie10a/index.pdf

Levac, D., Rivard, L., & Missiuna, C. (2012). Defining the active ingredients of interactive computer play interventions for children with neuromotor impairments: A scoping review. *Research in Developmental Disabilities, 33*(1), 214–223. doi:10.1016/j.ridd.2011.09.007 PMID:22093667

Lewis, K., Kaufman, J., Gonzalez, M., Wimmer, A., & Christakis, N. (2008). Tastes, ties, and time: A new social network dataset using facebook.com. *Social Networks, 30*(4), 330–342.

Li, S., Zhang, Y., & Sun, H. (2010). Mashup FOAF for video recommendation LightWeight prototype. In *Proceedings of Web Information Systems and Applications Conference (WISA),* (pp. 190-193). WISA. doi:10.1109/WISA.2010.49

Liang, X., Barua, M., Chen, L., Lu, R., Shen, X., Li, X., & Luo, H. Y. (2012). Enabling Pervasive Healthcare Through Continuous Remote Health Monitoring. *IEEE Wireless Communications, 19*(6), 10–18. doi:10.1109/MWC.2012.6393513

Liarokapis, F., Macan, L., Malone, G., Rebolledo-Mendez, G., & De Freitas, S. (2009). *A Pervasive Augmented Reality Serious Game.* Games and Virtual Worlds for Serious Applications.

Li, M., Lou, W., & Ren, K. (2010). Data Security and Privacy in Wireless Body Area Networks. *IEEE Wireless Communications, 17*(1), 51–58. doi:10.1109/MWC.2010.5416350

Limitations of the Kinect. (2010, December 17). Retrieved from I Heart Robotics: http://www.iheartrobotics.com/2010/12/limitations-of-kinect.html

Lin, K., Yuen, F., & Barth, T. (2008). *The Punch Meter.* Retrieved from http://processors.wiki.ti.com/index.php/The_Punch_Meter

Lin, S.-C., Chiang, Y.-L., Lin, H.-C., Hsu, J., & Wang, J.-F. (2009). Design and Implementation of a HL7-based Physiological Monitoring System for Mobile Consumer Devices. In *Proceedings of Consumer Electronics,* (pp. 1–2). ICCE. doi:10.1109/ICCE.2009.5012233

Linder, S. M., Reiss, A., Buchanan, S., Sahu, K., Rosenfeldt, A. B., & Clark, C. et al. (2013). Incorporating robotic-assisted telerehabilitation in a home program to improve arm function following stroke. *Journal of Neurologic Physical Therapy; JNPT, 37*(3), 125–132. doi:10.1097/NPT.0b013e31829fa808 PMID:23872687

Linder, S. M., Rosenfeldt, A. B., Reiss, A., Buchanan, S., Sahu, K., & Bay, C. R. et al. (2013). The home stroke rehabilitation and monitoring system trial: A randomized controlled trial. *International Journal of Stroke Rehabilitation, 8*(1), 46–53. doi:10.1111/j.1747-4949.2012.00971.x PMID:23280269

Lin, H., Shao, J., Zhang, C., & Fang, Y. (2013). Cam: Cloud-assisted privacy preserving mobile health monitoring. *IEEE Transactions on* Information Forensics and Security, 8(6), 985–997. doi:10.1109/TIFS.2013.2255593

Liu, J. G., Liu, J. C., Chen, Y. G., & Yuang, M. C. (1995). DMTS: A distributed multimedia teleworking system. In *Proceedings of Local Computer Networks,* (pp. 326-335). IEEE.

Liu, Y., & Li, F. (2006). PCA: A Reference Architecture for Pervasive Computing. In *Pervasive Computing and Applications,* (pp. 99–103). Academic Press. doi:10.1109/SPCA.2006.297550

Li, X., Feng, L., Zhou, L., & Shi, Y. (2009). Learning in an Ambient Intelligent World: Enabling Technologies and Practices. *IEEE Transactions on* Knowledge and Data Engineering, 21(6), 910–924.

Lockery, D., Peters, J. F., Ramanna, S., Shay, B. L., & Szturm, T. (2011). Store-and-Feedforward Adaptive Gaming System for Hand-Finger Motion Tracking in Telerehabilitation. *IEEE Transactions on Information Technology in Biomedicine, 15*(3), 467–473. doi:10.1109/TITB.2011.2125976 PMID:21536526

Loke, S. (2007). *Context-aware pervasive systems: Architectures for a new breed of applications.* Boca Raton, FL: Auerbach Publications.

Lombardi, A., Ferri, M., Rescio, G., Grassi, M., & Malcovati, P. (2009). Wearable wireless accelerometer with embedded fall-detection logic for multi-sensor ambient assisted living applications. In *Proceedings of IEEE Sensors.* IEEE. doi:10.1109/ICSENS.2009.5398327

Long, X., Yin, B., & Aarts, R. (2009). Single-accelerometer-based daily physical activity classification. In *Proceedings of International Conference of Engineering in Medicine and Biology Society,* (pp. 3-6). Academic Press.

Lounis, A., Hadjidj, A., Bouabdallah, A., & Challal, Y. (2012). Secure and Scalable Cloud-Based Architecture for e-Health Wireless Sensor Networks. In *Proceedings of Computer Communications and Networks (ICCCN),* (pp. 1–7). ICCCN. doi:10.1109/ICCCN.2012.6289252

Lowe, A. (2011). *Hacking on the rise – all around.* Retrieved from http://hexus.net/business/news/general-business/32399-hacking-rise-around/

Lu, B., & DeClue, T. (2011). *Teaching Agile Methodology In A Software Engineering Capstone Course.* Department of Computer and Information Sciences, Southwest Baptist University. Retrieved from http://db.grinnell.edu/ccsc/ccsc-cp2011/Program/viewAcceptedProposal.pdf?sessionType=paper&sessionNumber=13

Lu, C., Chang, M., Kinshuk, Huang, E., & Chen, C.-W. (2011). Architecture and collaborations among agents in mobile educational game. In *Proceedings of 2011 IEEE International Conference on Pervasive Computing and Communications Workshops (PERCOM Workshops)* (pp. 556–560). IEEE. doi:10.1109/PERCOMW.2011.5766951

Lu, L., Tamura, T., & Togawa, T. (1999). Detection of body movements during sleep by monitoring of bed temperature. Physiol. Meas., 137-148.

Lui, T. J., Stirling, W., & Marcy, H. O. (2010). Get smart. *IEEE Power and Energy Magazine, 8*(3), 66–78.

Lyons, K., Starner, T., & Harvel, L. (2000). A Context-Based Document System for Wearable Computers. In *Proceedings of 2012 16th International Symposium on Wearable Computers.* Academic Press.

Lyons, K., Skeels, C., & Starner, T. (2005). *Providing Support for Mobile Calendaring Conversations: A Wizard of Oz Evaluation of Dual-purpose Speech. In Proceedings of the 7th International Conference on Human Computer Interaction with Mobile Devices & Services* (pp. 243–246). New York, NY: ACM. doi:10.1145/1085777.1085821

Lyons, K., Skeels, C., Starner, T., Snoeck, C. M., Wong, B. A., & Ashbrook, D. (2004). *Augmenting Conversations Using Dual-purpose Speech. In Proceedings of the 17th Annual ACM Symposium on User Interface Software and Technology* (pp. 237–246). New York, NY: ACM.http://doi.acm.org/10.1145/1029632.1029674

Mabry, S. L., Schneringer, T., Etters, T., & Edwards, N. (2003). *Intelligent Agents for Patient Monitoring and Diagnostics* (pp. 257–262). SAC. doi:10.1145/952576.952585

Macarro, A., Pedrero, A., & Fraile, J. A. (2009). Multiagent-Based Educational Environment for Dependents. In J. Cabestany, F. Sandoval, A. Prieto, & J. M. Corchado (Eds.), *Bio-Inspired Systems: Computational and Ambient Intelligence* (pp. 602–609). Springer Berlin Heidelberg.

Mace, D., Gao, W., & Coskun, A. (2013). *Improving the accuracy and practicality of accelerometer based hand gesture*. Santa Monica, CA: International Conference on Intelligent User Interfaces.

Mack, D. C., Patrie, J. T., Suratt, P. M., Felder, R. A., & Alwan, M. (2009). Development and preliminary validation of heart rate and breathing rate detection using a passive, ballistocardiography-based sleep monitoring system. *IEEE Transactions on Information Technology in Biomedicine, 13*(1), 111–120. PMID:19129030

Madeira, R. N., Correia, N., Guerra, M., Postolache, O., Dias, A. C., & Postolache, G. (2011). Designing personalized therapeutic serious games for a pervasive assistive environment. In *Proceedings of 2011 IEEE 1st International Conference on Serious Games and Applications for Health (SeGAH)*. IEEE. doi:10.1109/SeGAH.2011.6165465

Magnussen, G. (1939). Vasomotorische Veränderungen in den Extremitäten im Verhältnis zu Schlaf und Schlafbereitschaft Acta. *Psychiatria et Neurologia, 14*, 39–54.

Majithia, V., & Geraci, A. (2007). Rheumatoid Arthritis: Diagnosis and Management. *The American Journal of Medicine, 44*(2), 936–939. doi:10.1016/j.amjmed.2007.04.005 PMID:17976416

Manning, P. (2002). *Electronic & Computer Music*. Oxford University Press.

Mano, C. D., DuHadway, L., & Striegel, A. (2006). A Case for Instilling Security as a Core Programming Skill. In *Proceedings of Frontiers in Education Conference*, (vol. 4, pp. 13-18). doi:10.1109/FIE.2006.322347

Marin-Garcia, J., & Mauri, J. (2007). Teamwork with University Engineering Students. Group Process Assessment Tool. In *Proceedings of the 3rd WSEAS/IASME International Conference on Educational Technologies*. Retrieved from http://personales.gan.upv.es/jlloret/pdf/edute2007-2.pdf

Marin-Garcia, J., et al. (2009). Enhancing motivation and satisfaction of students: analysis of quantitative data in three subjects of Industrial Engineering. *WSEAS Transactions on Advances in Engineering Education, 6*(1), 32-44. Retrieved from http://www.wseas.us/e-library/transactions/education/2009/28-854.pdf

Mark, D., Nutting, J., & LaMarche, J. (2011). *Beginning iPhone 4 Development Exploring the iOS SDK*. Apress Pub.

Marosi, I., & Bencsik, A. (2010). Teamwork in Higher Education: Teamwork as Chance of Success. *The International Journal of Learning, 16*(5), 167–174. Retrieved from http://ijl.cgpublisher.com/product/pub.30/prod.2156

Marotte, H., & Timbal, J. (1982). Circadian rhythm of temperature in man. Comparative study with two experimental protocols. *Chronobiologica, 8*, 87–100.

Martín, S., Peire, J., & Castro, M. (2010). M2Learn: Towards a homogeneous vision of advanced mobile learning development. In Proceedings of Education Engineering (EDUCON), (pp. 569–574). IEEE.

Maurtua, I., Kirisci, P. T., Stiefmeier, T., Sbodio, M. L., & Witt, H. (2007, March). A Wearable Computing Prototype for supporting training activities in Automotive Production. In *Proceedings of 4th International Forum on Applied Wearable Computing (IFAWC)*, (pp. 1-12). IFAWC.

McCarthy, J. F., Costa, T. J., & Liongosari, E. S. (2001). *UniCast, OutCast & GroupCast: Three Steps toward Ubiquitous Peripheral Displays.* Paper presented at the International Conference on Ubiquitous Computing. Atlanta, GA. doi:10.1007/3-540-45427-6_28

McCarthy, J. F., McDonald, D. W., Soroczak, S., Nguyen, D. H., & Rashid, A. M. (2004). *Augmenting the Social Space of an Academic Conference.* Paper presented at the CSCW. Chicago, IL.

McDonald, D. W., McCarthy, J. F., Soroczak, S., Nguyen, D. H., & Rashid, A. M. (2008). Proactive Displays: Supporting Awareness in Fluid Social Environments. *ACM Transactions on Computer-Human Interaction*, *14*(4), 1–31. doi:10.1145/1314683.1314684

McEuen, A. (2013). *Pink Floyd 360: Dark Side Of The Moon* [Video]. Starlight Productions. Presented at Dome Club [Audio-visual event series], January 24, 2013, The Old Custard Factory, Birmingham.

McGuinness, D. L., & Van Harmelen, F. (2004). OWL web ontology language overview. *W3C Recommendation*, *10*(2004-03), 10.

McIntyre, I. M., Norman, T. R., Burrows, G. D., & Armstrong, S. M. (1989). Human melatonin suppression by light is intensity dependent. *Journal of Pineal Research*, *6*(2), 149–156. PMID:2915324

McKenna. T., & The Shamen (1992). *Narration from Re:Evolution.* Retrieved September 2, 2013 from: http://deoxy.org/t_re-evo.htm

McKerracher, C., & Torriti, J. (2012). Energy consumption feedback in perspective: integrating Australian data to meta-analyses on in-home displays. *Energy Efficiency*, 1-19.

McLachlan, R., McGee-Lennon, M., & Brewster, S. (2012). *The sound of musicons: Investigating the design of musically derived audio cues.* Retrieved from http://hdl.handle.net/1853/44429

McLean, M. (Video artist), Scott, C. (Video artist), & Dougans, B. (Music). (1988). *Humanoid: Stakker Humanoid* [Video]. Retrieved August 27, 2013 from: http://www.youtube.com/watch?v=hxEoU-oE0j4

McPherson, M., Smith-Lovin, L., & Cook, J. M. (2001). Birds of a feather: Homophily in social networks. *Annual Review of Sociology*, *27*(1), 415–444. doi:10.1146/annurev.soc.27.1.415

Meerlo, P., Mistlberger, R. E., Jacobs, B. L., Heller, H. C., & McGinty, D. (2009). New neurons in the adult brain: The role of sleep and consequence of sleep loss. *Sleep Medicine Reviews*, *13*, 187–194. PMID:18848476

Mehta, N. A., Starner, T., Jackson, M. M., Babalola, K. O., & James, G. A. (2010). Recognizing Sign Language from Brain Imaging. In *Proceedings of the 2010 20th International Conference on Pattern Recognition* (pp. 3842-3845). Washington, DC: IEEE Computer Society. doi:10.1109/ICPR.2010.936

Meier, R. (2010). *Professional Android 2 Application Development.* Wiley Publishing Inc.

Memon, M., Wagner, S. R., Pedersen, C. F., Beevi, F. H. A., & Hansen, F. O. (2014). Ambient Assisted Living Healthcare Frameworks, Platforms, Standards, and Quality Attributes. *Sensors (Basel, Switzerland)*, *14*(3), 4312–4341. doi:10.3390/s140304312 PMID:24599192

Mendel, J. (1995). Fuzzy logic systems for engineering: A tutorial. *Proceedings of the IEEE*, *83*(3), 345–377. doi:10.1109/5.364485

Merians, A. S., Fluet, G. G., Qiu, Q., Saleh, S., Lafond, I., Davidow, A., & Adamovich, S. V. (2011). Robotically facilitated virtual rehabilitation of arm transport integrated with finger movement in persons with hemiparesis. *Journal of Neuroengineering and Rehabilitation*, 8(1), 27. doi:10.1186/1743-0003-8-27 PMID:21575185

Messer, A., Kunjithapatham, A., Sheshagiri, M., Song, H., Kumar, P., Nguyen, P., & Yi, K. H. (2006). *InterPlay: A middleware for seamless device integration and task orchestration in a networked home*. Paper presented at the Pervasive Computing and Communications, 2006. Washington, DC.

Metcalf, C. D., Robinson, R., Malpass, A. J., Bogle, T. P., Dell, T. A., Harris, C., & Demain, S. H. (2013). Markerless motion capture and measurement of hand kinematics: Validation and application to home-based upper limb rehabilitation. *IEEE Transactions on Bio-Medical Engineering*, 60(8), 2184–2192. doi:10.1109/TBME.2013.2250286 PMID:23475333

Micera, S., Cavallaro, E., Belli, R., Zaccone, F., Guliel-melli, E., Dario, P., et al. (2003). Functional assessment of hand orthopedic disorders using a sensorised glove. In *Proceedings of IEEE International Conference on Robotics and Automation*, (pp. 2212-2217). IEEE.

Michelis, D., & Müller, J. (2011). The Audience Funnel: Observations of Gesture Based Interaction With Multiple Large Displays in a City Center. *International Journal of Human-Computer Interaction*, 27(6), 562–579. doi:10.1080/10447318.2011.555299

Middleton, A. M., & Ward, T. E. (2012). The Pursuit of Flow in the Design of Rehabilitation Systems for Ambient Assisted Living: A Review of Current Knowledge. *International Journal of Ambient Computing and Intelligence*, 4(1), 54–65. doi:10.4018/jaci.2012010105

Miller, A. (2008). Distributed Agile Development at Microsoft patterns & practices. *MSDN white paper*. Retrieved from http://download.microsoft.com/download/4/4/a/44a2cebd-63fb-4379-898d-9cf24822c6cc/distributed_agile_development_at_microsoft_patterns_and_practices.pdf

Minter, J. (1990). *Virtual Light Machine* [Software]. Atari Jaguar. Retrieved August 28, 2013 from: http://www.youtube.com/watch?v=8CrQOk7TseY

Minter, J. (2005). *Neon* [Software]. X-Box 360.

Miranda, E., Durrant, S., & Anders, T. (2008). Toward Brain-Computer Music Interfaces: Progress and Challenges. In *Proceedings of the International Symposium on Applied Sciences in Biomedical and Communication Technologies* (ISABEL2008). Aalborg, Denmark: ISABEL.

Mislove, A., Marcon, M., Gummadi, K. P., Druschel, P., & Bhattacharjee, B. (2007). Measurement and analysis of online social networks. In *Proceedings of the 7th ACM SIGCOMM Conference on Internet Measurement*. ACM. doi:10.1145/1298306.1298311

Mitrovic, D., Zeppelzauer, M., & Breitender, C. (2010). Features for Content-Based Audio Retrieval. *Advances in Computers: Improving the Web, 78*.

Moe, K.E., Vitiello, M.V., Larsen, L.H., & Prinz, P.N. (1995). Sleep/wake patterns in Alzheimer's disease: relationships with cognition and function. *Journal of Sleep Research, 4*, 15-20.

Mohammed, S., Amirat, Y., & Rifai, H. (2012). Lower-Limb Movement Assistance through Wearable Robots: State of the Art and Challenges. *Advanced Robotics, 26*(1-2), 1–22. doi:10.1163/016918611X607356

Moncrieff, S., Venkatesh, S., & West, G. (2009). A Framework for the Design of Privacy Preserving Pervasive Healthcare. In *Proceedings of Multimedia and Expo*, (pp. 1696–1699). IEEE. doi:10.1109/ICME.2009.5202847

Moore, G.E. (1965, April 19). Cramming more components onto integrated circuits. *Electronics, 38*(8).

Morales-Aranda, A. H., & Mayora-Ibarra, O. (2007, June 19 -25). *A Context Sensitive Public Display for Adaptive Multi-User Information Visualization* Paper presented at the Third International Conference on Autonomic and Autonomous Systems. Athens, Greece. doi:10.1109/CONIELECOMP.2007.40

Morgenthaler, T., Alessi, C., Friedman, L., Owens, J., Kapur, V., & Boehlecke, B. et al. (2007). Practice Parameters for the Use of Actigraphy in the Assessment of Sleep and Sleep Disorders: An Update for 2007. *Sleep, 30*, 519–529. PMID:17520797

Moritz, W. (1997). The Dream of Colour Music and the Machines that Made it Possible. *Animation World Magazine, 2*(1). Retrieved August 27, 2013 from: http://www.awn.com/mag/issue2.1/articles/moritz2.1.html

Mortiz, W. (1999). *Stereoscopic abstract films* [PDF document]. Retrieved August 28, 2013 from: http://www.centerforvisualmusic.org/WMlecstereo.pdf

MOSA. (2010, January). *Mobile and open service access.* Retrieved from http://www.mosaproject.org/

Mozer, M. (2005). Lessons from an adaptive house. In D. Cook & R. Das (Eds.), *Smart Environments: Technologies, Protocols, and Applications* (pp. 273–294). Hoboken, NJ: Wiley.

Mukerjee, A., & Joe, G. (1990). A qualitative model for space. In *Proceedings of the 8th National Conference on Artificial Intelligence* (pp. 721–727). Palo Alto, CA: AAAI Press.

Muldoon, C., O'Hare, G. M., Collier, R., & O'Grady, M. J. (2006). *Agent factory micro edition: A framework for ambient applications. In Computational Science–ICCS 2006* (pp. 727–734). Springer.

Müller, J., Kruger, A., & Kuflik, T. (2007). *Maximizing the Utility of Situated Public Displays.* Paper presented at the Adjunct Proceedings of User Modeling. Corfu, Greece. doi:10.1007/978-3-540-73078-1_52

Mulvenna, M., Carswell, W., McCullagh, P., Augusto, J., Zheng, H., & Jeffers, P. et al. (2011). Visualization of data for ambient assisted living services. *IEEE Communications Magazine, 49*(1), 110–117. doi:10.1109/MCOM.2011.5681023

Murphy, P. J., & Campbell, S. S. (1997). Nighttime drop in body temperature: A physiological trigger for sleep onset? *Sleep, 20*(7), 505–511. PMID:9322266

Murthy, G. R., & Jadon, R. S. (2009). A review of vision based hand gestures recognition. *Internation Journal of Information Technology and Knowledge Management*, 405-410.

Muzet, A., Ehrhart, J., Candas, V., Libert, J. P., & Vogt, J. J. (1983). Rem Sleep and Ambient Temperature in Man. *The International Journal of Neuroscience, 18*, 117–125. PMID:6840976

Muzet, A., Libert, J. P., & Candas, V. (1984). Ambient temperature and human sleep. *Experientia, 40*, 425–429. PMID:6723903

Nachemson, A., & Elfström, G. (1970). Intravital dynamic pressure measurements in lumbar discs. A study of common movements, maneuvers, and exercises. *Scandinavian Journal of Rehabilitation Medicine, 1*, 1–40. PMID:4257209

NanaOn-Sha. (1996). *PaRappa the Rapper* [Video game]. PlayStation.

Nauck, D., & Kruse, R. (1993). A fuzzy neural network learning fuzzy control rules and membership functions by fuzzy error backpropagation. In *Proceedings of the IEEE International Conference on Neural Networks* (pp. 1022–1027). Los Alamitos, CA: IEEE Computer Society.

Nebusens. (2013). *n-Core®: A Faster and Easier Way to Create Wireless Sensor Networks*. Retrieved from http://www.nebusens.com

Nehmer, J., Becker, M., Karshmer, A., & Lamm, R. (2006). Living assistance systems - An ambient intelligence approach. In *Proceedings - International Conference on Software Engineering*. Academic Press.

Nehmer, J., Karshmer, A., Lamm, R., & Becker, M. (2006). Living assistance systems: an ambient intelligence approach. In *Proceedings of28th International Conference on Software Engineering (ICSE'06)* (pp. 43-50). ICSE. doi:10.1145/1134285.1134293

Neil, A., Ens, S., Pelletier, R., Jarus, T., & Rand, D. (2013). Sony PlayStation EyeToy elicits higher levels of movement than the Nintendo Wii: Implications for stroke rehabilitation. *European Journal of Physical and Rehabilitation Medicine, 49*, 13–21. PMID:23172403

Nejati, M. (2010). Teamwork Approach: An Investigation on Iranian Teamwork Attitudes. *Canadian Social Science, 6*(3), 104–113. Retrieved from http://cscanada.net/index.php/css/article/view/1058/1077

New Media Consortium. (2011). *The Horizon Report 2011 edition*. Available from: http://www.nmc.org/horizon-project/horizon-reports/horizon-report-k-12-edition

Newman, M. E. J. (2003). The structure and function of complex networks. *SIAM Review, 45*(2), 167–256. doi:10.1137/S003614450342480

Newton-Dunn, H., Nakano, H., & Gibson, J. (2003, May). Block jam: a tangible interface for interactive music. In *Proceedings of the 2003 conference on New interfaces for musical expression*, (pp. 170-177). National University of Singapore.

Neyem, A., Ochoa, S. F., Pino, J. A., & Guerrero, L. A. (2005). Sharing Information Resources in Mobile Ad-hoc Networks. In *Proceedings of 11th Workshop on Groupware, CRIWG05*, (pp. 351–358). CRIWG. doi:10.1007/11560296_28

Nguyen, H., Kreinovich, V., & Tolbert, D. (1993). On robustness of fuzzy logics. In *Proceedings of the IEEE International Conference on Fuzzy Systems* (pp. 543–547). Los Alamitos, CA: IEEE Computer Society.

Nichols, J., & Myers, B. A. (2009, November). Creating a Lightweight User Interface Description Language: An Overview and Analysis of the Personal Universal Controller Project. *ACM Transactions on Computer-Human Interaction, 16*(4), 17:1-17:37. http://doi.acm.org/10.1145/1614390.1614392

Nichols, J., Myers, B. A., Litwack, K., Higgins, M., Hughes, J., & Harris, T. K. (2004). Describing Appliance User Interfaces Abstractly with XML. In *Proceedings of Workshop on Developing User Interfaces with XML: Advances on User Interface Description Languages*. Academic Press.

Nichols, J., Rothrock, B., Chau, D. H., & Myers, B. A. (2006). *Huddle: Automatically Generating Interfaces for Systems of Multiple Connected Appliances. In Proceedings of the 19th Annual ACM Symposium on User Interface Software and Technology* (pp. 279–288). New York, NY: ACM. doi:10.1145/1166253.1166298

Nickel, C., & Busch, C. (2011). Classifying accelerometer data via Hidden Markov Models to authenticate people by the way they walk. In *Proceedings of International Carnahan Conference on Security Technology* (pp. 18-21). IEEE. doi:10.1109/CCST.2011.6095941

Nicolai, T., Sindt, T., Witt, H., Reimerdes, J., & Kenn, H. (2006, March). Wearable Computing for Aircraft Maintenance: Simplifying the User Interface. In *Proceedings of 3rd International Forum on Applied Wearable Computing (IFAWC)*, (pp. 1-12). IFAWC.

NIMO. (2014, September). *Nordic interaction and mobility research platform*. Retrieved from http://nimoproject.org/

Niyato, D., Xiao, L., & Wang, P. (2011). Machine-to-machine communications for home energy management system in smart grid. *IEEE Communications Magazine, 49*(4), 53–59.

Non-visual interfaces for wearable computers. (2000, January). *IET Conference Proceedings*, 6-6(1). Retrieved from http://digital-library.theiet.org/content/conferences/10.1049/ic_20000511

Nordin, A. M., Chee, P. S., Addi, M. M., & Che Harun, F. K. (2011). EZ430-Chronos watch as a wireless health monitoring device. In *Proceedings of International Conference on Biomedial Engineering*, (pp. 305-307). Kuala Lumpur: Academic Press. doi:10.1007/978-3-642-21729-6_79

Northern Ireland Council for Curriculum (NICC). (1989). *Nursery Education Guidelines - 'The Curriculum'*. Retrieved from http://www.deni.gov.uk/pre_school_guidance_pdf

Nukaya, S., Shino, T., Kurihara, Y., Watanabe, K., & Tanaka, H. (2012). Noninvasive bed sensing of human biosignals via piezoceramic devices sandwiched between the floor and bed. *IEEE Sensors Journal, 12*(3), 431–438.

O'Donoghue, P. (2010). *Chasing Waves* [Video]. Retrieved August 27, 2013 from: https://vimeo.com/10314195

O'Neill, G., Patel, H., & Artemiadis, P. (2013). An intrinsically safe mechanism for physically coupling humans with robots. In *Proceedings of IEEE International Conference on Rehabilitation Robotics*. IEEE. doi:10.1109/ICORR.2013.6650510

O'Neill, S. A., Nugent, C. D., Donnelly, M. P., McCullagh, P., & McLaughlin, J. (2012). Evaluation of connected health technology. *Technology and Health Care, 20*, 151–167. PMID:22735731

O'Donovan, T., O'Donoghue, J., Sreenan, C., Sammon, D., O'Reilly, P., & O'Connor, K. A. (2009). A context aware wireless body area network (BAN). In *Proceedings of Pervasive Computing Technologies for Healthcare,* (pp. 1-8). Academic Press.

O'Grady, M. J., Murdoch, O., Kroon, B., Lillis, D., Carr, D., Collier, R. W., & O'Hare, G. M. (2013). *Pervasive Sensing: Addressing the Heterogeneity Problem.* Paper presented at the Journal of Physics: Conference Series. New York, NY.

O'Hare, G. M. P., Collier, R. W., Dragone, M., O'Grady, M. J., Muldoon, C., & Montoya, A. D. J. (2012b). Embedding Agents within Ambient Intelligent Applications. In T. Bosse (Ed.), *Agents and Ambient Intelligence* (pp. 119–135). IOS Press.

O'Hare, G. M. P., Muldoon, C., O'Grady, M. J., Collier, R. W., Murdoch, O., & Carr, D. (2012a). Sensor web interaction. *International Journal of Artificial Intelligence Tools, 21*(02).

Okamoto, K., Mizuno, K., & Okudaira, N. (1997). The effects of a newly designed air mattress upon sleep and bed climate. *Applied Human Science, 16,* 161–166. PMID:9343865

Olindo, S., Signate, A., Richech, A., Cabre, P., Catonne, Y., Smadja, D., & Pascal-Mousselard, H. (2008). Quantitative assessment of hand disability by the Nine-Hole-Peg test (9-HPT) in cervical spondylotic myelopathy. *Journal of Neurology, Neurosurgery, and Psychiatry, 79*(8), 965–967. doi:10.1136/jnnp.2007.140285 PMID:18420728

Olsen, J. D., Jefferies, S., Nielsen, T., Moyes, W., & Fredrickson, P. (2000). *Cross-modal Interaction Using XWeb. In Proceedings of the 13th Annual ACM Symposium on User Interface Software and Technology* (pp. 191–200). New York, NY: ACM. doi:10.1145/354401.354764

Onias Kukkonen, H. (2003). *Developing successful mobile applications.* Stanford University.

Opus. (1998). *Fluid* [Video game]. Playstation.

Ortiz, M., Coghlan, N., Jaimovich, J., & Knapp, B. (2010). *Biosignal-drive Art: Beyond biofeedback. Sonic Ideas/ Ideas Sonicas, 3(2).*

Oskoui, M., Coutinho, F., Dykeman, J., Jetté, N., & Pringsheim, T. (2013). An update on the prevalence of cerebral palsy: A systematic review and meta-analysis. *Developmental Medicine and Child Neurology, 55*(6), 509–519. doi:10.1111/dmcn.12080 PMID:23346889

Oulasvirta, A., Tamminen, S., Roto, V., & Kuorelahti, J. (2005). *Interaction in 4-second Bursts: The Fragmented Nature of Attentional Resources in Mobile HCI. In Proceedings of the SIGCHI Conference on Human Factors in Computing Systems* (pp. 919–928). New York, NY: ACM. doi:10.1145/1054972.1055101

Paap, J. (Musical composer), & Pagano, S. (Video artist). (2007). *Umfeld* [Video]. Retrieved August 27, 2013 from: http://www.youtube.com/watch?v=_e_h9pyQwH4

Padovitz, A., Loke, S., & Zaslavsky, A. (2008). The ECO-RA framework: A hybrid architecture for context-oriented pervasive computing. *Pervasive and Mobile Computing, 4*(2), 182–215. doi:10.1016/j.pmcj.2007.10.002

Paksuniemi, M., Sorvoja, H., Alasaarela, E., & Myllyla, R. (2006). Wireless sensor and data transmission needs and technologies for patient monitoring in the operating room and intensive care unit. In *Proceedings of Engineering in Medicine and Biology Society,* (pp. 5182-5185). IEEE.

Palsbo, S. E., Marr, D., Streng, T., Bay, B. K., & Norblad, A. W. (2011). Towards a modified consumer haptic device for robotic-assisted fine-motor repetitive motion training. *Disability and Rehabilitation. Assistive Technology, 6*(6), 546–551. doi:10.3109/17483107.2010.532287 PMID:21091135

Panayi, G. (2003). *What is RA?* National Rheumatoid Arthritus Society.

Pangolin. (2013). *Laser light show software from Pangolin Laser Systems.* Retrieved August 28, 2013 from: http://www.pangolin.com/

Paquet, J., Kwainska, A., & Carrier, J., (2007). *Wake detection capacity of actigraphy during sleep.* Academic Press.

Parallaxis. (2010). *Parallaxis 3D audio-visual liveact // Track: Spiral* [Video]. Retrieved August 28, 2013 from: https://vimeo.com/11987591

Parameswaran, M., & Whinston, A. B. (2007). Research issues in social computing. *Journal of the Association for Information Systems, 8*(6), 336–350.

Parikh, P. P., Kanabar, M. G., & Sidhu, T. S. (2010). *Opportunities and challenges of wireless communication technologies for smart grid applications.* Paper presented at the Power and Energy Society General Meeting. New York, NY.

Parry, I., Carbullido, C., Kawada, J., Bagley, A., Sen, S., Greenhalgh, D., & Palmieri, T. (2013). Keeping up with video game technology: Objective analysis of Xbox Kinect™ and PlayStation 3 Move™ for use in burn rehabilitation. *Burns.* doi:10.1016/j.burns.2013.11.005

Parsons, S. (1994). Some qualitative approaches to applying the Dempster-Shafer theory. *Information and Decision Technologies, 19*, 321–337.

Payne, T., David, E., Jennings, N. R., & Sharifi, M. (2006). *Auction Mechanisms for Efficient Advertisement Selection on Public Displays.* Paper presented at the European Conference on Artificial Intelligence. Riva del Garda, Italy.

Pechacek, C. S., Andersen, M., & Lockley, S. W. (2008). Preliminary method for prospective analysis of the circadian efficacy of (day)light with applications to healthcare architecture. *LEUKOS, 5*(1), 1–26. doi:10.1080/155027 24.2008.10747625

Peltokangas, M., Verho, J., & Vehkaoja, A. (2012). Night-time EKG and HRV monitoring with bed sheet integrated textile electrodes. *IEEE Transactions on Information Technology in Biomedicine, 16*(5), 935–942. PMID:22829424

Peng, H., Hu, B., Liu, Q., Dong, Q., Zhao, Q., & Moore, P. (2011). User-centered Depression Prevention: An EEG Approach to Pervasive Healthcare. In *Proceedings of Pervasive Computing Technologies for Healthcare (PervasiveHealth),* (pp. 325–330). Academic Press.

Pessemier, T. D., Deryckere, T., & Martens, L. (2009). *Context aware recommendations for user-generated content on a social network site.* Paper presented at the 7th European Interactive Television Conference. Leuven, Belgium.

Pettey, C., & Goasduff, L. (2011). *Gartner Says Sales of Mobile Devices in Second Quarter of 2011 Grew 16.5 Percent Year-on-Year; Smartphone Sales Grew 74 Percent.* Retrieved from http://www.gartner.com/it/page.jsp?id=1764714

Pfeil, U., Arjan, R., & Zaphiris, P. (2009). Age differences in online social networking-A study of user profiles and the social capital divide among teenagers and older users in MySpace. *Computers in Human Behavior, 25*(3), 643–654. doi:10.1016/j.chb.2008.08.015

Pfeil, U., & Zaphiris, P. (2007). Patterns of empathy in online communication. In *Proceedings of the SIGCHI Conference on Human Factors in Computing Systems,* (pp. 919-928). ACM. doi:10.1145/1240624.1240763

Pfeil, U., & Zaphiris, P. (2009). Investigating social network patterns within an empathic online community for older people. *Computers in Human Behavior, 25*(5), 1139–1155. doi:10.1016/j.chb.2009.05.001

Picard, R. (2000). *Affective Computing.* MIT Press.

Pioggia, G., Tartarisco, G., Valenza, G., Ricci, G., Volpi, L., Siciliano, G., & Bonfiglio, S. (2010). A Pervasive Activity Management and Rehabilitation Support System for the Elderly. In Proceedings of PerCom Workshops (pp. 813–816). PerCom. doi:10.1109/PERCOMW.2010.5470548

Pollack, M. E., Brown, L., Colbry, D., McCarthy, C. E., Orosz, C., & Peintner, B. et al. (2003). Autominder: An intelligent cognitive orthotic system for people with memory impairment. *Robotics and Autonomous Systems, 44*(3-4), 273–282. doi:10.1016/S0921-8890(03)00077-0

Ponnekanti, S. R., Johanson, B., Kiciman, E., & Fox, A. (2003). Portability, extensibility and robustness in iROS. Pervasive Computing and Communications. 11-19.

Poole, S. (2004). *Trigger Happy: Videogames and Entertainment Revolution.* Arcade Publishing.

Porter, M. A., Onnela, J. P., & Mucha, P. J. (2009). Communities in networks. *Notices of the American Mathematical Society, 56*(9), 1082–1097.

Prescher, S., Bourke, A. K., Koehler, F., Martins, A., Sereno Ferreira, H., Boldt Sousa, T. ... Nelson, J. (2012). Ubiquitous Ambient Assisted Living Solution to Promote Safer Independent Living in Older Adults Suffering From Co-morbidity. In *Proceedings of Engineering in Medicine and Biology Society (EMBC)*, (pp. 5118–5121). IEEE. doi:10.1109/EMBC.2012.6347145

Profita, H. P., Clawson, J., Gilliland, S., Zeagler, C., Starner, T., Budd, J., & Do, E. Y.-L. (2013). *Don'T Mind Me Touching My Wrist: A Case Study of Interacting with On-body Technology in Public. In Proceedings of the 2013 International Symposium on Wearable Computers* (pp. 89–96). New York, NY: ACM. doi:10.1145/2493988.2494331

Psallidas, F., Ntoulas, A., & Delis, A. (2013). Soc web: Efficient monitoring of social network activities. In *Proceedings of the 14th International Conference on Web information systems Engineering–WISE 2013* (pp. 118-136) Nanjing, China: Springer. doi:10.1007/978-3-642-41154-0_9

Psygnosis. (1995). *Wipeout* [Video game]. PlayStation.

Q Entertainment. (2011). *Child of Eden* [Video game]. PlayStation 3.

Qian, K., & Cui, C. (2010). *Chronos Tennis*. Retrieved from http://processors.wiki.ti.com/index.php/Chronos_Tennis

Qnx. (n.d.). Retrieved from http://www.qnx.com/solutions/industries/medical/

Quinn, D. (2013). *Analysis of how young and older people interact using online social networks*. (PhD Dissertation). University of Ulster, Ulster, UK.

Quinn, D., Chen, L., & Mulvenna, M. (2011a). Does age make a difference in the behaviour of online social network users? In *Proceedings of Internet of Things (iThings/CPSCom), 2011 International Conference on and 4th International Conference on Cyber, Physical and Social Computing*, (pp. 266-272). Academic Press.

Quinn, D., Chen, L., & Mulvenna, M. (2011b). An examination of the behaviour of young and older users of facebook. In *Proceedings of 4th International Conference on eHealth*, (pp. 9-16). Academic Press.

Rabah, K. (2005). Secure Implementation of Message Digest, Authentication and Digital Signature. *Information Technology Journal, 4*(3), 204-221.

Rabiner, L. (1989). A tutorial on hidden markov models and selected applications in speech recognition. *Proceedings of the IEEE, 77*(2), 257–286. doi:10.1109/5.18626

Rakhecha, S., & Hsu, K. (2013). Reliable and Secure Body Fall Detection Algorithm in a wireless mesh network. Rochester, NY: Department of Computer Engineering, Kate Gleason College of Engineering, Rochester Insitute of Technology. doi:10.4108/icst.bodynets.2013.253528

Randell, D., Cui, Z., & Cohn, A. (1992). A spatial logic based on regions and connection. In *Proceedings of the 3rd International Conference on Principles of Knowledge Representation and Reasoning* (pp. 165–176). San Francisco, CA: Morgan Kaufmann.

Ranganathan, A., Shankar, C., & Campbell, R. (2005). Application polymorphism for autonomic ubiquitous computing. *Multiagent Grid Syst., 1*(2), 109–129.

Raymann, R. J. E. M., Swaab, D. F., & Van Someren, E. J. W. (2008). Skin deep: Enhanced sleep depth by cutaneous temperature manipulation. *Brain, 131*, 500–513. doi:10.1093/brain/awm315 PMID:18192289

Raymann, R. J. E. M., Swaab, D. F., & Van Someren, E. J. W. (2007b). Skin temperature and sleep-onset latency: Changes with age and insomnia. *Physiology & Behavior, 90*, 257–266. PMID:17070562

Raymann, R. J. E. M., & Van Someren, E. J. W. (2007a). Time-on-task impairment of psychomotor vigilance is affected by mild skin warming and changes with aging and insomnia. *Sleep, 30*, 96–103. PMID:17310870

Razmov, V., & Anderson, R. J. (2006). Experiences with Agile Teaching in Project-Based Courses. In *Proceedings of Annual Conference of the American Society for Engineering Education (ASEE)*. ASEE. Retrieved from http://www.cs.washington.edu/research/edtech/publications/RA06-ASEE_AgileTeaching.pdf

Reas, C., & Fry, C. (2013). *Processing* [Programming language]. Academic Press.

Rechtschaffen, A., & Kales, A. (1968). A manual of standardized terminology, techniques and scoring system for sleep stages of human subjects. In *National Institutes of Health Publications No. 204*. Washington, DC: U.S. Government Printing Office.

Reynolds, S. (2008). *Energy Flash: A Journey Through Rave Music and Dance Culture*. Picador.

Rheumatoid: Hand Exam. (2011). Retrieved December 08, 2011, from Clinical Exam: http://clinicalexam.com/pda/r_hand.htm

Rhodes, B. J. (1997). The wearable remembrance agent: a system for augmented memory. In *Proceedings of 2012 16th International Symposium on Wearable Computers*. Academic Press.

Rialle, V., Lamy, J.-B., Noury, N., & Bajolle, L. (2003). Telemonitoring of Patients at Home: A Software Agent Approach. *Computer Methods and Programs in Biomedicine*, *72*(3), 257–268. doi:10.1016/S0169-2607(02)00161-X PMID:14554139

Ribeiro, F. R., & José, R. (2007). *Proactive Scheduling for Situated Displays*. Paper presented at the Workshop on Ambient Intelligence Technologies and Applications. Guimarães.

Ribeiro, F. R., & José, R. (2009b). *Timeliness for dynamic source selection in situated public displays* Paper presented at the 5th Int. Conference on Web Information Systems and Technologies. Lisbon, Portugal.

Ribeiro, F. R., & José, R. (2009a). Place-aware content selection from dynamic web sources for public displays. In *Proceedings of 5th International Conference on Signal-Image Technology & Internet-Based Systems* (pp. 302-309). Marrakech: IEEE Computer Society Press. doi:10.1109/SITIS.2009.56

Ribeiro, F., & José, R. (2013). Smart content selection for public displays in ambient intelligence environments. *International Journal of Ambient Computing and Intelligence*, *5*(2), 35–55. doi:10.4018/jaci.2013040103

Richards, L., & Palmiter-Thomas, P. (1996). Grip strength measurement: A critical review of tools, methods and clinical utility. *Critical Reviews in Physical and Rehabilitation Medicine*, *32*(1), 87–109. doi:10.1615/CritRevPhysRehabilMed.v8.i1-2.50

Rico, J., & Brewster, S. (2010). *Usable Gestures for Mobile Interfaces: Evaluating Social Acceptability. In Proceedings of the SIGCHI Conference on Human Factors in Computing Systems* (pp. 887–896). New York, NY: ACM. doi:10.1145/1753326.1753458

Riemersma-van der Lek, R. F., Swaab, D. F., Twisk, J., Hol, E. M., Hoogendijk, W. J. G., & van Someren, E. J. W. (2008). Effect of bright light and melatonin on cognitive and noncognitive function in elderly residents of group care facilities. A randomized controlled trial. *Journal of the American Medical Association*, *299*(22), 2642–2655. doi:10.1001/jama.299.22.2642 PMID:18544724

Rimal, B., Choi, E., & Lumb, I. (2009). A taxonomy and survey of cloud computing systems. In *Proceedings of Inc, IMS and IDC, 2009* (pp. 44–51). IEEE. doi:10.1109/NCM.2009.218

Rivera-Illingworth, F., Callaghan, V., & Hagras, H. (2010). Detection of normal and novel behaviours in ubiquitous domestic environments. *The Computer Journal*, *53*(2), 142–151.

Roberts, P. (2012). *10 projection mapping demos that will blow your mind!* [Web log comment]. Retrieved August 28, 2013 from: http://www.creativebloq.com/video/projection-mapping-912849

Robins, G., Pattison, P., Kalish, Y., & Lusher, D. (2007). An introduction to exponential random graph (p*) models for social networks. *Social Networks*, *29*(2), 173–191. doi:10.1016/j.socnet.2006.08.002

Robinson, J. (2007, April 14). Tripping the Lights. *The Guardian*. Retrieved August 27, 2013 from: http://www.theguardian.com/artanddesign/2007/apr/14/art.culture/print

Roe, C., & Gonik, S. (2002). Server-side Design Principles for Scalable Internet Systems. *Software, IEEE*, *19*(2), 34–41. doi:10.1109/52.991330

Roman, G. (1985). A Taxonomy of Current Issues in Requirements Engineering. *IEEE Computer*, *28*(4), 14–21. doi:10.1109/MC.1985.1662861

Rosales, L., Skubic, M., Heise, D., Devaney, M. J., & Schaumburg, M. (2012). Heartbeat detection from a hydraulic bed sensor using a clustering approach. In *Proceedings of the 34th Annual Conference of the IEEE Engineering in Medicine and Biology Society (EMBS)*, (pp. 2383-2387). EMBS.

Roschelle, J. (2003). Unlocking the learning value of wireless mobile devices. *Journal of Computer Assisted Learning*, *19*(3), 260–272. doi:10.1046/j.0266-4909.2003.00028.x

Rouphael, T. J. (2008). *RF and Digital Signal Processing for Software-Defined Radio*. Newnes.

Russell, D. M., & Sue, A. (2003). Large Interactive Public Displays: Use Patterns, Support Patterns, Community Patterns. In K. O'Hara, M. Perry, E. Churchill, & D. Russell (Eds.), *Public and Situated Displays* (Vol. 2, pp. 3–17). Dordrecht, The Netherlands: Springer Netherlands. doi:10.1007/978-94-017-2813-3_1

Russell, J. A. (1980). A circumplex model of affect. *Journal of Personality and Social Psychology*, *39*(6), 1161–1178.

Russett, R., & Starr, C. (1976). *Experimental Animation: Origins of a New Art*. New York: Da Capo Press Inc.

Rutterford, A. (Video artist), & Autechre (Music). (2002). *Autechre: Gantz Graf* [Video]. Retrieved August 27, 2013 from: http://www.youtube.com/watch?v=nfwD05XA2YQ

Rutterford, A., & Kilroy, N. (2002). *Alex Rutterford on the creation of the Gantz Graf Video* [Web log comment]. Retrieved August 28, 2013 from: http://warp.net/records/autechre/alex-rutterford-on-the-creation-of-the-gantz-graf-video

Ruzzelli, A. G., Nicolas, C., Schoofs, A., & O'Hare, G. M. (2010). *Real-time recognition and profiling of appliances through a single electricity sensor*. Paper presented at the Sensor Mesh and Ad Hoc Communications and Networks (SECON). Washington, DC.

Sakagami, Y., Watanabe, R., Aoyama, C., Matsunaga, S., Higaki, N., & Fujimura, K. (2002). The intelligent ASIMO: system overview and integration. In *Proceedings of IEEE/RSJ International Conference on Intelligent Robots and Systems*. IEEE. doi:10.1109/IRDS.2002.1041641

Salazar, A. J., Silva, A. S., Borges, C. M., & Correia, M. V. (2010). An initial experience in wearable monitoring sport systems. In *Proceedings of Information Technology and Applications in Biomedicine (ITAB)*, (pp. 1-4). IEEE.

Salih, R. M., Othmane, L. B., & Lilien, L. (2011). Privacy Protection in Pervasive Healthcare Monitoring Systems with Active Bundles. In *Proceedings of Parallel and Distributed Processing with Applications Workshops (ISPAW)*, (pp. 311–315). IEEE. doi:10.1109/ISPAW.2011.60

Saposnik, G., & Levin, M.Outcome Research Canada. (2011). Virtual reality in stroke rehabilitation: A meta-analysis and implications for clinicians. *Stroke*, *42*(5), 1380–1386. doi:10.1161/STROKEAHA.110.605451 PMID:21474804

Saposnik, G., Teasell, R., Mamdani, M., Hall, J., McIlroy, W., & Cheung, D. et al. (2010). Effectiveness of Virtual Reality Using Wii Gaming Technology in Stroke Rehabilitation A Pilot Randomized Clinical Trial and Proof of Principle. *Stroke*, *41*(7), 1477–1484. doi:10.1161/STROKEAHA.110.584979 PMID:20508185

Sari, M. (2011). *LibHand: A library for Hand Articulations*. Retrieved from http://www.libhand.org/

Satoh, I. (2005). Self-deployment of distributed applications. In N. Guelfi, G. Reggio, & A. Romanovsky (Eds.), Scientific engineering of distributed java applications (Vol. 3409, p. 48-57). Springer Berlin/Heidelberg.

Satyanarayanan, M., Kozuch, M. A., Helfrich, C. J., & O'Hallaron, D. R. (2005). Towards seamless mobility on pervasive hardware. *Pervasive and Mobile Computing*, *1*(2), 157–189. doi:10.1016/j.pmcj.2005.03.005

Scardamalia, M., Bereiter, C., McLean, R. S., Swallow, J., & Woodruff, E. (1989). Computer-Supported Intentional Learning Environments. *Journal of Educational Computing Research*, *5*(1), 51–68.

Schmidt, H., Kapitza, R., & Hauck, F. J. (2007). Mobile-process-based ubiquitous computing platform: a blueprint. *In Proceedings of the 1st Workshop on Middleware-Application Interaction: In Conjunction with Euro-Sys 2007* (pp. 25–30). New York, NY: ACM.

Schnars, U., & Jueptner, W. (2005). *Digital holography.* Springer Berlin Heidelberg.

Schofield, P., Aveyard, B., & Black, C. (2007). *Management of Pain in Older People.* Keswick: M&K Publishing.

Scott, J. (2000). Social network analysis: A handbook (2nd ed.). London: Sage Publications.

Scott, K. (2013). *Harmony* [Software]. Not publically available. Retrieved August 28, 2013 from: http://www.digitalchaotics.com/harmony/

Segers, E., & Verhoeven, L. (2003). Effects of vocabulary training by computer in kindergarten. *Journal of Computer Assisted Learning, 19*(3), 557–566. doi:10.1046/j.0266-4909.2003.00058.x

Semiconductors, V. (2013). *Data Formats for IR Remote Control* (Document Number: 80071). Retrieved from MCS electronics: http://www.vishay.com/docs/80071/dataform.pdf

Seo, J., & Croft, W. B. (2007). *UMass at TREC 2007 Blog Distillation Task.* Paper presented at the Text Retrieval Conference. Gaithersburg, MD.

Shafer, G. (1976). *A Mathematical Theory of Evidence.* Princeton, NJ: Princeton University Press.

Shapiro, C. M., Bortz, R., Mitchell, D., Bartel, P., & Jooste, P. (1981). Slow-wave sleep: A recovery period after exercise. *Science, 214*(4526), 1253–1254. doi:10.1126/science.7302594 PMID:7302594

Sharples, M., Taylor, J., & Vavoula, G. (2010). A Theory of Learning for the Mobile Age. In B. Bachmair (Ed.), *Medienbildung in neuen Kulturräumen* (pp. 87–99). Wiesbaden: VS Verlag für Sozialwissenschaften. doi:10.1007/978-3-531-92133-4_6

Shikder, S., Mourshed, M., & Price, A. (2012). Therapeutic lighting design for the elderly: A review. *Perspectives in Public Health, 132*(6), 282–291. doi:10.1177/1757913911422288 PMID:23111083

Shin, J. H., Chee, Y. J., Jeong, D. U., & Park, K. S. (2010). Nonconstrained sleep monitoring system and algorithms using air-mattress with balancing tube method. *IEEE Transactions on Information Technology in Biomedicine, 14*(1), 147–156. PMID:19846378

Shuler, C. (2009). Pockets of potential: Using mobile technologies to promote children's learning. *Joan Ganz Cooney Centre.* Retrieved from http://www.joanganzcooneycenter.org/upload_kits/pockets_of_potential_1_.pdf

Siegenthaler, M., & Birman, K. (2009). Privacy Enforcement for Distributed Healthcare Queries. In *Proceedings of Pervasive Computing Technologies for Healthcare,* (pp. 1–6). Academic Press. doi:10.4108/ICST.PERVASIVEHEALTH2009.6016

Signore, J. D. (2007, April 2). Joshua White: The Joshua Light Show. *Gothamist.* Retrieved August 27, 2013 from: http://gothamist.com/2007/04/02/interview_joshu.php

Simmel, G. (1950). The sociology of georg simmel. (K. H. Wolff, Trans.). Simon and Schuster.

Simoncini, L. (2003). Architectural Challenges for "Ambient Dependability". In *Proceedings of Object-Oriented Real-Time Dependable Systems.* IEEE.

Simonea, L. S. (2007). A low cost instrumented glove for extended monitoring. *Journal of Neuroscience Methods, 160*(2), 335–348. doi:10.1016/j.jneumeth.2006.09.021 PMID:17069892

Sinoo, M. M., van Hoof, J., & Kort, H. S. M. (2011). Lighting conditions for older adults in the nursing home. Assessment of environmental illuminances and colour temperature. *Building and Environment, 46*(10), 1917–1927. doi:10.1016/j.buildenv.2011.03.013

Siu, P., Belaramani, N., Wang, C., & Lau, F. (2004). Context-aware state management for ubiquitous applications. In L. Yang, M. Guo, G. Gao, & N. Jha (Eds.), *Embedded and ubiquitous computing* (Vol. 3207, pp. 776–785). Springer Berlin Heidelberg. doi:10.1007/978-3-540-30121-9_74

Sky-Skan. (2013). *Definiti Theaters Powered by DigitalSky 2 | Sky-Skan.* Retrieved November 16, 2013 from: http://www.skyskan.com/definiti

Smalley, D. (1986). Spectro-morphology and Structuring Processes. In S. Emmerson (Ed.), *The Language of Electroacoustic Music* (pp. 61–93). London: Macmillan.

Smith, H. (1946-1957). *Early Abstractions* [Video]. Retrieved August 27, 2013 from: http://www.youtube.com/watch?v=-wYJ51nSXRQ

Sneha, S., & Varshney, U. (2013). A framework for enabling patient monitoring via mobile ad hoc network. *Decis. Support Syst., 55*(1), 218–234. DOI: 10.1016/j.dss.2013.01.024

Somers, V. K., Dyken, M. E., Mark, A. L., & Abboud, F. M. (1993). Sympathetic-nerve activity during sleep in normal subjects. *The New England Journal of Medicine, 328*, 303–307. PMID:8419815

Sommerville, I. (2004). *Software Engineering* (7th ed.). Pearson Addison Wesley.

Sonmisonmi. (2007). *Atari video music* [Video]. Retrieved August 28, 2013 from: http://www.youtube.com/watch?v=-NWwtZCpC2M

Son, Y.-S., Pulkkinen, T., Moon, K.-D., & Kim, C. (2010). Home energy management system based on power line communication. *IEEE Transactions on* Consumer Electronics, *56*(3), 1380–1386.

Spadotto, K. M. S. E., & Hawkins, J. (2009). ICT convergence, confluence and creativity: The application of emerging technologies for healthcare transformation. In *Proc. of the 3rd Int. Symp. on Medical Information and Communication Technology*. Academic Press.

Sprager, S., & Zazula, D. (2012). Heartbeat and respiration detection from optical interferometric signals by using a multimethod approach. *IEEE Transactions on Bio-Medical Engineering, 59*(10), 2922–2929. PMID:22907961

Spreeuwenberg, M. D., Willems, C., Verheesen, H., Schols, J., & de Witte, L. (2010). Dynamic lighting as a tool to influence the day-night rhythm of clients with psychogeriatric disorders: A pilot study in a Dutch nursing home. *Journal of the American Geriatrics Society, 58*(5), 981–982. doi:10.1111/j.1532-5415.2010.02825.x PMID:20722824

Stamatis, D. H. (2003). Failure mode and effect analysis: FMEA from theory to execution (2nd ed.). ASQ Quality Press.

Starner, T. (2008). Reading Your Mind: Interfaces for Wearable Computing. In *Proceedings ofInternational Symposium on Ubiquitous Virtual Reality*. Academic Press.

Starner, T. E. (1999). *Wearable Computing and Contextual Awareness*. Massachusetts Institute of Technology. Retrieved from http://hdl.handle.net/1721.1/9543

Starner, T., & Maguire, Y. (1999, March). Heat Dissipation in Wearable Computers Aided by Thermal Coupling with the User. *Mob. Netw. Appl., 4*(1), 3-13. 10.1023/A:1019113924178

Starner, T., Rhodes, B., Weaver, J., & Pentland, A. (1999). Everyday-use Wearable Computers. In *Proceedings ofInternational Symposium on Wearable Computers*. Academic Press.

Starner, T. (2001a, July). The challenges of wearable computing: Part 1. *Micro, IEEE, 21*(4), 44–52. doi:10.1109/40.946681

Starner, T. (2002, October). Attention, memory, and wearable interfaces. *Pervasive Computing, IEEE, 1*(4), 88–91. doi:10.1109/MPRV.2002.1158283

Starner, T. E. (2003). Powerful Change Part 1: Batteries and Possible Alternatives for the Mobile Market. *IEEE Pervasive Computing, 2*(4), 86–88. doi:10.1109/MPRV.2003.1251172

Starner, T. E., Snoeck, C. M., Wong, B. A., & McGuire, R. M. (2004). *Use of Mobile Appointment Scheduling Devices*. In Proceedings of CHI '04 Extended Abstracts on Human Factors in Computing Systems (pp. 1501–1504). New York, NY: ACM. http://doi.acm.org/10.1145/985921.986100

Starner, T., Leibe, B., Singletary, B., & Pair, J. (2000). *MIND-WARPING: Towards Creating a Compelling Collaborative Augmented Reality Game. In Proceedings of the 5th International Conference on Intelligent User Interfaces* (pp. 256–259). New York, NY: ACM. doi:10.1145/325737.325864

Starner, T., Weaver, J., & Pentland, A. (1998). *A Wearable Computer Based American Sign Language Recognizer. In Assistive Technology and Artificial Intelligence, Applications in Robotics, User Interfaces and Natural Language Processing* (pp. 84–96). London, UK: Springer-Verlag. http://dl.acm.org/citation.cfm?id=646629.696531

Stein, P. K., & Pu, Y. (2012). Heart rate variability, sleep and sleep disorders. *Sleep Medicine Reviews, 16*(1), 47–66. PMID:21658979

Stolterman, E., & Wiberg, M. (2010). Concept-driven interaction design research. *Human-Computer Interaction, 25*(2), 95–118. doi:10.1080/07370020903586696

Studio! K7. (Record Label). (1993-1998). *X-Mix* [Video series]. Retrieved August 27, 2013, from http://www.youtube.com/watch?v=izelmqskjaA&list=PLEA51AB0E440929B2

Sun, H., De Florio, V., Gui, N., & Blondia, C. (2007). Promises and Challenges of Ambient Assisted Living Systems. In *Proceedings of Information Technology: New Generations,* (pp. 1201–1207). ITGN. doi:10.1109/ITNG.2009.169

Sunil Kumar, C., Guru Rao, C. V., & Govardhan, A. (2010). A Framework for Interoperable Healthcare Information Systems. In *Proceedings of Computer Information Systems and Industrial Management Applications (CISIM),* (pp. 604–608). CISIM. doi:10.1109/CISIM.2010.5643522

Tablado, A., Illarramendi, A., Bagüés, M. I., Bermúdez, J., & Goñi, A. (2004). Aingeru: an Innovating System for Tele Assistance of Elderly People. In Proceedings of TELECARE (pp. 27–36). Academic Press.

Tan, Q., Kinshuk, Kuo, Y.-H., Jeng, Y.-L., Wu, P.-H., Huang, Y.-M., … Chang, M. (2009). Location-Based Adaptive Mobile Learning Research Framework and Topics. In *Proceedings of International Conference on Computational Science and Engineering,* (Vol. 1, pp. 140–147). IEEE. doi:10.1109/CSE.2009.96

Tanaka, F. (2014). Robotics for Supporting Childhood Education. In Y. Sankai, K. Suzuki, & Y. Hasegawa (Eds.), *Cybernics* (pp. 185–195). Springer Japan. doi:10.1007/978-4-431-54159-2_10

Tapia, E., Intille, S., & Larson, K. (2004). Activity recognition in the home using simple and ubiquitous sensors. In D. Hutchison, T. Kanade, J. Kittler, J. M. Kleinberg, A. Kobsa, F. Mattern, … G. Weikum (Eds.), *Pervasive Computing: 2nd International Conference, PERVASIVE 2004* (LNCS) (Vol. 3001, pp. 158–175). Berlin, Germany: Springer.

Tapia, D. I., Abraham, A., Corchado, J. M., & Alonso, R. S. (2009). Agents and ambient intelligence: Case studies. *Journal of Ambient Intelligence and Humanized Computing, 1*(2), 85–93. doi:10.1007/s12652-009-0006-2

Tapia, D. I., Bajo, J., Sánchez, J. M., & Corchado, J. M. (2008). An Ambient Intelligence Based Multi-Agent Architecture. In *Developing Ambient Intelligence* (pp. 68–78). Paris: Springer Paris. doi:10.1007/978-2-287-78544-3_7

Task Force of the European Society of Cardiology and the North American Society of Pacing and Electrophysiology. (1996, March). Heart rate variability: Standards of measurement, physiological interpretation and clinical use. *Circulation, 93*(5), 1043–1065. PMID:8598068

Tavenard, R., Salah, A., & Pauwels, E. (2007). Searching for temporal patterns in AmI sensor data. In B. Schiele, A. K. Dey, H. Gellersen, M. Tscheligi, R. Wichert, E. Aerts, & A. Buchmann (Eds.), *Ambient Intelligence: European Conference, AmI 2007* (LNCS) (Vol. 4794, pp. 53–62). Berlin, Germany: Springer.

The Eudaemons' Shoe. (1998). *The Eudaemons' Shoe.* Retrieved from http://wearcam.org/historical/node3.html

The National Sleep Foundation. (2012). *What makes a good night's sleep.* Available: http://www.sleepfoundation.org

Thelwall, M. (2008). Social networks, gender, and friending: An analysis of MySpace member profiles. *Journal of the American Society for Information Science and Technology, 59*(8), 1321–1330. doi:10.1002/asi.20835

Thompson, S. M., & Dean, M. D. (2009). Advancing information technology in health care. *Communications of the ACM, 52*(6), 118–121. doi:10.1145/1516046.1516077

Thorp, E. O. (1998). *The Invention of the First Wearable Computer. In Proceedings of the 2nd IEEE International Symposium on Wearable Computers* (p. 4). Washington, DC: IEEE Computer Society.http://dl.acm.org/citation.cfm?id=857199.858031

Threadx. (n.d.). Retrieved from http://www.qnx.com/solutions/industries/medical/

Tikuisis, P., & Ducharme, M. B. (1996). The effect of postural changes on body temperatures and heat balance. *European Journal of Applied Physiology, 72*, 451–459. PMID:8925816

Toivonen, R., Kovanen, L., Kivelä, M., Onnela, J. P., Saramäki, J., & Kaski, K. (2009). A comparative study of social network models: Network evolution models and nodal attribute models. *Social Networks, 31*(4), 240–254. doi:10.1016/j.socnet.2009.06.004

Toivonen, R., Onnela, J. P., Saramäki, J., Hyvönen, J., & Kaski, K. (2006). A model for social networks. *Physica A:Statistical and Theoretical Physics, 371*(2), 851–860. doi:10.1016/j.physa.2006.03.050

Tölgyessy, M., & Hubinský, P. (2011). *The Kinect Sensor in Robotics Education*. Bratislava: Slovak University of Technology. doi:10.1016/j.talanta.2011.09.055

Tomas, M., & Castro, D. (2011). Multidimensional Framework for the Analysis of Innovations at Universities in Catalonia. *Educational Policy, 19*(27), 48-60.

Toninelli, A., Montanari, R., & Corradi, A. (2009). Enabling Secure Service Discovery in Mobile Healthcare Enterprise Networks. *IEEE Wireless Communications, 16*(3), 24–32. doi:10.1109/MWC.2009.5109461

Toole, J., King, A., & He, L. (2011). *MSP430_Flying_Mouse*. Retrieved from MSP430_Flying_Mouse: http://processors.wiki.ti.com/index.php/MSP430_Flying_Mouse

Tran, N. X., Phan, H., & Dinh, V. V. (2009). Lecture Notes in Computer Science (Vol. 5611). Springer Berlin Heidelberg. doi:10.1007/978-3-642-02577-8_30

Traud, A. L., Kelsic, E. D., Mucha, P. J., & Porter, M. A. (2008). Community structure in online collegiate social networks. *ArXiv, 809*

Traynor, D., Xie, E., & Curran, K. (2010). Context-Awareness in Ambient Intelligence. *International Journal of Ambient Computing and Intelligence, 2*(1), 13–23. doi:10.4018/jaci.2010010102

Triantafyllidis, A., Koutkias, V., Chouvarda, I., & Maglaveras, N. (2012). A pervasive health system integrating patient monitoring, status logging and social sharing. *IEEE Transactions on Information Technology in Biomedicine.* PMID:23193318

Trifonova, A., & Ronchetti, M. (2006). Hoarding content for mobile learning. *International Journal of Mobile Communications, 4*(4), 459–476. doi:10.1504/IJMC.2006.008952

Trip Hackers. (2013). *Trip Hackers* [Facebook Group]. Retrieved November 19, 2013 from: https://www.facebook.com/TRIPHACKERS.RU?fref=ts

Trowell, I. (2001). Auto Synthesis. *Organised Sound, 6*(3).

Trumbull, D. (1968). Creating Special Effects for 2001: A Space Odyssey. *American Cinematographer, 49*(6). Retrieved August 27, 2013 from: http://www.visual-memory.co.uk/sk/2001a/page3.html

United Game Artists. (2001). *Rez* [Video game]. Dreamcast.

Unity Technologies. (2013). *Unity3D* [video game engine]. Author.

US Centre for Disease Control and Prevention. (2010). *Stroke Statistics: Internet Stroke Center.* Author.

Uslu, G., Altun, O., & Baydere, S. (2011). A Bayesian approach for indoor human activity monitoring. In *Proceedings of International Conference on Hybrid Intelligent systems* (pp. 324-327). Melacca: IEEE. doi:10.1109/HIS.2011.6122126

Vadas, K., Lyons, K. M., Ashbrook, D., Yi, J. S., Starner, T., & Jacko, J. A. (2006). *Reading on the go: An evaluation of three mobile display technologies*. Retrieved from http://hdl.handle.net/1853/13112

Vadas, K., Patel, N., Lyons, K., Starner, T., & Jacko, J. (2006). *Reading On-the-go: A Comparison of Audio and Hand-held Displays. In Proceedings of the 8th Conference on Human-computer Interaction with Mobile Devices and Services* (pp. 219–226). New York, NY: ACM. doi:10.1145/1152215.1152262

Van Cleave, D., & Rattan, K. (2000). Tuning of fuzzy logic controller using neural network. In *Proceedings of the IEEE National Conference Aerospace and Electronics* (pp. 305–312). Los Alamitos, CA: IEEE Computer Society.

Van Deun, D., Verhaert, V., Willemen, T., Buys, K., Haex, B., & Vander Sloten, J. (2013). Automatic modeling of customized human avatars using contour information. In *Proceedings of the International Digital Human Modeling Symposium* (pp. 1-6). Academic Press.

Van Deun, D., Verhaert, V., Willemen, T., Wuyts, J., Verbraecken, J., & Exadaktylos, V. et al. (2012). Biomechanics-based active control of bedding support properties and its influence on sleep. *Work (Reading, Mass.), 41*(Suppl. 1), 1274–1280. PMID:22316894

Van Halteren, A., Bults, R., Wac, K., Konstantas, D., Widya, I., Dokovski, N., et al. (2004). *Mobile Patient Monitoring: The Mobihealth System*. Academic Press.

van Hoof, J., Aarts, M. P. J., Rense, C. G., & Schoutens, A. M. C. (2009). Ambient bright light in dementia: Effects on behavior and circadian rhythmicity. *Building and Environment, 44*(1), 146–155. doi:10.1016/j.buildenv.2008.02.005

van Hoof, J., Kort, H. S. M., Duijnstee, M. S. H., Rutten, P. G. S., & Hensen, J. L. M. (2010). The indoor environment and the integrated building design of homes for older people with dementia. *Building and Environment, 45*(5), 1244–1261. doi:10.1016/j.buildenv.2009.11.008

van Hoof, J., Schoutens, A. M. C., & Aarts, M. P. J. (2009). High colour temperature lighting for institutionalised older people with dementia. *Building and Environment, 44*(9), 1959–1969. doi:10.1016/j.buildenv.2009.01.009

van Hoof, J., Westerlaken, A. C., Aarts, M. P. J., Wouters, E. J. M., Schoutens, A. M. C., Sinoo, M. M., & Aries, M. B. C. (2012). Light therapy: Methodological issues from an engineering perspective. *Health Care and Technology, 20*, 11–23. PMID:22297710

van Hoof, J., Wouters, E. J. M., Schräder, B., Weffers, H. T. G., Aarts, M. P. J., Aries, M. B. C., & Westerlaken, A. C. (2013). Intelligent light therapy for older adults: Ambient assisted living. In A. Agah (Ed.), *Medical Applications of Artificial Intelligence* (pp. 341–351). Boca Raton, FL: CRC Press/Taylor & Francis Group. doi:10.1201/b15618-22

Van Marken Lichtenbelt, W. D., Daanen, H. A., Wouters, L., Fronczek, R., Raymann, R. J., & Severens, N. M. et al. (2006). Evaluation of wireless determination of skin temperature using iButtons. *Physiology & Behavior, 88*, 489–447. PMID:16797616

Van Someren, E. J. W. (2006). Mechanisms and functios of coupling between sleep and temperature rhythms. *Brain Research, 153*, 309–324. PMID:16876583

van Someren, E. J. W., Kessler, A., Mirmiran, M., & Swaab, D. F. (1997). Indirect bright light improves circadian rest-activity rhythm disturbances in demented patients. *Biological Psychiatry, 41*(9), 955–963. doi:10.1016/S0006-3223(97)89928-3 PMID:9110101

Varshney, U. (2007). Pervasive Healthcare and Wireless Health Monitoring. *Mobile Networks and Applications, 12*(2-3), 113–127. doi:10.1007/s11036-007-0017-1

Vasiliou, A., & Economides, A. A. (2007). Mobile collaborative learning using multicast manets. *International Journal of Mobile Communications, 5*(4), 423–444. doi:10.1504/IJMC.2007.012789

Venkatasubramanian, K. K., Banerjee, A., & Gupta, S. K. S. (2010). PSKA: Usable and Secure Key Agreement Scheme for Body Area Networks. *IEEE Transactions on Information Technology in Biomedicine, 14*(1), 60–68. doi:10.1109/TITB.2009.2037617

Verhaert, V. et al. (2011b). The use of a generic human model to personalize bed design. In *Proceedings of 1st International Symposium on Digital Human Modeling*. Accepted for publication.

Verhaert, V., Druyts, H., Van Deun, D., Exadaktylos, V., Verbraecken, J., & Vandekerckhove, M. et al. (2012). Estimating spine shape in lateral sleep positions using silhouette-derived body shape models. *International Journal of Industrial Ergonomics, 42*(5), 489–498.

Verhaert, V., Haex, B., De Wilde, T., Berckmans, D., Vandekerckhove, M., Verbraecken, J., & Vander Sloten, J. (2011). Unobtrusive assessment of motor patterns during sleep based on mattress indentation measurements. *IEEE Transactions on Information Technology in Biomedicine, 15*(5), 787–794. PMID:21435985

Verhaert, V., Van Deun, D., Verbraecken, J., Vandekerckhove, M., Exadaktylos, V., Haex, B., & Vander Sloten, J. (2013). Smart control of spinal alignment through active adjustment of mechanical bed properties during sleep. *Journal of Ambient Intelligence and Smart Environments, 5*(4), 369–380.

Vidal, M., Turner, J., Bulling, A., & Gellersen, H. (2012). Wearable Eye Tracking for Mental Health Monitoring. *Computer Communications, 35*(11), 1306–1311. doi:10.1016/j.comcom.2011.11.002

VIDVOX, LLC. (2013). *VDMX5* [Software]. Mac. Retrieved August 28, 2013 from: http://vidvox.net

Volk, J. (2010). *Make Money Online With Affiliate Marketing*. Retrieved from www.jonathanvolk.com/4Xel2Sf9mj/jvolkaffiliateguide.pdf

Volz, A., Blum, R., Hberling, S., & Khakzar, K. (2007). Automatic, body measurements based generation of individual avatars using highly adjustable linear transformation. In *Proceedings of Digital Human Modelling*, (pp. 453-459). ICDHM.

VVVV Group. (2013). *VVVV* [Programming language]. PC.

Wagner, A. (Music), & Minter, J. (Video artist). (2005). *Merak* (Motion picture). DVD version of VHS PAL release, 1988. UK: Media Quest Production. Retrieved August 27, 2013 from: http://www.adrianwagner.com/awmerak.html

Wagner, M., & Carroll, S. (2001). DeepWave: Visualizing Music with VRML. In *Proceedings of the Seventh International Conference on Virtual Systems and Multimedia* (VSMM'01). doi:10.1109/VSMM.2001.969717

Wang, M., Boring, S., & Greenberg, S. (2012). *Proxemic peddler: a public advertising display that captures and preserves the attention of a passerby*. Paper presented at the 2012 International Symposium on Pervasive Displays. Porto, Portugal. doi:10.1145/2307798.2307801

Wan, J., O'Grady, M. J., & O'Hare, G. M. P. (2013). Bootstrapping Activity Modeling for Ambient Assisted Living. In D. Zeng, C. C. Yang, V. S. Tseng, C. Xing, H. Chen, F.-Y. Wang, & X. Zheng (Eds.), *Smart Health* (LNCS), (pp. 96–106). Springer Berlin Heidelberg. doi:10.1007/978-3-642-39844-5_12

Wasserman, A. (2010). *Software Engineering Issues for Mobile Application Development*. ACM Digital Library.

Wasserman, S., & Faust, K. (1994). *Social network analysis methods and applications*. Cambridge, UK: Cambridge University Press. doi:10.1017/CBO9780511815478

Webb, A. R. (2006). Considerations for lighting in the built environment: Non-visual effects of light. *Energy and Building, 38*(7), 721–727. doi:10.1016/j.enbuild.2006.03.004

Wees, W. C. (1992). Making Films for the Inner Eye: Jordan Belson, James Whitney, Paul Sharits. In *Light Moving in Time: Studies in the Visual Aesthetics of Avant-garde Film*. University of California Press.

Weichert, F., Bachmann, D., Rudak, B., & Fisseler, D. (2013). Analysis of the Accuracy and Robustness of the Leap Motion Controller. *Sensors (Basel, Switzerland), 13*(5), 6380–6393. doi:10.3390/s130506380 PMID:23673678

Weick, K. E. (1989). Theory construction as disciplined imagination. *Academy of Management Review, 14*(4), 516–531.

Weinel, J. (2011a). Tiny Jungle: Psychedelic Techniques in Audio-Visual Composition. In *Proceedings of the International Computer Music Conference 2011*. Retrieved August 27, 2013 from: http://www.jonweinel.com/wp-content/uploads/2011/08/JW_ICMC2011-Tiny_Jungle.pdf

Weinel, J. (2013). *Mezcal Animations #1-3* [Video]. Retrieved August 27, 2013 from: http://vimeo.com/69790818

Weinel, J., Cunningham, S., Roberts, N., Roberts, S., & Griffiths, D. (2013). *Psych Dome* [Video installation]. Retrieved August 27 2013 from: https://vimeo.com/78153713

Weiser, M. (1993). Hot topics-ubiquitous computing. *Computer, 26*(10), 71–72. doi:10.1109/2.237456

Weiser, M. (1993). Some Computer Science Issues in Ubiquitous Computing. *Communications of the ACM, 36*(7), 75–84. doi:10.1145/159544.159617

Weiser, M. (1994). The world is not a desktop. *Interaction, 1*(1), 7–8. doi:10.1145/174800.174801

Wellman, B. (1983). Network analysis: Some basic principles. *Sociological Theory*, *1*, 155–200. doi:10.2307/202050

Wenger, E. (2012). *ArtMatic* [Software]. Mac. Retrieved August 28, 2013 from: http://uisoftware.com

Whitney, J. (1961). *Catalogue* [Video]. Retrieved August 27, 2013 from: http://www.youtube.com/watch?v=TbV7loKp69s

Whitney, J. (1972). *Matrix III* [Video]. Retrieved August 27, 2013 from: http://www.youtube.com/watch?v=ZrKgyY5aDvA

Whitney, J. (1981). *Digital Harmony: On The Complementarity of Music and Visual Art*. McGraw-Hill Inc.

Wiegers, K. (2003). *Software Requirements*. Redmond: Microsoft.

Wijckmans, J., Van Deun, D., Buys, K., Vander Sloten, J., & Bruyninckx, H. (2013). Parametric Modeling of the Human Body Using Kinect Measurements. In *Proceedings on 4th International Conference and Exhibition on 3D Body Scanning Technologies* (pp. 117-126). Long Beach, CA: Academic Press.

Willemen, T., Van Deun, D., Verhaert, V., Vandekerckhove, M., Exadaktylos, V., & Verbraecken, J. et al. (2013). *An evaluation of cardio-respiratory and movement features with respect to sleep stage classification. IEEE Journal of Biomedical and Health Informatics*.

Wilson, D. (2012). *Circitified: Circuit Bending Workshop* [Lecture slides online]. Retrieved November 19, 2013 from: http://www.slideshare.net/circitfied/circuit-bending-workshop

Wilson, C., Boe, B., Sala, A., Puttaswamy, K. P. N., & Zhao, B. Y. (2009). User interactions in social networks and their implications. In *Proceedings of the 4th ACM European Conference on Computer Systems*, (pp. 205-218.) ACM. doi:10.1145/1519065.1519089

Wilson, G., Halvey, M., Brewster, S. A., & Hughes, S. A. (2011). *Some Like It Hot: Thermal Feedback for Mobile Devices*. In *Proceedings of the SIGCHI Conference on Human Factors in Computing Systems* (pp. 2555–2564). New York, NY: ACM. doi:10.1145/1978942.1979316

Winters, R. M., & Wanderley, M. M. (2013). Sonification of Emotion: Strategies for Continuous Display of Arousal and Valence. In *Proceedings of the 3rd International Conference on Music & Emotion (ICME3)*. University of Jyväskylä, Department of Music.

Witt, H. (2005). A Toolkit for Context-aware User Interface Development for Wearable Computers. In *Proceedings of Doctoral Colloquium at the 9th International Symposium on Wearable Computers (ISWC)*. ISWC.

Witt, H. (2007). *Human-Computer Interfaces for Wearable Computers: A Systematic Approach to Development and Evaluation*. (Ph.D. dissertation). Bremen.

Witt, H., Nicolai, T., & Kenn, H. (2006). Designing a Wearable User Interface for Hands-free Interaction in Maintenance Applications. In *Proceedings of IEEE International Conference on Pervasive Computing and Communications Workshops*, (pp. 652-655). IEEE. doi:10.1109/PERCOMW.2006.39

Witt, H., Nicolai, T., & Kenn, H. (2007, June). The WUI-Toolkit: A Model-Driven UI Development Framework for Wearable User Interfaces. In *Proceedings of 27th International Conference on Distributed Computing Systems Workshops, 2007* (pp. 43-43). ICDCSW. doi:10.1109/ICDCSW.2007.80

Worden, J. (2011). *Rheumatoid Arthritis*. Retrieved from BBC Health: http://www.bbc.co.uk/health/physical_health/conditions/in_depth/arthritis/aboutarthritis_rheumatoid.shtml

World, O. N. (2010). *The Smart Energy Home Market to Reach $3 Billion in 2014*. Retrieved from http://www.onworld.com/news/newssmartenergy.htm

Xu, L., Guo, D., Tay, F. E. H., & Xing, S. (2010). A wearable vital signs monitoring system for pervasive healthcare. In *Proceedings of Sustainable Utilization and Development in Engineering and Technology (STUDENT)*, (pp. 86 –89). IEEE. doi:10.1109/STUDENT.2010.5687003

Yaghmaie, M., & Bahreininejad, A. (2011). A context-aware adaptive learning system using agents. *Expert Systems with Applications*, *38*(4), 3280–3286. doi:10.1016/j.eswa.2010.08.113

Yakushev, A. V., Boukhanovsky, A. V., & Sloot, P. M. (2013). Topic crawler for social networks monitoring. *Knowledge Engineering and the Semantic Web, 394,* 214-227.

Yang, S., Peng, S., Song, A., Li, J., (2011). An one to many telerehabilitation training robot system based on virtual reality. *Gaojishu Tongxin/Chinese High Technology Letters, 21,* 191–195. doi:10.3772/j.issn.1002-0470.2011.02.014

Yan, H., Huo, H., Xu, Y., & Gidlund, M. (2010). Wireless sensor network based e-health system implementation and experimental results. *IEEE Transactions on* Consumer Electronics, *56*(4), 2288–2295. doi:10.1109/TCE.2010.5681102

Yu, M., Rhuma, A., Naqvi, S. M., Wang, L., & Chambers, J. (2012). A Posture Recognition-Based Fall Detection System for Monitoring an Elderly Person in a Smart Home Environment. *IEEE Transactions on* Information Technology in Biomedicine, *16*(6), 1274–1286. doi:10.1109/TITB.2012.2214786

Zafrulla, Z., Brashear, H., Starner, T., Hamilton, H., & Presti, P. (2011). *American Sign Language Recognition with the Kinect. In Proceedings of the 13th International Conference on Multimodal Interfaces* (pp. 279–286). New York, NY: ACM. http://doi.acm.org/10.1145/2070481.2070532

Zaphiris, P., & Sarwar, R. (2006). Trends, similarities, and differences in the usage of teen and senior public online newsgroups. *ACM Transactions on Computer-Human Interaction (Tochi), 13*(3), 422. doi:10.1145/1183456.1183461

Zhang, H., Wang, F.-Y., & Ai, Y. (2005). *An OSGi and agent based control system architecture for smart home.* Paper presented at the Networking, Sensing and Control, 2005. Washington, DC.

Zhang, Y., & Xiao, H. (2009). Bluetooth-based sensor networks for remotely monitoring the physiological signals of a patient. *Trans. Info. Tech. Biomed., 13.*

Zhang, Y., Huang, G., Zhang, W., Liu, X., & Mei, H. (2012). Towards module-based automatic partitioning of java applications. *Frontiers of Computer Science, 6*(6), 725–740.

Zhao, P., Simões, M. G., & Suryanarayanan, S. (2010). *A conceptual scheme for cyber-physical systems based energy management in building structures.* Paper presented at the 9th IEEE/IAS International Conference on Industry Applications (INDUSCON). Washington, DC.

Zhou, Y., Cao, J., Raychoudhury, V., Siebert, J., & Lu, J. (2007). A middleware support for agent-based application mobility in pervasive environments. In *Proceedings of the 32nd International Conference on Distributed Computing Systems Workshops* (p. 9). Los Alamitos, CA: IEEE Computer Society. doi:10.1109/ICDCSW.2007.12

Zhu, M., Zhang, D., Zhang, J., & Lim, B.Y. (2007). *Context-Aware Informative Display.* Paper presented at the International Conference on Multimedia and Expo. Beijing, China.

Zhu, X., Chen, W., Nemoto, T., Kanemitsu, Y., Kitamura, K., Yamakoshi, K., & Wei, D. (2006). Real-time monitoring of respiration rhythm and pulse rate during sleep. *IEEE Transactions on Bio-Medical Engineering, 53*(12), 2553–2563. PMID:17153213

Zsiga, K., Edelmayer, G., Rumeau, P., Péter, O., Tóth, A., & Fazekas, G. (2013). Home care robot for socially supporting the elderly: Focus group studies in three European countries to screen user attitudes and requirements. *International Journal of Rehabilitation Research. Internationale Zeitschrift fur Rehabilitationsforschung. Revue Internationale de Recherches de Readaptation, 36*(4), 375–378. doi:10.1097/MRR.0b013e3283643d26 PMID:24189106

Zurita, G., Baloain, N., & Baytelman, F. (2008). Using Mobile Devices to Foster Social Interactions in the Classroom. In *Proceedings of Computer Supported Cooperative Work in Design.* CSCW. doi:10.1109/CSCWD.2008.4537123

About the Contributors

Kevin Curran is a Reader in Computer Science at the University of Ulster and group leader for the Ambient Intelligence Research Group. His achievements include winning and managing UK and European Framework projects and Technology Transfer Schemes. Dr. Curran has made significant contributions to advancing the knowledge and understanding of computer networking and systems, evidenced by over 700 published works. He is perhaps most well known for his work on location positioning within indoor environments, pervasive computing, and Internet security. His expertise has been acknowledged by invitations to present his work at international conferences, overseas universities, and research laboratories. He is a regular contributor to BBC radio and TV news in the UK and is an IEEE Technical Expert for Internet/Security matters.

* * *

Mariëlle P. J. Aarts graduated at the department of the Built Environment at the Eindhoven University of Technology on Office Lighting. Her research was part of a bigger project at Philips Lighting where light preferences of office workers were analyzed. After being a light-consultant for 7 years, she returned to the now called Building Lighting chair. She teaches students how to integrate lighting in their building design. Knowledge of (day)light physics, electric lighting, as well as human responses to light are essential to determine solutions. Currently, light for elderly people and specifically people with dementia and schoolchildren are her research specialization. In her research, she tries to establish the relation between the physical aspects of light and its health related effects. Aarts is an assistant professor at the Eindhoven University of Technology; chair Building Lighting, unit Building Physics and Services, Department of the Built Environment.

Claas Ahlrichs is a student of the University Bremen. He enrolled in 2007, started to study computer science and is currently preparing for graduation. He is working as a student assistant at the Centre for Computing Technology (TZI) in the field of wearable computing.

Ricardo S. Alonso is a doctoral candidate at the Faculty of Sciences of the University of Salamanca (Spain). His research interests include wireless sensor networks, embedded devices, distributed systems, and AI techniques. He received a MSc in Intelligent Systems from the University of Salamanca (Spain) in 2009, and a graduate engineering degree in Telecommunications from the University of Valladolid (Spain) in 2007.

Myriam Aries holds a MSc in Building Technology (TU Delft, 2001) and a PhD in Building Physics/ Lighting (TU Eindhoven, 2005). After completion of her PhD she has worked as a post-doctoral fellow of Lighting (NRC Canada, 2005-2007), as an Indoor Environment and Health researcher (TNO Built Environment and Geosciences, 2007-2009), and currently as an assistant professor Lighting Technology (TU Eindhoven, 2010 - present). Myriam has expertise in the field of daylight application, visual comfort, and human light and health demands in the built environment. She uses statistical models next to computer modeling and simulation in order to investigate the relationship between physical (light) aspects of the built environment, overall environmental satisfaction, visual comfort, visual performance, and health. She is secretary of the Dutch Light and Health Research Foundation (SOLG) and chairs the program committee of the LICHT2014 conference. She is also member of the TU/e Intelligent Lighting Institute (ILI).

Aaron Bond holds a first class honours degree in Computing from the University of Ulster. He is currently employed in the Northern Ireland IT industry and his research interests include programming, vision systems, and networking.

Stefano Bromuri is a senior research scientist at HES-SO, and he obtained his PhD at Royal Holloway university of London in October 2009, with a thesis on distributed agent environments titled Generalised Ontological Environments for Multiagent Systems (GOLEM). Dr. Bromuri was directly involved with the EU FP6 ARGUGRID project where he was in charge of the implementation and testing of the infrastructure. In particular, Dr. Bromuri expertise lays in distributed multi-agent systems with particular focus on the concept of agent environment, combining the concept of agent environment with multiple areas such as pervasive computing for assisted living, Semantic Web combined with argumentation theory and distributed event-based systems. At HES-SO, he is working as a working package leader in the EU FP7 COMMODITY12 project, in which he also leads the technical development of the project. Furthermore, Dr. Bromuri works on innovative ways to manage pervasive healthcare environments for assisted living as co-investigator of the project G-DEMANDE and MONDAINE.

Albert Brugués obtained the degree in Telecommunications Engineering from Autonomous University of Barcelona (UAB) in 2008, and the MSc in Telemedicine and Biomedical Engineering from Polytechnic University of Madrid (UPM) in 2010. Currently he is a researcher at HES-SO, where he is working on the application of the agent technology in the field of pervasive healthcare. Previously he was at Polytechnic University of Catalonia (UPC) involved in the definition of a network protocol based on agents for the secure exchange of clinical data.

Sean Carlin has a first class honours degree in Computing from the University of Ulster. He is experienced in aspects of computing such as computer hardware, operating systems, and Web development. He has a strong interest in dynamic Website development and Web 2.0 technologies and uses many Web-based technologies such as HTML, XML, CSS, RSS, including server-side script technologies such as PHP, ASP.NET 3.5 coupled with client-side technologies such as Javascript. He is highly proficient in using SQL and database applications such as MySQL and SQL server 2008 and enjoys application development using Java and C++.

Liming Chen is a reader within the School of Computing and Mathematics, University of Ulster, UK. He received a BSc and MSc in Computing Engineering from Beijing Institute of Technology, China, and DPhil in Artificial Intelligence from De Montfort University, UK. His current research interests include semantic technologies, knowledge management, intelligent agents, pervasive computing, and social computing and their applications in smart homes and intelligent environments. He has published widely in above areas.

Marcello Cinque graduated with honours from University of Naples, Italy, in 2003, where he received the PhD degree in Computer Engineering in 2006. Currently, he is Assistant Professor at the Department of Computer and Systems Engineering (DIS) of the University of Naples Federico II. Dr. Cinque is chair and/or TPC member of several tecnica conferences and workshops on dependable, mobile, and pervasive systems, including IEEE PIMRC, DEPEND, and ACM ICPS. His research interests include dependability analysis of mobile and sensor systems, and middleware solutions for mobile ubiquitous systems.

Aodhán Coffey studied Electronic Engineering in NUI Maynooth from 2006-2010, where he obtained a first class honours degree. He is currently a member of the Biomedical Engineering research group at NUI Maynooth as a PhD student. The title of his PhD is "Technology Derived Solutions for Improving the Efficacy of Unsupervised Physical Rehabilitation Post Stroke" and is supervised by Dr Tomás Ward. This project is funded by a John Hume scholarship and an Enterprise Ireland grant. This research focuses is to explore the potential of wearable sensors and smart technology for improving patient compliance with unsupervised physical therapy and in enhancing the outcome of recovery by diffusing rehabilitation into the activities of daily living.

Juan M. Corchado is Dean at the Faculty of Sciences and leader of the BISITE Research Group of the University of Salamanca, Spain. His research interests include hybrid AI and distributed systems. He received a PhD in Computer Science from the University of Salamanca (Spain) in 1998 and a PhD in Artificial Intelligence (AI) from the University of Paisley, Glasgow (UK) in 2000.

Antonio Coronato is a researcher at the Institute of High-Performance Computing and Networking (ICAR) of the National Research Council (CNR) of Italy. His research focuses on pervasive computing and component-based architectures. Coronato received an MSc in computer engineering from "Federico II" University in Naples. He is a member of the ACM.

Stuart Cunningham joined Glyndŵr University in 2003, where he is currently Head of the Department of Creative Industries. He was awarded the BSc degree in Computer Networks in 2001, and in 2003 was awarded the MSc Multimedia Communications degree with Distinction, both from the University of Paisley (UK). In 2009, he was awarded the degree of PhD in Data Reduced Audio Coding by the University of Wales (UK). His research interests cover a broad range of computing and creative hybrids and include audio compression techniques, human-computer interaction, and sound design. He currently serves on the BCS Computer Arts Society committee. Stuart was a member of the MPEG Music Notation Standards (MPEG-SMR) working group.

Giuseppe De Pietro is a Senior Researcher at the Institute of High Performance Computing and Networking(ICAR) of the National Research Council (CNR). He is a contract professor of Information Systems at the Università Partenope of Naples. His research interests cover pervasive computing, multimodal, health monitoring, and virtual reality environments. He is member of the IEEE.

Óscar García is a PhD student researching in the area of e-learning and ambient intelligence at the Faculty of Sciences of the University of Salamanca (Spain). His research interests include ubiquitous communications, wireless technologies and distributed systems. He received a graduate degree in Telecommunications from the University of Valladolid (Spain) in 2006.

Hans Guesgen holds a diploma in Computer Science and Mathematics of the University of Bonn, a Doctorate in Computer Science of the University of Kaiserslautern, and a higher Doctorate (Habilitation) in Computer Science of the University of Hamburg, Germany. He worked as a research scientist at the GMD in Sankt Augustin from 1983 to 1992, primarily in the area of artificial intelligence and expert systems. During this period, he held a one-year post-doctoral fellowship at the International Computer Science Institute in Berkeley, California, where his research focus changed to spatial and temporal reasoning. In 1992, he joined the Computer Science Department of the University of Auckland, where for almost 15 years he led the AI research group and was involved in projects on constraint satisfaction, spatio-temporal reasoning, fuzzy logic, heuristic search, computer games, health informatics, and others. In 2007, he was appointed Chair of Computer Science in the School of Engineering and Advanced Technology at Massey University.

Bart Haex, after obtaining his PhD degree in the field of Biomedical Engineering, has been active in the creation of interdisciplinary research and innovation collaboration platforms, bringing together people with backgrounds in medicine, engineering, and humanities. His research is dedicated to ergonomic aspects of sleeping. As a professor, he is teaching biomedical engineering at both Leuven University (Belgium) and Maastricht University (Netherlands). At the latter university, he is Director of Research Policy.

Richard Harte is a PhD candidate in the Bio-electronics Research Cluster in the College of Engineering of Informatics at NUI Galway under Professor Gearóid O Laighin. His research is funded by the FP7 backed WIISEL project (www.wiisel.eu) and focuses on the design and use of connected health devices in the home by older adults, particularly in the area of fall prevention and disease management. Richard completed his MEng at NUI Maynooth in 2010 in Electronic Engineering, writing his thesis on the design of a haptic robotic device for stroke rehabilitation. He then worked for 18 months in Ryanair as a materials engineer before taking up his fellowship at NUI Galway.

Thomas Holz is a research assistant in the Autonomic Home Area Network Infrastructure (AUTHENTIC) project. He is also completing a PhD at University College Dublin on the topic of "Mixed Reality Agents." His research interests include augmented reality and the difference of human reactions to virtual and physical agents. He is a graduate of the University of Applied Sciences Harz, Germany, and worked on augmented reality at the Fraunhofer Institute for Computer Graphics in Darmstadt, Germany, in the GEIST project. He also reviews extensively for the *Journal of Social Robotics* and has guest lectured repeatedly on the topic of human-robot interaction.

Hendrik Iben studied Computer Science at the University Bremen and received his diploma (Diplom in Informatik, Dipl.Inf.) in 2007. He participated in the student project PEnG (Physical Environment Games) were he first published in the field of wearable computing. Since then he has been working as a PhD student in Prof. Herzog's wearable computing workgroup at the TZI. He is currently engaged in the BMWi project SiWear where wearable computing equipment is used to improve the workflow in industrial picking and service scenarios.

Dan Johansson holds a PhD in the subject Mobile Systems from Luleå University of Technology, Sweden. He works at the Department of Computer Science, Electrical, and Space Engineering, and his research interests include mobile systems, application mobility, context-awareness, mobile services and applications, as well as e-Services and emerging Web technologies.

Rui José is an Assistant Professor at the University of Minho, in Portugal, where he leads the Ubicomp research group. Rui José received his PhD in Computer Science from Lancaster University in 2001. His research interests are in ubiquitous systems in general and particularly on the design and development of ubiquitous information services that are situated within particular physical and social settings. In recent years, he has been focusing on public digital displays and how they can be transformed into a new open communication medium for public and semi-public spaces. He has been PI or co-PI in multiple international research projects (FP7, Portugal/CMU partnership) and also national projects (QREN, FCT) on this topic. Rui José has also authored over 100 publications, half of which related with public displays. In 2012, he hosted the first Symposium on Pervasive Displays, which is now the key world event for public displays research. Rui José is a member of ACM and its SIGCHI. Contact him at rui@dsi.uminho.pt.

Michael Lawo is with TZI (Centre for Computing Technology) of Universitaet Bremen since 2004. He is professor for Applied Computer Science involved in numerous projects of wearable computing and artificial intelligence. He is a 1975 graduate of Ruhr-Universitaet-Bochum, got his PhD in 1981 from Essen University and became professor there in 1992. He has more than 15 years of experience in the IT industry in different management positions, and is author, co-author and co-publisher of 8 books and more than 120 scientific papers on numerical methods and computer applications also in healthcare, optimization, IT-security, and wearable computing.

David Lillis graduated from University of Limerick with a BA (Hons) in Law and Accounting in 2002. Since then, he has also received a HDip, MSc, and PhD in Computer Science, from University College Dublin. He worked as a Post-Doctoral Research Fellow for the CLARITY: Centre for Sensor Web Technologies. He is currently a Lecturer in Computer Science at University College Dublin, where his research interests include Multi Agent Systems and Information Retrieval.

Stephen Marsland has a BA (Hons) in Mathematics from the University of Oxford and a PhD in "Self-Organisation and Novelty Detection" from the University of Manchester, which he completed in 2002. Since then he has spent time at the Santa Fe Institute, the University of Bremen and the University of Manchester, where he was a lecturer in computer science and a researcher in the division of Imaging Science and Biomedical Engineering. He moved to Massey University in 2004, and was awarded an Early Career research award there in 2005. He is currently a professor and the postgraduate director of the School of Engineering and Advanced Technology at Massey University.

Niall McCarroll is a PhD Researcher at the ISRC centre, University of Ulster, Magee, researching bio-inspired solutions for face detection and recognition using spiking neural networks. Niall holds a First Class Honours degree in Computer Science from University of Ulster and a First Class Honours degree in Psychology from Queen's University, Belfast. He is experienced in aspects of computing such as Web development, graphic and multimedia design. He has a strong interest in dynamic website development and Web 2.0 technologies and uses many Web based technologies such as HTML5, XML, CSS3, RSS, and client-side technologies such as Javascript and JQuery. He is highly proficient in application development using Java, C++, and C#.

Nigel McKelvey (MSc, BSc, PGCE, MICS) is a lecturer in Computing at the Letterkenny Institute of Technology and specialises in teaching secure programming techniques at both undergraduate and postgraduate level. Other areas of interest include ethical gaming, performance-based programming, and digital forensics. Nigel is currently completing a Doctorate in Education focusing on adopting heuristic programming techniques within the classroom.

Joseph McMahon (BSc) is a graduate in Computer Science of the University of Ulster. He is presently working in the IT industry and his research interests include distributed systems, mobile and Internet Technologies.

Anthea Middleton received BE and ME degrees in Electronic Engineering in 2009 and 2010, respectively. She then worked as a researcher in the field of motion tracking for movement-based rehabilitation. In 2013, she took up a position as system engineer at Valeo Vision Systems, where she develops system architecture for vision-based automotive applications. Her research interests lie in computer vision techniques, novel interfaces for rehabilitation, pervasive computing, and game development.

Conor Muldoon is a Research Scientist in University College Dublin (UCD) with research interests in Wireless Sensor Networks, Multi-Agent Systems, Machine Learning, and Ubiquitous Computing. He holds a PhD in Computer Science and a first class BSc (Honours) degree in Computer and Software Engineering. From 2009 to 2012, he was an INSPIRE IRCSET Marie Curie Research Fellow hosted in the University of Oxford from 2009 to 2011 and UCD in 2012. Prior to this, from 2007 to 2009, he was a Government of Ireland Embark Fellow in UCD. He has over 50 publications and was a winner of the Cooperative Information Agents System Innovation Award in Helsinki, Finland, in 2003.

Maurice Mulvenna is Professor of Computer Science in the School of Computing and Mathematics at the University of Ulster, UK, and a senior member of both the Institute of Electrical and Electronics Engineers and the Association for Computing Machinery. He is also a chartered member of the British Computer Society.

Michael O'Grady is a Postdoctoral Researcher at the School of Computer Science and Informatics at University College Dublin. His research interests include Ambient Intelligence, Mobile Computing, and Multimedia Systems. He has spent over a decade working in the software and telecommunications industries. In his research career, he has authored and contributed to over 110 publications in the broad area of ambient Intelligence, and has served in a variety of roles in conference organization and review committees. Dr. O'Grady is a senior member of the ACM and IEEE. He is a member of the editorial board of the *Journal of Ambient Intelligence and Humanized Computing*.

Gregory O'Hare completed his studies at the University of Ulster graduating with a BSc, MSc, and PhD. He held the position of Head of the Department of Computer Science at University College Dublin (UCD) 2001-2004. Prior to joining UCD, he has been on the Faculty of the University of Central Lancashire (1984-86) and the University of Manchester (1986-1996). He is an Associate Professor within the School of Computer Science and Informatics at UCD. He has published over 350 refereed publications in Journals and International Conferences, 7 books, and has won significant grant income (ca €28.00M). O'Hare is an established researcher of international repute. His research interests are in the areas of Distributed Artificial Intelligence and Multi-Agent Systems (MAS), and Mobile and Ubiquitous Computing, Autonomic Systems and Wireless Sensor Networks.

Tadhg O'Sullivan received his PhD on the topic of "Visualisation and Quantification of HIV-Associated-Lipodystrophy from Magnetic Resonance Images" from University College Dublin in 2012. He holds an honours degree in Psychology from the American College Dublin and an honours degree in Computer Science from University College Dublin. He is currently a postdoctoral researcher in the Autonomic Home Area Network Infrastructure (AUTHENTIC) project and has previously guest lectured in University College Dublin. His research interests include 3D visualisation, image processing, interface design, and machine learning.

Josep Pegueroles was born in Tortosa (Spain) in 1974. He received the MS degree in Telecommunications Engineering in 1999, and the PhD degree in 2003, both from the Polytechnic University of Catalonia (UPC). In 1999, he joined the Information Security Workgroup (ISG) within the Telematics Services Research Group (SERTEL) at the Department of Telematics Engineering (ENTEL) of the UPC. Currently, he works as assistant professor at the Telecommunications Engineering School in Barcelona (ETSETB). His research interests include security for multimedia networked services and secure group communications.

Richard Picking, BSc (Hons), MSc (Sheff), PhD (Lough), is Reader in Human-Computer Interaction at Glyndwr University, Wrexham, Wales. He is also the Director of the Glyndwr University Centre for Creative and Applied Research for the Digital Society (CARDS) and Chair of the British Computer Society (BCS) Specialist Group for Health in Wales, UK. He specializes in user interface design and evaluation, and was the lead designer and technical manager for User Experience on the FP6 EU-funded programme: "Easyline+: Low Cost Advanced White Goods for a Longer Independent Life of Elderly People." He has extensive experience in both academia and industry, and has worked as a user interface design expert on many projects in a wide range of industries, such as engineering, logistics, security, production control, healthcare, and e-commerce. He is Chair of the International Conference on Internet Technologies and Applications (ITA) and has over 50 publications in quality journals and conference proceedings, and is also the author of *Get on up with Java*, a computer programming text book.

Darren Quinn is a business analyst with a global bank who has attained a BSc (Hons) and a PhD from the school of Computing and Mathematics, University of Ulster, UK. His core research interests are in social computing, gerontechnology, and human computer interaction with a focus on how systems impact upon Quality of Life. Recent studies have evaluated the real life impact of social network usage, determining impact upon Quality of Life. Darren has published research in a number of industry publications and presented at several international conferences. Further interests include the concept of big data and how it may be leveraged to reveal new insights.

Fernando Reinaldo Ribeiro is an adjunct professor at the Informatics Department on Polytechnic Institute of Castelo Branco, PT. He holds a PhD in Information and Communication Technologies from University of Minho. He graduated in Electrotechnical Engineering at the UTAD, PT. He completed his MSc in Computer and Electrotechnical Engineering at the University of Porto, PT. He is also a researcher in the Mobile and Ubiquitous Systems Group at University of Minho. His research interests include ubiquitous computing, context-aware systems, pervasive advertising, environment intelligence, and public displays systems.

Björn Schrader is the head of the interdisciplinary focus Licht@hslu of the University of Applied Science and Arts Lucerne Engineering and Architecture, in Horw/Luzern, Switzerland. His main research interest concerns lighting engineering, energy efficiency, daylight and artificial light, nonvisual effects of light. He graduated in electro-technics main focus lighting technology and media technologies from the Technische Universität Ilmenau, in Ilmenau, Germany. He gathered industrial experience as a senior lighting consultant by Amstein and Walthert and Zumtobel AG in Zürich, Switzerland.

Michael Ignaz Schumacher is a full Professor in the Institute of Business Information Systems at the University of Applied Sciences Western Switzerland (HES-SO) since 2007. Previously, he held positions at the Swiss Federal Institute of Technology Lausanne (EPFL), where he was responsible for the FP6 European project CASCOM, and at the Robotics Institute in Carnegie Mellon University in Pittsburgh (USA) as a visiting researcher. He has worked in project management in an international Swiss foundation committed in social investment. He holds a PhD and an MSc in Computer Science and Biology from the University of Fribourg in Switzerland. In 2009, he founded the Applied Intelligent Systems Lab (AISLab) that focuses on distributed information systems and artificial intelligence applied to healthcare. He is currently working on multi-parametric analysis for diabetes type 1 and 2 in the framework of the European FP7 project COMMODITY12, on the Nano-Tera GDEMANDE and the Hasler Foundation MONDAINE projects that develop platforms to monitor gestational diabetes, and on several medical interoperability projects (such as FNS SemHealthCoord), that define solutions to exchange medical information between caretakers. He will also be working in the Nano-Tera project Theraper (Therapeutic Drug Monitoring for Personalized Medicine), providing an intelligent agent based cloud infrastructure. He is member of the commission "Architecture and Standards" of the Swiss eHealth strategy. In 2012, the startup company Fairtrace was founded by a research project led by AISLab.

Dante I. Tapia is a researcher at the BISITE Research Group of the University of Salamanca, Spain. His research interests include ubiquitous computing, wireless technologies, distributed architectures, and middleware systems. He received a PhD in Computer Science from the University of Salamanca (Spain) in 2009.

Alessandro Testa received in 2008 his MS degree in Computer Engineering from the University of Naples "Federico II," Italy. He is a PhD student in the MobiLab Group at the Computer and Systems Engineering Department of the University of Naples "Federico II." He is a research fellow at the Italian National Research Council (CNR) - Institute for High-Performance Computing and Networking (ICAR), where he is involved in the design of RunTime Verification Techniques in the Ambient Intelligence Systems used in the Healthcare Field. Alessandro Testa's research interests focus on analysis and implementation of platforms for monitoring of Wireless Sensor Networks. He is an IEEE Member since 2009.

Dorien Van Deun (1986, Geel, Belgium) received the BSc degree in Mechanical Engineering from KU Leuven, Belgium, in July 2007, and the MSc degree in Biomedical Engineering from KU Leuven, Belgium, in July 2009. She is currently working as a Doctoral student at the Biomechanics section of the Mechanical Engineering Department, KU Leuven, Belgium, to study and optimize ergonomics in sleep by means of integrated measurement tools and actuators in bedding systems.

Joost van Hoof, PhD, MSc, Eur Ing (1980), has a background in building physics and systems, with a specialisation in dementia, housing, and technology. He works with the Institute of Allied Health Professions of Fontys University of Applied Sciences in Eindhoven. Van Hoof is involved in the development of an interfacultary centre for education and research in the field of healthcare and technology.

Sabine Van Huffel received the MD in Computer Science Engineering in June 1981, the MD in Biomedical Engineering in July 1985, and the PhD in Electrical Engineering in June 1987, all from KU Leuven, Belgium. She is full professor at the department of Electrical Engineering, KU Leuven, Belgium, and also PI of the iMinds Medical IT Department. In April 2013, she received an honorary doctorate from Eindhoven University of Technology, together with an appointment as a distinguished professor. She is heading the Biomedical Data Processing Research Group with focus on the development of numerically reliable and robust algorithms for improving medical diagnostics.

Jos Vander Sloten, MSc, PhD (°1962, Leuven, Belgium) is full professor at the Division of Biomechanics at KU Leuven. He also chairs the Leuven Medical Technology Centre (L-MTC), which he founded in 2008. His teaching assignments include basic engineering courses and biomedical engineering courses. From 2006 to 2012 he served as program director of the Master in Biomedical Engineering at KU Leuven. His research interests are computer applications in musculoskeletal biomechanics and computer integrated surgery, on which he authored more than 160 journal papers. He is member of the council of the Belgian Society for Medical and Biological Engineering and Computing, and a former council member of the European Society of Biomechanics. In the European Alliance for Medical and Biological Engineering and Science (EAMBES) he served as secretary-general (2003-2004), president-elect (2005) and president (2006). He was recently elected Founding Fellow of EAMBES. He is a co-founder of the spin-off company Custom8 and member of the board of directors of the company Materialise NV.

Vincent Verhaert (1983, Belgium) received his MSc degree in Mechanical Engineering in 2006 and started working on the topic of ergonomics in sleep research back in 2007. After obtaining his PhD degree in 2011, he focused on integrating his academic know-how into actual consumer products that improve sleep, effectively building the foundations of IRISI. IRISI stands for Innovative Research In Sleep Improvement and develops scientific-based products and applications that improve sleep quality (www.irisi.be).

Tomas Ward is Senior Lecturer in Electronic Engineering at NUI Maynooth (since 1999) and leads the Biomedical Engineering Research Group. Dr. Ward holds BE (Electronic Engineering), MEngSc (Rehabilitation Engineering), and PhD (Biomedical Engineering) degrees from University College, Dublin. His current research includes the application of brain computer interfaces for neurorehabilitation, particularly in stroke and signal processing for connected health. Dr. Ward serves on the Engineering Sciences committee of the Royal Irish Academy and previously on the Irish Research Council He is a Senior Member of the IEEE since 2011. Dr. Ward has authored more than 200 peer-reviewed publications and has supervised to completion 20 research students (12 PhD). He has licensed a range of technologies to industry since 2009 including sensor-streaming technologies for e-health, over the air programming, and mobile health applications.

H.T.G. Weffers received his M.Sc. degree in Computer Science from Eindhoven University of Technology in 1993 and his PDEng (Professional Doctorate in Engineering) degree in Software Technology from Eindhoven University of Technology in 1995. After having worked for the Royal Netherlands Navy and for Philips, in 1998 he joined the Department of Mathematics and Computer Science of Eindhoven University of Technology where he has worked ever since in various positions related to industry-university collaboration and consequently he has been involved in many projects with industry. Since 2013 he is also affiliated with the Intelligent Lighting Institute of Eindhoven University of Technology.

Jonathan Weinel was awarded a 1st Class BA (Hons) degree in Music Technology and Visual Arts (2005) and MRes Music with Distinction (2006), both from Keele University. He received his Arts and Humanities Research Council funded PhD in Music from Keele University (2012), regarding the use of altered states of consciousness as a principle for the composition of electroacoustic music. He has taught at Manchester Metropolitan University, Keele University, and currently holds a Postdoctoral Research Associate position at Glyndŵr University. He has presented both creative works and academic research internationally at conferences such as the International Computer Music Conference, Audio Mostly and in Sonic Ideas, eContact!, and the ACM Digital Library. His research currently focuses on representations of altered states of consciousness in sound and computer graphics, in the context of interactive artworks and video games.

Nancy Westerlaken (1977) obtained her Master's in Building Physics and Systems from the Eindhoven University of Technology. She worked at Eindhoven University of Technology on the topic of indoor ambient lighting applications and user demands after graduating in 2003. In 2007 she started working at The Netherlands Organization for Applied Scientific Research-TNO as a researcher and project manager, having a particular interest in the integrated approach of energy-saving and lighting, including the focus on user demands for well-being of users and their support in an optimal way. Furthermore she is a board member of the Dutch Light and Health Foundation and is associated in standardization activities (guide lines, NEN). Also she is secretary of the Roadmap Healthcare of the High Tech Systems and Materials 'Topsector' of the Dutch government.

Mikael Wiberg, PhD, is Head of Department and Full Professor in Informatics at Umeå University, Sweden. His research interests include mobile and ubiquitous systems, Mobile IT for group collaboration, and novel approaches to interaction design.

Tim Willemen (1987, Wilrijk, Belgium) received the BSc degree in Electrical Engineering from KU Leuven, Belgium, in 2008, and the Erasmus Mundus MSc degree in Nanoscience and Nanotechnology from KU Leuven, Belgium, and Chalmers University of Technology, Sweden, in 2010. He is currently working towards his PhD degree at the Biomechanics section, Mechanical Engineering Department, KU Leuven, Belgium, and at STADIUS, Electrical Engineering Department, KU Leuven, Belgium. His research interests include biomedical data processing, data mining, unobtrusive monitoring, and sleep.

Lyall Williams was awarded a BA (Hons) degree in Music Technology and Philosophy in 2005, and MRes Music Technology in 2006, from Keele University. He has presented at conferences on a range of video game audio topics, both in the UK and internationally, including at Audio Mostly. Though no longer directly involved in academia, he still enjoys any excuse to talk about games.

Eveline Wouters, PhD, MD, MSc, is medical doctor and professor of Health Innovations and Technology in the Faculty of allied health professions, Fontys University of Applied Sciences. Her research focus is on technology development, acceptance, and implementation of technology in healthcare from the point of view of patients, family, and healthcare professionals and organisations. In this, she works together with technological faculties. Together with Dr. Joost van Hoof, EurIng, she was editor on a *Dutch Handbook on Smart Living and Health*. Dr. Wouters has written several other textbooks, book chapters, and many peer-reviewed articles on a diversity of health-related subjects. Key words of the research subjects are: technology, healthcare, professional- and patient-centeredness, acceptance. Research originates from professional practice, and generates knowledge, skills, and instruments directly applicable for professional and educational purposes.

Index